★ **British Museum** ④
See pages 126–9

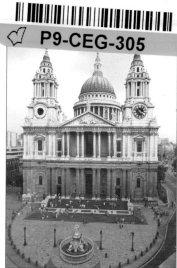

★ **Tower of London** ⑫
See pages 154–7

★ **St. Paul's** ⑩
See pages 148–51

★ **Houses of Parliament** ⑧
See pages 72–3

Smithfield and Spitalfields

⑪

⑩

The City

T H A M E S

⑫

Southwark and Bankside

0 kilometers 1

0 miles 0.5

N

Greenwich and Blackheath

★ **Museum of London** ⑪
See pages 166–7

★ **Westminster Abbey** ⑦
See pages 76–9

LONDON

EYEWITNESS *TRAVEL GUIDES*

LONDON

Main Contributor: MICHAEL LEAPMAN

A DK PUBLISHING BOOK

PROJECT EDITOR Jane Shaw
ART EDITOR Sally Ann Hibbard
EDITOR Tom Fraser
US EDITOR Mary Ann Lynch
DESIGNERS Pippa Hurst, Robyn Tomlinson
DESIGN ASSISTANT Clare Sullivan

MANAGING EDITOR Douglas Amrine
MANAGING ART EDITOR Geoff Manders
SENIOR EDITOR Georgina Matthews
SERIES DESIGN CONSULTANT Peter Luff
EDITORIAL DIRECTOR David Lamb
ART DIRECTOR Anne-Marie Bulat

PRODUCTION CONTROLLER Hilary Stephens
PICTURE RESEARCH Ellen Root
DTP EDITOR Siri Lowe

CONTRIBUTORS
Christopher Pick, Lindsay Hunt

MAPS
Andrew Heritage, James Mills-Hicks, Chez Picthall,
John Plumer (Dorling Kindersley Cartography)

PHOTOGRAPHERS
Philip Enticknap, John Heseltine,
Stephen Oliver

ILLUSTRATORS
Brian Delf, Trevor Hill, Robbie Polley

•

This book was produced with the assistance of
Websters International Publishers.

Film outputting bureau Cooling Brown (London)
Reproduced by Colourscan (Singapore)
Printed and bound by Graphicom (Italy)

First American edition 1993
6 8 10 9 7
Published in the United States by
DK Publishing, Inc.,
95 Madison Avenue, New York, New York 10016

Copyright 1993, 1996 © Dorling Kindersley Limited, London
Visit us on the World Wide Web at http://www.dk.com

Library of Congress Cataloging-in-Publication Data

Leapman, Michael, 1938–
London/Michael Leapman. – – 1st American ed.
p.   cm. – – (Eyewitness travel guides)
ISBN 1–56458–183–7
1. London (England) – – Guidebooks.   I. Title.   II. Series.
DA679.L43 1992   92–53470
914.21'204859 – – dc20   CIP

•

Every effort has been made to ensure that the information in this book is as
up-to-date as possible at the time of going to press. However, details such
as telephone numbers, opening hours, prices, gallery hanging arrangements
and travel information are liable to change. The publishers cannot accept
responsibility for any consequences arising from the use of this book.

We would be delighted to receive any corrections and suggestions for
incorporation in the next edition. Please write to the Managing Editor,
Eyewitness Travel Guides
Dorling Kindersley
9 Henrietta Street, London WC2E 8PS, UK.

THROUGHOUT THIS BOOK, FLOORS ARE REFERRED TO IN ACCORDANCE WITH BRITISH
USAGE, I.E. THE "FIRST FLOOR" IS ONE FLIGHT UP.

CONTENTS

HOW TO USE
THIS GUIDE 6

Portrait of Sir Walter Raleigh (1585)

INTRODUCING
LONDON

PUTTING LONDON
ON THE MAP 10

THE HISTORY OF
LONDON 14

LONDON
AT A GLANCE 34

LONDON THROUGH
THE YEAR 56

A RIVER VIEW
OF LONDON 60

Bedford Square doorway (1775)

The Broadwalk at Hampton Court (c.1720)

Bandstand in St. James's Park

Beefeater at the Tower of London

Houses of Parliament

St. Paul's Church: Covent Garden

HOW TO USE THIS GUIDE

THIS EYEWITNESS TRAVEL GUIDE helps you get the most from your stay in London with the minimum of difficulty. The opening section, *Introducing London*, locates the city geographically, places modern London in its historical context and describes the regular highlights of the London year. *London at a Glance* is an overview of the city's attractions. Section two, *London Area by Area*, guides you through the city's main sightseeing areas, describing all the main sights with maps, photographs and detailed illustrations. In addition, five planned walks take you step-by-step through London's special areas.

Well-researched tips on where to stay, eat, shop, and go for entertainment are in section three, *Travelers' Needs*. *Children's London* is geared for young visitors, and section four, *Survival Guide*, tells you essentials such as how to use the Underground.

LONDON AREA BY AREA

The city has been divided into 17 sightseeing areas, each described separately in the guide. Each area opens with a portrait, summing up the area's character and history and listing all the sights to be covered. Sights are numbered and clearly located on an *Area Map*. After this comes a large-scale *Street-by-Street Map* focusing on the most interesting part of the area. Finding your way around the area is made simple by the numbering system. This refers to the order in which sights are described on the pages following.

Sights at a Glance lists the sights in the area by category: Historic Streets and Buildings; Churches; Museums and Galleries; Monuments; Parks and Gardens and so forth.

The area covered in greater detail on the *Street-by-Street Map* is shaded red.

Numbered circles pinpoint all the listed sights on the *Area Map*. St. Margaret's Church, for example, is ❻.

1 The Area Map

For easy reference, the sights in each area are numbered and located on an Area Map. *The map also shows Underground and mainline stations and parking garages.*

Photographs of facades and distinctive details of buildings help you locate the sights.

Color-coding on each page makes the area easy to find in the book.

2 The Street-by-Street Map

This gives a bird's-eye view of the heart of each sightseeing area. The most important buildings are highlighted in stronger color, to help you spot them as you walk around.

A locator map shows you where you are in relation to surrounding areas. The area of the *Street-by-Street Map* is shown in red.

Travel tips help you reach the area quickly by public transportation.

A suggested route for a walk takes in the most attractive and interesting streets in the area.

St. Margaret's Church is shown on this map as well.

Red stars indicate the sights that no visitor should miss.

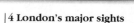

LONDON AT A GLANCE

Each map in this section concentrates on a specific theme: *Celebrated Londoners; Museums and Galleries; Churches; Parks and Gardens* and *Ceremonies.* Major sights are shown on the map; others are described on the following two pages and cross-referenced to their full entries in the *Area by Area* section.

Each sightseeing area is color-coded.

The theme is explored in greater detail on the pages following the map.

3 Detailed information on each sight

All important sights in each area are described in depth in this section. They are listed in order, following the numbering on the Area Map. Practical information is also provided.

4 London's major sights

These are given two or more full pages in the sightseeing area in which they are found. Historic buildings are dissected to reveal their interiors; museums and galleries have color-coded floor plans to help you find important exhibits.

PRACTICAL INFORMATION

Each entry provides all the information needed to plan a visit to the sight. The key to the symbols is inside the back cover.

Telephone number

Address

Map reference to Street Finder at back of book

St. Margaret's Church ⑥ — Sight Number

Parliament Sq SW1. **Map** 13 B5.
📞 071-222 5152. ➤ *Westminster.*
Open 9:30am–5:30pm Mon–Sat,
1–5:30pm Sun. ✝ 11am Sun.
🚫 ♿ 🔲 **Concerts.**

Opening hours

Services and facilities available

Nearest Underground station

The Visitors' Checklist provides the practical information you will need to plan your visit.

The facade of each major sight is shown to help you spot it quickly.

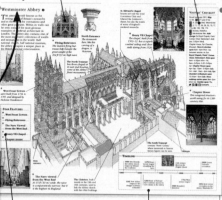

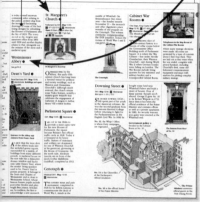

Red stars indicate the most interesting architectural details of the building and the most important works of art or exhibits to be seen inside.

A timeline charts the key events in the history of the sight.

INTRODUCING LONDON

Putting London on the Map

L ONDON, THE CAPITAL of the United
Kingdom, is a city of seven million
people covering 601 square miles
(1,580 sq km) of southeast England. It is
built on the River Thames at the center
of the UK road and rail networks. From
London visitors can easily reach the
country's other main tourist attractions.

View east over the Thames from Southwark

NORWAY

SWEDEN

DENMARK

REPUBLIC
OF
IRELAND

UNITED
KINGDOM

London

NETHERLANDS

BELGIUM

GERMANY

LUXEMBOURG

FRANCE

SWITZERLAND

AUSTRIA

ITALY

SPAIN

PORTUGAL

The Midlands

*The Midlands
The North*

Stratford-
upon-Avon

M40

A43

A40

Thames

Oxford

M40

C h i l t e r n   H i l l s

Western Europe

*London is in northwest
Europe, on the same
latitude as Warsaw. It
is Europe's biggest city
and the business center
of the continent. London
has five airports and is
about an hour's flying
time from Scandinavia,
Germany, Holland and
France. It is also linked
to northern Europe
through nearby ports.*

The West

M4

Bath

Stonehenge

A36

Salisbury

A30

The West

A34

M4

M4

Reading

Windsor

M3

A30

Winchester

S
o
D
o

A3(M)

A35

Southampton

M27

Portsmouth

Aerial view of central London

Poole

Isle of Wight

Le H

Channel Islands

Cherbourg

St Malo

Cherbourg

Caen

E N G L I S

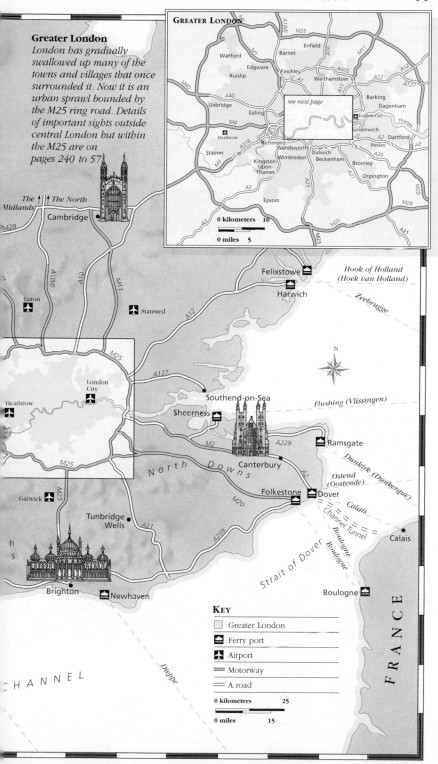

Greater London
*London has gradually
swallowed up many of the
towns and villages that once
surrounded it. Now it is an
urban sprawl bounded by
the M25 ring road. Details
of important sights outside
central London but within
the M25 are on
pages 240 to 57.*

GREATER LONDON

see next page

Watford
Enfield
Barnet
Edgware
Ruislip
Finchley
Walthamstow
Uxbridge
Ealing
Barking
Dagenham
London City
Greenwich
Heathrow
Richmond
Wandsworth
Dartford
Staines
Wimbledon
Dulwich
Bexley
Kingston-Upon-Thames
Beckenham
Bromley
Orpington
Epsom

0 kilometers 10
0 miles 5

The Midlands — The North

Cambridge

A428

Luton

Stansted

Felixstowe
Harwich

Hook of Holland
(Hoek van Holland)

Zeebrugge

London City

Heathrow

Southend-on-Sea
Sheerness

Flushing (Vlissingen)

Gatwick

Canterbury

Ramsgate

Dunkirk (Dunkerque)

North Downs

Folkestone
Dover

Ostend
(Oostende)

Calais

Tunbridge Wells

Channel Tunnel

Calais

Brighton
Newhaven

Strait of Dover

Boulogne

Boulogne

CHANNEL

Dieppe

F R A N C E

KEY

Greater London
Ferry port
Airport
Motorway
A road

0 kilometers 25
0 miles 15

Central London

$\mathbf{M}$OST OF THE SIGHTS described in this guide lie within 14 areas of central London plus 2 outlying districts of Hampstead and Greenwich. Each of these areas is described separately in the Area by Area section of this guide. If you're short of time, restrict yourself to the five areas that are packed with many famous sights: Whitehall and Westminster, the City, Bloomsbury and Fitzrovia, Soho and Trafalgar Square, and South Kensington and Knightsbridge.

PAGES 216–23
*Street Finder maps
3–4, 11–12*

PAGES 232–9
*Street Finder maps
23–24*

Hampstead

PAGES 224–31
*Street Finder maps
1–2*

*Regent's Park
and
Marylebone*

*Greenwich and
Blackheath*

PAGES 210–15
*Street Finder maps
9–10, 17*

*Kensington
and
Holland Park*

*South Kensington
and
Knightsbridge*

*Piccadilly
and
St. James*

Chelsea

PAGES 194–209
*Street Finder maps
10–11, 18–19*

PAGES 188–93
*Street Finder maps
18–19*

0 kilometers   1

0 miles   0.5

PAGES 98–109
Street Finder maps 12–13

PAGES 120–31
Street Finder maps 4–5, 13

PAGES 110–19
Street Finder maps 13–14

PAGES 132–41
Street Finder maps 5–6, 13–14

N

Bloomsbury and Fitzrovia

Smithfield and Spitalfields

PAGES 160–71
Street Finder maps 6–7, 14, 16

ho and rafalgar square

Holborn and the Inns of Court

Covent Garden and the Strand

The City

RIVER THAMES

South Bank

Southwark and Bankside

PAGES 142–59
Street Finder maps 14–16

Whitehall and Westminster

PAGES 68–85
Street Finder maps 13, 20–1

PAGES 86–97
Street Finder maps 12–13, 20

PAGES 180–7
Street Finder maps 13–14, 21–2

PAGES 172–9
Street Finder maps 6, 16

THE HISTORY OF LONDON

IN 55 BC, JULIUS CAESAR'S Roman army invaded England, landed in Kent and then marched northwest until it reached the broad River Thames at what is now called Southwark. There were a few tribesmen living on the opposite bank but no major settlement. However, by the time of the second Roman invasion 88 years later, a small port and mercantile community had been established there. The Romans bridged the river and built their administrative headquarters on the north bank, calling it Londinium – a version of its old Celtic name.

The griffon: the City of London's symbol

LONDON AS CAPITAL

London was soon the largest city in England, and by the time of the Norman Conquest in 1066, it was the obvious choice for the national capital.

Settlement slowly spread beyond the original walled city, which was virtually wiped out by the Great Fire of 1666. The post-Fire rebuilding formed the basis of the area we know today as the City, but by the 18th century, London enveloped the settlements around it. These included the royal city of Westminster, which had long been London's religious and political center. The explosive growth of commerce and industry in the 18th and 19th centuries made London the biggest and wealthiest city in the world, creating a prosperous middle class who built fine houses that still grace parts of the capital. The prospect of riches also lured many dispossessed from the countryside and from abroad. They moved into insanitary dwellings, many just east of the City, where docks provided employment.

By the end of the 19th century, 4.5 million people lived in inner London; another 4 million nearby. Bombing in World War II devastated many central areas and led to rebuilding in the second half of the 20th century, when the docks and other Victorian industries disappeared.

The following pages illustrate London's history by giving snapshots of significant periods in its evolution.

A map of 1580 showing the City of London and, towards the lower-left corner, the City of Westminster

A 15th-century manuscript showing the Tower of London with London Bridge in the background

Roman London

1st-century Roman coin

W
HEN THE ROMANS invaded Britain in the
1st century AD, they already controlled
vast areas of the Mediterranean, but fierce
opposition from local tribes (such as Queen
Boadicea's Iceni) made Britain difficult to
control. The Romans persevered, however,
and had consolidated their power by the
end of the century. Londinium, with its port, developed
into a capital city; by the 3rd century, there were some
50,000 people living there. But, as the Roman Empire
crumbled in the 5th century, the garrison pulled out,
leaving the city to the Saxons.

EXTENT OF THE CITY

☐ *125 AD*   ☐ *Today*

Site of present-day Museum of London

Public Baths
*Bathing was an
important part
of Roman life.
This pocket-sized
personal hygiene
kit (including a
nail pick) and
bronze pouring
dish date from
the 1st century.*

Roman fort

Site of present-day St. Paul's

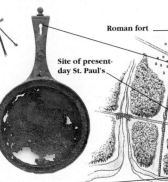

Basilica

Forum

LONDINIUM
*Roman London was an
important center on the site
of the present-day City (see
pp142–59). On the Thames,
it was in a good position
to trade with the rest
of the Empire.*

Temple of Mithras
*Mithras protected the
good from evil. This
2nd-century head
was in his temple.*

Forum and Basilica
*About 600 ft (200 m)
from London Bridge was
the forum (the chief market
and meeting place) and the
basilica (the town hall and
court of justice).*

TIMELINE

55 BC Julius Caesar invades Britain	**200** City wall built	**410** Roman troops begin to leave
AD 61 Boadicea attacks		
100	200	300	400
AD 43 Claudius establishes Roman London and builds the first bridge		

☐ **Roman London**

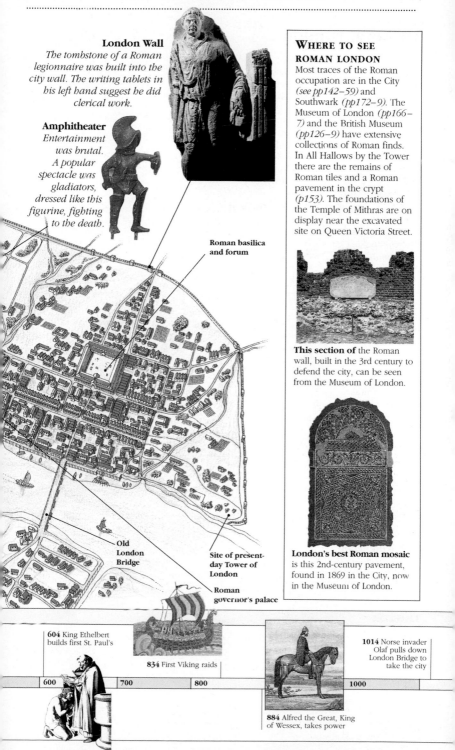

London Wall
The tombstone of a Roman legionnaire was built into the city wall. The writing tablets in his left hand suggest he did clerical work.

Amphitheater
Entertainment was brutal. A popular spectacle was gladiators, dressed like this figurine, fighting to the death.

Roman basilica and forum

Old London Bridge

Site of present-day Tower of London

Roman governor's palace

WHERE TO SEE ROMAN LONDON
Most traces of the Roman occupation are in the City *(see pp142–59)* and Southwark *(pp172–9)*. The Museum of London *(pp166–7)* and the British Museum *(pp126–9)* have extensive collections of Roman finds. In All Hallows by the Tower there are the remains of Roman tiles and a Roman pavement in the crypt *(p153)*. The foundations of the Temple of Mithras are on display near the excavated site on Queen Victoria Street.

This section of the Roman wall, built in the 3rd century to defend the city, can be seen from the Museum of London.

London's best Roman mosaic is this 2nd-century pavement, found in 1869 in the City, now in the Museum of London.

604 King Ethelbert builds first St. Paul's

834 First Viking raids

884 Alfred the Great, King of Wessex, takes power

1014 Norse invader Olaf pulls down London Bridge to take the city

| 600 | 700 | 800 | | 1000 |

Medieval London

THE HISTORIC DIVISION between London's centers of commerce (the City) and government (Westminster) started in the mid-11th century when Edward the Confessor established his court and sited his abbey *(see pp76–9)* at Westminster. Meanwhile, in the City, tradesmen set up their own institutions and guilds, and London appointed its first mayor, in 1191. But disease was rife, and the population never rose much above 50,000, London's peak population in Roman times.

EXTENT OF THE CITY

▨ *1200*   ☐ *Today*

LONDON BRIDGE

The first stone bridge was built in 1209 and lasted 600 years. It was the only bridge across the Thames in London until Westminster Bridge (1750).

The Chapel of St. Thomas, erected the year the bridge was completed, was one of its first buildings.

Iron railings

St. Thomas à Becket
As Archbishop of Canterbury he was murdered in 1170 at the request of Henry II, with whom he was quarreling. Thomas was made a saint and pilgrims still visit his Canterbury shrine.

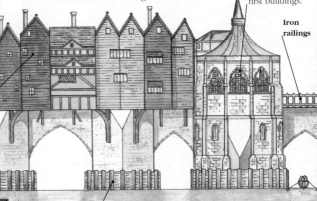

Houses and shops projected over both sides of the bridge. Shopkeepers made their own merchandise on the premises and lived above their shops. Apprentices did the selling.

THE HOUSE OF
RICHARD
WHITTINGTON
MAYOR OF LONDON
STOOD ON THIS SITE
1423

Dick Whittington
The 15th-century trader was thrice mayor of London (see p39).

The piers were made from wooden stakes rammed into the riverbed and filled with rubble.

Stag Hunting
Such sports were the chief recreation of wealthy landowners.

The arches ranged from 15 ft (4.5 m) to 35 ft (10 m) in width.

TIMELINE

1042 Edward the Confessor becomes king	**1086** Domesday Book, England's first survey, published		**1191** Henry Fitzalwin becomes London's first mayor	**1215** King John's Magna Carta gives the City more powers	
1050	1100	1150	1200		1250
1066 William I crowned in Abbey		**1176** Work starts on the first stone London Bridge		**1240** First Parliament sits at Westminster	
1065 Westminster Abbey completed					

☐ **Medieval London**

Chivalry
Medieval knights were idealized for their courage and honor. Edward Burne-Jones (1833–98) painted George, patron saint of England, rescuing a maiden from this dragon.

Geoffrey Chaucer
This poet and customs controller (see p39) *is best remembered for his* Canterbury Tales, *which creates a rich picture of 14th-century England.*

WHERE TO SEE MEDIEVAL LONDON
There were only a few survivors of the Great Fire of 1666 *(see pp22–3)* – the Tower *(pp154–7)*, Westminster Hall *(p72)* and Abbey *(pp76–9)* and a few churches *(p46)*. The Museum of London *(pp166–7)* has artifacts, while the Tate *(pp82–5)* and National Gallery *(pp104–7)* have paintings. Manuscripts, including the *Domesday Book*, are at the British Library *(p129)* and the Public Record Office *(p137)*.

The Tower of London was started in 1078 and became one of the few centers of royal power in the largely self-governing City.

A 14th-century rose window is all that remains of Winchester Palace near the Clink *(see p177)*.

Plan of the Bridge
The bridge had 19 arches to span the river making it, for many years, the longest stone bridge in England.

Many 13th-century pilgrims went to Canterbury.

	1348 Black Death kills thousands	**1394** Westminster Hall remodeled by Henry Yevele	*The Great Seal of Richard I shows us what medieval kings looked like.*
1350		**1400**	**1450**
	1381 Peasant's Revolt defeated	**1397** Richard Whittington becomes mayor	**1476** William Caxton sets up first printing press at Westminster

Elizabethan London

IN THE 16TH CENTURY the monarchy was stronger than ever before. The Tudors established peace throughout England, allowing art and commerce to flourish. This Renaissance reached its zenith under Elizabeth I as explorers opened up the New World, and English theater, the nation's most lasting contribution to world culture, was born.

EXTENT OF THE CITY
◼ *1561*   ☐ *Today*

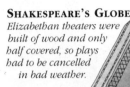

SHAKESPEARE'S GLOBE
Elizabethan theaters were built of wood and only half covered, so plays had to be cancelled in bad weather.

Curtain

A balcony on the stage was part of the scenery.

The apron stage had a trap door for special effects.

Death at the Stake
The Tudors dealt harshly with social and religious dissent. Here Bishops Latimer and Ridley die for so-called heresy in 1555, when Elizabeth's half-sister, Mary I, was queen. Traitors could expect to be hung, drawn and quartered.

In the pit, below the level of the stage, commoners stood to watch the play.

Hunting and Hawking
Popular 16th-century pastimes are shown on this cushion cover.

TIMELINE

Rat catchers, and other pest controllers, could not prevent epidemics of plague

1535 Sir Thomas More executed for treason

1536 Henry VIII's second wife, Anne Boleyn, executed

1530

1534 Henry VIII breaks with the Roman Catholic church

1547 Henry dies; succeeded by his son, Edward VI

1550

1553 Edward dies; succeeded by his sister, Mary I

☐ Elizabethan London

The galleries were for rich theatergoers who could watch from the comfort of seats.

Elizabeth I
The "Virgin Queen" sat for this portrait to celebrate victory over the Spanish in 1588.

Tilting Spurs
The aim of this high-speed sport, popular among noblemen, was to knock opponents off their horses.

Steps allowed tiered seating.

Astronomical Clock
Made in 1540 at Hampton Court, it shows the sun moving around the earth.

Audience entrance

WHERE TO SEE ELIZABETHAN LONDON

The Great Fire of 1666 wiped out the City. Fortunately, Middle Temple Hall *(see p139)*, Staple Inn *(p141)* and the Lady Chapel inside Westminster Abbey *(pp76–9)* were beyond its reach. The Museum of London *(pp166–7)*, the Victoria and Albert *(pp198–201)*, and the Geffrye Museum *(p244)* have fine furniture and artifacts. Out of town are Hampton Court *(pp250–3)* and Sutton House *(p244)*.

Elizabeth I watched *Twelfth Night* by Shakespeare under the hammerbeam roof of Middle Temple Hall in 1603.

The Parr Pot, now in the Museum of London, was made by Venetian craftsmen in London in 1547.

53 Plague
eps Europe

58 Mary I's death
kes Elizabeth queen

1570 Francis Drake makes first voyage to the West Indies

1584 Walter Raleigh's first attempt to colonize America

1588 Drake defeats Spanish Armada

1591 First play by Shakespeare produced

| 1560 | 1570 | 1580 | 1590 |

Gloves made from imported silk and velvet

1603 Elizabeth dies; James I accedes

Restoration London

CIVIL WAR HAD BROKEN OUT in 1642 when the mercantile class demanded that some of the monarch's power be passed to Parliament. The subsequent Commonwealth was dominated by Puritans under Oliver Cromwell. The Puritans outlawed simple pleasures, such as dancing and theater, so it was small wonder that the restoration of the monarchy under Charles II in 1660 was greeted with rejoicing and the release of pent-up creative energies. The period was, however, also marked with two major tragedies: the Plague (1665) and the Great Fire (1666).

EXTENT OF THE CITY

☐ *1680* ☐ *Today*

St. Paul's was destroyed in the fire that raged as far east as Fetter Lane *(map 14 E1)*.

London Bridge itself survived, but many of the buildings on it were burned down.

Oliver Cromwell
He led the Parliamentarian army and was Lord Protector of the Realm from 1653 until his death in 1658. At the Restoration, his body was dug up and hung from the gallows at Tyburn, (near Hyde Park, see p207).

Charles I's Death
The king was beheaded for tyranny on a freezing day (January 30, 1649) outside Banqueting House (see p80).

Charles I
His belief in the Divine Right of Kings angered Parliament and was one of the causes of civil war.

TIMELINE

1605 Guy Fawkes leads failed attempt to blow up the King and Parliament

1620

1623 Shakespeare's first folio published

1625 James I dies; succeeded by his son, Charles I

Feathered helmet worn by Royalist cavaliers

1640

1642 Civil war starts when Parliament defies king

1649 Charles I executed; Commonwealth established

1650

☐ **Restoration London**

Newton's Telescope
Physicist and astronomer Sir Isaac Newton (1642–1727) discovered the law of gravity.

Samuel Pepys
His exuberant diaries tell us much about courtly life of the time.

The Tower of London was just out of the fire's reach.

WHERE TO SEE RESTORATION LONDON
Wren's churches and his St. Paul's Cathedral *(see p47 and pp148–51)* are, with Inigo Jones's Banqueting House *(p80)*, London's most famous 17th-century buildings. On a more modest scale are Lincoln's Inn *(p136)* and Cloth Fair *(p165)*. There is a fine period interior at the Museum of London *(pp166–7)*. The British Museum *(pp126–9)* and the Victoria and Albert *(pp198–201)* have pottery, silver and textile collections.

Ham House *(p248)* was built in 1610 but much enlarged later in the century. It has the finest interior of its time in England.

THE GREAT FIRE OF 1666
An unidentified Dutch artist painted this view of the fire that burned for 5 days, destroying 13,000 houses.

The Plague
During 1665, carts collected the dead and took them to communal graves outside the city.

Peter Paul Rubens painted the ceiling in 1636 for Inigo Jones's Banqueting House *(p80)*. This is one of its panels.

1664–5 Plague kills 100,000

1666 Great Fire

1685 Charles II dies; Catholic James II becomes king

1692 First insurance market opens at Lloyd's

1660 1670 1690

1660 Monarchy restored under Charles II

A barber's bowl made by London potters in 1681

1688 James ousted in favor of Protestant William of Orange

1694 First Bank of England set up by William Paterson

Georgian London

THE FOUNDING of the Bank of England in 1694 spurred the growth of London, and by the time George I came to the throne in 1714, London had become an important financial and commercial center. Aristocrats with West End estates began laying out elegant squares and terraces to house newly rich merchants. Architects such as the Adam brothers, John Soane and John Nash developed stylish medium-scale housing. They drew inspiration from the great European capitals, as did English painters, sculptors, composers and craftsmen.

George I (reigned 1714–27)

EXTENT OF THE CITY

☐ 1810   ☐ Today

Manchester Square was laid out from 1776 to 1778.

Portman Square was on the town's out-skirts when it was started in 1764.

Great Cumberland Place
Built in 1790, it was named after a royal duke and military commander.

Grosvenor Square
Few of the original houses remain here, one of the oldest and largest Mayfair squares (1720).

Docks
Shipping docks handled the growth in world trade.

TIMELINE

1714 George I becomes king

1727 George II becomes king

1717 Hanover Square built; start of West End development

1720

1729 John Wesley (1703–91) founds the Methodist Church

1740

1759 Kew Gardens established

1760

1760 George III becomes king

1768 Royal Academy of Art established

☐ Georgian London

John Nash

Stylish Nash shaped 18th-century London with variations on Classical themes, such as this archway in Cumberland Terrace, near Regent's Park.

WHERE TO SEE GEORGIAN LONDON

The portico of the Theatre Royal, Haymarket *(see pp326–7)*, gives a taste of the style of fashionable London in the 1820s. In Pall Mall *(p92)*, Charles Barry's Reform and Travellers' Clubs are equally evocative. Most West End squares have some Georgian buildings, while Fournier Street *(p170)* has good small-scale domestic architecture. The Victoria and Albert Museum (V&A, *pp198–201*) has silver, as do the London Silver Vaults *(p141)*, where it is for sale. Hogarth's pictures, at the Tate *(pp82–5)* and Sir John Soane's Museum *(pp136–7)*, show the social conditions.

This English long case clock
(1725), made of oak and pine with Chinese designs, is in the V&A.

GEORGIAN LONDON

The layout of much of London's West End has remained very similar to how it was in 1828, when this map was published.

Captain Cook
This Yorkshire-born explorer "discovered" Australia during a world voyage from 1768 to 1771.

Berkeley Square
Built in the 1730s and 1740s on the grounds of the former Berkeley House, several characteristic original houses remain on its west side.

Ironwork
Crafts flourished. This ornate railing is on Manchester Square.

Signatories of the American Declaration of Independence.

1811 George III goes mad; his son George is made Regent

1820 George III dies; Prince Regent becomes George IV

1830 George IV dies; brother William IV is king

| 1800 | 1810 | 1820 | 1830 |

1776 Britain loses American colonies with Declaration of Independence

1802 Stock Exchange formally established

1829 London's first horse bus

Victorian London

Queen Victoria in her coronation year (1838)

Much of London today is Victorian. Until the early 19th century, the capital had been confined to the original Roman city, plus Westminster and Mayfair to the west, ringed by fields and villages such as Brompton, Islington and Battersea. From the 1820s these green spaces filled rapidly with terraces of houses for the growing numbers attracted to London by industrialization. Rapid expansion brought challenges to the City. The first cholera epidemic broke out in 1832, and in 1858 came the Great Stink, when the smell from the Thames became so bad that Parliament had to go into recess. But Joseph Bazalgette's sewage system (1875), involving banking both sides of the Thames, eased the problem.

EXTENT OF THE CITY

☐ 1900   ☐ Today

The building was 1,850 ft (560 m) long and 110 ft (33 m) high.

Nearly 14,000 exhibitors came from all over the world, bringing more than 100,000 exhibits.

Pantomime
The traditional family Christmas entertainment (still popular today – see p326) started in the 19th century.

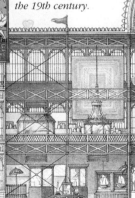

Soldiers marched and jumped on the floor to test its strength before the exhibition opened.

Massive elm trees growing in Hyde Park were left standing, and the exhibition was erected around them.

The Crystal Fountain was 27 ft (8 m) high.

Carpets and stained glass were hung from the galleries.

TIMELINE

1837 Victoria becomes queen

1851 Great Exhibition

Season ticket for Great Exhibition

A Wedgwood plate in typical florid Victorian style

1861 Prince Albert dies

1860

1836 First London rail terminus opens at London Bridge

1840 Rowland Hill introduces Penny Post

1863 Metropolitan Railway, world's first Underground system, is opened

1870 First Peabo Buildings, to hou the poor, built Blackfriars Ro

☐ **Victoria's reign**

Railways
By 1900 fast trains, such as this Scotch Express, *were crossing the country.*

WHERE TO SEE VICTORIAN LONDON
Grandiose buildings best reflect the spirit of the age, notably the rail termini, the Kensington Museums *(see pp194–209)* and the Royal Albert Hall *(p203)*. Leighton House *(p214)* has a well-preserved interior. Pottery and fabrics are in the Victoria and Albert Museum, and the London Transport Museum *(p114)* has buses, trams and trains.

Telegraph
Newly invented communications technology, like this telegraph from 1840, made business expansion easier.

Crystal Palace
Between May and October 1851, six million people visited Joseph Paxton's superb feat of engineering. In 1852 it was dismantled and reassembled in south London, where it remained until it was destroyed by fire in 1936.

The Victorian Gothic style suited buildings like the Public Record Office *(p137)*.

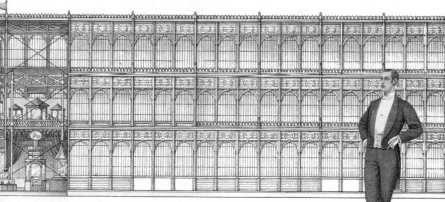

GREAT EXHIBITION OF 1851
The exhibition, held in the Crystal Palace in Hyde Park, celebrated industry, technology and the expanding British Empire.

Formal Dress
Under Victoria, elaborate men's attire was replaced by more restrained evening wear.

A special box for carrying top hats

1889 London County Council (LCC) established

1891 First LCC public housing built, in Shoreditch

1899 First motor buses introduced

1901 Queen Victoria dies; Edward VII accedes

1880

1890

1900

1890 First electric Underground line, from Bank to Stockwell, opens

Commemorative fan from the Boer War, which ended in 1903

London Between the World Wars

Art Deco china by Clarice Cliff

THE SOCIETY THAT emerged from World War I grasped eagerly at the innovations of early 20th-century London – the motor car, the telephone and commuter transportation. Movies brought transatlantic culture, especially jazz and swing music. Victorian restraints were discarded as people flocked to dance in clubs and dance halls. Many left the crowded inner city for new suburban estates. Then came the 1930s global Depression, whose effects had barely worn off when World War II began.

EXTENT OF THE CITY

| 1938 | Today |

METRO·LAND
PRICE TWO·PENCE

Commuting
London's new outer suburbs were made popular by the underground railway. In the north was "Metroland," named after the Metropolitan line that reached Hertfordshire.

High Fashion
The sleek, flowing new styles contrasted with the fussy elaboration of the Victorians and Edwardians. This tea gown is from the 1920s.

Formal evening wear, including hats for both sexes, was still compulsory when going to smart West End nightspots.

A LONDON STREET SCENE
Maurice Greiflenhagen's painting (1926) captures the bustle of London after dark.

Medals, like this from 1914, were struck during the campaign for women's votes

1921 North Circular Road links northern suburbs

1922 First BBC national radio broadcast

1910

1920

1910
George V succeeds Edward VII

Cavalry was still used in the Middle Eastern battles of World War I (1914–18)

 Interwar period

Early Movies
London-born Charlie Chaplin (1889–1977), seen here in City Lights, *was a popular star of both silent and talking pictures.*

Seven new theaters were built in central London from 1924 to 1931.

George VI
Oswald Birley painted this portrait of the king, who became a model for wartime resistance and unity.

Early motor buses had open tops, like the old horse-drawn buses.

Communications
The radio provided home entertainment and information. This is a 1933 model.

Throughout the period newspaper circulations increased massively. In 1930 *The Daily Herald* sold 2 million copies a day.

WORLD WAR II AND THE BLITZ
World War II saw large-scale civilian bombing for the first time, bringing the horror of war to Londoners' doorsteps. Thousands were killed in their homes. Many people took refuge in underground stations, and children were evacuated to the safety of the country.

WOMEN OF BRITAIN
COME INTO THE FACTORIES

As in World War I, women were recruited for factory work formerly done by men who were away fighting.

Bombing raids in 1940 and 1941 (the Blitz) caused devastation all over the city.

1929 US stock market crash brings world Depression

1939 World War II begins

1930

1927 First talking pictures

1936 Edward VIII abdicates to marry US divorcée Wallis Simpson. George VI accedes

1940 Winston Churchill becomes Prime Minister

Postwar London

THOUGH MUCH OF LONDON was flattened by World War II bombs, remarkable architecture has survived. Postwar rebuilding was often unimaginative, and some buildings have already been razed. More traditional design has returned, but so have skyscrapers. By the 1960s, London was thriving, and such a dynamic world leader in fashion and popular music that *Time* magazine dubbed it "swinging London." It remains a leading European city.

EXTENT OF THE CITY

▨ *1959*	☐ *Today*

The Beatles
The Liverpool pop group, pictured in 1965, had rocketed to stardom two years earlier with songs of appealing freshness and directness. The group symbolized carefree 1960s London.

Margaret Thatcher
Britain's first woman Prime Minister (1979–90) promoted the market-led policies that fueled the 1980s boom.

Festival of Britain
After wartime, the city's morale was lifted by the Festival, marking the 1851 Great Exhibition's centenary (see pp26–7).

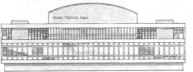

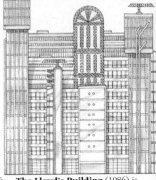

The Royal Festival Hall (1951) was the Festival's centerpiece and is still a landmark *(see pp184–5).*

Telecom Tower (1964), at 580 ft (180 m) high, dominates the Fitzrovia skyline.

The Lloyd's Building (1986) is Richard Rogers's Post-Modernist emblem *(see p159).*

TIMELINE

1948 Olympic Games held in London

1952 George VI dies; his daughter Elizabeth II accedes

Minis became a symbol of the 1960s; they typified the go-as-you-please mood of the decade.

1945	1950	1955	1960	1965

1951 Festival of Britain

1954 Food rationing, introduced during World War II, abolished

1963 National Theatre founded at the Old Vic

1945 End of World War II

☐ **Postwar London**

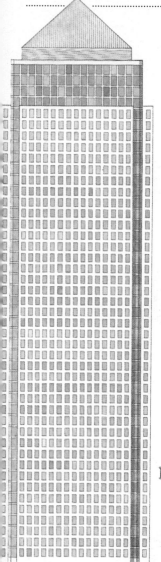

Docklands Light Railway
In the 1980s, new, driver-less trains started to transport people to the developing Docklands.

POST-MODERN ARCHITECTURE
The new wave of archi-tects since the 1980s are reacting against the bleak and stark shapes of the Modernists. Some, like Richard Rogers, are masters of high-tech, emphasizing structural features in their designs. Others, Terry Farrell, for example, adopt a more playful approach using pastiches of Classical features, such as columns.

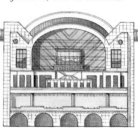

Canada Tower (1991) is London's tallest building and was designed by César Pelli *(see p245)*.

Charing Cross (1991) has Terry Farrell's glasshouse on top of the Victorian station *(see p119)*.

YOUTH CULTURE
With their new-found mobility and spending power, young people assumed an influence in the development of British popular culture in the years after World War II. Music, fashion and design were increasingly geared to their rapidly changing tastes.

Punks were a phenomenon of the 1970s and 1980s. Their clothes, music, hair and habits were designed to shock.

The Prince of Wales
As heir to the throne, he is outspokenly critical of much of London's recent architecture. He prefers Classical styles.

	1977 Queen's Silver Jubilee; work starts on Jubilee line Underground route		**1984** Thames Barrier completed	*Vivienne Westwood's clothes won prizes in the 1980s and 1990s.* **1986** Greater London Council abolished

1970	1975	1980	1985	1990

1971 New London Bridge built

1982 Last of the London docks closes

1985 Ethiopian famine led to the massive Live Aid relief campaign

1992 Canary Wharf development opens

Kings and Queens in London

L ONDON HAS BEEN the royal capital of England
since 1066, when Willliam the Conqueror began
the tradition of holding coronations in Westminster
Abbey. Since then, successive kings and queens
have left their mark on London and many of the
places described in this book have royal
associations: Henry VIII hunted at
Richmond, Charles I was executed
on Whitehall and the young Queen
Victoria rode on Queensway.
Royalty is also celebrated in
many of London's traditional
ceremonies – for more details
on these turn to pages 52–5.

1413–22 Henry V

1509–47 Henry VIII

1399–1413 Henry IV

1485–1509 Henry VII

1066–87 William the Conqueror

1087–1100 William II

1100–35 Henry I

1135–54 Stephen

1327–77 Edward III

1483–5 Richard III

1050	1100	1150	1200	1250	1300	1350	1400	1450	1500
NORMAN		PLANTAGENET					LANCASTER	YORK	TUDOR
1050	1100	1150	1200	1250	1300	1350	1400	1450	1500

1154–89 Henry II

1189–99 Richard I

1199–1216 John

1216–72 Henry III

1307–27 Edward II

1272–1307 Edward I

1461–70 and 1471–83 Edward IV

1422–61 and 1470–1 Henry VI

1377–99 Richard II

Matthew Paris's 13th-century chronicle showing Kings Richard I, Henry II, John and Henry III

1483 Edward V

1553–8 Mary I

1660–85 Charles II

1685–8 James II

1689–1702
William and Mary

1702–14
Anne

1714–27
George I

1603–25
James I

1936 Edward VIII

1952– Elizabeth II

1837–1901 Victoria

1901–10
Edward VII

1727–60 George II

550	1600	1650	1700	1750	1800	1850	1900	1950	2000
	STUART			**HANOVER**			**WINDSOR**		
550	1600	1650	1700	1750	1800	1850	1900	1950	2000

1649–60 The Common-
wealth under Oliver
Cromwell

1830–37
William IV

1820–30
George IV

1936–52 George VI shown
on the George Cross medal

1910–36
George V

1625–49 Charles I

1558–1603 Elizabeth I

1760–1820 George III

547–53 Edward VI

LONDON AT A GLANCE

THERE ARE NEARLY 300 places of interest described in the *Area by Area* section of this book. These range from the delightful Museum of the Moving Image *(see p184)* to the gruesome Old St. Thomas's Operating Theatre *(p176)*, and from the ancient Charterhouse *(p164)* to the modern Canary Wharf *(p245)*. To help you make the most of your stay, the following 20 pages are a time-saving guide to the best London has to offer. Museums, galleries, churches, parks and gardens are listed and described and there are guides to famous Londoners and ceremonies in London. Each sight mentioned is cross-referenced to its own full entry later in the guide. Below are the top-ten tourist attractions to start you off.

LONDON'S TOP-TEN TOURIST ATTRACTIONS

St. Paul's
See pp148–51.

Hampton Court
See pp250–3.

Changing of the Guard
Buckingham Palace, see pp94–5.

British Museum
See pp126–9.

National Gallery
See pp104–7.

Westminster Abbey
See pp76–9.

Madame Tussaud's
See p220.

Houses of Parliament
See pp72–3.

Tower of London
See pp154–7.

Victoria and Albert Museum
See pp198–201.

Westminster Bridge and the Houses of Parliament

Celebrated Visitors and Residents

MANY FAMOUS LONDONERS are famous for *being* Londoners – Samuel Pepys, Christopher Wren, Dr. P. Samuel Johnson, Charles Dickens and countless others *(see pp38–9)*. However, as a center of international culture, commerce and politics, the English capital has also always attracted celebrated people from overseas. Some famous visitors were escaping war or persecution at home, others came to work or study, or as tourists. In some cases, their association with London is little-known and surprising.

Mary Seacole *(1805–81)*
The Jamaican-born writer and nurse in the Crimean War lodged first in Tavistock Street, then Cambridge Street, Paddington.

Regent's Park and Marylebone

Richard Wagner
(1813–83)
In 1877 the German opera composer lived at No. 12 Orme Square, Bayswater, from where he would walk across the park to conduct at the Royal Albert Hall (see p203).

Kensington and Holland Park

South Kensington and Knightsbridge

Henry James *(1811–1916)*
The American novelist lived at No. 3 Bolton Street, Mayfair, then at No. 34 de Vere Gardens, Kensington (1886–92). He died at Carlyle Mansions, Cheyne Walk.

Dwight Eisenhower
(1890–1969)
During World War II he planned the North African invasion in a house on Grosvenor Square, Mayfair.

Chelsea

Jenny Lind /
(1827–87)
The "Swedish Nightingale" lived for a time at No. 189 Old Brompton Road, Kensington.

Mark Twain
(1835–1910)
Huckleberry Finn's American creator lived from 1896 until 1897 at No. 23 Tedworth Square.

Giuseppe Mazzini

(1805–72)
The architect of Italian unity was exiled to London in 1837 and lived at No. 183 Gower Street until 1840. He founded a school for Italian immigrants at No. 5 Hatton Garden.

Karl Marx *(1818–83)*

The German philosopher lived at No. 28 Dean Street, and wrote Das Kapital *in the British Library Reading Room (see p129).*

Bloomsbury and Fitzrovia

Smithfield and Spitalfields

Holborn and the Inns of Court

Soho and Trafalgar Square

Covent Garden and the Strand

The City

R I V E R   T H A M E S

South Bank

Southwark and Bankside

cadilly nd St mes's

Whitehall and Westminster

0 kilometers 1

0 miles 0.5

Mahatma Gandhi

(1869–1948) Founder of independent India, he studied law at Inner Temple (see p139) in 1889 and ate at the Central, a vegetarian restaurant in St. Bride's Lane.

GREATER LONDON COUNCIL
GENERAL
CHARLES DE GAULLE
President of the
French National Committee
set up
the Headquarters of the
Free French Forces
here in
1940

Charles de Gaulle *(1890–1970)*

In World War II he organized the French Resistance from Carlton House Terrace.

Charlie Chaplin *(1889–1977)*

America's greatest screen comedian was born in south London and lived at No. 287 Kennington Road. He began his career in London's music halls.

Remarkable Londoners

LONDON HAS ALWAYS been a gathering place for the most prominent and influential people of their times. Some of these figures have come to London from other parts of Britain or from countries farther afield; others have been Londoners, born and bred. All of them have left their mark on London, by designing great and lasting buildings, establishing institutions and traditions and writing about or painting the city they knew. Most of them have also had an influence on their times that spread out from London to the rest of the world.

Caricature of the Duke of Wellington

Venus Venticordia by Dante Gabriel Rossetti

ARCHITECTS AND ENGINEERS

John Nash's Theatre Royal Haymarket (1821)

A NUMBER OF PEOPLE who built London still have works standing. Inigo Jones (1573–1652), London-born, was the father of English Renaissance architecture. He was also a landscape painter and stage designer. Jones lived and worked at Great Scotland Yard, Whitehall, then the residence of the royal architect – the post in which he was later succeeded by Sir Christopher Wren (1632–1723).

Wren's successors as the prime architects of London were his protégé Nicholas Hawksmoor (1661–1736) and James Gibbs (1682–1754). Succeeding generations of architects were to stamp their genius on the city: in the 18th century there were brothers Robert (1728–92) and James Adam (1730–94), John Nash (1752–1835), Sir Charles Barry (1795–1860) and Decimus Burton (1800–81). Famous Victorians were Alfred Waterhouse (1830–1905),

Norman Shaw (1831–1912) and Sir George Scott (1811–78). Engineer Sir Joseph Bazalgette (1819–91) built London's sewer system and the Thames Embankment.

ARTISTS

PAINTERS IN LONDON, as elsewhere, often lived in enclaves, for mutual support and because they had common priorities. During the 18th century, artists clustered around the court at St. James's

to be near their patrons. Thus both William Hogarth (1697–1764) and Sir Joshua Reynolds (1723–92) lived and worked in Leicester Square, while Thomas Gainsborough (1727–88) lived in Pall Mall. (Hogarth's Chiswick house was his place in the country.)

Later, Cheyne Walk in Chelsea, with its river views, became popular with artists, including the masters J. M. W. Turner (1775–1851), James McNeill Whistler (1834–1903), Dante Gabriel Rossetti (1828–82), Philip Wilson Steer (1860–1942) and

---

HISTORIC LONDON HOMES

Four writers' homes that have been re-created and are open to visitors are those of the romantic poet **John Keats** (1795–1821), where he fell in love with Fanny Brawne; the historian **Thomas Carlyle** (1795–1881); the lexicographer **Dr. Samuel Johnson** (1709–84); and the prolific and popular novelist **Charles Dickens** (1812–70). The house that the architect **Sir John Soane** (1753–1837) designed for himself remains largely as it was when he died, as does the house where the neurologist **Sigmund Freud** (1856–1939) settled after fleeing from the Nazis before the outbreak of World War II.

Dicken's House

The Hyde Park Corner house of the **Duke of Wellington** (1769–1852), hero of the Battle of Waterloo, is now being refurbished. Finally, the rooms of Sir Arthur Conan Doyle's fictional detective **Sherlock Holmes** have been created in Baker Street.

Carlyle's House

PLAQUES

All over London the former homes of well-known figures are marked by plaques. Watch for these, especially in Chelsea, Kensington and Mayfair, and see how many names you recognize.

No. 3 Sussex Square, Kensington

No. 50 Lawford Road, Islington

No. 56 Oakley Street, Chelsea

---

the sculptor Sir Jacob Epstein (1880–1959). Augustus John (1879–1961) and John Singer Sargent (1856–1925) had studios in Tite Street. John Constable (1776–1837) is best known as a Suffolk painter, but lived for a while at Hampstead from where he painted many fine views of the heath.

WRITERS

G EOFFREY CHAUCER (1345?–1400), author of *The Canterbury Tales*, was born in Upper Thames Street, the son of an inn-keeper. Both the playwrights William Shakespeare (1564–1616) and Christopher Marlowe (1564–93) were associated with the theaters in Southwark and may have lived nearby.

The poets John Donne (1572–1631) and John Milton (1608–74) were both born in Bread Street in the City. Donne, after a profligate youth, became Dean of St. Paul's. The diarist Samuel Pepys (1633–1703) was born off Fleet Street.

The young novelist Jane Austen (1775–1817) lived briefly off Sloane Street, near the Cadogan Hotel, where the flamboyant Oscar Wilde (1854–1900) was arrested in 1895 for homosexuality. Playwright George Bernard Shaw (1856–1950) lived at No. 29 Fitzroy Square in Bloomsbury. Later the same house was home to Virginia Woolf (1882–1941) and

George Bernard Shaw

became a meeting place for the Bloomsbury Group of writers and artists, which included Vanessa Bell, John Maynard Keynes, E. M. Forster, Roger Fry and Duncan Grant.

LEADERS

I N LEGEND, a penniless boy named Dick Whittington came to London with his cat seeking streets paved with gold and later became Lord Mayor. In fact, Richard Whittington (1360?–1423), Lord Mayor three times between 1397 and 1420 and one of London's most celebrated early politicians, was the son of a noble. Sir Thomas More (1478–1535), a Chelsea resident, was Henry VIII's Chancellor until they quarreled over the king's break with the Catholic Church and Henry ordered More's execution. More was canonized in 1935. Sir Thomas Gresham (1519?–79) founded the Royal Exchange. Sir Robert Peel (1788–1850) started the London police force, who were known as "bobbies" after him.

ACTORS

N ELL GWYNNE (1650–87) won more fame as King Charles II's mistress than as an actress. However, she did appear on stage at Drury Lane Theatre; she also sold oranges there. The Shakespearean actor Edmund Kean (1789–1833) and the great

tragic actress Sarah Siddons (1755–1831) were more distinguished players at Drury Lane. So were Henry Irving (1838–1905) and Ellen Terry (1847–1928), whose stage partnership lasted 24 years. Charlie Chaplin (1889–1977, born in Kennington, had a poverty-stricken childhood in the slums of London.

In the 20th century, a school of fine actors blossomed at the Old Vic, including Sir John Gielgud (1904–), Sir Ralph Richardson (1902–83), Dame Peggy Ashcroft (1907–91) and Laurence (later Lord) Olivier (1907–89), who was appointed the first director of the National Theatre.

Laurence Olivier

WHERE TO FIND HISTORIC LONDON HOMES

London's Best: Museums and Galleries

LONDON'S MUSEUMS ARE FILLED with an astonishing diversity of treasures from all over the world. This map highlights 15 of the city's most important galleries and museums, whose exhibits will satisfy most interests. Some of these collections started from the legacies of 18th- and 19th-century explorers, traders and collectors. Others specialize in one aspect of art, history, science or technology. A more detailed overview of London's museums and galleries is on pages 42 and 43.

British Museum
This Anglo-Saxon helmet is part of a massive collection of antiquities.

Wallace Collection
Frans Hals's Laughing Cavalier *is a star attraction in this museum of art, furniture, armor and objets d'art.*

Regent's Park and Marylebone

Royal Academy of Arts
Major international art exhibitions are held here, and the renowned Summer Exhibition, when works are on sale, takes place every year.

Kensington and Holland Park

South Kensington and Knightsbridge

Piccadilly and St. James

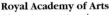

Science Museum
Newcomen's steam engine of 1712 is just one of the many exhibits suited to both novice and expert.

Chelsea

Natural History Museum
All of life is here, with vivid displays on everything from dinosaurs (like this Triceratops skull) to butterflies.

Victoria and Albert
It is the world's largest museum of decorative arts. This Indian vase is 18th-century.

0 kilometers   1

0 miles   0.5

National Portrait Gallery

Important British figures are documented in paintings and photographs. This is Vivien Leigh, by Angus McBean (1954).

National Gallery

The world-famous paintings in its collection are mainly European and date from the 15th to the 19th century.

Museum of London

London's history since prehistoric times is told with exhibits like this 1920s elevator.

Tower of London

The Crown Jewels and the Royal Armories are here. This armor was worn by a 14th-century Italian knight.

Design Museum

New inventions and prototypes sit next to familiar, every-day objects from the past and present.

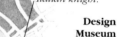

Bloomsbury and Fitzrovia

Holborn and the Inns of Court

Smithfield and Spitalfields

Soho and Trafalgar Square

Covent Garden and the Strand

The City

South Bank

Southwark and Bankside

Whitehall and Westminster

RIVER THAMES

Courtauld Institute

Well-known works, such as Manet's Bar at the Folies Bergère, *line its galleries.*

Tate Gallery

Two outstanding national collections, British art from 1550 and international modern art, are housed here.

Imperial War Museum

It uses displays, films and special effects to re-create 20th-century battles. This is one of the earliest tanks.

Museum of the Moving Image

Actors and life-sized models, like this film director, bring films to life.

Exploring Museums and Galleries

Austin Mini, exhibited at the Design Museum

L ONDON BOASTS astonishingly rich and diverse museums, the products, in part, of centuries at the hub of world-wide trade and a far-flung empire. The world-renowned collections cannot be missed, but do not neglect the city's range of smaller museums. From buses to fans, these cover every imaginable specialty and are often more peaceful than their grander counterparts.

Geffrye Museum: Art Nouveau Room

ANTIQUITIES AND ARCHAEOLOGY

S OME OF THE most celebrated artifacts of ancient Asia, Egypt, Greece and Rome are housed in the **British Museum**. Other antiquities, including books, manuscripts, paintings, busts and gems, are displayed in **Sir John Soane's Museum**, which is one of the most idiosyncratic to be found in London.

The **Museum of London** contains much of archae-ological interest from all periods of the city's history.

Eclectic collection at Sir John Soane's Museum

FURNITURE AND INTERIORS

T HE MUSEUM OF LONDON re-creates typical domestic and commercial interiors from the Roman period right up to the present day. The **Victoria and Albert Museum** (V&A) contains complete rooms rescued from now-vanished buildings, plus a magnificent collection of furniture ranging from 16th-century pieces to contemporary designers' work.

Design Museum display of chairs

On a more modest scale, the **Geffrye Museum** consists of fully furnished period rooms dating from 1600 to the 1930s. Writers' houses *(see p38)* such as the **Freud Museum** give insights into the furniture of specific periods, while the **Linley Sambourne House** offers visitors a perfectly preserved example of a late Victorian interior.

COSTUMES AND JEWELRY

T HE V&A'S VAST collections include English and European clothes of the last 400 years and some stunning jewelry from China, India and Japan. The priceless Crown Jewels, at the **Tower of London**, should not be missed. **Kensington Palace's** Court Dress Collection opens a window on court uniforms and protocol from about 1750. The **Theatre Museum** has displays of costumes, props and other memorabilia, while the **Museum of Mankind** displays Aztec, Mayan and African costumes.

CRAFTS AND DESIGN

O NCE AGAIN, the **V&A** is the essential first port of call; its collections in these fields remain unrivaled. The more specialized **William Morris Gallery** shows every aspect of this designer's work within the Arts and Crafts movement. For more modern craft and design, the **Design Museum** focuses on mass-produced goods, while the **Crafts Council Gallery** and **Contemporary Applied Arts** display (and sometimes sell) contemporary British craftwork.

MILITARY ARTIFACTS

T HE NATIONAL ARMY MUSEUM uses vivid models and displays to narrate the history of the British Army from the reign of Henry VII to to the present. The crack regiments of Foot Guards, who are the elite of the British Army, are the main focus of the **Guards' Museum**. The Royal Armouries in the **Tower of London**, Britain's oldest public museum, hold the national collection of arms and armor; the **Wallace Collection** also has a display. In the **Imperial War Museum** re-creations of World War I trenches and the 1940 Blitz show war as it really was. The **Florence Nightingale Museum** illustrates the hardships of 19th-century warfare.

TOYS AND CHILDHOOD

TEDDY BEARS, toy soldiers, dolls' houses and Dinky cars are just some of the toys in the **London Toy and Model Museum**. **Pollock's Toy Museum** offers a similar collection, including Eric, "the oldest known teddy-bear." The **Bethnal Green Museum of Childhood** and the **Museum of London** are slightly more formal, but still fun, and illustrate aspects of the social history of childhood.

SCIENCE AND NATURAL HISTORY

COMPUTERS, ELECTRICITY, space exploration, industrial processes, and transportation are all featured at the **Science Museum**. Enthusiasts are also catered to at the **London Transport Museum**, where visitors can clamber on subway trains, buses and trams. There are more specialized museums, such as the **Faraday Museum**, of the development of electricity; the **Kew Bridge Steam Museum**; the **National Maritime Museum**; and the **Museum of the Moving Image**. The **Natural History Museum** mixes displays of

animal and bird life with innovative ecological exhibits. The **Museum of Garden History** is devoted to what is said to be the British people's favorite pastime.

Imperial War Museum

VISUAL ARTS

THE PARTICULAR STRENGTHS of the **National Gallery** are early Renaissance Italian and 17th-century Spanish painting and a wonderful collection of Dutch masters. The **Tate Gallery** specializes in 20th-century art from both Europe and America, and British paintings of all periods; the Clore Gallery is devoted to the work of Turner. The **V&A** is strong on European art from 1500 to 1900 and British art from 1700 to 1900. The **Royal Academy** and the **Hayward**

Stone Dancer (1913) **by Gaudier-Brzeska at the Tate Gallery**

Gallery specialize in major temporary exhibitions. The **Courtauld Institute** contains Impressionist and Post-Impressionist works, while the **Wallace Collection** has 17th-century Dutch and 18th-century French paintings. The **Dulwich Picture Gallery** includes works by Rembrandt, Rubens, Poussin and Gainsborough. **Kenwood House** is home to paintings by Reynolds, Gainsborough and Rubens in fine Adam interiors. Details of temporary exhibitions are in listings magazines *(see p324)*.

WHERE TO FIND THE COLLECTIONS

Samson and Delilah (1620) **by Van Dyck at the Dulwich Picture Gallery**

London's Best: Churches

IT IS WORTH stopping to look at London's churches and going in if they're open. They have a special atmosphere unmatched elsewhere, and they can often yield an intimate glimpse of the past. Many churches have replaced earlier buildings in a steady succession dating back to pre-Christian times. Some began life in outlying villages beyond London's fortified center and were absorbed into suburbs when the city expanded in the 18th century. The memorials in the capital's churches and churchyards are a fascinating record of local life, liberally peppered with famous names. A more detailed overview of London churches is on pages 46–7.

All Souls
This plaque comes from a tomb in John Nash's Regency church of 1824.

St. Paul's, Covent Garden
Inigo Jones's Classical church was known as "the handsomest barn in England."

Regent's Park and Marylebone

Bloomsbury and Fitzrovia

Soho and Trafalgar Square

Piccadilly and St. James's

St. Martin-in-the Fields
James Gibbs's church of 1722 to 1726 was originally thought "too gay" for Protestant worship.

South Kensington and Knightsbridge

| 0 kilometers | 1 |
| 0 miles | 0.5 |

Whitehall and Westminster

Westminster Cathedral
This Italian-Byzantine Catholic cathedral's red-and-white brick exterior conceals a rich interior of multicolored marbles.

Westminster Abbey
The famous abbey has the most glorious medieval architecture in London, plus highly impressive tombs and monuments.

Brompton Oratory
This sumptuous Baroque church was decorated with works by Italian artists.

St. Mary-le-Strand
Now on a traffic island, this shiplike church was built by James Gibbs from 1714 to 1717 to a lively Baroque design. Featuring high windows and rich interior detailing, it was made solid enough to keep out street noise.

Smithfield and Spitalfields

St. Mary Woolnoth
The jewel-like interior of Nicholas Hawksmoor's small Baroque church (1716–27) appears larger than the outside.

Holborn and the Inns of Court

Covent Garden and the Strand

The City

St. Stephen Walbrook
Wren was at his best with this domed interior of 1672 to 1677. Its carvings include Henry Moore's austere modern altar.

South Bank

Southwark and Bankside

St. Paul's
At 360ft (110m) high, the dome of Wren's cathedral is the world's second largest after St. Peter's in Rome.

Temple Church
Built in the 12th and 13th centuries for the Knights Templar, this is one of the few circular churches to survive in England.

Southwark Cathedral
This largely 13th-century priory church was not designated a cathedral until 1905. It has a fine medieval choir.

Exploring Churches

THE CHURCH SPIRES that punctuate London's skyline span nearly a thousand years of the city's history. They form an index to many of the events that have shaped the city – the Norman Conquest (1066); the Great Fire of London (1666); the great restoration, led by Wren, that followed it; the Regency period; the confidence of the Victorian era; and the devastation of World War II. Each has had its effect on the churches, many designed by the most influential architects of their times.

St. Paul's, Covent Garden

MEDIEVAL CHURCHES

THE MOST FAMOUS old church to survive the Great Fire of 1666 is the superb 13th-century **Westminster Abbey**, the church of the Coronation, with its tombs of British monarchs and heroes. Less well known are the well-hidden Norman church of **St. Bartholomew-the-Great**, London's oldest church, (1123), the circular **Temple Church** founded in 1160 by the Knights Templar, and **Southwark Cathedral**, set amid Victorian railroad lines and warehouses. **Chelsea Old Church** is a charming village church near the river.

CHURCHES BY JONES

INIGO JONES (1573–1652) was Shakespeare's contemporary, and his works were almost as revolutionary as the great dramatist's. Jones's Classical churches of the 1620s and 1630s shocked a public used to conservative Gothic finery. By far the best known is **St. Paul's Church** of the 1630s, the centerpiece of Jones's Italian-style piazza in Covent Garden. **Queen's Chapel, St. James**, was built in 1623 for Queen Henrietta Maria, the Catholic wife of Charles I. It was the first Classical church in England and has a magnificent interior but is, unfortunately, usually closed to the public.

CHURCHES BY HAWKSMOOR

NICHOLAS HAWKSMOOR (1661–1736) was Wren's most talented pupil, and his churches are among the finest

SPIRES

Look out for London's richly decorated church steeples. Here are four of the city's most distinctive to get you started.

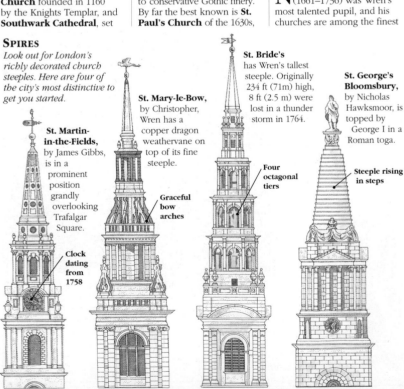

St. Martin-in-the-Fields, by James Gibbs, is in a prominent position grandly overlooking Trafalgar Square.

Clock dating from 1758

St. Mary-le-Bow, by Christopher, Wren has a copper dragon weathervane on top of its fine steeple.

Graceful bow arches

St. Bride's has Wren's tallest steeple. Originally 234 ft (71m) high, 8 ft (2.5 m) were lost in a thunder storm in 1764.

Four octagonal tiers

St. George's Bloomsbury, by Nicholas Hawksmoor, is topped by George I in a Roman toga.

Steeple rising in steps

British Baroque buildings.
St. George's, Bloomsbury
(1716–31), has an unusual
centralized plan and a
pyramid steeple topped by a
statue of King George I. **St.
Mary Woolnoth** is a tiny
jewel of 1716 to 1727, and
further east **Christ Church,
Spitalfields** is a Baroque
tour-de-force of 1714 to 1729,
now being restored.

Among Hawksmoor's East
End churches are the stunning
St. Anne's, Limehouse and
St. Alfege, of 1714 to 1717,
which is across the river in
Greenwich. The tower on this
templelike church was added
later by John James in 1730.

St. Anne's, Limehouse

CHURCHES BY GIBBS

JAMES GIBBS (1682–1754)
more conservative than his
Baroque contemporaries,
such as Hawksmoor, and he
also kept his distance from
the Neoclassical trend so
popular after 1720. His
idiosyncratic London
churches were enormously
influential. **St. Mary-le-
Strand** (1714–17) is an island
church that appears to be
sailing down the Strand. The
radical design of **St. Martin-
in-the-Fields** (1722–26)
predates its setting, Trafalgar
Square, by a hundred years.

REGENCY CHURCHES

THE END OF the Napoleonic
Wars in 1815 brought a
flurry of church building.
The need for churches in
London's new suburbs
inspired a growth of Greek

CHRISTOPHER WREN

Sir Christopher Wren
(1632–1723) was
leader among the
many architects
who helped restore
London after the
Great Fire of
London. He devised
a new city plan,
replacing the narrow
streets with wide avenues
radiating from piazzas. His
plan was rejected, but he
was commissioned to build
52 new churches; 31 have
survived various threats of
demolition and the bombs
of World War II, although 6
are shells. Wren's great
masterpiece is the massive

St. Paul's, while
nearby is splendid
**St. Stephen
Walbrook**, his
domed church of
1672 to 1677.
Other landmarks
are **St. Bride's**, off
Fleet Street, said to
have inspired the
traditional shape of wedding
cakes, **St. Mary-le-Bow** in
Cheapside and **St. Magnus
Martyr** in Lower Thames
Street. Wren's own favorite
was **St. James's, Piccadilly**
(1683–4). Smaller gems are
St. Clement Danes, Strand
(1680–82) and **St. James,
Garlickhythe** (1674–87).

Revival styles. The results
may lack the exuberance of
Hawksmoor's work, but they
have an austere elegance. **All
Souls, Langham Place**
(1822–24), at the north end of
Regent Street, was built by the
Prince Regent's favorite, John
Nash, who was ridiculed at the
time for its unusual
combination of design styles.
Also worth visiting is
St. Pancras, a Greek Revival
church (1819–22), which is
typical of the period.

VICTORIAN CHURCHES

LONDON HAS SOME of the
finest 19th-century
churches in Europe. Grand
and colorful, they bear
riotous decoration that is in
marked contrast to the chaste
Neoclassicism of the
preceding Regency era.
Perhaps the best of the
capital's late Victorian
churches is **Westminster**

Brompton Oratory

Cathedral, a stunning
Italianate Catholic cathedral
built from 1895 to 1903, with
architecture by J. F. Bentley
and *Stations of the Cross*
reliefs by Eric Gill. **Brompton
Oratory** is a grand Baroque
revival, based on a church in
Rome and filled with
magnificent furnishings from
all over Catholic Europe.

WHERE TO FIND THE CHURCHES

London's Best: Parks and Gardens

SINCE MEDIEVAL TIMES London has had large expanses of green. Some of these, such as Hampstead Heath, were originally common land, where those lacking sufficient space could graze their animals. Other areas such as Richmond Park and Holland Park, were royal hunting grounds or estate gardens; several still have formal features dating from those times. Today you can cross much of central London by walking from St. James's Park in the east to Kensington Gardens in the west. Formal parks, like Battersea, and botanical gardens, like Kew, appeared later.

Hampstead Heath
This breezy open space is located in the midst of north London. Nearby Parliament Hill offers views of St. Paul's, the City and the West End.

Kensington Gardens
This plaque is from the Italian Garden, one of the features of this elegant park.

Holland Park
The former grounds of one of London's grandest homes are now its most romantic park.

Kew Gardens
The world's premier botanical garden is a must for anyone with an interest in plants, exotic or mundane.

| 0 kilometers | 1 |
| 0 miles | 0.5 |

Richmond Park
The biggest royal park in London remains largely unspoiled, with deer and magnificent river views.

Regent's Park
In this civilized park surrounded by fine Regency buildings, you can stroll around the rose garden, visit the open-air theater, or simply sit and admire the view.

Greenwich Park
Its focal point is the National Maritime Museum, well worth a visit for its architecture as well as its exhibits. There are also fine views.

Hyde Park
The Serpentine is one of the highlights of a park that also boasts restaurants, an art gallery and Speakers' Corner.

gent's rk and rylebone

Bloomsbury and Fitzrovia

Holborn and the Inns of Court

Smithfield and Spitalfields

Soho and Trafalgar Square

Piccadilly

The City

R I V E R T H A M E S

The South-bank

Southwark and Bankside

Whitehall and Westminster

Greenwich and Blackheath

N

Green Park
Its leafy paths are favored by early-morning joggers from the Mayfair hotels.

Battersea Park
Visitors can rent a rowboat for the best view of the Victorian landscaping around the lake.

St. James's Park
People come here to feed the ducks or watch the pelicans. A band plays throughout the summer.

Exploring Parks and Gardens

LONDON HAS ONE of the the world's greenest city centers, full of tree-filled squares and grassy parks. From the intimacy of the the Chelsea Physic Garden, to the wild, open spaces of Hampstead Heath, every London park has its own charm and character. For those looking for a specific outdoor attraction – such as sports, wildlife or flowers – here is a list of the most interesting London parks.

Camilla japonica

FLOWER GARDENS

THE BRITISH are famed for their gardens and love of flowers, and this is reflected in several of London's parks. Really avid gardeners will find all they ever wanted to know at **Kew Gardens** and at the **Chelsea Physic Garden**, which is especially strong on herbs. Closer to the center of town, **St. James's Park** boasts some spectacular flower beds, filled with bulbs and bedding plants, which are changed every season. **Hyde Park** sports a magnificent show of daffodils and crocuses in the spring, and London's best rose garden is Queen Mary's

situated in **Regent's Park**. **Kensington Gardens'** flower walk has an exemplary English mixed border, and there is also a delightful small 17th-century garden at the **Museum of Garden History**. **Battersea Park** also has a charming flower garden, and indoor gardeners should head to the **Barbican Centre's** well-stocked conservatory.

FORMAL GARDENS

THE MOST SPECTACULAR formal garden is at **Hampton Court**, which has a network of gardens from different periods, starting with Tudor. The gardens at **Chiswick**

Embankment Gardens

House remain dotted with their 18th-century statuary and pavilions. Other restored gardens include 17th-century **Ham House** and **Osterley Park**, whose 18th-century layout was retraced through the art of dowsing. **Fenton House** has a really fine walled garden; **Kenwood** is less formal, with its woodland area. **The Hill** is great in summer. The sunken garden at **Kensington Palace** has a formal layout and **Holland Park** has flowers around its statues.

RESTFUL CORNERS

LONDON'S SQUARES are cool, shady retreats, but, sadly, many are reserved for key-holders, usually residents of the surrounding houses. Of those open to all, **Russell Square** is the largest and most secluded. **Berkeley Square** is open but barren. **Green Park**, with its shady trees and deck chairs, offers a cool picnic spot right in central London. The Inns of Court provide some really pleasant havens: **Gray's Inn** gardens, **Middle Temple**

Sunken garden at Kensington Palace

GREEN LONDON

In Greater London there are 1,700 parks covering a total of 67 sq miles (174 sq km). This land is home to some 2,000 types of plants and 100 bird species who breed in the trees. Trees help the city to breathe, manu-facturing oxygen from the polluted air. Here are some of the species most likely to be seen in London.

The London plane, now the most common tree in London, grows along many streets.

The English oak grows all over Europe. The Royal Navy used to build ships from it.

gardens and **Lincoln's Inn Fields**. **Soho Square,** which is surrounded by streets, is more urban and animated.

Music in Summer

S TRETCHING OUT on the grass or in a deck chair to listen to a band is a British tradition. Military and other bands give regular concerts throughout the summer at **St. James's** and **Regent's parks** and also at **Parliament Hill Fields**. The concert schedule will usually be found posted up close to the bandstand in the park.

Open-air festivals of classical music are held in the summer in several parks (*see p331*).

Wildlife

T HERE IS A LARGE and well-fed collection of ducks and other water birds, even including a few pelicans, in **St. James's Park**. Duck lovers will also appreciate **Regent's, Hyde** and **Battersea Parks,** as well as **Hampstead Heath.** Deer roam in **Richmond** and **Greenwich Parks.** For a wide variety of captive animals, **London Zoo** is in **Regent's Park**, and there are aviaries or aquariums at several parks and gardens, including **Kew Gardens** and **Syon House**.

Geese in St. James's Park

HISTORIC CEMETERIES

In the late 1830s a ring of private cemeteries was established around London to ease the pressure on the monstrously overcrowded and un-healthy burial grounds of the inner city. Today some of these (notably **Highgate Cemetery** and **Kensal Green** – Harrow Road W10) are worth visiting for their air of repose and their Victorian monuments. The older **Bunhill Fields** was first used during the plague of 1665.

Kensal Green cemetery

Boating pond at Regent's Park

Sports

C YCLING IS NOT universally encouraged in London's parks, and footpaths tend to be too bumpy to allow much rollerskating. However, most parks have tennis courts, which normally have to be reserved in advance with the attendant. Rowboats may be rented at **Hyde, Regent's** and **Battersea Parks,** among others. Athletics tracks are at both Battersea Park and also **Parliament Hill**. The public may swim at the ponds on **Hampstead Heath** and in the Serpentine in Hyde Park. Hampstead Heath is also ideal kite-flying territory.

WHERE TO FIND THE PARKS

The common beech has a close relation, the copper beech, with reddish purple leaves.

The horse chestnut's hard round fruits are used by children for a game called conkers.

London's Best: Ceremonies

MUCH OF LONDON'S rich inheritance of tradition and ceremony centers on royalty. Faithfully enacted today, some of these ceremonies date back to the Middle Ages, when the ruling monarch had absolute power and had to be protected from opponents. This map shows the venues for some of the most important ceremonies in London. For more details on these and other ceremonies, please turn to pages 54 and 55; information on various events taking place in London throughout the year can be found on pages 56 to 59.

St. James's Palace and Buckingham Palace
Members of the Queen's Life Guard stand in front of the two royal palaces. The Guard is changed daily in summer.

Bloomsbury and Fitzroy

Soho and Trafalgar Square

South Kensington and Knightsbridge

Piccadilly and St. James's

Whitehall and Westminster

Hyde Park
A Royal Salute is fired from a cannon in the park on six royal anniversaries each year and also on other special occasions.

Chelsea

Chelsea Hospital
In 1651, Charles II hid from parliamentary forces in an oak tree. On Oak Apple Day, Chelsea Pensioners decorate his statue with oak leaves and branches.

Horse Guards
At Trooping the Colour, the most elaborate of London's royal ceremonies, the Queen salutes as a battalion of Foot Guards parades its colors before her.

The City and Embankment
At the Lord Mayor's Show, pikemen and musketeers escort the newly elected Lord Mayor through the City in a gold state coach.

The Cenotaph
On Remembrance Sunday, the Queen pays homage to the nation's war dead.

Holborn and the Inns of Court

vent en and Strand

The City

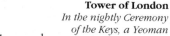

R I V E R   T H A M E S

South Bank

Southwark and Bankside

Tower of London
In the nightly Ceremony of the Keys, a Yeoman Warder locks the gates. A military escort ensures the keys are not stolen.

0 kilometers	1
0 miles	0.5

Houses of Parliament
Each autumn, the Queen goes to Parliament in the Irish State Coach to open the new parliamentary session.

Attending London's Ceremonies

Royalty and commerce provide the two principal sources of London's rich calendar of ceremonial events. Quaint and old-fashioned these events may be, but what may seem arcane ritual has real historical meaning – many of the capital's ceremonies originated in the the Middle Ages.

ROYAL CEREMONIES

Although the Queen's role is now largely symbolic, the Guard at Buckingham Palace still actively patrols the palace grounds. The impressive ceremony of **Changing of the Guard** – dazzling uniforms, shouted commands, martial music – consists of the Old Guard, which forms up in the palace forecourt, going off duty and handing over to the New Guard. The Guard consists of 3 officers and 40 men when the Queen is in residence, but only 3 officers and 31 men when she is away. The ceremony takes place in full public view, right in front of the palace. The Guard is also changed at Horse Guards and on Tower Green, at the Tower of London.

One of the Queen's Life Guards

A Queen's Guard in winter

The **Ceremony of the Keys** at the Tower of London is one of the capital's most timeless ceremonies. After each of the Tower gates has been locked, the last post is sounded by a trumpeter before the keys are secured in the Queen's House.

The Tower of London and Hyde Park are also the scene of **Royal Salutes** which take place on birthdays and other occasions throughout the year. At such times 41 rounds are fired in Hyde Park at noon and 62 rounds at the Tower at 1pm. The spectacle in Hyde Park is a stirring one as 71 horses and six 13-pounder cannons swirl into place and the roar of the guns begins.

The combination of pageantry, color and music makes the annual **Trooping the Colour** the high point of London's ceremonial year. The Queen takes the Royal Salute, and after her troops have marched past, she leads them to Buckingham Palace, where a second march past takes place. The best place to watch this spectacle is from the Horse Guards Parade side of St. James's Park.

Bands of the Household Cavalry and the Foot Guards stage the ceremony of **Beating the Retreat** at Horse Guards Parade. This takes place three or four evenings a week in the two weeks before the **Trooping the Colour**. The spectacular **State Opening of Parliament**, when the Queen opens the annual parliamentary session in the House of Lords – usually in November – is not open to the general public, although it is now televised. The huge royal procession, which moves from Buckingham Palace to Westminster, is a magnificent sight, with the Queen traveling in the highly ornate Irish State Coach drawn by four horses.

MILITARY CEREMONIES

The cenotaph in Whitehall is the setting for a ceremony held on **Remembrance Sunday**, to give thanks to those who died fighting in the two world wars.

National **Navy Day** is commemorated by a parade down the Mall, followed by a service held at Nelson's Column in Trafalgar Square.

Royal salute, Tower of London

Changing the Guard, Tower of London

Silent Change Ceremony in Guildhall for the new Lord Mayor

CEREMONIES IN THE CITY

NOVEMBER IS THE focus of the City of London's ceremonial year. At the **Silent Change** in Guildhall, the outgoing Lord Mayor hands over symbols of office to the new mayor in a virtually wordless ceremony. The following day sees the rumbustious **Lord Mayor's Show**. Accompanying the Lord Mayor in his gold state coach, a procession of bands, decorated floats and military detachments makes its way through from Guildhall past the Mansion House to the Law Courts and back again along the Embankment.

Lord Mayor's chain of office

Many of the ceremonies that take place in the City are linked to the activities of the Livery Companies (see p152). These include the Worshipful Companies of **Vintners' and Distillers'** annual celebration of the wine harvest and the Stationers' **Cakes and Ale Sermon**, held in St. Paul's. Cakes and ale are provided according to the will of a 17th-century stationer.

NAME-DAY CEREMONIES

EVERY MAY 21 **King Henry VI**, who was murdered in the Tower of London in 1471, is still remembered by the members of his two famous foundations, Eton College and King's College, Cambridge, who meet for a ceremony at the Wakefield Tower, where he was killed. **Oak Apple Day** commemorates King Charles II's lucky escape from the Parliamentary forces of Oliver Cromwell in 1651. The King managed to conceal himself in a hollow oak tree, and today Chelsea Pensioners honor his memory by decorating his statue at Chelsea Hospital with oak leaves and branches. On December 18, the diarist **Dr Johnson** is commemorated in an annual service held at Westminster Abbey.

INFORMAL CEREMONIES

EACH JULY, six guildsmen from the Company of Watermen compete for the prize in **Doggett's Coat and Badge Race**. In autumn, the **Pearly Kings and Queens**, representatives of east London's traders, meet at St. Martin-in-the-Fields. In March children get fruit at the **Oranges and Lemons service** at St. Clement Danes Church. In February, clowns attend a service for famous clown **Joseph Grimaldi** (1779–1837) at the Holy Trinity Church in Dalston E8.

Pearly Queen

WHERE TO FIND THE CEREMONIES

Beating the Retreat
Horse Guards p80, date arranged during first two weeks of June.

Cakes and Ale Sermon
St. Paul's pp148–51, Ash Wed.

Ceremony of the Keys
Tower of London pp154–7, 9:30pm daily. Tickets from the Tower, but reserve well in advance.

Changing of the Guard
Buckingham Palace pp94–5, Apr–Jul: 11:30am daily; Aug–Mar: alternate days. Horse Guards p80, 1pm daily. Tower of London pp154–7, noon daily.

Doggett's Coat and Badge Race
From London Bridge to Cadogan Pier, Chelsea pp189 –93, July.

Dr Johnson Memorial
Westminster Abbey pp76–9, Dec 18.

Joseph Grimaldi Memorial
Holy Trinity Church, Dalston E8, Feb 7.

King Henry VI Memorial
Wakefield Tower, Tower of London pp154–7, May 21.

Lord Mayor's Show
The City pp143–53, second Sat Nov.

Navy Day
Trafalgar Sq p102, Oct 21.

Oak Apple Day
Royal Hospital p193, Thu after May 29.

Oranges and Lemons Service
St. Clement Danes p138, Mar.

Pearly Kings and Queens Harvest Festival
St. Martin-in-the-Fields p102, autumn.

Remembrance Sunday
Cenotaph p74, Sun nearest Nov 11.

Royal Salutes
Hyde Park p207, royal anniversaries and other state occasions.

Silent Change
Guildhall p159, second Fri in Nov.

State Opening of Parliament, Houses of Parliament pp72–3, Oct–Nov. Procession from Buckingham Palace pp94–5 to Westminster.

Trooping the Colour
Horse Guards p80, 2nd Sat Jun (rehearsals on previous two Sats). Limited tickets from headquarters Household Division, Horse Guards.

Vintners' and Distillers' Wine Harvest
St. Olave's Church, Hart St EC3, second Tue in Oct.

LONDON THROUGH THE YEAR

SPRINGTIME IN London carries an almost tangible air of a city waking up to longer days and outdoor pursuits. The cheerful yellow daffodil blooms stud the parks, and less-hardy Londoners take their first jog of the year, finding themselves in the wake of serious runners in training for the Marathon. As spring turns into summer, the royal parks reach their full glory, and in Kensington Gardens, nannies gather to chat under chestnut trees. As autumn takes hold, those same trees blaze with red and gold, and Londoners' thoughts turn to afternoons in museums and art galleries, followed by tea in a café. The year draws to a close with Guy Fawkes parties and holiday shopping in the West End. Contact the London Tourist Board *(see p345)* or check the magazines *(p325)* for details of seasonal events.

SPRING

THE WEATHER during the spring months may be raw, and an umbrella is a necessary precaution. Druids celebrate the equinox in a subdued ceremony on Tower Hill. Painters compete to have their works hung at the Royal Academy. Footballers (soccer players) close their season with the FA Cup Final at Wembley, while cricketers begin theirs. Oxford and Cambridge universities hold their annual boat race along the Thames, and Marathon runners pound the streets.

Runners in the London Marathon passing Tower Bridge

MARCH

Chelsea Antiques Fair *(second week)*, Chelsea Old Town Hall, King's Rd SW3.
Ideal Home Exhibition *(second week)*, Earl's Court, Warwick Rd SW5. It is a long-established show with the latest in domestic gadgetry and state-of-the-art technology.
Oranges and Lemons Service, St. Clement Danes *(p55)*. Service for school-children; each child is given an orange and a lemon.
Oxford vs. Cambridge boat race *(Sat before Easter, or Easter)*, Putney to Mortlake *(p337)*.
Spring Equinox celebration *(Mar 21)*, Tower Hill EC3. Subdued pagan ceremony with modern-day druids.

EASTER

Good Friday and Monday are public holidays. **Easter parades**, Covent Garden *(p114)*, Battersea Park *(p247)*.

Kite flying, Blackheath *(p239)* and Hampstead Heath *(p230)*.
Easter procession and hymns *(Easter Mon)*, Westminster Abbey *(pp76–9)*. One of London's most evocative religious celebrations.
International Model Railway Exhibition *(Easter weekend)*, Royal Horticultural Hall, Vincent Sq SW1. Of real interest to everyone, not just railroad enthusiasts.

A London park in the spring

APRIL

Queen's Birthday gun salutes *(Apr 21)*, Hyde Park, Tower of London *(p54)*.
London Marathon *(Sun in Apr or May)*, Greenwich to Westminster *(p337)*.

MAY

First and last Mondays are public holidays.
FA Cup Final, Wembley. Football (Soccer) season's climax *(p336)*.
Henry VI Memorial *(p55)*.
Beating the Bounds *(Ascension Day)*, throughout the City. Young boys from the City parish hit certain buildings, marking parish boundaries.
Oak Apple Day, at the Royal Hospital, Chelsea *(p55)*.
Funfairs *(late May public hol weekend)*, various commons.
Chelsea Flower Show *(late May)*, Royal Hospital, Chelsea.
Beating the Retreat *(p54)*.
Royal Academy Summer Exhibition *(May–Jul)*, Piccadilly *(p90)*.

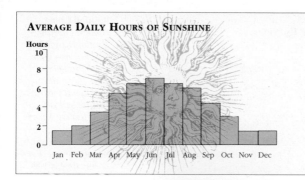

AVERAGE DAILY HOURS OF SUNSHINE

Hours

Jan Feb Mar Apr May Jun Jul Aug Sep Oct Nov Dec

Sunshine Chart
London's longest and hottest days fall between May and August. In the height of summer, daylight hours can extend from well before 5am to after 9pm. Daytime is much shorter in the winter, but London can be stunning in the winter sunshine.

SUMMER

LONDON'S SUMMER season is packed full of indoor and outdoor events. The weather is very unreliable, even at the height of summer, but unless you are notably unlucky, there should be enough fine days to sample what is available.

The selection includes many traditional events, such as the Wimbledon tennis championships and the many cricket test matches at Lord's and the Oval. Well out of view from the general public and prying photographers, the Queen holds garden parties for favored subjects on the splendid grounds of Buckingham Palace. Summertime public holidays are also studded with fairs in most of London's parks.

JUNE

Morris dancing *(Wed eves, all summer)*, Westminster Abbey *(pp76–9)*. Traditional English folk dancing.
Coronation Day gun salutes *(Jun 2)*, Hyde Park and Tower of London *(p54)*.
Ceramics fair, Dorchester Hotel, Park Lane W1.
Fine Art and Antiques fair, Olympia, Olympia Way W14.
Trooping the Colour, Horse Guards *(p54)*.
Charles Dickens memorial service *(Jun 9)*, Westminster Abbey *(pp76–9)*. Celebration of London's famous author.
Duke of Edinburgh's Birthday gun salutes *(Jun 10)*, Hyde Park and Tower of London *(p54)*.
Wimbledon Lawn Tennis Championships *(two weeks in late Jun; p336)*.

Revelers at Notting Hill Carnival

Cricket test match, Lord's *(p336)*.
Open-air theater Shakespeare season *(throughout the summer)*, Regent's Park and Holland Park. The perfect opportunity for a picnic *(p326)*.
Open-air concerts, Kenwood, Hampstead Heath, Crystal Palace, Marble Hill, St. James's Park *(p331)*.
Street theater festival *(Jun–Jul)*, Covent Garden *(p114)*. Street performers of every kind gather to flaunt their various talents.
Summer festivals *(late Jun)*, Greenwich, Spitalfields and Primrose Hill. Contact the London Tourist Board *(p345)* or see the listings magazines *(p325)* for times and venues of all these events.

JULY

Summer festivals, City of London and Richmond.
Sales. Price reductions across London's shops *(p311)*.

Doggett's Coat and Badge Race *(p55)*.
Hampton Court Flower Show, Hampton Court Palace *(pp250–3)*.
Royal Tournament *(mid-Jul)*, Earl's Court, Warwick Rd SW5. Impressive military spectacle put on by members of the combined armed forces.
Capital Radio Jazz Festival, Royal Festival Hall *(p184)*.
Henry Wood Promenade Concerts *(late Jul–Sep)*, Royal Albert Hall *(p203)*.

AUGUST

Last Monday is a public holiday.
Queen Mother's Birthday gun salutes *(Aug 4)*, Hyde Park and Tower of London *(p54)*.
Notting Hill Carnival *(late Aug holiday weekend)*. Organized by the area's ethnic communities *(p215)*.
Funfairs *(Aug holiday)*, throughout London's parks.

Regimental band, St. James's Park

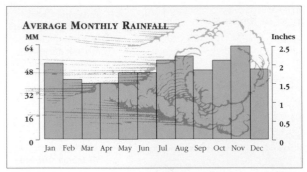

Rainfall Chart
*London's average
monthly rainfall
remains much the
same throughout the
year. July and August,
the capital's warmest
months, are also two
of its wettest. Rain is
less likely in spring,
but visitors should be
prepared for a shower
at any time of year.*

AUTUMN

THERE IS A SENSE of purpose about London in autumn. The build-up to the busiest shopping season, the start of the academic year and the new parliamentary session, opened by the Queen, inject some life into the colder months. The cricket season comes to an end in mid-September, while food-lovers may be interested in the spectacular displays of fresh fish that are laid out in the vestry of St. Mary-at-the-Hill, celebrating the harvest of this island nation.

Memories of a more turbulent opening of Parliament are revived on November 5, when there are bonfires and fireworks to commemorate the failure of a conspiracy led by Guy Fawkes to blow up the Palace of Westminster in 1605. A few days later, the dead of two world wars are commemorated at a ceremony held in Whitehall.

Pearly Kings gathering for the harvest festival at St. Martin-in-the-Fields

SEPTEMBER

National Rose Society Annual Show, Royal Horticultural Hall, Vincent Sq W1.
Chelsea Antiques Fair *(third week)*, Chelsea Old Town Hall, King's Road SW3.
Last Night of the Proms *(late Sep)*, Royal Albert Hall *(p203)*.

OCTOBER

Pearly Harvest Festival *(Oct 3)*, St. Martin-in-the-Fields *(p55)*.
Punch and Judy Festival *(Oct 3)*, Covent Garden WC2. Celebration of puppet duo.
Horse of the Year Show *(early Oct)*, Wembley *(p337)*. London's equestrian showpiece.
Harvest of the Sea *(second Sun)*, St. Mary-at-Hill Church *(p152)*.
Vintners' and Distillers' Wine Harvest *(p55)*.
Navy Day *(p54)*.

State Opening of Parliament *(p54)*.

NOVEMBER

Guy Fawkes Night *(Nov 5)*. Magazines give details of fireworks displays *(p324)*.
Remembrance Day Service *(p54)*.
Silent Change *(p55)*.
Lord Mayor's Show *(p55)*.
London to Brighton veteran car run *(first Sun)*. Starts in Hyde Park *(p207)*.
Christmas lights *(late Nov–Jan 6)*, West End *(p313)*.

London-to-Brighton veteran car run

Autumn colors in a London park

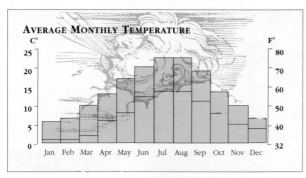

AVERAGE MONTHLY TEMPERATURE

Temperature Chart
The chart shows the average minimum and maximum temperatures for each month. Top temperatures averaging 22° C (75° F) belie London's reputation for year-round chilliness, although November through February see icy conditions.

WINTER

SOME OF THE most striking images of London are drawn from winter: paintings of frost fairs in the 17th and 18th centuries, when the River Thames froze over completely; and Claude Monet's views of the river and its bridges.

For centuries thick "pea-souper" fogs were an inevitable part of winter, until the Clean Air Act of 1956 barred coalburning in open grates.

Christmas trees and lights twinkle everywhere – from the West End shopping streets to construction sites. The scent of roasting chestnuts pervades as street peddlers sell them from glowing mobile braziers.

Seasonal menus feature roast turkey, mince pies and rich, dark Christmas pudding. Traditional fare in theaters includes colorful family pantomimes (where the customary cross-dressing between the sexes baffles many visitors – *p326*) and popular ballets such as *Swan Lake* and *The Nutcracker*.

Skaters use the open-air rink at the Broadgate Centre in the City, and sometimes it is safe to venture onto the frozen lakes in the parks.

PUBLIC HOLIDAYS
New Year's Day (Jan 1); **Good Friday; Easter Monday; May Day** (first Monday in May); **Whit Monday** (last Monday in May); **August Bank Holiday** (last Monday in August); **Christmas** (December 25–26).

Winter in Kensington Gardens

DECEMBER

Oxford vs. Cambridge rugby union match *(mid-Dec)*, Twickenham *(p337)*.
Dr. Johnson memorial service *(Dec 18)*, Westminster Abbey *(p55)*.

CHRISTMAS AND NEW YEAR

Dec 25–26 and Jan 1 are public hols. There is no train service on Christmas Day.
Carol services *(each*

evening leading up to Christmas)*, Trafalgar Square *(p102)*, St. Paul's *(pp148–51)*, Westminster Abbey *(pp76–9)* and other churches.
Turkey auction *(Dec 24)*, Smithfield Market *(p164)*.
Christmas Day swim Serpentine, Hyde Park *(p207)*.
New Year's Eve celebrations *(Dec 31)*, Trafalgar Square, St. Paul's.

JANUARY

Sales *(p311)*.
International Boat Show, Earl's Court, Warwick Rd SW5.
International Mime Festival *(mid Jan– early Feb)*, various venues.
Charles I Commemoration *(last Sun)*, procession from St. James's Palace *(p91)* to Banqueting House *(p80)*.
Chinese New Year *(late Jan–early Feb)*, Chinatown *(p108)* and Soho *(p109)*.

FEBRUARY

Clowns' Service *(first Sun)*, Dalston *(p55)*.
Queen's Accession gun salutes *(Feb 6)*, 41-gun salute Hyde Park; 62-gun salute Tower of London *(p54)*.
Pancake races *(Shrove Tue)*, Lincoln's Inn Fields *(p137)* and Covent Garden *(p114)*.

Christmas illuminations in Trafalgar Square

A River View of London

IN OLD Celtic, the word for river was *teme*, and the Romans adopted this as the name for the great waterway upon which they founded the city of *Londinium (see pp16–17)* nearly 2,000 years ago. The Roman settlers built their new city along the most easterly point at which the river could be bridged using the technology of the time. Since then, the Thames has continued to play a critical role in London's history. It was the route taken by the Viking invaders of the 8th and 9th centuries, the birthplace of the Royal Navy in Tudor times, and the artery for much of the country's commerce until well into the 1950s.

Now, changing trade patterns have caused the big ships to move elsewhere, and the river has become the capital's foremost leisure

Decoration on Southwark Bridge

amenity instead. Where once stood wharves and many warehouses, today there are riverside walks, marinas, bars and restaurants.

One of the most interesting ways of seeing the capital is by boat, and several companies offer sightseeing cruises from central London. These vary in length from 30 minutes to 4 hours. The most popular section of the river to travel runs downstream from the Houses of Parliament to Tower Bridge. A river view gives you a very different perspective of London's major sites, including Traitors' Gate, the infamous river entrance to the Tower of London, which was used for prisoners brought from trial in Westminster Hall *(see pp72–3)*. You can also take longer journeys past the varied architectural styles found between Hampton Court and the Thames Barrier.

The Thames in London
Passenger boat services cover about 30 miles (50 km) of the Thames, from Hampton Court in the west to the Thames Barrier in the former Docklands of the east.

Houseboats at Chelsea

TOUR COMPANIES

Most of these services run from May 6 until the end of October, when they revert to winter schedules, but call first because some change earlier. During the winter there are no upriver services.

A circular cruise on *Mercedes*

Westminster Pier
Map 13 C5.
🚇 *Westminster.*

Downriver to Tower Pier
☎ 0171-515 1415.

Departures 10:20am, 10:40am, 11am, 11:30am and noon. Then every 20 minutes until 3pm. Then every 30 minutes until 5pm (every 30 minutes until 6pm during peak season).
Duration 30 minutes.

Downriver to Greenwich ·
☎ 0171-930 4097.
Departures every 30 minutes, 10:30am–4pm (5pm peak season).
Duration 40–50 minutes.

Downriver to the Thames Barrier
☎ 0171-930 3373.
Departures 10:15am, 11:15am, 12:45pm, 1:45pm and 3:15pm.
Duration 75 mins each way.

Private party on a chartered boat

Upriver to Kew
☎ 0171-930 4721.
Departures 10:30am, 11:15am, noon, 2pm and 2:30pm.
Duration about 90 minutes.

Upriver to Richmond
☎ 0171-930 4721.
Departures 10:30am and noon.
Duration about 3 hours.

Upriver to Hampton Court
☎ 0171-930 4721.
Departures 11:15am and noon.

The River Thames is at its most romantic at dusk. The view east from Waterloo Bridge shows St. Paul's and the City on the north bank and the Oxo Tower on the south.

N

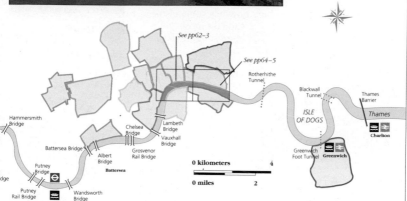

See pp62–3

See pp64–5

Rotherhithe Tunnel

Blackwall Tunnel

Thames Barrier

ISLE OF DOGS

Thames

Charlton

Hammersmith Bridge

Chelsea Bridge

Lambeth Bridge

Vauxhall Bridge

Battersea Bridge

Albert Bridge

Grosvenor Rail Bridge

Battersea

Greenwich Foot Tunnel Greenwich

Putney Bridge

Putney Rail Bridge

Wandsworth Bridge

Putney

nes l Bridge

0 kilometers   4

0 miles   2

KEY

Underground station

British Rail station

River boat stop

The river at Twickenham

The view from Richmond Hill

Open-decked boat

Duration 3–4¹/₂ hours.
Circular lunchtime cruise
0171-839 3572.
12:45pm Sun.
Duration 2 hours.
Circular supper cruise
0171-839 3572.
9pm Wed, Fri, Sun.
Duration 90 minutes.
Circular evening cruise
0171-930 2062.
7:30 and 8:30pm.
Duration 45 minutes.

Charing Cross Pier
Map 13 C3.
Charing Cross, Embankment.

Downriver to Tower Pier
0171-839 3572.
Departures every 30 minutes, 10:30am–4pm.
Duration 20 minutes.

Downriver to Greenwich
0171-839 3572.
Departures every 30 minutes, 10:30am–4pm.
Duration 45–60 minutes.

Circular evening cruise
0171-839 3572.
6:30, 7:30 and 8:30pm.
Duration 45 minutes.

Tower Pier
Map 16 D3. Tower Hill.

Upriver to HMS Belfast
0181-468 7201.
Departures every 15 minutes, 11am–6pm.

Downriver to Greenwich
0171-839 3572.
Departures every 30 minutes, 10:30am–4:30pm.
Duration 35 minutes.

Sightseeing boat

Westminster Bridge to Blackfriars Bridge

U NTIL WORLD WAR II, this stretch of the Thames marked the division between rich and poor London. On the north bank were the offices, shops, luxury hotels and apartments of Whitehall and the Strand, the Inns of Court and the newspaper district. To the south were smoky factories and slum dwellings. After the war, the Festival of Britain in 1951 started the revival of the South Bank (see pp181–7), which now has some of the capital's most interesting modern buildings.

Savoy Hotel
This hotel is on the site of a medieval palace (p116).

Shell Mex House
Offices for the oil company were built in 1931 on the site of the vast Cecil Hotel.

Somerset House is an office complex built in 1786 *(p117)*.

Cleopatra's Needle was made in ancient Egypt and given to London in 1819 *(p118).*

Embankment Gardens is the site of many open-air concerts held in the bandstand during the summer months *(p118).*

Ⓔ Charing Cross

Ⓔ Embankment
Charing Cross Pier
Hungerford Railway Bridge

Waterloo Bridge

Festival Pier

The South Bank Centre was the site of the 1951 Festival of Britain and is London's most important arts complex. It is dominated by the Festival Hall, the National Theatre and the Hayward Gallery *(pp181–7).*

Charing Cross
The rail terminus is encased in a Post-Modernist office complex with many shops (p119).

The Banqueting House is one of Inigo Jones's finest works, built as part of Whitehall Palace *(p80).*

The Ministry of Defense is a bulky white fortress completed in the 1950s.

Westminster Ⓔ
Westminster Bridge

County Hall
Built early this century as the seat of London's government, the hall is now being turned into a hotel (p185).

Temple and the Inns of Court
These historic buildings have been the offices of lawyers and barristers for over 500 years (pp136–9).

St. Paul's
Christopher Wren's masterwork, finished in 1708, formerly dominated the London skyline (pp148–51).

Blackfriars

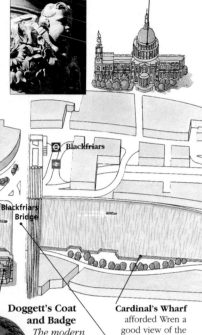

Blackfriars Bridge

Gabriel's Wharf

Doggett's Coat and Badge
The modern pub here is named after a river race in which boatmen compete for this huge badge (p187).

Cardinal's Wharf
afforded Wren a good view of the building of St. Paul's *(p178).*

OXO Tower
The windows were designed to spell the brand name of a popular meat extract.

Blackfriars Bridge
The logo of a former railway company adorns the bridge.

St. Paul's
The cathedral dominates views from the South Bank.

Gabriel's Wharf
A lively craft market operates where once there were warehouses (p187).

KEY
🚇 Underground station

🚆 British Rail station

🚢 Riverboat boarding point

Southwark Bridge to St. Katharine's Dock

FOR CENTURIES, THE STRETCH just east of London
Bridge was the busiest part of the Thames, with
ships of all sizes jostling for position to unload at
the wharves on both banks. Then, in the 19th
century, the construction of the docks to the east
eased congestion. Today most landmarks on this
section harken back to that commercial past.

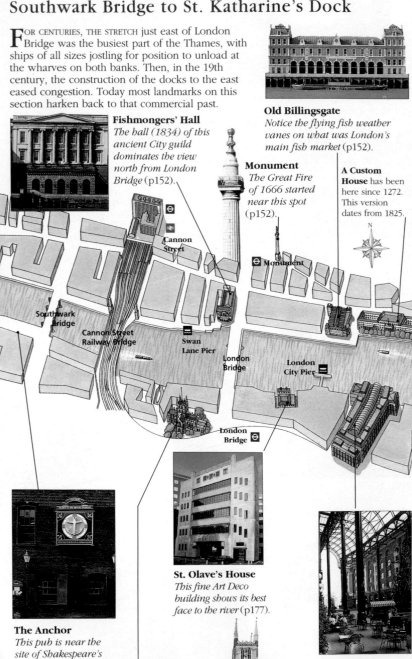

Old Billingsgate
*Notice the flying fish weather
vanes on what was London's
main fish market (p152).*

Fishmongers' Hall
*The hall (1834) of this
ancient City guild
dominates the view
north from London
Bridge (p152).*

Monument
*The Great Fire
of 1666 started
near this spot
(p152).*

**A Custom
House** has been
here since 1272.
This version
dates from 1825.

Cannon
Street

Monument

Southwark
Bridge

Cannon Street
Railway Bridge

Swan
Lane Pier

London
Bridge

London
City Pier

London
Bridge

The Anchor
*This pub is near the
site of Shakespeare's
Globe Theatre (p178).*

St. Olave's House
*This fine Art Deco
building shows its best
face to the river (p177).*

Southwark Cathedral
*Parts of this building date from
the 12th century. It contains
memorials to Shakespeare (p176).*

Hay's Galleria
*Once a wharf for
unloading food, it
has been covered to
house shops and
restaurants (p177).*

Southwark Wharves
Now there are walkways with river views where ships used to dock.

Tower Bridge
It still opens to let tall ships pass, but not as often as it did when cargo vessels came through (p153).

Tower of London
Don't miss seeing Traitors' Gate, where prisoners would be taken into the Tower by boat (pp154–7).

St. Katharine's Dock
The former dock is now a lively attraction for visitors. Its yacht marina is a highlight (p158).

Tower Pier

Tower Bridge

Victorian warehouses on Butlers Wharf have been converted into apartments.

HMS *Belfast*
The World War II cruiser has been a museum since 1971 (p179).

Design Museum
Opened in 1989, this shiplike building is a shining example of Docklands' renaissance (p179).

London Area by Area

WHITEHALL AND WESTMINSTER

WHITEHALL AND WESTMINSTER have been at the center of political and religious power in England for a thousand years. King Canute, who ruled at the beginning of the 11th century, was the first monarch to have a palace on what was then an island in the swampy meeting point of the Thames and its now-vanished tributary, the Tyburn. Canute built his palace beside the church that, some 50 years later, Edward the Confessor would enlarge into England's greatest abbey, giving the area its name. (A *minster* is an abbey church.) Over the following centuries the offices of state were established in the vicinity. All this is still reflected in Whitehall's heroic statues and massive government buildings. But, to its north, Trafalgar Square marks the start of the West End entertainment district.

Horse Guard on Whitehall

SIGHTS AT A GLANCE

Historic Streets and Buildings
Houses of Parliament pp72–3 ❶
Big Ben ❷
Jewel Tower ❸
Dean's Yard ❺
Parliament Square ❼
Downing Street ❾
Cabinet War Rooms ❿
Banqueting House ⓫
Horse Guards ⓬
Queen Anne's Gate ⓮
St. James's Park Station ⓰
Blewcoat School ⓱

Churches, Abbeys and Cathedrals
Westminster Abbey pp76–9 ❹
St Margaret's Church ❻
Westminster Cathedral ⓲
St. John's, Smith Square ⓳

Museums and Galleries
Guards' Museum ⓯
Tate Gallery pp82–5 ⓴

Theaters
Whitehall Theatre ⓭

Monuments
Cenotaph ❽

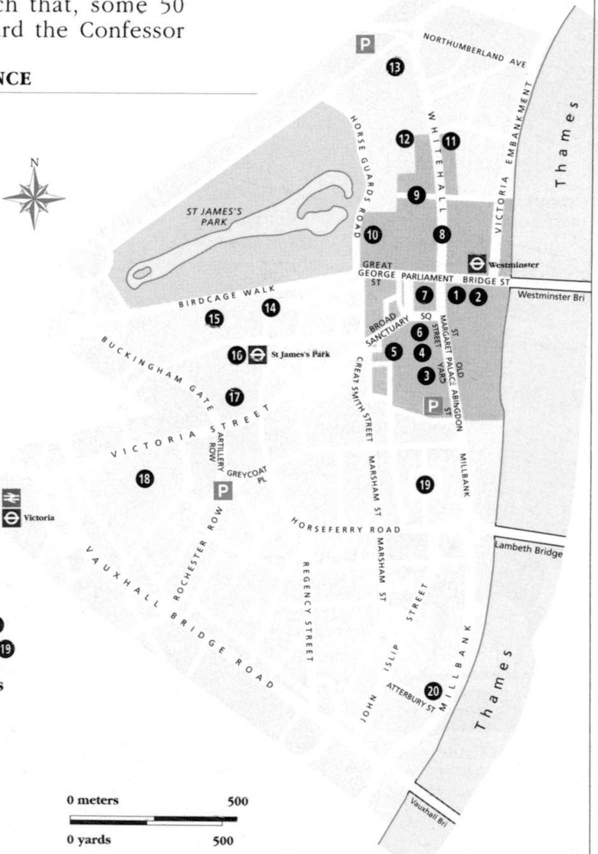

GETTING THERE
British Rail and the Victoria, District and Circle lines all serve the area. Bus numbers 3, 11, 12, 24, 29, 53, 77, 77A, 88, 109, 159, 170 and 184 go to Whitehall; 2, 2B, 16, 25, 36A, 38, 39, 52, 52A, 73, 76, 135, 507 and 510 serve Victoria.

0 meters 500
0 yards 500

KEY

	Street-by-Street map
Ⓔ	Underground station
⇄	British Rail station
P	Parking

SEE ALSO
- *Street Finder*, maps 13, 20, 21
- *Where to stay* pp276–7
- *Restaurants* pp292–4

Looking down Whitehall towards Big Ben

Street by Street: Whitehall and Westminster

COMPARED WITH MANY capital cities, London has little awe-inspiring monumental architecture. Here however, at the historic seat both of the government and of the established church, is an area reminiscent of the broad, stately avenues of Paris, Rome and Madrid. On weekdays the streets are crowded with members of the civil service, as most of their work is based in this area. On weekends, however, it is deserted, apart from tourists visiting some of London's most famous sights.

Earl Haig, the British World War I chief, was sculpted by Alfred Hardiman in 1936.

Downing Street
British Prime Ministers have lived here since 1732 ❾

Central Hall is a florid example of the Beaux Arts style, built in 1911 as a Methodist meeting hall. In 1946 the first General Assembly of the United Nations was held here.

★ Cabinet War Rooms
Now open to the public, these were Winston Churchill's World War II headquarters ❿

★ Westminster Abbey
The Abbey is London's oldest and most important church ❹

The Sanctuary
was a medieval safe-place for those escaping the law.

Dean's Yard
Westminster School was founded here in 1540 ❺

Richard I's Statue, by Carlo Marochetti (1860), depicts the 12th-century *Coeur de Lion* (Lionheart).

Jewel Tower
Kings once stored their most valuable possessions here ❸

The Burghers of Calais
is a cast of Auguste Rodin's original in Paris.

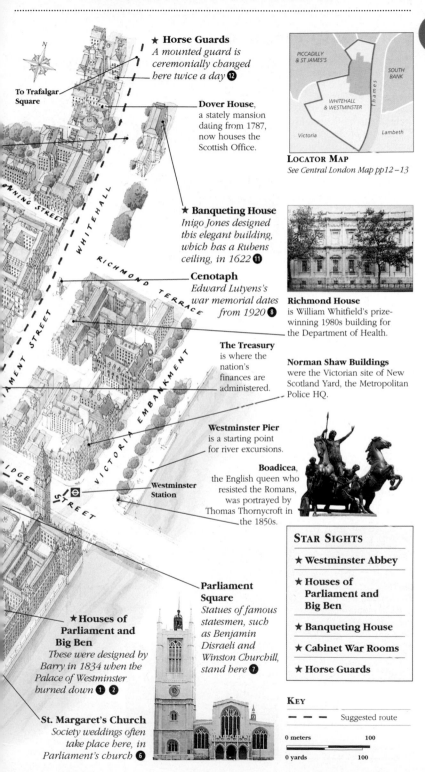

★ Horse Guards
*A mounted guard is
ceremonially changed
here twice a day* **⑫**

**To Trafalgar
Square**

Dover House,
a stately mansion
dating from 1787,
now houses the
Scottish Office.

*PICCADILLY
& ST JAMES'S*

*SOUTH
BANK*

*WHITEHALL
& WESTMINSTER*

Victoria

Lambeth

LOCATOR MAP
See Central London Map pp12–13

★ Banqueting House
*Inigo Jones designed
this elegant building,
which has a Rubens
ceiling, in 1622* **⑪**

Cenotaph
*Edward Lutyens's
war memorial dates
from 1920* **⑧**

Richmond House
is William Whitfield's prize-
winning 1980s building for
the Department of Health.

The Treasury
is where the
nation's
finances are
administered.

Norman Shaw Buildings
were the Victorian site of New
Scotland Yard, the Metropolitan
Police HQ.

Westminster Pier
is a starting point
for river excursions.

**Westminster
Station**

Boadicea,
the English queen who
resisted the Romans,
was portrayed by
Thomas Thornycroft in
the 1850s.

**Parliament
Square**
*Statues of famous
statesmen, such
as Benjamin
Disraeli and
Winston Churchill,
stand here* **⑦**

**★ Houses of
Parliament and
Big Ben**
*These were designed by
Barry in 1834 when the
Palace of Westminster
burned down* **❶ ❷**

St. Margaret's Church
*Society weddings often
take place here, in
Parliament's church* **❻**

STAR SIGHTS

★ Westminster Abbey

**★ Houses of
Parliament and
Big Ben**

★ Banqueting House

★ Cabinet War Rooms

★ Horse Guards

KEY

– – – Suggested route

0 meters	100
0 yards	100

Houses of Parliament ❶

SINCE 1512 the Palace of Westminster has been the seat of the two Houses of Parliament, called the Lords and the Commons. The Commons is made up of elected Members of Parliament (MPs) of different political parties; the party with the most MPs forms the Government, and its leader becomes Prime Minister. MPs from other parties make up the Opposition. Commons' debates can become heated and are impartially chaired by an MP designated as Speaker. The Commons formulates legislation that is first debated in both Houses before becoming law.

The mock-Gothic building was designed by Victorian architect Sir Charles Barry. Victoria Tower, on the left, contains 1.5 million Acts of Parliament passed since 1497.

★ **Commons' Chamber**
The room is upholstered in green with the Government sitting on the left, the Opposition on the right, and the Speaker presiding between them.

Members' entrance

Big Ben
The vast bell was hung in 1858 and chimes on the hour; four smaller ones ring on the quarter hours (see p74).

STAR FEATURES

★ **Westminster Hall**

★ **Lords' Chamber**

★ **Commons' Chamber**

★ **Westminster Hall**
The only surviving part of the original Palace of Westminster, it dates from 1097; its hammerbeam roof is from the 14th century.

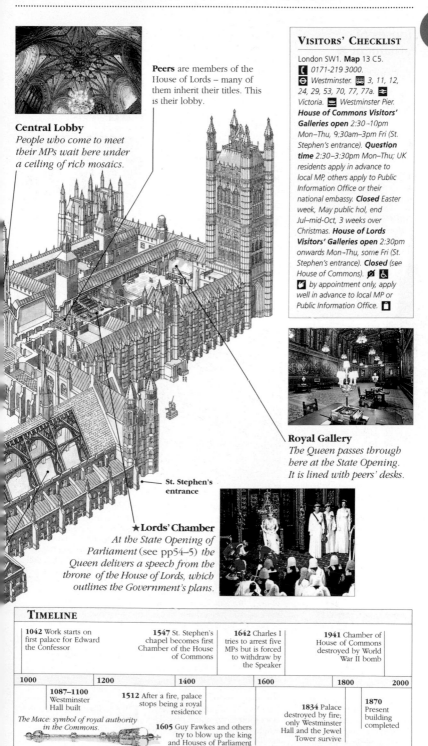

Central Lobby
*People who come to meet
their MPs wait here under
a ceiling of rich mosaics.*

Peers are members of the
House of Lords – many of
them inherit their titles. This
is their lobby.

St. Stephen's
entrance

★**Lords' Chamber**
*At the State Opening of
Parliament (see pp54–5) the
Queen delivers a speech from the
throne of the House of Lords, which
outlines the Government's plans.*

Royal Gallery
*The Queen passes through
here at the State Opening.
It is lined with peers' desks.*

VISITORS' CHECKLIST

London SW1. **Map** 13 C5.
☎ 0171-219 3000.
⊖ *Westminster.* 🚌 *3, 11, 12,
24, 29, 53, 70, 77, 77a.* 🚆
Victoria. 🚤 *Westminster Pier.*
**House of Commons Visitors'
Galleries open** 2:30 –10pm
Mon–Thu, 9:30am–3pm Fri (St.
Stephen's entrance). **Question
time** 2:30–3:30pm Mon–Thu; UK
residents apply in advance to
local MP, others apply to Public
Information Office or their
national embassy. **Closed** Easter
week, May public hol, end
Jul–mid-Oct, 3 weeks over
Christmas. **House of Lords
Visitors' Galleries open** 2:30pm
onwards Mon–Thu, some Fri (St.
Stephen's entrance). **Closed** (see
House of Commons). 📷 ♿
📋 by appointment only, apply
well in advance to local MP or
Public Information Office. 📱

TIMELINE

1042 Work starts on first palace for Edward the Confessor		**1547** St. Stephen's chapel becomes first Chamber of the House of Commons	**1642** Charles I tries to arrest five MPs but is forced to withdraw by the Speaker	**1941** Chamber of House of Commons destroyed by World War II bomb

1000	1200	1400	1600	1800	2000

1087–1100 Westminster Hall built

The Mace: symbol of royal authority in the Commons.

1512 After a fire, palace stops being a royal residence

1605 Guy Fawkes and others try to blow up the king and Houses of Parliament

1834 Palace destroyed by fire; only Westminster Hall and the Jewel Tower survive

1870 Present building completed

Houses of Parliament ❶

See pp72–3.

Big Ben ❷

Bridge St SW1. **Map** 13 C5.
📞 *0171-222 2219.* 🚇 *Westminster.*
Not open *to the public.*

To BE PRECISE, Big Ben is not the name of the world-famous four-faced clock in the 320-ft (106-m) tower that rises above the Houses of Parliament, but of the resonant bell on which the hours are struck. It was named after Sir Benjamin Hall, Chief Commissioner of Works when the bell was hung in 1858. Cast at Whitechapel, it was the second giant bell made for the clock, the first having become cracked during a test ringing. (The present bell also has a slight crack.) The clock is the largest in Britain, its four dials 24 ft (7.5 m) in diameter and the minute hand 14 ft (4.25 m) long, are made in hollow copper for lightness. It has kept exact time for the nation more or less continuously since it was first set in motion in May 1859. The deep chimes have become a symbol of Britain worldwide and are broadcast daily on BBC radio.

Jewel Tower ❸

Abingdon St SW1. **Map** 13 B5.
📞 *0171-222 2219.* 🚇 *Westminster.*
Open *Apr–Sept: 10am–6pm daily;*
Oct–Mar: 10am–4pm daily. **Closed**
1–2pm daily, Jan 1, Dec 24–26, for
state occasions. **Adm**
charge.

THIS AND WESTMINSTER HALL *(see p72)* are the only vestiges of the old Palace of Westminster. The tower was built in 1366 as a stronghold for Edward III's treasure and

is today a small museum containing relics relating to the palace, pottery dug from the moat and fascinating drawings of some of the best losing designs for rebuilding the Houses of Parliament after the fire of 1834. The tower served as the weights and measures office from 1869 until 1938 and another display relates to that. Alongside are the remains of the moat and a medieval quay.

Westminster Abbey ❹

See pp76–9.

Dean's Yard ❺

Broad Sanctuary SW1. **Map** 13 B5.
🚇 *Westminster.* **Buildings not open**
to the public.

Entrance to the Abbey and cloisters from Dean's Yard

AN ARCH NEAR the west door of the Abbey leads into this secluded grassy square, surrounded by a jumble of buildings from many different periods. A medieval house on the east side has a distinctive dormer window and backs onto Little Dean's Yard, where the monks' living quarters used to be. Dean's Yard is private property. It belongs to the Dean and Chapter of Westminster and is close to Westminster School, whose famous former pupils include poet John Dryden and playwright Ben Jonson. Scholars are, by tradition, the first to acknowledge a new monarch.

St. Margaret's Church ❻

Parliament Sq SW1. **Map** 13 B5.
📞 *0171-222 5152.* 🚇 *Westminster.*
Open *9:30am–5pm daily;*
1–5:30pm Sun. 🕆 *11am Sun.*
🚫 ♿ 🎵 *Concerts.*

Statue of Charles I overlooking St Margaret's doorway

OVERSHADOWED by the Abbey, this early-15th-century church has long been a favored venue for political and society weddings, such as Winston and Clementine Churchill's. Although much restored, the church retains some Tudor features, notably a stained-glass window that celebrates the engagement of Catherine of Aragon to Arthur, Henry VIII's eldest brother.

Parliament Square ❼

SW1. **Map** 13 B5. 🚇 *Westminster.*

LAID OUT IN THE 1840s to provide a more open view for the new Houses of Parliament, the square became Britain's first official traffic circle in 1926. Today it is hemmed in by heavy traffic. Statues of statesmen and soldiers are dominated by one of Winston Churchill in his greatcoat, glowering at the House of Commons. On the north side, Abraham Lincoln sits in front of the mock-Gothic Middlesex Guildhall, completed in 1913.

Cenotaph ❽

Whitehall SW1. **Map** 13 B4.
🚇 *Westminster.*

THIS SUITABLY BLEAK and pale monument, completed in 1920 by Sir Edwin Lutyens to commemorate the dead of World War I, stands in the middle of Whitehall. On Remembrance Day every year – the Sunday nearest November 11 – the monarch and other dignitaries place wreaths of red poppies on the Cenotaph. This solemn ceremony, commemorating the 1918 armistice, honors the victims of World Wars I and II *(see pp54–5).*

The Cenotaph

Cabinet War Rooms ⑩

Clive Steps, King Charles St SW1. **Map** 13 B5. (*0171-930 6961.* ⊖ *Westminster.* **Open** *10am–6pm daily.* **Closed** *Jan 1, Dec 24-26.* **Adm charge.**

T HIS INTRIGUING slice of 20th-century history is a warren of cellar rooms below the Government Office Building north of Parliament Square. It is where the War Cabinet – first under Neville Chamberlain, then Winston Churchill – met during World War II when German bombs were falling on London. The War Rooms include living quarters for key ministers and military leaders and a soundproofed Cabinet Room,

Telephones in the Map Room of the Cabinet War Rooms

where many strategic decisions were made. All rooms are protected by a layer of concrete about 3 feet (1m) thick. They are laid out as they were when the war ended, complete with period furniture, including Churchill's desk, some old-fashioned communications equipment and maps with markers for plotting complex military strategy.

Downing Street ⑨

SW1. **Map** 13 B4. ⊖ *Westminster.* **Not open** to the public.

S IR GEORGE DOWNING (1623– 84) spent part of his youth in the American colonies. He was the second graduate from the nascent Harvard College before returning to fight for the Parliamentarians in the English Civil War. In 1680 he

bought some land near Whitehall Palace and built a street of houses. Four of these survive, though much altered. George II gave No. 10 to Sir Robert Walpole in 1732. Since then it has been the official residence of the Prime Minister and contains offices as well as a private apartment. In 1989, for security reasons, iron gates were erected at the Whitehall end.

The famous front door of No. 10

Government policy is decided in the Cabinet Room at No. 10.

No. 12, the Whips' Office, is where Party campaigns are organized.

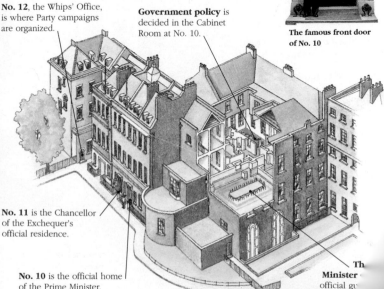

No. 11 is the Chancellor of the Exchequer's official residence.

No. 10 is the official home of the Prime Minister.

Th
Minister
official gu
State Di

Westminster Abbey ❹

THE ABBEY is world famous as the resting place of Britain's monarchs and as the setting for coronations and other great pageants. Within its walls can be seen some of the most glorious examples of medieval architecture in London. The Abbey also contains one of the most impressive collections of tombs and monuments in the world. Half national church, half national museum, the abbey occupies a unique place in the British national consciousness.

★ **Flying Buttresses**
The massive flying buttresses help transfer the great weight of the 102 ft (31 m) high nave.

North Entrance
The stonework here, like this carving of a dragon, is Victorian.

The North Transept *has three chapels at its east end housing some of the Abbey's finest monuments.*

★ **West Front Towers**
were built from 1734 to 1745, and designed by Nicholas Hawksmoor.

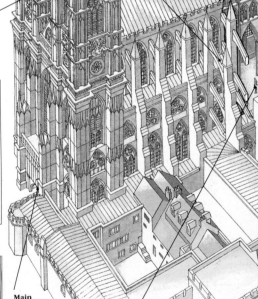

STAR FEATURES

★ **West Front Towers**

★ **Flying Buttresses**

★ **The Nave Viewed from the West End**

★ **Henry VII Chapel**

★ **Chapter House**

Main entrance

★ **The Nave viewed from the West End**
At 35 ft (10 m) wide, the nave is comparatively narrow, but it is the highest in England.

The Cloisters, built mainly in the 13th and 14th centuries, used to link the Abbey church with the other buildings.

St. Edward's Chapel
houses not only the royal
Coronation Chair and
Edward the Confessor's
shrine, but also the tombs
of many of England's
medieval monarchs.

★ Henry VII Chapel
*The chapel, built from
1503–12, has a superb
vaulted ceiling and choir
stalls dating from 1520.*

VISITORS' CHECKLIST

Broad Sanctuary SW1. **Map**
13 B5. 0171-222 5152.
St. James's Park, Westminster.
3, 11, 12, 24, 29, 53, 70, 77,
77a, 88, 109, 159, 170.
Victoria, Waterloo.
Westminster Pier. **Adm
charge** for Royal Chapels, Poets'
Corner, Choir, Statesmen's Aisle
(exc 7:45pm Wed),
Chapter House, Pyx Chamber,
Museum. **Nave & cloisters
open** 8am–6pm Mon–Sat,
between services on Sun.
**Royal Chapels, Poets' Corner,
Choir, Statesmen's Aisle open**
9am–4:45pm Mon–Fri,
9am–2:45pm, 3:45–5:45pm
Sat. **Chapter House open**
Apr–Sep: 10am–5:45pm daily;
Oct–Mar: 10am–4pm daily. **Pyx
Chamber & Museum open**
10:30am–4pm daily. **Brass
rubbing center open** 9am–5pm
Mon–Sat. **Garden open** Thu.
Concerts.

★ Chapter House
*This octagonal structure is
worth seeing for its 13th-
century tiles.*

The South Transept
contains "Poets' Corner,"
where memorials to famous
literary figures can be seen.

Museum

TIMELINE

*13th-century
tile from the
Chapter House*

1050 New Benedictine abbey church begun by Edward the Confessor	**1376** Henry Yevele begins rebuilding the nave			**1838** Queen Victoria's coronation	
1000	**1200**	**1400**	**1600**	**1800**	**2000**
1245 New Abbey begun to the designs of Henry of Rheims	**1269** Body of Edward the Confessor moved to new shrine in the abbey	**1540** Monastery dissolved	**1734** West towers begun	**1953** Most recent coronation in the Abbey: Elizabeth II's	

A Guided Tour of Westminster Abbey

T HE ABBEY'S INTERIOR presents an exceptionally diverse array of architectural and sculptural styles. These range from the austere French Gothic of the nave to the stunning complexity of Henry VII's Tudor chapel and the riotous invention of the later 18th-century monuments. Many English monarchs are buried here; some of their tombs are deliberately plain, while others are lavishly decorated. At the same time, there are monuments to a number of Britain's greatest public figures – ranging from politicians to poets – crowded into the aisles and transepts.

② **Lady Nightingale's Memorial**
The North Transept chapels contain some of the abbey's finest monuments – this one, by Roubiliac, is for Lady Nightingale (1761).

North entrance

① **The Nave**
Enter the abbey and walk along the nave, which is 35 ft (10.5 m) wide and 100 ft (31 m) high. It took 150 years to build.

The Choir houses a gilded 1840s screen, which contains remnants of the 13th-century original.

HISTORICAL PLAN OF THE ABBEY
The first Abbey church was established as early as the 10th century, when St. Dunstan brought a group of Benedictine monks to the area. The present structure dates largely from the 13th century; the new, French-influenced design was begun in 1245 at the behest of Henry III. Because of its unique role as the royal coronation church, the Abbey survived Henry VIII's mid-16th-century onslaught on Britain's monastic buildings.

KEY
- Built before 1400
- Added in 15th century
- Built from 1503–19
- Completed in 1745
- Completed after 1850

⑧ **The Cloisters**
A brass rubbing center in the cloisters invites visitors to create personal souvenirs of the Abbey – perhaps a rubbing of a knight's tomb.

Main entrance

The Jerusalem Chamber has a 17th-century fireplace, fine 1540s tapestries and an interesting painted ceiling.

The Jericho Parlor, added in the early 16th century, contains some impressive paneling.

The Deanery is where the monastery's abbot used to live.

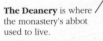

CORONATION

The abbey has been the fittingly sumptuous setting for all royal coronations since 1066. The last occupant of the Coronation Chair was the present monarch, Elizabeth II. She was crowned in 1953 during the first televised coronation.

The Chapel of St. John the Baptist is full of tombs dating from the 14th to the 19th centuries.

The St. Faith Chapel contains works of art that date back to the 13th century.

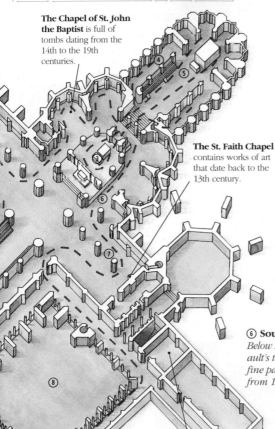

③ **St. Edward's Chapel**
Contained here are the royal Coronation Chair, the shrine of the Saxon king Edward the Confessor and the tombs of many medieval monarchs.

④ **Tomb of Elizabeth I**
Inside the Henry VII Chapel is Elizabeth I's (reigned 1558–1603) huge tomb. The chapel also houses the body of her sister, "Bloody" Mary I.

⑤ **Henry VII Chapel**
The undersides of the choir stalls, dating from 1512, are beautifully carved with exotic and fantastic creatures.

⑥ **South Ambulatory**
Below Philippa of Hainault's tomb are some fine painted panels from 1270.

The Pyx Chamber's gaunt columns date from the 11th century.

Dean's Yard entrance

KEY

– – – Tour route

⑦ **Poets' Corner**
Take time to explore the memorials to countless literary giants, such as Shakespeare and Dickens, that are gathered here.

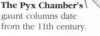

Banqueting House ⑪

Whitehall SW1. **Map** 13 B4.
【 *0171-839 7569.* **⊖** *Charing Cross, Embankment, Westminster.* **Open** *10am–5pm Mon–Sat (last adm: 4:30).* **Closed** *Jan 1, Dec 24-26 & for ceremonies.* **Adm charge.**
⚪ ⬛ ⬛ ⬛ *Video presentations.*

T his delightful building is of great architectural importance. It was the first in central London to embody the Classical Palladian style that designer Inigo Jones brought back from his travels in Italy. Completed in 1622, its disciplined stone facade marked a startling change from the Elizabethans' fussy turrets and unrestrained external decoration. It was the sole survivor of the fire that destroyed most of the old Whitehall Palace in 1698.

The ceiling paintings by Rubens, a complex allegory on the exaltation of James I, were commissioned by his son, Charles I, in 1630. This blatant glorification of royalty was despised by Oliver Cromwell and the Parliamentarians, who executed King Charles I on a scaffold outside Banqueting House in 1649. Ironically, Charles II celebrated his restoration to the throne here 20 years later. The building is occasionally used for official functions.

Mounted sentries stationed outside Horse Guards

Horse Guards ⑫

Whitehall SW1. **Map** 13 B4.
【 *0171-930 4466.* **⊖** *Westminster, Charing Cross.* **Closed** *Sats in June.* **Changing of the Guard** *11am Mon–Sat, 10am Sun.* **Dismounting Ceremony** *4pm daily.* **Trooping the Colour** *see* **Ceremonial London** *pp52–5.*

O nce Henry VIII's tiltyard (tournament ground), the Changing of the Guard still takes place here every day. The elegant buildings, completed in 1755, were designed by William Kent. On the left, as you enter the parade ground, is the Old Treasury, also by Kent, and the back of Dover House, completed in 1758 and now used as the Scottish Office. Nearby, in a corner of the parade ground, is a trace of the "real tennis" court where Henry VIII is said to have played the ancient precursor of modern lawn tennis. On the opposite side, the view is dominated by the ivy-covered Citadel. This is a bombproof structure that was erected in 1940 beside the Admiralty. During World War II it was used as a communications headquarters by the Navy.

Whitehall Theatre ⑬

Whitehall SW1. **Map** 13 B3.
【 *0171-867 1119.* **⊖** *Charing Cross.* **Open** *for performances only. See* **Entertainment** *pp326–7.*

Detail of a Whitehall Theatre box

B uilt in 1930, the plain white front seems to emulate the Cenotaph *(see p74)* at the other end of the street, but inside, the theater boasts excellent Art Deco detailing. From the 1950s to the 1970s, it was noted for staging a wide range of farces.

Queen Anne's Gate ⑭

SW1. **Map** 13 A5. **⊖** *St. James's Park.*

T he spacious terraced houses at the west end of this well-preserved enclave date from 1704 and are notable for the ornate canopies over their front doors. At the other end are houses built some 70 years later, sporting blue plaques that record former residents, such as Lord Palmerston, the Victorian Prime Minister. Until recently, the British Secret Service, MI5, was allegedly based in this unlikely spot. A small statue of Queen Anne stands in front of the wall separating Nos. 13 and 15. To the west, situated at the corner of Petty France, Sir Basil Spence's Home Office building (1976),

Panels from the Rubens ceiling, Banqueting House

is an architectural incongruity. Cockpit Steps, leading down to Birdcage Walk, mark the site of a 17th-century venue for the popular, yet blood-thirsty, sport of cockfighting.

Guards Museum ⓯

Birdcage Walk SW1. **Map** 13 A5.
📞 *0171-930 4466 x 3271.* Ⓔ *St. James's Park.* **Open** *10am– 4pm Sat–Fri.* **Closed** *Jan 1, Dec 24-26 & ceremonies.* **Adm charge.** 📷 ⓰

E NTERED FROM Birdcage Walk, the museum is under the parade ground of Wellington Barracks, head-quarters of the five Guards regiments. A must for military buffs, the museum uses tableaux and dioramas to illustrate various battles in which the Guards have taken part, from the English Civil War (1642– 8) to the present. Weapons and row after row of colorful uniforms are on display, as well as a fascin-ating collection of models.

St. James's Park Station ⓰

55 Broadway SW1. **Map** 13 A5.
Ⓔ *St. James's Park.*

Epstein sculpture outside St. James's Park Station

T HE STATION is built into Broadway House, Charles Holden's 1929 headquarters for London Transport. It is notable for its sculptures by Jacob Epstein and reliefs by Henry Moore and Eric Gill.

Blewcoat School ⓱

23 Caxton St SW1. **Map** 13 A5.
📞 *0171-222 2877.* Ⓔ *St. James's Park.* **Open** *10am –5:30pm Mon– Wed, Fri; 10am –7pm Thu.*

Statue of a Blewcoat pupil above the Caxton Street entrance

A RED-BRICK GEM hemmed in by the office towers of Victoria Street, it was built in 1709 as a charity school to teach pupils how to "read, write, cast accounts and the catechism." It remained as a school until 1939, then became an army store during World War II and was bought by the National Trust in 1954. The beautifully proportioned interior now serves as a National Trust gift shop.

Westminster Cathedral ⓲

Ashley Pl. SW1. **Map** 20 F1.
📞 *0171-834 7452.* Ⓔ *Victoria.* **Open** *6:45am–8pm daily.* **Adm charge** *for bell tower lift (Apr–Oct: 9am–1pm, 2–5pm).* ✝ *5:30pm Mon–Fri, 10:30am Sat & Sun, sung Mass.* ⓰ **Concerts.**

O NE OF LONDON'S rare Byzantine buildings, it was designed by John Francis Bentley for the Catholic diocese and completed in 1903 on the site of a former prison. Its 285-ft (87-m) high, red-brick tower, with horizontal stripes of white stone, stands out on the skyline in sharp contrast to the Abbey nearby. A restful piazza on the north side offers a good view of the

cathedral from Victoria Street. The rich interior decoration, with marble of varying colors and intricate mosaics, makes the domes above the nave seem incongruous. They were left bare because the project ran out of money before it could be completed.

Eric Gill's dramatic reliefs of the 14 Stations of the Cross, created during World War I, adorn the pier of the nave. The organ is one of the finest in Europe, and a series of concerts is held here every second Tuesday from June until September.

St. John's, Smith Square ⓳

Smith Sq SW1. **Map** 21 B1.
📞 *0171-222 1061.* Ⓔ *Westminster.* **Open** *10am–5pm and for evening concerts.* 🚫 🍴 ⓰ **Concerts.** *See* **Entertainment** *pp330–1.*

Premiere Ensemble at St. John's, Smith Square

D ESCRIBED BY artist and art historian Sir Hugh Casson as one of the masterpieces of English Baroque architecture, Thomas Archer's plump church, with its turrets at each corner, looks as if it is trying to burst from the confines of the square, and overpowers the pleasing 18th-century houses on its north side. It has an accident-prone history: completed in 1728, it was burned down in 1742, struck by lightning in 1773 and destroyed again by a World War II bomb in 1941. There is a reasonably priced restaurant in the basement – a rarity in this area – that is open daily for lunch and on the evenings of concerts.

Tate Gallery ⓴

See pp82–5.

Tate Gallery ⑳

ORIGINALLY BUILT through the philanthropy of the sugar magnate Sir Henry Tate, the Tate now holds an extensive range of British works from the 16th to the 20th centuries. It is also London's leading international modern art museum. In the adjoining Clore Gallery is the magnificent Turner Bequest, left to the nation by the landscape artist J.M.W. Turner himself.

The portico of the Tate building, which dates from 1897, overlooks the Thames.

GALLERY GUIDE

Most of the collection is housed in 30 rooms on the ground floor. Works on paper and temporary exhibitions are downstairs. The paintings are hung chronologically, tracing British art from 1550 (Room 1) to contemporary British and foreign art (Rooms 27–30). The display changes annually, in order to emphasize different aspects of the collection. Note that not all of the works illustrated here will be on exhibit.

Stairs to lower galleries

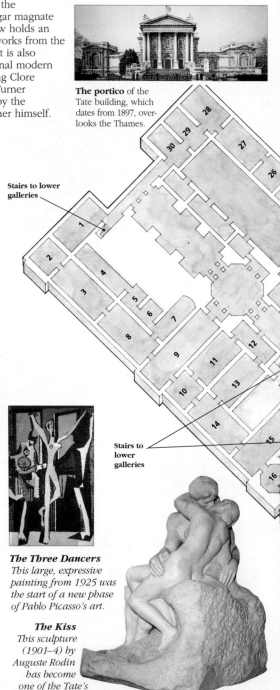

Stairs to lower galleries

★ *Peace – Burial at Sea*
This is J.M.W. Turner's tribute to his friend and rival David Wilkie. It was painted in 1842, the year after Wilkie died at sea.

The Three Dancers
This large, expressive painting from 1925 was the start of a new phase of Pablo Picasso's art.

The Kiss
This sculpture (1901–4) by Auguste Rodin has become one of the Tate's most popular works.

KEY TO FLOOR PLAN

- ☐ Sculpture Gallery
- ☐ Temporary exhibitions
- ☐ Paintings
- ☐ Clore Gallery (Turner)
- ☐ Non-exhibition space

THE ART OF GOOD FOOD

The Tate boasts both a coffee bar and a licensed restaurant on the lower floor, decorated with a lavish mural by Rex Whistler. It tells the story of the inhabitants of the mythical Epicurania, and their pursuit of exotic foods to revive their jaded palates. The restaurant is well worth a visit for lunch, but it is not open for dinner *(see pp306–7)*.

VISITORS' CHECKLIST

Millbank SW1. **Map** 21 B2.
📞 0171-821 1313. 📠 0171-821 7128. ⊖ *Pimlico.* 🚌 *77a, 88, C10 or 2, 2b, 3, 36, 36b, 159, 185 (to Bessborough Gardens), 507.* 🚆 *Victoria, Vauxhall.* **Open** *10am–5:50pm Mon–Sat; 2–5:50pm Sun.* **Closed** *Jan 1, Dec 24–26, Good Fri, May Day.* **Adm charge** *for major exhibitions.* 📷 ♿ *Atterbury St.* 🎫 🍴 🖥 🛍

Disabled entrance on ground floor ♿

Entrance to Clore Gallery via Room 18

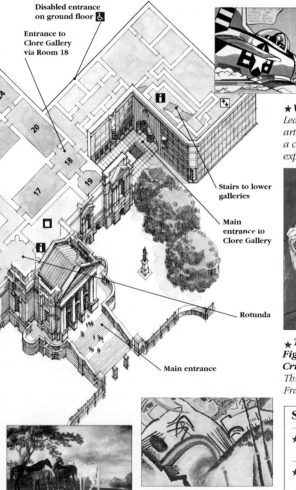

Stairs to lower galleries

Main entrance to Clore Gallery

Rotunda

Main entrance

★ Whaam !
Leading American Pop artist Roy Lichtenstein used a comic-strip source for this explosive image from 1963.

★ Three Studies for Figures at the Base of a Crucifixion* (1944)
This is the central panel of Francis Bacon's triptych.

★ Mares and Foals
George Stubbs's work (from 1762–8) is characterized by perfect anatomical detail.

Cossacks
Painted in 1911 by Wassily Kandinsky, this was a major step in the development of Abstract art.

STAR PAINTINGS

★ **Mares and Foals** by George Stubbs

★ **Burial at Sea** by J.M.W. Turner

★ **Three Studies** by Francis Bacon

★ **Whaam!** by Roy Lichtenstein

Exploring the Tate's Collection

THE TATE'S COLLECTION comprises three basic elements: British art from 1550 to the present day, international 20th-century art and the Turner Collection, housed entirely in the Clore Gallery.

16TH- AND 17TH-CENTURY BRITISH

Endymion Porter (1643–45) by William Dobson

FORMAL PORTRAITS dominate this period of British art. The earliest painting in the Tate, *A Man in a Black Cap*, painted by John Bettes in 1545, reveals the influence of Hans Holbein, who brought Renaissance art to England. Holbein's meticulous, linear style is echoed in many works. One of England's first home-grown artistic geniuses was the miniaturist Nicholas Hilliard. He is represented here by a rare, full-size portrait of Elizabeth I, a typically jeweled icon of exquisite quality. In the 17th century, under the influence of Sir Anthony Van Dyck, a new grandly elegant style of portraiture emerged. Van

Dyck's *Lady of the Spencer Family* and William Dobson's *Endymion Porter* are excellent examples. Two non-portrait gems include Francis Barlow's *Monkeys and Spaniels Playing*, a charming early animal painting, and Jan Sibrecht's *Landscape with Rainbow, Henley-on-Thames*, which marks the birth of the English landscape tradition.

18TH-CENTURY BRITISH

ALONG WITH the early 18th-century illustrative paintings, the collection also boasts some fine examples of "conversation pieces" (people in an informal setting). These include the elegant, doll-like *James Family* by Arthur Devis, and William Hogarth's vivid painting of *The Strode Family at Breakfast*. Hogarth, the leading figure in British art in the 18th century, is very well known for his satirical works. From the late 18th century, the "Grand Style" of Joshua Reynolds can be compared with the feathery brushwork of portraits by his rival, Thomas Gainsborough. Richard Wilson's work from the same era shows the same Grand Style in landscape, while George Stubbs is well represented by countryside pictures and equine portraits of astonishing beauty.

19TH-CENTURY BRITISH

Satan Smiting Job with Sore Boils (c.1826) by William Blake

THE TATE HOLDS a large number of works by the visionary genius of the 19th century, William Blake. And there are pictures by Blake's followers, including Samuel Palmer, whose intimate, pastoral scenes are imbued with mystic intensity. The two greatest landscape artists of the century are also well represented: the Turners (in the Clore) far outnumber the Constables, but a good variety of John Constable's paintings are on exhibit. Both sketches and finished works such as the famous *Flatford Mill*. Landscapes by Crome, Cotman, Bonington and others can also be seen. The collection reveals the variety of content and style found in Victorian art. It ranges from the very sentimental "subject paintings" such as *The Blind Fiddler* by Wilkie, whose death is commemorated in Turner's *Peace (see p82)*, to William Frith's view of *Derby Day* and the highly colored, emotionally intense images of the Pre-Raphaelites.

TURNER AT THE CLORE GALLERY

When J.M.W. Turner (1775–1851) left his works to the nation, it was on condition that they were kept together. In 1910, a suite of rooms at the Tate was devoted to some of his oil paintings, but it was not until the Clore Gallery was opened in 1987 that the entire bequest, including thousands of studies, came together. The gallery also houses Turner's watercolors, including *A City on a River at Sunset*, part of his *Great Rivers of Europe* project.

A City on a River at Sunset (1832)

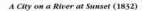

IMPRESSIONISM AND POST-IMPRESSIONISM

The Gardener (1906) by Paul Cézanne

MANY OF THE important Impressionist and Post-Impressionist works have now been transferred over to the National Gallery *(see pp104–7)* but the Tate still maintains a selection from the major figures, and these mark the beginning of modern art. Renoir, Pissarro, Sisley, Degas, Toulouse-Lautrec, Van Gogh, Gauguin and Seurat are all represented. Highlights here include Claude Monet's grid like *Poplars on the Epte* and Cézanne's *The Gardener*, both using radically new methods of painting that led to Abstract art.

EARLY 20TH CENTURY

THE 20TH CENTURY opens with the intimate, decorative scenes of Nabis, Vuillard and Bonnard. Then come avant-garde paintings, starting with the Fauves (the word means "wild animals"), exemplified by Henri Matisse's portrait of his fellow Fauve, Derain. All the major movements of the early century are here: the revolutionary Cubism of Picasso, Braque and Leger; the dynamic, machine-inspired Futurism of artists such as Severnini and Boccioni; the disturbing works of Munch, Kirchner, Beckman and the other German Expressionists; as well as the more traditional art styles that flourished in Britain after World War I.

Most notable in this area are some works by Sir Stanley Spencer, including the massive *Resurrection, Cookham.* There are also major works by the Central Abstract artists – like Kandinsky, Mondrian and Malevich – and by British Abstract artists such as Ben Nicholson. The sculpture includes major works by Rodin, Brancusi, Hepworth and Moore. The Surrealists are well in evidence – the most popular being the Dalis.

Madame Derain in a White Shawl (1919–20) by André Derain

LATE 20TH CENTURY

THE RANGE OF styles and "schools" in the post-World War II collection is vast, reflecting international developments in Abstract and Figurative painting and sculpture. The effects of World War II can be seen directly and indirectly in the works of the 1940s and 1950s, from Paul Nash's eerie wartorn landscape *Totes Meer* (Dead Sea), to the disturbing "new images of man" created by Giacometti, Dubuffet and Bacon. Late works by Picasso, Matisse and Leger reflect the Expressionist and Abstract developments of the postwar period. One of the most magnificent images is Matisse's gigantic collage of cut-out paper, *Snail*. The Tate also contains some impressive paintings by the American Abstract Expressionists of the 1940s and 1950s: de Kooning, Newman, Pollock and Rothko. It later acquired related works, such as Morris Louis's huge drip-stained canvases.

Op (Optical) Art and Kinetic (moving) Art were two movements of the 1960s which, like Anthony Caro's amazing bright red sheet-steel sculpture *Early One Morning*, reflect a move away from the Expressionism of the 1950s. The art movement that is probably most associated with the 1960s is Pop Art. The Tate contains some key works by both American and British exponents – including Blake's *Toy Shop*, Lichtenstein's *Whaam!* and Andy Warhol's *Marilyn Diptych*.

There are many significant works of recent British figure painting: Freud, Auerbach, Kossoff, Kitaj, Hockney and Bacon can all be seen. More controversial are Minimalist works – the American Carl André's *Equivalent VIII* (made out of bricks) is an extreme example. A wide variety of Conceptual Art is on display, including Richard Long's landscape art in which maps, photos and printed words codify the artist's response to nature. The Tate's huge collection continues to grow and reflect new developments in contemporary art.

Mr and Mrs Clark and Percy (1970–1) by David Hockney

PICCADILLY AND ST. JAMES'S

PICCADILLY is the main artery of the West End. Once called Portugal Street, it acquired its present name from the ruffs, or pick-adills, worn by 17th-century dandies. St. James's still bears traces of the 18th century, when it surrounded the royal residences and denizens of the court and society shopped and amused

Buckingham Palace decorative lock

themselves there. Two shops in St. James's Street – Lock the hatter and Berry Bros. the vintners – recall that era. Fortnum and Mason, on Piccadilly, has served high-quality food for nearly 300 years. Mayfair to the north is still the most fashionable address in London, while Piccadilly Circus marks the start of Soho.

SIGHTS AT A GLANCE

Historic Streets and Buildings
Piccadilly Circus **1**
Albany **3**
Burlington Arcade **6**
Ritz Hotel **7**
Spencer House **8**
St. James's Palace **9**
St. James's Square **10**
Royal Opera Arcade **11**
Pall Mall **12**
The Mall **15**
Marlborough House **16**
Clarence House **18**
Lancaster House **19**
Buckingham Palace pp94–5 **20**
Royal Mews **22**
Wellington Arch **23**
Shepherd Market **25**

Museums and Galleries
Royal Academy of Arts **4**
Museum of Mankind **5**
Institute of Contemporary Arts **13**
Queen's Gallery **21**
Royal Mews **22**
Apsley House **24**
Faraday Museum **27**

Churches
St. James's Church **2**
Queen's Chapel **17**

Parks and Gardens
St. James's Park **14**
Green Park **26**

SEE ALSO

• *Street Finder*, maps 12, 13

• *Where to Stay* pp276–7

• *Restaurants* pp292–4

GETTING THERE
The Piccadilly line serves Hyde Park Corner, Piccadilly Circus and Green Park. The Bakerloo and Jubilee lines serve Charing Cross, which is also a major BR terminus. The area is served by bus Nos. 6, 9, 15, 23 and 139.

KEY

▨	Street-by-Street map
⊖	Underground station
⊒	British Rail station
🅿	Parking

0 meters		500
0 yards		500

Piccadilly Arcade with its many fine shops

Street by Street: Piccadilly and St. James's

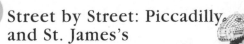

As soon as Henry VIII built St. James's Palace in the 1530s, the area around it became the center of fashionable London, and it has remained so ever since. The most influential people in the land stroll its historic streets on their way to lunch in their clubs, to shop in the capital's oldest and most exclusive stores or to visit one of the many art galleries.

★ **Museum of Mankind**
This ivory leopard is in the museum's collection of primitive art ❺

The Albany
It has been one of London's smartest addresses since it opened in 1774 ❸

★ **Royal Academy of Arts**
Sir Joshua Reynolds founded the Academy in 1768. Now it mounts large popular exhibitions ❹

★ **Burlington Arcade**
Uniformed beadles discourage unruly behavior in this 19th-century mall ❻

Fortnum and Mason
was founded in 1707 by one of Queen Anne's footmen *(see p311)*.

The Ritz
Named after César Ritz, and opened in 1906, it still lives up to his name ❼

Spencer House
An ancestor of the Princess of Wales built this house in 1766 ❽

St. James's Palace
This Tudor palace is still the Court's official headquarters ❾

To the Mall

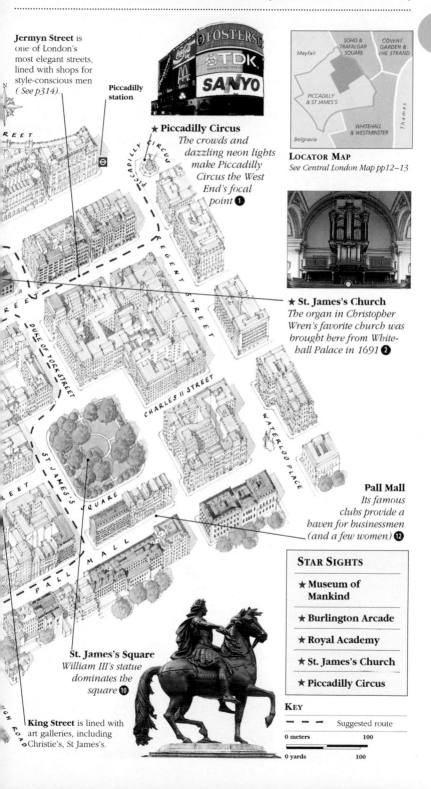

Jermyn Street is one of London's most elegant streets, lined with shops for style-conscious men *(See p314).*

Piccadilly station

LOCATOR MAP
See Central London Map pp12–13

★ **Piccadilly Circus**
The crowds and dazzling neon lights make Piccadilly Circus the West End's focal point ❶

★ **St. James's Church**
The organ in Christopher Wren's favorite church was brought here from Whitehall Palace in 1691 ❷

Pall Mall
Its famous clubs provide a haven for businessmen (and a few women) ⑫

St. James's Square
William III's statue dominates the square ❿

King Street is lined with art galleries, including Christie's, St James's.

STAR SIGHTS

★ **Museum of Mankind**

★ **Burlington Arcade**

★ **Royal Academy**

★ **St. James's Church**

★ **Piccadilly Circus**

KEY

— — — Suggested route

0 meters   100

0 yards   100

Piccadilly Circus ❶

W1. **Map** 13 A3. 🚇 *Piccadilly Circus.*

Alfred Gilbert's statue of Eros

FOR YEARS PEOPLE have congregated beneath the symbolic figure of Eros, originally intended to be an angel of mercy but renamed after the Greek god of love. Poised delicately with his bow, Eros has become almost a trademark for the capital. It was erected in 1892 as a memorial to the Earl of Shaftesbury, the Victorian philanthropist. Part of Nash's master plan for Regent's Street *(see p220)*, Piccadilly Circus has been considerably altered in recent years and consists chiefly of shopping malls. One of them can be found behind the facade of the London Pavilion (1885), once a popular music hall. The circus has London's gaudiest array of neon advertising signs marking the entrance to the city's lively entertainment district with cinemas, theaters, nightclubs, restaurants and pubs.

St. James's Church ❷

197 Piccadilly W1. **Map** 13 A3. 📞 *0171-734 4511.* 🚇 *Piccadilly Circus, Green Park.* **Open** 8:30am–7pm daily. **Closed** public hols. **Crafts market** 9:30am–6pm Thu, Fri and Sat except Easter. 🚫 *during services.* 🍴 **Concerts, lectures.**

AMONG THE many churches Wren designed *(see p47)*, this is said to be one of his favorites. It has been altered over the years and was half-wrecked by a bomb in 1940, but it maintains the essential features from 1684 – its tall arched windows; thin spire (a 1966 fiberglass replica of the original); and light, dignified interior. The ornate screen behind the altar is one of the finest works of the 17th-century master carver Grinling Gibbons, who also made the exquisite marble font, with a scene depicting Adam and Eve standing by the Tree of Life. Artist and poet William Blake and Prime Minister Pitt the Elder were both baptized here. More of Gibbons's carvings can be seen above the grandiose organ, made for Whitehall Palace chapel but installed here in 1691. Today the church has a full calendar of events and runs the vegetarian Wren Coffee House.

Albany ❸

Albany Court Yard, Piccadilly W1. **Map** 12 F3. 🚇 *Green Park, Piccadilly Circus.*

THESE DESIRABLE and discreet bachelor apartments, half-hidden through an entrance off Piccadilly, were built in 1803 by Henry Holland. Notable residents have included the poet Lord Byron, novelist Graham Greene, two Prime Ministers (William Gladstone and Edward Heath) and the actor Terence Stamp. Married men were admitted in 1878 but could not bring their wives to live with them until 1919. Women are now allowed to live here in their own right.

Lord Byron lived in Albany

Royal Academy of Arts ❹

Burlington House, Piccadilly W1. **Map** 12 F3. 📞 *0171-439 7438.* 🚇 *Piccadilly Circus, Green Park.* **Open** 10am–6pm daily (last adm: 5:30pm). **Closed** Good Fri & Dec 24–25. **Adm charge**. 🚫 ♿ 📷 📹 🍴 📖 **Lectures**.

Michelangelo's Madonnna and Child

THE COURTYARD in front of Burlington House, one of the West End's few surviving mansions from the early 18th century, is often crammed with people waiting to get into one of the prestigious visiting art exhibitions at the Royal Academy (founded 1768). The famous annual summer exhibition, which has now been held for over 200 years, comprises about 1,200 new works by both established and unknown painters, sculptors and architects. Any artist, regardless of background, can submit work.

The airy Sackler Galleries (1991), designed by Norman Foster in the former diploma galleries, show visiting exhibitions. There are permanent items in the sculpture promenade outside the galleries, notably a Michelangelo relief of the Madonna and Child (1505). The exceptional permanent collection (not all on display) includes one work by each current and former academician. On the first floor is a good shop that sells cards and other items that are designed by Academy members for the RA.

Museum of Mankind **5**

6 Burlington Gdns W1. **Map** 12 F3.
🕻 *0171-437 2224.* ⊖ *Piccadilly
Circus, Green Park.* **Open** *10am–5pm
Mon–Sat, 2:30–6pm Sun.* **Closed** *Jan 1,
Good Fri, 1st Mon in May & Dec
24–26.* 🖾 🕭 🔄 🖋 ⅋ 🖳 🛢
Lectures, film presentations.

THE SMALL, well-organized
ethnographic section of
the British Museum *(see
pp126–9)* occupies an 1860s
back extension of Burlington
House (the Royal Academy).
Highlights of the museum's
excellent collection, from
both ancient and modern
cultures, are displayed on the
first floor. These include
figures, masks, ornaments
and a number of giant
statues. Among the West
African treasures are a pair of
ivory leopards from Benin
and an intricately carved
Yoruba door panel. The
ground floor houses
changing exhibitions
about particular
cultures, which often
include reconstructed
buildings and villages.
The Colombian
coffee shop provides a
welcome and often
uncrowded refuge for
refreshments, soup and
light meals. The
entrance is flanked by
enormous casts of two
Mayan pillars.

**Hawaiian war god in the
Museum of Mankind**

Burlington Arcade **6**

Piccadilly W1. **Map** 12 F3. ⊖ *Green
Park, Piccadilly Circus. See* **Shops and
Markets** *p318.*

THIS IS ONE OF three 19th-
century arcades of small
shops selling traditional
British luxuries. (The others,
Piccadilly and Princes
arcades, are on the south side
of Piccadilly.) It was built for
Lord Cavendish in 1819 to
stop passers-by from throwing
rubbish into his garden. The
arcade is still patrolled by
beadles who ensure that
decorum is maintained.

Afternoon tea served in the opulent Palm Court of the Ritz

Ritz Hotel **7**

Piccadilly W1. **Map** 12 F3. 🕻 *0171-
493 8181.* ⊖ *Green Park.* **Open** *to
nonresidents for tea or restaurant
meals.* 🕭 🖾 *See* **Where to Stay** *p282
and* **Restaurants and Pubs** *p306.*

CESAR RITZ, the Swiss
hotelier who inspired
the word ritzy, had
virtually retired by
1906, when this hotel
was built and named
after him. The colon-
naded front of the
dominant château-style
building was meant to
suggest Paris, where
the grandest hotels
were to be found at
the turn of the
century. It manages to
maintain its Edward-
ian air of opulence
and is a popular stop,
among those who are suitably
dressed, for afternoon tea.

Spencer House **8**

27 St. James's Pl SW1. **Map** 12 F4.
🕻 *0171-499 8620.* ⊖ *Green Park.*
Open *10:45am–5:30pm Sun (last
adm: 4:45pm).* **Closed** *Jan & Aug.*
Adm charge. Children *under 10 not
welcome.* 🖾 🕭 🖋 *compulsory.* ⅋

THIS PALLADIAN PALACE was
finished in 1766 for the
first Earl Spencer, an ancestor
of the Princess of Wales.
Today it has been restored to
its 18th-century splendor and
contains fine paintings and
contemporary furniture; one

of the highlights is the
beautifully decorated painted
room. The house is open to
the public for guided tours,
receptions or meetings.

St. James's Palace **9**

The Mall SW1. **Map** 12 F4. ⊖ *Green
Park.* **Not open** *to the public.*

BUILT BY HENRY VIII in the
late 1530s on the site of a
former leper hospital, it was a
primary royal residence only
briefly, mainly during the
reign of Elizabeth I and
during the late 17th and early
18th centuries. In 1952 Queen
Elizabeth II made her first
speech as queen here, and
foreign ambassadors are still
officially accredited to the
Court of St. James. Its
northern gatehouse, seen
from St. James's Street, is one
of London's most evocative
Tudor landmarks. The palace
buildings behind it are now
occupied by privileged
Crown servants.

St. James's Tudor gatehouse

Royal Opera Arcade

St. James's Square ⑩

SW1. **Map** 13 A3. ⊖ *Green Park, Piccadilly Circus.*

ONE OF LONDON'S earliest squares, this was laid out in the 1670s and lined by exclusive houses for those whose business made it vital for them to live near St. James's Palace. Many of the buildings date from the 18th and 19th centuries and have had many illustrious residents. During World War II Generals Eisenhower and de Gaulle both had headquarters here.

Today No. 10 on the north side is Chatham House (1736), home of the Royal Institute for International Affairs, and in the northeast corner can be found the London Library (1896), a private lending library founded in 1841 by historian Thomas Carlyle *(see p192)* and others. The private gardens in the middle contain an equestrian statue of William III that has been here since 1808.

Royal Opera Arcade ⑪

SW1. **Map** 13 A3. ⊖ *Piccadilly Circus.*

LONDON'S FIRST shopping arcade, this was designed by John Nash and completed in 1818, behind the Haymarket Opera House (now called Her Majesty's Theatre). It preceded the Burlington Arcade *(see p91)* by a year or so. Farlows, on the Mall side of this arcade, sells shooting equipment, fishing tackle, including the famous Hunter's green Wellington boots, and a broad range of other essentials for traditional country living.

Pall Mall ⑫

SW1. **Map** 13 A4. ⊖ *Charing Cross, Green Park.*

The Duke of Wellington (1842): a frequent visitor to Pall Mall

THIS DIGNIFIED street is named after the game of *palle-maille*, a cross between croquet and golf, which was played here in the early 17th century. For more than 150 years Pall Mall has been the heart of London's clubland. Here exclusive gentlemen's clubs were formed to provide members with a refuge from their womenfolk.

The club houses now amount to a showcase of the most fashionable architects of the era. From the east end, on the left is the colonnaded entrance to No. 116, Nash's United Services Club (1827). This was the favorite club of the Duke of Wellington and it now houses the Institute of Directors. Facing it, on the other side of Waterloo Place, is the Athenaeum (No. 116), designed three years later by Decimus Burton and long the powerhouse of the British establishment. Next door are two clubs by Sir Charles Barry, architect of the Houses of Parliament: *(see pp72–3)*; the Travelers' is at No. 106 and the Reform at No. 104. The clubs' stately interiors are well preserved, but only members and their guests are admitted.

Institute of Contemporary Arts ⑬

The Mall SW1. **Map** 13 B3.
🕻 *0171-930 3647.* ⊖ *Charing Cross, Piccadilly Circus.* **Open** *noon–1am daily.* **Closed** *Christmas week, public hols.* **Adm charge.** ⬥ *notify in advance.* ▦ ▯ ⑪ ▯
Concerts, theater, dance, lectures.
See **Entertainment** *pp332–3.*

THE INSTITUTE (ICA) was established in 1947 in an effort to offer British artists some of the facilities that were available to US artists at the Museum of Modern Art in New York. Originally on Dover Street, it has been incongruously situated in part of John Nash's Classical Carlton House Terrace (1833) since 1968.

With its entrance on the Mall, this extensive warren contains a cinema, an auditorium, a bookshop, an art gallery, bar and an excellent restaurant. It offers lively and often avant-garde exhibitions, talks, concerts, films and plays. Nonmembers pay a nominal charge.

Institute of Contemporary Arts, Carlton House Terrace

St. James's Park ⑭

SW1. **Map** 13 A4. ☏ *0171-930 1793*. ⊖ *St. James's Park*. **Open** *6am–midnight daily*. ☐ **Open** *10am–6pm daily*. ♿ **Concerts** *twice daily in summer*. **Bird collection**.

IN SUMMER office workers enjoy sunbathing between the dazzling flower beds of this, the capital's most ornamental park. In winter overcoated civil servants discuss affairs of state as they stroll by the lake with its numerous ducks, geese and pelicans.

Originally a marsh, the park was drained by Henry VIII and incorporated into his hunting grounds. Later Charles II redesigned it for pedestrian pleasures, with an aviary along its southern edge (hence Birdcage Walk, the street where the aviary was). It is still a popular place to enjoy the outdoors, with an appealing view of Whitehall rooftops. In the summer there are concerts at the bandstand.

The Mall ⑮

SW1. **Map** 13 A4. ⊖ *Charing Cross, Green Park, Piccadilly Circus*.

THIS BROAD triumphal approach to Buckingham Palace was created by Aston Webb when he redesigned the front of the palace and the Victoria Monument in 1911 (*see picture p96*). It follows the course of the old path at the edge of St. James's Park, laid out in the reign of Charles II, when it became London's most fashionable promenade. On the flagpoles down both sides of the Mall fly national flags of foreign heads of state during official visits.

Marlborough House ⑯

Pall Mall SW1. **Map** 13 A4. ☏ *0171-839 3411*. ⊖ *St. James's Park, Green Park*. **Closed** *until Autumn 1995 for restoration*.

MARLBOROUGH HOUSE was designed by Christopher Wren (*see p47*) for the Duchess of Marlborough and was finished in 1711. It was substantially enlarged in the 19th century and used by members of the royal family. It was the social center of London and home to the Prince and Princess of Wales from 1863 untill 1903, when the Prince became Edward VII. An Art Nouveau memorial in the Marlborough Road wall of the house commemorates Edward's queen, Alexandra. The building now houses the Commonwealth Secretariat.

Queen's Chapel ⑰

Marlborough Rd SW1. **Map** 13 A4. ⊖ *Green Park*. **Not open** *to the public*.

THIS EXQUISITE WORK of the architect Inigo Jones was built for Charles I's French wife, Henrietta Maria, in 1627 and was the first Classical church in England. It was initially intended to be part

Queen's Chapel

of St. James's Palace but is now separated from it by Marlborough Gate. George III married his queen, Charlotte of Mecklenburg-Strelitz (who was to bear him 15 children), here in 1761.

The interior of the chapel, with its wonderful Annibale Caracci altarpiece and glorious 17th-century trim, is, unfortunately, open to regular worshipers only during the spring and early summer.

Early summer in St. James's Park

Buckingham Palace ⑳

BUCKINGHAM PALACE is the headquarters of the British monarchy. It doubles as an office and a home, and is also used for ceremonial state occasions such as banquets for visiting heads of state. About 300 people work at the palace. These include officers of the Royal Household, who organize the Queen's official affairs, as well as domestic staff.

John Nash converted the original Buckingham House into a palace for George IV (reigned 1820–30). Because both he and his brother, William IV (reigned 1830–7), died before work was completed, Queen Victoria was the first monarch to live at the palace. The present east front, facing the Mall, was added in 1913.

Music Room
State guests are presented and royal christenings take place in this room, which boasts a beautiful, original parquet floor by Nash.

The Picture Gallery houses a selection of the Queen's priceless collection of paintings.

The State Dining Room is the location for meals that are less formal than state banquets.

Kitchen and staff quarters

Blue Drawing Room
Imitation onyx columns, created by John Nash, decorate this room.

Private post office

State Ballroom
The Georgian baroque ballroom is used for state banquets and investitures.

Changing of the Guard
During the summer the palace guard is changed every day in a colorful ceremony. (See p52–5.)

The White Drawing Room is where the Royal Family assemble before passing into the State Dining Room or Ball Room.

The garden is a haven for wild life and is visible from most of the lavishly decorated state rooms at the back of the palace.

A swimming pool and a private cinema are on the palace grounds.

The Throne Room is illuminated by seven magnificent chandeliers.

The Green Drawing Room is the first of the state rooms entered by guests at royal functions.

VISITORS' CHECKLIST

SW1. **Map** 12 F5. ☎ 0171-930 5526. ⊖ St. James's Park, Victoria. 🚌 2B, 11, 16, 24, 25, 36, 38, 52, 73, 135, C1. 🚆 Victoria. **State rooms open** Aug–Sep: 9:30am–5:30pm daily. **Adm charge.** 🚫 **Changing of the Queen's Guard**: May–Aug: 11:30am daily; Sep–Apr: alternate days but subject to change without notice.

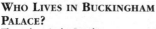

Queen's Audience Chamber
This is one of the Queen's 12 private rooms on the first floor of the palace.

The Royal Standard flies while the Queen is in residence.

View Over Mall
Traditionally, the Royal Family waves to eager crowds from the palace balcony.

WHO LIVES IN BUCKINGHAM PALACE?

The palace is the London residence of the Queen and her husband, the Duke of Edinburgh. Prince Edward also has an apartment here, as do Princess Anne and the Duke of York. About 50 domestic staff have rooms in the palace. There are more staff homes situated in the Royal Mews (see p96).

Clarence House ⑱

Stable Yard SW1. **Map** 12 F4.
🚇 *Green Park, St. James's Park.*
Not open to the public.

OVERLOOKING THE MALL, this was designed in 1827 by John Nash for Queen Victoria's predecessor, William, Duke of Clarence, who lived here after he became king in 1830. It is now the Queen Mother's London home.

Lancaster House ⑲

Stable Yard SW1. **Map** 12 F4.
🚇 *Green Park, St. James's Park.*
Not open to the public.

Lancaster House

THIS ROYAL residence was built for the Duke of York by Benjamin Wyatt, architect of Apsley House, in 1825. In 1848 Chopin played here for Queen Victoria, Prince Albert and the Duke of Wellington. It is now a conference center.

Buckingham Palace ⑳

See pp94–5.

Queen's Gallery ㉑

Buckingham Palace Rd SW1.
Map 12 F5. 📞 *0171-799 2331.*
🚇 *St. James's Park, Victoria.* **Open** 10:30am–5pm Tue–Sat, 2–5pm Sun. **Closed** Jan 1 & Dec 24–26. **Adm charge.** 📷 🚻

THE QUEEN POSSESSES one of the finest and most valuable collections of paintings in the world, rich in the work of the old masters – for instance, Vermeer and da Vinci. (For 30 years her art adviser was Sir Anthony Blunt, until he was exposed as a Soviet spy in 1979 and stripped of his knighthood.)

A selection of the works is on display in this small gallery (at the side of the palace), which was used as a conservatory until 1962. The building was once also used as a chapel, and there is still an area devoted to private worship that is screened off from the public. The exhibitions here are based on a specific theme and change regularly. A shop sells a variety of royal memorabilia.

Royal Mews ㉒

Buckingham Palace Rd SW1.
Map 12 E5. 📞 *0171-799 2331.*
🚇 *St. James's Park, Victoria.* **Open** noon–4pm Wed, plus other days during summer. Subject to closure at short notice (phone first). **Adm charge.** ♿ 📷

ALTHOUGH OPEN for only a few hours a week, the mews is worth a visit for all lovers of horses and of royal pomp. The stables and coach houses, designed by Nash in 1825, accommodate the horses and coaches used by the royal family on state occasions, as well as the Rolls-Royce limousines with transparent tops that allow their royal occupants to

Fabergé egg, Queen's Gallery

be seen by bystanders. The star exhibit is the gold state coach, built for George III in 1761, with its panels painted by Giovanni Cipriani. Among the other vehicles on view are the Irish state coach, bought by Queen Victoria for the State Opening of Parliament; the open-topped royal landau; and the glass coach used for royal weddings and for transporting foreign ambassadors. The elaborate harnesses of the horses are also on display, and so are some of the splendid animals that wear them.

The mews remains open during the week of the Royal Ascot race meeting in June. For this event, however, the Mews vehicles go to the Berkshire course, where they convey the royal party past the grandstand before the first race.

The Victoria Monument outside Buckingham Palace

Wellington Arch ㉓

SW1. **Map** 12 D4. ⊖ *Hyde Park Corner.* **Open** *5am–midnight daily.*

Aᴛᴇʀ ɴᴇᴀʀʟʏ ᴀ century of debate about what to do with the patch of land that lies in front of Apsley House, a vast archway, designed by Decimus Burton and called Wellington Arch, was erected in 1828. The sculpture, by Adrian Jones, was added later, in 1912. Before it was installed on the arch, Jones managed to seat eight people for dinner in the hollow, boat-shaped body of one of the horses.

Until 1992 London's second smallest police station (the smallest can be found on Trafalgar Square) used to be located inside the arch, which is sometimes referred to as Constitution Arch.

Wellington Arch

Apsley House ㉔

149 Piccadilly W1. **Map** 12 D4. ☎ *0171-499 5676.* ⊖ *Hyde Park Corner.* **Closed** *for refurbishment until June 1995.* **Normally open** *11am–5pm Tue–Sun (last adm: 4:30pm).* **Closed** *Jan 1 & Dec 24–26, Good Fri, May Day, public hols.* **Adm charge.** ◻ ▨ *alternate Thu pm.*

Aᴘsʟᴇʏ ʜᴏᴜsᴇ, on the south-east corner of Hyde Park, was completed by Robert Adam for Baron Apsley in 1778. Fifty years later it was enlarged and altered by the architects Benjamin and Philip Wyatt to provide a suitably grand home for the Duke of Wellington, hero of the Battle of Waterloo (1815) against Napoleon. Later Wellington became Prime Minister. It is now a museum of fascinating Wellington

Interior of Apsley House

memorabilia and some of his trophies, and is dominated by Canova's startling, twice-life-size statue of Napoleon, who was Wellington's arch-enemy, wearing only a fig leaf. This once stood in the Louvre in Paris. Most of the paintings are of Wellington's contemporaries and victories, but there are also some old masters from his collection. The few remaining Adam interiors are worth seeing.

Shepherd Market ㉕

W1. **Map** 12 E4. ⊖ *Green Park.*

Tʜɪs ᴛᴀsᴛᴇꜰᴜʟ pedestrianized enclave of small shops, restaurants and outdoor cafés, between Piccadilly and Curzon Street, was named after Edward Shepherd, who built it in the mid-18th century. During the 17th century the annual 15-day May Fair (from which the area's name is derived) was held on this site, and today Shepherd Market is still very much the center of Mayfair.

Green Park ㉖

SW1. **Map** 12 E4. ☎ *0171-930 1793.* ⊖ *Green Park, Hyde Park Corner.* **Open** *5am–midnight daily.*

Oɴᴄᴇ ᴘᴀʀᴛ ᴏꜰ Henry VIII's hunting ground, it was, like St. James's Park, adapted for public enjoyment by Charles II in the 1660s and is a natural, undulating landscape of grass and trees

(with a good spring show of daffodils). It was a favorite site for duels during the 18th century; in 1771 the poet Alfieri was wounded here by his mistress's husband, Viscount Ligonier, but then rushed back to the Haymarket Theatre still in time to catch the last act of a play. Today the park is popular with guests staying at the Mayfair hotels as a place to jog.

Faraday Museum ㉗

The Royal Institution, 21 Albemarle St W1. **Map** 12 F3. ☎ *0171-409 2992.* ⊖ *Green Park.* **Open** *10am–6pm Mon–Fri.* **Adm charge.** ◻ ▨ ▯ .

Mɪᴄʜᴀᴇʟ ꜰᴀʀᴀᴅᴀʏ was a 19th-century pioneer of the uses of electricity. His laboratory of the 1850s has been reconstructed in the basement of the Royal Institution and is on display together with a small museum showing some of Faraday's scientific apparatus and personal effects.

Michael Faraday

SOHO AND TRAFALGAR SQUARE

SOHO HAS BEEN renowned for pleasures of the table, the flesh and the intellect ever since it was first developed in the late 17th century. For its first century the area was one of London's most fashionable, and Soho residents of the time have gone down in history for their extravagant parties.

Today the area is the capital's best-known red-light district, even though most of the prostitutes were forced

Clock on Liberty department store

from the streets by legislation in 1959. There is also a fertile subculture of artists and writers in the dingy pubs, clubs and cafés.

Soho is one of London's most multicultural districts. The first immigrants were 18th-century Huguenots from France *(see Christ Church, Spitalfields p170)*. They were followed by people from all over the rest of Europe, but today Soho is famous for its Chinatown.

SIGHTS AT A GLANCE

Historic Streets and Buildings

Trafalgar Square **1**
Admiralty Arch **2**
Leicester Square **6**
Shaftesbury Avenue **8**
Chinatown **9**
Charing Cross Road **10**
Soho Square **12**
Carnaby Street **14**

Shops and Markets

Berwick Street Market **13**
Liberty **15**

Churches

St. Martin-in-the-Fields **4**

Museums and Galleries

National Gallery pp104–7 **3**
National Portrait Gallery **5**
Design Council **7**

Theaters

Palace Theatre **11**

GETTING THERE

This area is served by the Central, Piccadilly, Bakerloo, Victoria, Northern and Jubilee lines. Many buses pass through Trafalgar Square. British Rail trains run from Charing Cross.

KEY

▢	Street-by-Street map
⊖	Underground station
⯊	British Rail station
▣	Parking

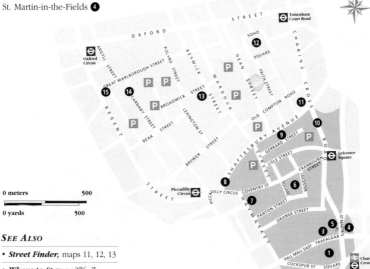

SEE ALSO

The fountains of Trafalgar Square

Street by Street: Trafalgar Square

Theaters, cinemas, night clubs and restaurants make this London's prime area for entertainment; there are also vast official buildings and narrow, shop-lined streets nearby.

To Tottenham Court Road station

Charing Cross Road
The shops here are a feast for booklovers ⑩

Shaftesbury Avenue
Theaterland's main artery is lined with posters for current shows ⑧

★ Chinatown
An area of Chinese restaurants and shops, it is home to many Chinese-speaking people ⑨

The Blue Posts pub stands on the site of a pick-up point for sedan chairs in the 18th century.

Guinness World of Records reveals the best, worst and most of anything and everything *(see p340)*.

Mechanized pop stars wave from the balcony of Rock Circus, in the former London Pavilion.

Design Council
The best in British design can be seen and bought here ⑦

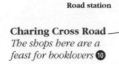

Leicester Square
Film pioneer Charlie Chaplin stands in the traffic-free square ⑥

The Theatre Royal, on the site of an older theater, is graced by John Nash's portico.

STAR SIGHTS

★ **National Gallery**

★ **National Portrait Gallery**

★ **St. Martin-in-the-Fields**

★ **Chinatown**

★ **Trafalgar Square**

KEY

– – – Suggested route

0 meters   100

0 yards   100

Notre Dame, once a theater, was converted into a church in 1855. The Jean Cocteau murals inside date from 1960.

LOCATOR MAP
See Central London Map pp12–13

The Hippodrome, a disco and nightclub *(see pp334–5)*, was once a variety theater.

Cecil Court is lined with shops selling old books and prints *(see p317)*.

★ **National Gallery**
The national collection of art is housed in these buildings ❸

Leicester Square station

★ **St. Martin-in-the-Fields**
James Gibbs's masterpiece set the US "Colonial" style ❹

★ **National Portrait Gallery**
Portraits of prominent Britons from Tudor times to the present day adorn the walls here ❺

Charing Cross station

Admiralty Arch
The Mall's regal entrance was built in 1910 ❷

★ **Trafalgar Square**
Millions of tourists come here to feed the pigeons and admire the fountains ❶

Nelson's Column

Trafalgar Square ❶

WC2. **Map** 13 B3. 🚇 *Charing Cross.*

L ONDON'S MAIN venue for
rallies and outdoor public
meetings, the square was
conceived by John Nash and
was mainly constructed
during the 1830s. The 165-ft
(50-m) column commemorates
Admiral Lord Nelson, Britain's
most famous sea lord, who
died heroically at the Battle of
Trafalgar against Napoleon in
1805. It dates from 1842; 14
stonemasons held a dinner on
its flat top before the statue of
Nelson was finally installed.
Edwin Landseer's four
impassive lions were added
to guard its base 25 years
later. The north side of the
square is now taken up by
the National Gallery and its
annex *(see pp104–7)*, with
Canada House on the
west side, and South
Africa House on the
east. The restored Grand
Buildings on the south
side, with their fine
arcade, were built in
1880 as the Grand
Hotel. Today the
pigeon-filled square
is a popular rallying
point for demonstra-
tions, and for raucous
New Year's Eve
celebrations.

**Nelson's statue over-
looking the square**

Admiralty Arch ❷

The Mall SW1. **Map** 13 B3.
🚇 *Charing Cross.*

D ESIGNED IN 1911, this triple
archway was part of
Aston Webb's scheme to
rebuild the Mall as a grand
processional route honoring
Queen Victoria. The arch
effectively seals the eastern
end of the Mall, although
traffic passes through the
smaller side gates, and
separates courtly London
from the hurly-burly of
Trafalgar Square. The central
gate is opened only for royal
processions, making a fine
setting for the coaches and
horses trotting through.

Filming *Howard's End* at Admiralty Arch

National Gallery ❸

See pp104–7.

St. Martin-in-the-Fields ❹

Trafalgar Sq WC2. **Map** 13 B3.
📞 *0171-930 1862.* 🚇 *Charing
Cross.* **Open** 8am–6pm daily. ✝
11:30 am Sun. ♿ 🅿 🛍 **London
Brass Rubbing Center** 📞 *0171-437
6023.* **Open** 10am–6pm Mon–Sat,
noon–6pm Sun. **Concerts** *see
Entertainment pp330–1.*

T HERE HAS BEEN a church on
this site since the 13th
century. Many famous people
were buried here, including
Charles II's mistress, Nell
Gwynn, and the painters
William Hogarth and Joshua
Reynolds. The present church
was designed by James Gibbs
and completed in 1726. In
architectural terms it was one
of the most influential ever
built; it was much copied in
the United States where it
became a model for the
Colonial style of church-
building. An unusual feature
of St. Martin's spacious interior
is the royal box at gallery
level on the left of the altar.
   From 1914 until 1927 the
crypt was opened as a shelter
for homeless soldiers and
down-and-outs; during World
War II it was an air-raid
shelter. Today it still plays a
role, helping the homeless
and providing a lunchtime
soup kitchen for them. It also
houses a café and a religious
bookshop as well as the

London Brass Rubbing
Center. There is a good craft
market in the yard outside
(see p323) and regular lunchtime and evening concerts are
held in the church.

National Portrait Gallery ❺

2 St. Martin's Pl WC2. **Map** 13 B3.
📞 *0171-306 0055.* 🚇 *Leicester Sq,
Charing Cross.* **Open** 10am–6pm
Mon–Sat; noon–6pm Sun. **Closed**
Jan 1, Good Fri, May Day, Dec 24–25.
🚫 ♿ *limited.* 📷 *during August.*
🛍 **Lectures.**

T OO OFTEN IGNORED in favor
of the National Gallery
next door, this fascinating
museum recounts British
history through portraits of its
main characters. There are
pictures of kings, queens,
poets, musicians, artists,
thinkers, heroes and villains
from all periods since the late
14th century. The oldest

**Rodrigo Moynihan's portrait of
Margaret Thatcher (1984)**

works, on the fourth floor, include a Hans Holbein cartoon of Henry VIII and paintings of several of his unfortunate wives. The Elizabethans, a floor higher, feature probably the only surviving portrait of Shakespeare taken from life. Lower floors continue the collection chronologically, with works from such artists as van Dyck, Reynolds, Gainsborough and Sargent.

The 20th century is represented on the first floor where there are as many photographs as paintings. Here musicians Elton John and Mick Jagger, and fashion designers Mary Quant and Katharine Hamnett hang around the corner from the Royal Family and politicians.

The gallery also houses temporary exhibitions and has an excellent shop selling books on art and literature, as well as an extensive range of cards, prints and posters featuring pictures from the main collection.

Leicester Square ❻

WC2. **Map** 13 B2. 🚇 *Leicester Sq, Piccadilly Circus.*

IT IS HARD to imagine that this, the perpetually animated heart of the West End entertainment district, was once a fashionable place to live. Laid out in 1670 south of Leicester House, a long-gone royal residence, the square's early occupants included the scientist Isaac Newton and later the artists Joshua Reynolds and William Hogarth. (Hogarth's house, in the southeast corner, became the Hôtel de la Sablonère in 1801, probably the area's first public restaurant.)

In Victorian times several of London's most popular music halls were established here, including the Empire (today the cinema on the same site perpetuates the name) and the Alhambra, replaced in 1937 by the Art Deco Odeon. The center of the square has recently been refurbished and includes a booth selling cut-price theater tickets *(see*

pp326–7). There is also a statue of Charlie Chaplin (by John Doubleday), unveiled in 1981. The Shakespeare fountain dates from an earlier renovation in 1874.

Design Council ❼

28 Haymarket SW1. **Map** 13 A3. ☎ *0171-839 8000.* 🚇 *Leicester Sq, Piccadilly Circus.* **Open** *10am-6pm Mon–Sat.* **Closed** *public hols.* 📷 ♿ 🛒

FOUNDED IN 1944 as the Council for Industrial Design, this center was the only permanent showcase for modern British design until the recent opening of the Design Museum in Bermondsey *(see p179)*. Its display changes periodically and winners of the Design Council's annual awards are shown in the Awards Gallery. The bookshop has books on all aspects of design.

Shaftesbury Avenue ❽

W1. **Map** 13 A2. 🚇 *Piccadilly Circus, Leicester Sq.*

THE MAIN ARTERY of London's theaterland, Shaftesbury Avenue has six theaters and two cinemas, all on its north side. This street was cut through an area of terrible slums between 1877 and 1886 in order to improve communications across the city's busy West End; it follows the route of a much earlier highway. It is named after the Earl of Shaftesbury (1801–85), whose attempts to improve housing conditions had helped some of the local poor. (The Earl is also commemorated by the Eros statue in Piccadilly Circus – *see p90*). The Lyric Theatre, which was designed by C. J. Phipps, has been open for almost the same length of time as the avenue.

London's West End: the Globe Theatre (now known as the Gielgud)

National Gallery ❸

Trafalgar Square facade

THE NATIONAL GALLERY has flourished since its inception in the early 19th century. In 1824 George IV persuaded a reluctant government to buy 38 major paintings, including works by Raphael and Rembrandt, and these became the start of a national collection. The collection grew over the years as rich benefactors contributed works and money. The main gallery building was designed in Neoclassical style by William Wilkins and built from 1834 to 1838. To its left lies the new Sainsbury Wing, financed by the grocery family and completed in 1991. It houses some spectacular early Renaissance art.

GALLERY GUIDE

Most of the collection is housed on one floor divided into four wings. The paintings hang chronologically, with the earliest works (1260–1510) in the Sainsbury Wing. The North, West and East Wings cover 1510–1600, 1600–1700 and 1700–1920. Lesser paintings of all periods are on the lower floor.

Stairs to lower galleries

Orange St entrance ♿

Stairs to lower floor 🚻 ♿ 🚹 🚺

Link to main building

Stairs to lower galleries 🖼 🚻 ♿ 🚹 🚺

★ **Leonardo Cartoon** *(1510s)*
The genius of Leonardo da Vinci glows through this chalk drawing of the Virgin and Child with St. Anne and John the Baptist.

KEY TO FLOORPLAN

⬜	Painting 1260–1510
⬜	Painting 1510–1600
⬜	Painting 1600–1700
⬜	Painting 1700–1920
⬜	Non-exhibition space
⬜	Special exhibitions

Main entrance to Sainsbury Wing ♿

Doge Leonardo Loredan *(1501)*
Giovanni Bellini portrays this Venetian head of state as a serene father figure.

★ Rokeby Venus (1649)
Diego Velázquez painted it
to match a lost
Venetian
nude.

★ The Haywain (1821)
John Constable brilliantly
caught the effect of distance
and the changing light and
shadow of a typically
English cloudy summer day
in this famous classic.

VISITORS' CHECKLIST

Trafalgar Sq WC2. **Map** 13 B3.
☎ 0171-839 3321. ☎ 0171-
389 1785. ⊖ Charing Cross,
Leicester Sq, Piccadilly Circus.
🚌 3, 6, 9, 11, 12, 13, 15, 23,
24, 29, 30, 53, 77a, 88, 94, 109,
159, 176, 177, 184, 196.
🚆 Charing Cross. **Open** 10am–
6pm Mon–Sat, 2–6pm Sun.
Closed Jan 1, Good Friday, Dec
24–26 and public hols. 🚫
♿ Orange St and Sainsbury
Wing entrances. 📷 ▯ 🍴 🛍
**Lectures, film presentations,
videos, exhibitions, events.**

Bathers at Asnières (1884)
Georges Seurat experiments here
with millions of little dots of color,
to create a Neoclassical portrayal
of modern urban life.

Stairs to
lower floor
▯ 🚹 🛗

★ The Ambassadors
The strange shape in the
foreground of this Hans
Holbein portrait (1533)
is a foreshortened skull,
a symbol of mortality.

Trafalgar Square
entrance

★ Baptism of Christ
Piero della Francesca
painted this tranquil
masterpiece (1450s) of
early Renaissance
perspective for a church
in his native Umbria.

Arnolfini Marriage
The woman in Jan van
Eyck's famous painting
(1434) is not pregnant –
her rotund shape
conforms to period ideas
of female beauty.

STAR PICTURES

★ **Baptism of Christ**
by Piero della
Francesca

★ **Cartoon** by
Leonardo da Vinci

★ **Rokeby Venus** by
Diego Velázquez

★ **The Ambassadors**
by Hans Holbein

★ **The Haywain** by
John Constable

Exploring the National Gallery

T HE NATIONAL GALLERY IS London's leading art museum, with over 2,200 paintings, most kept on permanent display. The collection includes everything from early works by Giotto, in the 13th century, to 20th-century Picassos, but its particular strengths are in Dutch, early Renaissance Italian and 17th-century Spanish painting. The bulk of the modern and British collections are housed in the Tate Gallery *(see pp82–5).*

The Adoration of the Kings (1564) by Pieter Brueghel the Elder

EARLY RENAISSANCE (1260–1510): ITALIAN AND NORTHERN PAINTING

T HREE LUSTROUS PANELS from the *Maestà*, Duccio's great altarpiece in the Siena cathedral, are among the earliest paintings here. Other Italian works of the period include his *Madonna*.

The fine *Wilton Diptych* portraying England's Richard II is probably by a French artist. It displays the lyrical elegance of the International Gothic style that swept Europe.

Italian masters of this style include Pisanello and Gentile da Fabriano, whose *Madonna* often hangs beside another, by Masaccio – both date from 1426. Also shown are works by Masaccio's pupil, Filippo Lippi, as well as Botticelli and Uccello. Umbrian paintings include Piero della Francesca's *Nativity* and *Baptism* and an excellent collection of Mantegna, Bellini and other works from the Venetian and Ferrarese schools. Antonello da Messina's *St. Jerome in His Study* has been mistaken for a van Eyck; it is not hard to see why, when you compare it with van Eyck's *Arnolfini Marriage.* Important

Netherlandish pictures, including some by Rogier van der Weyden and his followers, are also here, in the new Sainsbury Wing.

HIGH RENAISSANCE (1520–1600): ITALIAN, NETHERLANDISH AND GERMAN PAINTING

Christ Mocked (1490–1500) by Hieronymus Bosch

S EBASTIANO DEL PIOMBO'S *The Raising of Lazarus* was painted, with Michelangelo's assistance, to rival Raphael's great *Transfiguration*, which hangs in the Vatican in Rome.

These and other well-known names of the High (or late) Renaissance are extremely well represented, often with massive works. Watch for Parmigianino's *Madonna and Child with Saints*, Leonardo da Vinci's black chalk cartoon of the *Virgin and Child* (a full-sized drawing used for copying as a painting) and his second version of the *Virgin of the Rocks*. There are also tender and amusing works by Piero di Cosimo and several Titians, including *Bacchus and Ariadne* – which the public found too bright and garish when it was first cleaned by the gallery in the 1840s.

The Netherlandish and German collections are weaker. Even so, they include *The Ambassadors*; a fine double portrait by Holbein; and Altdorfer's superb *Christ Bidding Farewell to His Mother*, bought by the gallery in 1980. There is also a Hieronymus Bosch of *Christ Mocked* (sometimes known as *The Crowning with Thorns*), and an excellent Brueghel, *The Adoration of the Kings.*

The Annunciation (1448) by Filippo Lippi

THE SAINSBURY WING

Plans for this new wing, opened in 1991, provoked a storm of dissension. An incensed Prince Charles dubbed an early design "a monstrous carbuncle on the face of a much-loved friend." The final building, by Robert Venturi, has drawn criticism, from other quarters, for being a derivative compromise.

Inside is the Micro Gallery, a computerized database of the collection from which you can print out floorplans and illustrated information.

DUTCH, ITALIAN, FRENCH AND SPANISH PAINTING (1600–1700)

THE SUPERB DUTCH collection gives two entire rooms to Rembrandt. There are also works by Vermeer, Van Dyck (among them his equestrian portrait of King Charles I) and Rubens (including the popular *Chapeau de Paille*).

From Italy, the works of Carracci and Caravaggio are strongly represented, and Salvatore Rosa has a glowering self-portrait.

French works on show include a magnificent portrait of Cardinal Richelieu by Philippe de Champaigne. Claude's seascape, *The Embarkation of the Queen of Sheba*, hangs beside Turner's rival painting *Dido Building Carthage*, as Turner himself had instructed.

The Spanish school has works by Murillo, Velázquez, Zurbarán and others.

Young Woman Standing at a Virginal (1670) by Jan Vermeer

The Scale of Love (1715–18) by Jean Antoine Watteau

VENETIAN, FRENCH AND ENGLISH PAINTING (1700–1800)

ONE OF THE GALLERY's most famous 18th-century works is Canaletto's *The Stone-Mason's Yard*. Other Venetians here are Longhi and Tiepolo.

The French collection includes Rococo masters such as Chardin, Watteau and Boucher, as well as landscapists and portraitists.

Gainsborough's early, gauche *Mr. and Mrs. Andrews* and *The Morning Walk* are favorites with visitors; his rival, Sir Joshua Reynolds, is represented by some of his most Classical work and by more informal portraits.

ENGLISH, FRENCH AND GERMAN PAINTING (1800–1900)

THE GREAT AGE of 19th-century landscape painting is amply represented here, with fine works by Constable and Turner as well as by the French artists Corot and Daubigny.

Of Romantic art, there is Géricault's vivid work, *Horse Frightened by Lightning*, and several interesting paintings by Delacroix. In contrast, the society portrait of *Mme. Moitessier* by Ingres, though still Romantic, is more restrained and Classical.

Impressionists and other French avant-garde artists are well represented. Highlights include *Waterlilies* by Monet, Renoir's *Umbrellas*, Van Gogh's *Sunflowers*, Seurat's *Bathers at Asnières* and Rousseau's *Tropical Storm with Tiger*.

Klimt's *Hermione Gallia* is one of only four German paintings in the gallery, while most English works of the period are in the Tate Gallery (see pp82–5).

Umbrellas (1881–6) by Pierre-Auguste Renoir

Chinatown 9

Streets around Gerrard St W1.
Map 13 A2. ⊖ *Leicester Sq,*
Piccadilly Circus.

THERE HAS BEEN a Chinese
community in London
since the 19th century.
Originally it was concentrated
around the East End docks at
Limehouse, where the opium
dens of Victorian melodrama
were located. As the number
of immigrants increased in the
1950s, many moved into Soho
where they created an ever-
expanding Chinatown. It
contains scores of restaurants,
and mysterious aroma-filled
shops selling Asian produce.
Three Chinese arches straddle
Gerrard Street, where a vibrant,
colorful street festival, held
every year, celebrates Chinese
New Year *(see p59).*

Charing Cross Road 10

WC2. **Map** 13 B2. ⊖ *Leicester Sq.*
See **Shops and Markets** *p316.*

**Antiquarian books from the
shops on Charing Cross Road**

THE ROAD is a mecca for
booklovers, with a row of
second-hand bookstores
south of Cambridge Circus
and, north of these, a group
of shops that collectively
should be able to supply
almost any recently published
volume. Be sure to visit the
giants: chaotic Foyle's and
user-friendly Waterstones, and
Collet's international bookstore, which specializes in
European politics and
literature. At the junction with
New Oxford Street rises the
1960s skyscraper, Center
Point. It lay empty for nearly
ten years after it was built; its
owners found this more
profitable than renting it out.

At the Palace Theatre in 1898

Palace Theatre 11

Shaftesbury Ave W1. **Map** 13 B2.
[**Box office** *0171-434 0909.*
⊖ *Leicester Sq.* **Open** for
performances only. See
Entertainment *pp326–7.*

MOST WEST END theaters
are disappointingly
plain. This one, which
dominates the west side
of Cambridge Circus, is a
splendid exception, with its
sparkling terracotta exterior
and opulent furnishings.
Completed as an opera house
in 1891, it became a music
hall the following year. The
ballerina Anna Pavlova made
her London debut here in
1910. Now the theater, owned
by Andrew Lloyd Webber
whose own musicals are all
over London, stages hit
shows such as *Les Miserables*.

Soho Square 12

W1. **Map** 13 A1. ⊖ *Tottenham
Court Rd.*

SOON AFTER it was laid out
in 1681 this enjoyed a brief
reign as the most fashionable
address in London. Originally
it was called King Square,
after Charles II whose statue
was erected in the middle. The
square went out of fashion by
the late 18th century and is
now surrounded by bland
office buildings. The mock-
Tudor garden shed in the
center was added much later
in Victorian times.

Berwick Street Market 13

W1. **Map** 13 A1. ⊖ *Piccadilly
Circus.* **Open** *9am–6pm Mon–Sat.*
See **Shops and Markets** *p322.*

THERE HAS BEEN a market
here since the 1840s.
Berwick Street trader Jack
Smith introduced grapefruit to
London in 1890. Today this is
the West End's best street
market, at its cheeriest and
most crowded during the
lunch hour. The freshest and
least expensive produce for
miles around is to be had
here. There are also many
interesting shops, notably
Camisa, a delectable Italian
delicatessen, and Borovick's,
which sells extraordinary
fabrics. At its southern end
the street narrows into an
alley where Raymond's Revue
Bar (the comparatively
respectable face of Soho
sleaze) has presented its
festival of erotica since 1958.

Some of London's cheapest produce at Berwick Street Market

Carnaby Street ⓮

W1. **Map** 12 F2. 🚇 *Oxford Circus.*

During the 1960s this street was so much the center of swinging London that the Oxford English Dictionary recognized the noun "Carnaby Street" as meaning "fashionable clothing for young people." Today the street caters more to tourists than to the truly fashionable. England's oldest pipe maker, Inderwick's, founded in 1797, is located at No. 45. There are some interesting young designers' shops selling very stylish clothing in nearby backstreets, notably those on Newburgh Street *(see pp314–15).*

Liberty's mock-Tudor façade

Liberty ⓯

Regent St W1. **Map** 12 F2. 🚇 *Oxford Circus. See **Shops and Markets** p311.*

Arthur Lasenby Liberty opened his first shop, selling silks from the Far East on Regent Street in 1875. Among his first customers were the artists Ruskin, Rossetti and Whistler. Soon Liberty prints and designs, by artists such as William Morris, became a strong influence on the Arts and Crafts movement of the late 19th and early 20th centuries. They are still very fashionable today.

The present mock-Tudor building with its country-house feel dates from 1925, and was built specifically to house the store.

Today the shop maintains its strong links with the East. The basement Oriental Bazaar and the top floor, which is crammed with period Art Nouveau and Arts and Crafts furniture, are worth visiting.

The Heart of Soho

Old Compton Street is Soho's High Street. Its shops and restaurants reflect the variety of people who have lived in the area over the centuries. These include many great artists, writers and musicians.

Bar Italia is a coffee shop situated under the room where John Logie Baird first demonstrated television in 1926. As a child, Mozart stayed next door with his family in 1764 and 1765.

Wheeler's opened in 1929 as part of the London-wide fish restaurant chain *(see p301).*

Ronnie Scott's opened in 1959, and nearly all the big names of jazz have played here *(see pp333–5).*

The Coach and Horses pub has been a center of bohemian Soho since the 1950s and is still popular.

Patisserie Valerie is a Hungarian-owned café serving delicious pastries *(see pp306–7).*

St. Anne's Church Tower is all that remained after a bomb destroyed the church in 1940.

The French House was frequented by Maurice Chevalier and General de Gaulle.

The Palace Theatre has hosted many successful musicals.

COVENT GARDEN AND THE STRAND

T HE OPEN-AIR cafés, novelty street entertainers, stylish shops and markets make this area a magnet for visitors. At its center is the Piazza, which sheltered a wholesale market until 1974. Since then, the pretty Victorian buildings here and in the surrounding streets have been converted into one of the city's liveliest districts. In medieval times, the area was occupied by a convent garden that supplied Westminster Abbey with produce. Then in the 1630s,

Inigo Jones laid out the Piazza as London's first square, with its west side dominated by St. Paul's Church.

Dried flowers from the Piazza

The Piazza was commissioned as a residential development by the Earl of Bedford, owner of one of the mansions that lined the Strand. Before the Embankment was built, the Strand ran along the river.

SIGHTS AT A GLANCE

Historic Streets and Buildings
The Piazza and Central Market ❶
Neal Street and Neal's Yard ❼
Savoy Hotel ❽
Somerset House ❿
Roman Bath ⓲
Bush House ⓳
Adelphi ⓴
Charing Cross ㉓

Museums and Galleries
London Transport Museum ❸
Theatre Museum ❹
Contemporary Applied Arts ❽
Photographers' Gallery ⓫
Courtauld Institute Galleries ⓰

Churches
St. Paul's Church ❷
Savoy Chapel ⓮
St. Mary-le-Strand ⓱

Monuments and Statues
Seven Dials ❾
Cleopatra's Needle ⓴

Parks and Gardens
Victoria Embankment Gardens ㉑

Famous Theaters
Theatre Royal ❺
Royal Opera House ❻
Adelphi Theatre ⓬
The London Coliseum ㉔

Historic Pubs and Restaurants
Lamb and Flag ❿

0 meters	500
0 yards	500

GETTING THERE

Covent Garden, Leicester Square and Charing Cross Underground stations are all nearby. There are frequent buses: 9, 11, 15 and 30 to the Strand or 14, 19, 22b, 24, 29, 38 and 176 to Shaftesbury Avenue. Charing Cross British Rail station is a short walk.

KEY

▨	Street-by-Street map
❷	Undergound station
≋	British Rail station
P	Parking

SEE ALSO

• **Street Finder**, maps 13, 14
• **Where to Stay** pp276–7
• **Restaurants** pp292–4

The old vegetable market, now converted into shops and bars

Street by Street: Covent Garden

ONCE AN AREA of decaying streets and
warehouses, Covent Garden came
alive only after dark when the fruit and
vegetable market traders went
about their business. Now it
is completely revitalized.
Day and night visitors,
residents and street-
entertainers of every
type throng the
piazza, much as
they would have
done several
centuries ago.

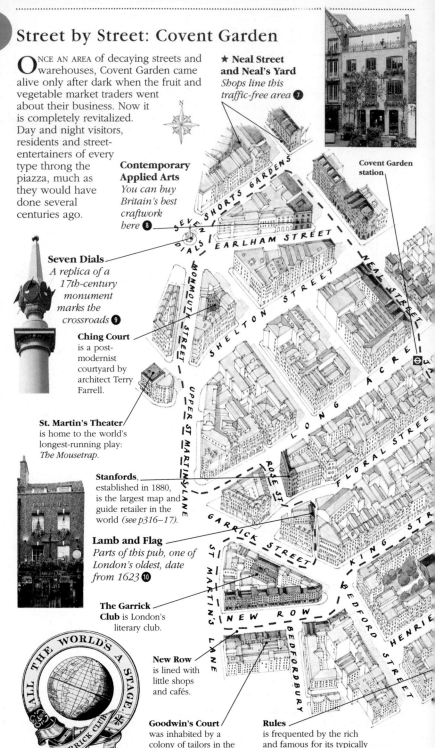

**★ Neal Street
and Neal's Yard**
*Shops line this
traffic-free area* ❼

**Covent Garden
station**

**Contemporary
Applied Arts**
*You can buy
Britain's best
craftwork
here* ❽

Seven Dials
*A replica of a
17th-century
monument
marks the
crossroads* ❾

Ching Court
is a post-
modernist
courtyard by
architect Terry
Farrell.

St. Martin's Theater
is home to the world's
longest-running play:
The Mousetrap.

Stanfords,
established in 1880,
is the largest map and
guide retailer in the
world *(see p316–17).*

Lamb and Flag
*Parts of this pub, one of
London's oldest, date
from 1623* ❿

**The Garrick
Club** is London's
literary club.

New Row
is lined with
little shops
and cafés.

Goodwin's Court
was inhabited by a
colony of tailors in the
18th century.

Rules
is frequented by the rich
and famous for its typically
English food *(see p295).*

ALL THE WORLD'S A STAGE

GARRICK CLUB

★ The Piazza and Central Market
Performers of all kinds–jugglers, clowns, acrobats and musicians–entertain the crowds in the square ❶

Royal Opera House
Most of the world's greatest singers and dancers have appeared on its stage ❻

Bow Street Police Station housed London's first police force, the Bow Street Runners, in the 18th century. It closed in 1992.

Floral Hall used to sell exotic fruit as well as fresh flowers.

★ Theatre Museum
A collection of theatrical memorabilia is housed here ❹

Theatre Royal
The old theater now presents extravagant musicals ❺

Boswells, now a coffeehouse, is where Dr. Johnson first met his biographer, Boswell.

Jubilee Market sells clothes and bric-a-brac.

★ St. Paul's Church
Despite appearances, Inigo Jones's church faces away from the piazza– the entrance is through a churchyard ❷

★ London Transport Museum
The history of the city's subways and buses is brought to life in this museum ❸

LOCATOR MAP
See Central London Map pp12–13

BLOOMSBURY & FITZROVIA
HOLBORN & THE INNS OF COURT
SOHO & TRAFALGAR SQUARE
COVENT GARDEN & THE STRAND
Thames
PICCADILLY & ST JAMES'S
WHITEHALL & WESTMINSTER
SOUTH BANK

STAR SIGHTS

* ★ The Piazza and Central Market
* ★ St. Paul's Church
* ★ The London Transport Museum
* ★ Theatre Museum
* ★ Neal Street and Neal's Yard

KEY

— — —   Suggested route

0 meters	100
0 yards	100

The Piazza and Central Market ❶

Covent Garden WC2. **Map** 13 C2.
⊖ *Covent Garden.*   🅱 *but cobbled streets.* **Street performers**
10am–dusk daily. See **Shops and Markets** *p323.*

THE 17TH-CENTURY architect Inigo Jones originally planned this area to be an elegant residential square, modeled on the piazza at Livorno in northern Italy. Today the buildings on and around the Piazza are almost entirely Victorian. The covered central market was designed by Charles Fowler in 1833 for fruit and vegetable wholesalers, the glass-and-iron roof anticipating the giant rail termini built later in the century – for instance, St. Pancras *(see p130)* and Waterloo *(see p187)*. It now makes a magnificent arena for an array of small shops selling designer clothes, books, arts, crafts, decorative items and antiques, all surrounded by market stalls that overflow north into the adjacent streets and south into Jubilee Hall, which was built in 1903.

The colonnaded Bedford Chambers, on the north side, give a hint of Inigo Jones's plan, although even they are not original; they were rebuilt and partially modified in 1879.

Street entertainment is a tradition of the area; in 1662, diarist Samuel Pepys wrote of watching a Punch and Judy show under the portico of St Paul's Church.

West entrance to St. Paul's

St. Paul's Church ❷

Bedford St WC2. **Map** 13 C2.
📞 *0171-836 5221.* ⊖ *Covent Garden.* **Open** *8:30am–4:30pm Mon–Fri, 10am–1pm Sun.*
✝ *11am Sun.* 🅾 🅱

INIGO JONES built this church (completed in 1633) with the altar at the west end, so as to allow his grand portico, with its two square and two round columns, to face east into the new Piazza. Clerics objected to this unorthodox arrangement, and the altar was moved to its conventional position at the east end. Jones still went ahead with his original exterior design. Thus the church is entered from the west, and the east portico is essentially a fake door, used now as an impromptu stage for street entertainers. In 1795 the interior was destroyed by fire but was rebuilt in Jones's airy, uncomplicated style. Today the church is all that is left of Jones's original plan for the Piazza. St. Paul's has long been called "the actors' church," and plaques commemorate men and women of the theater. A 17th-century carving by Grinling Gibbons, on the west screen, is a memorial to the architect.

Punch and Judy performer

London Transport Museum ❸

The Piazza WC2. **Map** 13 C2.
📞 *0171-379 6344.* ⊖ *Covent Garden.* **Open** *10am–6pm daily (last adm: 5:15pm).* **Closed** *Dec 24–26.* **Museum closed** *Mar–Dec 1993 for refurbishment. Please call for further details.* **Adm charge.**
🅾 🅱 🅿

London Transport Museum

YOU DO NOT have to be an ardent traveler or collector to enjoy this exhibition. Since 1980 the intriguing collection has been housed in the picturesque Victorian Flower Market, built in 1872, and it features past and present examples of public transportation.

The history of London's public transportation is in essence its social history. Bus, tram and underground route patterns first reflected the city's growth and then promoted it: the northern and western suburbs began to develop only after their tube (subway) connections were built. The museum houses a fine collection of 20th-century commercial art. London's bus and train companies have been, and still are, prolific patrons of contemporary artists, and copies of some of the finest posters on display can be bought at the well-stocked museum shop. They include the innovative Art Deco designs of E. McKnight Kauffer, as well as work by renowned artists of the 1930s, such as Graham Sutherland and Paul Nash.

This museum is excellent for children. There are plenty of hands-on exhibits, and these include the opportunity for children to put themselves in the driver's seat of a London bus, or a train from the underground system.

A mid-18th-century view of the Piazza

Theatre Museum ❹

7 Russell St WC2. **Map** 13 C2.
📞 *0171-836 7891.* ⊖ *Covent
Garden.* **Open** *11am–7pm Tue–Sun.*
Closed *Jan 1, Dec 25–26, & public
hols.* **Adm charge.** 🚻 📷 🏛
**Studio theater performances,
events.**

A LARGE GOLD statue of the
Spirit of Gaiety, which
once stood on the roof of
the long-gone Gaiety variety
theater, lures you down into
the museum's subterranean
galleries with their fascinating
collection of theatrical
memorabilia. This includes
playbills, programs, props
and costumes from historic
productions; bits of interior
decor from vanished theaters;
and paintings of actors and
scenes from plays. A display
illustrates the development of
theater from Shakespeare's
time to the present, with
models of auditoriums
through the ages. Exhibitions
are held in the Gielgud and
Irving galleries, and young
companies mount produc-
tions in the theater inside.

Theatre Royal ❺

Catherine St WC2. **Map** 13 C2.
📞 *0171-494 5040.* ⊖ *Covent
Garden, Holborn, Temple.* **Open**
*for performances only. See
Entertainment pp326–7*

T HE FIRST THEATER on this
site was built in 1663 as
one of only two venues
in London where drama
could legally be staged.
Nell Gwynn, King
Charles II's mistress,
acted here. Three of the
theaters built on this site
since then burned down,
including one designed
by Sir Christopher Wren
(see p47). The present
building, by Benjamin
Wyatt, was completed in
1812 and has one of the
city's largest auditoriums.
In the 1800s it was
famous for pantomimes –
now it specializes in
blockbuster musicals. It
is called the Theatre
Royal, Drury Lane, even
though its entrance is
on Catherine Street.

The Royal Opera House, designed by E. M. Barry in 1858

Royal Opera House ❻

Covent Garden WC2. **Map** 13 C2.
📞 *0171-240 1066.* ⊖ *Covent
Garden.* **Open** *for performances only.
See* **Entertainment** *p330.*

T HE FIRST THEATER on this
site was built in 1732 and
staged plays as well as
concerts. However, like its
neighbor the Theatre Royal, it
proved prone to fire and was
destroyed in 1808 and again
in 1856. The present opera
house was designed in 1858
by E. M. Barry (son of the
architect of the Houses of
Parliament). John Flaxman's
portico frieze, of tragedy and
comedy, survived from the
previous building of 1809.
The Opera House has
had both high and low
points during its history.
In 1892, the first British
performance of Wagner's
Ring was conducted
here by Gustav Mahler.
Later, during World War I,
the opera house was
used as a storehouse by
the government.
The siting of a fine
opera house next to a
busy produce market
was exploited by
George Bernard Shaw in
1913 for his *Pygmalion*,
on which the musical
My Fair Lady is based.
The building is now
the home of the Royal
Opera and Royal Ballet
companies – the best

tickets cost over £100 (about
$200) and are hard to acquire.
Recently some performances
have been televised free on
giant screens to very large
audiences in the Piazza.

Neal Street and Neal's Yard ❼

Covent Garden WC2. **Map** B1 13.
⊖ *Covent Garden. See* **Shops and
Markets** *pp312–13.*

A specialty shop on Neal Street

I N THIS ATTRACTIVE street,
former warehouses from
the 19th century can be
identified by the hoisting
mechanisms high on their
exterior walls. The buildings
have been converted into
attractive shops, art galleries
and restaurants. Off Neal
Street is Neal's Yard, a mock
rustic cornucopia for lovers of
wholefoods, farmhouse
cheeses and yogurts, salads,
herbs and fresh-baked
breads. Above the Wholefood
Warehouse is a bizarre and
entertaining water clock
designed by Tim Hunkin.

Modern ceramics in Contemporary Applied Arts

Contemporary Applied Arts ❽

43 Earlham St WC2. **Map** 13 B2.
📞 0171-836 6993. ⊖ *Covent
Garden*. **Open** *10am–6pm
Mon–Wed, Fri, Sat, 10am–7pm Thu.*
Closed *public hols.* ✍ ♿ *ground
floor only.* 🏛 **Exhibitions.** *See*
Shops and Markets *p319.*

PREVIOUSLY THE British Craft
Centre, the ground floor
showcases the best of British
contemporary crafts including
furniture, ceramics, textiles,
glass and jewelry. The shop
sells crafts and books.

Seven Dials ❾

Monmouth St WC2. **Map** 13 B2.
⊖ *Covent Garden, Leicester Sq.*

THE PILLAR at this junction of
seven streets incorporates
six sundials (the central spike
acts as the seventh). It was

installed in 1989 and is a copy
of a 17th-century monument.
The original was removed in
the 19th century because it
had become a notorious
meeting place for criminals.

Lamb and Flag ❿

33 Rose St WC2. **Map** 13 B2.
📞 0171-497 9504. ⊖ *Covent
Garden, Leicester Sq.* **Open**
*11am–11pm Mon–Sat, noon–3pm &
7–10:30pm Sun. See* **Restaurants
and Pubs** *p309.*

THERE HAS BEEN an inn here
since the 16th century,
and the cramped barrooms
are still largely unmodernized.
A plaque commemorates the
satirist John Dryden, who was
viciously attacked in the alley
outside in 1679, probably
because he lampooned the
Duchess of Portsmouth (one
of Charles II's mistresses) in
scurrilous verses.

Photographers' Gallery ⓫

5 & 8 Great Newport St WC2.
Map 13 B2. 📞 0171-831 1772.
⊖ *Leicester Sq.* **Open** *11am–6pm
Tue–Sat.* 🖥 🏛

THIS ENTERPRISING gallery is
London's leading venue
for photographic exhibitions,
which change periodically.
There are occasional lectures
and theatrical events, and
visitors can browse in the
specialized photography
bookshop, buy original prints
or meet fellow enthusiasts in

Photographers' Gallery

the café. The plaque outside
commemorates Sir Joshua
Reynolds, the founder of the
Royal Academy *(see p90),* who
lived here in the 18th century.

Adelphi Theatre ⓬

Strand WC2. **Map** 13 C3.
📞 0171-836 7611. ⊖ *Charing
Cross, Embankment.*
Open *for performances only.*
See **Entertainment** *pp326–7.*

BUILT IN 1806, the Adelphi
was opened by John
Scott, a wealthy tradesman
who was helping to launch
his daughter on the stage. It
was remodeled in 1930 in Art
Deco style. Note the highly
distinctive lettering on the
frontage and the well-kept
lobby and auditorium, with
their stylized motifs.

Adelphi Theatre (1840)

Savoy Hotel ⓭

Strand WC2. **Map** 13 C2.
📞 0171-836 4343. ⊖ *Charing
Cross, Embankment. See* **Where to
Stay** *p285.*

THE SAVOY was opened in
1889 on the site of the
medieval Savoy Palace. One
of London's grandest hotels,
it pioneered en suite bathrooms and electric lighting.
The forecourt is the only
street in Britain where traffic
drives on the right. Attached
to the hotel are the Savoy
Theatre, built for D'Oyly Carte
opera, Simpson's traditional
English restaurant specializing
in roast beef *(see p295);* and
the Savoy Taylor's Guild with

Front entrance to the Savoy Hotel

its Art Nouveau shop front.
Next door is Shell Mex House,
which replaced the Cecil Hotel
while keeping its Strand facade.

Savoy Chapel ⑭

Strand WC2. **Map** 13 C2.
[0171-836 7221.] Charing
Cross, Embankment. **Open** 11:30am–
3:30pm Tue–Fri. **Closed** Aug–Sep.
⛪ 11am Sun. ∅ ⬛

THE FIRST SAVOY CHAPEL was
founded during the 16th
century as the chapel for the
hospital established on the
site of the old Savoy Palace.

Parts of the outside walls date
from 1502, but most of the
present building dates from
the mid-19th century. In 1890
it was London's first church
to be electrically lit. It became
the chapel of the Royal
Victorian Order in 1936, and
is now a private chapel of the
Queen. Nearby on Savoy Hill
were the first studios of the
BBC from 1922 until 1932.

Somerset House ⑮

Strand WC2. **Map** 14 D2.
[0171-438 6622.] Temple,
Embankment, Charing Cross
Not open to the public.

THE IMPOSING Classical
compound by William
Chambers was built during
the 1770s on the site of the
Renaissance palace of the
Earls of Somerset. It was the
first major building designed
specifically to house offices
and is like four extremely
grand mansions of the period
grouped around a courtyard.
Before the river embankment
was built in the late 19th
century, Somerset House
stretched down to the water
line. You can still see old

mooring rings on the arched
southern frontage. The
courtyard is open to visitors,
but most of the interiors, still
used by the Civil Service, are
private. The exception is the
block known as the Fine
Rooms, built for the Royal
Academy of Arts. It is now the
Courtauld Institute.

Somerset House: Strand facade

Courtauld Institute Galleries ⑯

Somerset House, Strand WC2.
Map 14 D2. [0171-873 2526.
] Temple, Embankment, Charing
Cross. **Open** 10am–6pm Mon–Sat,
2–6pm Sun (last adm: 5:15pm).
Closed Jan 1, Good Fri. & Dec 24–26.
Adm charge. ∅ ♿ ⬛ ⬛

LONDON'S MOST spectacular
small collection of
paintings has been housed
since 1990 in Somerset House.
The Institute was established
in 1931 by the textile magnate
Samuel Courtauld, and its
holdings are based on his
collection of Impressionist
and Post-Impressionist
paintings. These have since
been added to by donations,
making the collection more
representative of post-
Renaissance European art.
    The early galleries display
work by Botticelli, Brueghel,
Bellini, Rubens and Tiepolo.
The Impressionists remain the
chief attraction, and this
collection includes Manet's
Bar at the Folies-Bergère; one
of the two versions of *Le
Déjeuner sur l'Herbe*; Van
Gogh's *Self-Portrait with
Bandaged Ear*; and works
by Renoir, Monet, Degas,
Gauguin, Cézanne and
Toulouse-Lautrec. The gallery
also houses a fine collection
of 20th-century British art.

Van Gogh's *Self-Portrait with Bandaged Ear* (1889) at the Courtauld

St. Mary-le-Strand ⑰

The Strand WC2. **Map** 14 D2.
☎ 0171-836 3126. ⊖ Temple,
Holborn. **Open** 11am–3:30pm
Mon–Fri,10am–1pm Sun.
✝ 11am Sun. ◉ ▯

Now beached on a road island at the east end of the Strand, this pleasing church was completed in 1717. It was the first public building by James Gibbs, who designed St. Martin-in-the-Fields *(see p102)*. Gibbs was influenced by Christopher Wren, but the exuberant external decorative detail here was inspired by the Baroque churches of Rome, where Gibbs studied. Its multiarched tower is layered like a wedding cake and culminates in a cupola and lantern. St. Mary-le-Strand is now the official church of the Women's Royal Naval Service.

St. Mary-le-Strand

Roman Bath ⑱

5 Strand Lane WC2. **Map** 14 D2.
☎ 0171-798 2063. ⊖ Temple,
Embankment, Charing Cross. **Open**
only by prior request. ♿ through
Temple Pl.

This little bath and its surroundings may be seen from a full-length window on Surrey Street by pressing a light switch on the outside wall. It is almost certainly not Roman, for there is no other

Bush House from Kingsway

evidence of Roman habitation in the immediate area. It is more likely to have been part of Arundel House, one of several palaces that stood on the Strand from Tudor times until the 17th century, when they were demolished for new buildings. In the 19th century the bath was open to the public for cold plunges, believed to be healthy.

Bush House ⑲

Aldwych WC2. **Map** 14 D2.
⊖ Temple, Holborn. **Not open** to the public.

Situated at the center of the Aldwych Crescent, this Neoclassical building was first designed as manufacturers' showrooms by an American, Irving T. Bush, and completed in 1935. It appears especially imposing when viewed from Kingsway, its dramatic north entrance graced with various statues symbolizing Anglo-American relations. Since 1940 it has been used as radio studios and is the head-quarters of the BBC World Service, which is due to be relocated to West London within a few years.

Cleopatra's Needle ⑳

Embankment WC2. **Map** 13 C3.
⊖ Embankment, Charing Cross.

Erected in Heliopolis in about 1500 BC, this incongruous pink granite monument is much older than London itself. Its inscriptions

celebrate the deeds of the pharaohs of ancient Egypt. It was presented to Britain by the then Viceroy of Egypt, Mohammed Ali, in 1819 and erected in 1878, shortly after the Embankment was built. It has a twin in New York's Central Park, behind the Metropolitan Museum of Art. The bronze sphinxes, added in 1882, are not Egyptian.

In its base is a Victorian time capsule of artifacts of the day, such as the day's newspapers, a train timetable and photographs of 12 beautiful women.

Victoria Embankment Gardens ㉑

WC2. **Map** 13 C3. ⊖ Embankment,
Charing Cross. **Open** 7:30am–dusk,
daily. ♿ ▯

This narrow sliver of a public park, created when the Embankment was built, boasts well-maintained flower beds, a group of statues of British worthies (including the Scottish poet Robert Burns) and, in summer, a season of concerts. Its main historical feature is the northwest corner's water gate, which was built as a triumphal entry to the Thames for the Duke of Buckingham in 1626. It is a relic of York House, which used to stand on this site and was the home first of the Archbishops of York and then of the Duke. It is still in its original position, and although the water used to lap against it, because of the Thames's Embankment the gate is now a good 330 ft (100 m) from the river's edge.

Victoria Embankment Gardens

The new shopping and office block above Charing Cross

Adelphi ㉒

Strand WC2. **Map** 13 C3.
⊖ *Embankment, Charing Cross.*
Not open to the public.

John Adam Street, Adelphi

A DELPHI IS A PUN on *adelphoi*, the Greek word for brothers – this area was once an elegant riverside residential development designed in 1772 by brothers Robert and John Adam. The name now refers to the Art Deco office block, its entrance adorned with N.A.Trent's heroic reliefs of workers at toil; in 1938 this block replaced the Adams' Palladian-style apartment complex. That destruction is now viewed as one of the worst acts of 20th-century official vandalism. A number of the Adams' surrounding buildings fortunately survive, notably the ornate Royal Society for the Encourage-ment of Arts, Manufactures and Commerce just opposite. Equally exuberant are Nos. 1–4 Robert Street, where Robert Adam lived for a time, and No. 7 Adam Street, decorated with honeysuckle reliefs.

Charing Cross ㉓

Strand WC2. **Map** 13 C3.
⊖ *Charing Cross, Embankment.*

T HE NAME DERIVES from the last of the 12 crosses erected by Edward I to mark the funeral route in 1290 of his wife, Eleanor of Castile, from Nottinghamshire to Westminster Abbey. Today a 19th-century replica stands in the forecourt of Charing Cross Station. Both the cross and the Charing Cross Hotel, built into the station frontage, were designed in 1863 by E.M.Barry, architect of the Royal Opera House *(see p115)*.
Above the station platforms has risen a prominent shopping center and office block, completed in 1991. Designed by Terry Farrell, it resembles a giant ocean liner, with portholes looking out onto Villiers Street. The new building is best seen from the river, where it dominates its neighbors. The railway arches at the rear of the station have been modernized as a suite of small shops and cafés, as well as a new venue for the Players Theatre, the last repository of Victorian music hall fare.

London Coliseum ㉔

St Martin's Lane WC2. **Map** 13 B3.
📞 *0171-836 3161.* ⊖ *Leicester Sq, Charing Cross.* **Open** for perfor-mances only. 🚫 ♿ 🖥 🎧 **Lectures**.
See **Entertainment** pp330–1.

L ONDON'S LARGEST theater and one of its most elaborate, this flamboyant building, topped with a huge globe, was designed in 1904 by Frank Matcham and was equipped with London's first revolving stage. It was also the first theater in Europe to have elevators and has a capacity of over 2,500. Once a famous variety house, it had a brief spell as a movie theater from 1961 to 1968. Today it is the home of the English National Opera and worth visiting to view the largely unaltered Edwardian interior, with its gilded cherubs and heavy scarlet curtains.

London Coliseum

BLOOMSBURY AND FITZROVIA

SINCE THE BEGINNING of the 20th century, both Bloomsbury and Fitzrovia have been synonymous with literature, art and learning. The Bloomsbury Group of writers and artists was active from the early 1900s until the 1930s; the name Fitzrovia was invented by writers

Carving in Russell Square

such as Dylan Thomas, who drank in the Fitzroy Tavern. Bloomsbury still boasts the University of London, the British Museum and many fine Georgian squares. But it is now also noted for its Charlotte Street restaurants and the furniture and electrical shops lining Tottenham Court Road.

SIGHTS AT A GLANCE

Historic Streets and Buildings
Bloomsbury Square **2**
Bedford Square **4**
Russell Square **5**
Queen Square **6**
St. Pancras Station **9**
Woburn Walk **11**
Fitzroy Square **13**
Charlotte Street **15**

Museums
British Museum pp126–9 **1**
Dickens House Museum **7**
Thomas Coram Foundation Museum **8**

Percival David Foundation of Chinese Art **12**
Pollock's Toy Museum **16**

Churches
St. George's, Bloomsbury **3**
St. Pancras Parish Church **10**

Pubs
Fitzroy Tavern **14**

SEE ALSO

- *Street Finder*, maps 4, 5, 6, 13
- *Where to Stay* pp276–7
- *Restaurants* pp292–4

GETTING THERE

This area is served by the Circle, Northern, Hammersmith and City, and Central lines. Useful buses include Nos. 8 and 98. Major BR stations are at Euston, St. Pancras and King's Cross.

KEY

▨	Street-by-Street map
⊖	Underground station
⇄	British Rail station
P	Parking

0 meters 500

0 yards 500

A grand Georgian house in Bedford Square

Street by Street: Bloomsbury

THE BRITISH MUSEUM dominates Bloomsbury. Its earnestly intellectual atmosphere spills over into the surrounding streets, and to its north lies the main campus of London University. The area has been home to writers and artists and is a traditional center of the book trade. Most of the publishers have left, but there are still many bookshops around.

The Senate House (1932) is the administrative headquarters of the University of London. It holds a priceless library.

Bedford Square
Uniform doorways in this square (1775) are fringed in artificial stone ❹

★ British Museum and Library
Designed in the mid-19th century, it is London's most popular attraction, with some 5 million visitors a year ❶

Museum Street is lined with small cafés and shops selling old books, prints and antiques.

Pizza Express occupies a charming and little-altered Victorian dairy.

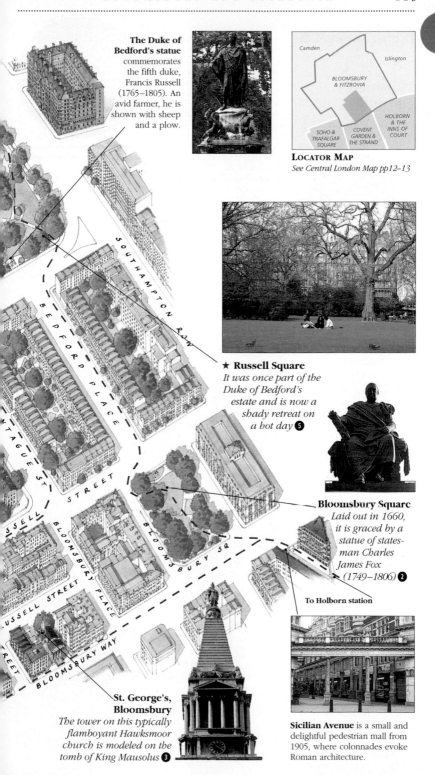

The Duke of Bedford's statue commemorates the fifth duke, Francis Russell (1765–1805). An avid farmer, he is shown with sheep and a plow.

LOCATOR MAP
See Central London Map pp12–13

★ **Russell Square**
It was once part of the Duke of Bedford's estate and is now a shady retreat on a hot day **5**

Bloomsbury Square
Laid out in 1660, it is graced by a statue of states-man Charles James Fox (1749–1806) **2**

To Holborn station

St. George's, Bloomsbury
The tower on this typically flamboyant Hawksmoor church is modeled on the tomb of King Mausolus **3**

Sicilian Avenue is a small and delightful pedestrian mall from 1905, where colonnades evoke Roman architecture.

British Museum ❶

See pp126–9.

Bloomsbury Square ❷

WC1. **Map** 5 C5. 🔵 *Holborn.*

Novelist Virginia Woolf, a Bloomsbury resident

THIS IS THE OLDEST of the Bloomsbury squares. It was laid out in 1661 by the Earl of Southampton, who owned the land. None of the original buildings survive, and the square's shaded garden is encircled by a busy one-way traffic system. (Unusual for London, one can always find parking space in the garage under the square.)

The square has had many famous residents; a plaque commemorates the literary and artistic Bloomsbury Group, whose members lived in the area during the early decades of this century. The group included novelist Virginia Woolf; biographer Lytton Strachey; and artists Vanessa Bell, Duncan Grant and Dora Carrington. Look for their individual plaques throughout the area.

St. George's, Bloomsbury ❸

Bloomsbury Way WC1. **Map** 13 B1. 📞 *0171-405 3044.* 🔵 *Holborn, Tottenham Court Rd.* **Open** *10:30am–3pm Mon–Fri.* 🔼 *10am Sun.* **Recitals, exhibitions.**

A SLIGHTLY ECCENTRIC church, St. George's was designed by Nicholas Hawksmoor, Wren's pupil,

and completed in 1730. It was built as a place of worship for the prosperous residents of newly developed, fashionable Bloomsbury. The layered tower, modeled on the tomb of King Mausolus (the original mausoleum in Turkey) and topped by a statue of George I, was for a long time an object of derision – the king's presentation was considered a bit too heroic. There is some good original plasterwork here, especially in the apse.

Bedford Square ❹

WC1. **Map** 5 B5. 🔵 *Tottenham Court Rd, Goodge St.*

BUILT IN 1775, this is one of the best preserved of London's 18th-century squares. All the entrances to its brick houses are adorned with Coade stone, a durable artificial stone made in Lambeth (in

HERE AND
IN NEIGHBOURING
HOUSES DURING
THE FIRST HALF OF
THE 20TH CENTURY
THERE LIVED SEVERAL
MEMBERS OF THE
BLOOMSBURY GROUP
INCLUDING
VIRGINIA WOOLF
CLIVE BELL AND
THE STRACHEYS

A plaque in Bloomsbury Square commemorating famous residents

south London) from a formula that remained secret for generations. The stately houses were once inhabited by the aristocracy. The buildings now contain offices, many of which were occupied until recently by publishers; most of these have moved to less expensive premises. Many of London's best known architects have passed through the Architectural Association at Nos. 34 – 36, including Richard Rogers who designed the Lloyd's Building (*see p159*).

Bedford Square's lush private gardens

Russell Square ⑤

WC1. **Map** 5 B5. ⊖ *Russell Sq.*
⬛ *Opening hours flexible.*

THIS IS ONE OF LONDON'S largest squares, and the east side boasts perhaps the best of the Victorian grand hotels to survive in the capital. Charles Doll's Hotel Russell *(see p284),* which was opened in 1900, is a wondrous confection of red terra cotta, with colonnaded balconies and prancing cherubs beneath the main columns. The exuberance is continued in the lobby, faced with marble of many colors.

The garden is open to the public. Poet T.S.Eliot worked in the square, from 1925 to 1965, in what were the offices of publishers Faber and Faber.

The flamboyant Hotel Russell on Russell Square

Queen Square ⑥

WC1. **Map** 5 C5. ⊖ *Russell Sq.*

IN SPITE OF being named after Queen Anne, this square contains a statue of Queen Charlotte. Her husband, George III, stayed at the house of a doctor here when he became ill with the hereditary disease that drove him mad before his death in 1820. Today the square is surrounded chiefly by hospital buildings and there are early Georgian houses on its west side.

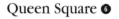

Queen Charlotte's statue in Queen Square

Dickens House Museum ⑦

48 Doughty St WC1. **Map** 6 D4.
📞 *0171-405 2127.* ⊖ *Chancery Lane, Russell Sq.* **Open** *10am–5pm Mon–Sat (last adm: 4:30pm).* **Closed** *Christmas week–New Year, public hols.* **Adm charge.** ✍ ⬛

THE NOVELIST Charles Dickens lived in this early-19th-century terraced house for three of his most productive years, from 1837 to 1839. The popular works *Oliver Twist* and *Nicholas Nickleby* were written here, and *The Pickwick Papers* was finished. Although Dickens had many London homes throughout his lifetime, this is the only one to have survived. In 1923 it was acquired by the Dickens Fellowship, and it is now a well-conceived museum with some of the principal rooms laid out exactly as they were in Dickens's time. Others have been adapted to display a varied collection of articles associated with him. The exhibits include letters, papers, portraits and pieces of furniture taken from his other London homes as well as first editions of many of his best-known works.

Thomas Coram Foundation Museum ⑧

40 Brunswick Sq WC1. **Map** 5 C4.
📞 *0171-278 2424.* ⊖ *Russell Sq.* **Open** *1:30–4:30pm Mon and Fri.* **Closed** *2 weeks over Christmas, public hols.* **Adm charge.** ✍ ⬛

THOMAS CORAM WAS an 18th-century sea captain who in 1739 was granted a charter by King George II to establish a hospital for the care and education of deserted young children. Coram asked prominent artists to become governors, and one of the first to do so was the painter William Hogarth, who gave his portrait of Thomas Coram to the hospital.

The foundation owns many other treasures. In the picture gallery are Handel's own copy of *The Messiah,* together with the uniforms worn by the children and some of the mementos left with them at the hospital gates. The hospital buildings were demolished in 1926, and their Court Room and oak staircase are now here. The children were moved out of London to Hertfordshire. Today the foundation survives – its aim is still the care of children, in particular those under five.

Hogarth's portrait of Thomas Coram

British Museum and Library ❶

THE BRITISH MUSEUM, founded in 1753, is the oldest museum in the world. Its rich collection of artifacts was started by the physician Sir Hans Sloane (1660–1753), who also helped establish the Chelsea Physic Garden *(see p193)*.

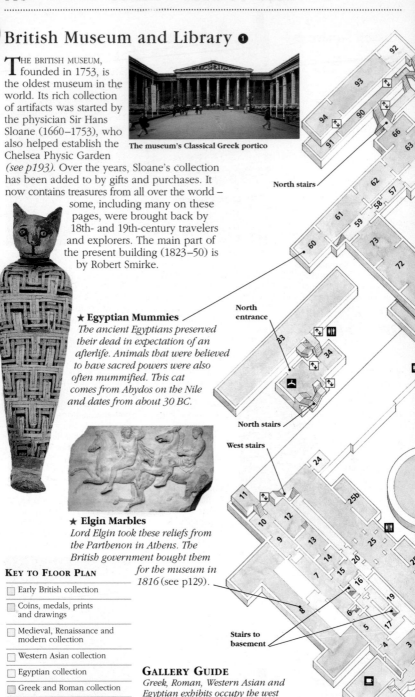

The museum's Classical Greek portico

Over the years, Sloane's collection has been added to by gifts and purchases. It now contains treasures from all over the world – some, including many on these pages, were brought back by 18th- and 19th-century travelers and explorers. The main part of the present building (1823–50) is by Robert Smirke.

★ Egyptian Mummies

The ancient Egyptians preserved their dead in expectation of an afterlife. Animals that were believed to have sacred powers were also often mummified. This cat comes from Abydos on the Nile and dates from about 30 BC.

★ Elgin Marbles

Lord Elgin took these reliefs from the Parthenon in Athens. The British government bought them for the museum in 1816 (see p129).

North stairs

North entrance

North stairs

West stairs

Stairs to basement

KEY TO FLOOR PLAN

☐ Early British collection

☐ Coins, medals, prints and drawings

☐ Medieval, Renaissance and modern collection

☐ Western Asian collection

☐ Egyptian collection

☐ Greek and Roman collection

☐ Oriental collection

☐ British Library

☐ Temporary exhibitions

☐ Non-exhibition space

GALLERY GUIDE

Greek, Roman, Western Asian and Egyptian exhibits occupy the west side of the ground floor; the British Library exhibits are on the east, and the rest of the floor is taken up with library reading rooms. The collections continue on the first floor and in the basement.

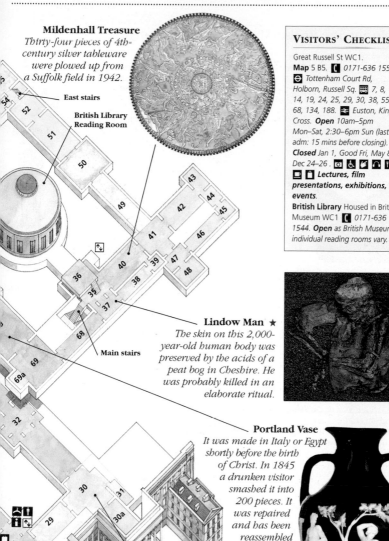

Mildenhall Treasure
Thirty-four pieces of 4th-century silver tableware were plowed up from a Suffolk field in 1942.

East stairs

British Library Reading Room

Main stairs

Main entrance

Main stairs

VISITORS' CHECKLIST

Great Russell St WC1.
Map 5 B5. 0171-636 1555.
Tottenham Court Rd, Holborn, Russell Sq. 7, 8, 10, 14, 19, 24, 25, 29, 30, 38, 55, 68, 134, 188. Euston, King's Cross. **Open** 10am–5pm Mon–Sat, 2:30–6pm Sun (last adm: 15 mins before closing). **Closed** Jan 1, Good Fri, May 8, Dec 24–26. **Lectures, film presentations, exhibitions, events.**
British Library Housed in British Museum WC1 0171-636 1544. **Open** as British Museum; individual reading rooms vary.

Lindow Man ★
The skin on this 2,000-year-old human body was preserved by the acids of a peat bog in Cheshire. He was probably killed in an elaborate ritual.

Portland Vase
It was made in Italy or Egypt shortly before the birth of Christ. In 1845 a drunken visitor smashed it into 200 pieces. It was repaired and has been reassembled twice since then.

Lindisfarne Gospels ★
The gospels were written in Latin and illuminated in 698 by a monk called Eadfrith. Lindisfarne island is off northeast England.

STAR EXHIBITS

★ Elgin Marbles

★ Lindow Man

★ Egyptian Mummies

★ Lindisfarne Gospels

Exploring the British Museum's Collections

THE MUSEUM'S immense hoard of treasure spans two million years of world history and civilization. There are 94 galleries, covering 2.5 miles (4 km), which are divided into the following specialized sections.

Ornamental detail from a Sumerian Queen's lyre

PREHISTORIC AND ROMAN BRITAIN

1st-century BC bronze helmet dredged up from the Thames

SIX GALLERIES cover the period from man's first, prehistoric, efforts at toolmaking in Africa's Olduvai Gorge up until Christianity overtook Britain's Roman overlords. The first exhibit, which stands at the top of the main stairs, is a vast mosaic of Christ, dating from Roman times, which was dug up in an English field.

The remains of an Iron Age human sacrifice are in Room 37: "Lindow Man," who was probably slain in the 1st century AD, lay preserved in a bog until 1984.

Rooms 38 and 39 contain Celtic artifacts; Room 40 has the silver Mildenhall Treasure and Roman pieces, often made by British craftsmen.

MEDIEVAL, RENAISSANCE AND MODERN OBJECTS

THE SPECTACULAR Sutton Hoo ship treasure, the burial hoard of a 7th-century Anglo-Saxon king, is on display in Room 41; this superb jewelry, made from pure gold and garnets, is unblemished.

The medieval carved walrus-tusk chessmen from the island of Lewis off Scotland are in Room 42. Room 44 has a fine collection of clocks, watches and scientific instruments. Timepieces have often inspired the most exquisite

craftsmanship and some grand designs – a 400-year-old table clock made for a Holy Roman Emperor is an ornate golden galleon that pitched, played music and fired a cannon. Room 45 is an Aladdin's cave housing part of Baron Ferdinand Rothschild's diverse treasure. Artifacts from the Renaissance and later are on display in Room 47, and the museum's modern collection is in Room 48.

Late 16th-century gilded brass ship clock from Prague

WESTERN ASIA

THERE ARE 18 galleries on all 3 floors devoted to the Western Asian collections, which cover 7,000 years of history from an area stretching from Afghanistan to Phoenicia. The most prized part of the collection is probably the 7th-century BC Assyrian reliefs from King Ashurbanipal's palace at Nineveh, in Room 21. Two large human-headed bulls from 7th-century BC Khorsabad are in Room 16; there are more fine reliefs in Rooms 17, 19, 20 and 89. Room 19 also houses the famous inscribed Black

Obelisk of King Shalmaneser III. Room 51 houses part of the Oxus Treasure, a large hoard of gold and silver, buried for over 2,000 years. The museum's collection of clay cuneiform tablets are in Room 55. This was the first form of writing, developed when civilization began 5,000 years ago. Room 56 contains treasures from ancient Sumeria.

ANCIENT EGYPT

THE MUSEUM'S Egyptian sculptures are in Room 25, a giant gallery just off the front hall. The Rosetta Stone, the famous key to the Egyptian hieroglyphs, is near the main entrance. In a side gallery is a fine New Kingdom royal head in green schist, dated 1490 BC, with a wonderful tomb painting of a hunt on the far wall. Don't miss the bronze cat with its gold nose ring, in the center of the main hall; the huge statue of Rameses II is impossible to miss. The amazing mummies, jewelry and Coptic art are in Rooms 60 to 66 upstairs.

Part of a colossal granite statue to Rameses II, the 13th-century BC Egyptian monarch

GREECE AND ROME

THE GREEK and Roman collections, in 30 galleries, include the museum's most famous treasure, the Elgin Marbles in Room 8. These 5th-century BC reliefs from the Parthenon once made up a marble frieze, with sculptured pediments and panels, which went around Athena's temple on the Acropolis in Athens. Much of it was destroyed in battle in 1687, and most of what survived was removed between 1801 and 1804 by British diplomat Lord Elgin and sold to the British nation.

Ancient Greek vase illustrating the mythical hero Hercules's fight with a bull

The Greek government wants it back. However, it is still here. You can rent a recorded commentary at the entrance. Don't miss the Nereid Monument in Room 7, or, in Room 12, the 350 BC sculpture and friezes from the Mausoleum at Halicarnassus, one of the Seven Wonders of the Ancient World. The 1st-century BC Portland Vase, which was smashed by a drunken visitor in 1845 and then lovingly reassembled, is located in the Roman Empire collection upstairs in Room 70.

ORIENTAL ART

THE ORIENTAL department's magnificent Chinese collection is especially strong on fine porcelain and ancient Shang bronzes. Gallery 33, newly refurbished, features these and much other Chinese art, along with exhibits from the finest collection of South Asian sculpture outside India. Splendid Buddhist temple reliefs from Amaravati are in Room 33a. Islamic art is in Room 34, including a fine jade terrapin, found in a water tank. Room 91 houses temporary exhibitions, and

Rooms 92–4 are the new Japanese galleries, with a Classical teahouse in Room 92 and netsuke (small ivory carvings) in the lobby.

Statue of the Hindu God Shiva Nataraja, also known as the Lord of the Dance (11th century AD)

BRITISH LIBRARY

THE BEAUTIFUL 7th-century illuminated gospels of Lindisfarne are on display in Room 30a, and the Magna Carta is in Room 30. Fine manuscripts and bindings from many lands are on display in the magnificent King's Library, Room 32.

THE BRITISH LIBRARY READING ROOM

The British Library was established by an Act of Parliament in 1973. But though the library has only been in existence for two decades, its origins can be traced to the foundation of the British Museum in 1753. The vast Round Reading Room was designed by Sir Robert Smirke, architect of the museum. He based his designs on a sketch by chief librarian Sir Anthony Panizzi. Completed in 1857, it was built to give "all studious and curious persons" access to the library collections. Twenty cast-iron pillars support the great roof, and 20 tall, arched windows rise above these. Visitors are admitted from Monday to Friday at 2, 3 and 4pm. You can stand among the 30,000 reference works and think of Karl Marx, Mahatma Gandhi, or George Bernard Shaw, all of whom worked here.

The dome of the reading room is wider than that of St. Peter's in Rome.

There are three levels of book-shelves up the library walls.

The massive and derelict hotel above St. Pancras Station

St. Pancras Station ❾

Euston Rd NW1. **Map** 5 B2.
📞 *0171-387 7070 (British Rail
inquiries).* 🚇 *King's Cross, St.
Pancras.* **Open** *5am–11pm daily. See
Getting to London pp358–9.*

Easily the most spectacular of the three rail termini along Euston Road, St. Pancras has an extravagant frontage, in red-brick gingerbread Gothic, that is not part of the station. It was really Sir George Gilbert Scott's Midland Grand Hotel, opened in 1874 with 250 rooms as one of the most sumptuous and modern hotels of its time. In 1890 London's first smoking room for women was opened here. From 1935 until the early 1980s the building contained

Figures on St. Pancras Church

offices; it now lies empty and its future is undecided. The vast train shed behind it is an outstanding example of Victorian engineering, with a roof that is 700 ft (210 m) long and 100 ft (30 m) high.

St. Pancras Parish Church ❿

Euston Rd NW1. **Map** 5 B3.
📞 *0171-387 8250.* 🚇 *Euston.*
Open *8am–noon Mon,
8am–6pm Wed–Sat,
8am–noon, 4–6:30pm Sun.*
✝ *10am Sun* 📷 ♿
Recitals *Mar–Sep: 1:15pm Thu.*

This is a stately Greek Revival church of 1822 by William Inwood and his son, Henry, both great enthusiasts for Athenian architecture. The design is based on that of the Erectheum on the Acropolis in Athens, and even the wooden pulpit stands on miniature Ionic columns of its own. The long, galleried interior has a dramatic severity appropriate to the church's style. The female figures on the northern outer wall were originally taller than they are now; a section had to be taken out of each to make them fit under the roof they were made to support.

Woburn Walk ⓫

WC1. **Map** 5 B4. 🚇 *Euston,
Euston Sq.*

A well-restored street of bow-fronted shops, Woburn Walk was designed by Thomas Cubitt in 1822. The high pavement on the east side protected shop fronts from mud thrown up by carriages. Poet W.B.Yeats lived at No. 5 from 1895 to 1919.

Percival David Foundation of Chinese Art ⓬

53 Gordon Sq WC1. **Map** 5 B4.
📞 *0171-387 3909.* 🚇 *Russell Sq,
Euston Sq, Goodge St.* **Open**
10:30am–5pm Mon–Fri. **Closed**
*Christmas week–New Year, Maundy
Thu–Easter Mon, public hols.* ♿ 📷

Particularly interesting to those with a specialized interest in Chinese porcelain, this is an important collection of exquisite wares made between the 10th and the 18th century. Percival David presented his collection, much of it uniquely well preserved, to the University of London in 1950, and it is now administered by the School of Oriental and African Studies. The foundation includes a research library and houses occasional special exhibitions of East Asian art as well as the permanent collection.

**Blue temple vase from
David's collection**

Fitzroy Square ⓭

W1. **Map** 4 F4. 🚇 *Warren St,
Great Portland St.*

This square was designed by Robert Adam in 1794, and its south and east sides survive in their original form, in Portland stone. Blue plaques record the homes of many artists, writers and statesmen: George Bernard Shaw and Virginia Woolf lived at No. 29 – but not at the same time. Shaw gave money to the artist Roger Fry to establish the Omega workshop at No. 33 in 1913. Here young artists were paid a fixed wage to produce Post-Impressionist furniture, pottery, carpets and paintings for sale to the public.

No. 29 Fitzroy Square

Fitzroy Tavern ⓮

16 Charlotte St W1. **Map** 4 F5.
🕻 *0171-580 3714.* ⊖ *Goodge St.*
Open *11am–11pm Mon–Sat,
noon–3pm, 7–10:30pm Sun.* ♿ *See*
Restaurants and Pubs *pp308–9.*

THIS TRADITIONAL PUB was a meeting place between World Wars I and II for a group of writers and artists who dubbed the area around Fitzroy Square and Charlotte Street "Fitzrovia." The basement "Writers and Artists Bar" contains pictures of former customers, including the writers Dylan Thomas and George Orwell and the artist Augustus John.

Charlotte Street ⓯

W1. **Map** 5 A5. ⊖ *Goodge St.*

AS THE UPPER CLASSES moved west from Bloomsbury in the early 19th century, a flood of artists and European immigrants moved in, turning the area into a northern appendage to Soho *(see pp98–109).* The artist John Constable lived and worked for many years at No. 76. Some of the new residents established small workshops

to service the clothing shops on Oxford Street and the furniture stores on Tottenham Court Road. Others set up reasonably priced restaurants. The street still boasts a great variety of eating places. It is overshadowed from the north by the 580-ft (180-m) Telecom Tower, built in 1964 as a vast TV, radio and telecommunications aerial *(see p30).*

Telecom Tower

Pollock's Toy Museum ⓰

1 Scala St W1. **Map** 5 A5.
🕻 *0171-636 3452.* ⊖ *Goodge St.*
Open *10am–5pm Mon–Sat.* **Closed**
public hols. **Adm charge.** ♿ 🛍

BENJAMIN POLLOCK was a renowned maker of toy theaters in the late 19th and early 20th centuries – the

novelist Robert Louis Stevenson was an enthusiastic customer. The museum opened in 1956, and one room is devoted to stages and puppets from Pollock's theaters, together with a reconstruction of his workshop. This is a child-sized museum contained in two largely unaltered 18th-century houses. The small rooms are filled with a fascinating assortment of historic toys from all over the world. There are dolls, puppets, trains, cars, construction sets, a fine rocking horse and a splendid collection of mainly Victorian dolls' houses. Toy theater performances are held here during school holidays, and children can play board games at no charge. Parents should beware – the exit passes through a very tempting toyshop.

Pearly king and queen dolls from Pollock's Museum

HOLBORN AND THE INNS OF COURT

THIS AREA IS traditionally home to the legal and journalistic professions. The law is still here, in the Royal Courts of Justice and the Inns of Court, but most national newspapers left Fleet Street in the 1980s. Several buildings here predate the Great Fire of 1666 *(see pp22–3)*. These

Royal crest at Lincoln's Inn

include the superb facade of Staple Inn, Prince Henry's Room and the interior of Middle Temple Hall. Holborn used to be one of the capital's main shopping districts. Times have changed, but the jewelry and diamond dealers of Hatton Garden are still here, as well as the London Silver Vaults.

SIGHTS AT A GLANCE

Historic Buildings, Sights and Streets
Lincoln's Inn ❷
Old Curiosity Shop ❹
Royal Courts of Justice ❼
Fleet Street ❾
Prince Henry's Room ❿
Temple ⓫
Dr. Johnson's House ⓮
Holborn Viaduct ⓰
Hatton Garden ⓲
Staple Inn ⓳
Gray's Inn ㉑

Museums and Galleries
Sir John Soane's Museum ❶
Public Record Office Museum ❺

Churches
St. Clement Danes ❻

St. Bride's ⓬
St. Andrew, Holborn ⓯
St. Etheldreda's Chapel ⓱

Monuments
Temple Bar Memorial ❽

Parks and Gardens
Lincoln's Inn Fields ❸

Pubs
Ye Olde Cheshire Cheese ⓭

Shops
London Silver Vaults ⓴

KEY

	Street-by-Street map
🚇	Underground station
🚄	British Rail station
🅿	Parking

GETTING THERE

This area is served by the Circle, Central, District, Metropolitan and Piccadilly lines. Buses 17, 18, 45, 46, 171, 243 and 259 are among many in the area, and British Rail runs from a number of mainline stations inside or close to the area.

SEE ALSO

- **Street Finder,** maps 6, 13, 14
- **Where to stay** pp276–7
- **Restaurants** pp292–4

The Royal Courts of Justice on the Strand

Street by Street: Lincoln's Inn

THIS IS CALM, dignified, legal London, packed with history and interest. Lincoln's Inn, adjoining one of the city's first residential squares, has buildings dating from the late 15th century. Dark-suited lawyers carry bundles of briefs between their offices here and the Neo-Gothic law courts. Nearby is the Temple, another historic legal district with a famous 13th-century round church.

★ Sir John Soane's Museum
The Georgian architect made this his London home and left it, with his collection, to the nation ❶

To Kingsway

LINCOLN'S INN FIELDS

LINCOLN'S INN FIELDS

★ Lincoln's Inn Fields
The mock-Tudor archway, leading to Lincoln's Inn and built in 1845, overlooks the fields ❸

Old Curiosity Shop
This is a rare 17th-century, pre-Great Fire building that used to be a shop ❹

PORTSMOUTH ST

PORTUGAL STREET

CAREY

The Royal College of Surgeons was designed in 1836 by Sir Charles Barry. Inside there are laboratories for research and teaching as well as a museum of anatomical specimens.

STAR SIGHTS

- ★ Sir John Soane's Museum
- ★ Temple
- ★ Lincoln's Inn Fields
- ★ Lincoln's Inn

KEY

– – – Suggested route

0 meters   100

0 yards   100

Twinings has been selling tea from here since 1706. The doorway dates from 1787, when the shop was called the Golden Lion.

The Gladstone Statue was erected in 1905 to commemorate William Gladstone, the Victorian statesman who was Prime Minister four times.

★ Lincoln's Inn
The Court of Chancery sat here, in Old Hall, from 1835 until 1858. Sir John Taylor Coleridge was a well-known judge of the time **2**

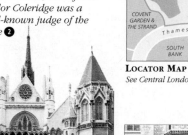

LOCATOR MAP
See Central London Map pp12–13

Royal Courts of Justice
The country's main court for civil cases and appeals was built in 1882. It is made out of 35 million bricks faced with Portland stone **7**

Public Record Office
A display of documents here includes Shakespeare's will and the Domesday Book **5**

Fleet Street
For two centuries this was the center of the national press. Today the newspaper offices are gone **9**

El Vino's is a venerable wine bar, where journalists still mingle with lawyers.

Prince Henry's Room
There is an authentic 17th-century room in this former gatehouse **10**

St. Clement Danes
Designed by Wren (1679), it is the Royal Air Force church **6**

Temple Bar Memorial
A griffin marks where the city of London meets Westminster **8**

★ Temple
This was built for the Knights Templar in the 13th century, but today lawyers stroll here **11**

Wigged barristers on their way to their offices in Lincoln's Inn

Lincoln's Inn ❷

WC2. **Map** 14 D1. 📞 *0171-405 1393*.
🚇 *Holborn, Chancery Lane*. **Grounds
open** *9am–6pm Mon–Fri*. **Chapel
open** *12:30–2pm Mon–Fri*. **Hall**
enquire at Porter's lodge. 📞 *0171-
405 6360.* ♿ *grounds only.* ▢

SOME OF THE BUILDINGS in
Lincoln's Inn, the best-
preserved of London's Inns of
Court, go back to the late
15th century. The coat of
arms above the arch of the
Chancery Lane gatehouse is
Henry VIII's, and the heavy
oak door is of the same
vintage. Shakespeare's
contemporary, Ben Jonson, is
believed to have laid some of
the bricks of Lincoln's Inn
during the reign of Elizabeth I.
The chapel is early-17th-
century Gothic. Women were
not allowed burial here until
1839, when the grieving Lord
Brougham petitioned to have
the rule changed so that his
beloved daughter could be
interred in the chapel, to wait
for him to join her.
Lincoln's Inn has its share
of famous alumni. Oliver
Cromwell and John Donne,

Sir John Soane's Museum ❶

13 Lincoln's Inn Fields WC2.
Map 14 D1. 📞 *0171-430 0175.*
🚇 *Holborn.* **Open** *10am–5pm
Tue–Sat, 6–9pm 1st Tue of month.*
Closed *Jan 1, Dec 24–26 & Easter*
♿ *ground floor only.*
📷 *Sat 2:30pm.*

ONE OF THE MOST surprising
museums in London, this
house was left to the nation
by Sir John Soane in 1837,
with a stipulation that nothing
should be changed. One of
Britain's leading 19th-century
architects, responsible for
designing the Bank of England,
Soane was the son of a brick-
layer. After marrying the niece
of a wealthy builder, whose
fortune he inherited, he bought
and reconstructed No. 12
Lincoln's Inn Fields. In 1813
he and his wife moved into
No. 13, and in 1824 he rebuilt
No. 14. Today, true to
Soane's wishes, the collec-

tions are much as he left
them – an eclectic gathering
of beautiful, peculiar and
often instructional objects.
The building itself is full of
architectural surprises and
illusions. In the main ground-
floor room, with its color
scheme of deep red and green,
cunningly placed mirrors play
tricks with light and space. The
upstairs picture gallery is lined
with layers of folding panels to
increase its capacity. The
panels open out to reveal
galleried extensions to the
room itself. Among other
works here are many of
Soanes's own exotic designs,
including those for Pitshanger
Manor *(see p254)* and the
Bank of England *(see p147)*.
Here also is William Hogarth's
Rake's Progress series and
several other of his paintings.
In the centre of the low-
ceilinged basement an atrium
stretches up to the roof. A
glass dome lights galleries, on
every floor, that are laden with
Classical statuary.

A glass dome allows
light into the basement.

A vast sarcophagus
stands on the floor of
the crypt.

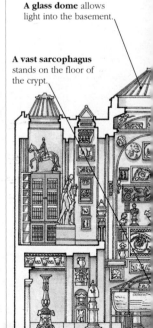

the 17th-century poet, were both students here, as was William Penn, founder of the state of Pennsylvania.

Lincoln's Inn Fields ❸

WC2. **Map** 14 D1. 🚇 *Holborn.* **Open** *8am–dusk daily.* **Public tennis courts** 📞 *0171-278 4444.*

THIS USED TO BE a public execution site. Under the Tudors and the Stuarts, many religious martyrs, and those suspected of treachery to the Crown, died here.

When the developer William Newton wanted to build here in the 1640s, students at Lincoln's Inn and other residents made him promise that the land in the center would remain a public area forever. Thanks to this early environmental pressure group, lawyers today play tennis here throughout the summer or read their briefs in the fresh air. In recent years it has also become the site of a "tent city" for some of London's homeless.

Old Curiosity Shop sign

Old Curiosity Shop ❹

13–14 Portsmouth St WC2. **Map** 14 D1. 🚇 *Holborn.* **Closed** *and changing ownership.*

WHETHER IT IS or is not the original for Charles Dickens's novel of the same name, this is a genuine 17th-century building and it's almost certainly the oldest shop in central London. With its overhanging first floor, it gives a rare impression of a London streetscape from

before the Great Fire of 1666. Recently it has sold antiques and, although it is presently unoccupied, a preservation order guarantees its future, most likely as a shop.

Public Record Office Museum ❺

Chancery Lane WC2. **Map** 14 E1. 📞 *0181-876 3444.* 🚇 *Chancery Lane, Holborn, Temple.* **Open** *9:30am–5pm Mon–Fri.* **Closed** *public hols, 1st 2 weeks Oct.* 🚫 📷 ▯

RECORDS OF THE official actions and decisions of central government and the law courts are kept here. There is a small changing exhibition of some of the seminal documents from all periods in British history since the Norman Conquest of 1066. The collection includes the *Domesday Book* (England's first census of land and people, made in 1086), Sir Francis Drake's report on his defeat of the Spanish Armada in 1588, Shakespeare's will, and a letter from George Washington to George III.

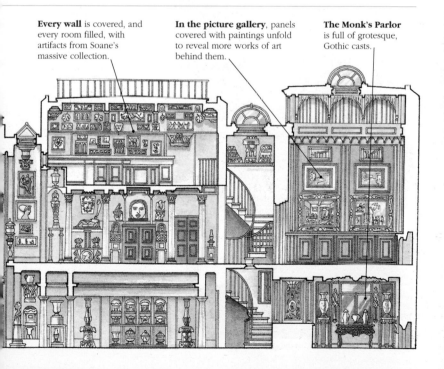

Every wall is covered, and every room filled, with artifacts from Soane's massive collection.

In the picture gallery, panels covered with paintings unfold to reveal more works of art behind them.

The Monk's Parlor is full of grotesque, Gothic casts.

St. Clement Danes ⑥

Strand WC2. **Map** 14 D2.
📞 0171-242 8282. ⊖ Temple.
Open 8am–5pm daily. **Closed** noon
Dec 25–27. ✝ 11am Sun.
See **Ceremonial London** p55.

CHRISTOPHER WREN designed
this wonderful church in
1680. Its name derives from
an earlier church built here
by the descendants of Danish
invaders whom Alfred the
Great had allowed to remain
in London in the 9th century.
 During the 17th, 18th and
19th centuries many people
were buried in the crypt. The
chain now hanging on the
crypt wall was probably used
to secure coffin lids against
body snatchers who stole
fresh corpses and sold them
to the teaching hospitals.
 St. Clement Danes sits
proudly isolated on a traffic
island. It is now the church of
the Royal Air Force (RAF),
and the interior decor is
dominated by
RAF symbols,
memorials and
monuments.

Clock at the Victorian law courts

Outside, to the east, is a 1910
statue of Dr. Samuel Johnson
(*see p140*), who, during the
18th century, often came to
services here. The church
bells are rung to the tune of
the English nursery rhyme,
"Oranges and Lemons" at
9am, noon, 3pm and 6pm
daily and there is an
annual oranges and
lemons service.

The griffon, symbol of the City, at the entrance to the City at Temple Bar

Royal Courts of Justice (the Law Courts) ⑦

Strand WC2. **Map** 14 D2.
📞 0171-936 6000. ⊖ Holborn,
Temple, Chancery Lane. **Open**
9am–4:30pm Mon–Fri. **Closed** public
hols. ♿ limited. 📷

GROUPS OF demonstrators
and television cameras
can often be seen outside this
sprawling, fanciful Victorian
Gothic building, awaiting the
controversial case. These are
the nation's main civil courts,
dealing with such matters as
divorce, libel, civil liability
and appeals. Criminals are
dealt with at the Old Bailey
(*see p147*), ten minutes' walk
to the east. The public are
admitted to all the court-
rooms, and a roster lists court
assignments. The massive,
Gothic building was
completed in 1882. It is
said to contain 1,000
rooms and 3.5 miles (5.6
km) of corridors.

Temple Bar Memorial ⑧

Fleet St EC4. **Map** 14 D2.
⊖ Holborn, Temple, Chancery Lane.

THIS MONUMENT in the
middle of Fleet Street,
outside the Law Courts, dates
from 1880 and marks the
entrance to the City of
London. On state occasions
the monarch traditionally
has to pause here and ask
permission of the Lord Mayor
to enter. Temple Bar, an
archway designed by Wren,
used to stand here. You can
see what it used to look like
from one of the four reliefs
that surround the base of the
present monument.

Fleet Street ⑨

EC4. **Map** 14 E1. ⊖ Temple,
Blackfriars, St. Paul's.

ENGLAND'S FIRST printing
press was set up here in
the late 15th century by
William Caxton's assistant,

William Capon's engraving of Fleet Street in 1799

and Fleet Street has been a center of London's publishing industry ever since. Playwrights Shakespeare and Ben Jonson were patrons of the old Mitre Tavern, now No. 37 Fleet Street. In 1702 the first newspaper, *The Daily Courant*, was issued from Fleet Street – convenient to both the City and Westminster, the main sources of news. In time, the street became synonymous with the press.

The printing presses underneath the newspaper offices were abandoned in 1987, when new technology made it easy to produce papers away from the centre of town in areas such as Wapping and the Docklands. Today the newspapers have left their Fleet Street offices, and only the agencies, Reuters and the Press Association, remain.

El Vino's wine bar, at the western end opposite Fetter Lane, is a traditional haunt of journalists and lawyers.

Effigies in Temple Church

Prince Henry's Room ❿

17 Fleet St. EC4. **Map** 14 E1.
🕾 0171-936 2710. ⊖ *Temple, Chancery Lane.* **Open** 11am–2pm Mon–Sat. **Closed** Jan 1, Good Friday, Dec 24–26, public hols. 🄾

BUILT IN 1610 as part of a Fleet Street tavern, this gets its name from the Prince of Wales's coat of arms and the initials *PH* in the center of the ceiling. They were probably put there to mark the investiture of Henry (James I's eldest son) as Prince of Wales, who died before he became king. The fine half-timbered front, alongside the gateway to Inner Temple, is original, and so is some of the room's oak paneling. It contains an exhibition about the diarist Samuel Pepys.

Temple ⓫

Inner Temple, King's Bench Walk EC4. **Map** 14 E2. 🕾 0171-353 1736. ⊖ *Temple.* **Open** 10am–4pm Wed–Sat, 12:45–4pm Sun. 🄾 ♿ **Middle Temple Hall**, Middle Temple Lane EC4. **Map** 14 E2. 🕾 0171-353 4355. ⊖ *Temple.* **Open** 10am–4pm Mon–Fri. **Closed** for functions. 🄴 🄾

THIS EMBRACES TWO of the four Inns of Court, the Middle Temple and the Inner Temple. (The remaining two are Lincoln's and Gray's Inns – *see p136 and p141.*)

The name derives from the Knights Templar, a chivalrous order that specialized in the protection of pilgrims to the Holy Land. The order was based here from 1185 until suppressed by the Crown in 1312 – its power was viewed as a threat to the throne. Secret initiation rites into the order probably took place in the crypt of Temple Church and there are 13th-century effigies of Knights Templar in the nave.

Among other interesting and ancient buildings in this area is Middle Temple Hall. Its Elizabethan interior has survived – Shakespeare's *Twelfth Night* was performed here in 1601. Behind Temple, peaceful lawns stretch down to the Embankment.

St. Bride's ⓬

Fleet St. EC4. **Map** 14 F2. 🕾 0171-353 1301. ⊖ *Blackfriars, St. Paul's.* **Open** 8:30am–5pm Mon–Fri, 9am–4:30pm Sat, 9am–7:30pm Sun. **Closed** public hols. 🄾 ♿ ✝ 11:30am Sun. **Concerts.**

St. Bride's, church of the press.

ST. BRIDE'S IS ONE OF Wren's best-loved churches. Its position just off Fleet Street has made it the traditional venue for memorial services for departed journalists. Wall plaques commemorate Fleet Street journalists and printers.

The marvelous octagonal, layered spire has been the model for tiered wedding cakes since shortly after it was added in 1703. Bombed in 1940, the interior was faithfully restored after World War II. The fascinating crypt contains remnants of earlier churches on the site and a section of Roman pavement.

Ye Olde Cheshire Cheese ⑬

Wine Office Court, 145 Fleet St EC4.
Map 14 E1. ℂ *0171-353 6170.*
⊖ *Blackfriars.* **Open** *11:30am–11pm
Mon–Sat, noon–3pm, 6–10pm Sun.
See* **Restaurants and Pubs** *pp308–9.*

THERE HAS BEEN an inn here
for centuries; parts of this
building date back to 1667,
when the Cheshire Cheese
was rebuilt after the Great
Fire. The diarist Samuel Pepys
drank here in the 17th
century, but it was Dr. Samuel
Johnson's association with
"the Cheese" that made it a
place of pilgrimage for 19th-
century literati. These included
novelists Mark Twain and
Charles Dickens, who was a
frequent customer.
   Today it is one of the few
pubs that has not altered its
layout. It has kept the
comfortable 18th-century
arrangement of small rooms
featuring fireplaces, tables
and benches.

Dr. Johnson's House ⑭

17 Gough Sq EC4. **Map** 14 E1.
ℂ *0171-353 3745.* ⊖ *Blackfriars,
Chancery Lane, Temple.* **Open**
*May–Sep: 11am–5:30pm Mon–Sat;
Oct–Apr: 11am–5pm Mon–Sat.*
Closed *Jan 1, Dec 24–26, Good
Friday, public hols.* **Adm charge.** ⊚
small charge. ▯ ▧

DR. SAMUEL JOHNSON was an
18th-century scholar
famous for the many witty
(and often contentious)

19th-century St. Andrew schoolgirl

remarks that his biographer,
James Boswell, recorded and
published. Johnson lived here
from 1748 to 1759. He
compiled the first definitive
English dictionary (published
in 1755) in the attic, where
six scribes and assistants
stood all day at high desks.
   The house, built before
1700, is sparsely furnished
with 18th-century pieces and
a small collection of exhibits
relating to Johnson and the
times in which he lived. These
include a tea set belonging to
his friend Mrs. Thrale and
pictures of the great man
himself, his contemporaries
and their houses.

Reconstructed interior of Dr. Johnson's house

St. Andrew, Holborn ⑮

Holborn Circus EC4. **Map** 14 E1.
ℂ *0171-353 3544.* ⊖ *Chancery
Lane.* **Open** *8am–5pm Mon–Fri.* ⊚

THE MEDIEVAL CHURCH here
survived the Great Fire of
1666. In 1686 Christopher
Wren was commissioned to
redesign it, and the lower part
of the tower is virtually all that
remains of the earlier church.
One of Wren's most spacious
churches, it was gutted during
World War II but faithfully
restored as the church of the
London trade guilds. Prime
Minister, Benjamin Disraeli,
born to Jewish parents, was
baptized here in 1817, at the
age of 12. In the 19th century
a charity school was attached
to the church.

Holborn Viaduct ⑯

EC1. **Map** 14 F1. ⊖ *Farringdon, St.
Paul's, Chancery Lane.*

Civic symbol on Holborn Viaduct

THIS PIECE of Victorian
ironwork was erected in
the 1860s as part of a much-
needed traffic system. It is
best seen from Farringdon
Street, which is linked to the
bridge by a staircase. Climb
up and see the statues of City
heroes and bronze images of
Commerce, Agriculture,
Science and Fine Arts.

St. Etheldreda's Chapel ⑰

14 Ely Place EC1. **Map** 6 E5.
ℂ *0171-405 1061.* ⊖ *Chancery
Lane, Farringdon.* **Open** *8am–6pm
daily.* ⊚ ▯ *noon–2pm Mon–Fri.*

THIS IS A RARE 13th-century
survivor, the chapel and
crypt of Ely House, where the
Bishops of Ely lived until the

Reformation. Then it was acquired by an Elizabethan courtier, Sir Christopher Hatton, whose descendants demolished the house but kept the chapel and turned it into a Protestant church. It passed through various hands and, in 1874, reverted to the Catholic faith.

Hatton Garden ⑱

EC1. **Map** 6 E5. 🚇 *Chancery Lane, Farringdon.*

BUILT ON LAND that used to be the garden of Hatton House, this is London's diamond and jewelry district. Gems ranging from the priceless to the mundane are traded in scores of small shops with sparkling window displays, and even from the sidewalks. One of the City's few remaining pawnbrokers is here – look for its traditional sign of three brass balls above the door.

Staple Inn ⑲

Holborn WC1. **Map** 14 E1. ☎ *0171-242 5240.* 🚇 *Chancery Lane.* **Courtyard open** *9am–5pm Mon–Fri.* 📷 🚻

ONCE THE WOOL supply center, where wool was weighed and taxed, the frontage overlooks Holborn and is the only real example of Elizabethan half-timbering left in central London. Although now much restored, it would still be recognizable by someone who had known it in 1586, when it was built. The shops at street level have the feel of the 19th century, and there are some 18th-century buildings in the courtyard.

London Silver Vaults ⑳

53–64 Chancery Lane WC2. **Map** 14 D1. 🚇 *Chancery Lane. See* **Shops and Markets** *pp322–3.*

THE LONDON SILVER VAULTS originate from the Chancery Lane Safe Deposit Company, established in

Staple Inn, a survivor from 1586

1885. At the bottom of the staircase formidable steel security doors open to reveal a nest of underground shops sparkling with antique and modern silverware. London silver makers have been renowned for centuries; their finest works were produced in the Georgian era. The best examples sell for many thousands of pounds, but most shops also offer modest pieces at realistic prices.

Coffee pot (1716): Silver Vaults

Gray's Inn ㉑

Gray's Inn Rd WC1. **Map** 6 D5. ☎ *0171-405 8164.* 🚇 *Chancery Lane, Holborn.* **Open** *10am–4pm Mon–Fri.* **Grounds open** *24 hrs daily.* 📷 ♿

THIS ANCIENT LEGAL center and law school dates from the 14th century. Like many of the buildings in this area, it was badly damaged by World War II bombs, but much of it has been faithfully rebuilt. At least one of William Shakespeare's plays (*A Comedy of Errors*) was first performed in the now-restored Gray's Inn hall in 1594. Only a 16th-century interior screen survives from the original hall.

The young Charles Dickens was employed as a clerk at Gray's in 1827 and 1828. Today its stately garden, once a convenient site for duels, is open to lunchtime strollers for part of the year and typifies the cloistered calm of the four Inns of Court. The buildings may be visited only by appointment.

THE CITY

L ONDON'S FINANCIAL dis-
trict is built on the site
of the original Roman
settlement. Its full title is the
City of London, but it is usually referred to as the City.
Most traces of the early City
were obliterated by the Great
Fire of 1666 and World War II
(see pp22–3 and 31). Today
glossy modern offices stand

**Traditional bank sign
on Lombard Street**

contrast between dour, warren-
like Victorian buildings and
shiny new ones that gives
the City its distinctive character. Though it hums with
activity in business hours,
few people have lived here
since the 19th century, when it
was one of London's main
residential centers. Today
only the churches, many of

among a plethora of banks, with marbled halls and stately pillars. It is the

them by Christopher Wren *(see p47),*
are a reminder of those past times.

SIGHTS AT A GLANCE

**Historic Streets and
Buildings**
Mansion House **1**
Royal Exchange **3**
Old Bailey **7**
Apothecaries' Hall **8**
Fishmongers' Hall **9**
Tower of London pp154-7 **16**
Tower Bridge **17**
Lloyd's of London **22**
Stock Exchange **24**
Guildhall **25**

Museums and Galleries
Bank of England Museum **4**
Tower Hill Pageant **19**

Historic Markets
Billingsgate **12**
Leadenhall Market **23**

Monuments
Monument **11**

Churches and Cathedrals
St. Stephen Walbrook **2**
St. Mary-le-Bow **5**
St. Paul's Cathedral pp148-51 **6**
St. Magnus the Martyr **10**
St. Mary-at-Hill **13**
St. Margaret Pattens **14**
All Hallows by the Tower **15**
St. Helen's Bishopsgate **20**
St. Katharine Cree **21**

Dock
St. Katharine's Dock **18**

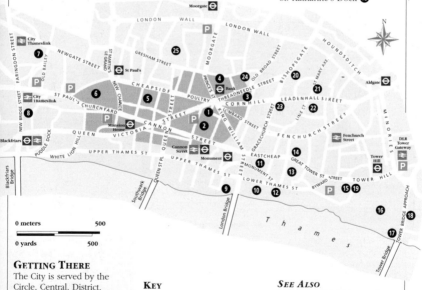

GETTING THERE
The City is served by the
Circle, Central, District,
Northern and Metropolitan
Underground lines, and bus
numbers 6, 8, 9, 11, 15, 15B,
22B, 25, 133 and 501. There
are many Thameslink and
mainline British Rail stations.

KEY

▢ Street-by-Street map

🔵 Underground station

🔀 British Rail station

🅿 Parking

SEE ALSO

• *Street Finder,* maps 14, 15, 16

• *Where to Stay* pp276–7

• *Restaurants* pp292–4

St. Paul's Cathedral with the NatWest Tower (1980) to its left

Street by Street: The City

THIS IS THE BUSINESS CENTER of London, home to vast financial institutions such as the Stock Exchange and the Bank of England. But in contrast to these 19th- and 20th-century buildings are the older survivors. A walk through the City is in part a pilgrimage through the architectural visions of Christopher Wren, England's most sublime and probably most prolific architect. After the Great Fire of 1666 he supervised the rebuilding of 52 churches within the area, and enough survive to testify to his genius.

St. Mary-le-Bow
Anyone born within earshot of the bells of this Wren church (the historic Bow Bells) is said to be a true Londoner or Cockney **5**

The Temple of Mithras is an important Roman relic whose foundations were revealed by a World War II bomb.

★ St. Paul's
Wren's masterpiece still dominates the City skyline **6**

St. Paul's station

NEW CHANGE

WATLING STREET

BREAD STREET

ST PAUL'S CHURCHYARD

CANNON STREET

FRIDAY ST

Mansion House station

QUEEN VICTORI

The College of Arms received its royal charter in 1484 from Richard III. Still active today, it assesses who has a legitimate claim to a British family coat of arms.

COLLEGE · OF · ARMS

St. Nicholas Cole was the first church Wren built in the City (in 1677). Like many others, it had to be restored after World War II bomb damage.

St. James Garlickhythe contains unusual sword rests and hat stands, beneath Wren's elegant spire of 1717.

KEY

– – –   Suggested route

| 0 meters | 100 |
| 0 yards | 100 |

Skinners' Hall is the Italianate 18th-century guild hall for the leather trade.

Mansion House
*The official home of London's
mayor, this building
contains a small prison* ❶

★ **Bank of England Museum**
*The intriguing story of England's
financial system is vividly
displayed here* ❹

LOCATOR MAP
See Central London Map pp12–13

**Bank
station**

**Royal
Exchange**
*Since its
foundation in
Tudor times,
this has been
at the heart of
London's
commerce* ❸

Lombard Street
is named after Italian
bankers who left
Lombardy to settle   here
in the 13th century. It is
still a banking center.

St. Mary Abchurch
owes its unusually
spacious feel to
Wren's large dome.
The altar carving is
by Grinling Gibbons.

St. Mary Woolnoth is a
characteristically powerful
work by Wren's pupil,
Nicholas Hawksmoor.

★**St. Stephen
Walbrook**
*Experimenting for
St. Paul's, Wren created
its unique steeple. The
interior contains
original features,
such as this font* ❷

Mansion House ❶

Walbrook EC4. **Map** 15 B2.
☎ 0171-626 2500. ⊖ Bank, Mansion
House. **Not open** to the public.

THE OFFICIAL RESIDENCE of the
Lord Mayor, it was
completed in 1753 to the
design of George Dance the
Elder, whose designs can now
be seen in John Soane's
Museum (see pp136 −7). The
Palladian front with its six
large Corinthian columns is
one of the most familiar City
landmarks. The state rooms

are of a splendor and dignity
appropriate to the office of
mayor. One of the most
spectacular rooms the 90-ft
(27-m) Egyptian Hall.

Hidden from view are 11
holding cells (10 for men and
1, "the birdcage," for women),
a reminder of the building's
other function as a magistrate's court. The Mayor is
chief magistrate of the city
during his special year of
office. Emmeline Pankhurst,
who campaigned for women's
suffrage in the early 20th
century, was once held here.

Egyptian Hall in Mansion House

St. Stephen Walbrook ❷

39 Walbrook EC4. **Map** 15 B2. ☎
0171-283 4444. ⊖ Bank, Cannon St.
Open 10am–4pm Mon–Thu,
10am–3pm Fri. ✝ 12:45pm Thu,
sung Mass. 📷 **Organ recitals** Fri.

THE LORD MAYOR'S parish
church was built by
Christopher Wren in 1672–9.
Architectural writers consider
it to be the finest of his City
churches (see p47). The deep,
coffered dome, with its ornate
plasterwork, was a forerunner
of St. Paul's. St. Stephen's airy
columned interior comes as a
surprise after its plain exterior.
The font cover and pulpit
canopy are decorated with

exquisite carved figures that
contrast strongly with the
stark simplicity of Henry
Moore's massive white stone
altar (1987).

However, perhaps the most
moving monument of all is a
telephone in a glass box. This
is a tribute to Rector Chad
Varah who, in 1953, founded
the Samaritans, a voluntarily
staffed telephone help-line
for people in emotional need.

*The Martyrdom of St.
Stephen*, which hangs on the
north wall, is by American
painter Benjamin West, who
became a Royal Academician
(see p90) in 1768.

The spire was
added in 1717.

The dome
makes this
small church
light and airy.

Wren's
original altar
and screen
are still here.

Wren's pulpit
has a delicate
canopy.

Henry Moore's
polished stone altar
was added in 1987.

Royal Exchange ❸

EC3. **Map** 15 C2. ☎ *0171-623 0444.*
🚇 *Bank.* **Not open to the public.**

Sir Thomas Gresham, the Elizabethan merchant and courtier, founded the Royal Exchange in 1565 as a center for commerce of all kinds. The original building was centered on a vast courtyard where merchants and tradesmen did business. Queen Elizabeth I gave it its royal title and it is still one of the sites from which new kings and queens are announced. Dating from 1844, this is the third splendid building on the site since Gresham's.

Britain's first public lavatories (for men only) were erected in the forecourt of the Royal Exchange in 1855.

Bank of England Museum ❹

Bartholomew Lane EC2. **Map** 15 B1.
☎ *0171-601 5545.* 📠 *0171-601 5792.* 🚇 *Bank.* **Open** *10am–5pm Mon–Fri.* **Closed** *public hols Oct 1–Easter.* 📷 ♿ *(loop system).* 🎧 📺 **Filmshows, lectures.**

The Duke of Wellington (1884) opposite the Bank of England

The Bank of England was set up in 1694 to raise money for foreign wars. It grew to become Britain's central bank, and also issues currency notes.

Sir John Soane *(see pp136–7)* was the architect of the 1788 bank building on this site, but only the exterior wall of his design has survived. The rest was destroyed in the 1920s and 1930s when the Bank

The facade of William Tite's Royal Exchange of 1844

was enlarged. There is now a reconstruction of Soane's stock office of 1793.

Glittering gold bars, silver plated decoration and a Roman mosaic floor, discovered during the rebuilding, are among the items on display. The museum illustrates the work of the bank and the financial system. The gift shop sells paperweights which are made out of used banknotes.

St. Mary-le-Bow ❺

(Bow Church) Cheapside EC2.
Map 15 A2. ☎ *0171-248 5139.*
🚇 *Mansion House.* **Open** *6:30am–6pm Mon, Wed and Fri; 6:30am–7pm Thu; 6:30am–4pm Fri.* ✝ *5:45pm Thu.* 🍴

The church takes its name from the bow arches in the Norman crypt. When Wren rebuilt the church (in 1670–80) after the Great Fire *(see pp22–3)*, he continued this architectural pattern through the graceful arches on the steeple. The weathervane, dating from 1674, is an enormous dragon.

The church was destroyed by bombs in 1941, leaving only the steeple and two outer walls standing. It was restored in 1956–62 when the bells were recast and rehung. Bow bells are important to Londoners: traditionally only those born within their sound can claim to be true Cockneys.

St. Paul's ❻

See pp148–51.

Old Bailey ❼

EC4. **Map** 14 F1. ☎ *0171-248 3277.*
🚇 *St. Paul's.* **Open** *10:30am–1pm, 2–4:30pm Mon–Fri (but opening hours vary from court to court).* **Closed** *Christmas, New Year, Easter, public hols.* 📷

Old Bailey's rooftop Justice

This short street has a long association with crime and punishment. The new Central Criminal Courts opened here in 1907 on the site of the notorious and malodorous Newgate prison (on special days in the legal calendar judges still carry small posies to court as a reminder of those times). Across the road, the Magpie and Stump served "execution breakfasts" until 1868, when mass public hangings outside the prison gates were stopped.

Today, when the courts are in session, they are open to members of the public.

St. Paul's Cathedral ⑥

Fᴏʟʟᴏᴡɪɴɢ ᴛʜᴇ Great Fire of London in 1666, the medieval cathedral of St. Paul's was left in ruins. The authorities turned to Christopher Wren to rebuild it, but his ideas met with considerable resistance from the conservative, tightfisted Dean and Chapter. Wren's 1672 Great Model plan, now on display in the crypt, was not at all popular, and a watered-down plan was agreed on in 1675. Wren's determination paid off, though, as can be seen from the grandeur of the present cathedral.

Stone statuary outside the South Transept

★ **The Inner and Outer Dome**
At 360 ft (110 m) high it is the second biggest dome in the world, after St. Peter's in Rome, as spectacular from inside as outside.

The balustrade along the top was added in 1718 against Wren's wishes.

The pediment carvings, dating from 1706, show the Conversion of St. Paul.

★ **The West Front and Towers**
The towers were not on Wren's original plan – he added them in 1707, when he was 75 years old. Both were designed to have clocks.

Flying buttresses support the nave walls and the dome.

The West Portico comprises two tiers of columns rather than the single colonnade that Wren intended.

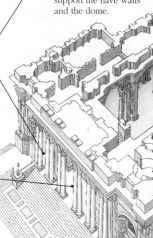

Star Sights

★ **The West Front and Towers**

★ **The Inner and Outer Dome**

★ **Whispering Gallery**

The West Porch, approached from Ludgate Hill, is the main entrance to St. Paul's.

Queen Anne's Statue
An 1886 copy of Francis Bird's 1712 original now stands in the forecourt.

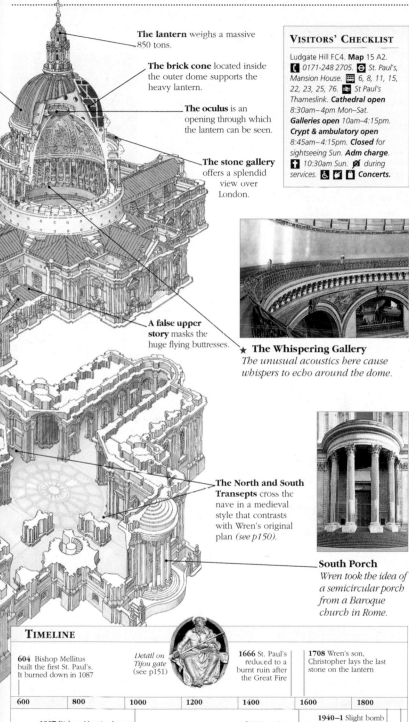

The lantern weighs a massive 850 tons.

The brick cone located inside the outer dome supports the heavy lantern.

The oculus is an opening through which the lantern can be seen.

The stone gallery offers a splendid view over London.

VISITORS' CHECKLIST

Ludgate Hill EC4. **Map** 15 A2.
[] 0171-248 2705. [] St. Paul's,
Mansion House. [] 6, 8, 11, 15,
22, 23, 25, 76. [] St Paul's
Thameslink. **Cathedral open**
8:30am–4pm Mon–Sat.
Galleries open 10am–4:15pm.
Crypt & ambulatory open
8:45am–4:15pm. **Closed** for
sightseeing Sun. **Adm charge.**
[] 10:30am Sun. [] during
services. [] [] [] **Concerts.**

A false upper story masks the huge flying buttresses.

★ **The Whispering Gallery**
The unusual acoustics here cause whispers to echo around the dome.

The North and South Transepts cross the nave in a medieval style that contrasts with Wren's original plan *(see p150)*.

South Porch
Wren took the idea of a semicircular porch from a Baroque church in Rome.

TIMELINE

Detail on Tijou gate (see p151)

600	800	1000	1200	1400	1600	1800

604 Bishop Mellitus built the first St. Paul's. It burned down in 1087

1666 St. Paul's reduced to a burnt ruin after the Great Fire

1708 Wren's son, Christopher lays the last stone on the lantern

1087 Bishop Maurice began Old St. Paul's: a Norman cathedral of stone

1675 Foundation stone of Wren's design laid

1940–1 Slight bomb damage to the cathedral

1981 Prince Charles marries Lady Diana Spencer

A Guided Tour of St. Paul's

T HE VISITOR TO ST. PAUL'S will be immediately
impressed by its cool, beautifully ordered and
extremely spacious interior. The nave, transepts and
choir are arranged in the shape of a cross, as in a
medieval cathedral, but Wren's Classical vision shines
through this conservative floor plan, forced on him by
the cathedral authorities. Aided by some of the finest
craftsmen of his day, he created an interior of grand
majesty and Baroque splendor, a worthy setting for the
many great ceremonial events that have taken
place here. These include the funeral of Winston
Churchill in 1965
and the wedding of
Prince Charles and
Lady Diana
Spencer in 1981.

The mosaics on the
choir ceiling were
completed in the
1890s by William
Richmond.

② The North Aisle
*Walking along the North
Aisle, look above: the aisles
are vaulted with small
domes mimicking those of
the nave ceiling.*

① The Nave
*Take in the full glory of the massive
arches and the succession of
saucer domes that open out into a
huge space below the main dome.*

⑨ South Aisle
*From here the brave can
ascend the 259 steps to the
Whispering Gallery and
test the acoustics.*

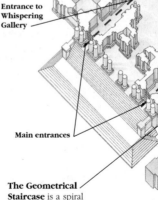

**Entrance to
Whispering
Gallery**

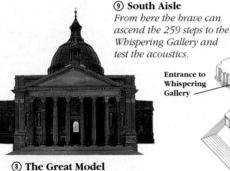

⑧ The Great Model
*A model of Wren's original
design was carved in 1672.
The plan was rejected as being
too revolutionary for its time.*

Main entrances

**The Geometrical
Staircase** is a spiral
of 92 stone steps
giving access to the
cathedral library.

⑦ Wren's Tomb
*Wren's burial place is marked
by a slab. The inscription states:
"Reader, if you seek his
memorial look all around you."*

KEY

– – – Tour route

③ **The Crossing**
The climax of Wren's interior is this great open space. The vast dome is decorated with monochrome frescoes by Sir James Thornhill, the leading architectural painter of Wren's time.

Entrance to crypt

④ **The Choir**
Jean Tijou, a Huguenot refugee, created much of the cathedral's fine wrought iron-work, such as these screens in the choir aisles.

John Donne's tomb, from 1631, was the only monument to survive the Great Fire of 1666. The poet posed for it in his lifetime.

⑤ **The High Altar**
The canopy over the altar was replaced after World War II. It is based on Wren's original Baroque drawings.

Grinling Gibbons's work can be found on the choir stalls, with typically intricate carvings of cherubs, fruits and garlands.

⑥ **The Crypt**
Memorials to famous figures and popular heroes, such as Lord Nelson, can be seen in the crypt.

Lawrence of Arabia, the adventurer, is commemorated by this bust in the crypt.

Apothecaries' Hall ⑧

Blackfriars Lane EC4. **Map** 14 F2.
☎ *0171-236 1189.* ⊖ *Blackfriars.*
Courtyard open 9am–5:30pm
Mon–Fri. **Closed** public hols. **Hall**
closed to the public. &

Apothecaries' Hall, rebuilt in 1670

LONDON HAS had livery companies, or guilds, to protect and regulate specific trades since early medieval times. The Apothecaries' Society was founded in 1617 for those who prepared, prescribed or sold drugs. It has some surprising alumni, including Oliver Cromwell and the poet John Keats. Now nearly all the members are physicians or surgeons.

Fishmongers' Hall ⑨

London Bridge EC4. **Map** 15 B3.
☎ *0171-626 3531.* ⊖ *Monument.*
Not open to the public.

THIS IS ONE of the oldest livery companies, established in 1272. Lord Mayor Walworth, a member of the Fishmongers' Company, killed Wat Tyler, leader of the Peasants' Revolt, in 1381 *(see p162)*. Today it still fulfils its original role; all fish sold in the city must be inspected by Company officials. The building dates from 1834.

St. Magnus the Martyr ⑩

Lower Thames St EC3. **Map** 15 C3.
☎ *0171-626 4481.* ⊖ *Monument.*
🕇 *11am Sun* ∅.

THERE HAS BEEN a church here for more than 1,000 years. Its patron saint, St. Magnus, was a Norwegian Earl of the Orkney Islands off the north coast of Scotland. He was a highly regarded Christian leader, murdered by his cousin in 1110.

When Christopher Wren built this church from 1671–6, it was at the foot of old London Bridge, until 1738 the only bridge across the Thames in London. Anyone going south from the city would have passed under Wren's magnificent arched porch spanning the flagstones leading to the old bridge.

Highlights of the church include the carved musical instruments that decorate the organ case. Wren's pulpit, with its slender supporting stem, was restored in 1924.

Monument ⑪

Monument St EC3. **Map** 15 C2.
☎ *0171-626 2717.* ⊖ *Monument.*
Open Apr–Sep: 9am–5:40pm
Mon–Fri; 2–5:40pm Sat–Sun;
Oct–Mar: 9am–3:40pm Mon–Sat.
Adm charge. 📷 **Closed** for
renovation until mid 1995.

THE COLUMN, designed by Christopher Wren to commemorate the Great Fire of London in September 1666, is the tallest isolated stone column in the world. It is 205 ft (62 m) high and is said to be 205 ft west of where the fire started in Pudding Lane. It was sited on the direct approach to old London Bridge, which was a few steps downstream from the present one. Reliefs around

The altar of St. Magnus the Martyr

the column's base show Charles II restoring the city. The 311 steps to the top lead to a platform with fine views. In 1842 this was enclosed with railings after a suicide.

Billingsgate ⑫

Lower Thames St EC3. **Map** 15 C3.
⊖ *Monument.* **Not open to the**
public.

Fish weathervane at Billingsgate

LONDON'S MAIN fish market was based here for 900 years, on one of the city's earliest quays. During the 19th and early 20th centuries, 400 tons of fish were sold here every day, much of it delivered by boat. It was London's noisiest market, renowned, even in Shakespeare's day, for foul language. In 1982 the market moved from this building (1877) to the Isle of Dogs.

St. Mary-at-Hill ⑬

Lovat Lane EC3. **Map** 15 C2.
☎ *0171-626 4184.* ⊖ *Monument.*
Concerts. Open 10am–1pm Mon–Fri.

THE INTERIOR and east end of St. Mary-at-Hill were Wren's first church designs (1670–6). The Greek cross design was a prototype for his St. Paul's proposals.

Ironically, the delicate plasterwork and rich 17th-century fittings, which had survived both the Victorian mania for renovation and the bombs of World War II, were lost in a fire in 1988. The building was then restored to its original appearance, only to be damaged again, this time by an IRA bomb in 1992.

St. Margaret Pattens ⑭

Rood Lane and Eastcheap EC3. **Map** 15 C2. 🕿 *0171-623 6630.* ⊖ *Monument.* **Open** *8am–4pm Mon–Fri.* **Closed** *Christmas week, 3 weeks Aug.* ✝ *1pm Wed.*

WREN'S CHURCH from 1684–7 was named after a type of overshoe made near here. Its Portland stone walls are a good contrast to the Georgian stucco shopfront in the forecourt. The simple interior retains 17th-century canopied pews and an ornate font.

All Hallows by the Tower ⑮

Byward St EC3. **Map** 16 D3. 🕿 *0171-481 2928.* ⊖ *Tower Hill.* **Open** *9am–6pm Mon–Fri; 10am–5pm Sun.* **Closed** *Jan 1, Dec 26–27.* ♿ ✝ *11am Sun.* 🅿

THE FIRST CHURCH on this site was Saxon. The arch in the southwest corner, which contains Roman tiles, dates from that period and so do some crosses now in the crypt. There is also a well-preserved Roman pavement in the crypt that at times is open to the public. Most of the interior has been altered by restoration, but a limewood font cover, carved by Grinling Gibbons in 1682, still survives.

Roman tile from All Hallows

William Penn (founder of Pennsylvania) was baptized here in 1644 and John Quincy Adams married in 1797 before he was US president. Samuel Pepys watched the Great Fire of 1666 from the church tower.

Tower of London ⑯

See pp154–7.

Tower Bridge ⑰

SE1. **Map** 16 D3. 🕿 *0171-403 3761.* ⊖ *Tower Hill.* **Open** *Apr–Oct: 10am–6:30pm daily; Nov–Mar: 10am–4:45pm daily (last adm: 45 mins before closing).* **Closed** *Jan 1, Good Fri, Dec 24–26.* **Adm charge.** 📷 ♿ *Video* 🅿

COMPLETED IN 1894, this flamboyant piece of Victorian engineering quickly became a symbol of London. Its pinnacled towers and linking catwalk support the mechanism for raising the roadway when big ships have to pass through, or for special occasions, such as the return

of the *Gipsy Moth* (see p237). This is an impressive sight.

The bridge now houses a museum of its history, with fine river views from the catwalk. Also on display is the steam engine that powered the lifting machinery until 1976, when the system was electrified.

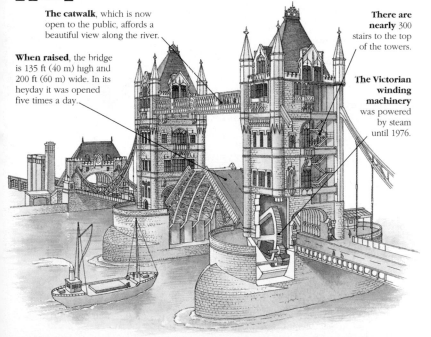

The catwalk, which is now open to the public, affords a beautiful view along the river.

When raised, the bridge is 135 ft (40 m) high and 200 ft (60 m) wide. In its heyday it was opened five times a day.

There are nearly 300 stairs to the top of the towers.

The Victorian winding machinery was powered by steam until 1976.

Tower of London 16

For much of its 900-year history, the Tower was an object of fear. Those who had offended the monarch were held within its dank walls. A lucky few lived in comparative comfort, but the majority had to put up with appalling conditions. Many did not get out alive and were tortured before meeting cruelly violent deaths on nearby Tower Hill.

★ **The White Tower**
When it was finished in 1097, it was the tallest building in London – 90 ft (30 m) high.

★ **The Jewel House** is where the magnificent English Crown Jewels are housed *(see p156)*.

"Beefeaters"
Forty-two Yeoman Warders guard the Tower and live there.

Beauchamp Tower
Many high-ranking prisoners were held here, often with their own retinues of servants.

Tower Green was where the most favored prisoners were executed, away from the ghoulish crowds on Tower Hill. Only seven people died here – including two of Henry VIII's six wives – but hundreds had to bear more public executions.

Main entrance

STAR BUILDINGS

★ **The White Tower**

★ **The Jewel House**

★ **Chapel of St. John**

★ **The Martin Tower**

THE RAVENS

The Tower's most celebrated residents are a colony of eight ravens. It is not known when they first settled here, but there is a legend that should they desert the Tower, the kingdom will fall. In fact, the birds have their wings clipped on one side, making flight impossible. The Ravenmaster, one of the Yeoman Warders, looks after the birds.

A memorial in the moat commemorates some of the ravens who have died at the Tower since the 1950s.

Queen's House
This is the private home of the Tower's governor.

★ **The Martin Tower**
Instruments of torture and the executioner's ax and block are displayed here.

★ **Chapel of St. John**
The stone for this austerely beautiful Romanesque chapel was brought from France.

VISITORS' CHECKLIST

Tower Hill EC3. **Map** 16 D3.
0171-709 0765. ⊖ *Tower Hill.* 15, X15, 25, 42, 78, 100. ⊕ *Fenchurch Street.*
Docklands Light Railway
Tower Gateway. **Open** *Mar–Oct:*
9:30am–6pm Mon–Sat, 10am–
6pm Sun; Nov–Feb: 9:30am–
5pm Mon–Sat. **Tower closed**
Jan 1, Good Fri, Dec 24–26.
Jewel House closed *Jan.* **Adm charge.** & *except to Crown Jewels exhibition.* ☑ *Ceremony of the Keys 9:30pm daily (see pp52–5).* ☐ ☐

Wakefield Tower
has been reconstructed to match its appearance in the 13th century.

The Bloody Tower
is named after its association with the two young princes who disappeared from here in 1483 *(see p157).*

Traitors' Gate
The Tower's boat entry for prisoners, many on their way to die.

TIMELINE

1078 The White Tower started	**1536** Anne Boleyn executed	**1810–15** Mint moves from the Tower and arms stop being manufactured here
	1483 Princes disappeared from the Tower	
	1553–4 Lady Jane Grey held and executed	

1050	1250	1450	1650	1850	1950

1066 William I erects a temporary castle	**1530s** Castle stops being a royal palace	**1671** Crown Jewels stolen by "Colonel" Blood
	1534–5 Thomas More imprisoned and executed	**1834** Menagerie moves out of Tower
		1603–16 Walter Raleigh imprisoned in Tower
		1941 Rudolph Hess is the last prisoner held in Queen's House

Inside the Tower

THE TOWER HAS been a tourist attraction since the reign of Charles II (1660–85), when both the Crown Jewels and the collection of armor were first shown to the public. They remain powerful reminders of royal might and wealth.

The Orb, symbolizing the power and Empire of Christ the Redeemer

THE CROWN JEWELS

THE CROWN JEWELS comprise the regalia of crowns, scepters, orbs and swords used at coronations and other state occasions. They are impossible to price, but their worth is irrelevant beside their enormous significance in the historical and religious life of the kingdom. Most of the Crown Jewels date from 1661, when a new set was made for the coronation of Charles II; Parliament had destroyed the previous crowns and scepters after the execution of Charles I in 1649. Only a few pieces survived, hidden by the clergy of Westminster Abbey until the Restoration.

The Coronation Ceremony
Many elements in this solemn and mystical ceremony date from the days of Edward the · Confessor. The king or queen proceeds to Westminster Abbey, accompanied by parts of the regalia, including the State Sword, which represents the monarch's own sword. He or she is then annointed with holy oil, to signify divine approval, and invested with ornaments and royal robes. Each of the jewels represents an aspect of the monarch's role as head of the state and church. The climax comes when St. Edward's Crown is placed on the sovereign's head; there is a cry of "God Save the King" (or Queen), the trumpets sound and guns at the Tower are fired. The last coronation was Elizabeth II's in 1953.

The Imperial State Crown, made for Queen Victoria in 1837, containing 2,800 diamonds and other gems

The crowns
There are 12 crowns on display at the Tower. Many of these have not been worn for years, but the Imperial State Crown is in constant use. The Queen wears it at state events, such as the Opening of Parliament (*see p73*). The crown was made in 1837 for the coronation of 18-year-old Queen Victoria. The sapphire that is set in the cross is said to have been worn in a ring by Edward the Confessor (who ruled from 1042–66). The most recent crown is not at the Tower, however. It was made for Prince Charles's investiture as Prince of Wales and is kept at Caernavon Castle in north Wales, where the ceremony took place in 1969. The Queen Mother's crown was made for the 1937 coronation of her husband, George VI. It is made out of platinum – all the other crowns at the Tower are gold.

Other regalia
Apart from the crowns, there are other pieces of the Crown Jewels that are essential to coronations. Among these are three Swords of Justice, symbolizing mercy, spiritual and temporal justice. The orb is a hollow gold sphere encrusted with jewels and weighing about 3 lbs (1.5 kg). The Scepter of the Cross contains the biggest cut diamond in the world, the 530-carat First Star of Africa. The rough stone it came from weighed 3,106 carats.

The Sovereign's Ring, sometimes referred to as "the wedding ring of England"

The Plate Collection
The Jewel House also holds a collection of elaborate gold and silver plate. The Maundy Dish is still used on Maundy Thursday, when the monarch distributes money to selected old people. The Exeter Salt (a very grand salt cellar from the days when salt was a valuable commodity) was given by the citizens of Exeter, in west England, to Charles II; during the 1640s' Civil War Exeter was a Royalist stronghold.

The Scepter with the Cross (1660), redesigned in 1910 when Edward VII was presented with the First Star of Africa diamond.

The hilt and solid-gold scabbard of the Jeweled State Sword, one of the most valuable swords in the world

ROYAL ARMORIES

THE ROYAL ARMORIES are the nation's largest and most important collection of arms and armor. There are about 40,000 objects in the collection, including sporting pieces as well as the weapons of warfare. It was organized by Henry VIII soon after he came to the throne in 1509 and ordered the Tower arsenal to be re-equipped with the latest weapons and armor. The present collection grew over the centuries as surplus weapons and booty accumulated from Britain's imperial conquests were added.

Early weaponry

All four floors of the White Tower are devoted to this collection. On the first is sporting and tournament armor. The sporting gallery contains crossbows, hunting spears and swords and sporting guns. From about 1400 tournaments were primarily social occasions where knights sparred with one another against a background of much feasting and music, not to mention a little chivalric courting. Armor worn at tournaments was elaborately decorated but still functional. The second floor is devoted to medieval and Renaissance armor. Be sure to see the etched-and-gilt three-quarter armor made for the Earl of Southampton in 1598 and the wonderful 15th-century armed horse and rider. The medieval, English shaffron, or head defense, which is displayed nearby is one of the the oldest pieces of horse armor in the world. It dates from about 1400.

Arms since the Tudors

Tudor and Stuart armor is found on the third floor. Among the highlights are two armors made for Henry VIII in 1520 and 1540 (observe how much weight the king put on between the two). A boy's light field armor was probably made for Edward VI, Henry's son; there is another even smaller armor, about 3 feet (1 m) tall. Other Tower treasures include richly decorated swords and a variety of pistols.

In the basement are swords, armor and cannons. Here also are the remains of the Line of Kings, established under Charles II. This was a collection of models of selected kings of England, wearing 16th-century armor. Some of the models' horses were made by the well-known wood carver, Grinling Gibbons.

16th-century greave (leg guard) and sabaton (foot guard)

The New Armories

Collections in the New Armories, built as a storehouse in the 17th century, concentrate on 18th- and 19th-century weapons. There are some early machine guns (including a Gatling and a Maxim) and a fine pair of dueling pistols made in 1834 by Purdey, the English gunsmith. Here also are miniature guns, swords for children and the smallest German automatic pistol, which was made around 1913.

The Martin Tower

Some of the most gruesome exhibits in the armories are on display in the Martin Tower, where the instruments of torture used to extract confessions from prisoners are housed. Many of the victims of the rack (for stretching the body) and the scavenger's daughter (for compressing the body) suffered for beliefs at odds with those of the monarch.

Flintlock pistols (1695)

Henry VIII's armor (1540)

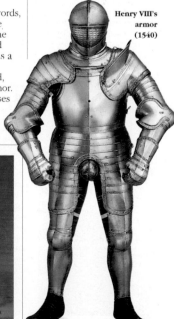

THE PRINCES IN THE TOWER

One of the Tower's darkest mysteries concerns two child princes, sons and heirs of Edward IV. They were put into the Tower by their uncle, Richard of Gloucester, when their father died in 1483. Neither was seen again, and Richard was crowned later that year. In 1674 the skeletons of two children were found nearby.

The yacht haven of the restored St. Katharine's Dock

St. Katharine's Dock 🔞

E1. **Map** 16 E3. 🛈 *0171-488 2400.*
🚇 *Tower Hill.* ♿ 🍴 🛒 📷

THIS MOST CENTRAL of all
London's docks was
designed by Thomas Telford
and opened in 1828 on the
site of St. Katharine's hospital.
Commodities as diverse as
tea, marble and live turtles
(turtle soup was a Victorian
delicacy) were unloaded here.

During the 19th and early
20th centuries the docks
flourished, but by the mid-
20th century cargo ships were
delivering vast, bulky cargoes
in massive containers. The old
docks became too small and
new ones had to be built
downstream. St. Katharine's
closed in 1968 and the others
followed within 15 years.

St. Katharine's is now one
of London's most successful
developments, with
commercial, residential and
entertainment facilities,
including a hotel and a yacht

haven. Old warehouse
buildings have shops and
restaurants on their ground
floors, and offices above.

On the north side is the
London FOX (Futures and
Options Exchange), trading in
commodities such as coffee
and oil. There is no public
gallery but, if you ask at the
door, you may be allowed
entry to the glass-walled
reception area to look down
upon the frenzied trading
floors. The dock is worth a
visit after seeing the Tower or
Tower Bridge *(see pp154 – 7
and p153)*.

Tower Hill Pageant 🔟

Tower Hill Terrace EC3. **Map** 16 D2.
🛈 *0171-709 0081.* 🚇 *Tower Hill.*
Open *Apr–Oct: 9:30am–5:30pm
daily; Nov–Mar: 9:30am–4:30pm
daily.* **Adm charge.** ♿
Filmshows. 🛒 📷

THIS UNDERGROUND ride
offers a whirlwind account
of London's history, with an
emphasis on its role as a port.
The story is told through life-
sized tableaux with visual and
sound effects. After the ride,
the viewing cars deposit
visitors in a fascinating small
exhibition, organized by the
Museum of London. It shows
objects dug up from the river
(including long-sunken boats)
and explains how archae-
ologists make deductions
from them about life in earlier
times. In many ways, the
exhibition is of more interest
(for adults at least) than the
ride itself. A large shop sells,
among many other things,
reproductions of Roman
jewelry found in London.

St. Helen's Bishopsgate 🔂

Great St. Helen's EC3. **Map** 15 C1.
🛈 *0171-283 2810.* 🚇 *Liverpool St.*
Closed *for repairs until autumn 1995.*

THE CURIOUS, bisected
appearance of this 13th-
century church is due to its
origins as two places of
worship: one, a parish church
and, the other, the chapel of
a long-gone nunnery next
door. (The medieval nuns of
St. Helen's were notorious for
the amount of "secular
kissing" they indulged in.)

Among the church's many
interesting monuments is the
tomb of Sir Thomas Gresham,
who founded the Royal
Exchange *(see p147)*.

St. Katharine Cree 🔃

86 Leadenhall St EC3. **Map** 16 D1.
🛈 *0171-283 5733.* 🚇 *Aldgate,
Tower Hill.* **Open** *8:30am–6pm Mon–
Fri.* **Closed** *Christmas, Easter.*
🚫 *during services.* 🕐 *1:05pm Thu.*

The organ at St. Katharine Cree

A RARE PRE-WREN 17th-century
church with a medieval
tower, this was one of only
eight churches in the city to
survive the fire of 1666. Some
of the elaborate plasterwork
on and beneath the high
ceiling of the nave depicts
the coats of arms of the
guilds closely associated with
the church. The 17th-century
organ, supported on
magnificent carved wooden
columns, was played by both
Purcell and Handel.

St. Helen's Bishopsgate

Lloyd's of London 22

1 Lime St EC3. **Map** 15 C2.
📞 0171-327 6210. 🚇 *Bank,
Monument, Liverpool St, Aldgate.*
Not open *to the public.*

Lloyd's was founded in the late 17th century and takes its name from the coffeehouse where underwriters and shipowners used to meet to arrange marine insurance contracts. Lloyd's soon became the world's main insurers, issuing policies on everything from oil tankers to Betty Grable's legs.

The present building, by Richard Rogers, dates from 1986 and is one of the most interesting modern buildings in London *(see p30)*. Its exaggerated stainless steel external piping and high-tech ducts echo Rogers's forceful Pompidou Center in Paris. Lloyd's is a far more elegant building and particularly worth seeing floodlit at night.

Leadenhall Market 23

Whittington Ave EC3. **Map** 15 C2.
🚇 *Bank, Monument.* **Open**
7am–4pm Mon–Fri. See **Shops and
Markets** *pp322–3.*

There has been a food market here, on the site of the Roman forum *(see pp16 – 17)*, since the Middle Ages. Its name derives from a lead-roofed mansion that stood nearby in the 14th century. The ornate, Victorian-covered shopping precinct that is here today was designed in 1881 by Sir Horace Jones, the architect of Billingsgate fish market *(see p152)*. The shopping precinct is at its best at Christmastime when all the stores are decorated.

Stock Exchange 24

Old Broad St EC4. **Map** 15 B1.
🚇 *Bank.* **Not open** *to the public.*

The first stock exchange was established in Threadneedle Street in 1773. Before that, in the 17th and

Leadenhall Market in 1881

18th centuries, stockbrokers met and dealt in city coffee-houses. Until 1914 the London Stock Exchange was the biggest in the world; now it is third to Tokyo and New York. The building, which dates from 1969, used to house the frenzied trading floor, but in 1986 the business was computerized and the floor effectively made redundant. The former public viewing gallery stayed open for a while, but was closed after a terrorist bomb attempt.

Guildhall 25

Gresham St EC2. **Map** 15 B1.
📞 *0171-606 3030.* 🚇 *St Paul's.*
Not open *to the public.* **Clock
Museum** *Aldermanbury St EC2.*
Open *9:30am–5pm Mon–Sat.* 🚻

This has been the administrative center of the city for at least 800 years. The crypt and great hall in the present building date from the 15th century.

For centuries the hall was used for trials, and many were condemned to death here, including Henry Garnet, one of the Gunpowder Plot conspirators *(see p22)*. Today its role is less bloody; in November, a few days after the Lord Mayor's parade takes place *(see pp54 – 5)*, the Prime Minister addresses a banquet here.

The adjoining public library houses the collection of the Clockmakers' Company. This includes some 600 watches and 30 clocks dating from the 16th to the 19th centuries. Mary Queen of Scots's skull-shaped watch is also here.

Richard Rogers's Lloyd's building illuminated at night

SMITHFIELD AND SPITALFIELDS

THE AREAS JUST north of the City walls have historically provided refuge for people and institutions that did not want to come under the City's jurisdiction, or were not welcome there. These included religious orders; dissenters; the earliest theaters; French Huguenots in the 17th century; and, in the 19th and 20th centuries, other immigrants from Europe and, later, from Bengal. They established workshops, small factories and restaurants and brought with them their ethnic traditions and places of worship. The name Spitalfields derives from the medieval priory of St. Mary Spital. Middlesex Street off Aldgate became known as Petticoat Lane in the 16th century, when a market for clothing was established there; it remains the hub of a popular and crowded Sunday-morning street market that spreads as far east as Brick Lane, today lined with aromatic Bengali food shops. The wholesale fruit-and-vegetable market at Spitalfields survived until 1991, when it moved to the eastern suburbs. The meat market at Smithfield, however-er, is still going strong. The area around Smithfield adjoining the City is dominated by the Barbican, a modern residential complex with an arts and conference center.

Tower: Smithfield Market

Columbia Road flower and plant market

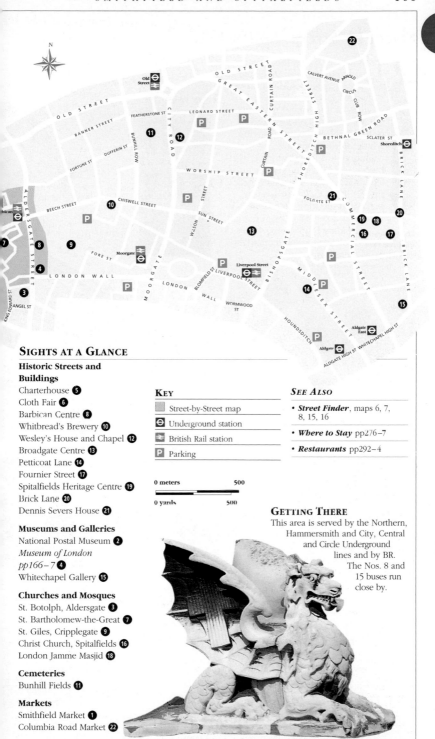

SIGHTS AT A GLANCE

Historic Streets and Buildings

Charterhouse **5**
Cloth Fair **6**
Barbican Centre **8**
Whitbread's Brewery **10**
Wesley's House and Chapel **12**
Broadgate Centre **13**
Petticoat Lane **14**
Fournier Street **17**
Spitalfields Heritage Centre **19**
Brick Lane **20**
Dennis Severs House **21**

Museums and Galleries

National Postal Museum **2**
Museum of London pp166–7 **4**
Whitechapel Gallery **15**

Churches and Mosques

St. Botolph, Aldersgate **3**
St. Bartholomew-the-Great **7**
St. Giles, Cripplegate **9**
Christ Church, Spitalfields **16**
London Jamme Masjid **18**

Cemeteries

Bunhill Fields **11**

Markets

Smithfield Market **1**
Columbia Road Market **22**

KEY

▢	Street-by-Street map
Ⓔ	Underground station
▆	British Rail station
P	Parking

0 meters   500

0 yards   500

SEE ALSO

GETTING THERE

This area is served by the Northern, Hammersmith and City, Central and Circle Underground lines and by BR. The Nos. 8 and 15 buses run close by.

Stone dragon in Smithfield Market

Street by Street: Smithfield

The Fat Boy:
the Great Fire
ended here

THIS AREA IS AMONG the most historic in London. It contains one of the capital's oldest churches, some rare Jacobean houses, vestiges of the Roman wall (near the Museum of London) and central London's only surviving wholesale food market.

Smithfield's long history is also bloody. In 1381 the rebel peasant leader Wat Tyler was killed here by an ally of Richard III, as he presented the king with demands for lower taxes. Later, in the reign of Mary I (1553–8), scores of Protestant religious martyrs were burned at the stake here.

The Fox and Anchor pub is open from 7am for hearty breakfasts washed down with ale, enjoyed by the market traders of Smithfield.

★ **Smithfield Market**
A contemporary print shows Horace Jones's stately building for the meat market when it was completed in 1867 ❶

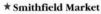

Fat Boy

The Saracen's Head, a historic inn, stood on this site until the 1860s, when it was demolished to make way for Holborn Viaduct (*see p140*).

St. Bartholomew-the-Less has a 15th-century tower and vestry. Links to the hospital are shown by this 20th-century stained glass panel of a nurse; a gift of the Worshipful Company of Glaziers.

St. Bartholomew's
Hospital has stood on this site since 1123. Some of the existing buildings date from 1759.

KEY

– – –   Suggested route

0 meters   100

0 yards   100

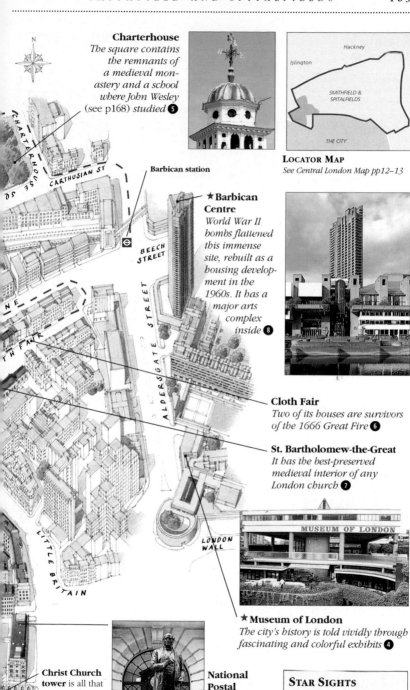

N

Charterhouse
The square contains the remnants of a medieval monastery and a school where John Wesley (see p168) studied **5**

LOCATOR MAP
See Central London Map pp12–13

Hackney

Islington

SMITHFIELD & SPITALFIELDS

THE CITY

CHARTERHOUSE SQ

CARTHUSIAN ST

Barbican station

BEECH STREET

★Barbican Centre
World War II bombs flattened this immense site, rebuilt as a housing development in the 1960s. It has a major arts complex inside **8**

ALDERSGATE STREET

LANE

TH FAIR

LITTLE

BRITAIN

LONDON WALL

Cloth Fair
Two of its houses are survivors of the 1666 Great Fire **6**

St. Bartholomew-the-Great
It has the best-preserved medieval interior of any London church **7**

MUSEUM OF LONDON

★Museum of London
The city's history is told vividly through fascinating and colorful exhibits **4**

Christ Church tower is all that remains of one of Wren's most splendid churches (1704).

To St. Paul's station

National Postal Museum
The statue of Rowland Hill, inventor of the Penny Post, is outside **2**

STAR SIGHTS

★**Museum of London**

★**Barbican Centre**

★**Smithfield Market**

Smithfield Market ❶

Charterhouse St EC1. **Map** 6 F5.
🚇 *Farringdon, Barbican.* **Open**
5–9am Mon–Fri.

Until the mid-19th century, live cattle were sold here when it was the smooth field from which its name probably derives. Smithfield is still London's main meat market, but since 1855 it has confined itself mainly to wholesale trading in dead meat and poultry. The old buildings are by Sir Horace Jones, the Victorian architect who specialized in markets, but there are 20th-century additions. Some pubs in the area keep market hours and, from dawn, serve substantial breakfasts, with ale, to market traders and office workers.

Smithfield Market central tower

National Postal Museum ❷

King Edward Bldg, King Edward St
EC1. **Map** 15 A1. 📞 *0171-239
5420.* 🚇 *Barbican, St. Paul's.* **Open**
9:30am–4:30pm Mon–Fri. **Closed**
public hols. 📷

THE HEADQUARTERS of the Post Office stands on the site of the old Bull and Mouth Inn, behind St. Paul's, where in the 18th century the first

Stamp commemorating the 1953 Coronation: National Postal Museum

mail coaches would leave for cities across the country. The museum itself contains a comprehensive collection of British and overseas stamps, including some great rarities. There is also a collection of post office equipment, which includes early letter boxes and franking machines.

St. Botolph, Aldersgate ❸

Aldersgate St EC1. **Map** 15 A1.
📞 *0171-606 0684.* 🚇 *St. Paul's.*
Open *11am–3pm Mon–Fri.*
🕐 *1:10pm Thu.* ♿

A MODEST LATE Georgian exterior (completed 1791) conceals a flamboyant, well-preserved interior which has a finely decorated plaster ceiling, a rich brown wooden organ case and galleries and an oak pulpit resting on a carved palm tree. The original box pews have been kept in the galleries but not in the body of the church. Some memorials come from a 14th-century church on the site.

The former churchyard alongside was converted in 1880 into a relaxing green space known as Postman's Park, because it was used by workers from the nearby Post Office headquarters. In the late 19th century, Victorian artist G.F.Watts dedicated one of the walls to a quirky collection of plaques that commemorate acts of bravery and self-sacrifice by ordinary people; some of these are still there. In 1973 a powerful, modern bronze minotaur, the work of sculptor Michael Ayrton, was erected.

Museum of London ❹

See pp166–7.

Charterhouse ❺

Charterhouse Sq EC1. **Map** 6 F5.
📞 *0171-253 9503.* 🚇 *Barbican.*
Open *Apr–Jul: 2:15pm Wed.* **Adm
charge.** 📷 📹

THE 14TH-CENTURY gateway on the north side of the square leads to the site of a former Carthusian monastery dissolved under Henry VIII. In 1611 the buildings were converted into a hospital for poor pensioners and a charity school – called Charterhouse – whose pupils included John Wesley *(see p168)*; writer William Thackeray; and Robert Baden-Powell, the founder of the Boy Scouts. In 1872 the school, now a boarding school for fee-paying boys, moved to Godalming in Surrey. The site was subsequently taken over by St. Bartholomew's Hospital medical school. Some of the old buildings survived, including the chapel and part of the cloisters.

Charterhouse: stone carving

Cloth Fair ❻

EC1. **Map** 6 F5. 🚇 *Barbican*.

THIS PRETTY STREET is named after the notoriously rowdy Bartholomew Fair, which was the main cloth fair in medieval and Elizabethan England, held annually at Smithfield until 1855. Nos. 41 and 42 are fine 17th-century houses and have distinctive two-story wooden bay windows; however, their ground floors have since been modernized. The former poet laureate John Betjeman, who died in 1984, lived in No. 43 for most of his life. It has now been turned into a wine bar named after him.

17th-century houses: Cloth Fair

St. Bartholomew-the-Great ❼

West Smithfield EC1. **Map** 6 F5.
📞 *0171-606 5171*. 🚇 *Barbican*.
Open *8:30am–4:30pm (4pm in winter), Mon–Fri.* 🕦 *11am Sun.*
📷 ♿ 📹 🎵 *Concerts.*

ONE OF LONDON'S OLDEST churches was founded in 1123 by a monk named Rahere, whose tomb is inside. Once Henry I's court jester, he became a monk after having a dream in which St. Bartholomew saved him from a winged monster.

The 13th-century arch used to be the door to an earlier church on the site, whose nave was taken down when Henry VIII dissolved the priory. Today the arch leads from Little Britain to the small

burial ground – the gatehouse above it is from a later period. The church retains its original crossing and chancel, with its round arches and other fine Norman detailing. There are also some fine examples of Tudor and other monuments. The painter William Hogarth *(see p257)* was baptized in the font here in 1697.

From time to time parts of the church were used for secular purposes, including housing a blacksmith's forge and a hop store. In 1725 US statesman Benjamin Franklin worked for a printer in the Lady Chapel.

Barbican Centre ❽

Silk St EC2. **Map** 7 A5. 📞 *0171-638 8891.* 🎫 *0171-628 2295.*
🚇 *Barbican, Moorgate.* **Open** *9am–8pm Mon–Sat, noon–11pm Sun, public hols.* ♿ *induction loop.* 📷 📹 🍴 🎵 *Films, concerts, exhibitions.* See *Entertainment pp324–37.*

AN AMBITIOUS PIECE of 1960s city planning, this large residential, commercial and arts complex was begun in 1962 on a site devastated by World War II bombs and not completed for nearly 20 years. Tall residential tower blocks surround an arts center, which also includes an ornamental lake, fountains and lawns.

The old city wall turned a corner here, and substantial remains are still clearly visible (particularly from the Museum of London – *see pp166–7*). The word *barbican* means a defensive tower over a gate – perhaps the architects were

St. Bartholomew's gate house

trying to live up to the name when they designed this self-sufficient community with formidable defenses against the outside world. Obscure entrances and raised walkways remove pedestrians from the cramped bustle of the City, but, in spite of the signs and yellow lines on the pavement, the center can be difficult to navigate.

In addition to two theaters and a concert hall, the Barbican includes movie theaters, one of London's largest art galleries for major exhibitions, a convention and exhibition hall, a library and a music school (the Guildhall School of Music). There is also a surprising conservatory above the arts center.

The well-stocked conservatory at the Barbican Centre

Museum of London ❹

O PENED IN 1976 on the edge of the Barbican,
this museum provides a lively account of
London life from prehistoric times to the present
day. Reconstructed interiors and street scenes are
alternated with displays of original domestic
artifacts and items found in the museum's
archeological digs. Be sure to see the
working model of the Great Fire of 1666,
accompanied by readings from Samuel
Pepys's eyewitness account.

GALLERY GUIDE
*The chronological
arrangement of the
galleries creates an
easy route that
takes about 90
minutes to
complete.*

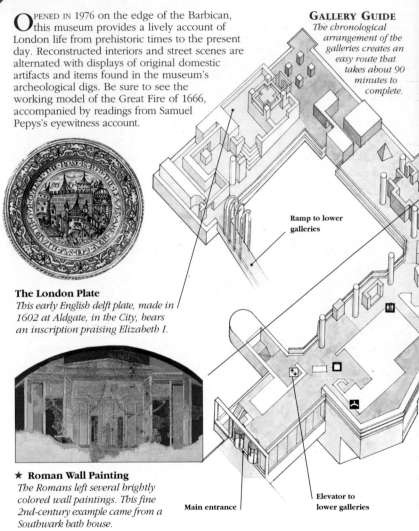

Ramp to lower
galleries

The London Plate
*This early English delft plate, made in
1602 at Aldgate, in the City, bears
an inscription praising Elizabeth I.*

★ Roman Wall Painting
*The Romans left several brightly
colored wall paintings. This fine
2nd-century example came from a
Southwark bath house.*

Main entrance

Elevator to
lower galleries

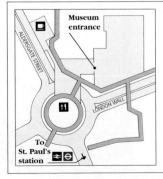

Museum
entrance

ALDERSGATE STREET

LONDON WALL

To
St. Paul's
station

STAR EXHIBITS

★ **Roman Wall
Painting**

★ **Late Stuart Interior**

★ **Victorian Shop
Fronts**

ORIENTATION
The museum is in a
modern building above
street level where
Aldersgate Street meets
London Wall. Access is
by signposted steps
and ramps.

KEY

☐ Museum buildings

■ Raised walkways

☐ Roads

★ **Victorian Shop Fronts**
The atmosphere of 19th-century London is re-created by several authentic shop interiors, like this grocer's.

Twentieth-century London is illustrated by displays exploring the major historical events of this century. The suffragette movement, World War II, the rise of cinema and the Swinging 1960's are all here.

Garden

18th-Century Dress
Luxuriously worked Spitalfields silk was used to make this dress in 1753. It was worn over light-weight cane hoops.

Elevator to upper galleries

KEY TO FLOOR PLAN

- ☐ Prehistoric London
- ☐ Roman London
- ☐ Dark Age and Saxon London
- ☐ Medieval London
- ☐ Tudor and Early Stuart London
- ☐ Late Stuart London
- ☐ 18th-Century London
- ☐ Victorian London and the Imperial Capital
- ☐ 20th-Century London
- ☐ Lord Mayor's coach
- ☐ Temporary exhibitions
- ☐ Non-exhibition space

★ **Late Stuart Interior**
Outstanding features from several grand houses of the late 17th century were used to reconstruct this room.

St. Giles, Cripplegate ⑨

Fore St EC2. **Map** 7 A5.
📞 0171-606 3630. 🚇 Barbican, Moorgate. **Open** Apr–Oct: 9:30am–5:30pm daily; Nov–Mar: 9:30am–4:30pm daily. 🕐 10am Sun.
♿ ✔

COMPLETED IN 1550, this church managed to survive the ravages of the Great Fire in 1666 but was badly damaged by a World War II bomb; only the tower survived. St Giles was refurbished during the 1950s to serve as the parish church of the Barbican development and now stands awkwardly amid the uncompromising modernity of the Barbican.

Oliver Cromwell married Elizabeth Bourchier here in 1620, and the poet John Milton was buried here in 1674. Well-preserved remains of London's Roman and medieval walls are displayed to the church's south.

Whitbread's Brewery ⑩

Chiswell St EC1. **Map** 7 B5.
🚇 Barbican, Moorgate. **Not open** to the public.

IN 1736, WHEN HE was only 16 years old, Samuel Whitbread became an apprentice brewer in Bedford. By the time of his death in 1796, his Chiswell Street brewery (which he had

Blake's gravestone at Bunhill Fields

bought in 1750) was brewing 240,000 gal (909,200 liters) a year – a record for London. The building has not been used as a brewery since 1976 when it was converted into rooms rented out for private functions – they are no longer open to the public. The Porter Tun room, which is now used as a banqueting suite, boasts the largest timber-post roof in Europe, and has a huge span of 60 ft (18 m).

The 18th-century buildings on both sides of the street are well-preserved examples of their period and are worth a look from the outside. A plaque on the outside of one commemorates a visit to the brewery in 1787 by George III and Queen Charlotte.

Bunhill Fields ⑪

City Rd EC1. **Map** 7 B4.
📞 0181-472 3584. 🚇 Old St. **Open** noon–5:30pm Sat, Sun, public hols. **Closed** Jan 1 & Dec 25–26.
📷 ♿

IT WAS FIRST designated a cemetery after the Great Plague of 1665 (see p23), when it was enclosed by a brick wall and gates. Twenty years later it was allocated to religious Nonconformists,

who were banned from being buried in churchyards because of their refusal to use the Church of England prayer book when carrying out their religious services. Visitors to this pleasant spot, shaded by large plane trees and on the edge of the bustling City, can see monuments to the writers Daniel Defoe, John Bunyan and William Blake, as well as to members of the Cromwell family.

John Milton wrote his famous epic poem *Paradise Lost* while he lived in Bunhill Row, on the west side of the cemetery, in the years leading up to his death in 1674.

Wesley's House and Chapel ⑫

49 City Rd EC1. **Map** 7 B4.
📞 0171-253 2262. 🚇 Old St. **House open** 10am–4pm Mon–Sat. **Adm charge.** 📷 ♿ 🕐 11am Sun.
✔ 🔲 Films, exhibitions.

Wesley's Chapel

JOHN WESLEY, the founder of the Methodist Church, laid the chapel's foundation stone in 1777. He preached here until his death in 1791 and is buried behind the chapel. Next door is the house where he lived, and today some of his furniture, books and other assorted possessions can be seen on display.

The chapel, adorned in a spartan style in accordance with Wesley's austere religious principles, has columns made from ships' masts. Beneath it is a small museum that explores the history of the Methodist church. Margaret Thatcher, the first British woman Prime Minister, in office from 1979 to 1990, was married in the chapel.

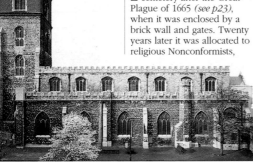

St Giles, Cripplegate

Broadgate Centre 🅱

Exchange Sq EC2. **Map** 7 C5.
📞 0171-588 6565. 🚇 Liverpool St.
♿ 🅿 🖥 🏧

Broadgate Centre skating rink

SITUATED ABOVE and around Liverpool Street station, the terminus for trains to eastern England, this is one of the most successful recent (1985–91) shop-and-office developments. Each of the squares has its own distinctive character. Broadgate Arena emulates New York's Rockefeller Center, doubling as a skating rink in winter and a venue for refreshments and entertainment in summer.

Among the many sculptures dotted about the complex are George Segal's *Rush Hour Group* and Barry Flanagan's *Leaping Hare on Crescent and Bell*. Don't miss the spectacular view of Liverpool Street station and its glass-roofed train shed, seen from Exchange Square to the north.

Petticoat Lane 🅐

Middlesex St E1. **Map** 16 D1.
🚇 Aldgate East, Aldgate, Liverpool St. **Open** 9am–2pm Sun. See **Shops and Markets** pp322–3.

IN QUEEN VICTORIA'S prudish reign the name of this street, long famous for its market, was changed to the respectable but colorless Middlesex Street. That is still its official designation, but the old name, derived from its many years as a center of the clothing trade, has stuck and

is now applied to the market held every Sunday morning in this and the surrounding streets. Numerous attempts have been made to stop the market, but with no success. An enormous variety of goods is sold, but there is still a bias toward clothing, especially leather coats. The atmosphere is noisy and cheerful, with Cockney stall-holders making use of their wit and insolence to attract customers. There are scores of snack bars, and many of these sell such traditional Jewish food as salt-beef sandwiches and bagels with smoked salmon.

Whitechapel Art Gallery 🅔

Whitechapel High St E1. **Map** 16 E1.
📞 0171-377 0107. 🚇 Aldgate East, Aldgate. **Open** 11am–5pm Tue–Sun, 11am–8pm Wed. **Closed** Jan 1, Dec 25–26 & for exhibitions.
Occasional adm charge. ♿ 🎬 🅿
🖥 🅘 ***Films, lectures.***

A STRIKING ART NOUVEAU facade by C.Harrison Townsend fronts this light, airy gallery founded in 1901.

Entrance to Whitechapel Gallery

Its aim is to bring art to the people of East London. Today this independent gallery enjoys an excellent international reputation for high-quality shows of major contemporary artists; these are interspersed with exhibitions reflecting the rich cultural origins of the people in the local community. In the 1950s and 1960s the likes of Jackson Pollock, Robert Rauschenberg, Anthony Caro and John Hoyland all displayed their work here. In 1970 David Hockney's first exhibition was held here.

The gallery also has a well-stocked arts bookshop, and there is a café here, serving a range of appetizing and healthy food and drink in a relaxed atmosphere.

Bustling Petticoat Lane Market

18th-century Fournier Street

Christch Church, Spitalfields 16

Commercial St E1. **Map** 8 E5.
[0171-247 7202. ⊖ Aldgate
East, Liverpool St. **Open** noon–
2:30pm Mon–Fri. ✚ 10:30am Sun.
& **Concerts** in June.

THE FINEST of Nicholas
Hawksmoor's six London
churches, started in 1714
and completed in 1729, was
changed by Victorian alterations
started in 1866. But Christ
Church still dominates the
surrounding narrow streets. Its
portico and spire are best seen
from the western end of
Brushfield Street, from which
visitors can see the four Tuscan
columns on pediments
supporting the arched roof of
the portico.

Christ Church was com-
missioned by parliament in
the Fifty New Churches Act of
1711. The act's purpose was
to combat the spread of Non-
conformism (to the estab-
lished Church of England),
and a church needed to make
a strong statement here, in an
area that was fast becoming a
Huguenot stronghold. The
Protestant Huguenots had fled
from religious persecution in
Catholic France and came to
Spitalfields to work in the
local silkweaving industry.

The church's impression of
size and strength is reinforced
inside by the high ceiling, the
sturdy wooden canopy over
the west door and the gallery.
In Hawksmoor's original plan
the gallery extends around the
north and south sides joining

the organ gallery at the west
end. The organ dates from
1735; the royal coat of arms,
in Coade stone, from 1822.

During the 19th century the
hand silkweaving industry
declined as machinery took
over and Spitalfields became
too poor to maintain a church.
By the early 20th century Christ
Church had fallen into disrepair
and, in 1958, it was closed for
public worship. Restoration
began in 1964 and the church
reopened in 1987. Since 1965
the crypt has been a home for
rehabilitated alcoholics.

Fournier Street 17

E1. **Map** 8 E5. ⊖ Aldgate East,
Liverpool St.

THE 18TH-CENTURY houses
on the north side of this
street have attics with broad
windows that were designed
to give maximum light to the
silkweaving French Huguenot
community who lived here.
Even now, the textile trade
lives on, in this and nearby
streets, still dependent on
immigrant labor. Today it is
Bengalis who toil at sewing
machines in workrooms that
are as cramped as they were
when the Huguenots used
them. Working conditions are
improving, however, and
many of the sweatshops have
been converted into show-
rooms for companies that
now have modern factories
away from the town center.

Christ Church, Spitalfields

Bengali sweet factory, Brick Lane

London Jamme Masjid 18

Brick Lane E1. **Map** 8 E5.
⊖ Liverpool St, Aldgate East.

LOCAL MUSLIMS NOW worship
here, in a building whose
life story reflects the history
of immigration into the area.
Built in 1743 as a Huguenot
chapel, it became a synagogue
in the 19th century, was used
as a Methodist chapel in the
early 20th century and is now
a mosque. The sundial above
the entrance bears the Latin
inscription *Umbra sumus* –
"We are shadows."

Spitalfields Heritage Centre 19

19 Princelet St E1. **Map** 8 E5.
[0171-377 6901. ⊖ Aldgate East,
Liverpool St. **Open** 10am–5pm (not
guaranteed, phone first). **Exhibitions,
theater performances.**

THIS HOUSE, built in 1719, still
has a silkweavers' attic. Its
most intriguing feature is a
synagogue built in the garden
in 1870 and used for worship
until the 1960s. Its balconies
are inscribed with Hebrew
texts and names of benefactors.

Brick Lane 20

E1. **Map** 8 E5. ⊖ Liverpool St,
Aldgate East, Old St. **Market open**
dawn–noon Sun. See **Shops and
Markets** pp322–3.

ONCE A LANE running through
brickfields, this is now
the busy center of London's
Bengali district. Its shops and

The grand bedroom of Dennis Severs House

houses, some dating from the 18th century, have seen waves of immigrants of many nationalities, and most now sell food, spices, silks and saris. The first Bengalis to live here were sailors who came in the 19th century. In those days it was a predominantly Jewish quarter, and there are still a few Jewish shops left, including a popular 24-hour bagel shop at No. 159.

On Sundays a large market is held here and in the surrounding streets, complementing that in Petticoat Lane (see p169). At the northern end of Brick Lane is the former Black Eagle Brewery, a medley of 18th- and 19th-century industrial architecture, now reflected in, and set off by, a sympathetic mirror-glassed extension.

Dennis Severs House ㉑

18 Folgate St E1. **Map** 8 D5.
📞 0171-247 4013. ⊖ Liverpool St.
Open first Sun of month 2–5pm
Adm charge. Evening performances.

AT NO. 18 FOLGATE STREET, built in 1724, Dennis Severs, a designer and performer, has re-created an historical interior that takes you on a journey from the 17th to the 19th centuries. It offers what he calls "an adventure of the imagination… a visit to a time-mode rather than… merely a look at a house." The rooms are like a series of *tableaux vivants*, as if the occupants had simply left for a moment. There is broken bread on the plates, wine in the glasses and fruit in the

18th-century portrait: Dennis Severs House

bowl; the candles flicker and horses' hooves clatter on the cobbles outside. Mr. Severs presents a more elaborate, three-hour version of the visit on some weekday evenings, with 18th-century music, drinks and snacks. These theatrical evenings are for groups of up to eight and are not suitable for children under 12. Reservations need to be made three weeks in advance.

Around the corner on Elder Street are two of London's earliest surviving terraces, also built in the 1720s, where many of the orderly Georgian red-brick houses have been carefully restored.

Columbia Road Flower Market ㉒

Columbia Rd E2. **Map** 8 D3.
⊖ Liverpool St, Old St, Bethnal Green. **Open** 8:30am–1pm Sun.
See **Shops and Markets** pp322–3.

A VISIT TO this flower-and-plant market is one of the most delightful things to do on Sunday mornings in London, whether or not you actually buy any of the exotic species there. Set in a well-preserved street of small Victorian shops, it is a lively, sweet-smelling and colorful event. Apart from the stalls, there are several shops selling, among other things, home-made bread and farmhouse cheeses, plus antiques and interesting objects, many flower-related. There is also a Spanish delicatessen and an excellent snack bar that sells bagels and welcome mugs of hot chocolate on chilly winter mornings.

Columbia Road flower market

SOUTHWARK AND BANKSIDE

SOUTHWARK ONCE offered an escape route from the City, where many forms of pleasure were banned. Borough High Street was once lined with taverns in the medieval courtyards still standing today. The George survives as the only galleried London inn. Prostitution thrived in houses facing the river, and theaters and bear gardens *(see picture p178)* were established here in the late 16th century.

Shakespeare window at Southwark Cathedral

Shakespeare's company was based at the Globe Theatre and also performed at the Rose nearby. The palace of the Bishops of Winchester – from which a magnificent rose window survives – was best known for its notorious Clink prison. Today the wharves are closed and the river is lined with a pleasant walkway linking its attractions and giving tremendous views across the river to the City.

SIGHTS AT A GLANCE

Historic Streets and Buildings
Hop Exchange **2**
Old St. Thomas's Operating Theatre **5**
Hay's Galleria **6**
St. Olave's House **7**
Cardinal's Wharf **11**

Museums and Galleries
Clink Exhibition **8**

Shakespeare's Globe Museum **10**
Bankside Gallery **12**
London Dungeon **14**
Design Museum **15**

Cathedrals
Southwark Cathedral **1**

Pubs
George Inn **4**
The Anchor **9**

Markets
Borough Market **3**
Bermondsey Antiques Market **13**

Historic Ships
HMS *Belfast* **16**

0 meters	500
0 yards	500

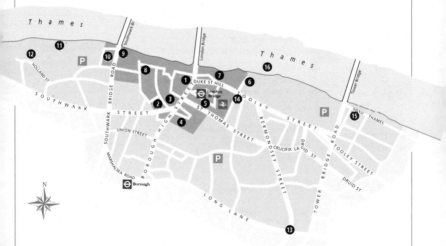

GETTING THERE
The Northern line runs a regular Underground service to this area. Nearly every BR train from Charing Cross or Cannon Street stops at London Bridge. Taking a bus from the city center is very confusing because you have to change.

SEE ALSO
• **Street Finder**, maps 14, 15, 16
• **Where to Stay** pp276–7
• **Restaurants** pp292–4

KEY
▢ Street-by-Street map
Ⓔ Underground station
⊞ British Rail station
Ⓟ Parking

View from the riverside walkway

Street by Street: Southwark

Southwark Bridge was opened in 1912 to replace a bridge from 1819.

FROM MEDIEVAL TIMES until the 18th century, Southwark was a popular venue for the pursuit of illicit pleasures – including the Elizabethan theater. It was south of the Thames and out of the jurisdiction of the City authorities. The 18th and 19th centuries brought docks, warehouses and factories, while railroads carved a swathe through the area. Today it has been developed with offices.

★ Shakespeare's Globe Museum

A museum of Elizabethan theaters stands near the site of the Globe (shown in 1612) ❿

Hop Exchange

It used to be the main trading center for hops used by brewers. The building is now used as offices ❷

The Anchor

For centuries it has been a favorite riverside pub with fine views ❾

Clink Exhibition

A museum on the site of the notorious old prison looks back at Southwark's colorful past ❽

Borough Market

There has been a market on or near this site since 1276. Now it sells wholesale fruits and vegetables ❸

The War Memorial, commemorating soldiers who fell in World War I, was erected in 1924 on Borough High Street, where it has become a powerful landmark.

THE GEORGE

★ George Inn

This is London's only surviving traditional, galleried inn ❹

Southwark Quayside

LOCATOR MAP
See Central London Map pp12–13

London Bridge, in its various forms, was the only river crossing in London from Roman times until 1750. The present bridge, completed in 1972, replaced the one of 1831 now in Arizona.

KEY

– – – Suggested route

| 0 meters | 100 |
| 0 yards | 100 |

★ **Southwark Cathedral**
Despite major alterations, it still contains medieval elements **1**

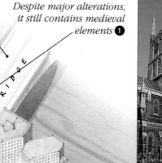

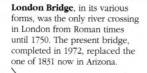

MONTAGUE CLOSE

LONDON BRIDGE

TOOLEY STREET

ST THOMAS'S STREET

St. Olave's House
These Art Deco offices for Hay's Wharf were built in 1932 **7**

London Bridge station

Old St. Thomas's Operating Theatre
The gory days of surgery without anesthetic are reconstructed in this perfectly preserved room **5**

STAR SIGHTS

★ **Southwark Cathedral**

★ **George Inn**

★ **Shakespeare's Globe Museum**

Southwark Cathedral ❶

Montague Close SE1. **Map** 15 B3.
📞 *0171-407 2939.* 🚇 *London Bridge.* **Open** *7:30am–6pm daily.*
✝ *11am Sun.* 🎵 **Concerts.**

THIS CHURCH DID not become a cathedral until 1905. However, some parts of the building date back to the 12th century, when it was attached to a priory, and many of its original medieval features remain. The memorials are especially interesting. The wooden effigy of a knight is late 13th century, and another medieval gem is the tomb, dating from 1408, of John Gower, poet and contemporary of Geoffrey Chaucer *(see p39).*

The monument to William Shakespeare, shown in front of a relief of 17th-century Southwark, was carved in 1912. Shakespeare's brother Edmond, also an actor, is buried here, and so is Philip Henslowe, who was in charge of the nearby Rose Theatre in Shakespeare's day. John Harvard, founder of Harvard University in the United States, was baptized here in 1607 and there is a chapel named after him.

Shakespeare Window in Cathedral

Hop Exchange ❷

Southwark St SE1. **Map** 15 B4. 🚇 *London Bridge.* **Not open to the public.**

SOUTHWARK, with its easy access to Kent where hops are grown, was a natural venue for brewing beer and trading hops. In 1866 this building was constructed as the center of that trade. Now

The George Inn, now owned by the National Trust

offices, it retains its original pediment complete with carved scenes showing the hop harvest, and iron gates with a hop motif.

Borough Market ❸

Stoney St SE1. **Map** 15 B4.
🚇 *London Bridge.* **Open** *midnight–10am Mon–Sat.*

THIS SMALL WHOLESALE fruit and vegetable market spreads out in an L-shape beneath the railway tracks. It is the successor to a medieval market, held on London Bridge, which was moved to Borough High Street in 1276 to avoid congestion. It was moved again in 1756, for the same reason, to its present location where the buildings date from 1851. Today its future is uncertain.

George Inn ❹

77 Borough High St SE1. **Map** 15 B4.
📞 *0171-407 2056.* 🚇 *London Bridge, Borough.* **Open** *11am–11pm Mon–Fri; noon–3pm, 6–11pm Sat; noon–3pm, 7–10:30pm Sun.* 🍴 *See* **Restaurants and Pubs** *pp308–9.*

DATING FROM THE 17th century, this building is the only example of a traditional galleried coaching inn left in London. It was rebuilt after the Southwark fire of 1676 in a style that dates back to the Middle Ages. Originally

there would have been three wings around a courtyard where plays were staged in the 17th century. In 1889 the north and east wings were demolished to make room for the railway, so only one wing has survived.

The inn, now owned by the National Trust, still operates as a pub and restaurant. Plays, morris dancing and other entertainments are sometimes performed in the yard during the summer.

Old St. Thomas's Operating Theater ❺

9a St. Thomas St SE1. **Map** 15 B4.
📞 *0171-955 4791.* 🚇 *London Bridge.* **Open** *12am–4pm Mon–Fri.* **Closed** *Christmas week–New Year, public hols.* **Adm charge.**

ST. THOMAS'S HOSPITAL, one of the oldest in Britain, stood here from its foundation in the 12th century until it was moved west in 1862. At that time nearly all of its buildings were demolished in order to make way for the railway.

19th-century surgical tools

The women's operating theater survived only because it was located away from the main buildings in a garret over the hospital church (now the Chapter House of Southwark Cathedral). It lay, bricked over and forgotten, until the 1950s. It has since been restored to what it would have been in the early 19th century, before the discovery of either anesthetics or antiseptics.

The display shows how patients were blindfolded, gagged and bound to the wooden operating table, while a box of sawdust underneath was used to catch the blood.

Hay's Galleria ⑥

Tooley St SE1. **Map** 15 C3.
Ⓔ London Bridge.

The Galleria's atrium

THIS IS A well-conceived development of upmarket shops, restaurants, offices and private apartments on what used to be Hay's Wharf. The wharf was built by Thomas Cubitt in 1857 and was used for unloading tea and various other provisions for the London trade. It was one of the first places to use cold storage, importing New Zealand cheese and butter from 1867. Now covered by a high glass roof on iron columns, the former warehouses are occupied by a variety of eating and drinking places, offices and some shops. There are also market

St. Olave's House, Hay's Wharf: an Art Deco gem

stalls, street entertainers and, in the center, David Kemp's intriguing moving sculpture *The Navigators*, which incorporates water jets, fountains and a glorious mixture of nautical symbols.

Hay's Galleria has become the focal point of London Bridge City, the name that covers all the new office developments in this area.

St. Olave's House ⑦

Tooley St SE1. **Map** 15 C3.
Ⓔ London Bridge.

WHEN IT WAS COMPLETED in 1932, H. S. Goodhart-Rendel's innovative Art Deco office building was considered controversial. Nowadays it is recognized as being one of the finest such buildings in London and has been carefully restored. It was the headquarters of Hay's Wharf, whose name is spelled out in thick gold lettering along the top of the riverfront. Below this are three large bronze reliefs by sculptor Frank Dobson symbolizing capital, labor and commerce. These are surrounded by smaller reliefs.

Clink Exhibition ⑧

1 Clink St SE1. **Map** 15 B3.
📞 0171-403 6515. Ⓔ London Bridge. **Open** 10am–6pm daily, some evenings until 9pm (phone first). **Closed** Dec 25–26. **Adm charge**.

THE CLINK was the popular name for the prison attached to Winchester House, a large palace which was the

home of the Bishops of Winchester from the 12th century until 1626. In the 16th century Protestant and Catholic prisoners of conscience were detained in the prison. The surrounding area was under the jurisdiction of the bishop rather than the City of London and was called "The Liberty of the Clink." It was London's red-light district, and rather than condemning prostitution, as happened in the City, the bishops licensed the brothels, regulating their opening hours.

The prison was one of five in Southwark and the first in which women were regularly confined. No doubt some of them were "Winchester geese" – prostitutes – who had broken the strict rules of their profession.

Along with displays on the history of prostitution, there are exhibits about the Clink prison. Britain's only working armory, where arms and armor are still mended and made, is also here.

Also situated in the "liberty" was the Globe Theatre *(see p178)*, venue for many of William Shakespeare's plays. This was a round wooden theater, and took its name from its sign showing Hercules carrying the world on his shoulders. Shakespeare was a shareholder and a player here. The plays written by him and performed here include *Romeo and Juliet, King Lear, Othello,* and *Macbeth,* but there is no complete record.

The only surviving part of Winchester House is a 14th-century rose window, which stands a few steps to the east of here. It was revealed when a fire broke out in 1814.

Replica of Civil War trouper's pot helmet, made in the Clink

The Anchor ⑨

34 Park St SE1. **Map** 15 A3.
📞 *0171-407 1577*. 🚇 *London
Bridge.* **Open** *11:30am–11pm
Mon–Sat; noon–3pm, 6:30–
10:30pm Sun.*

Pub sign at the Anchor Inn

T HIS IS ONE OF London's
most famous riverside
pubs. It dates from after the
Southwark fire of 1676, which
devastated the area much as
the Great Fire across the river
had done 10 years before *(see
pp22–3)*. The present building
is 18th century but traces of
much earlier hostelries have
been found beneath it. The
inn was once connected with
a brewery on the other side
of the road that belonged to
Henry Thrale, a close friend
of Dr. Samuel Johnson *(see
p140)*. When Thrale died in
1781, Dr. Johnson went to the
brewery sale and encouraged
the bidders with a phrase that
has passed into the English
language: "The potential of

growing rich beyond the
dreams of avarice."
   A platform by the Thames
offers patrons of the pub fine
views across the river to the
City as they sip their drinks
on long summer evenings.

Shakespeare's Globe Museum ⑩

New Globe Walk SE1. **Map** 15 A3.
📞 *0171-620 0202.* 🚇 *London
Bridge.* **Open** *10am–5pm Mon–Sun.*
Closed *Christmas week–Jan 2, public
hols.* **Adm charge.** 🚫 ⬛
Concerts, events.

T HE MUSEUM is in a ware-
house on the site of
Davies Amphitheatre, a 17th-
century venue for bear-
baiting. Diarist Samuel Pepys
saw bull-baiting here (he
called it "a very rude and
nasty pleasure") as well as
two prize fights. The museum
has exhibits on those vicious
pastimes as well as on the
Elizabethan theaters that
thrived in the neighborhood.
   The Globe Theatre, headquarters of the band of
players for whom William
Shakespeare wrote his plays,
is being reconstructed just
east of its original site. There
are interesting displays in the
museum which illustrate the
history of both the Globe and
the Rose Theatres, where
Shakespeare also acted.
   The museum hosts a lively
program of lunchtime events
including poetry, jazz and
Elizabethan music.

Davies Amphitheatre, on the site of Shakespeare's Globe Museum

Cardinal's Wharf ⑪

SE1. **Map** 15 A3. 🚇 *London Bridge.*

A SMALL GROUP OF 17th-
century houses today
survives here in the shadow
of the now-abandoned power
station. A plaque commem-
orates Christopher Wren's stay
while St. Paul's Cathedral *(see
pp148–51)* was being built.
He would have had a particularly fine view of the
construction in progress just
across the water.

Bankside Gallery ⑫

48 Hopton St SE1. **Map** 14 F3.
📞 *0171-928 7521.* 🚇 *Blackfriars,
Waterloo.* **Open** *10am–8pm Tue;
10am–5pm Wed–Fri; 1–5pm Sun.*
Closed *Christmas week–Jan 2, Easter.*
Adm charge. ♿ 📷 ⬛ **Lectures**.

View from the Founders' Arms

T HIS MODERN RIVERSIDE
gallery is the headquarters
of the Royal Watercolor
Society and the Royal Society
of Painter-Printmakers. Its
permanent collection is not
on show here but there are
changing exhibitions of
watercolors and engravings,
with many pieces for sale.
There is also an excellent
specialty shop that sells
books and art supplies.
   There is an unparalleled
view of St. Paul's Cathedral
from the nearby Founders'
Arms – built on the site of the
foundry where St. Paul's bells
were cast. South of here, on
Hopton Street, are some
almshouses dating from 1752.

Bermondsey Antiques Market 13

(New Caledonian Market) Long Lane and Bermondsey St SE1. **Map** 15 C5. 🚇 *London Bridge, Borough.* **Open** *5am–2pm Fri, starts closing midday. See* **Shops and Markets** *pp322–3.*

ONE OF LONDON'S main markets for antiques, Bermondsey market was established here in the 1960s when the old Caledonian Market site in Islington was redeveloped. Each Friday at dawn, serious antique dealers trade their latest acquisitions at Bermondsey. The press reports the occasional long-lost masterpiece changing hands here for a song, and early-rising optimists can try their luck and judgment. However, trading starts very early, and the best bargains go long before most tourists are likely to be awake.

Several nearby antique shops are open all week. The most interesting of these are situated in a row of old warehouses on Tower Bridge Road, piled high with furniture and knickknacks of mixed vintage, condition and price.

London Dungeon 14

Tooley St SE1. **Map** 15 C3. 📞 *0171-403 0606.* 🚇 *London Bridge.* **Open** *Apr–Sep: 10am–6:30pm daily (last adm: 5:30pm); Oct–Mar: 10am–5:30pm daily (last adm: 4:30pm).* **Closed** *Dec 24–26.* **Adm charge.** ♿ 🖼 📷

IN EFFECT a much expanded version of the chamber of horrors at Madame Tussaud's *(see p220)*, this museum is a great hit with ghoulish children. It illustrates the most bloodthirsty events in British history. It is played strictly for terror, and screams and moans abound as Druids perform a human sacrifice at Stonehenge, Anne Boleyn is beheaded on the orders of her husband Henry VIII, and a room full of people die in agony during the Great Plague of 1665. Torture, murder and witchcraft fill the gaps between these spectacles.

Antiques stall at Bermondsey Market

Design Museum 15

Butlers Wharf, Shad Thames SE1. **Map** 16 E4. 📞 *0171-407 6261.* 🚇 *Tower Hill, London Bridge.* **Open** *11:30am–6pm Mon–Fri; 12pm–6pm Sat and Sun.* **Closed** *Jan 1 & Dec 24–26.* **Adm charge.** ♿ 🖼 🍴 📷

THIS MUSEUM was the first in the world to be devoted solely to the design of mass-produced everyday objects. This permanent collection offers a nostalgic look at furniture, office equipment, cars, radio and TV sets and household utensils from the past. Temporary exhibitions of international design in

Eduardo Paolozzi sculpture (1986), outside Design Museum

the Review and Collections galleries provide a taste of what may become common in the future.

Located on the first floor of the museum is the Blueprint Café, a restaurant that has a wonderful view of the Thames, especially when the river is lit up at night.

HMS *Belfast* 16

Morgan's Lane, Tooley St SE1. **Map** 16 D3. 📞 *0171-407 6434.* 🚇 *London Bridge, Tower Hill.* ⚓ *Tower Pier.* **Open** *Mar 1–31 Oct: 10am–6pm daily; 1 Nov–Mar 1: 10am–5pm daily.* **Closed** *Jan 1 & Dec 25–26.* **Adm charge.** 📷 ♿ *except for café.* 🏠 🖼 📷

SINCE 1971, this Royal Navy cruiser has been used as a floating naval museum. Part of it has been re-created to show what the ship was like in 1943 when it participated in sinking the German cruiser *Scharnhorst.* Displays portray life on board during World War II and there are general exhibits relating to the history of the Royal Navy.

SOUTH BANK

FOLLOWING the Festival of Britain in 1951, the South Bank arts center grew up around the newly erected Royal Festival Hall. The architecture of some buildings has been criticized, especially that of the chunky concrete Hayward Gallery. But the area functions well and is crowded with culture seekers most evenings and afternoons. The bordering areas of Waterloo and Lambeth are both down-to-earth, working-class areas. Lambeth is celebrated in the song "The Lambeth Walk" from the 1930s musical *Me and My Girl*. The gatehouse of Lambeth Palace, situated on the southern edge of the area, is one of London's finest Tudor buildings.

Signpost at the South Bank Centre

SIGHTS AT A GLANCE

Historic Streets and Buildings
County Hall ⑥
Lambeth Palace ⑨
Waterloo Station ⑫
Gabriel's Wharf ⑭

Museums and Galleries
Museum of the Moving Image ②
Hayward Gallery ③
Florence Nightingale Museum ⑦
Museum of Garden History ⑧
Imperial War Museum ⑩

Churches
St. John's, Waterloo Road ⑬

Gardens
Jubilee Gardens ⑤

Theaters and Concert Halls
National Theatre ①
Royal Festival Hall ④
Old Vic ⑪

Pubs
Doggett's Coat and Badge ⑮

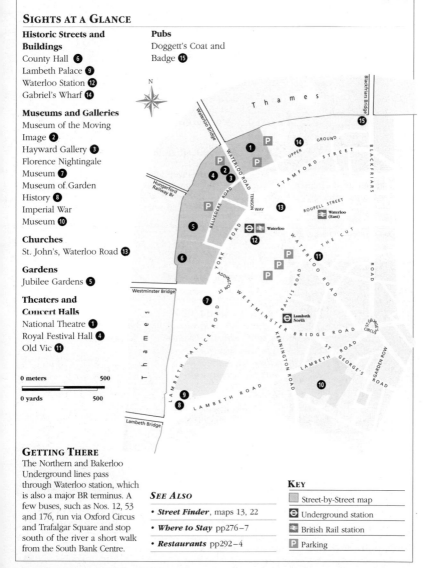

| 0 meters | 500 |
| 0 yards | 500 |

GETTING THERE

The Northern and Bakerloo Underground lines pass through Waterloo station, which is also a major BR terminus. A few buses, such as Nos. 12, 53 and 176, run via Oxford Circus and Trafalgar Square and stop south of the river a short walk from the South Bank Centre.

SEE ALSO

• *Street Finder*, maps 13, 22

• *Where to Stay* pp276–7

• *Restaurants* pp292–4

KEY

▨ Street-by-Street map
🚇 Underground station
🚆 British Rail station
P Parking

Thameside promenade at the South Bank Centre

Street by Street: South Bank Centre

ORIGINALLY THIS WAS an area of wharves and factories that was much damaged by bombing during World War II. Then it was chosen as the site of the Festival of Britain *(see p30)*, celebrating the centenary of the Great Exhibition *(see pp26–7)*. The Royal Festival Hall is the only building from 1951 to remain, but since then London's main arts center has been created around it, including the national showplaces for theater, music and film, plus a major art gallery.

Memorial to the International Brigade of the Spanish Civil War

To the Strand

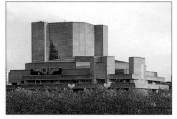

★ Royal National Theatre
Its three auditoriums offer a choice of plays – ranging from the classics to the sharpest modern writing **❶**

The National Film Theatre
was established in 1953 to show historic films *(see pp328–9)*.

Festival Pier

The Queen Elizabeth Hall
stages more intimate concerts than the Festival Hall. The adjoining Purcell Room is for chamber music *(see pp330–1)*.

Hayward Gallery
The concrete interior of this venue for important exhibitions is well suited to many modern works **❸**

★ Royal Festival Hall
The London Philharmonic is one of many world-class orchestras to perform here in the focal point of the South Bank Centre **❹**

Hungerford Bridge
was built in 1864 to carry both trains and pedestrians to Charing Cross.

STAR SIGHTS

★ **Museum of the Moving Image**

★ **Royal National Theatre**

★ **Royal Festival Hall**

KEY

– – – Suggested route

0 meters   100

0 yards   100

★ Museum of the Moving Image
This all-action history of the cinema offers a lively family outing **❷**

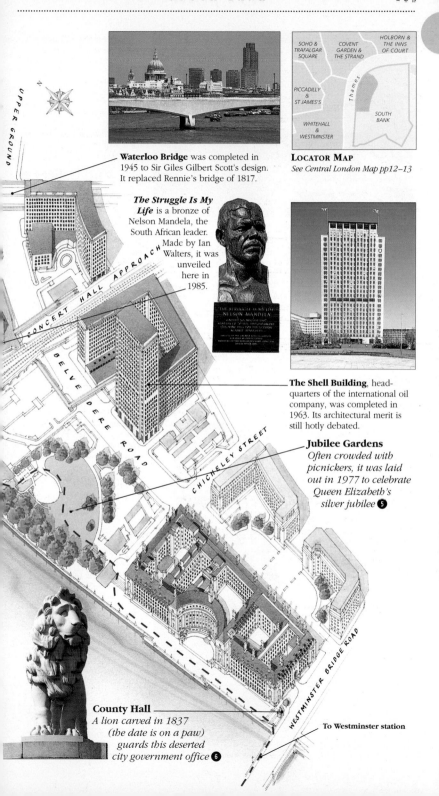

Waterloo Bridge was completed in 1945 to Sir Giles Gilbert Scott's design. It replaced Rennie's bridge of 1817.

LOCATOR MAP
See Central London Map pp12–13

The Struggle Is My Life is a bronze of Nelson Mandela, the South African leader. Made by Ian Walters, it was unveiled here in 1985.

THE STRUGGLE IS MY LIFE
NELSON MANDELA

The Shell Building, head-quarters of the international oil company, was completed in 1963. Its architectural merit is still hotly debated.

Jubilee Gardens
Often crowded with picnickers, it was laid out in 1977 to celebrate Queen Elizabeth's silver jubilee ❺

County Hall
A lion carved in 1837 (the date is on a paw) guards this deserted city government office ❻

To Westminster station

The stark concrete façade of the Hayward Gallery

Royal National Theatre ❶

South Bank Centre SE1. **Map** 14 D3.
📞 *0171-928 2252.* 🚇 *Waterloo.*
Open *10am–11pm Mon–Sat.* **Closed**
Dec 24–25. 📷 *during performances.*
Concerts *at 6pm,* **exhibitions.** ♿
🍴 🖥 🎭 *See* **Entertainment**
pp326–7.

E VEN IF YOU DON'T want to see
a play, this well-appointed
complex is worth a visit. Sir
Denys Lasdun's building was
opened in 1976 after 200 years
of debate about whether there
should be a national theater
and where it should be
located. The company was
formed in 1963, under
Laurence (later Lord) Olivier,
Britain's leading 20th-century
actor. The largest of the three
theaters is named after him; the
Cottesloe and the Lyttleton,
commemorate administrators.

Museum of the Moving Image ❷

South Bank Centre SE1. **Map** 14 D3.
📞 *0171-401 2636.* 🚇 *Waterloo.*
Open *10am–6pm daily (last adm:
5pm).* **Closed** *Dec 24–26.* **Adm
charge.** *Events, lectures, films.* ♿
🍴 🖥 🎭

M OMI is an enthralling
experience for both
adults and children as well
as an invaluable resource
for television and cinema
students. The museum traces
the history of film from the
first experiments with

zoetropes, magic lanterns,
lenses and cameras. The
exhibition bursts into life with
the coming of silent cinema.
A display devoted to Charlie
Chaplin, born in nearby
Kennington *(see p37),* is
illustrated with clips from his
films and artifacts from his
era. In small viewing areas
visitors watch historic scenes
from films in different genres
including French and Russian
cinema, documentaries and
newsreels. Actors wander
around in the guise of starlets,

A "Dalek" robot: MOMI

cowboy heroes and ushers,
engaging visitors in banter
and luring them to take part
in movie scenes. You can be
interviewed onscreen in a
studio, draw your own cartoons, read the news from an
autocue and watch yourself
fly over the Thames. You
should allow at least 2 hours
for a visit here.

Hayward Gallery ❸

South Bank Centre SE1. **Map** 14 D3.
📞 *0171-928 3144.* 📠 *0171-261
0127.* 🚇 *Waterloo.* **Open** *10am–8pm
Tue–Wed, 10am–6pm Thu–Mon.*
Closed *Jan 1 & Dec 24–26, Good Fri,
May Day, between exhibitions.* **Adm
charge.** 📷 ♿ 🎭 🖥 🎭

T HE HAYWARD GALLERY is one
of London's main venues
for large art exhibitions. Its
slabby gray concrete exterior
is too starkly modern for some
tastes and there has been
pressure for it to be
demolished or completely
redone almost ever since it
opened in October 1968.
   Hayward exhibitions cover
classical and contemporary
art, but the work of British
contemporary artists is particularly well represented.
You may have to wait on line,
especially on weekends.

Royal Festival Hall ❹

South Bank Centre SE1. **Map** 14 D4.
📞 *0171-928 3191.* 🚇 *Waterloo.*
Open *10am–10pm daily.* **Closed** *Dec
25.* 📷 *during performances.* **Pre-
concert talks, exhibitions, free
concerts.** ♿ 🍴 🖥 🎭 *See*
Entertainment *p330.*

T HIS WAS THE ONLY structure
in the 1951 Festival of
Britain *(see p30)* designed for
permanence. Sir Robert
Matthew and Sir Leslie
Martin's concert hall was the
first major public building in
London following World War
II. It has stood the test of time
so well that many of the
capital's major arts institutions
have gathered around it. The
hall's interior has always
attracted much admiration; its
sweeping staircases lead up

majestically from the lobby to create a tremendous sense of elegance while also remaining highly functional. The stage has hosted tributes to the cellist, Jacqueline du Pré, and the conductor, Georg Solti. The organ was installed in 1954. There are a variety of cafés, bars and music and book stalls on the lower floors. Backstage tours are available.

Festival of Britain: symbol of 1951

Jubilee Gardens ❺

South Bank SE1. **Map** 14 D4.
🚇 *Waterloo.*

THIS PLEASANT riverside space was laid out in 1977 to mark the Silver Jubilee of the Queen's accession to the throne. In summer it is a favorite spot for sandwich-munching office workers and a venue for concerts and festivals. Sculptures include a memorial to the International Brigade who fought in the Spanish Civil War (1936–9).

County Hall ❻

York Rd SE1. **Map** 13 C4.
🚇 *Waterloo, Westminster.* **Not open to the public.**

THIS VAST, EMPTY building used to be the headquarters of the old London County Council (LCC). It was started in 1912 but, interrupted by two World Wars, was not completed until 1958. The best views of its curved, colonnaded central section are from the river.

The LCC became the Greater London Council (GLC) in 1965, but in 1986 this London-wide authority was abolished and its powers dispersed. The future of County Hall is now uncertain.

Florence Nightingale Museum ❼

2 Lambeth Palace Rd SE1. **Map** 14 D5.
📞 *0171-620 0374.* 🚇 *Waterloo, Westminster.* **Open** *10am–4pm Tue–Sun, public hols.* **Closed** *Jan 1, Good Fri, Easter Sun & Dec 25–26.*
Adm charge. Videos. 🚫 ♿ 🖥 🛗

THIS DETERMINED woman captured the nation's imagination as the "Lady of the Lamp," who nursed the wounded soldiers of the Crimea War (1853 – 6). She also founded Britain's first school of nursing at old St. Thomas's Hospital in 1860.

Obscurely located near the entrance to new St. Thomas's Hospital, the museum is worth seeking out. It gives a

Florence Nightingale

fascinating account of Florence Nightingale's career through original documents, photographs and personal memorabilia. Vivid displays illustrate her life and the developments she continued to make in health care and sanitation, until her death in 1910, at the age of 90.

Museum of Garden History ❽

Lambeth Palace Rd SE1. **Map** 21 C1.
📞 *0171-261 1891.* 📠 *0171-373 4030.* 🚇 *Waterloo, Vauxhall, Lambeth North, Westminster.* **Open** *11am–3pm Mon–Fri, 10:30am–5pm Sun.* **Closed** *2nd Sun Dec–1st Sun Mar.* 🅿 *small charge.* **Lectures, films.** ♿ 🍴 🖥 🛗

HOUSED IN AND AROUND the 14th-century tower of St. Mary's Church, this museum opened in 1979. In the church-yard is the tomb of a father and son both called John Tradescant. The Tradescants were gardeners to the 17th-century monarchs and were also pioneer plant hunters in the Americas, Russia and Europe. Their collection of rarities formed the basis of the Ashmolean Museum, Oxford.

The museum here consists of a history of gardening in Britain, illustrated by ancient implements, plans and documents. A knot garden outside is devoted to plants from the Tradescants' era. There is a shop with a stock of garden-related items.

County Hall: seeking a new role

The Tudor gatehouse

Lambeth Palace **9**

SE1. **Map** 21 C1. 🚇 *Lambeth North, Westminster, Waterloo, Vauxhall.* **Not open** to the public.

THIS HAS BEEN the London base of the Archbishop of Canterbury, the senior cleric in the Church of England, for 800 years. The chapel and its undercroft contain elements from the 13th century, but a large part of the rest of the building is far more recent. It has been frequently restored, most recently by Edward Blore in 1828–34. The Tudor gatehouse, however, dates from 1485 and is one of London's most pleasing and familiar riverside landmarks.

Until the first Westminster Bridge was built, the horse ferry that operated between here and Millbank was a principal river crossing. The revenues from it went to the Archbishop, who received compensation for loss of business when the bridge opened in 1750.

Imperial War Museum **10**

Lambeth Rd SE1. **Map** 22 E1. 📞 *0171-416 5000.* 📠 *0171-820 1683.* 🚇 *Lambeth North, Elephant & Castle.* **Open** 10am–6pm daily. **Closed** Jan 1, Dec 24–26. **Adm charge.** 📷 ♿ *Films, lectures.* 🍴 📖 🛍

IN SPITE OF THE TWO colossal guns that point up the drive from the main entrance, this is not just a display of the engines of modern warfare. Massive tanks, artillery, bombs and aircraft are on display, yet some of the most fascinating exhibits in the museum relate more to the social effects of 20th-century wars and their impact on the lives of people at home than to the actual business of fighting. There are displays about food rationing, air raid precautions, censorship and morale-boosting.

The arts are well represented, with extracts from wartime films, radio programs and literature, plus many hundreds of photographs, paintings by Graham Sutherland and Paul Nash and sculpture by Jacob Epstein. Henry Moore did some evocative drawings of life during the Blitz of 1940, when many Londoners slept in underground stations in order to protect themselves from falling bombs.

The museum is kept up to date with exhibits relating to recent military engagements of British forces, including the Gulf War of 1991. It is housed in part of what used to be Bethlehem Hospital for the Insane ("Bedlam"), built in 1811. In the 19th century, visitors would come for the afternoon to enjoy the antics of the patients. The hospital moved out to new premises in Surrey in 1930, leaving this vast building empty. Its two large, flanking wings were demolished and this central building converted into the museum, which moved here from its former South Kensington site in 1936.

Old Vic **11**

Waterloo Rd SE1. **Map** 14 E5. 📞 *0171-928 7616.* 📠 *0171-928 7618.* 🚇 *Waterloo.* **Open** for performances and guided tours only. 🎭 *See* **Entertainment** *pp326–7.*

The Old Vic's facade from 1816

THIS SPLENDID building dates from 1816, when it was opened as the Royal Coburg Theatre. In 1833 the name was changed to the Royal Victoria in honor of the future queen. Shortly after this the theater became a center for "music hall," the immensely popular Victorian entertainment in which singers, comedians and other acts were introduced by a chairman, who needed a booming voice to control unruly audiences.

In 1912 Lillian Baylis took over as manager and in 1914 introduced Shakespearean plays to the Old Vic. Between 1963 and 1976 it was the first home of the National Theatre (*see p184*). In 1983 it was restored; since then it has operated as a conventional West End theater.

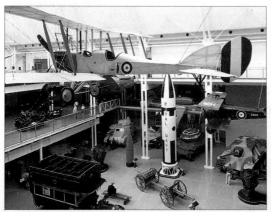

The machinery of war through the ages

Waterloo Station ⑫

York Rd SE1. **Map** 14 D4.
☎ 0171-928 5100 ⊖ *Waterloo.*
See ***Getting to London*** *pp358–9.*

THE TERMINAL FOR trains to southwest England, Waterloo is being enlarged to become London's main link to the Channel Tunnel. It was originally built in 1848 but completely remodeled in the early 20th century, with a grand formal entrance on the northeast corner. Today the spacious concourse, lined with shops, makes it one of the most practical of the London rail stations.

St. John's, Waterloo Road ⑬

SE1. **Map** 14 E4. ☎ 0171-633 9819.
⊖ *Waterloo.* **Open** *11:45am–1pm
Mon–Fri; 10am–noon Sat; at other
times phone first.* ✝ *10:30am Sun.*

ST. JOHN'S IS ONE of four "Waterloo churches" that was commissioned in 1818, after the Napoleonic Wars. They are often thought to have been built as a thanks-giving for Britain's victory in these wars, but it is more likely that they were built to serve Lambeth's rapidly growing population. The church's portico, with its six Doric columns supporting a pediment, is in the Greek Revival style popular at the time. Damaged by wartime bombing, St. John's was restored in time to become the official church for the Festival of Britain in 1951 *(see p30).*

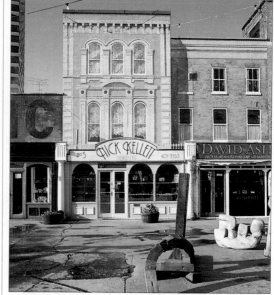

Illusionistic painting on the buildings around Gabriel's Wharf

Gabriel's Wharf ⑭

56 Upper Ground SE1. **Map** 14 E3.
⊖ *Waterloo. See **Shops and
Markets** pp322–3.*

THIS PLEASANT enclave of boutiques, craft shops and cafés was the product of a long and stormy debate over the future of what was once an industrial riverside area. Residents of Waterloo strongly opposed various schemes for office developments before a community association was able to acquire the site in 1984 and build cooperative housing around the wharf. Adjoining the market is a small garden and a riverside walkway with views of northern London. The tower to the east, built in 1928, incorporates an ingenious way of avoiding advertising restrictions. Its windows spell *Oxo,* the brand name of a popular meat extract.

Doggett's Coat and Badge ⑮

1 Blackfriars Bridge SE1. **Map** 14 F3.
☎ 0171-633 9081. ⊖ *Blackfriars.*
Open *normal licensing hours Mon–
Sat.* **Closed** *Dec 25.* 🔟 *See
Ceremonial London p55.*

A MODERN RIVERSIDE pub next to Blackfriars Bridge, Doggett's is named after an historic annual boat race. The race was instituted in 1716 for the boatmen who used to row passengers across the river. Its patron was Thomas Doggett, an actor who was grateful for the services of the watermen; they were held in low esteem because of their vulgarity and coarse language.

The coat and ceremonial arm badge are still competed for today in a boat race between London Bridge and Cadogan Pier, Chelsea.

The memorial to the dead of World War I at Waterloo Station

CHELSEA

THE FLASHY young shoppers who paraded along the King's Road from the Swinging 1960s until the 1980s are more or less gone, along with Chelsea's reputation for extreme behavior established by the bohemian Chelsea Set of writers and artists in the 19th century. Formerly a riverside village, Chelsea became fashionable in Tudor times. Henry VIII liked it so much that he built a small palace (long vanished) here. Artists, including Turner, Whistler and Rossetti, were attracted by the river

Cow's head outside the Old Dairy on Old Church Street

views from Cheyne Walk. The historian Thomas Carlyle and the essayist Leigh Hunt arrived in the 1830s and began a literary tradition continued by writers such as the poet Swinburne. Yet Chelsea has always had a raffish element, too: in the 18th century the pleasure gardens were noted for beautiful courtesans, and the Chelsea Arts Club has had riotous balls for nearly a century. Chelsea is far too expensive for most artists now, but the artistic connection remains with its galleries and antiques shops.

SIGHTS AT A GLANCE

Historic Streets and Buildings
King's Road ❶
Carlyle's House ❷
Cheyne Walk ❺
Royal Hospital ❽
Sloane Square ❾

Museums
National Army Museum ❼

Churches
Chelsea Old Church ❸

Gardens
Roper's Garden ❹
Chelsea Physic Garden ❻

GETTING THERE
The District and Circle Underground lines serve Sloane Square; the Piccadilly line passes just outside this area, through South Kensington. Buses 11, 19 and 22 all stop on the King's Road.

SEE ALSO

- *Street Finder*, maps 19, 20
- *Where to Stay* pp276–7
- *Restaurants* pp292–4
- *Chelsea and Battersea Walk* pp266–7

No. 56 Oakley Street, where the polar explorer R. F. Scott once lived

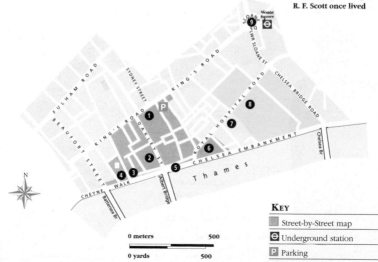

KEY

	Street-by-Street map
⊖	Underground station
P	Parking

Picturesque Chelsea residences in a cul-de-sac off the King's Road

Street by Street: Chelsea

ONCE A PEACEFUL riverside village, Chelsea has been fashionable since Tudor times when Sir Thomas More, Henry VIII's Lord Chancellor, lived here. Artists, including Turner, Whistler and Rossetti, were attracted by the views from Cheyne Walk, before a busy main road disturbed the area's peace. Chelsea's artistic connection is maintained by its galleries and antiques shops, while enclaves of 18th-century houses preserve its old village atmosphere.

King's Road
In the 1960s and 1970s it was the boutique-lined center of fashionable London and is still a main shopping street ❶

To King's Road

The Old Dairy, at 46 Old Church Street, was built in 1796, when cows still grazed in the surrounding fields. The tiling is original.

Carlyle's House
The historian and philosopher lived here from 1834 until his death in 1882 ❷

Chelsea Old Church
Although severely damaged during World War II, it still holds some fine Tudor monuments ❸

Roper's Garden
It includes a sculpture by Jacob Epstein, who had a studio here ❹

Thomas More, sculpted in 1969 by L. Cubitt Bevis, gazes calmly across the river near where he lived.

STAR SIGHT

★ **Chelsea Physic Garden**

KEY

– – – Suggested route

0 meters 100

0 yards 100

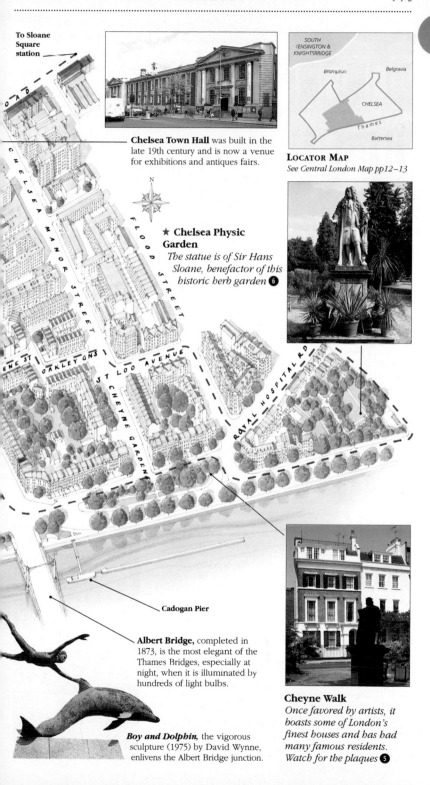

To Sloane Square station

Chelsea Town Hall was built in the late 19th century and is now a venue for exhibitions and antiques fairs.

SOUTH KENSINGTON & KNIGHTSBRIDGE

Brompton

Belgravia

CHELSEA

Thames

Battersea

LOCATOR MAP
See Central London Map pp12–13

★ **Chelsea Physic Garden**
The statue is of Sir Hans Sloane, benefactor of this historic herb garden ⑥

Cadogan Pier

Albert Bridge, completed in 1873, is the most elegant of the Thames Bridges, especially at night, when it is illuminated by hundreds of light bulbs.

Boy and Dolphin, the vigorous sculpture (1975) by David Wynne, enlivens the Albert Bridge junction.

Cheyne Walk
Once favored by artists, it boasts some of London's finest houses and has had many famous residents. Watch for the plaques ⑤

The Pheasantry, King's Road

King's Road **❶**

SW3 and SW10. **Map** 19 B3.
🚇 *Sloane Square. See **Shops and
Markets** pp310–23.*

THIS IS CHELSEA's central
artery, with its wealth of
small fashion shops packed
with young people looking
for avant-garde fashions. The
miniskirt revolution of the
1960s began here, and so
have many subsequent style
trends, perhaps the most
famous of them being punk.
　Watch for the Pheasantry at
No. 152, with its columns and
statuary. It was built in 1881
as the shopfront of a furniture
maker's premises but now
conceals a modern restaurant.
Antiques lovers will find three
warrens of stalls on the south
side of the King's Road:
Antiquarius at No. 137, the
Chenil Galleries at Nos. 181–3
and the Chelsea Antiques
Market at No. 253.

Carlyle's House **❷**

24 Cheyne Row SW3. **Map** 19 B4.
📞 *0171-352 7087.* 🚇 *Sloane Square,
South Kensington.* **Open** *Apr–Oct:
11am–5pm Wed–Sun, public hols (last
adm: 4:30pm).* **Closed** *Good Fri.*
Adm charge. 🚫

THE HISTORIAN and founder
of the London Library *(see
St James's Square p96)* Thomas
Carlyle moved into this modest
18th-century house in 1834,
and he wrote many of his
best-known books here, most
notably *The French Revolution*

and *Frederick the Great*. His
presence made Chelsea more
fashionable, and the house
became a mecca for some of
the great literary figures of the
19th century. The novelists
Charles Dickens and William
Thackeray, poet Alfred, Lord
Tennyson, naturalist Charles
Darwin and philosopher John
Stuart Mill were all regular
visitors here. The house has
been restored so that it looks
as it did during Carlyle's
lifetime, and is now a museum
dedicated to his life and work.

Chelsea Old Church **❸**

Cheyne Walk SW3. **Map** 19 A4.
📞 *0171-352 7978.* 🚇 *Sloane
Square, South Kensington.* **Open**
10am–1pm, 2–5pm daily (phone first).
🚫 ♿ 📷 *most days.* ✝ *11am Sun.*

Chelsea Old Church in 1860

REBUILT AFTER World War II,
this square-towered
building does not look old
from the outside. However,
early prints confirm that it is a
careful replica of the medieval
church that was destroyed by
World War II bombs.
　The glories of this church
are its Tudor monuments. One
to Sir Thomas More, who
built a chapel here in 1528,
contains an inscription he
wrote (in Latin), asking to be
buried next to his wife.
Among other monuments is a
chapel to Sir Thomas
Lawrence, who was an
Elizabethan merchant, and a
17th-century memorial to
Lady Jane Cheyne, after whose
husband Cheyne Walk was
named. Outside is a statue of
Sir Thomas More, "statesman,
scholar, saint," gazing piously
across the river.

Roper's Garden **❹**

Cheyne Walk SW3. **Map** 19 A4.
🚇 *Sloane Square, South Kensington.*

THIS IS A SMALL PARK outside
Chelsea Old Church. It is
named after Margaret Roper,
Sir Thomas More's daughter,
and her husband, William,
who wrote More's biography.
The sculptor Sir Jacob Epstein
worked at a studio on the site
between 1909 and 1914, and
there is a stone carving by
him commemorating the fact.
The park also contains a
figure of a nude woman by
Gilbert Carter.

Cheyne Walk **❺**

SW3. **Map** 19 B4. 🚇 *Sloane Square,
South Kensington.*

UNTIL CHELSEA Embankment
was constructed in 1874,
Cheyne Walk was a pleasant
riverside promenade. Now it
overlooks a busy road that
has destroyed much of its
charm. Many of the 18th-
century houses remain,
though, bristling with blue
plaques noting some of its
famous residents. Most were
writers and artists – including
J. M. W. Turner, who lived
incognito at No. 119; George
Eliot, who died at No. 4; and
a circle of well-known writers
(Henry James, T. S. Eliot and
Ian Fleming) who lived in
Carlyle Mansions.

Thomas More on Cheyne Walk

Chelsea Physic Garden ⑥

Swan Walk SW3. **Map** 19 C4.
📞 *0171-352 5646.* 🚇 *Sloane Square.* **Open** *Apr–Oct: 2–5pm Wed, Sun.* **Adm charge.**
♿ 🖵 *3:15–4:45pm.* 🏛 **Annual exhibition** *during Chelsea Flower Show, see p56.*

E STABLISHED BY the Society of Apothecaries in 1673 to study plants for medicinal use, this garden has survived to the present day. It was saved from closure in 1722 by a gift from Sir Hans Sloane, whose statue adorns it. The garden has since broadened its range of plants, but parts of it would be recognizable to Sir Hans today.

Many new varieties have been nurtured in its glasshouses, including cotton sent to the plantations of the southern United States. Today, visitors can see ancient trees, an historical walk and one of Britain's first rock gardens, installed in 1772.

Chelsea Physic Garden

National Army Museum ⑦

Royal Hospital Rd SW3. **Map** 19 C4.
📞 *0171-730 0717.* 🚇 *Sloane Square.* **Open** *10am–5:30pm daily.* **Closed** *Jan 1, Good Fri, Dec 24–26, May Day.* ♿ 🖵 🏛

A VIVID AND LIVELY account of the history of British land forces from 1485 to the present can be found here. Tableaux, dioramas and archive film clips illustrate major engagements and give a taste of what life behind the lines was like. There are fine paintings of battle scenes as well as portraits of soldiers. The museum shop offers a good selection of military books and model soldiers.

Royal Hospital ⑧

Royal Hospital Rd SW3. **Map** 20 D3.
📞 *0171-730 0161.* 🚇 *Sloane Square.* **Open** *10am–noon, 2–4pm Mon–Sat, 2–4pm Sun.*

T HIS GRACEFUL COMPLEX was commissioned by Charles II from Christopher Wren in 1682 as a retirement home for old or wounded soldiers, who have been known as Chelsea Pensioners ever since. The hospital opened 10 years later and is still home to about 400 retired soldiers, who are instantly recognizable in their scarlet coats and tricorne hats, a distinctive uniform which dates from the 17th century. Flanking the

A Chelsea Pensioner in uniform

northern entrance are Wren's two main public rooms: the chapel, which is notable for its wonderful simplicity, and the paneled Great Hall, still used today as the dining room. A small museum explains the history of the Pensioners.

A statue of Charles II by Grinling Gibbons is to be found on the terrace outside, and there is a fine view of the remains of Battersea Power Station across the river.

Sloane Square ⑨

SW1. **Map** 20 D2. 🚇 *Sloane Square.*

Sloane Square fountain

T HIS PLEASANT SMALL square (rectangle to be precise) has a paved center with a flower stall and fountain depicting Venus. Laid out in the late 18th century, it was named after Sir Hans Sloane, the wealthy physician and collector who bought the manor of Chelsea in 1712. Opposite Peter Jones, the 1936 department store on the square's west side, is the Royal Court Theatre, which for over a century has fostered new drama.

SOUTH KENSINGTON AND KNIGHTSBRIDGE

BRISTLING WITH embassies and consulates, South Kensington and Knightsbridge are still among London's most desirable and well-kept areas. The proximity of Kensington Palace, still a royal residence, means the area has remained relatively unchanged. It vies with Mayfair as the most expensive place to live in London. The elite shops of Knightsbridge, led by Harrods, serve its wealthy residents. With Hyde Park to the north and the museums that once celebrated Victorian learning and self-confidence at its heart, visitors to this part of London can expect to find a unique combination of the serene and the grandiose.

Façade of the Victoria and Albert Museum

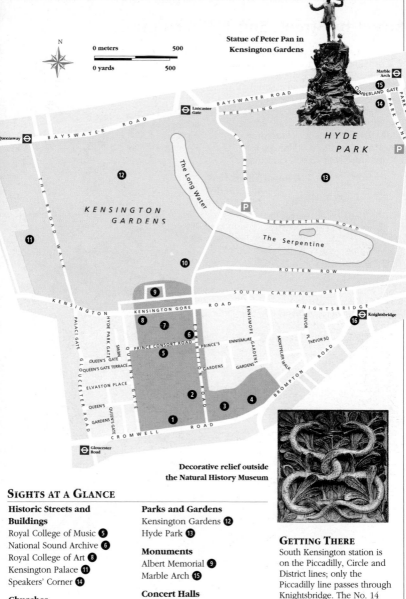

Statue of Peter Pan in Kensington Gardens

Decorative relief outside the Natural History Museum

SIGHTS AT A GLANCE

Historic Streets and Buildings
Royal College of Music ⑤
National Sound Archive ⑥
Royal College of Art ⑧
Kensington Palace ⑪
Speakers' Corner ⑭

Churches
Brompton Oratory ④

Museums and Galleries
Natural History Museum pp204–5 ①
Science Museum pp208–9 ②
Victoria and Albert Museum pp198–201 ③
Serpentine Gallery ⑩

Parks and Gardens
Kensington Gardens ⑫
Hyde Park ⑬

Monuments
Albert Memorial ⑨
Marble Arch ⑮

Concert Halls
Royal Albert Hall ⑦

Shops
Harrods ⑯

SEE ALSO

GETTING THERE

South Kensington station is on the Piccadilly, Circle and District lines; only the Piccadilly line passes through Knightsbridge. The No. 14 bus runs directly from Piccadilly Circus to South Kensington, via Green Park and Knightsbridge.

KEY

Street-by-Street map
Underground station
Parking

Street by Street: South Kensington

A GROUP OF MUSEUMS and colleges provide this area with its dignified character. The Great Exhibition of 1851 in Hyde Park was so successful that in the following years smaller exhibitions were held here, just to its south. By the end of the 19th century some of these had become permanent museums, housed in grandiose buildings celebrating Victorian self-confidence.

Royal College of Art
David Hockney and Peter Blake are among the great artists who trained here **8**

The Royal College of Organists was decorated by F. W. Moody in 1876.

★ **Royal Albert Hall**
Opened in 1870, the Hall was partly funded by selling seats on a 999-year lease **7**

Royal College of Music
Historic musical instruments, like this harpsichord (1531) are exhibited here **5**

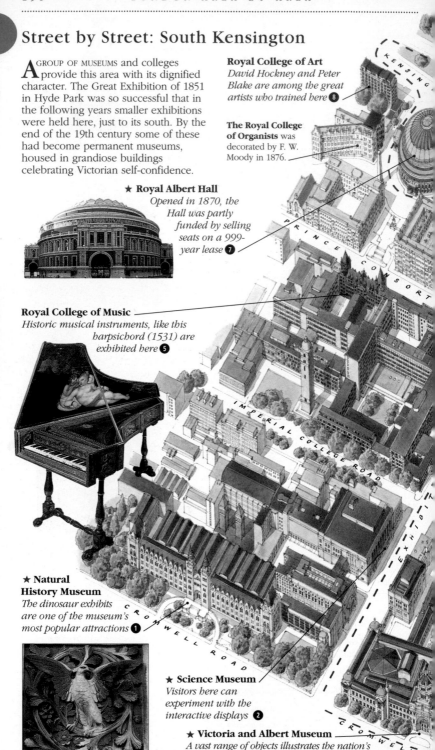

★ **Natural History Museum**
The dinosaur exhibits are one of the museum's most popular attractions **1**

★ **Science Museum**
Visitors here can experiment with the interactive displays **2**

★ **Victoria and Albert Museum**
A vast range of objects illustrates the nation's history of design and decoration **3**

Albert Memorial
This memorial was built to commemorate Queen Victoria's consort **9**

The Albert Hall Mansions, built by Norman Shaw in 1879, started a fashion for red brick.

N

LOCATOR MAP
See Central London Map pp12–13

KEY

– – – Suggested route

0 meters	100
0 yards	100

The Royal Geographical Society was founded in 1830. Scottish missionary and explorer David Livingstone (1813–73) was a member.

National Sound Archive
You can listen to a recording of Queen Victoria's voice here **6**

Imperial College, part of London University, is one of the country's leading scientific institutions.

Brompton Oratory
The Oratory was built during the 19th-century Catholic revival **4**

Brompton Square, begun in 1821, established this as a fashionable residential area.

Holy Trinity Church dates from the 19th century and is located in a calm backwater among cottages.

To Knightsbridge station

STAR SIGHTS

★ **Victoria and Albert Museum**

★ **Natural History Museum**

★ **Science Museum**

★ **Royal Albert Hall**

Victoria and Albert Museum ❸

Main entrance

THE VICTORIA AND ALBERT (or V&A) contains one of the world's widest collections of fine and applied arts. The exhibits range from early Christian devotional objects to Doc Marten boots, from the paintings of John Constable to the mystical art of Southeast Asia. The V&A also houses collections of sculpture, watercolors, jewelry and musical instruments. The building was originally opened in 1857 after nearly 25 years of planning and construction.

★ Twentieth-Century Gallery
This gallery shows modern design, like Daniel Weil's Radio in a Bag *(1983).*

GALLERY GUIDE

The V&A consists of 7 miles (11 km) of galleries that occupy four main-floor levels. The key to understanding the labyrinthine layout is in the division of galleries devoted to art and design and those concentrating on materials and techniques. In the former, many different kinds of artifacts are assembled to illustrate the art and design of a particular period or place – for example, Europe 1600–1800. The materials and techniques galleries contain collections of particular forms of art – porcelain, tapestries and so on. The art and design galleries occupy most of the ground floor, with British arts situated on the first floor. The Henry Cole Wing is situated on the northwest side of the main building and contains the museum's collections of paintings, drawings, prints and photographs. It also houses the new Frank Lloyd Wright Gallery.

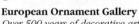

European Ornament Gallery
Over 500 years of decorative art is shown here. This sculpture, made for Marie Antoinette, represents the five orders of classical architecture.

Constable Collection
John Constable (1776–1837) vividly captured the East Anglian landscape. This painting is called A Windmill Among Houses.

Henry Cole Wing

Exhibition Road entrance

KEY TO FLOOR PLAN

- ▢ Lower ground floor
- ▢ Ground floor
- ▢ Upper ground floor
- ▢ First floor
- ▢ Upper first floor
- ▮ Second floor
- ▮ Henry Cole Wing

STAR EXHIBITS

- ★ **Medieval Treasury**
- ★ **Nehru Gallery of Indian Art**
- ★ **Dress Collection**
- ★ **Morris and Gamble Rooms**
- ★ **Twentieth-Century Gallery**

★ **Morris and Gamble Rooms**
The Victorian decorations here draw on past styles and the modern materials of an industrial age.

VISITORS' CHECKLIST

Cromwell Rd SW7. **Map** 19 A1.
📞 0171-938 8500. 🚇 0171-938 8441. ⊖ South Kensington.
🚌 14, 45A, 49, 74, 349, C1.
Open noon–5:50pm Mon, 10am–5:50pm Tue–Sun. **Closed** Jan 1, Good Friday, May Day hol & Dec 24–26. 🚻 🚷 🍴 🛍 📷
Lectures, film shows, presentations, concerts, exhibitions, events.

T.T. Tsui Gallery of Chinese Art
This ancestor portrait, in watercolor on silk, is from the Qing Dynasty (1644–1912).

Pirelli Garden

★ **Medieval Treasury**
The Eltenberg Reliquary (c. 1180) is one of the museum's masterpieces of medieval craftsmanship.

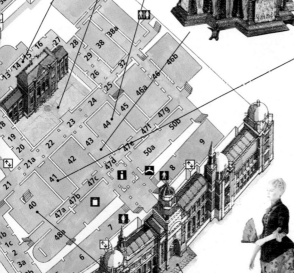

Main entrance

★ **Dress Collection**
Clothing here dates from 1600 to the present. This dress is from the 1880s.

★ **Nehru Gallery of Indian Art**
Much of this collection dates from when Britain ruled India. The Emperor Shah Jehan's jade wine cup was made in 1657.

Exploring the V&A's Collections

THE V&A WAS FOUNDED in 1852 as the Museum of Manufactures to inspire students of design. It was renamed by Queen Victoria, in memory of Prince Albert, in 1899. Many of the exhibits originate from parts of the British Empire, and among the wealth of artifacts is the greatest collection of Indian art outside India. The museum houses the National Art Library, which contains works on aspects of art and design, items illustrating the art of book production from the Middle Ages onward and artists' diaries and correspondence.

German Castle Cup (15th century)

SCULPTURE

THERE ARE 26 galleries devoted to Postclassical sculpture, alabasters and ivories, bronzes and casts. The superb Renaissance collection includes a marble relief of *The Ascension* by Donatello. At the museum's Exhibition Road entrance stand 17 pieces by Auguste Rodin, presented by the sculptor in 1914. There are also collections of sculpture from India, the Middle East and the Far East.

CERAMICS AND GLASS

EXAMPLES OF 2,000 years of craftsmanship in pottery, porcelain and glass from Europe and the Near and Far East are exhibited across 21 galleries. These contain superb porcelain from all the major European china factories, such as Meissen, Sèvres, Royal Copenhagen and Royal Worcester; stained glass, including some lovely medieval "Labours of the Months"; studio pottery, with rare pieces by such masters as William de Morgan, Picasso and Bernard Leach; rich and intricately patterned Persian and Turkish tiles; and a wide selection of Chinese pieces.

FURNITURE AND DESIGN

THERE ARE 37 galleries containing a vast array of furniture and interior design, with especially outstanding collections of 18th-century French and English pieces. Fully furnished interiors offer a vivid re-creation of social life through their displays of furniture, paintings, pottery and other domestic objects – one fine example is a room from La Tournerie, near Alençon, in France (Room 3A). The V&A also has a wide collection of musical instruments including virginals, lutes, flutes, barytons, musical boxes, harps and a Dutch "giraffe" piano with six percussion pedals that ring bells, drum and buzz.

Russian porcelain (1862)

METALWORK

INTRICATELY WROUGHT CUPS and decanters, medals, snuff-boxes, arms and armor, hunting horns, watches and clocks are among more than 35,000 objects from Europe and the Near East that are displayed across 22 of the museum's galleries. Highlights include the 16th-century Burghley Nef (Room 26), a great silver salt cellar that was used to indicate the position of the host at the dinner table; the 15th-century German Castle Cup (Room 27), a castellated, turreted copper-gilt extravaganza; and the Ashburnham Centrepiece, an 18th-century silver tureen in Rococo style.

THE GREAT BED OF WARE

Made in about 1590 of oak with inlaid and painted decoration, the Great Bed of Ware measures some 12 by 12 ft (3.6 by 3.6 m) and is 8 ft 9 inches (2.6 m) high. It is the V&A's most celebrated piece of furniture. Elaborately carved and decorated, the bed is a superb example of the art of the English wood-worker. Its name derives from the town of Ware in Hertfordshire, about a day's ride north of London, where it resided in a number of inns. The Great Bed's enormous size made it an early tourist attraction, and no doubt interest in it was boosted by Shakespeare's reference to it in *Twelfth Night*, which he wrote in 1601.

The bed was draped with curtains when in use.

Tippoo's Tiger, carved in wood for the Sultan of Mysore in about 1790, is depicted mauling an Englishman.

INDIAN ART

THE NEHRU GALLERY of Indian Art forms the centerpiece of the museum's extensive collection of Indian art from 1550 to 1900, a period that includes the opulent Mughal Empire and the India of the British Raj. Textiles, weapons, jewelry, metalwork, glass and paintings, both secular and religious, are on display. One particular highlight of the collection is a Mughal tent of hanging painted cotton (1640) decorated with birds, trees and a double-headed eagle (Room 41). Also look for an 11th-century bronze depicting the Hindu deity Shiva as Lord of the Eternal Dance (Room 47B).

Indian panel of painted and dyed cotton from the 18th century

TEXTILES AND DRESS

THE WORLD-RENOWNED Dress Collection, displayed in Room 40, is devoted to fashionable clothing from about 1600 to the present day. The figures are fully dressed, complete with accessories; in addition, small cases display collections of such items as buttons, shoes, hats and parasols. The scope of the textile collection, displayed in 18 galleries, is worldwide,

starting with ancient Egypt. English textiles of the last three centuries are particularly well represented.

The four great medieval tapestries in Room 94, from the collection of the Duke of Devonshire, depict fascinating scenes of courtly pastimes, while the Syon Cope, from 1300–1320, is an exquisite example of *opus anglicanum*, a type of English embroidery that was popular in Europe during the Middle Ages.

FAR EASTERN ART

EIGHT GALLERIES are devoted to the arts of China, Japan, Korea and other Far Eastern countries. Under a dramatic arc of burnished-steel fins representing the spine of a Chinese dragon, the T T. Tsui Gallery of Chinese Art shows how the artifacts displayed would have been used in everyday life. Among the highlights of the collection are a giant Buddha's head from 700 to 900 AD, a huge Ming canopied bed and rare jade and ceramics (Room 44). Japanese art is concentrated in the Toshiba Gallery, which is particularly notable for lacquer, ceramics, textiles,

Mantle for Buddhist priest from the mid-19th century

Samurai armor and woodblock prints. Especially fine exhibits include a 17th-century wooden writing table inlaid with gold and silver lacquer and the Akita Armor, dating from 1714, both in Room 38A.

PAINTINGS, PRINTS, DRAWINGS AND PHOTOGRAPHS

THESE COLLECTIONS are housed in the Henry Cole Wing. The highlights include British paintings from 1700 to 1900 some wonderful English portrait miniatures, European paintings between 1500 and 1900 and the largest collection of paintings and drawings by John Constable. The Print Room is a public study room for the museum's collection of more than half a million watercolors, engravings, etchings and even playing cards and wallpapers.

Nicholas Hilliard's *A Young Man Among Roses* **(1588)**

Natural History Museum ❶

See pp204–5.

Relief: Natural History Museum

Science Museum ❷

See pp208–9.

Victoria and Albert Museum ❸

See pp198–201.

Brompton Oratory ❹

Brompton Rd SW7. **Map** 19 A1.
[0171-589 4811. ⊖ South
Kensington. **Open** 6:30am–8pm daily.
✝ 11am Sun (sung Latin Mass.) &

THIS ITALIANATE Oratory, or
church, famous for its
splendid musical tradition, is
a rich monument to the
English Catholic revival of the
late 19th century. The Oratory
was established in 1884 by
John Henry Newman (who
later became Cardinal
Newman). Its origins began
with Father Frederick William
Faber (1814–63) who
founded a London community
of priests at Charing Cross.
The community moved to
Brompton, then an outlying
London district, to found an
oratory, that is, a community
of secular scholars living
together without vows. This
concept of oratory started
with the 16th-century Italian
St. Philip Neri. Newman
and Faber, both Anglican
converts to Catholicism,
were following the example
of St. Neri.

The present church was
opened in 1884. Its facade
and dome were added in
the 1890s, and the interior
has been progressively
enriched ever since.
Herbert Gribble, the
architect, yet another
convert to Catholicism,
was 29 when he
designed it.

Many of the most
important treasures
predate the church
and were bought
from churches in
Italy. Giuseppe
Mazzuoli carved the
huge marble figures of the
12 apostles for Siena
Cathedral in the late 17th
century. The elaborate Lady
Altar was created in 1693 for
the Dominican church in
Brescia, and the 18th-century
altar in St. Wilfrid's Chapel is
from Rochefort in Belgium.

Royal College of Music ❺

Prince Consort Rd SW7. **Map** 10 F5.
[0171-589 3643. ⊖ High St
Kensington, Knightsbridge, South
Kensington. **Museum of Musical
Instruments open** 2–4:30pm Wed in
term time. **Adm charge.** ∅ ▣

SIR ARTHUR BLOMFIELD
designed the turreted
Gothic palace, with Bavarian
overtones, that has housed
this distinguished institution
since 1894. The college was
founded in 1882 by George
Grove, who also compiled
the famous *Dictionary of
Music*; famous pupils have
included English composers
Benjamin Britten and Ralph
Vaughan Williams.

Fortunate visitors may
visit the Museum of Musical
Instruments, which is rarely
open; if you do manage
to get in, you will see
instruments dating
from the earliest times
and from many parts
of the world. Some of
the exhibits were
played by great
musicians, such as
Handel and Haydn.

**17th-century viol at the
Royal College of Music**

National Sound Archive ❻

29 Exhibition Rd SW7. **Map** 11 A5.
[0171-589 6603. ⊖ South
Kensington. **Open** 10am–5pm
Mon–Fri, 10am–9pm Thu (last adm:
4:45pm). **Closed** public hols. ▣

THIS BRANCH OF the British
Library contains 900,000
discs, some dating from the
very start of recording in the
1890s. The 80,000 hours of
tape and 6,000 videos include
an 1880s recording of Queen
Victoria. The archive has a
reference library, and anything in the collection can be
heard by prior appointment.
There is a small exhibition of
early gramophones, phon-
ographs and other objects,
including a German machine
for children that played
chocolate records (1903).

The sumptuous interior of Brompton Oratory

Joseph Durham's statue of Prince Albert (1858) by the Royal Albert Hall

Royal Albert Hall ●

Kensington Gore SW7. **Map** 10 F5.
[0171-589 3203. ● High St
Kensington, South Kensington
Knightsbridge. **Open** for
performances and guided tours
[0171-589 8212. ⊘ ⅋ ▣ See
Entertainment pp330–1.

DESIGNED BY AN engineer,
Francis Fowke, and
completed in 1871, this huge
concert hall was modeled on
Roman amphitheaters and is
an attractive Victorian
structure. On the red-brick
exterior the only ostentation is
a handsome frieze symbolizing
the triumph of arts and science.
In plans the building was
called the Hall of Arts and
Science, but Queen Victoria
named it the Albert Hall, in
memory of her husband,
when she laid the foundation
stone in 1868.

The hall is often used for
Classical concerts, most
famously the "Proms," but it
also accommodates every
other kind of large gathering
– from boxing matches (first
held here in 1919) to major
business conferences.

Royal College of Art ●

Kensington Gore SW7. **Map** 10 F5.
[0171-584 5020. ● High St
Kensington, South Kensington,
Knightsbridge. **Open** 8:30am–10pm
Mon–Fri (call first). ▣ ▯ **Lectures,
events, film presentations,
exhibitions.**

SIR HUGH CASSON'S mainly
glass-fronted building
(1973) is in stark contrast to
the Victoriana around it. The
college was founded in 1837
as a school of design and
practical art for the manufacturing industries. It became
noted for modern art in the
1950s and 1960s when David
Hockney, Peter Blake and
Eduardo Paolozzi were there.

Albert Memorial ●

South Carriage Drive, Kensington
Gdns SW7. **Map** 10 F5. ● High St
Kensington, Knightsbridge, South
Kensington. Undergoing restoration
until 1995.

THIS GRANDIOSE memorial to
Queen Victoria's beloved
consort was completed in
1876. Albert was a German
prince and a cousin of Queen
Victoria's. When he died from
typhoid in 1861, he was 41,
and they had been happily
married for 21 years and had
nine children. It is fitting that
the monument is near the site
of the 1851 Exhibition (see
pp26–7), for Prince Albert was
closely identified with it and
with the scientific advances it
celebrated. The larger-than-
life statue, by John Foley,
shows him with an exhibition
catalog on his knee.

The desolate Queen chose
Sir George Gilbert Scott to
design the monument that
stands 175 ft (55 m) high. It is
loosely based on a medieval
market cross – although many
times more elaborate, with a
gilded black spire, multicolored marble canopy,
stones, mosaics, enamels,
wrought iron and nearly 200
sculpted figures. The steps
around it are guarded by four
groups symbolizing Europe,
Africa, America and Asia. In
the corners Engineering,
Agriculture, Manufacturing
and Commerce are shown.

**Victoria and Albert at the Great
Exhibition opening (1851)**

Natural History Museum ❶

Museum's main entrance

L IFE ON EARTH and the Earth
itself are vividly explained
at the Natural History Museum.
Combining the latest interactive
techniques with traditional displays, the exhibits tackle many
fundamental issues, such as the
delicate ecology of our planet
and its gradual evolution over
millions of years, the origin of
species and how human beings
evolved. The vast cathedral-like
museum building is a masterpiece
in itself. It opened in 1881 and was designed by Alfred
Waterhouse using revolutionary Victorian building
techniques. It is built on an iron-and-
steel framework concealed behind
arches and columns, richly
decorated with sculptures
of plants and animals.

★ **Creepy Crawlies**
*Eight out of ten animal species
are arthropods from the world
of insects and spiders,
like this tarantula.*

First floor

Ground floor

★ **New Dinosaur
Exhibition**
*The killer dinosaur
Deinonychus is one
of the life-size robotic
models in the display,
opened in 1992.*

GALLERY GUIDE
*The museum is divided into
Life Galleries and Earth
Galleries, with the Life
Galleries in the main body of
the building. An 85-ft (26-m)
skeleton of the dinosaur
Diplodocus dominates the
entrance hall (10). To the left
are Dinosaurs, Human
Biology (22), Marine Inverte-
brates (23), and Discovering
Mammals (24). To the right
are Ecology (32) and Creepy
Crawlies (33). Reptiles and
Fish (12) are behind the main
hall. The basement has a
children's Discovery Center.
   On the first floor are found
Origin of Species (105) and the
Mammal Balcony (107).
British Natural History (202)
is on the second floor.
   The Earth Galleries are to
the right of the entrance hall
in a separate wing and house
Treasures of the Earth (73)
and The Story of the Earth (71).*

Main entrance

**Access to
basement**

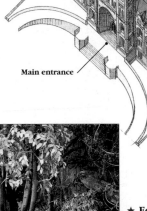

★ **Ecology Gallery**
*A moonlit rain forest buzzing
with the sounds of life begins
an exploration of the complex
web of the natural world and
human interaction.*

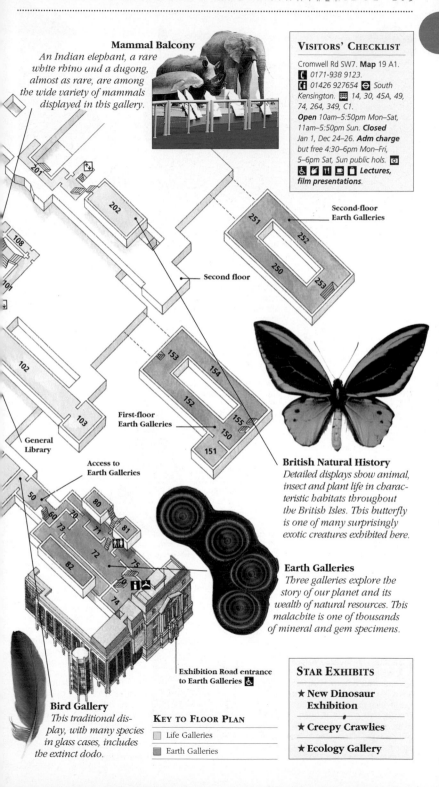

Mammal Balcony
An Indian elephant, a rare white rhino and a dugong, almost as rare, are among the wide variety of mammals displayed in this gallery.

VISITORS' CHECKLIST

Cromwell Rd SW7. **Map** 19 A1.
0171-938 9123.
01426 927654 South Kensington. 14, 30, 45A, 49, 74, 264, 349, C1.
Open 10am–5:50pm Mon–Sat, 11am–5:50pm Sun. **Closed** Jan 1, Dec 24–26. **Adm charge** but free 4:30–6pm Mon–Fri, 5–6pm Sat, Sun public hols.
Lectures, film presentations.

Second-floor Earth Galleries

Second floor

First-floor Earth Galleries

General Library

Access to Earth Galleries

British Natural History
Detailed displays show animal, insect and plant life in characteristic habitats throughout the British Isles. This butterfly is one of many surprisingly exotic creatures exhibited here.

Earth Galleries
Three galleries explore the story of our planet and its wealth of natural resources. This malachite is one of thousands of mineral and gem specimens.

Exhibition Road entrance to Earth Galleries

Bird Gallery
This traditional display, with many species in glass cases, includes the extinct dodo.

KEY TO FLOOR PLAN

☐ Life Galleries
☐ Earth Galleries

STAR EXHIBITS

★ **New Dinosaur Exhibition**

★ **Creepy Crawlies**

★ **Ecology Gallery**

Statue of young Queen Victoria by her daughter Princess Louise outside Kensington Palace

Serpentine Gallery ⑩

Kensington Gdns W2. **Map** 10 F4.
📞 0171-402 6075. ⊖ Lancaster
Gate, South Kensington. **Open**
10am–6pm daily. **Closed** for
exhibition installations, Christmas
week. 🚻 🏛 **Lectures** on current
exhibition 3pm Sun.

IN THE SOUTHEAST corner of
Kensington Gardens is the
Serpentine Gallery, which
houses temporary exhibitions
of contemporary painting and
sculpture. The building is a
former tea pavilion built in
1912; exhibits often spill out
into the surrounding park. Its
tiny bookshop has a remarkable stock of art books.

Kensington Palace ⑪

Kensington Palace Gdns W8.
Map 10 D4. 📞 0171-937 9561.
⊖ High St Kensington, Queensway.
Open 9am–5pm Mon–Sat, 11am–
5pm Sun (last adm: 4:15pm). **Closed**
Jan 1, Good Fri & Dec 24–26, **Adm
charge.** 🚫 🚻 ground floor only. 📷
🏛 **Exhibitions, holiday activities.**

HALF OF THIS SPACIOUS palace
is used as lavish royal
apartments: Princess Margaret
has a base here. The other
half, which includes the 18th-
century state rooms, is open
to the public. When William III
and his wife, Mary, came to the
throne in 1689, they bought a
mansion, dating from 1605,

and commissioned Christopher
Wren to convert it into a royal
palace. He created separate
suites of rooms for the king
and queen, and today visiting
members of public use the
queen's entrance – note the
William and Mary monogram
over the door.

The palace has seen some
important royal events. In
1714 Queen Anne died here
from a fit of apoplexy
brought on by overeating,
and on June 20, 1837,
Princess Victoria of Kent
was awakened at 5am
to be told that her uncle
William IV had died
and she was now
queen – the start of
her 64-year reign.

Highlights of the
palace are the
finely decorated
state rooms and,
on the ground   **Detail of the Coalbrookdale**
floor, a fascinating **gate, Kensington Gardens**
exhibition of court
dress from 1760 to the
present, culminating in the
Princess of Wales's wedding
dress from 1981.

Henry Moore's *Arch* **(1979),
Kensington Gardens**

Kensington Gardens ⑫

W8. **Map** 10 E4. 📞 0171-262 5484.
⊖ Bayswater, High St Kensington,
Queensway, Lancaster Gate. **Open**
5am–midnight daily.

THE FORMER GROUNDS of
Kensington Palace became
a public park in 1841 and
now merge imperceptibly
into Hyde Park to the east.
The gardens are full of
charm, starting with Sir
George Frampton's
statue (1912) of J. M.
Barrie's fictional Peter
Pan, the boy who
never grew up,
playing his pipes
to the bronze fairies
and animals that
cling to the
column below
him. Often
surrounded by
parents, nannies
and their charges, the statue
stands near the west bank of
the Serpentine, not far from
where Harriet, wife of the
poet Percy Bysshe Shelley
drowned herself in 1816.

Just north of here are the
ornamental fountains and
statues, including Jacob
Epstein's *Rima*, at the lake's
head. George Frederick
Watts's statue of a muscular
horse and rider, *Physical
Energy*, stands to the south.
Not far away are a
summerhouse designed by
William Kent in 1735 and the
Serpentine Gallery.

The Round Pond, created in 1728 just east of the palace, is often packed with model boats navigated by children and older enthusiasts. In winter it is occasionally suitable for skating. In the north, near Lancaster Gate, is a dogs' cemetery, started in 1880 by the Duke of Cambridge while mourning one of his pets.

Hyde Park ⓭

W2. **Map** 11 B3. ☏ 0171-262 5484. ⊖ Hyde Park Corner, Knightsbridge, Lancaster Gate, Marble Arch. **Open** 5am–midnight daily. ▯ **Sporting facilities**. See also **Five Guided Walks** pp 260–1.

Riding on Rotten Row, Hyde Park

THE ANCIENT MANOR of Hyde was part of the lands of Westminster Abbey seized by Henry VIII at the Dissolution of the Monasteries in 1536. It has remained a royal park ever since. Henry used it for hunting, but James I opened it to the public in the early 17th century, and it became one of the city's most prized public spaces. The Serpentine, an artificial lake used for boating and bathing, was created when Caroline, George II's queen, dammed the flow of the Westbourne River in 1730.

In its time the park has been a venue for dueling, horse racing, highwaymen, political demonstrations, music (Mick Jagger and Luciano Pavarotti have each had a concert here) and parades. The 1851 Exhibition was held here in a vast glass palace (see pp26–7). The aristocracy drove their carriages on the outer roads.

Speakers' Corner ⓮

Hyde Park W2. **Map** 11 C2. ⊖ Marble Arch.

AN 1872 LAW made it legal to assemble an audience and address them on whatever topic you chose; since then this corner of Hyde Park has become the established venue for budding orators and a fair number of eccentrics. It is well worth spending time here on a Sunday: speakers from fringe groups and one-member political parties reveal their plans for the betterment of humankind while the assembled onlookers heckle them without mercy.

Marble Arch ⓯

Park Lane W1. **Map** 11 C2. ⊖ Marble Arch.

JOHN NASH designed the arch in 1827 as the main entrance to Buckingham Palace. It was, however, too narrow for the grandest coaches and was moved here in 1851. Now, only senior members of the royal family and one of the royal artillery regiments are allowed to pass under it.

The arch stands near the site of the old Tyburn gallows (marked by a plaque), where until 1783 the city's most notorious criminals were hanged in front of crowds of bloodthirsty spectators.

An orator at Speakers' Corner

Harrods ⓰

Knightsbridge SW1. **Map** 11 C5. ☏ 0171-730 1234. ⊖ Knightsbridge. **Open** 10am–6pm Mon–Tue & Thu–Sat, 10am–7pm Wed–Sat. ✂ 丙 ▯ ▯ See **Shops and Markets** p311.

LONDON'S MOST FAMOUS department store had beginnings in 1849 when Henry Charles Harrod opened a small grocery shop nearby on Brompton Road. By concentrating on good quality and impeccable service (rather than on low prices), the store was soon popular enough to expand over the surrounding area.

It used to be claimed that Harrods could supply anything from a packet of pins to an elephant – that is not quite true today, but the range of goods is still phenomenal.

Harrods at night, lit by 11,500 lights

Science Museum ❷

CENTURIES OF CONTINUING scientific
and technological development
lie at the heart of the Science Museum's massive collections. The
hardware displayed is magnificent:
steam engines, the earliest and the
latest computers, spacecraft – the
list is endless. Equally important is
the social context of science – what
discoveries and inventions mean for
day-to-day life – and the process of
discovery itself. Exciting interactive
displays enable visitors to take part
in scientific inquiry themselves.

Science Museum facade

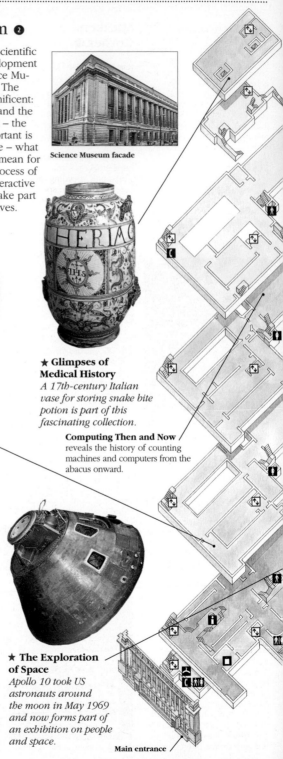

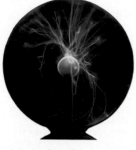

★ Launch Pad
*A plasma ball is one of
many hands-on exhibits for
children in this first-floor
gallery where basic scientific
principles are demonstrated.*

★ Glimpses of
Medical History
*A 17th-century Italian
vase for storing snake bite
potion is part of this
fascinating collection.*

Computing Then and Now
reveals the history of counting
machines and computers from the
abacus onward.

GALLERY GUIDE
*There are five floors. In the
basement is the Children's
Gallery, with many working
demonstrations; there are
also displays of domestic
appliances through the ages.
Big machines – steam engines,
locomotives, cars – dominate
the ground floor; here, too,
are displays on space
exploration and fire-fighting.
The first floor has exhibits on
telecommunications, iron
and steel, gas and food. On
the second floor are such
diverse galleries as nuclear
power, ships, printing and
computing. On the third floor
is the new flight gallery that
opened in 1992, along with
photography, optics and
electricity. The smaller fourth
and fifth floors house the
medical galleries, featuring
many fascinating full-scale
reconstructions.*

★ The Exploration
of Space
*Apollo 10 took US
astronauts around
the moon in May 1969
and now forms part of
an exhibition on people
and space.*

Main entrance

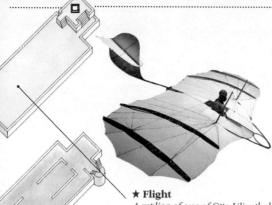

★ Flight
*A replica of one of Otto Lilienthal's
gliders (1895) is one of the displays
that range from man's early
dreams of flight to today's jets.*

Navigation and Surveying
*The display of historic
navigational and surveying
aids includes this decorated
circumferentor (1676) by
architect Joannes Macarius.*

Food for Thought
*The science of food is explored
through demonstrations and
historic reconstructions, such as
this 18th-century kitchen.*

Meteorology
*Here is a rich collection of
weather instruments and other
exhibits, like this 16th-century
watercolor of a comet.*

★ Land Transport
*Exhibits here include early
cars, motorcycles, a tram
and this prototype British
Deltic locomotive (1956).*

KEY TO FLOOR PLAN

- ☐ Basement
- ☐ Ground floor
- ☐ First floor
- ☐ Second floor
- ☐ Third floor
- ☐ Fourth floor
- ☐ Fifth floor

STAR EXHIBITS

★ **Launch Pad**

★ **The Exploration
of Space**

★ **Land Transport**

★ **Flight**

★ **Glimpses of
Medical History**

KENSINGTON AND HOLLAND PARK

THE WESTERN and northern perimeters of Kensington Gardens form a rich residential area including many foreign embassies. The shops on Kensington High Street are almost as smart as the ones on Knightsbridge, and Kensington Church Street is a good source of quality antiques. Around Holland Park are some magnificent late Victorian houses, two open to the public. But as you cross into Bayswater and Notting Hill, you enter a more vibrant, cosmopolitan part of London. Its stucco terraces are lined with medium-price hotels and a huge number of inexpensive restaurants. There has always been

Tiled crest from Holland House

something rather furtive about Bayswater: Victorian men would keep mistresses in its terraces; the Profumo sex scandal (1963) that toppled a government occurred here, and today prostitution remains a major, if discreet, local industry. Its main street, Queensway, is a center of club life and café society, while farther west, Portobello Road is a popular street market. Many West Indians settled in Notting Hill in the 1950s, and for three days every August its streets are home to a lively Caribbean carnival *(see p57)*.

SIGHTS AT A GLANCE

Historic Streets and Buildings
Holland House ➋
Leighton House ➌
Commonwealth Institute ➍
Linley Sambourne House ➎
Kensington Square ➏
Kensington Palace Gardens ➐
Queensway ➑

Parks and Gardens
Holland Park ➊

Markets
Portobello Road ➒

Historic Areas
Notting Hill ➓

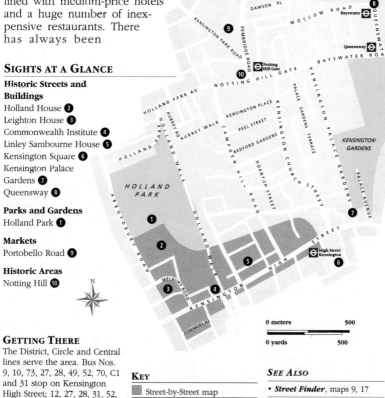

SEE ALSO

• *Street Finder*, maps 9, 17
• *Where to Stay* pp276–7
• *Restaurants* pp292–4

GETTING THERE

The District, Circle and Central lines serve the area. Bus Nos. 9, 10, 73, 27, 28, 49, 52, 70, C1 and 31 stop on Kensington High Street; 12, 27, 28, 31, 52, 70 and 94 go to Notting Hill Gate; and 70, 7, 15, 23, 27, 36, 12 and 94 cross Bayswater.

Entrance to a house in Edwardes Square, Kensington

Street by Street: Kensington and Holland Park

ALTHOUGH NOW PART OF central London, this was a country village of market gardens and mansions as recently as the 1830s. Outstanding among these was Holland House; part of its grounds are now Holland Park. The area grew up rapidly in the mid-19th century, and most of its expensive apartments, mansion flats and fashionable shops date from then.

Holland House
The rambling Jacobean mansion, started in 1605 and pictured here in 1795, was largely demolished in the 1950s 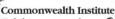 ❷

★ **Holland Park**
Parts of the old formal gardens of Holland House have been retained to grace this delightful public park ❶

The Orangery, now a restaurant, has parts that date from the 1630s, when it was in the grounds of Holland House.

Melbury Road is lined with large, Victorian houses. Many were built for fashionable artists of the time.

Commonwealth Institute
Exhibits capture the exotic flavor of the countries that were once British colonies ❹

The Victorian letter box on the High Street is one of the oldest in London.

★ **Leighton House**
It is preserved as it was when the Victorian painter Lord Leighton lived here. He had a passion for Middle Eastern tiles ❸

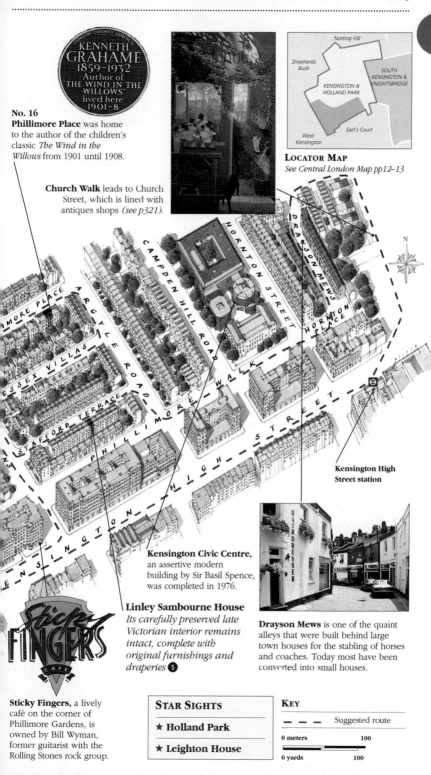

KENNETH GRAHAME
1859–1932
Author of
"THE WIND IN THE
WILLOWS"
lived here
1901–8

No. 16
Phillimore Place was home to the author of the children's classic *The Wind in the Willows* from 1901 until 1908.

LOCATOR MAP
See Central London Map pp12–13

Notting Hill

Shepherds Bush

SOUTH KENSINGTON & KNIGHTSBRIDGE

KENSINGTON & HOLLAND PARK

West Kensington

Earl's Court

Church Walk leads to Church Street, which is lined with antiques shops *(see p321).*

CAMPDEN HILL ROAD

HORNTON STREET

DRAYSON MEWS

HORNTON PLACE

PHILLIMORE PLACE

ARGYLE ROAD

ESSEX VILLAS

STAFFORD TERRACE

PHILLIMORE WALK

PHILLIMORE GARDENS

KENSINGTON HIGH STREET

N

Kensington High Street station

Kensington Civic Centre, an assertive modern building by Sir Basil Spence, was completed in 1976.

Linley Sambourne House
Its carefully preserved late Victorian interior remains intact, complete with original furnishings and draperies ❺

Drayson Mews is one of the quaint alleys that were built behind large town houses for the stabling of horses and coaches. Today most have been converted into small houses.

Sticky FINGERS CAFÉ

Sticky Fingers, a lively café on the corner of Phillimore Gardens, is owned by Bill Wyman, former guitarist with the Rolling Stones rock group.

STAR SIGHTS
★ Holland Park
★ Leighton House

KEY
– – – Suggested route
0 meters   100
0 yards   100

Holland Park ❶

Abbotsbury Rd W14. **Map** 9 B4.
📞 *0171-602 9487.* 🚇 *Holland Park,
High St Kensington, Notting Hill Gate.*
Open *Apr–late Oct: 7:30am–10pm
daily (but flexible); late Oct–Mar:
7:30am–4:30pm (11pm floodlit areas).*
🎭 🖥 **Open-air opera, theater,
dance. Art exhibitions** *Apr–Oct.
See* **Entertainment** *pp326–7.*

T HIS SMALL but delightful
park, more wooded and
intimate than the large royal
parks to its east (Hyde Park
and Kensington Gardens,
see pp206–7), was opened in
1952 on what remained of the
grounds of Holland House –
the rest had been sold off in
the late 19th century, and large
houses and terraces were built
on the northern and western
parts. The park still contains
some of the formal gardens,
laid out in the early 19th
century for Holland House.
There is also a Japanese
garden, created for the 1991
London Festival of Japan. The
park has an abundance of
wildlife, including peacocks.

The café in Holland Park

Holland House ❷

Holland Park W8. **Map** 9 B5. **Youth
Hostel** 📞 *0171-937 0748.* 🚇
Holland Park, High St Kensington. See
Where to Stay *p275.* ♿

Original tiling in Holland House

D URING ITS HEYDAY in the
19th century, this was a
noted center of social and
political intrigue. Statesmen
such as Lord Palmerston
mingled here with the likes of
the poet Byron. What remains
of the house is now used as a
youth hostel.
    The outhouses have various
uses: Exhibitions are held in
the orangery and the ice
house (a forerunner of the
fridge), and the old Garden
Ballroom is now a restaurant.

Leighton House ❸

12 Holland Park Rd W14. **Map** 17 B1.
📞 *0171-602 3316.* 🚇 *High St
Kensington.* **Open** *11am–5:30pm
Mon–Sat.* **Closed** *public hols.*
📷 🎫 📅 **Concerts, exhibitions.**

B UILT FOR Pre-Raphaelite
painter Lord Leighton in
1866, the house has been
preserved, with its opulent
decoration almost intact, as
an extraordinary monument
to the Victorian Aesthetic
movement. The highlight is
the Arab hall, which Leighton
added in 1879 to house his
stupendous collection of
Islamic tiles, some of which
are inscribed with quotations
from the Koran. The best
paintings, including some by
Edward Burne-Jones, John
Millais and Lord Leighton
himself, can be seen in the
downstairs reception room.

Commonwealth
Institute ❹

Kensington High St W8. **Map** 9 C5.
📞 *0171-603 4535.* 🚇 *High St
Kensington.* **Open** *10am–5pm
Mon–Sat, 2–5pm Sun.* **Closed** *Dec
24–26, Jan 1, Good Fri, May Day.*
♿ *phone first.* 🎭 📅 📷 📅
Lectures, concerts, workshops.

I N 1962, the Commonwealth
Institute replaced the old
Imperial Institute (founded in
1887). It is housed in a tent-
like building, erected in 1962,
and includes displays on the
history, industries and culture
of the 50 member nations of
the Commonwealth. In

addition to the permanent
displays, there are temporary
art exhibits and live music by
Commonwealth groups.

Linley Sambourne
House ❺

18 Stafford Terrace W8. **Map** 9 C5.
📞 *0181-994 1019.* 🚇 *High St
Kensington.* **Open** *Mar 1–Oct 31:
10am–4pm Wed, 2–5pm Sun.* **Closed**
Nov 1–Feb 28. **Adm charge.** 🚫 📷

T HIS HOUSE, built in about
1870, has hardly changed
since Linley Sambourne
furnished it in the cluttered
Victorian manner, with china
ornaments and heavy velvet
drapes. Sambourne was a
cartoonist for the satirical
magazine *Punch* and drawings,
including some of his own,
cram the walls. Some rooms
have William Morris wallpaper
(see p245), and even the
bathroom is a Victorian gem.

Logo for *Punch*
**magazine
(1841–1992)**

Kensington Square ⑥

W8. **Map** 10 D5. ⊖ *High St Kensington.*

THIS IS ONE of London's oldest squares. It was laid out in the 1680s, and a few early 18th-century houses still remain. (Nos. 11 and 12 are the oldest.) The renowned philosopher John Stuart Mill lived at No. 18, and the Pre-Raphaelite painter and illustrator Edward Burne-Jones occupied No. 41.

LCC
JOHN STUART MILL
1806-1873
Philosopher Lived Here

Resident's plaque in Kensington Square

Kensington Palace Gardens ⑦

W8. **Map** 10 D3. ⊖ *High St Kensington, Notting Hill Gate, Queensway.*

THIS PRIVATE ROAD of luxury mansions is on the site of the former kitchen gardens of Kensington Palace *(see p206).*

It changes its name halfway down; the southern part is known as Palace Green. It is open to pedestrians but closed to cars except those on official business. Most of the houses are occupied by embassies and their staff. At the cocktail hour, watch the black limousines with their diplomatic license plates go under the raised barriers at each end of the road.

Queensway ⑧

W2. **Map** 10 D2. ⊖ *Queensway, Bayswater.*

ONE OF LONDON'S most cosmopolitan streets, Queensway has the heaviest concentration of eating places anywhere except Soho. At newsstands, you may see more Arabic and European than British newspapers on sale. At the northern end is the domed Whiteley's shopping center. Founded by

Queensway shopfront

William Whiteley, who was born in Yorkshire in 1863, it was probably the world's first department store. The present building dates from 1911.

The street is named after Queen Victoria, who rode here as a princess.

Portobello Road ⑨

W11. **Map** 9 C3. ⊖ *Notting Hill Gate, Ladbroke Grove. **Antiques market open** 9:30am–4pm Fri, 8am–5pm Sat. See also **Shops and Markets** p323.*

THERE HAS been a market here since 1837. The southern end today consists almost exclusively of stalls selling antiques, jewelry, souvenirs and many other collectibles that are popular with tourists. The market is crowded on summer weekends, but is worth visiting for its bustling and cheerful atmosphere, if only to browse. Real bargains are hard to find, since the stallholders have a sound idea of the value of their goods.

Notting Hill ⑩

W11. **Map** 9 C3. ⊖ *Notting Hill Gate.*

NOW THE HOME of Europe's biggest street carnival, most of this area was farmland until the 19th century.

In the 1950s and 1960s Notting Hill became a center for the Caribbean community, many of whom made this their first home in Britain. The carnival started in 1966 and takes over the area every August over the holiday weekend *(see p57),* when costumed paraders flood all of the streets.

Antiques shop on Portobello Road

REGENT'S PARK AND MARYLEBONE

THE AREA south of Regent's Park, incorporating the medieval village of Marylebone, boasts London's highest concentration of quality Georgian housing. It was developed by Robert Harley, Earl of Oxford, as London's borders shifted west in the 18th century. Terraces by John Nash adorn the southern edge of Regent's Park, the busiest of the royal parks, while to its northwest lies St. John's Wood, a smart inner suburb.

GETTING THERE

Regent's Park and Great Portland Street are the nearest tube stations. Marylebone is served by tube and British Rail. Buses 13, 139 and 159 run from Trafalgar Square to near Baker Street, and numerous buses run along Oxford Street.

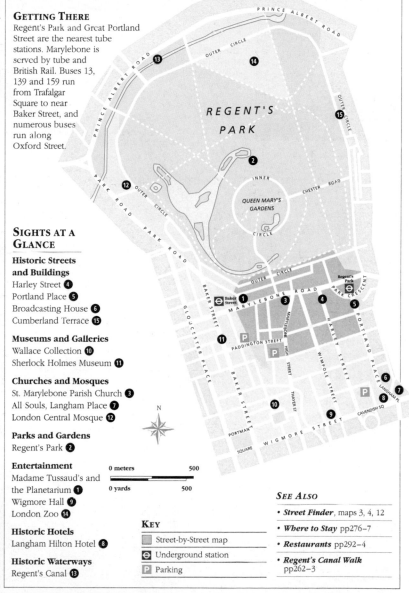

SIGHTS AT A GLANCE

Historic Streets and Buildings
Harley Street **4**
Portland Place **5**
Broadcasting House **6**
Cumberland Terrace **15**

Museums and Galleries
Wallace Collection **10**
Sherlock Holmes Museum **11**

Churches and Mosques
St. Marylebone Parish Church **3**
All Souls, Langham Place **7**
London Central Mosque **12**

Parks and Gardens
Regent's Park **2**

Entertainment
Madame Tussaud's and the Planetarium **1**
Wigmore Hall **9**
London Zoo **14**

Historic Hotels
Langham Hilton Hotel **8**

Historic Waterways
Regent's Canal **13**

| 0 meters | 500 |
| 0 yards | 500 |

KEY

Street-by-Street map

Ⓔ Underground station

Ⓟ Parking

SEE ALSO

St. Andrew's Place, Regent's Park

Street by Street: Marylebone

SOUTH OF REGENT'S PARK, the medieval village of Marylebone (originally Maryburne, the stream by St. Mary's Church) has London's highest concentration of genteel Georgian housing. Until the 18th century it was surrounded by fields and a pleasure garden, but these were built over as fashionable London drifted west. In the mid-19th century, professional people, especially doctors, used the spacious houses to receive wealthy clients. The area has maintained both its medical connection and its elegance.

Tiananmen Square memorial: Portland Place

★ **Regent's Park**
John Nash laid out the royal park in 1812 as a setting for classically designed villas and terraces ❷

The Royal Academy of Music, England's first music academy, was founded in 1774. The present brick building, with its own concert hall, is from 1911.

★ **Madame Tussaud's and the Planetarium**
The wax museum of famous people, historical and contemporary, is one of London's most popular attractions. Next door, a planetarium shows models of the sky at night ❶

To Regent's Park

St. Marylebone Parish Church
Poets Robert Browning and Elizabeth Barrett married in this church ❸

KEY

– – – Suggested route

0 meters   100
0 yards   100

Baker Street station

Park Crescent's breathtaking facades by Nash have been preserved, although the interiors were rebuilt as offices in the 1960s. The crescent seals the north end of Nash's ceremonial route from St. James's to Regent's Park, via Regent Street and Portland Place.

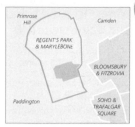

LOCATOR MAP
See Central London Map pp12–13

The London Clinic is one of the best-known private hospitals in this medical district.

Regent's Park station

Portland Place
In the center of this broad street stands a statue of Field Marshal Sir George Stuart White, who won the Victoria Cross for gallantry in the Afghan War of 1879 ❺

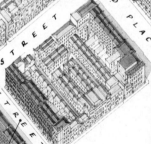

The Royal Institute of British Architects is housed in a controversial Art Deco building designed by Grey Wornum in 1934.

Harley Street
Consulting rooms of eminent medical specialists have been here for more than a century ❹

STAR SIGHTS

★ **Madame Tussaud's and the Planetarium**

★ **Regent's Park**

Mme. Tussaud's and the Planetarium ❶

Marylebone Rd NW1. **Map** 4 D5.
📞 *0171-935 6861.* 🚇 *Baker St.*
Open *9:30am–5:30pm daily.*
Closed *Dec 25.* **Adm charge.**
♿ *call first.* 📷 🖥 🚻

MADAME TUSSAUD began her
wax-modeling career
taking death masks of many
of the best-known victims of
the French Revolution. In
1835 she set up an exhibition
of her work in Baker Street,
not far from the collections
present site.

The 1990s collection still
relies upon traditional wax-
modeling techniques to re-
create the razzmatazz of
politicians, film and television
actors, rock stars and sporting
heroes.

The main sections of the
exhibition are the "Garden
Party," where visitors mingle
with extraordinarily lifelike
models of celebrities; "Super
Stars," devoted to the giants
of the entertainment world;

**Traditional wax-modeling at
Madame Tussaud's**

and the "Grand Hall," containing a collection of royalty,
statesmen and world leaders,
writers and artists. Where else
do Lenin, Martin Luther King
and William Shakespeare all
rub shoulders?

The Chamber of Horrors is
the most-renowned part of
Madame Tussaud's. It
includes re-creations of the
most gruesome episodes in
the grim catalog of crime and
punishment: the murderers
Dr. Crippen and Ethel le

Nève; Gary Gilmore facing a
firing squad; and the chill
gloom of a Victorian street in
Jack the Ripper's London.

The "Spirit of London" is a
grand finale. Visitors travel in
stylized London taxis and
participate in momentous
events of the city, from the
Great Fire of 1666 to 1960s
Swinging London.

Situated next door, and part
of the same great
complex, is the
London Planetarium,
where a spectacular
star show explores
and reveals some
of the mysteries
of the planets
and the solar
system. The
interactive Space
Trail exhibition
contains many
detailed models
of the planets,
satellites and
spacecraft.

**Waxwork of
Elizabeth II**

Tulip time at Queen Mary's Gardens in Regent's Park

Regent's Park ❷

NW1. **Map** 3 C2. 📞 *0171-486 7905.*
🚇 *Regent's Park, Baker St, Great
Portland St.* **Open** *5am–dusk daily.*
♿ 🖥 **Open-air theater.** See
Entertainment *pp326–8.*

THIS AREA OF land became
enclosed as a park in
1812. John Nash designed
the scheme and originally
envisaged a kind of garden
suburb, dotted with 56 villas
in a variety of Classical styles,

with a pleasure palace for the
Prince Regent. At the end of
the day only eight villas – but
no palace – were built inside
the park (three survive round
the edge of the Inner Circle).

The boating lake, which has
many varieties of water birds,
is marvelously romantic,
especially when music drifts
across from the bandstand in
the distance. Queen Mary's
Gardens are a mass of
wonderful sights and smells
in summer, when visitors

can enjoy Shakespeare
productions at the open-air
theater nearby. Broad Walk
provides a picturesque stroll
north from Park Square.

Nash's master plan for
Regent's Park continues just
beyond its northeastern edge
in Park Village East and West.
These captivating buildings in
elegant stucco were completed
in 1828, some adorned with
Wedgwood-style medallions.

St. Marylebone
Parish Church ❸

Marylebone Rd NW1. **Map** 4 D5.
📞 *0171-935 7315.* 🚇 *Regent's Park.*
Open *12:30–1:30pm Mon–Fri, Sun
mornings.* ♿ 📷 ✝ *11am Sun.* 🎵

THIS IS WHERE the poets
Robert Browning and
Elizabeth Barrett were married
in 1846 after eloping from the
home of her strict family on
nearby Wimpole Street. The
large, stately church by
Thomas Hardwick was
consecrated in 1817 after the
former church, where Lord
Byron was christened in 1778,

had become too small. Hardwick was determined that the same should not happen to his new church – so everything is on a grand scale.

Commemorative window in St. Marylebone Parish Church

Harley Street ➍

W1. **Map** 4 E5. ⊖ *Regent's Park, Oxford Circus, Bond St, Great Portland St.*

THE LARGE HOUSES on this late 18th-century street were popular with successful doctors and specialists in the middle of the 19th century when it was a rich residential area. The doctors' practices stayed and lend the street an air of hushed order, unusual in central London. There are very few private houses or apartments here now, but William Gladstone lived at No. 73 from 1876 to 1882.

Portland Place ➎

W1. **Map** 4 E5. ⊖ *Regent's Park.*

THE ADAM BROTHERS, Robert and James, originally laid this street out in 1773. Only a few of their original houses remain, the best being Nos. 27 to 47 on the west side, south of Devonshire Street. John Nash added the street to his processional route that ran from Carlton House to Regent's Park and sealed its northern end with the Park Crescent.

The building of the Royal Institute of British Architects (1934) at No. 66 is adorned with symbolic statues and reliefs. Its bronze front doors depict London's buildings and the River Thames.

Broadcasting House ➏

Portland Place W1. **Map** 12 E1. ⊖ *Oxford Circus.* **Not open** to *the public.*

THIS IS THE HEADQUARTERS of the BBC's national radio services and of its senior management; the television service is located in west London, at White City. It was constructed in 1931 as a suitably modern Art Deco headquarters for the brand-new medium of broadcasting. Its front, curving with the street, is dominated by sculptor Eric Gill's stylized relief of *Prospero and Ariel,* and more Gill ornament can be seen higher up. The lobby has been carefully restored to something close to its 1930s' appearance.

All Souls, Langham Place ➐

Langham Place W1. **Map** 12 F1. 🕻 *0171-580 3522.* ⊖ *Oxford Circus.* **Open** *9:30am–6pm Mon–Fri, 9am–9pm Sun.* ♿ ✝ *11am Sun.* 📷

JOHN NASH designed this church in 1824. Its quirky round frontage is best seen from Regent Street. When it was first built, the spire was ridiculed as it appeared too slender and flimsy. The only Nash church in London, it has

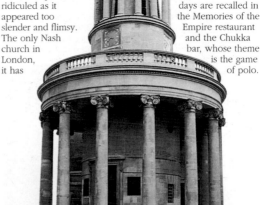

All Souls, Langham Place (1824)

Relief on the Royal Institute of British Architects on Portland Place

close links with the BBC opposite at Broadcasting House, and often doubles as a recording studio for the daily broadcast service.

Langham Hilton Hotel ➑

1 Portland Place W1. **Map** 12 E1. 🕻 *0171-636 1000.* ⊖ *Oxford Circus. See* **Where to Stay** *p284.*

THIS WAS LONDON'S grandest hotel after it was opened in 1865. The writers Oscar Wilde and Mark Twain and composer Antonin Dvořák were among its many distinguished guests. The hotel was, for a time, used by the BBC but since then has been restored behind its original facade. Its marble-lined entrance hall leads into the Palm Court, where there is piano music at teatime. Colonial days are recalled in the Memories of the Empire restaurant and the Chukka bar, whose theme is the game of polo.

Wigmore Hall ❾

36 Wigmore St W1. **Map** 12 E1.
🔲 *0171-935 2141.* ⊖ *Bond St.*
See *Entertainment p331.*

T HIS APPEALING little concert
hall for chamber music
was designed by T. E. Collcutt,
architect of the Savoy Hotel
(see p285), in 1900. At first it
was called Bechstein Hall
because it was attached to the
Bechstein piano showroom:
the area used to be the heart
of London's piano trade.
Opposite is the white-tiled Art
Nouveau emporium built in
1907 as Debenham and
Freebody's department store –
the forerunner of today's
Debenham's on Oxford Street.

Wallace
Collection ❿

Hertford House, Manchester Square
W1. **Map** 12 D1. 🔲 *0171-935 0687.*
⊖ *Bond St.* **Open** *10am–5pm
Mon–Sat, 2–5pm Sun.* **Closed** *Jan 1,
Good Friday, May Day & Dec 24–26.*
🚫 ♿ 📷 🏛 **Lectures.**

**16th-century Italian dish from
the Wallace Collection**

T HIS IS ONE OF the world's
finest private collections
of art. It has remained intact
since it was bequeathed to
the government in 1897 with
the stipulation that it should
go on permanent public
display with nothing added or
taken away. The product of
passionate collecting for four
generations of the Hertford
family, it is a must for anyone
with even a passing interest
in the progress of European
art up to the late 19th century.
   Most of its highlights are in
gallery 22, which contains
some 70 masterworks. Frans
Hals's *The Laughing Cavalier*

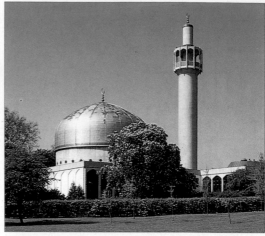

The Mosque on the edge of Regent's Park

and Rembrandt's *Titus* are
here, along with Titian's
Perseus and Andromeda and
Nicolas Poussin's *A Dance to
the Music of Time.* There are
also superb English portraits
by Reynolds, Gainsborough
and Romney. The 25 galleries
contain fine Sèvres porcelain
and sculpture by Houdon,
Roubiliac and Rysbrack. There
is also an armor collection.

Sherlock Holmes
Museum ⓫

221b Baker St NW1. **Map** 3 C5.
🔲 *0171-935 8866.* ⊖ *Baker St.*
Open *10am–6pm daily.* **Closed** *Dec
25.* **Adm charge.** 📷 📷 🏛 🏛

S IR ARTHUR CONAN DOYLE'S
fictional detective was
supposed to have lived at
221b Baker Street – this

Conan Doyle's Sherlock Holmes

museum, which boasts the
right number, actually sits
between Nos. 237 and 239.
Visitors are greeted by
Holmes's "housekeeper" and
shown to his re-created rooms
on the first floor. The fourth
floor shop sells copies of the
stories and deerstalker hats.

London Central
Mosque ⓬

146 Park Rd NW8. **Map** 3 B3.
🔲 *0171-724 3363.* ⊖ *Marylebone,
St. John's Wood, Baker St.* **Open**
dawn–dusk daily. ♿ 🏛 **Lectures.**

S URROUNDED BY TREES on the
edge of Regent's Park, this
large, golden-domed mosque
was designed by Sir Frederick
Gibberd and completed in
1978. It was built to cater to
the increasing number of
Muslim residents and visitors
in London. The mosque's
main hall of worship, which
is capable of holding 1,800
people, is a plain square
chamber with a domed roof.
It is sparsely furnished apart
from a magnificent carpet and
a colossal chandelier. The
dome is lined in a traditional
Islamic pattern of broken
shapes, predominantly blue.
Visitors must remove their
shoes before entering the
mosque, and women, for
whom there is a separate
gallery, should also remember
to cover their heads.

Regent's Canal ⑬

NW1 & NW8. **Map** 3 C1. **C** 0171-
482 0523. ☺ Camden Town,
St. John's Wood, Warwick Ave. **Canal
towpaths open** dawn–dusk daily.
See **Five Guided Walks** pp262–3.

A boat trip on Regent's Canal

JOHN NASH was extremely
enthusiastic about this
waterway, opened in 1820 to
link the Grand Junction Canal,
which ended at Little Venice
in Paddington in the west,
with the London docks at
Limehouse in the east. He
saw it as an added attraction
for his new Regent's Park and
originally wanted the canal to
run through the middle of
that park. He was dissuaded
by those who thought that
the bargees' bad language
would offend the genteel
residents of the area. Perhaps
this was just as well – the
steam tugs that hauled the
barges were dirty and
sometimes dangerous.

In 1874 a barge carrying
gunpowder blew up in the
cutting by London Zoo,
killing the crew, destroying
a bridge and terrifying the
populace and the animals.
After an initial period of
prosperity, the Canal began
to be hit by increasing
competition from the new
railroads and so gradually
slipped into decline.

Today it has been revived
for leisure activities: the towpath is paved as a pleasant
walkway, and short boat trips
are offered between Little
Venice and Camden Lock,
where there is a thriving
crafts market. Visitors to the
zoo can use the landing
platform alongside.

London Zoo ⑭

Regent's Park NW1. **Map** 4 D2.
C 0171-722 3333. ☺ Camden
Town. **Open** 10am–5:30pm daily.
Adm charge. 🍴 ▣ 🚻 **Filmshows**
in summer.

OPENED IN 1828, the zoo
has been one of London's
biggest tourist attractions ever
since, and also has become a
major research center.
However, spectacular TV
programs on wildlife, and
doubts about the ethics of
keeping animals in cages,
have caused attendance at the

**London Zoo's aviary designed by
Lord Snowdon (1964)**

zoo to drop from their 1950s
peak of 3 million visitors a year.
In recent years the future of
the zoo has been subject to a
great deal of uncertainty.

Cumberland
Terrace ⑮

NW1. **Map** 4 E2. ☺ Great Portland
St, Regent's Park.

JAMES THOMSON is credited
with the detailed design of
this, the longest and most
elaborate of the Nash terraces
around Regent's Park. Its
imposing central block of
raised Ionic columns is topped
with a decorated triangular
pediment. Completed in 1828,
the terrace was designed to
be visible from the palace
Nash planned for the Prince
Regent (later George IV). The
palace was never built; the
Prince was too busy with
plans for Buckingham Palace
(see pp94–5).

Nash's Cumberland Terrace, dating from 1828

HAMPSTEAD

AMPSTEAD HAS ALWAYS seemed aloof from London, looking down from its site on the high ridge north of the metropolis. Today it is essentially a Georgian village. The heath separating Hampstead from Highgate reinforces its appeal, isolating it further from the hurly-burly of the modern city. A stroll around the charming village streets, followed by a walk across the heath, makes for one of the finest walks in London.

SIGHTS AT A GLANCE

Historic Streets and Buildings
Flask Walk and Well Walk ❶
Church Row ❺
Downshire Hill ❻
Vale of Health ❸

Museums and Galleries
Burgh House ❷
Fenton House ❹
Keats House ❼
Kenwood House ❿

Parks and Gardens
Hampstead Heath ❽
Parliament Hill ❾
The Hill ⓬

Pubs and Restaurants
Jack Straw's Castle ❸
Spaniards Inn ⓫

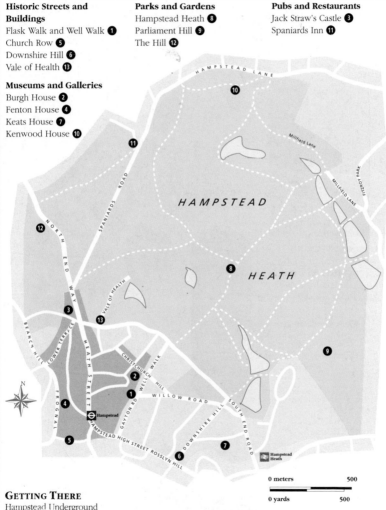

GETTING THERE
Hampstead Underground station lies on the Edgware branch of the Northern line, and there is a BR service, which stops at Hampstead Heath. Bus No. 24 operates a daily service from Victoria to Hampstead Heath, via Trafalgar Square and Tottenham Court Road.

SEE ALSO
• **Street Finder**, maps 1, 2
• **Where to Stay** pp276–7
• **Restaurants** pp292–4

KEY
▢ Street-by-Street map
🚇 Underground station
🚆 British Rail station

0 meters　　500
0 yards　　500

View across Hampstead Heath from Holly Hill

Street by Street: Hampstead

PERCHED AWKWARDLY on a hilltop, with its broad heath to the north, Hampstead has kept its villagelike atmosphere and sense of being aloof from urban pressures. This has attracted artists and writers since Georgian times and made it one of London's most desirable residential areas. Its mansions and town houses are perfectly maintained, and a stroll through Hampstead's narrow streets is one of London's quieter pleasures.

Jack Straw's Castle
The pub on the edge of the Heath is named after a 14th-century rebel ❸

★ **Hampstead Heath**
A welcome retreat from the city, it has broad open spaces that include bathing ponds, meadows and lakes ❽

Whitestone Pond takes its name from the old white milestone nearby. It is 4.5 miles (7 km) from Holborn *(see pp132–41).*

Grove Lodge was home to novelist John Galsworthy (1867–1933), author of *The Forsyte Saga*, for the last 15 years of his life.

Admiral's House dates from about 1700. Built for a sea captain, its name derives from its external maritime motifs. No admiral ever actually lived in it.

STAR SIGHTS

★ **Burgh House**

★ **Hampstead Heath**

★ **Fenton House**

★ **Church Row**

KEY

− − − Suggested route

| 0 meters | 100 |
| 0 yards | 100 |

★ **Fenton House**
Summer visitors should seek out this late 17th-century house and its exquisite walled garden, which are well hidden in the jumble of streets near the heath ❹

★ Burgh House
Built in 1702 but much altered since, this house contains an intriguing local history museum and a café overlooking the small garden ❷

LOCATOR MAP
See Greater London Map pp10–11

The New End Theatre
produces rare but significant work. The building used to be a morgue.

No. 40 Well Walk is where artist John Constable lived while working on his many Hampstead pictures.

Flask Walk and Well Walk
An alley of charming specialty shops broadens into a residential village street ❶

The Everyman Cinema
has been an art cinema since 1933.

Hampstead station

★ Church Row
The tall houses are rich in original detail. Notice the superb ironwork on what is probably London's finest Georgian street ❺

Jack Straw's Castle in the 19th century

Flask Walk and Well Walk ❶

NW3. **Map** 1 B5. ⊖ *Hampstead.*

FLASK WALK IS named after the Flask pub. Here, in the 18th century, therapeutic spa water from what was then the separate village of Hampstead was put into flasks and sold to visitors or sent to London. The water, rich in iron salts, came from nearby Well Walk, where a non-working fountain now marks the site of the well. The Wells Tavern, almost opposite the spring, used to be a hostelry that specialized in accommodating those who engaged in the illicit liaisons for which the spa became notorious.

In later times, there were many notable residents of Well Walk, including artist John Constable (at No. 40), novelists D. H. Lawrence and J. B. Priestley and the poet John Keats, before he moved to his better-known house in what is now Keats Grove.

Site of the well on Well Walk

At the High Street end, Flask Walk is narrow and lined with old shops. Beyond the pub (note the Victorian tiled panels outside) it broadens into a row of Regency houses, one of which used to be home to the novelist Kingsley Amis.

Burgh House ❷

New End Sq NW3. **Map** 1 B4.
📞 *0171-431 0144.* ⊖ *Hampstead.*
Open *noon–5pm Wed–Sun, 2–5pm public hols.* **Closed** *Good Fri, Christmas week.* 🅾 🏊 🛗 **Music recitals.**

THE LAST PRIVATE tenant of Burgh House was the son-in-law of the writer Rudyard Kipling, who visited here occasionally in the last years of his life until 1936. After a period under the ownership of Hampstead Borough Council, the house was leased to the independent Burgh House Trust. Since 1979 the Trust has run it as the Hampstead Museum, which is devoted to the history of the area, concentrating on some of its most celebrated residents.

One room is devoted entirely to the life of John Constable, who painted an extraordinary series of studies of clouds from Hampstead Heath. The house also has sections on Lawrence, Keats, the artist Stanley Spencer and others who lived and worked in the area. There is a display about Hampstead as a spa in the 18th and 19th centuries, which is also well worth a visit. Burgh House regularly offers exhibitions by contemporary local artists. The house itself was built in

1703 but is named after a 19th-century resident, the Reverend Allatson Burgh. It has been much altered inside, and today the marvelously carved staircase is a highlight of the interior. Also worth seeing is the music room, which was reconstructed in 1920 but contains good 18th-century pine paneling from another house. In the 1720s Dr. William Gibbons, chief physician to the then-thriving Hampstead spa, lived here.

There is a moderately priced café in the basement, with a terrace that overlooks the house's pretty garden.

Burgh House staircase

Jack Straw's Castle ❸

12 North End Way NW3. **Map** 1 A3.
📞 *0171-435 8374.* ⊖ *Hampstead.*
Open *licensed pub hours (see p308).*
♿ 🏊

THIS PUB IS NAMED after one of Wat Tyler's lieutenants in the Peasants' Revolt of 1381 *(see p162).* Jack Straw is believed to have built an encampment here, from which he planned to march on London. Instead, he was captured and hanged by the king's men. There has certainly been a pub here for many years – Charles Dickens was a customer – but the present building, a mock castle, dates only from 1962. It is a huge place, and there are good views across the Heath from the restaurant and Turret Bar on the second floor.

Fenton House ➍

20 Hampstead Grove NW3.
Map 1 A4. **[** 0171-435 3471.
⊖ Hampstead. **Open** 1–5:30pm
Mon–Wed, 11am–5:30pm Sat, Sun,
public hols. **Closed** Nov–Feb. **Adm
charge. ∅ Summer concerts**
8pm Wed.

BUILT IN 1693, this splendid
William and Mary house is
the oldest mansion in
Hampstead. It contains two
specialized exhibitions that
are open to the public during
the summer: the Benton-
Fletcher collection of early
keyboard instruments, which
includes a harpsichord dating
from 1612, said to have been
played by Handel; and a fine
collection of porcelain. The
instruments are kept in full
working order and are
actually used for concerts held
in the house. The porcelain
collection was largely
accumulated by Lady
Binning, who, in 1952,
bequeathed the house
and all of its contents
to the National Trust.

Church Row ➎

NW3. **Map** 1 A5. **⊖** Hampstead.

THE ROW IS ONE of the most
complete Georgian streets
in London. Much of its
original detail has survived,
notably the ironwork.
   At the west end is St. John's,
Hampstead's parish church,
built in 1745. The iron gates
are earlier and come from
Canons Park in Edgware.
Inside the church is a bust of
John Keats. John Constable's
grave is in the churchyard,
and many Hampstead
luminaries are buried in the
adjoining cemetery.

Downshire Hill ➏

NW3. **Map** 1 C5. **⊖** Hampstead.

A BEAUTIFUL STREET of mainly
Regency houses, it lent its
name to a group of artists,
including Stanley Spencer and
Mark Gertler, who often
gathered at No. 47 between
the two World Wars. Number
47 was also earlier the meeting
place of Pre-Raphaelite artists,
among them Dante Gabriel
Rossetti and Edward Burne-
Jones. A more recent resident,
at No. 5, was Jim Henson, the
creator of the television
puppets, *The Muppets.*
   The church on the corner
(the second Hampstead church
to be called St. John's) was
built in 1823 to serve the
Hill's residents. Inside, it still
has its original box pews.

Keats House ➐

Keats Grove NW3. **Map** 1 C5.
[0171-435 2062. **⊖** Hampstead,
Belsize Park. **Open** Apr–Oct: 10am–
1pm, 2–6pm Mon–Fri; Nov–Mar:
1–5pm Mon –Fri; all year: 10am–1pm,
2–5pm Sat; 2–5pm Sun, public hols.
Closed Jan 1, Easter, May Day & Dec
24–26,. **⬛ Poetry readings, talks.**

Lock of John Keats's hair

THESE WERE ORIGINALLY two
semi-detached houses
built in 1816; Keats was
persuaded to move into the
smaller one in 1818 by his

St John's, Downshire Hill

friend Charles Armitage
Brown. Keats spent two
productive years here: "Ode
to a Nightingale," perhaps his
most celebrated poem, was
written under a plum tree in
the garden. The Brawne
family moved into the larger
house a year later, and Keats
became engaged to their
daughter, Fanny. However,
the marriage never took place
because Keats died of
consumption in Rome before
two years had passed. He
was only 25 years old.
   One of Keats's love letters
to Fanny, the engagement
ring he offered her and a
lock of her hair are among
the mementoes that are now
on display at the house, first
opened to the public in 1925.
Visitors are also able to see
some of Keats's original
manuscripts and books, part
of a collection that serves as a
tribute to Keats's life and work.

Fenton House's 17th-century facade

View over London from Hampstead Heath

Hampstead Heath **8**

NW3. **Map** 1 C2. **Fi** *0181-348 9945.*
⊖ *Belsize Park, Hampstead.* **Open**
24hrs daily. **Special walks** *on
Sundays.* **Concerts, poetry readings
& children's activities** *in summer.*
Sports facilities, bathing ponds.
Sports **Fi** *0181-458 4548.*

Tᴴᴱ ʙᴇꜱᴛ ᴛɪᴍᴇ to stride
across these broad 3 sq
miles (8 sq km) is Sunday
afternoon, when the local
residents walk off their roast-
beef lunches, discussing the
contents of the Sunday
papers. Separating the hilltop
villages of Hampstead and
Highgate *(see p242),* the Heath
was made from the grounds
of several formerly separate
properties and embraces a
variety of landscapes –
woods, meadows, hills, ponds
and lakes. It remains
uncluttered by the haphazard
buildings and statues that
embellish the central London
parks and its open spaces
have become increasingly
precious to Londoners as
the areas around it get more
crowded. There are ponds for
bathing and fishing and, on
three holiday weekends –
Easter, late spring and late
summer – the southern part of
the Heath is taken over by a
popular fun fair *(see pp56–9).*

Parliament Hill **9**

NW3. **Map** 2 E4. **Fi** *0171-485 4491.*
⊖ *Belsize Park, Hampstead.*
♿ Concerts & children's activities
in summer. **Sporting facilities**. **▢**

Aɴ ᴜɴʟɪᴋᴇʟʏ ʙᴜᴛ romantic
explanation for the area's
name is that it is where Guy
Fawkes's fellow plotters
gathered on November 5,
1605 in the vain hope of
watching the Houses of
Parliament blow up after they
had planted gunpowder there
(see p22). More probably it
was a gun emplacement for
the Parliamentary side during
the Civil War 40 years later.
The gunners would have

Kenwood House **10**

Hampstead Lane NW3. **Map** 1 C1.
Fi *0181-348 1286.* **Fi** *0171-973
3427.* **⊖** *Highgate, Archway.* **Open**
*Apr–Sep: 10am–6pm daily; Oct–Mar:
10am–4pm daily.* **Closed** *Dec 24–25.*
♿ ⌀ 🎵 Lakeside concerts *in
summer.* **Exhibitions, poetry
readings, recitals.** **🍴 ▢ 🎁**
See **Entertainment** *pp330–31.*

Tʜɪꜱ ɪꜱ ᴀ ᴍᴀɢɴɪꜰɪᴄᴇɴᴛ Adam
mansion, filled with Old
Master paintings, including
works by Vermeer, Turner
and Romney (who lived in
Hampstead). It is situated on
landscaped grounds high on
the edge of Hampstead
Heath. There has been a
house here since 1616 – the
present one was remodeled
by Robert Adam in 1764 for
the Earl of Mansfield, the Lord
Chancellor. Adam remodeled
existing rooms and added to
the original building. Most of
his interiors have survived,
the highlight being the library.
A Rembrandt self-portrait is
the collection's star attraction,
and there are also works by
Van Dyck, Hals and Reynolds.

The orangery is
now used for
occasional concerts
and recitals.

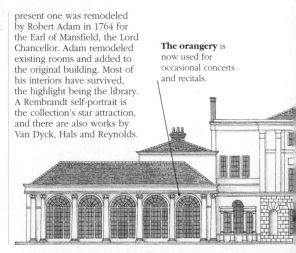

enjoyed a broad view across London. Today it provides one of the most spectacular views over the capital — from here you can see the dome of St. Paul's in the City.

In addition to wonderful views, Parliament Hill is also a popular place for flying kites or sailing model boats.

Spaniards Inn ⓫

Spaniards Rd NW3. **Map** 1 B1.
📞 0181-455 3276. 🚇 *Hampstead, Golders Green.* **Open** *11am–11pm Mon–Sat, noon– 3pm, 7–10pm Sun.*
♿ *See* **Restaurants and Pubs** *pp308–9.*

The historic Spaniards Inn

DICK TURPIN, the notorious 18th-century highwayman, is said to have frequented this pub. When he wasn't holding up stage coaches on their way to and from London, he stabled his horse, Black Bess, at the stables nearby. The building certainly dates from Turpin's time and, although the bar downstairs has been altered frequently, the small upstairs Turpin Bar is original. A pair of guns over the bar were reputedly taken from anti-Catholic rioters, who came to Hampstead to burn the Lord Chancellor's house at Kenwood during the Gordon Riots of 1780. The landlord detained them by offering pint after pint of free beer and, when they were drunk, disarmed them.

Among the pub's noted patrons have been the poets Shelley, Keats and Byron, the actor David Garrick; and the artist Sir Joshua Reynolds.

The toll house has been restored; it juts into the road so that, in the days when tolls were levied, traffic could not race past without paying.

The Hill ⓬

North End Way NW3. **Map** 1 A2.
📞 0181-455 5183. 🚇 *Hampstead, Golders Green.* **Open** *9am–dusk daily.*

THIS CHARMING garden was created by the Edwardian soap manufacturer and patron of the arts, Lord Leverhulme. It was originally the grounds to his house, now a hospital, and is now part of Hampstead Heath. Its highlight is a pergola walkway, best seen in summer when many of the plants are in flower; the garden also has a beautiful formal pond.

The pergola walk at The Hill

Vale of Health ⓭

NW3. **Map** 1 B4. 🚇 *Hampstead.*

THIS AREA was famous as a distinctly unhealthy swamp before it was drained in 1770; Until then it was known as Hatches Bottom, but its newer name may derive from people fleeing here from cholera in London at the end of the 18th century. It also could have been so named by a property developer in 1801, when the area was first recorded.

The poet James Henry Leigh Hunt put the area on the literary map when he moved here in 1815, and played host to Coleridge, Byron, Shelley and Keats.

Other famous residents have included D. H. Lawrence and neurologist Sigmund Freud.

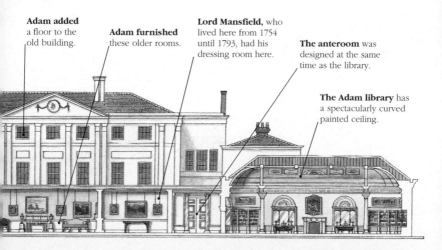

Adam added a floor to the old building.

Adam furnished these older rooms.

Lord Mansfield, who lived here from 1754 until 1793, had his dressing room here.

The anteroom was designed at the same time as the library.

The Adam library has a spectacularly curved painted ceiling.

GREENWICH AND BLACKHEATH

BEST KNOWN AS the place from which the world's time is measured, Greenwich marks the historic eastern approach to London by land and by water. Home to the National Maritime Museum and the exquisite Queen's House, Greenwich avoided the 19th-century industrialization of its neighbors and today remains an elegant oasis of bookshops, antiques shops and markets. Blackheath lies just to its south.

SIGHTS AT A GLANCE

Historic Streets and Buildings
Queen's House **2**
Royal Naval College **7**
Old Royal Observatory **9**
Croom's Hill **12**

Museums
National Maritime Museum **1**
Fan Museum **13**

Churches
St. Alfege Church **3**

Parks and Gardens
Greenwich Park **10**
Blackheath **11**

Walkway
Greenwich Foot Tunnel **6**

Pubs and Restaurants
Trafalgar Tavern **8**

Ships
Gipsy Moth IV **4**
Cutty Sark **5**

GETTING THERE
The best way is by BR from Charing Cross, Cannon Street or London Bridge station. The 188 bus goes five times an hour to Greenwich from Euston. There are also numerous river boats *(pp60–5)*.

SEE ALSO

• *Street Finder*, maps 23, 24

• *Where to Stay* pp276–7

• *Restaurants* pp292–4

KEY

Street-by-Street map

British Rail station

P Parking

Street by Street: Greenwich

THIS HISTORIC TOWN marks the eastern approach to London and is best visited by river *(see pp60–5)*. In Tudor times it was the site of a palace much enjoyed by Henry VIII, near a fine hunting ground and his naval base. He and his daughters, Elizabeth I and Mary, were born here, but the old palace is gone, leaving Inigo Jones's exquisite Queen's House, built for James I's wife. Museums, book and antiques shops, markets, Wren's architecture and the magnificent park make Greenwich an enjoyable day's excursion.

Greenwich Foot Tunnel
Leading to the Isle of Dogs, this is the only Thames tunnel built solely for pedestrians **6**

Greenwich Pier provides a boarding point for boat services to Westminster and the Thames Barrier.

Gipsy Moth IV
Sir Francis Chichester sailed single-handedly around the world in this little yacht **4**

Cutty Sark
Majestic clipper ships, such as this, once traded across the oceans **5**

Goddard's Pie and Eel House is a rare survivor of a London tradition *(see p307)*.

Greenwich Market sells crafts, antiques and books at weekends. It is especially popular on Sundays.

St. Alfege Church
There has been a church here since 1012 **3**

Spread Eagle Yard was a stopping point for horse-drawn carriages. The ticket office is now a shop for secondhand books.

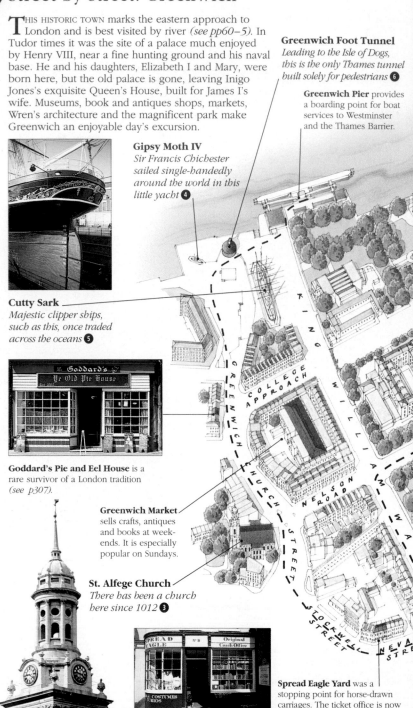

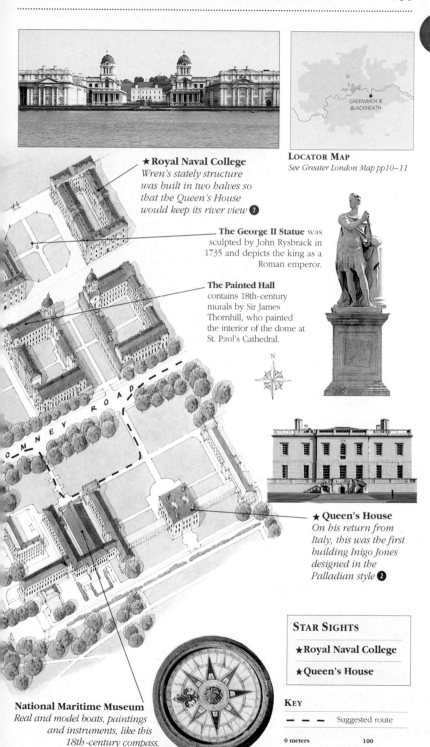

★ Royal Naval College
*Wren's stately structure
was built in two halves so
that the Queen's House
would keep its river view* ⑦

The George II Statue was
sculpted by John Rysbrack in
1735 and depicts the king as a
Roman emperor.

The Painted Hall
contains 18th-century
murals by Sir James
Thornhill, who painted
the interior of the dome at
St. Paul's Cathedral.

★ Queen's House
*On his return from
Italy, this was the first
building Inigo Jones
designed in the
Palladian style* ②

National Maritime Museum
*Real and model boats, paintings
and instruments, like this
18th-century compass,
illustrate naval history* ①

STAR SIGHTS

★ Royal Naval College

★ Queen's House

KEY

━ ━ ━ Suggested route

0 meters   100

0 yards   100

National Maritime Museum **1**

Romney Rd SE10. **Map** 23 C2.
(*0181-858 4422.* **≋** *Maze Hill.*
Open *Apr–Sep: 10am–6pm Mon–Sat,
noon–6pm Sun; Oct–Mar: 10am–5pm
Mon–Sat, noon–5pm Sun (last adm:
30 mins before closing).* **Closed**
Dec 24–26 . **Adm charge.** 🅾
🕭 *to most of museum.* **Lectures,
exhibitions.** 💻 📷

The sea has always played an extremely important role in British history, and this extensive museum celebrates the "island nation's" seafaring heritage. The exhibits include everything from the earliest coracles (primitive hollow canoes made from wood and leather), to early models of Elizabethan galleons to modern cargo, passenger and naval ships. There are sections devoted to trade and empire, the exploratory expeditions of Captain Cook and others and the Napoleonic Wars.

One of the star exhibits is the uniform that Lord Nelson was wearing when he was shot at the Battle of Trafalgar in October 1805. Clearly visible are the bullet hole and bloodstains. Rather more spectacular, however, are the royal barges in the basement, most notably one that was built for Prince Frederick in 1732, elaborately decorated with gilded mermaids, shells, garlands and his Prince of Wales feathers on the stern. Throughout the museum, which was built in the 19th century as a school for sailors' children, are scores of exquisitely crafted models of ships and historic paintings.

**Prince Frederick's barge at the
National Maritime Musueon**

St. Alfege's altar with rails by Jean Tijou

Queen's House **2**

Romney Rd SE10. **Map** 23 C2.
(*0181-858 4422.* **≋** *Maze Hill,
Greenwich.* **Open** *Apr–Sep:
10am–6pm Mon–Sat, noon–6pm
Sun; Oct–Mar: 10am–5pm Mon–Sat,
noon–5pm Sun (last adm: 30 mins
before closing).* **Adm charge.** 🅾 📷
🍴 💻 📷 **Lectures,
concerts, exhibitions.**

This house was designed by Inigo Jones after his return from Italy and completed in 1637. It was originally meant as the home of Anne of Denmark, wife of James I, but she died while it was being built. It was finished for Charles I's queen, Henrietta Maria, who loved it and called it her house of delights. After the English Civil War it was briefly occupied by Henrietta as dowager queen, but was not much used by the royal family after that.

It has recently been restored and furnished as it would have been in the late 17th century, with brightly colored wallhangings and fabrics. The house was built as two halves, one on each side of the road from Woolwich to Deptford, linked by a bridge. Later the road was diverted; its former course is marked by cobbles in the courtyard. The main hall is a perfect cube, 40 ft (12 m) in all three dimensions. Another feature is the spiral "tulip staircase" (named after the design on its balustrades), curving sinuously upward without a central support.

St. Alfege Church **3**

Greenwich Church St SE10.
Map 23 B2. **(** *0181-853 0687.*
≋ *Greenwich.* **Open** *12:30–4:30pm
daily.* 🕭 *9:30am Sun.* 🅾 🕭 📷
Concerts, exhibitions.

This is one of Nicholas Hawksmoor's distinctive and powerful designs, with its gigantic columns and

pediments topped by urns. It
was completed in 1714 on the
site of an older church that
marked the martyrdom of St.
Alfege, Archbishop of
Canterbury, who was killed on
this spot by the Danes in 1012.

Some of the carved wood
inside is by Grinling Gibbons,
but much of it was badly
damaged by a World War II
bomb and has been restored.
The wrought iron of the altar
and gallery rails is original,
attributed to Jean Tijou. Also
notice the reproduction of the
register entry recording the
baptism of Henry VIII in the
former church and a brass
plate denoting the tomb of
General Wolfe, who died
fighting the French in Quebec
in 1759. A window commem-
orates Thomas Tallis, the 16th-
century composer and
organist, who is buried here.

Gipsy Moth IV ❹

King William Walk SE10. **Map** 23 B2.
[0181-858 2698. **☎** Greenwich,
Maze Hill. **☎** Greenwich Pier. **Open**
Apr–Sep: 10am–6pm Mon–Sat,
noon–6pm Sun. **Closed** Nov–Mar.
Adm charge. ◙ ♿

Gipsy Moth IV

SIR FRANCIS CHICHESTER sailed
by himself around the world
in this little yacht. The journey,
from 1966 to 1967, took him
226 lonely days to cover the
30,000 miles (48,000 km). He
had to endure very cramped
conditions on this 54 ft (16 m)
vessel. The Queen knighted
him onboard using the sword
with which Elizabeth I had
knighted that earlier English
seaman, Sir Francis Drake.

**The domed terminal of the
Greenwich Foot Tunnel**

Cutty Sark ❺

King William Walk SE10. **Map** 23 B2.
[0181-858 2698. **[** 0181-853
3589. **☎** Greenwich, Maze Hill.
☎ Greenwich Pier. **Open** Apr–Sep:
10am–6pm Mon–Sat, noon–6pm
Sun; Oct–Mar: 10am–5pm Mon–Sat,
noon–5pm Sun, public hols (last adm:
30 mins before closing). **Closed**
Dec 24–26. **Adm charge.** ◙ ♿
restricted. ▨ 🎞 **Filmshows, videos.**

THIS MAJESTIC vessel is a
survivor of the clippers that
crossed the Atlantic and Pacific
oceans in the 19th century.
Launched in 1869 as a tea
carrier, it won the annual
clippers' race from China to
London in 1871, taking 107
days. It made its last sea
voyage in 1938 and was put
on display here in 1957. On
board, visitors can see where
merchant seamen slept, ate
and lived. Exhibits illustrate
the history of sailing and the
Pacific trade, and include a
tremendous collection of
carved ships' figureheads.

Greenwich Foot Tunnel ❻

Between Greenwich Pier SE10 and Isle
of Dogs E14. **Map** 23 B1. **☎** Maze
Hill, Greenwich. **Docklands Light
Railway** Island Gardens. **☎**
Greenwich Pier. **Open** 24hrs daily.
Elevators open 5am–9pm daily. ◙
♿ when elevators open.

THIS TUNNEL, 1,200 ft (370 m)
long, was opened in 1902
to allow south London
laborers to walk to work in

Millwall Docks. Today it is
worth crossing for the
wonderful views, across the
river, of Christopher Wren's
Old Royal Naval College and
Inigo Jones's Queen's House.

Matching round red-brick
terminals, with glass domes,
mark the top of the elevator
shafts on either side of the
river. The tunnel is about 9 ft
(2.5 m) high and is lined with
200,000 tiles. The north end,
on the southern tip of the
Isle of Dogs, is close to the
terminus of the Docklands
Light Railway, with its trains
to Canary Wharf *(see p245)*,
Limehouse, East London and
the City. Although there are
security cameras, the tunnel
can be eerie at night.

**A late 19th-century figurehead
in the *Cutty Sark***

Royal Naval College ❼

Greenwich SE10. **Map** 23 C2.
📞 0181-858 2154. 🚊 Greenwich,
Maze Hill. **Open** 2:30pm–5pm
Fri–Wed. 📷

THESE AMBITIOUS buildings
by Sir Christopher Wren
were built on the site of the
old 15th-century royal palace,
where Henry VIII, Mary I and
Elizabeth I lived. Only the
chapel and hall of the college
are open to the public. The
west front was completed by
Sir John Vanbrugh.

The chapel, by Wren, was
destroyed by fire in 1779.
The present Rococo interior,
designed by James Stuart, is
marvelously light and airy,
and has dainty plasterwork
decorations on the ceilings
and walls. The altar rail and
communion table, as well as
the candelabra, are gilded.

The Painted Hall was
opulently decorated by Sir
James Thornhill in the first
quarter of the 18th century.
The magnificent ceiling
paintings are supported by
his illusionistic pillars and
friezes. At the foot of one of
his paintings on the west
wall, the artist himself is
shown, apparently extending
his hand for more money.

Trafalgar Tavern ❽

Park Row SE10. **Map** 23 C1.
📞 0181-858 2437. See **Restaurants
and Pubs** pp308–9.

THIS CHARMING paneled pub
was built in 1837 and
quickly became established,
along with other waterside

Thornhill's painting of King William in the Hall of the Naval College

inns in Greenwich, as a
venue for "whitebait dinners."
Government ministers, legal
luminaries and the like would
arrive from Westminster and
Charing Cross by water on
celebratory occasions and
feast on the tiny fish, which
could in those days be caught
locally. The last such meeting
of government ministers was
held here in 1885. The pub's
menu still features whitefish
when it is in season – though
they are no longer caught
in the now over-polluted
river Thames.

This is another of Charles
Dickens's haunts. He drank
here with one of his novels'
most famous illustrators, the
engraver George Cruickshank.

In 1915 the pub became an
institution for old merchant
seamen. It was restored in 1965
after a spell when it was used
as a club for working men.

Old Royal Observatory ❾

Greenwich Park SE10. **Map** 23 C3.
📞 0181-858 4422. 🚊 Maze Hill,
Greenwich. **Open** Apr–Sep: 10am–
6pm Mon–Sat, noon–6pm Sun;
Oct–Mar: 10am–5pm Mon–Sat,
2–5pm Sun. **Adm charge.** 📷 🚻

THE MERIDIAN (0° longtitude)
that divides the earth's
eastern and western hemi-
spheres passes through here,
and millions of visitors have
been photographed standing
with a foot on either side of
it. In 1884, Greenwich Mean
Time became the basis of time
measurement for most of the
world following an important
international agreement.

The original building
designed by Wren still stands.
It is named Flamsteed House
after Flamsteed, the first
astronomer royal, appointed
by Charles II. The house has a
distinctive octagonal room at
the top, hidden by square
outer walls and crowned with
two turrets. Above one of
them is a ball on a rod that
has dropped at 1pm every
day since 1833, so that sailors
on ships on the Thames, and
makers of chronometers
(navigators' clocks), could set
their clocks by it.

This was the official
government observatory from
1675 until 1948, when the

Trafalgar Tavern viewed from the Thames

lights of London became too bright and the astronomers moved to darker Sussex. Today the Astronomer Royal is based in Cambridge, and in the old Observatory there is an intriguing exhibition of astronomical instruments, chronometers and clocks.

A rare 24-hour clock at the Old Royal Observatory

Greenwich Park ⑩

SE10. **Map** 23 C3. 【 *0181-858 2608.* ⇒ *Greenwich, Blackheath, Maze Hill.* **Open** *6am–dusk daily, pedestrians.* 🚻 **Children's shows, music, sports. Ranger's House,** *Chesterfield Walk, Greenwich Park SE10* **Map** 23 C4. 【 *0181-853 0035.* **Open** *Good Fri– Sep 30: 10am–1pm, 2–6pm Wed–Sun; Oct 31–Maundy Thu: 10am–1pm, 2–4pm Wed–Sun.* **Closed** *Dec 24–25.* 🚻 *ground floor only.*

O RIGINALLY THE GROUNDS of a royal palace and still owned by the Crown, the park was enclosed in 1433 and its brick wall built in the reign of James I. Later, in the 17th century, the French royal landscape gardener André Le Nôtre, who laid out the gardens at Versailles, was invited to design one at Greenwich. The broad avenue, rising south up the hill, was part of

his plan. There are great river views from the hilltop and on a fine day most of London can be seen. On the southeast edge of the park is the Ranger's House (1688), allotted in 1815 to the Park Ranger, but today housing the

Ranger's House in Greenwich Park

fine Suffolk Collection of 17th-century English portraits by William Larkin, Sir Peter Lely and others, as well as a display of historic musical instruments.

Blackheath ⑪

SE3. **Map** 24 D5. ⇒ *Blackheath.*

T HIS OPEN HEATH used to be a rallying point for large groups entering London from the east, including Wat Tyler's band of rebels at the time of the Peasants' Revolt in 1381. It is also the place where James I introduced the game of golf, from his native Scotland, to the then largely sceptical English.

Today the heath is well worth exploring for the stately Georgian houses and terraces that surround it. In the area named Tranquil Vale to the south, there are shops selling books, prints and antiques.

Croom's Hill ⑫

SE10. **Map** 23 C3. ⇒ *Greenwich.*

T HIS IS ONE of the best kept 17th- to early 19th-century streets in London. The oldest buildings are at the southern end, near

Blackheath: the Manor House of 1695; near it, No. 68, from about the same date; and No. 66 the oldest of all.

Famous residents of Croom's Hill have included General James Wolfe (buried in St. Alfege) and the English actor Daniel Day Lewis.

Fan Museum ⑬

12 Croom's Hill SE10. **Map** 23 B3. 【 *0181-858 7879.* ⇒ *Greenwich.* **Open** *11am–4:30pm Tue–Sat, noon–4:30pm Sun.* **Adm charge** *but free to pensioners and disabled 2–4:30pm Tue.* 🔲 🚻 📷 📱 **Lectures, fan-making workshops.**

O NE OF LONDON'S most unusual museums – the only one of its kind in the world – was opened here in 1989. It owes its existence and appeal to the enthusiasm of Helene Alexander, whose personal collection of 2,000 fans from the 17th century onward has been augmented by gifts, including several fans that were made for the stage. Exhibitions change regularly to highlight various aspects of this unique craft embracing miniature painting and carving and embroidery. If there, Ms. Alexander will happily guide you around all the exhibits.

Stage fan used in a D'Oyly Carte operetta

FARTHER AFIELD

MANY OF THE GREAT houses originally built as country retreats for London's high and mighty were overrun by sprawling suburbs in the Victorian era. Fortunately, several have survived as museums in these now less rustic surroundings. Most are less than an hour's journey from central London. Richmond Park and Wimbledon Common give a taste of the country, while a trip to Canary Wharf is an adventure.

SIGHTS AT A GLANCE

Historic Streets and Buildings
Sutton House ⑪
Charlton House ⑱
Eltham Palace ⑲
Ham House ㉘
Orleans House ㉙
Hampton Court pp250–53 ㉗
Marble Hill House ㉚
Syon House ㉜
Osterley Park House ㉞
Pitshanger Manor Museum ㉟
Strand on the Green ㊳
Chiswick House ㊴
Fulham Palace ㊶

Churches
St. Mary, Rotherhithe ⑬
St. Mary's, Battersea ㉓
St. Anne's, Limehouse ⑭

Museums and Galleries
Lord's Cricket Ground ①
Saatchi Collection ②
Freud Museum ③
St. John's Gate ⑦
Crafts Council Gallery ⑧
Geffrye Museum ⑩
Bethnal Green Museum of Childhood ⑫
William Morris Gallery ⑯
Horniman Museum ⑳
Dulwich Picture Gallery ㉑
Wimbledon Lawn Tennis Museum ㉔
Wimbledon Windmill Museum ㉕
Musical Museum ㉝
Kew Bridge Steam Museum ㊱
Hogarth's House ㊵
London Toy and Model Museum ㊸

Parks and Gardens
Battersea Park ㉒
Richmond Park ㉖
Kew Gardens pp256–7 ㊲

Cemeteries
Highgate Cemetery ⑤

Modern Architecture
Canary Wharf ⑮
Chelsea Harbour ㊷

Historic Districts
Highgate ④
Clerkenwell ⑥
Islington ⑨
Richmond ㉛

Modern Technology
Thames Barrier ⑰

All the sights in this section lie inside the M25 motorway *(see pp10–11)*.

0 kilometers 5
0 miles 3

KEY
▢ Main sightseeing areas
═ Motorway

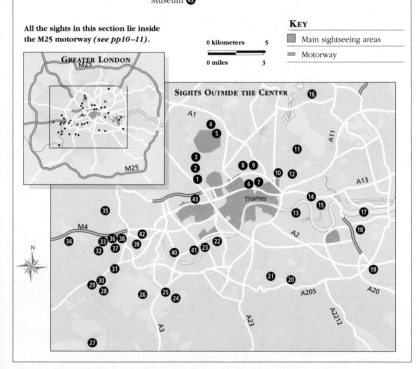

Victorian tombs in Highgate Cemetery, North London

North of the Center

Lord's Cricket Ground ●

NW8. **Map** 3 A3. **[** 0171-289 1611. ● St. John's Wood. **Open** summer: 10am–5pm match days; winter: tours only. **Closed** Dec 25. **Adm charge**. ▣ & ▮ noon, 2pm daily. ▯ See **Entertainment** pp336–7.

THE HEADQUARTERS of Britain's chief summer sport contains a suitably eccentric museum, including a mounted sparrow killed by a cricket ball in play and the Ashes (burned wood in an urn), the object of ferocious competition between the English and Australian national teams. The museum explains the history of the game, while paintings and mementoes of notable cricketers make it a place of pilgrimage for devotees of the sport.

Cricket pioneer Thomas Lord moved his ground to this site in 1814. The Pavilion (1890), with its weather vane depicting Old Father Time, is a late Victorian confection. There are guided tours of Lord's even when there is no game being played.

The Ashes at Lord's

Saatchi Collection ●

98a Boundary Rd NW8. **[** 0171-624 8299. ● St. John's Wood, Swiss Cottage. **Open** noon–6pm Fri, Sat and Sun. ▯ **Lectures**.

CHARLES SAATCHI, who is an advertising executive, and his former wife established this gallery of contemporary art in a converted warehouse. (There is no sign outside so take care not to miss it.) It includes close to 600 works by renowned artists such as Andy Warhol, Carl André and Frank Stella, and selections of these are put on display in exhibitions that are changed every few months.

Sigmund Freud's famous couch

Freud Museum ●

20 Maresfield Gdns NW3. **[** 0171-435 2002. ● Finchley Rd. **Open** noon–5pm Wed–Sun. **Adm charge**. ▣ & ▯ **Lectures, videos, evening classes**.

IN 1938 SIGMUND FREUD, the founder of psychoanalysis, fled from Nazi persecution in Vienna to this Hampstead house. Making use of the possessions he brought with him, his family re-created the atmosphere of Freud's Vienna consulting rooms. After Freud died in 1939 his daughter, Anna (who was a pioneer of child psychoanalysis), kept the house as it was. In 1986, four years after Anna's death, the house was opened as a museum dedicated to Freud. The most famous item is the couch on which patients lay for analysis. A compilation of 1930s home movies includes cheerful moments with his dog as well as scenes of Nazi attacks on his apartment. The museum's bookshop stocks many of his works.

Highgate ●

N6. ● Highgate.

THERE HAS BEEN a settlement here since at least the early Middle Ages, when an important staging post on the Great North Road from London was established here with a gate to control access. Like Hampstead across the Heath (see pp228–31), it soon became fashionable for its unpolluted air, and noblemen built country houses here. It still has an exclusive feel, with a Georgian High Street and expensive houses. On Highgate Hill, a statue of a black cat marks the spot where a dejected Richard Whittington and his pet are said to have paused. He was about to leave London, when he heard the sound of Bow Bells telling him to turn back – to become Lord Mayor three times (see p39).

Highgate Cemetery ●

Swain's Lane N6. **[** 0181-340 1834. ● Archway. **Eastern Cemetery open** Apr–Oct: 10am–5pm daily; Nov–Mar: 10am–4pm daily. **Western Cemetery open ▮ only** Apr–Oct: noon, 2pm & 4pm Mon–Fri, 11am–4pm Sat, Sun; Nov–Mar: noon, 2pm & 3pm Mon–Fri, 11am–3pm Sat, Sun. **Closed** Dec 25–26, during funerals. **Adm charge**. &

THE WESTERN part of this early Victorian delight opened in 1839. Its graves and tombs perfectly reflect high Victorian taste. For many years it lay neglected, until a voluntary group, called the Friends of Highgate Cemetery stepped in. They have restored the Egyptian Avenue, a street of family vaults, built in a style based on that of ancient Egyptian tombs, and the Circle of Lebanon, more vaults in a ring, topped by a cedar tree. In the eastern section lies Karl Marx, beneath a gigantic black bust of himself. The novelist George Eliot (real name, Mary Anne Cross) is also buried here.

George Wombwell's Memorial at Highgate Cemetery

St. John's Priory: today, only the gatehouse remains intact

with special exhibitions. There is a reference library and information service and a well-stocked bookshop that also sells good examples of modern crafts.

Clerkenwell ❻

EC1. **Map** 6 D4. 🚇 *Farringdon. See Entertainment p332.*

Sadler's Wells poster

T HE CLERKS IN the name of this area were parish clerks from the City. St. John's Priory dominated the area until Henry VIII dissolved the monasteries in 1536. It became a fashionable suburb but declined after the Plague of 1665 *(see p22).* Then French Huguenot refugees moved in, opening jewelry and silver workshops. Later it became a center for clockmaking. In Victorian times Clerkenwell had many slums, described by Dickens in *Oliver Twist.* More recently, the area became known as Little Italy, after the Italian immigrants who moved here from the late 19th century up until the 1930s.

On Rosebery Avenue is Sadler's Wells Theatre, where Thomas Sadler built a "musick house" in 1683, next to a well with "healthful" properties. It was rebuilt in 1927 by Lilian Baylis, who was also a

benefactor of the Old Vic *(see p186),* and was home to the Sadler's Wells Royal Ballet Company until 1990.

St. John's Gate ❼

St. John's Square EC1. **Map** 6 F4. 📞 *0171-253 6644.* 🚇 *Farringdon.* **Museum open** *10am–5pm Mon–Fri, 10am–4pm Sat.* **Closed** *Easter, Dec 25, public hols.* **Adm charge.** 📷 📹 *11am, 2:30pm Tue, Fri & Sat.* 📷

T HE TUDOR GATEHOUSE and parts of the 12th-century church are all that remain of the priory of the Knights of St. John, which flourished here for 400 years and was the precursor of the St. John Ambulance Brigade. Over the years, the priory buildings have had many uses. These include times as offices for Elizabeth I's Master of the Revels, a pub, a coffee shop run by artist William Hogarth's father, and the offices of Edward Cave's *Gentlemen's Magazine* (1731–54). A museum of the order's history is open daily, but to see the rest of the building, join a guided tour.

Crafts Council Gallery ❽

44a Pentonville Rd N1. **Map** 6 D2. 📞 *0171-278 7700.* 🚇 *Angel.* **Open** *11am–6pm Tue–Sat, 2–6pm Sun.* 👥 📹 📷 *Lectures.*

T HE COUNCIL is the national body for promoting the creation and appreciation of crafts in Britain. It has a collection of contemporary British crafts, some of which are displayed here, along

Islington ❾

N1. **Map** 6 E1. 🚇 *Angel, Highbury & Islington.*

I SLINGTON WAS ONCE a highly fashionable spa, but the rich began to move out in the late 18th century, and the area deteriorated rapidly. During the 20th century, writers such as Evelyn Waugh, George Orwell and Joe Orton lived here. Now Islington has again returned to fashion as one of London's first areas to become "gentrified," with many young professionals buying and refurbishing old houses.

An older relic is Canonbury Tower, the remains of a medieval manor house converted into apartments in the 18th century. Writers such as Washington Irving and Oliver Goldsmith lived here, and today it houses the Tower Theatre. On Islington Green there is a statue of Sir Hugh Myddleton, who built a canal through Islington in 1613 to bring water to London from Hertfordshire; today a pleasant landscaped walk along its banks runs between Essex Road and Canonbury British Rail stations *(see pp264–5).* There are two markets close to the Angel station *(see p322):* Chapel Road selling fresh food and cheap clothing, and the nearby Camden Passage, selling expensive antiques.

The Crafts Council Gallery

East of the Center

Geffrye Museum's Victorian Room

Geffrye Museum ⑩

Kingsland Rd E2. 📞 0171-739 9893.
🚇 Liverpool St, Old St. **Open**
10am–5pm Tue–Sat, 2–5pm Sun,
Mon & public hols. **Closed** Jan 1 &
Dec 24–26. ♿ 🔊 🖵 🎞
Exhibitions, lectures, events.

THIS COMPACT MUSEUM is
housed in an attractive set
of almshouses built in 1715
on land bequeathed by Sir
Robert Geffrye, a 17th-century
Lord Mayor of London who
made his fortune through
trade, including the slave
trade. The almshouses (built
for ironworkers and their
widows) have been adapted
into typical room settings of
specific periods, and provide
an insight into the history of
family life and the evolution
of interior design. The historic
room settings begin with
Elizabethan (which contains
magnificent paneling) and run
through various major styles
finishing with Art Nouveau
and the 1950s.

Each room contains splendid
examples of the furniture of
the period collected from all
over Britain. In the middle,
the chapel has not been
altered significantly from its
original appearance, with
box pews. The Creed, the
Commandments and the
Lord's Prayer are inscribed
on the alcove wall. Outside
the museum there are
attractive gardens, including a
walled herb garden.

Sutton House ⑪

2–4 Homerton High St E9.
📞 0181-986 2264. 🚇 Bethnal
Green then bus 253. **Open** 11:30am–
5:30pm Wed, Sun. **Closed** Dec, Jan,
Good Fri. **Adm charge.** 🚫 ♿ 🔊
🖵 🛈 *Concerts, lectures, films.*

THIS IS ONE OF THE FEW
London Tudor merchants'
houses to survive in
something like its original
form; it is now being restored.
It was built in 1535 for Ralph
Sadleir, a courtier to Henry
VIII, and was owned by
several wealthy families before
becoming a girls' school in
the 17th century. In the 18th
century the front was altered,
but the Tudor fabric remains
surprisingly intact, with much
original brickwork, large fireplaces and linenfold paneling.

Bethnal Green Museum of Childhood ⑫

Cambridge Heath Rd E2.
📞 0181-980 3204. 🚇 Bethnal
Green. **Open** 10am–5:50pm
Mon–Thu, Sat, 2:30–5:50pm Sun.
Closed Jan 1 & Dec 24–26, May Day.
📷 ♿ 🛈 *Workshop, children's
activities.*

THIS BRANCH of the Victoria
and Albert Museum *(see
pp198–201)* is better
described as a toy museum,
although there are plans to
broaden its range by showing
exhibits that illustrate the
social history of childhood. Its
very large array of dolls,
lavish dolls' houses (some

Tate "Baby" house made in 1760

donated by royalty), games,
model trains, theaters,
puppets and some large play
equipment are well explained
and enticingly displayed.

The toy collection began
early this century but Bethnal
Green did not become a
dedicated toy museum
until 1974. The museum
building itself was originally
erected on the V&A site but
in 1872, when the V&A was
extended, it was dismantled
and reassembled.

St. Mary, Rotherhithe ⑬

St Marychurch St SE16.
📞 0171-231 2465. 🚇 Rotherhithe.
Open 7am–6pm daily. ✝ 9:30am,
6pm Sun. 🚫 ♿ restricted.
Concerts, exhibitions.

St. Mary, Rotherhithe

THIS BRIGHT CHURCH was
built in 1715 on the site of
a medieval church, traces of
which remain in the tower. It
has various nautical elements,
most notably a memorial to
Christopher Jones, captain of
the *Mayflower* on which the
Founding Fathers sailed to
North America. The barrel
roof resembles an inverted
hull. The communion table
is made from the timbers of
the *Temeraire*, a warship
whose final journey to the
breaker's yard at Rotherhithe
was evocatively recorded in
Turner's painting at the
National Gallery *(see pp104–7).*

William Morris tapestry (1885)

St. Anne's, Limehouse ⓮

Commercial Rd E14.
【 0171-987 1502. **Docklands Light Railway** Westferry. **Open** 3–4:30pm Sun, key from rectory at other times, 5 Newell St, E14. **✚** 10:30am Sun.
◙ ▯ Concerts, lectures.

THIS IS ONE of the group of East End churches that were designed by Nicholas Hawksmoor. It was completed in 1724 and its 130 ft (40 m) tower soon became a landmark for ships using the East End docks – St. Anne's still has the highest church clock in London. The church was badly damaged by fire in 1850, and while it was being restored, the architect Philip Hardwick Victorianized its interior. It was bombed in World War II and is today in need of further restoration.

Canary Wharf ⓯

E14. **Docklands Light Railway** Canary Wharf. **& ▯ ▯ ▯**
Information center, concerts, exhibitions. See **The History of London** pp30–1.

LONDON'S MOST ambitious commercial development opened in 1991, when the first tenants moved into the

50-story Canada Tower, designed by US architect Cesar Pelli. At 800 ft (250 m) it dominates the city's eastern skyline and is the tallest office building in Europe. It stands on what was the West India Dock, closed, like all the London docks, during the 1960s to 1980s, when trade moved to the modern container port down river at Tilbury. When completed, Canary Wharf will have 21 office buildings plus shops and leisure facilities. However, it underwent serious financial difficulties in 1992 and its future is uncertain.

William Morris Gallery ⓰

Forest Rd E17. **【** 0181-527 3782.
⊖ Walthamstow Central. **Open** 10am–1pm & 2–5pm Tue–Sat, 10am–1pm & 2–5pm first Sun each month. **& ▯ Lectures**.

THE MOST influential designer of the Victorian era, born in 1834, lived as a youth in this imposing 18th-century house. It is now a beguiling and well-presented museum giving a full account of William Morris the artist, designer, writer, craftsman and pioneer socialist. It has choice examples of his work and that of various other members of the Arts and Crafts movement that he inspired – furniture by A. H. Mackmurdo, Kelmscott Press books, tiles by de Morgan, pottery by the Martin brothers and paintings by the Pre-Raphaelites.

Thames Barrier ⓱

Unity Way SE18. **【** 0181-854 1373.
➨ Charlton. **Open** 10am–5pm Mon–Fri, 10:30am–5:30pm Sat, Sun.
Closed Jan 1 & Dec 25.
Adm charge. ◙ & ▯ ▯
Multimedia show, exhibition.

Thames Barrier

IN 1236 THE THAMES rose so high that people rowed across Westminster Hall in boats; London was flooded again in 1663 and 1928. A tidal surge in 1953 caused great damage in the estuary below London. Something had to be done, and in 1965 the Greater London Council (see County Hall p183) invited proposals – nine years later work began on the barrier. It is 1,700 ft (520 m) across, and its 10 gates, which pivot from their normal position flat on the river bed, swing up to 6 ft (1.6 m) above the level reached by the tide in 1953. The barrier was opened in 1984 and seldom has to be raised more than once or twice a year. It is best visited by boat (see pp60–65).

Canada Tower at Canary Wharf

South of the Center

A Jacobean fireplace at Charlton House

Charlton House ⑱

Charlton Rd SE7. [0181-856 3951.
⚡ Charlton. **Open** 9am–11pm daily.
Closed public hols. 🔲 ♿ 🗎 🖥

THE HOUSE was completed in 1612 for Adam Newton, tutor to Prince Henry, the eldest son of James I. It has good river views and is the best-preserved Jacobean mansion in the London area. The house is now used as a community center. Inside, many of the original ceilings and fireplaces survive, as does the carved main staircase, all with an astonishing amount of ornament. Some parts of the wood paneling, too, are original. The ceilings have been restored by using the original molds, which were found in the basement. In the grounds there is a summer-house that may possibly have been designed by Inigo Jones and a mulberry tree (probably the oldest in England) planted by James I in 1608.

Rembrandt's *Jacob II de Gheyn* at Dulwich Picture Gallery

Eltham Palace ⑲

Court Yard SE9. [0181-781 4232.
⚡ Eltham. **Open** Oct–Mar:
10am–4pm Thu, Sun; Apr–Sep:
10am–6pm Thu, Sun. 🔲 🖥

IN THE 14TH CENTURY, kings traditionally spent Christmas here. The Tudors used the palace as a base to hunt deer, but it fell to ruin after the Civil War (1642–60). In 1934 Stephen Courtauld, from the textile family, restored the hall, which, apart from the bridge over the moat, was the only part to survive. Near the moat is the 15th-century house of Cardinal Wolsey (see p253).

Horniman Museum ⑳

100 London Rd SE23. [0181-699 2339. ⚡ Forest Hill. **Gardens open** 8am–dusk daily. **Museum open** 10:30am–5:30pm Mon–Sat, 2–5:30pm Sun. **Closed** Dec 24–26.
♿ 🗎 🖥 🍴 🔲 🖥
Concerts, lectures, events.

FREDERICK HORNIMAN, the tea merchant, had this museum built in 1901 to house the curios he had collected on his travels. It has a distinctly Victorian feel, from the inspirational mosaic on the front (representing Humanity in the House of Circumstance) to the overstuffed walrus inside. There is also an elaborate exhibition of tea-making paraphernalia.

Dulwich Picture Gallery ㉑

College Rd SE21. [0181-693 5254.
⚡ West Dulwich, North Dulwich.
Open 10am–1pm & 2–5pm Tue–Fri,
11am–5pm Sat, 2–5pm Sun (last adm: 4:45pm). **Closed** public hols.
Adm charge. 🖉 ♿ 🗎 3pm Sat, Sun. 🔲 **Concerts, events**.

ENGLAND'S OLDEST public art gallery, this was opened in 1817 and designed by Sir John Soane (see pp136–7). Its imaginative use of skylights

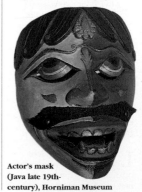

Actor's mask (Java late 19th-century), Horniman Museum

made it the prototype for most art galleries built after. The gallery was later commissioned to house the collection of nearby Dulwich College, a Victorian building designed by Charles Barry and opened in 1870.

The gallery has works by Rembrandt, including *Jacob II de Gheyn,* stolen from here four times; and Canaletto, Poussin, Watteau, Claude, Murillo and Raphael.

The building houses Soane's mausoleum to Desenfans and Bourgeois, original founders of the collection.

Tennis racket and net from 1888, Wimbledon Lawn Tennis Museum

Battersea Park **22**

Albert Bridge Rd SW11. **Map** 19 C5.
℡ *0181-871 7530.* **⊖** *Sloane Square then bus 137.* **≅** *Battersea Park.* **Open** *Dawn–dusk daily.* **Horticultural Therapy Garden ℡** *0171-720 2212.* **▣** *Events. See* **Five Guided Walks** *pp266–7.*

Peace Pagoda, Battersea Park

THIS WAS THE second public park created to relieve the growing urban stresses on Victorian Londoners (the first was Victoria Park in the East End). It opened in 1858 on the former Battersea Fields – a swampy area notorious for every kind of vice, centered around the Old Red House, a disreputable pub.

The park immediately became popular, especially for its newly created boating lake, with its romantic rocks, gardens and waterfalls. Later it became a great site for the new craze of cycling.

In 1985 a peace pagoda – one of more than 70 built throughout the world – was opened. Buddhist nuns and monks took 11 months to complete the monument, which is 100 ft (35 m) high.

St. Mary's, Battersea **23**

Battersea Church Rd SW11.
℡ *0171-228 9648.* **⊖** *Sloane Square then bus 19 or 219.* **Open** *noon–4pm Tue and Wed, otherwise key available from Vicarage, 32 Vicarage Crescent SW11.* **✝** *11am Sun.* **▣** *Concerts.*

THERE HAS BEEN a church here since at least the 10th century. The present brick building dates from 1775; but the 17th-century stained glass, commemorating Tudor monarchs, comes from the former church.

In 1782 the poet and artist William Blake was married in the church to the daughter of a Battersea market gardener. Later J.M.W. Turner painted some of his marvelous views of the Thames from the church tower. Nearby is Old Battersea House (1699).

Wimbledon Lawn Tennis Museum **24**

Church Rd SW19. **℡** *0181-946 6131.*
⊖ *Southfields.* **Open** *10:30am–5pm Tue–Sat, 2–5pm Sun.* **Adm charge.**
& **▣** **▯** *Exhibitions.*

EVEN THOSE with only a passing interest in the sport will find plenty to enjoy at this lively museum, on the site of the international tennis tournament. It traces tennis's development from its invention in the 1860s as a diversion for country house parties to the wealthy professional sport it is today. Alongside strange 19th-century equipment run

film clips showing great players of the past. More recent matches may be viewed in the video theater.

Wimbledon Windmill Museum **25**

Windmill Rd SW19. **℡** *0181-947 2825.* **⊖** *Wimbledon & then a 30-minute walk.* **Open** *Easter–Oct 31: 2–5pm Sat–Sun.* **Closed** *Nov 1–Easter.* **Adm charge.** **▣** **▯**

THE MILL on Wimbledon Common was built in 1817 and modified in 1893. The building at its base was converted into cottages in 1864. Lord Baden-Powell, founder of the Boy Scout movement, lived in the mill house. Now the site is a windmill museum.

St. Mary's, Battersea

West of the Center

Ham House

Richmond Park 26

Kingston Vale SW15.
🕿 0181-940 0654. 🚇 🚂 Richmond
then bus 65 or 71. **Open** Oct–Mar:
7:30am–dusk daily; Apr–Sep:
7am–dusk daily. **Fishing, golf.**

Deer in Richmond Park

CHARLES I, WHEN he was
Prince of Wales in 1637,
built a wall 8 miles (13 km)
around to enclose the royal
park as a hunting ground.
Deer still graze warily among
the chestnuts, birches and
oaks, no longer hunted but
still discreetly culled. They
have learned to coexist with
the many thousands of
human visitors who stroll
here on fine weekends.

In late spring the highlight
is the Isabella Plantation with
its spectacular display of
rhododendrons, while the
nearby Pen Ponds are very
popular with optimistic
anglers. (Adam's Pond is for
model boats.) The rest of the
park is heath, bracken and
trees. Richmond Gate, in
the northwest corner, was
designed by the landscape
gardener Capability Brown in
1798. Nearby is Henry VIII
Mound, where in 1536 the

king, staying in Richmond
Palace, awaited the signal that
his former wife, Anne Boleyn,
had been executed. The
Palladian White Lodge, built
for George II in 1729, is home
to the Royal Ballet School.

Hampton Court 27

See pp250–3.

Ham House 28

Ham St, Richmond. 🕿 0181-940
1950. 🚇 🚂 Richmond then bus 65
or 371. **Open** 1–5pm Mon–Wed,
1–5:30pm Sat, 11:30am–5.30pm Sun.

THIS MAGNIFICENT HOUSE by
the Thames was built in
1610 but had its heyday later
that century, when it became
the home of the Duke of
Lauderdale, confidant to
Charles II and Secretary of
State for Scotland. His wife,

Marble Hill House

the Countess of Dysart,
inherited the house from her
father who as a child had
been Charles I's "whipping
boy" – meaning that he was
punished for the future king's
misdemeanors. From 1672 the
duke and countess modern-
ized the house and grounds
until the estate became
regarded as one of the finest
in Britain. The diarist John
Evelyn praised the Lauderdales'
garden, now restored to its
17th-century form.

On some days in summer, a
foot passenger ferry runs from
here to Marble Hill House and
Orleans House at Twickenham.

Orleans House 29

Orleans Rd, Twickenham.
🕿 0181-892 0221. 🚇 🚂 Richmond
then bus 33, 90, 290, R68 or R70.
Open Apr–Sep: 1–5:30pm Tue–Sat,
2–5.30pm Sun, public hols. Oct–Mar:
1–4:30pm Tue–Sat, 2–4:30pm Sun,
public hols. **Closed** Dec 24–26 &
Good Fri. 🕭 restricted. 🚻
Concerts, lectures.

ONLY THE OCTAGON, designed
by James Gibbs for James
Johnson in 1720, remains of
this early 18th-century house.
It is named after Louis Philippe,
the exiled Duc d' Orléans,
who lived here between 1800
and 1817, before becoming
king of France in 1830. The
lively interior plasterwork of
the Octagon still remains
intact. The adjacent gallery
shows temporary exhibitions,
and these include some local
history displays of the area.

Marble Hill House 30

Richmond Rd, Twickenham.
🕿 0181-892 5115. 🚇 🚂 Richmond
then bus 33, 90, 290, R68 or R70.
Open Apr–Sep: 10am–6pm daily;
Oct–Mar: 10am–4pm daily. **Closed**
Dec 24–25. 🚫 🕭 restricted. 🎧
🍴 🚻 **Concerts, fireworks** on
summer weekends.
See **Entertainment** p331.

BUILT IN 1729 for George II's
mistress, the house and its
grounds have been open to the
public since 1903. It has now
been largely restored to its

Georgian appearance but is not yet fully furnished. Paintings include works by William Hogarth and Henry Kneller and a view of the river and house in 1762 by Richard Wilson, the father of English landscape painting.

Richmond ㉛

SW15. ⊖ ⊠ *Richmond.*

Richmond side street

THIS ATTRACTIVE London village took its name from the palace that Henry VII built here in 1500. Many early 18th-century houses survive near the river and off Richmond Hill, notably Maids of Honour Row, which was built in 1724. The classic view of the river from the top of the hill, that has been painted by numerous landscape artists, remains even now largely unspoiled.

Syon House ㉜

London Rd, Brentford. [0181-560 0881. ⊖ *Gunnersbury then bus 237 or 267.* **House open** *Apr–Sep: 11am–5pm Sat, Sun, public hols and by arrangement.* **House closed** *Oct–Mar.* **Gardens open** *10am–dusk daily.* **Adm charge.** ⊘ ♿ *to gardens only.* 📷 🎁 🍴 🛒 🚻

THE EARLS and Dukes of Northumberland have lived here for 400 years – it is the only large mansion in the London area still in its

hereditary ownership. The outbuildings accommodate a museum of 120 historic cars, a butterfly house, an art center, a garden center, a National Trust gift shop and two restaurants. However, the house itself remains the star exhibit, with lavish interiors created by Robert Adam. Some rooms have Spitalfields silk wall-hangings, and include many fine pictures. The gardens include a rose garden and a spectacular conservatory built in 1830.

Musical Museum ㉝

368 High St, Brentford. [0181-560 8108. ⊖ *Gunnersbury, South Ealing then bus 65, 237 or 267.* **Open** *Apr–Jun, Sep–Oct: 2–5pm Sat & Sun; Jul & Aug: 2–4pm Wed– Fri, 2–5pm Sat and Sun.* **Closed** *Nov–Mar.* **Adm charge.** 📷 ♿ 🎁 🚻

THE COLLECTION comprises chiefly large instruments, including player (or automatic) pianos and organs, miniature and cinema pianos and what is thought to be the only surviving self-playing Wurlitzer organ in Europe.

Drawing room: Osterley Park House

Osterley Park House ㉞

Isleworth. [0181-560 3918. ⊖ *Osterley.* **Open** *Apr 1–Oct 31: 1–5pm Wed–Sat, 11am–5pm Sun, public hols.* **Closed** *Nov 1–Mar 31, Good Fri.* 🚻

OSTERLEY is ranked among Robert Adam's finest works, especially for its colonnaded portico and multicolored library ceiling. Much of the furniture was designed by Adam. The garden and its temple are by William Chambers, architect of Somerset House *(see p117)*. The greenhouse is by Adam.

Robert Adam's red drawing room at Syon House

Hampton Court ⏳

Ceiling decoration from the Queen's drawing room

CARDINAL WOLSEY, powerful Archbishop of York to Henry VIII, began building Hampton Court in 1514. Originally it was not a royal palace but was intended as Wolsey's riverside country residence.

Later, in 1525, in the hope of retaining royal favor, Wolsey offered it to the king. After the royal takeover, Hampton Court was twice rebuilt and extended, first by Henry himself and then, in the 1690s, by William and Mary, who employed Christopher Wren as architect.

There is a striking contrast between Wren's classical royal apartments and the Tudor turrets, gables and chimneys elsewhere. The inspiration for the gardens as they are today comes largely from the time of William and Mary, for whom Wren created a vast formal Baroque landscape, with radiating avenues of majestic limes and many collections of exotic plants.

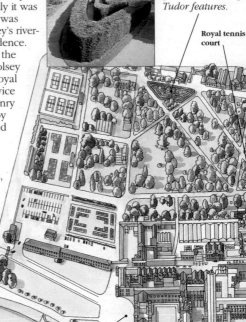

★ **The Maze**
You can lose yourself in one of the garden's surviving Tudor features.

Royal tennis court

Main entrance

River Thames

River boat pier

★ **The Great Vine**
The vine was planted in 1768, and, in the 19th century, produced up to 2,000 lbs (910 kg) of black grapes.

The Pond Garden
This sunken water garden was part of Henry VIII's elaborate designs.

★ **The Mantegna Gallery**
Andrea Mantegna's nine canvases depicting The Triumph of Julius Caesar *(1490s) are housed here.*

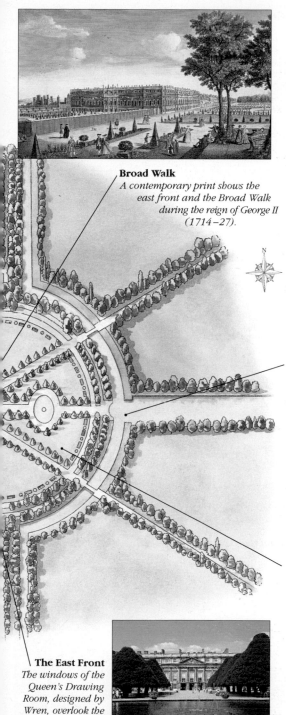

Broad Walk
A contemporary print shows the east front and the Broad Walk during the reign of George II (1714–27).

Long Water
An artificial lake runs parallel to the Thames, from the Fountain Garden across the Home Park.

Fountain Garden
A few of the clipped yews here were planted in the reign of William and Mary.

The East Front
The windows of the Queen's Drawing Room, designed by Wren, overlook the central avenue of the Fountain Garden.

STAR FEATURES

★ **The Great Vine**

★ **The Mantegna Gallery**

★ **The Maze**

Exploring the Palace

Carving on the roof of the Great Hall

As a historic royal palace, Hampton Court bears traces of all the kings and queens of England from Henry VIII to today's Elizabeth II. From the outside, the palace is a harmonious blend of Tudor and English Baroque architecture. Inside, visitors can see the Great Hall, built by Henry VIII, as well as state apartments of the Tudor court. Many of these apartments, including those above Fountain Court by Christopher Wren, are decorated with furniture, tapestries and old masters from the Royal Collection.

Queen's State Bedroom
William III bought the crimson bed from his Lord Chamberlain.

Queen's Presence Chamber

Queen's Guard Chamber

★ **Chapel Royal**
The Tudor chapel was redecorated by Wren, except for the carved and gilded vaulted ceiling.

Haunted gallery

★ **Great Hall**
The stained-glass window in the Tudor Great Hall shows Henry VIII flanked by the coats of arms of his six wives.

STAR FEATURES

★ **Great Hall**

★ **Fountain Court**

★ **Clock Court**

★ **Chapel Royal**

★ **Clock Court**
Anne Boleyn's Gateway is at the entrance to Clock Court. The Astronomical Clock, created for Henry VIII in 1540, is located here.

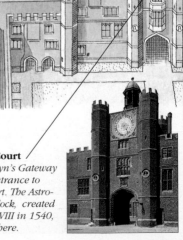

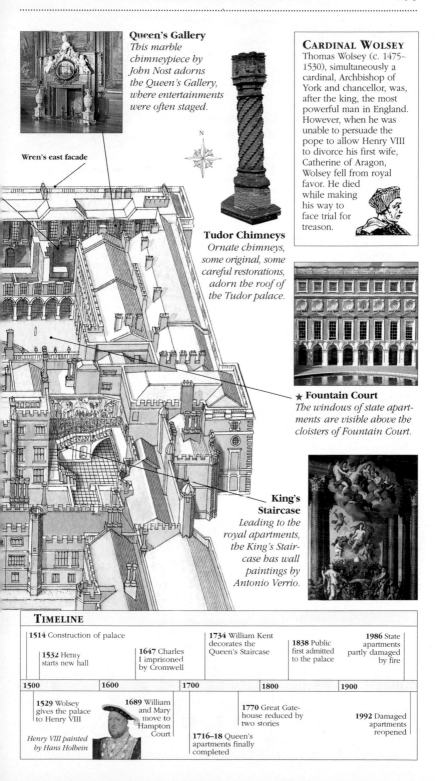

Queen's Gallery
This marble chimneypiece by John Nost adorns the Queen's Gallery, where entertainments were often staged.

Wren's east facade

N

Tudor Chimneys
Ornate chimneys, some original, some careful restorations, adorn the roof of the Tudor palace.

CARDINAL WOLSEY
Thomas Wolsey (c. 1475–1530), simultaneously a cardinal, Archbishop of York and chancellor, was, after the king, the most powerful man in England. However, when he was unable to persuade the pope to allow Henry VIII to divorce his first wife, Catherine of Aragon, Wolsey fell from royal favor. He died while making his way to face trial for treason.

★ Fountain Court
The windows of state apartments are visible above the cloisters of Fountain Court.

King's Staircase
Leading to the royal apartments, the King's Staircase has wall paintings by Antonio Verrio.

TIMELINE

1514 Construction of palace

1532 Henry starts new hall

1529 Wolsey gives the palace to Henry VIII

Henry VIII painted by Hans Holbein

1647 Charles I imprisoned by Cromwell

1689 William and Mary move to Hampton Court

1716–18 Queen's apartments finally completed

1734 William Kent decorates the Queen's Staircase

1770 Great Gatehouse reduced by two stories

1838 Public first admitted to the palace

1986 State apartments partly damaged by fire

1992 Damaged apartments reopened

| 1500 | 1600 | 1700 | 1800 | 1900 |

Pitshanger Manor Museum ㉟

Mattock Lane W5. ☎ *0181-567 1227.* ⊖ *Ealing Broadway.* **Open** *10am– 5pm Tue–Sat.* **Closed** *some public hols.* ⬛ ♿ ▢ *Exhibitions, concerts, lectures.*

SIR JOHN SOANE, architect of the Bank of England *(see p147)*, designed this house on the site of an earlier one. Completed in 1803, it was to become his own country residence. There are clear echoes of his elaborately constructed town house in Lincoln's Inn Fields *(see pp136–7)*, especially in the library, with its imaginative use of mirrors; in the darkly painted breakfast room opposite; and in the "monk's dining room," which is located on the basement level.

Soane retained two of the principal formal rooms: the drawing room and the dining room. These were designed in 1768 by George Dance the Younger, with whom Soane had worked before establishing his own reputation. The eating room has been extended consistent with the original design as a venue for concerts and poetry readings.

The house also contains a small exhibition of Martin-ware, highly decorated glazed pottery made in nearby Southall between 1877 and 1915 and fashionable in late

Martinware bird at Pitshanger Manor

Victorian times. The gardens of Pitshanger Manor make this a pleasant public park and provide a welcome contrast to the busy shopping center of nearby Ealing.

Kew Bridge Steam Museum ㊱

Green Dragon Lane, Brentford. ☎ *0181-568 4757.* ⊖ *Kew Bridge, Gunnersbury then bus 237 or 267.* **Open** *11am–5pm daily.* **Closed** *Good Friday & week before Christmas.* **Adm charge.** ⬛ ♿ 🚻 ▢ ▢ ▢

THE 19TH-CENTURY water pumping station, near the north end of Kew Bridge, this has now been opened as a museum of steam power. Its chief exhibits are five giant Cornish beam engines that used to pump the water here from the river Thames, to be distributed through London. The earliest engines, which date from 1820, were originally designed to pump water out of working Cornish tin and copper mines. An exhibition relates to the water supply.

Kew Gardens ㊲

See pp256–7.

City Barge: Strand on the Green

Strand on the Green ㊳

W4. ⊖ *Gunnersbury then bus 237 or 267.*

THIS CHARMING Thames-side walk passes some fine 18th-century houses as well as rows of more modest cottages once inhabited by fishermen. The oldest of its three pubs is the City Barge *(see pp308–9)*, parts of which date from the 15th century; the name is older and derives from when the Lord Mayor's barge was moored on the Thames outside.

Chiswick House ㊴

Burlington Lane W4. ☎ *0181-995 0508.* ⊖ *Chiswick.* **Open** *Apr–Sep: 10am–6pm daily; Oct–Mar: 10am– 4pm Wed–Sun.* **Closed** *1–2pm some days.* **Adm charge.** ⬛ ▢ ▢

COMPLETED IN 1729 to the design of the third Earl of Burlington, this is a textbook example of a Palladian villa. Burlington revered both Palladio and his disciple Inigo

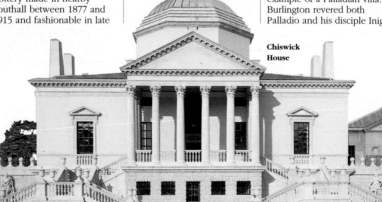

Chiswick House

...nes, and their statues stand outside. Built around a central octagonal room, the house is packed with references to ancient Rome and Palladian devices, such as rooms whose dimensions form perfect cubes.

Chiswick was Burlington's country residence, and this house was built as an annex to a larger, older house, which was later demolished. It was designed for recreation and entertaining – Lord Hervey, Burlington's enemy, dismissed it as "too little to live in and too big to hang on a watch chain." Some of the ceiling paintings are by William Kent, who also laid out the gardens.

The house was a private mental home from 1892 until 1928, when a long process of restoration began. The restorers are still searching for pieces of its original furniture, but the layout of the garden, now a public park, is much as Kent designed it.

Hogarth's House 40

Hogarth Lane, W4. ☎ 0181-994 6757. ⊖ Turnham Green. **Open** Apr–Sep: 11am–6pm Wed–Mon, 2–6pm Sun; Oct–Mar: 11am–4pm Wed–Mon, 2–4pm Sun. **Closed** first 2 wks in Sep, last 3 wks in Dec. 🎫 🅿️ 👟 ground floor only. 📷

W HEN THE PAINTER William Hogarth lived here from 1749 until his death in 1764, he called it "a little country box by the Thames" and painted bucolic views from its windows – he had moved

from Leicester Square (see p103). Today heavy traffic roars by along the Great West Road, on its way to and from Heathrow Airport – rush hour traffic is also notoriously bad here. In an environment as hostile as this, and following years of neglect and then bombing during World War II, the house has managed to survive. It has now been turned into a small museum and gallery, which is mostly filled with a collection of engraved copies of the moralistic cartoon-style pictures by which Hogarth made his name. Moralistic tales, such as *The Rake's Progress* (in Sir John Soane's Museum – see pp136–7), *Marriage à la Mode*, *An Election Entertainment* and many others, can all be seen here.

Plaque on Hogarth's House

Fulham Palace 41

Bishops Ave SW6. ☎ 0171-736 3233. ⊖ Putney Bridge. **Open** Wed–Sun, public hols Mon, Mar–Oct: 2–5pm; Nov–Mar: 1–4pm Thu–Sun. **Closed** Dec 25–26. **Park open** daylight hours. **Adm charge.** 👟 🎫 🅿️ 📷 **Events, concerts, lectures.**

T HE HOME of the Bishops of London from the 8th century until 1973, the oldest parts of Fulham Palace date from the 15th century. The rest of the building has been embellished in a mixture of styles by successive bishops. The palace stands in its own gardens in Bishop's Park west and north of Putney Bridge, where the annual Oxford versus Cambridge Boat Race begins (see p56).

Tudor entrance to Fulham Palace

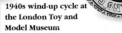

1940s wind-up cycle at the London Toy and Model Museum

Chelsea Harbour 42

SW10. ⊖ Fulham Broadway. 👟 **Exhibitions.** 💻 📷

T HIS IS AN impressive development of modern apartments, shops, offices, restaurants, a hotel and a marina. It is near the site of Cremorne Pleasure Gardens, which closed in 1877 after more than 40 years as a venue for dances and circuses. The centerpiece is the Belvedere, a 20-story apartment tower with an external glass elevator and pyramid roof with a golden ball on a rod that rises and falls with the tide.

London Toy and Model Museum 43

21–23 Craven Hill W2. **Map** 10 E2. ☎ 0171-402 5222. ⊖ Paddington. **Open** 10am–5:30pm Mon–Sat, 11am–5:30pm Sun (last adm: 4:30pm). **Adm charge.** 🅿️ 👟 💻 📷 **Annual exhibitions.**

A N ENORMOUS NUMBER of toys models and dolls, dating from the 18th century up to the present, are crammed into this house near Paddington Station. There is a room of model trains and another of cars; a teddy bears' picnic; and dolls' houses, the biggest of which is 8 ft (2.4 m) long and has 16 rooms. In the garden are a carousel and two model railroads, one of which offers rides. The museum provides many delights and activities for children as well as nostalgic adults.

Kew Gardens 🏷️

THE ROYAL BOTANIC GARDENS at Kew are the most complete public gardens in the world. Their reputation was first established by Sir Joseph Banks, the British naturalist and plant hunter, who worked here in the late 18th century. In 1841 the former royal gardens were given to the nation and now display about 40,000 different kinds of plant. Kew is also a center for scholarly research into horticulture and botany, and garden enthusiasts will want a full day for their visit.

Princess Augusta
King George III's mother established the first garden on a nine-acre (3.6 ha) site here in 1759.

Queen's Cottage

★ **Temperate House**
The building dates from 1899. Delicate woody plants are arranged here according to their geographical origins.

★ **Pagoda**
Britain's fascination with the Orient influenced William Chambers's pagoda, built in 1762.

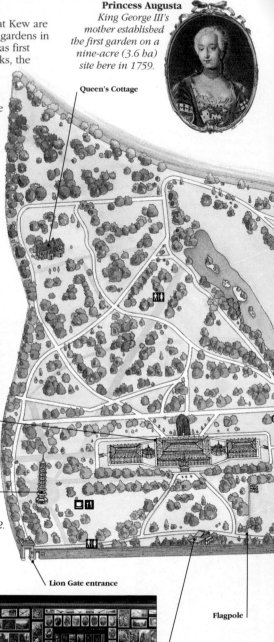

HIGHLIGHTS

Spring
Flowering cherries ①
Crocus "carpet" ②

Summer
Rock Garden ③
Rose Garden ④

Autumn
Autumn foliage ⑤

Winter
Alpine House ⑥
Witch Hazels ⑦

Lion Gate entrance

Flagpole

Marianne North Gallery
The Victorian flower painter Marianne North gave her works to Kew and paid for this gallery in 1882.

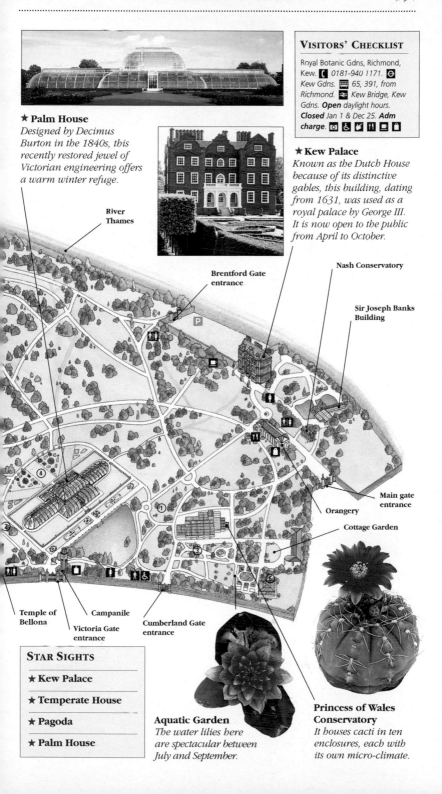

★ Palm House
Designed by Decimus Burton in the 1840s, this recently restored jewel of Victorian engineering offers a warm winter refuge.

River Thames

VISITORS' CHECKLIST

Royal Botanic Gdns, Richmond, Kew. **(** *0181-940 1171.* **⊖** *Kew Gdns.* **🚌** *65, 391, from Richmond.* **🚃** *Kew Bridge, Kew Gdns.* **Open** *daylight hours.* **Closed** *Jan 1 & Dec 25.* **Adm charge.** ⊙ & ✓ 🍴 ▢ ▢

★ Kew Palace
Known as the Dutch House because of its distinctive gables, this building, dating from 1631, was used as a royal palace by George III. It is now open to the public from April to October.

Brentford Gate entrance

Nash Conservatory

Sir Joseph Banks Building

Main gate entrance

Orangery

Cottage Garden

Temple of Bellona

Campanile

Victoria Gate entrance

Cumberland Gate entrance

Aquatic Garden
The water lilies here are spectacular between July and September.

Princess of Wales Conservatory
It houses cacti in ten enclosures, each with its own micro-climate.

FIVE GUIDED WALKS

LONDON IS AN EXCELLENT city for walkers. Although it is much more spread out than most European capitals, many of the main tourist attractions are fairly close to one another *(see pp12–13)*. Central London is full of parks and gardens *(see pp48–51)*, and there are also several walks planned by the tourist board and local history societies. These include footpaths along canals and the Thames, as well as the Silver Jubilee Walk. Planned in 1977 to commemorate the Queen's Silver Jubilee, the walk runs for 12 miles (19 km) between Lambeth Bridge in the west and Tower Bridge in the east; the London Tourist Board *(see p345)* has maps of the route, which is marked by silver-colored plaques placed at intervals on the pavement. Each of

Statue of boy and dolphin in Regent's Park

the 16 areas described in the *Area by Area* section of this book has a short walk marked on its *Street-by-Street* map. These walks will take you past many of the most interesting sights in that area. On the following ten pages are routes for five walks that take you through areas of London not covered in detail elsewhere. These range from the crowded 18th-century streets of Mayfair *(see pp260–61)* to the wide open spaces of riverside Richmond and Kew *(see pp268–9)*.

Several companies offer guided walks *(see below)*. Most of these have themes, such as ghosts or Shakespeare's London. Look in magazine listings *(see p324)* for details.

Useful numbers The Original London Walks **℡** *0171-624 3978.* City Walks **℡** *0171-700 6931.*

CHOOSING A WALK

The Five Walks
This map shows the location of the five guided walks in relation to the main sightseeing areas of London.

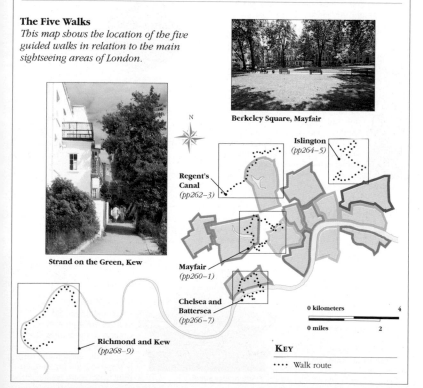

Berkeley Square, Mayfair

Strand on the Green, Kew

Islington *(pp264–5)*

Regent's Canal *(pp262–3)*

Mayfair *(pp260–1)*

Chelsea and Battersea *(pp266–7)*

Richmond and Kew *(pp268–9)*

N

0 kilometers 4

0 miles 2

KEY

•••• Walk route

Houseboats on Regent's Canal, Little Venice

A Two-Hour Walk through Mayfair

THIS WALK PENETRATES the heart of Mayfair and Knightsbridge, London's most elegant Georgian residential districts. It includes a bracing stroll through the green elegance of Hyde Park and, if you wish, a row on the gray waters of the Serpentine.

L'Artiste Musclé, Shepherd Market ⑦

Green Park to Berkeley Square

Leave Green Park station ① following the signs for Piccadilly North Side. With Green Park opposite you, turn left. Pass Devonshire House ②, a 1920s office block that replaced William Kent's 18th-century mansion for the dukes of Devonshire – only Kent's gates survive, now at the park entrance across Piccadilly. Turn left and walk up Berkeley Street to Berkeley Square ③. To the south, Lansdowne House

Nymph on Berkeley Square ③

TIPS FOR WALKERS

Starting point: Green Park Underground station.
Length: 3 miles (5 km).
Getting there: Green Park, Marble Arch, Hyde Park Corner and Knightsbridge Underground stations are all on the route. Bus Nos. 9, 14, 19, 22, 25 and 38 go to Green Park.
Stopping-off points: There are numerous pubs, cafés and restaurants in the area. The Dell Café on the Serpentine is open 8am–8pm.

---

by Robert Adam has been replaced by the headquarters of an advertising agency ④. There are still some splendid 18th-century houses to the west, including No. 45 ⑤, where the soldier and governor Clive of India lived.

Mayfair

Keep to the south of the square and turn onto Charles Street, noting the evocative lampholders at Nos. 40 and 41 ⑥. Turn left onto Queen Street and cross Curzon Street to enter Shepherd Market ⑦ *(see p97)* through Curzonfield House alleyway. Turning right up the pedestrian-only street, you come to Tiddy Dols Eating House ⑧. Turn right onto Hertford Street, passing the Curzon Cinema ⑨ on the corner of Curzon Street. Here you are almost facing Crewe House ⑩, built in 1730 by the Edward Shepherd who laid out the market.

Turn left and walk up Curzon Street, then turn right onto Chesterfield Street. A left turn at Charles Street brings you to Red Lion Yard ⑪, where a pub stands opposite one of the few weather-boarded buildings in the West End. Turn right into Hay's Mews and left up Chesterfield Hill. Cross Hill Street and South Street and head left until you reach an alley leading to the peaceful

Houses on Berkeley Square ③

0 meters		500
0 yards		500

Memorial on Grosvenor Square ⑭

South Audley Street

haven of Mount Street Gardens ⑫. It leads right up to the Church of the Immaculate Conception ⑬. Cross the garden and turn left onto Mount Street; then right onto South Audley Street and left at Grosvenor Square ⑭ onto Upper Grosvenor Street, passing to the left of the US Embassy (1961). Turn right up Park Lane and walk past the remnants of the houses ⑮ that lined what used to be London's most desirable residential street before the traffic got so heavy.

Hyde Park

Enter the pedestrian subway ⑯ at exit No. 6 and follow signs for Park Lane West Side, exit No. 5. You will emerge at Speakers' Corner ⑰ (see p207). Cross Hyde Park (see p207) south-southwest, making for the boat house ⑱ on the Serpentine, an artificial lake created by Queen Caroline in 1730. You could rent a boat or turn left and follow the path to the Dell Café ⑲. From there, take the stone bridge ⑳ and cross Rotten Row ㉑, where the most fashionable riders exercise their horses. Leave the park at Edinburgh Gate ㉒, where the road tunnels through Bowater House.

**Speakers'
Corner ⑰**

Motcomb Street. On your left is the Pantechnicon, an eccentric structure fronted by colossal Doric columns, built in 1830. A path beside it leads to Halkin Arcade ㉕, which is adorned by Geoffrey Wickham's fountain built in 1971.

Belgravia

Turn left out of the arcade onto Kinnerton Street, which boasts one of London's smallest pubs, the Nag's Head ㉖. Pretty mews run off the left of this street at its northern end: look for Ann's Close and Kinnerton Place North. Almost opposite the latter, the street makes a sharp right turn to emerge into Wilton Place opposite St. Paul's Church (1843). Turn right here and follow Wilton Crescent around to the left before turning left into Wilton Row, where there is another small pub, the Grenadier ㉗, once the officers' mess of the Guards' barracks and reputedly frequented by the Duke of Wellington. Up Old Barracks Yard to its right are some old officers' billets and a worn stone said to have been used by the duke for mounting his horses. The alley leads to a T-junction. Turn right onto Grosvenor Crescent Mews, then left onto Grosvenor Crescent, which leads you to Hyde Park Corner Underground station.

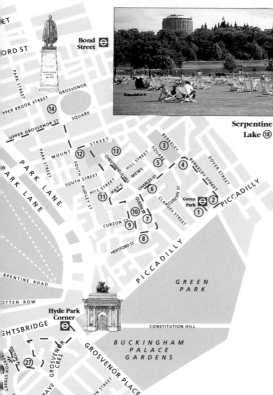

**Serpentine
Lake ⑱**

Knightsbridge

Resisting the temptations of two of London's great department stores – Harvey Nichols ㉓ on your left and Harrods ㉔ (see p207) to your right – cross Knightsbridge and head down Sloane Street to turn left at Harriet Street. At Lowndes Square turn right and leave the square on the far side, turning left on

Grenadier Pub ㉗

A Two-Hour Walk along the Regent's Canal

MASTER BUILDER John Nash wanted the Regent's Canal to pass through Regent's Park, but instead it circles north of the park. Opened in 1820, it is now no longer a commercial waterway but a location for leisure activity. This walk starts at Little Venice and ends at Camden Lock market, diverting briefly to take in the view from Primrose Hill. For more details on the sights near the Regent's Canal, see pages 216 to 223.

Houseboat on the canal ③

From Little Venice to Lisson Grove

At Warwick Avenue station ①, take the left exit and walk straight to the traffic lights by the canal bridge at Blomfield Road. Turn right and descend to the canal after passing through an iron gate ②, marked "Lady Rose of Regent," opposite No. 42. The basin with moored narrow boats is Little Venice ③. At the foot of the steps, turn left to walk back beneath the blue iron bridge ④. You soon have to climb to street level again because this stretch of the towpath is reserved for access to the

The Warwick Castle, near Warwick Avenue

barges. Cross Edgware Road and walk down Aberdeen Place. When the road turns left by a pub, Crockers ⑤, follow the signposted Canal Way down to the right of some modern apartment buildings. A short stretch of path is closed, but you can walk above the canal before rejoining the path down the ramp by the bus stop. The scenery is unremarkable until you reach the splash of green on the right, which is Regent's Park ⑥.

Houseboats moored at Little Venice ③

TIPS FOR WALKERS

Starting point: Warwick Avenue Underground station.
Length: 3 miles (5 km).
Getting there: Warwick Avenue and Camden Town Underground stations are at either end of the walk. Buses 16, 16A and 98 go to Warwick Avenue; 24, 29 and 31 go to Camden Town.
Stopping-off points: Crockers, Queens and The Princess of Wales (corner of Fitzroy and Chalcot roads) are good pubs. At the junction of Edgware Road and Aberdeen Place is Café La Ville. Camden Town has many cafés, restaurants and sandwich shops.

KEY

— Walk route

☼ Good viewing point

Ⓔ Underground station

🚆 British Rail

Regent's Park

Soon you'll see four mansions ⑦. A bridge on huge pillars marked "Coalbrookdale" ⑧ carries Avenue Road into the park. Cross the next bridge, with London Zoo ⑨ on your right, then turn left and go up a slope. A few steps later, take the right fork and turn left to cross Prince Albert Road. Turn right before entering Primrose Hill through the gate ⑩ on your left.

Mansion with riverside gardens ⑦

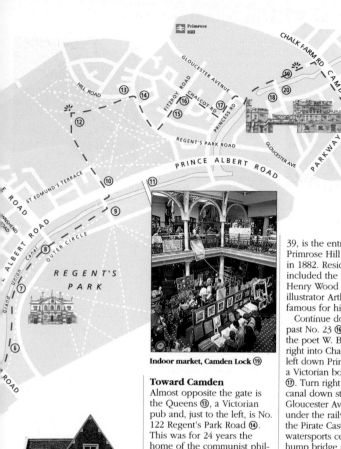

Primrose Lodge, Primrose Hill ⑩

Primrose Hill

From here there is a view of the zoo aviary ⑪, designed by Lord Snowdon and opened in 1965. Inside the park, keep to the left path and climb to the top of the hill then fork right to the summit, which offers a fine view of the city skyline. A viewing panel ⑫ identifies the landmarks but does not include the 1990 skyscraper at Canary Wharf, with its pyramid crown, on the left. Descend on the left, and head for the park gate at the junction of Regent's Park Road and Primrose Hill Road.

Indoor market, Camden Lock ⑲

Toward Camden

Almost opposite the gate is the Queens ⑬, a Victorian pub and, just to the left, is No. 122 Regent's Park Road ⑭. This was for 24 years the home of the communist philosopher Friedrich Engels; he was often visited there by his friend Karl Marx.

Turn to the right and walk down Regent's Park Road for 150 yd (135 m), then turn left up Fitzroy Road. On the right, between Nos. 41 and 39, is the entrance to Primrose Hill Studios ⑮, built in 1882. Residents have included the musician Sir Henry Wood and the illustrator Arthur Rackham, famous for his fairy pictures.

Continue down Fitzroy Road past No. 23 ⑯, once home to the poet W. B. Yeats, then go right into Chalcot Road and left down Princess Road, past a Victorian boarding school ⑰. Turn right and rejoin the canal down steps across Gloucester Avenue. Turn left under the railway bridge, past the Pirate Castle ⑱, a watersports center. Cross a hump bridge and enter Camden Lock Market ⑲ *(see p322)* through an arch on your left. After browsing there you can take the water bus ⑳ back to Little Venice or turn right into Chalk Farm Road and walk up to Camden Town Underground station.

Pedestrian bridge over the canal at Camden Lock ⑲

A Two-Hour Walk in Islington

THIS WALK OF CONTRASTS starts in the quiet streets of Canonbury, which have intriguing literary associations. It traces the route of a 17th-century artificial river, visits a canalside pub and ends among London's most concentrated array of antique shops.

Canonbury Grove houses

Canonbury Square

Turn right after leaving Highbury and Islington station ① and head southeast down Canonbury Road. The road soon dissects Canonbury Square ②, laid out in 1800. Turning left into the eastern half will take you through the garden with its flower beds and statue. The novelist Evelyn Waugh lived at No. 17a ③ in 1928, while the writer George Orwell lived at No. 27a ④ in 1945.

Canonbury

Leaving the square at the northeast corner, you face the late 18th-century Canonbury House ⑤. Other charming houses from the same period line the cul-de-sac to its right. Next to it is the historic Canonbury Tower ⑥, which is mainly 16th-century, although parts date from the 13th century, when the de Berners family built its manor

Statue in Canonbury Square

house here, in what was then countryside. Later it was occupied by the canons of St. Bartholomew, hence the name Canonbury. The tower, now the home of a theater company, served as an apartment house in the 18th century; the writers Oliver Goldsmith and Washington Irving were among its residents. Beyond the Tower, turn left into Canonbury Park North ⑦. Where the street meets St Paul's Road, opposite the New Crown Pub ⑧, turn right and, after a few steps, right again along a paved lane between trees. After 30 yd (25 m) go through the gate on the right into the New River Walk ⑨.

New River Walk

The New River was a real feat of engineering for its day. In the 17th century Sir Hugh Myddleton, a Welsh jeweler, cut a 40-mile (65-km) channel to bring water from Hertfordshire. Today, a landscaped park lines part of its course. Keep to the path until you go over a stone bridge ⑩ and reach Willow Bridge Road. Cross the road and turn left, reentering the river walk through a gate ⑪ in Canonbury Grove. You pass a round brick hut ⑫ just before exiting on Canonbury

View along the towpath of the Grand Union Canal ⑮

The river walk at Canonbury Grove ⑨ – ⑫

Grove. The final stretch of this walk ⑬ is in a park across Canonbury Road. Head southeast down Canonbury Road and into New North Road; after 500 yds (450 m) turn left into Shepperton Road ⑭. At the junction with Baring Street, go through the gate and down the steps to the towpath of the Grand Union Canal ⑮.

Along the Grand Union Canal

At the foot of the steps go straight ahead, with the canal on your left. This is a very different waterside walk from the bucolic New River; here the canal is lined with old industrial buildings and new housing estates. On weekends fishermen sit silently in hope, not

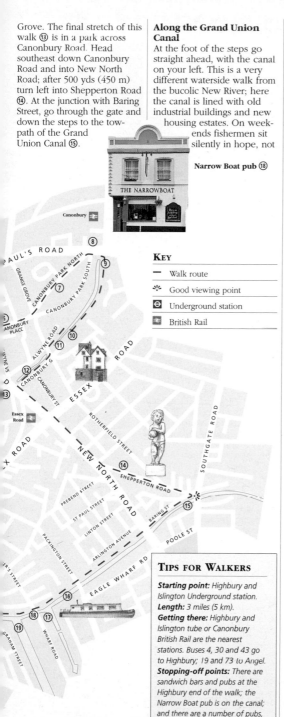

Narrow Boat pub ⑱

KEY

—	Walk route
☀	Good viewing point
Ⓔ	Underground station
⬛	British Rail

catching much. Soon Sturt's Lock ⑯ will come into view; beyond the lock are a few houseboats moored near the entrance to Wenlock Basin ⑰. On the right, the Narrow Boat Pub ⑱ is ideal for a refreshment stop.

Beyond the City Road Lock and Basin ⑲, the right of way switches to the opposite bank – this route must be taken to avoid a dead-end. Leave the towpath on Danbury Street and cross the bridge ⑳ to descend on the other side. You finally leave the canal at the entrance to the 800-yd (730-m) Islington Tunnel ㉑, climbing steps up to Colebrooke Row.

Camden Passage antiques shop

Islington

Turn right here, past some fine Georgian terraces ㉒, then go left at the Market Tavern into St. Peter's Street and left again at Islington Green ㉓, in Victorian times renowned as the site of the lively Collins' Music Hall. Just past the service station on your left, you can enter Camden Passage, the heart of a network of antiques shops, indoor markets and excellent restaurants.

After you have passed the Camden Head Pub ㉔, you will see, on the south end of the green, a statue of Sir Hugh Myddleton ㉕, whose river you explored earlier. Follow Islington High Street south; on the left, just before the junction with City Road, is the Angel Underground station, named after the coaching inn that used to stand nearby.

Sir Hugh Myddleton ㉕

TIPS FOR WALKERS

Starting point: Highbury and Islington Underground station.
Length: 3 miles (5 km).
Getting there: Highbury and Islington tube or Canonbury British Rail are the nearest stations. Buses 4, 30 and 43 go to Highbury; 19 and 73 to Angel.
Stopping-off points: There are sandwich bars and pubs at the Highbury end of the walk; the Narrow Boat pub is on the canal; and there are a number of pubs, cafés and restaurants clustered around the Angel.

0 meters   250
0 yards   250

A Three-Hour Walk in Chelsea and Battersea

THIS DELIGHTFUL CIRCULAR WALK begins on the grounds of the Royal Hospital and crosses the river to Battersea Park, with its romantic Victorian landscaping. It then returns through the narrow village streets of Chelsea and the stylish shops on King's Road. For more details on the sights in Chelsea see pages 188–93.

Royal Hospital ③

Sloane Square to Battersea Park

From the station ①, turn left and walk down Holbein Place named for the Renaissance painter who frequented Chelsea. Holbein was friends with Sir Thomas More, who lived nearby. Pass the cluster of good antiques shops ② at the turn onto Royal Hospital Road. Enter the grounds of the Royal Hospital ③, designed by Christopher Wren, and turn left into the informal Ranelagh Gardens ④. The small pavilion by John Soane ⑤ displays a history of the gardens as a Georgian pleasure resort – it was the most fashionable meeting place for London society.

Galleon on Chelsea Bridge

Charles II statue in Royal Hospital ⑥

Leave the gardens for fine views of the hospital and Grinling Gibbons's bronze of Charles II ⑥. The granite obelisk ⑦ commemorates the 1849 battle at Chilianwalla, in what is now Pakistan, and forms the center-piece of the main marquee at the Chelsea Flower Show *(see p56)*.

Battersea Park

When crossing the Chelsea Bridge ⑧ (1937), look up at the four gilded galleons on top of the pillars at each end. Turn into Battersea Park ⑨ *(see p247)*, one of London's liveliest, and follow the main path along the river to enjoy the excellent views of Chelsea. Turn left at the exotic Buddhist Peace Pagoda ⑩ to the main part of the park.

Past the bowling greens lies Henry Moore's carving of *Three Standing Figures* ⑪ (1948) and the lake, a favorite spot for birds and ducks. (There are boats for rent.) Just beyond the sculpture head northwest and, after crossing the central avenue, turn right toward the wooden gate into the rustic Old English Garden ⑫. Leave the garden by the metal gate and return to Chelsea via the Victorian Albert Bridge ⑬.

Three Standing Figures by Henry Moore ⑪

KEY

— Walk route

☀ Good viewing point

🚇 Underground station

TIPS FOR WALKERS

Starting point: *Sloane Square.*
Length: *4 miles (6.5 km).*
Getting there: *Sloane Square is the nearest tube. There are frequent buses 11, 19, 22 and 349 to Sloane Square and along the King's Road.*
Royal Hospital Grounds *are open only 10am–6pm Mon–Sat, 2–6pm Sun.*
Refreshment areas: *There is a café in Battersea Park, by the lake. The King's Head and Eight Bells, on Cheyne Walk, is a well-known local pub. There are several other pubs, restaurants and sandwich shops to be found along the King's Road. The Chelsea Farmers' Market on Sydney Street has several cafés.*

Old English Garden in Battersea Park ⑫

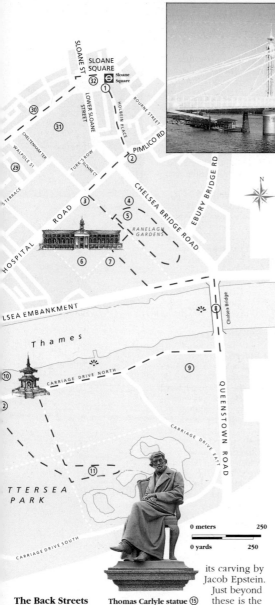

Albert Bridge ⑬

much of its original character. Where Glebe Place meets King's Road are three lovely, early 18th-century houses ㉓. Cross Dovehouse Green opposite (it used to be a burial ground), to Chelsea Farmers' Market ㉔, an enclave of cafés and crafts shops.

The King's Road

Leave the market on Sydney Street and cross into the garden of St. Luke's Church ㉕, where the writer Charles Dickens was married. The walk then winds through pretty back streets until it rejoins King's Road ㉖ (see p192), which was very fashionable in the 1960s. On the left is The Pheasantry ㉗. Look down the side streets on both left and right to see the squares and terraces: Wellington Square ㉘, then Royal Avenue ㉙, intended as a triumphal way to the Royal Hospital, and Blacklands Terrace ㉚, where book lovers will want to visit John Sandoe's shop. The Duke of York's Territorial Headquarters ㉛ (1803) on the right marks the approach to Sloane Square ㉜ and the Royal Court Theatre (see Sloane Square p193).

The Back Streets of Chelsea

Thomas Carlyle statue ⑮

Over the bridge is David Wynne's sculpture of a boy and dolphin ⑭ (1975). Pass the sought-after residences on Cheyne Walk and the statues of historian Thomas Carlyle ⑮, and Sir Thomas More ⑯. The area was renowned for gatherings of intellectuals. Past Chelsea Old Church ⑰ is Roper's Gardens ⑱, with

its carving by Jacob Epstein. Just beyond these is the old, medieval Crosby Hall ⑲. Justice Walk ⑳ has a nice view of two early Georgian houses – Duke's House and Monmouth House. Turn left to pass the site of the Chelsea porcelain factory ㉑, which used to make highly fashionable (and today very highly collectible) wares in the late 18th century. Glebe Place ㉒ has retained

Royal Court Theatre ㉜

A 90-Minute Walk around Richmond and Kew

THIS DELIGHTFUL RIVERSIDE walk begins in historic
Richmond by the remains of Henry VII's once-
splendid palace and ends at Kew, Britain's premier
botanical garden. For more details on the sights in
Richmond and Kew, turn to pages 248 to 254.

The river at low tide

Richmond Green
From Richmond station ①,
proceed to Oriel House ②,
which is practically opposite.
Take the alleyway beneath it,
and turn left toward the red-
brick-and-terra-cotta
Richmond Theatre
③, built in 1899.
The remarkable
Edmund Kean,
whose brief, meteoric
career in the early 19th
century had a lasting
impact on English
acting, was closely
associated with the
previous theater on
the site. Opposite is
Richmond Green ④. Cross it
diagonally and go through
the entrance arch ⑤ of the
old Tudor palace, which is
adorned with the arms of
Henry VII.

**Old Palace: carving
over entrance ⑤**

remnants, much modified, of
the 16th-century buildings.
Leave Old Palace Yard at
the right corner ⑥, following
a sign "To the River," and turn
left to pass the White Swan
pub ⑦. At the river,
go right along the
towpath under the
iron railway bridge
and then the concrete
Twickenham Bridge
⑧, completed in 1933,
to reach Richmond
Lock ⑨, with its
cast-iron footbridge
built in 1894. The
Thames is tidal as far
as Teddington, some 3 miles
(5 km) upstream, and the lock
is used to make the river
continuously navigable.

The Riverside
Do not cross the bridge but
continue along the wooded
path by the river to Isleworth
Ait ⑩, a large island where
herons may be standing
warily on the river bank. Just
beyond it, on the far shore, is
All Saints' Church ⑪, where
the 15th-century tower has
survived several rebuildings,
most recently in the 1960s.
Farther along, the inlet,
Isleworth ⑫, once
a small riverside
village with a
busy harbor,
is now a dormi-
tory for central
London. Here
there will be river
traffic to watch:
barges, yachts and,
in summer, the
passenger boats that ply
up-river to Hampton Court
(see pp60–61). Rowers
are out at most times
of year, training for
races and regattas. The most
prestigious occasions are the
Henley Regatta in July and the
Oxford versus Cambridge
boat race, that is held every
spring from Putney to
Mortlake (see p56).

Richmond Theatre ③

Richmond
Richmond owes much of its
importance – as well as its
name – to Henry, victor of the
Wars of the Roses and the
first Tudor monarch. On
becoming king in 1485, he
spent a lot of time at an
earlier residence on this site,
Sheen Palace, dating from the
12th century. The palace
burned down in 1499, and
Henry had it rebuilt, naming
it Richmond after the town in
Yorkshire where he held an
earldom. In 1603, Henry's
daughter, Elizabeth I, died
here. The houses inside the
archway on the left contain

**Herons fish
the river**

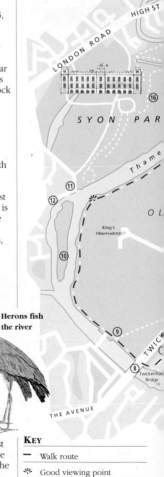

KEY

—	Walk route
☀	Good viewing point
Ⓔ	Underground station
⚏	British Rail

Kew

After a while, the iron railings on your right will signal you where Old Deer Park ⑬ turns into Kew Gardens ⑭ (more correctly the Royal Botanic Gardens; see pp256–7). There used to be a riverside entrance for visitors arriving on foot or by water, but the gate ⑮ is now closed, and the nearest

Kew Palace in Kew Gardens ⑲

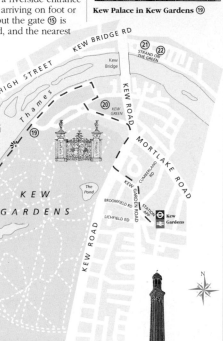

Steam Museum ⑱

0 meters	500
0 yards	500

Just beyond are modern waterside apartments at Brentford ⑰. This was originally an industrial suburb, sited where the Grand Union Canal runs into the Thames, and its residential potential has only recently been exploited. You can pick out the tall chimney of the waterworks ⑱, now a museum dedicated to steam power. On the right, behind the Kew Gardens parking lot, there is soon a view of Kew Palace ⑲, a gloomy edifice in red brick built in 1631.

Beyond the parking lot, leave the river by Ferry Lane and take it to Kew Green ⑳. You could spend the rest of the day in Kew Gardens or cross Kew Bridge and turn right on to Strand on the Green ㉑, a riverside walkway with atmospheric pubs, the oldest of them the City Barge ㉒ (see p256). Head south down Kew Road to get back, then turn left at Kew Gardens Road for Kew Gardens Underground station (District line).

TIPS FOR WALKERS

Starting point: Richmond station.
Length: 3 miles (5 km).
Getting there: Richmond Underground or British Rail station. Bus 415 comes from Victoria; 391 and R68 from Kew.
Stopping-off points: There are many cafés, pubs and tearooms in Richmond. The famous Maids of Honour tearoom is at Kew, as is Jasper's Bun in the Oven, a good restaurant.

entrance is to the north, near the parking lot. Across the river, there are magnificent views of Syon House ⑯, seat of the dukes of Northumberland since 1594. Part of the present house dates from the 16th century, but it was largely redesigned by Robert Adam in the 1760s. The garden across which you'll be looking was laid out by landscape gardener Capability Brown in the 18th century.

The riverbank between Richmond and Kew

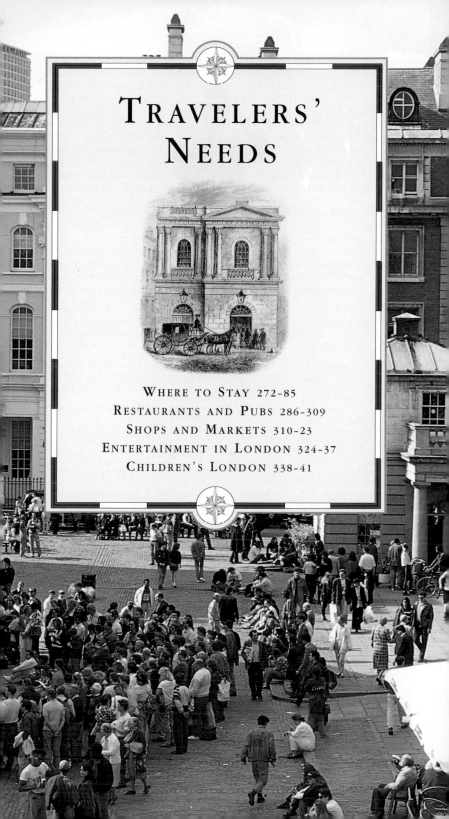

TRAVELERS' NEEDS

WHERE TO STAY

Lᴏɴᴅᴏɴ's ʜᴏᴛᴇʟs have had one of the worst reputations for value in Europe, but things are improving rapidly. At the top end of the market, there are the reliable, if expensive, international establishments and the pedigree hotels, such as the Savoy and the Ritz, for which London is renowned. Many of the mid-range hotels offer better value, although they tend to be slightly farther out of the center of town. There is, however, a distinct lack of appealing hotels at the lower end of the market, and budget hotels can be rather seedy and run down.

Hilton doorman

We have inspected more than 200 hotels across a wide range of price brackets and have selected 84 of them as offering visitors particularly good value. *Choosing a Hotel* on pages 276–7 will help you to narrow down your choice; for further details on each of the hotels turn to the listings, which are found on pages 278–85.

Apart from hotels, there are several other options worth considering. Furnished apartments and private homes *(see pp274–5)* are available at a wide range of prices, and there are camping sites, dorms and hostels for students and budget travelers *(see p275)*.

WHERE TO LOOK

Tʜᴇ ᴍᴏsᴛ ᴇxᴘᴇɴsɪᴠᴇ hotels tend to be in smart West End areas, such as Mayfair and Belgravia. Often large and opulent, with uniformed flunkies, they are not always the most relaxing places to stay. For smaller but still luxurious hotels, head for South Kensington or Holland Park.

The streets off Earl's Court Road are full of hotels at the bottom of the price range. Several of the big railroad stations are well served with smaller hotels, too. Try Ebury Street near Victoria or Sussex Gardens near Paddington. From Euston, head for Bloomsbury (avoiding the undesirable area behind King's Cross), where several modern hotels offer sensibly priced accommodations.

There are inexpensive hotels in the suburbs, such as Ealing, Hendon, Wembley and Harrow, where you can leave your car and get into town easily on public transportation (although it may take an hour or more to do so).

If you get stranded at an airport or have to catch a very early morning flight, consult the list on pages 356–7.

For further information, advice and reservation services, contact the **London Tourist Board,** which offers useful leaflets about all sorts of accommodations in central and Greater London.

DISCOUNT RATES

Pʀɪᴄᴇs ᴛᴇɴᴅ to be high all year round, but there are usually bargains to be had. Many hotels, including the big groups, reduce their rates on weekends and for special package deals *(see p274)*. Others work on a more ad hoc basis, depending on how busy they are. If a hotel isn't full, it is always worth trying to negotiate a discount.

Hotels in the lower price brackets often offer rooms without attached showers or bathrooms. These cost about 20% less than the full rates.

HIDDEN EXTRAS

Tʜᴇʀᴇ ɪs ᴀ tendency to quote rates exclusive of VAT (currently 17.5% – *see p310*), and the final bill can come as a shock. Read the small print carefully. Most hotels give room rates rather than rates per person, but check. You should also check the service charge, which is usually included in the quoted price but in some cases is added on. Beware of extras, such as a mark-up on telephone calls.

The Tearoom at the Waldorf Hotel *(see p284)*

The Hampshire Hotel *(see p283)*

Breakfast is likely to be charged on top of the room rate in more expensive hotels but tends to be included in the price in cheaper ones. Continental breakfast usually consists of coffee, fruit juice and a roll, toast or croissants with jam. English (or full) breakfast will see you through the busiest morning of sight-seeing. At its most basic it consists of cereal and fruit juice, followed by bacon, eggs and toast *(see p288)*.

Tipping is expected in the more expensive hotels. There is generally no need to tip staff other than porters, the exception being the concierge if, for example, he or she books theater tickets for you.

Single travelers are usually charged a "supplement" and end up paying about 80% of the double room rate, even if they are occupying a "single" room – so make sure you get a good one.

The elegant hallway of the Gore Hotel in Kensington *(see p279)*

FACILITIES

Rooms at all prices can be small (see the chart on pages 276–7 for hotels with larger-than-average rooms), but all except the most basic provide at least a telephone and television. In general, recently modernized hotels provide the most facilities at any price level, although in some small and very smart hotels you pay for atmosphere and pampering rather than for minibars and electronic gadgetry.

Whatever the hotel, you will be expected to vacate your room by noon on the day you leave, and sometimes even earlier.

HOW TO RESERVE

It is always advisable to make reservations well in advance, as room availability fluctuates. Reserving directly with the hotel can be done by letter, phone or fax and usually entails giving some kind of guarantee: either a credit-card number from which a cancellation fee can be deducted or a one-night deposit (some hotels will expect more for long stays).

The **London Tourist Board** provides a free reservation service. To take advantage of this, write at least six weeks in advance to the Accommodation Service's Advance Reservation Office stating how much you want to spend. Remember to confirm any reservations they make for you. If you give less than six weeks, notice, a small fee is charged, plus a deposit for your stay, which is deducted from the final bill. You can reserve by credit card over the phone or turn up at an LTB Tourist Information Centre in the Victoria or Liverpool Street station or at Heathrow (on the underground station concourse for terminals 1, 2 and 3). The LTB also has branches at Harrods, Selfridges and the Tower of London.

Accommodation reservation services are also available at the **British Travel Centre** on Regent Street. A number of non-LTB booking agencies

Hotel 167 *(see p278)*

operate from booths in the major railroad stations, too. Unidentified people, who hang around at railway and bus stations offering cheap accommodations to tourists should be avoided.

USEFUL RESERVATION ADDRESSES

British Hotel Reservation Centre
10 Buckingham Palace Rd,
SW1 0QP.
☎ 0171-828 2425.

British Travel Centre
4–12 Lower Regent St,
SW1Y 4PQ.
☎ 0171-930 0572.

Central London Accommodation System and Service
83 Addison Gdns, W14 0DT.
☎ 0171-602 9668.

Concordia Hotel Tourist Bookings Europoint
5–11 Lavington St, SE1 0NZ.
☎ 0171-945 6000.

London Accommodation Centre
22 Wardour St, W1V 3HH.
☎ 0171-287 6315.

London Tourist Board (LTB)
Accommodation Service's Advance Reservations Office
26 Grosvenor Gdns, SW1W 0DU.
☎ 0171-730 3488.
Credit Card Reservation Line
☎ 0171-824 8844 *(for reservations with less than six weeks' notice).*

SPECIAL DISCOUNTS

MANY TRAVEL agencies carry brochures from the major hotel chains listing special offers, which usually require a minimum two-night stay. Some are extraordinarily good value compared to the usual rates. For most travelers, this is the best way to take advantage of London hotels.

Other brochures are produced by independent travel agencies not tied to a single chain, and many privately owned hotels produce their own brochures of

1920s Savoy poster

special package deals. Ferry companies and airlines offer packages including hotel discounts. Sometimes the same hotel may be featured in several brochures at widely differing prices and special offers. It's worth asking the hotel directly what special rates it offers.

DISABLED TRAVELERS

OUR INFORMATION about wheelchair access to hotels was gathered by questionnaire and depends on the hotel's own assessment of its suitability. The **LTB** provides two useful leaflets: *Accessible Accommodation in London* and *London for All*. The booklet *Access in London* can be obtained from RADAR, 25 Mortimer Street, W1N 8AB (0171-637 5400).

TRAVELING WITH CHILDREN

LONDON HOTELS have long been notorious child-free zones, but some of them now try to accommodate children's needs. It is worth asking about deals for children; some hotels have special rates, or allow children to stay free in their parents' room. See *Choosing a Hotel* on pages 276–7 for hotels with facilities for children.

APARTMENTS

MANY AGENCIES offer accommodations in furnished apartments, usually for stays of a week or more. Prices, depending on size and location, start at about £300 per week.

The **Landmark Trust** rents apartments in historic or unusual buildings. These include rooms in Hampton Court *(see pp250–3)* and flats in a pretty 18th-century terrace in the City: one of them was the home of the late poet laureate Sir John Betjeman. A book of Landmark properties is available.

APARTMENT AGENCIES

Ashburn Gardens Apartments
3 Ashburn Gdns, SW7 4DG.
▐ 0171-370 2663.

Astons Budget Studios/ Luxury Apartments
39 Rosary Gdns, SW7 4NQ.
▐ 0171-370 0737.

Ealing Tourist Flats
94 Gordon Rd, W13 8PT.
▐ 0181-566 8187.

The Landmark Trust
Shottesbrooke, Maidenhead, Berkshire, SL6 3SW.
▐ 01628-825925.

Service Suites
42 Lower Sloane St, SW1W 8BP.
▐ 0171-730 5766.

STAYING IN PRIVATE HOMES

A NUMBER OF agencies arrange stays in private homes; several are registered with the **LTB**. Prices depend on the location and range from £15 to £60 per person per night. Sometimes you will stay with the family, but this isn't guaranteed, so you should make your preference clear when you reserve. Even though you are not making a hotel reservation, the same rules about deposits and cancellation fees may apply. Reservations can be made by credit card through LTB's telephone service *(see p273)*, or through any of the information centers listed under Self-catering. Several agencies have minimum stays of anything up to a week.

Wolsey Lodges, a consortium of private homes, offers pleasant hospitality and often a good dinner. It has four London properties.

AGENCIES FOR STAYS IN PRIVATE HOMES

Alma Tourist Services
21 Griffiths Rd, SW19 1SP.
▐ 0181-542 3771.

Anglo World Travel
123 Shaftesbury Ave, WC2H 8AD.
▐ 0171-436 3601.

At Home in London
70 Black Lion Lane, W6 9BE.
▐ 0181-748-1943.

Host and Guest Service
Harwood House, 27 Effie Rd, SW6 1EN.
▐ 0171-731 5340.

Classical opulence at Claridge's Hotel *(see p282)*

London Home to Home
19 Mount Park Crescent, W5 2RN.
[C] & [FAX] *0181-566 7976.*

Welcome Homes
6 Turnpin Lane, SE10 9JA.
[C] *0181-853 2706.*

Wolsey Lodges
17 Chapel St, Bildeston,
Suffolk, IP7 7EP.
[C] *0144-974 1297.*

BUDGET ACCOMMODATIONS

DESPITE THE generally high
cost of staying in London,
budget possibilities do exist,
and not only for the young.

Dormitory accommodations and youth hostels

These can be reserved
through LTB's information
center at Victoria Station *(see
p273)* for a small fee plus a
refundable deposit. There are
private hostels near Earl's
Court, where a dormitory bed
with breakfast can cost as little
as £10 a night. Don't expect
anything fancy, though. More
upmarket is the **Central Club**,
a Lutyens building run by the
YWCA but open to all. Single
rooms here cost about £30,
much less if you share.
    There are seven **Youth
Hostels Association** hostels
in London. Despite their
name, there is no age limit on
staying in these. One of the
most interesting is Holland
House, a Jacobean mansion
in Holland Park *(see p214).*
Reserve well in advance, as it
is deservedly popular.

HOSTEL ADDRESSES

Central Club
16–22 Great Russell St, WC1B 3LR.
[C] *0171-636 7512.*

Central London Hostel
28 Lancaster Gate, W2 3LP.
[C] *0171-706 1916. An independent
hostel.*

London Hostel Association
54 Eccleston Sq, SW1V 1PG.
[C] *0171-828 3263.*

Youth Hostels Association
Trevelyan House, 8 St Stephen's Hill,
St. Albans,Herts, AL1 2DY.
[C] *017278 55215.*

City of London Youth Hostel

Camping Sites

Tent City in East Acton
(open June-September) is
close to the underground, has
basic facilities and a 400-bed
tented hostel but can't take
trailers. Hackney, Edmonton,
Leyton, Chingford, Abbey
Wood and Crystal Palace sites
are farther from stations, but
have more trailer spaces. The
LTB has a camping leaflet.

CAMPING SITES

Tent City
Old Oak Common Lane, W3 7DP.
[C] *0181-749 9074.*

Halls of residence

Student rooms are available
from July to September at very
reasonable prices. Some of
these are in central locations,
such as South Kensington. It is
best to reserve in advance, but
King's College or **Imperial
College** can sometimes find
a place at short notice.

ADDRESSES FOR RESIDENCE HALLS

**City University Accom-
modation and Conference
Service**
Northampton Sq, EC1V 0HB.
[C] *0171-477 8037.*

**Imperial College Summer
Accommodation Centre**
Room 170, Sherfield Building,
Exhibition Rd, SW7 2AZ.
[C] *0171-594 9507.*

**King's Campus Vacation
Bureau**
King's College London, 552 King's Rd,
SW10 0UA.
[C] *0171-351 6011.*

Choosing a Hotel

THE 84 HOTELS listed on the following pages have all been inspected and assessed. This choosing chart shows a selection of factors affecting the choice of hotel. For more information on each hotel see pages 278–85. The hotels are listed by area and alphabetically within their price categories.

Hotel	Price	Number of Rooms	Large Rooms	Business Facilities	Children's Facilities	Recommended Restaurant	Close to Shops and Restaurants	Quiet Location	24-Hour Room Service
BAYSWATER, PADDINGTON *(see p278)*									
Byron	££	42		■	●			■	●
Delmere	££	38							
Mornington	££	68			●			■	
Whites	££££	54	●	■	●				●
KENSINGTON, HOLLAND PARK, NOTTING HILL *(see p278)*									
Abbey House	£	15					●	■	
Pembridge Court	££	21			●			■	●
Portobello	££	25						■	
Abbey Court	£££	22		■				■	●
Copthorne Tara	£££	825		■			●		●
Halcyon	£££££	44		■	●	■		■	●
SOUTH KENSINGTON, GLOUCESTER ROAD *(see pp278–9)*									
Hotel 167	£	19							
Swiss House	£	16		■					
Aster House	££	12			●			■	
Five Sumner Place	££	13						■	●
Number Sixteen	££	36			●			■	
Cranley	£££	36						■	●
Gore	£££	54		■		■		■	
Pelham	£££	37		■	●				●
Rembrandt	£££	195	●	■					●
Sydney House	£££	21						●	●
Blakes	£££££	52	●	■		■			●
KNIGHTSBRIDGE, BROMPTON, BELGRAVIA *(see pp279–81)*									
Executive	££	29					●		
Knightsbridge Green	££	24			●		●		
Beaufort	£££	28		■	●		●	■	
Basil Street	££££	96		■	●		●		●
Draycott	££££	25		■	●		●		●
Egerton House	££££	28		■			●		●
Eleven Cadogan Gardens	££££	61					●	■	●
Fenja	££££	13		■	●		●		●
Berkeley	£££££	160	●	■			●		●
Capital	£££££	48			●	■		■	●
Halkin	£££££	41	●	■		■			●
Hyatt Carlton Tower	£££££	224	●	■	●	■	●		●
Lowndes	£££££	78		■			●	■	●
WESTMINSTER, VICTORIA *(see p281)*									
Collin House	£	13							
Elizabeth	£	42			●			■	
Windermere	£	23							●
Woodville House	£	12							
Ebury Court	££	42		■					●
Royal Horseguards	£££	376		■				■	●
Stakis London St. Ermins	£££	290		■	●			■	●
Goring	££££	80	●					■	●
Scandic Crown	££££	210	●		●				●

<table>
<tr><td colspan="2">

Price categories for a standard double room per night including breakfast, tax and service:
£ under £70
££ £70–£100
£££ £100–£140
££££ £140–£190
£££££ over £190

CLOSE TO SHOPS AND RESTAURANTS Within a 5-minute walk of a good center for shops and restaurants.

</td><td colspan="2">

CHILDREN'S FACILITIES Family rooms and/or an extra bed in a double room, cribs, a baby-sitting service and children's portions and high chairs in the breakfast room or restaurant

BUSINESS FACILITIES Message-taking service, fax machine for guests, desk and telephone in each room and a meeting room within the hotel.

</td></tr>
</table>

		NUMBER OF ROOMS	LARGE ROOMS	BUSINESS FACILITIES	CHILDREN'S FACILITIES	RECOMMENDED RESTAURANT	CLOSE TO SHOPS AND RESTAURANTS	QUIET LOCATION	24-HOUR ROOM SERVICE
PICCADILLY, MAYFAIR *(see pp281–2)*									
Athenaeum	££££	112	●	■	●		●		●
Inn on the Park	££££	227		■	●	■	●		●
Twenty-two Jermyn St	££££	18	●	■	●		●	■	●
Brown's	£££££	120	●	■			●		●
Claridge's	£££££	190	●	■	●		●		●
Connaught	£££££	90	●			■	●		●
Dorchester	£££££	252	●	■	●	■	●		●
Dukes	£££££	64	●	■			●	●	●
Forty-seven Park Street	£££££	52	●	■		■	●		●
Grosvenor House	£££££	454	●	■	●	■	●		●
Ritz	£££££	129	●	■	●		●		●
SOHO, LEICESTER SQUARE, OXFORD STREET *(see p283)*									
Concorde	£	27			●		●		●
Edward Lear	£	31			●		●		
Parkwood	£	18			●		●	■	●
Bryanston Court	££	56		■			●		
Durrants	£££	96		■			●		
Hazlitt's	£££	23					●		
Marble Arch Marriott	££££	239	●	■	●				●
Hampshire	£££££	124	●	■	●		●		●
REGENT'S PARK, MARYLEBONE *(see pp283–4)*									
Blandford	£££	33						■	
La Place	£££	23		■	●			■	●
Dorset Square	£££	37	●		●			■	●
White House	££££	576		■	●			■	●
Langham Hilton	£££££	387	●	■	●		●		●
BLOOMSBURY, FITZROVIA, COVENT GARDEN, STRAND *(see pp284–5)*									
Mabledon Court	£	33							
Academy	££	33			●				●
Fielding	££	26		■			●		●
Bonnington	£££	215		■	●				●
Russell	£££	328	●	■	●				●
Mountbatten	££££	127	●	■	●		●		●
Waldorf	££££	292		■	●		●		●
Howard	£££££	135	●	■	●				●
Savoy	£££££	200	●	■	●	■	●		●
THE CITY *(see p285)*									
Great Eastern	£££	161		■					●
Tower Thistle	££££	808		■				■	●
FARTHER AFIELD *(see p285)*									
Chase Lodge	£	9			●			■	
La Reserve	££	40		■					●
Swiss Cottage	££	80		■	●			■	
Cannizaro House	£££	46	●	■				■	
Kingston Lodge	£££	62		■	●				
Sheraton Skyline	££££	354	●	■	●				●

BAYSWATER
PADDINGTON

Byron

36–8 Queensborough Terrace, W2 3SH. **Map** 10 E2. (0171-243 0987. FAX 0171-792 1957. TX 263431 BYRON G. **Rooms:** 42.
AE, DC, MC, V. £££

The decor is generally pleasant, ranging from traditional country-house style in the cozy lounge to unfussy simplicity in the bedrooms. The staff are young and pleasant, and the setting is peaceful. Expect nothing fancy in this very friendly and unpretentious hotel.

Delmere

130 Sussex Gdns, W2 1UB. **Map** 11 A2. (0171-706 3344. FAX 0171-262 1863. TX 8953857. **Rooms:** 38. DC, MC, V, JCB. £££

This well-kept building stands out in a line of lackluster neighbors. Furnishings can be pretentious in places, and some bedrooms have been shoe-horned into spaces scarcely adequate. Nonetheless, the hotel is well run and civilized. The comfortable sitting room downstairs has a gas-powered coal fire and supplies of daily newspapers.

Mornington

12 Lancaster Gate, W2 3LG. **Map** 10 F2. (0171-262 7361. FAX 0171-706 1028. TX 24281. **Rooms:** 68. AE, DC, MC, V. £££

This quiet hotel is run with courteous efficiency. The clubby intimacy of the book-lined library lounge provides a good contrast to the almost chilly Scandinavian austerity of the bedrooms. Both the sauna and smorgasbord breakfast reflect the hotel's Swedish ownership.

Whites

90 Lancaster Gate, W2 3NR. **Map** 10 F2. (0171-262 2711. FAX 0171-262 2147. TX 24771. **Rooms:** 54. AE, DC, MC, V. £££££

This large 19th-century hotel overlooking Kensington Gardens has a wedding-cake exterior that will remind you of the seaside. Inside, pretty chandeliers give the attractive public areas a festive and cheery air. The crystal look even extends to the bedrooms, where the decor is a mixture of Oriental, Louis XV and Belle Epoque themes. The historic appearance of these rooms is preserved by having hidden televisions that rise magically from cupboards at the press of a button.

KENSINGTON
HOLLAND PARK
NOTTING HILL

Abbey House

11 Vicarage Gate, W8 4AG. **Map** 10 D4. (0171-727 2594. **Rooms:** 15. £

The outside of this attractively located Victorian family home looks charming, and the proportions of the plant-filled stairwell hint at gracious living. But a no-frills bed-and-breakfast are what Abbey House offers. Bedrooms, though spacious, are very simply furnished, without in-suite bathrooms. The only public area is a bright, cheerful breakfast room in the basement.

Portobello

22 Stanley Gdns, W11 2NG. **Map** 9 B2. (0171-727 2777. FAX 0171-792 9641. **Rooms:** 25. AE, DC, MC, V. £££

This eccentric place around the corner from Portobello Road has a darkish and sophisticated decor that is a mix of Victorian Gothic and Edwardian. The tiniest single rooms have boxlike beds and minute, spartan bathrooms. Larger rooms are available, and for an exotic touch there is the Round Room (a round bed with free-hanging drapes). A casually chic restaurant is downstairs.

Abbey Court

20 Pembridge Gdns, W2 4DU. **Map** 9 C3. (0171-221 7518. FAX 0171-727 8166. TX 262167 ABBYCT. **Rooms:** 22. AE, DC, MC, V. £££

This lavishly decorated and well-kept town house provides a pleasing brand of luxury bed-and-breakfast. An elegant reception lounge and a conservatory break-fast room form the public areas. Bedrooms vary, but all include handsome Victorian-style bathroom fixtures and antiques. An unusually high percentage are singles – handy for lone travelers. Children over 12 are welcome.

Copthorne Tara

Scarsdale Pl, Wright's Lane, W8 5SR. **Map** 8 D1. (0171-937 7211. FAX 0171-937 7100. TX 918834 TARAHL G. **Rooms:** 825. AE, DC, MC, V, JCB. £££

The location, in a quiet side street just off Kensington High Street, is a strong point here. The style and facilities of this modern chain hotel are predictably comfortable and include a number of themed bars.

Pembridge Court

34 Pembridge Gdns, W2 4DX. **Map** 9 C3. (0171-229 9977. FAX 0171-727 4982. TX 298363. **Rooms:** 21. AE, DC, MC, V, JCB. £££

This elegant town-house hotel in a smart quiet street close to Notting Hill Gate is privately owned. It is comfortable and well maintained but not overly ornate. An interesting extra are the displays of costume accessories – gloves, fans, purses – in all the rooms. Caps Restaurant downstairs is an evening-only wine bar.

Halcyon

81 Holland Park, W11 3RZ. **Map** 9 A4. (0171-727 7288. FAX 0171-229 8516. TX 266721. **Rooms:** 44. AE, DC, MC, V. £££££

This is a luxurious hotel in the heart of Holland Park. Behind the splendid Belle Epoque exterior, the beautifully proportioned reception rooms retain all their original features. The bedrooms are hedonistic fantasies filled with canopies, swags and drapes. Bathrooms have whirlpool baths and bidets. The hotel cannot, in all honesty, be described as a bargain, but it does provide a feeling of comfortable opulence.

SOUTH KENSINGTON
GLOUCESTER ROAD

Hotel 167

167 Old Brompton Rd, SW5 0AN. **Map** 18 E3. (0171-373 3221. FAX 0171-373 3360. **Rooms:** 19. AE, DC, MC, V. £

Simple but refreshingly different, this little gem represents a unique brand of bed-and-breakfast. Large modern paintings catch the visitor's eye in the breakfast room and reception area, which doubles as a daytime lounge with its cushiony sofa. The bedrooms are stylishly practical, with small refrigerators, pleasant furnishings and some good bathrooms.

Swiss House

171 Old Brompton Rd, SW5 0AN. **Map** 18 E3. 0171-373 2769. FAX 0171-373 4983. **Rooms:** 16. 11. MC, V.

Trailing plants at the entrance give this tall terraced guesthouse an immediately welcoming look. Inside, the impression is reinforced by the cheerful, cottagey breakfast room – a pine dresser with china and dried-flower arrangements – and by the neat bedrooms, some of which are surprisingly spacious.

Aster House

3 Sumner Pl, SW7 3EE. **Map** 19 A2. 0171-581 5888. FAX 0171-584 4925. **Rooms:** 12. AE, DC, MC, V, JCB.

Several houses in this elegant South Kensington terrace are discreet, elegant hotels, but few have such reasonable rates. L'Orangerie, the hotel's stylish conservatory restaurant, serves health-conscious breakfasts. The bedrooms, all for nonsmokers, are individually decorated in varying degrees of sumptuousness. Children over 12 are welcome.

Five Sumner Place

5 Sumner Pl, SW7 3EE. **Map** 19 A2. 0171-584 7586. FAX 0171-823 9962. **Rooms:** 13. AE, DC, MC, V.

The winner of the British Tourist Association's Best Bed and Breakfast Award in 1991, this Victorian terraced town house is elegant and stylish. An eye-catching conservatory set with blue-skirted breakfast tables and fresh flowers overlooks a pretty patio garden. Upstairs, the bedrooms, all individually decorated, provide quiet, civilized havens from the bustle of central London.

Number Sixteen

16 Sumner Pl, SW7 3EG. **Map** 19 A2. 0171-589 5232. FAX 0171-584 8615. TX 266638. **Rooms:** 36. 34. AE, DC, MC, V.

The unmarked entrance here is typical of the fine little hotels along this smart street of white-painted Victorian houses. The ambience is understated but luxurious. Number Sixteen outdoes its neighbors with better facilities and more extensive public areas, including a conservatory leading to a charming garden with dribbling fountains. The bedrooms are spacious and imaginatively decorated, while the bathrooms are being upgraded. Children over 12 are welcome.

Cranley

10–12 Bina Gdns, SW5 0LA. **Map** 18 E2. 0171-373 0123. FAX 0171-373 9497. TX 991503. **Rooms:** 36. AE, DC, MC, V, JCB.

Antiques and designer fabrics abound in this grand American-owned town-house hotel, although not all of the rooms are particularly large. Discreetly concealed kitchenettes with refrigerators and microwaves are unusual features of the bedrooms. The drawing room is stunning.

Gore

189 Queen's Gate, SW7 5EX. **Map** 10 F5. 0171-584 6601. FAX 0171-589 8127. TX 296244. **Rooms:** 54. AE, DC, MC, V, JCB.

This idiosyncratic Victorian hotel is a sister to Hazlitt's (see p283). The trendy Kensington crowd hustle for tables at its chic Bistrot 190. Restaurant 190 is presided over by one of London's leading chefs, Antony Worrall-Thompson. Bedrooms vary from tiny singles with pine washstands to Tudor fantasies complete with their own minstrel's galleries; many bathrooms have Victorian and Edwardian furniture. Service is endearingly laid-back but always charming, and the rates will not make you gasp.

Pelham

15 Cromwell Pl, SW7 2LA. **Map** 19 A1. 0171-589 8288. FAX 0171-584 8444. TX 881 4714 TUDOR G. **Rooms:** 37. AE, MC, V.

Less than a minute from the South Kensington tube station, the Pelham looks like it's from the pages of a glossy magazine. From the 18th-century paneling in the drawing room to the flowers in the bedrooms, everything shows perfect housekeeping and exquisite (if opulent) taste. The restaurant (which also functions as lounge and bar) is particularly comfortable.

Rembrandt

11 Thurloe Pl, SW7 2RS. **Map** 19 A1. 0171-589 8100. FAX 0171-225 3363. TX 295828. **Rooms:** 195. AE, DC, MC, V, JCB.

This large hotel opposite the Victoria and Albert Museum is corporate in appearance but the atmosphere throughout its refurbished interior is peaceful. There is a pool downstairs.

Sydney House

9–11 Sydney St, SW3 6PU. **Map** 19 A1. 0171-376 7711. FAX 0171-376 4233. **Rooms:** 21. AE, DC, MC, V, JCB.

The palazzo wall treatments, Bugatti furniture and Baccarat chandeliers of the foyer set the tone here. Each room is a self-contained miniworld: Biedermeier here, Paris fabrics there. The sunny dining room features navy wicker. For this kind of style, the rates are reasonable.

Blakes

33 Roland Gdns, SW7 3PF. **Map** 18 F3. 0171-370 6701. FAX 0171-373 0442. TX 8813500. **Rooms:** 52. AE, DC, MC, V, JCB.

Designer Anouska Hempel's dashing establishment is a London legend. The racing-green facade distinguishes it instantly, and the exotic, scented interior declares that this is no ordinary hotel. Each bedroom is a unique extravaganza of deep colors, rich silks and opulent furnishings such as brocaded four-posters and antique lacquered chests.

KNIGHTSBRIDGE
BROMPTON
BELGRAVIA

Executive

57 Pont St, SW1X 0BD. **Map** 19 C1. 0171-581 2424. FAX 0171-589 9456. TX 9413498 EXECUT G. **Rooms:** 29. AE, DC, MC, V.

This unobtrusive historic town house lies a short stroll from some of London's most exclusive shops. Beyond the gracious entrance hall, bedrooms are modern but formally furnished. Downstairs, a buffet breakfast is served each morning in an attractive room of pink Chinese Chippendale.

Knightsbridge Green

159 Knightsbridge, SW1X 7PD.
Map 11 C5. 🅲 *0171-584 6274.*
📠 *0171-225 1635.* **Closed** *Dec 24–27.* **Rooms:** *24.*

Its proximity to Harrods, coupled with its reassuring ambience, makes this long-established, elegant bed-and-breakfast popular with women. Tea and coffee are available all day in the Club Room, where magazines lie on the large central coffee table. Most bedrooms have attached sitting rooms where breakfast is served. Decor is restful, and the practical details of lighting, soundproofing, and storage space are a plus.

Beaufort

33 Beaufort Gdns, SW3 1PP.
Map 19 B1. 🅲 *0171-584 5252.*
📠 *0171-589 2834.* 🆃 *929200.*
Rooms: *28.* AE, DC, MC, V, JCB.

Sheer elegance at least partially excuses the high rates of this classy little place tucked away in a leafy cul-de-sac near Harrods. Fresh flowers, stylish fabrics and floral watercolors characterize its delightful bedrooms. Downstairs, Harry (the hedonistic resident cat) may monopolize one of the luxurious sofas. Personal service and pampering are what you pay for, and neither is in short supply. Children over 10 are welcome.

Basil Street

Basil St, SW3 1AH. **Map** 11 C5.
🅲 *0171-581 3311.* 📠 *0171-581 3693.* 🆃 *28379.* **Rooms:** *96.* 73.
AE, DC, MC, V.

The civilized but unintimidating atmosphere of this old-fashioned privately owned hotel with an unpretentious Edwardian air explains its enduring popularity. The comfortable lounge bar is a perfect place to relax for afternoon tea. Its wine bar and upper carvery are excellent value for the area, and the unique Parrot Club for women (men can visit by invitation only) is an interesting answer to the leathery male bastions found elsewhere in London's hotels. Many of the regular "Basilites" are women.

Draycott

24–6 Cadogan Gdns, SW3 2RP.
Map 19 C2. 🅲 *0171-730 6466.*
📠 *0171-730 0236.* **Rooms:** *25.*
AE, DC, MC, V.

This unobtrusive Knightsbridge mansion is more like a residential club than a hotel. Downstairs by the entrance is a small paneled "smoking room" where blazing fires are lit in winter and newspapers are available year round, as though you're in some well-mannered private country house. Plants, antiques, prints and marble baths furnish the varying bedrooms, many of which have garden views.

Egerton House

17–19 Egerton Terrace, SW3 2BX.
Map 19 B1. 🅲 *0171-589 2412.*
📠 *0171-584 6540.* **Rooms:** *28.*
AE, DC, MC, V.

This smart, recently decorated town house provides high standards of both service and comfort. The style is urbane and professional. Although some of the furnishings have not yet achieved the patina of age, they certainly look good enough to stand alongside what are obviously genuine antiques.

Eleven Cadogan Gardens

11 Cadogan Gdns, SW3 2RJ.
Map 19 C2. 🅲 *0171-730 3426.*
📠 *0171-730 5217.* 🆃 *8813318.*
Rooms: *61.* AE, MC, V.

From the outside you would never guess that this red-brick mansion is a hotel. Perhaps it explains why so many famous people retreat here for peace and privacy when they become tired of being lionized by the public. An atmosphere of quiet good taste and unobtrusive service matches the paneling on the walls and the crisp sheets on the beds. Furnished with dignity and conservative elegance, the more mundane of hotel-type trappings are largely absent from this establishment.

Fenja

69 Cadogan Gdns, SW3 2RB.
Map 19 C2. 🅲 *0171-589 7333.*
📠 *0171-581 4958.* **Rooms:** *13.*
AE, DC, MC, V.

Hidden in a maze of Victorian mansions, this quietly grand bed-and-breakfast has the air of a private home. Paintings, antique busts and fine china fill the house, and many of the building's original features remain – including fireplaces, cornices and huge windows. Breakfast is served in the peaceful and comfortable bedrooms, and light meals can be ordered at other times of the day.

Berkeley

Wilton Pl, SW1X 7RL. **Map** 12 D5.
🅲 *0171-235 6000.* 📠 *0171-235 4330.* 🆃 *919252.* **Rooms:** *160.*
AE, DC, MC, V, JCB.

The discreet main entrance to this august member of the Savoy Group of hotels leads to a dignified hallway of marble and Lutyens paneling. The Buttery and Bar downstairs are slightly less formal, while bedrooms display unusual individuality.

Capital

22–4 Basil St, SW3 1AT. **Map** 11 C5.
🅲 *0171-589 5171.* 📠 *0171-225 0011.* **Rooms:** *48.*
AE, DC, MC, V.

The Capital is a small and distinctly luxurious hotel with a noted restaurant. Furnishings are imaginative and elaborate in a French fin-de-siècle mode. Its sister next door at No. 28, the equally stylish L'Hôtel (0171-589 6286), offers less expensive rooms but has fewer facilities and no room service.

Halkin

5 Halkin St, SW1X 7DJ. **Map** 12 D5.
🅲 *0171-333 1000.* 📠 *0171-333 1100.* **Rooms:** *41.*
AE, DC, MC, V, JCB.

For those weary of artificial period charm, the minimalism of the Halkin will come as a breath of fresh air. A restrained palette of blue and gray plus black and white creates a cool, sophisticated and utterly contemporary look. The bedrooms luxuriate in tawny marble, state-of-the-art bedside consoles and furniture in coppery veneers.

Hyatt Carlton Tower

Cadogan Pl, SW1X 9PY. **Map** 19 C1.
🅲 *0171-235 1234.* 📠 *0171-245 6570.* 🆃 *21944.* **Rooms:** *224.*
AE, DC, MC, V, JCB.

This large chain hotel avoids the usual soullessness of its type. The staff are well-trained and friendly. In some places the furnishings are predictable, but the Chinoiserie Lounge, where a harpist plays, is a wonderful place to rest weary feet after sightseeing or shopping. After tasting the wicked pastries you can head up to the health club to restore muscle tone.

Lowndes

Lowndes St, SW1X 9ES. **Map** 20 D1.
[0171-823 1234. FAX 0171-235
1154. TX 919065. **Rooms:** 78.
1 ⊞ 24 ✕ 🍽 🛏 🖪 🖬
🍷 ⊞ 🄴 AE, DC, MC, V, JCB.
£££££

This little sister of the Hyatt
Carlton Tower just around the
corner has a pleasant small-scale
feel, and guests can use the
larger hotel's excellent facilities at no
extra cost. The designer country-
house reception lounge provides
a relaxing place to read papers
over coffee. Bedrooms contain a
panoply of excellent facilities
amid smart contemporary decor.
The Biedermeier Suite is the most
expensive, with high-quality
reproduction furnishings.

WESTMINSTER
VICTORIA

Collin House

104 Ebury St, SW1W 9QD.
Map 20 E2. [0171-730 8031.
Closed 2 weeks at Christmas.
Rooms: 13. 🛏 8. 1 ⊞ £

This small guesthouse
distinguishes itself from its
similar neighbors by its pleasant
welcome, and if the decor is
scarcely fashionable, the rooms
are fresh and clean. A minute
breakfast room, cheered up by
landscape photographs and honey
pine, is the only public room.

Elizabeth

37 Eccleston Sq, SW1V 1PB.
Map 20 F2. [0171-828 6812.
FAX 0171-828 6814. **Rooms:** 42.
🛏 25. 1 ⊞ 🖪 🖬 🄴 £

This is a slightly shabby yet
respectable hotel. Public rooms
consist of armchairs and sofas
near reception, plus a somewhat
dark breakfast room downstairs.
Bedrooms are plain, but newer
ones have pine fixtures. The price
is astonishingly low for the area.

Windermere

142–4 Warwick Way, SW1V 4JE.
Map 20 E2. [0171-834 5163.
FAX 0171-630 8831. TX 94017182
WIRE G. **Rooms:** 23 🛏 19. 1 ⊞
24 ⊞ 🄴 AE, MC, V, JCB. £

The well-kept Victorian exterior
of this inexpensive, friendly hotel
stands out on a desolate and busy
road. Inside, the illusion is not
broken: it is as neat as a pin,
with a pleasant breakfast room
that doubles as a coffee shop;
snacks and drinks are available

there all day. Light, clean
bedrooms have curtains of heavy
glazed chintz plus some
modern furnishings.

Woodville House

107 Ebury St, SW1W 9QU.
Map 20 E2. [0171-730 1048.
FAX 0717-730 2574. **Rooms:** 12.
1 ⊞ ✕ 🖪 🄴 £

Though neither spacious nor
luxurious, this guesthouse, in a
Georgian building, is well kept,
personal and much frequented
by budget-conscious visitors. The
breakfast room is screened off
into intimate spaces; the bedroom
furnishings include tiny armchairs.

Ebury Court

28 Ebury St, SW1W 0LU. **Map** 20 E1.
[0171-730 8147. FAX 0171-823
5966. **Rooms:** 42. 🛏 21. 1 ⊞ 24
✕ 🖪 🖬 🍷 ⊞ 🄴 AE, DC,
MC, V. ££

Several adjacent town houses
make up this attractive privately
owned hotel. Family heirlooms
and pictures fill the cozy public
rooms. Labyrinthine passages and
stairways connect the rooms, most
of which are small and plain. The
price is very good for the area.

Royal Horseguards
Thistle

2 Whitehall Court, SW1A 2EJ.
Map 13 C4. [0171-839 3400.
FAX 0171-925 2263. TX 917096.
Rooms: 376. 🛏 1 ⊞ 24 ✕ 🍽 🌿
🖪 🖬 🍷 ⊞ 🄴 AE, DC, MC,
V, JCB. ££££

This grand 19th-century hotel
overlooks the river not far from
the Houses of Parliament. Potted
palms, chandeliers and ornate
plasterwork fill the lobby. Beyond,
the comfortable public rooms
include Granby's Restaurant,
handsome and formal in green
leather and a haunt of well-known
political faces. The style of all
the bedrooms varies from lovely
classical opulence to fresh
contemporary smartness.

Stakis London St.
Ermin's

Caxton St, SW1H 0QW. **Map** 13 A5.
[0171-222 7888. FAX 0171-222
6914. TX 917731. **Rooms:** 290. 🛏
1 ⊞ 24 ✕ 🍽 🖪 🖬 🍷
⊞ 🄴 AE, DC, MC, V, JCB. £££

This institutional-looking late-
Victorian hotel is close enough to
Westminster to have once had its
own tunnel link to the House of
Commons. The most striking
feature is a grand Baroque
staircase rearing from the main

lounge up toward the glittering
chandeliers, curving balustrades
and ornate plaster ceilings. The
bedrooms are furnished in a less
overbearing style than that in the
rest of the hotel.

Goring

Beeston Pl, Grosvenor Gdns, SW1W
0JW. **Map** 20 E1. [0171-396
9000. FAX 0171-834 4393. TX
919166. **Rooms:** 80. 🛏 1 ⊞ 24 ✕
🖪 🖬 🍷 P ⊞ 🄴 AE, DC,
MC, V. ££££

This imposing Edwardian building
is rare – a central London hotel
that is both grand and family-run.
The third-generation Gorings
maintain immaculate standards,
with meticulous attention to every
detail. The hotel exudes an air of
understated elegance. Exceptional
features include the bar lounge
and a delightful formal garden,
which, alas, can only be viewed,
not used.

Scandic Crown

2 Bridge Pl, SW1V 1QA. **Map** 20 F2.
[0171-834 8123. FAX 0171-828
1099. TX 914973. **Rooms:** 210. 🛏
1 ⊞ 24 ✕ 🍽 🖪 🖬 ⊞
🖪 🖬 🍷 ⊞ 🄴 AE, DC, MC,
V, JCB. ££££

This uncompromising modern
block that overlooks the train
marshaling yards of nearby
Victoria station is Swedish-owned.
The starkness of its chrome, glass
and plastic coffee shop is more
than offset by the friendly
Scandinavian welcome and the
stylish, well-equipped bedrooms.
One of the hotel's special
attractions is the wide variety of
health facilities that are available
to residents.

PICCADILLY
MAYFAIR

Athenaeum

116 Piccadilly, W1V 0BJ. **Map** 12 E4.
[0171-499 3464. FAX 0171-493
1860. TX 261589. **Rooms:** 112. 🛏
1 ⊞ 24 ✕ 🍽 🛏 🌿 🖪 🖪
🖬 🍷 ⊞ 🖬 🄴 AE, DC, MC, V,
JCB. ££££

Despite the prestigious Mayfair
location of this smart hotel, the
welcome is friendly and personal.
Tea or coffee served in the
relaxing Windsor lounge is a
particular delight. So, too, is the
vast range of malt Scotch whiskies
available in the cocktail bar. Some
bedrooms are perhaps too bland,
but all are comfortable and very
well furnished.

The Four Seasons

Hamilton Pl, Park Lane, W1A 1AZ.
Map 12 D4. **[** 0171-499 0888.
FAX 0171-493 6629. **TX** 227711.
Rooms: 227. *AE, DC, MC, V, JCB.* **£)£)£)£)£)**

The Four Seasons prides itself on individual service and understated luxury, and the overall effect is firmly traditional. In the opulent, well-equipped rooms, quieter styles are gradually replacing the Oriental birds and heavy chintzes, and the foyer and lounge areas glitter with Venetian crystal. At the top of the grand staircase, the elegant Four Seasons Restaurant and the less formal Lanes buffet provide arenas for splendid food.

Twenty-two Jermyn Street

22 Jermyn St, St. James's SW1Y 6HL.
Map 12 F3. **[** 0171-734 2353. **FAX** 0171-734 0750. **Rooms:** 18. *AE, DC, MC, V, JCB.* **£)£)£)£)**

An unobtrusive entrance leads to a complex of luxurious suites and studios that are perfect for the business visitor. They are very comfortable for anyone else, lavishly decorated and beautifully maintained. Round-the-clock room service, use of a nearby health club and an emphasis on security and privacy explain the hotel's steep rates.

Brown's

Albemarle and Dover Sts, W1A 4SW.
Map 12 F3. **[** 0171-493 6020.
FAX 0171-493 9381. **TX** 28686.
Rooms: 120. *AE, DC, MC, V, JCB.* **£)£)£)£)£)** *See Restaurants and Pubs pp306–7.*

Some of the urbane charm of the original Mr. Brown (who must have been the perfect gentleman's gentleman) still lingers here in one of London's oldest and most traditional hotels. The legendary afternoon teas are served in the chintz-filled lounge. Bedrooms are generally large, with charming, slightly outmoded decor.

Claridge's

Brook St, W1A 2JQ. **Map** 12 E2.
[0171-629 8860. **FAX** 0171-499 2210. **TX** 218762 CLRDGS G.
Rooms: 190. *AE, DC, MC, V, JCB.* **£)£)£)£)£)**

So much a part of the establishment that it functions virtually as an annex to Buckingham Palace, Claridge's favors tradition – yet the atmosphere is surprisingly unstarchy. Art Deco blends with the classical grandeur of marble mosaic, chandeliers, and a staircase wide enough for two full ballgowns to pass unhindered. Hungarian musicians play in the foyer; waiters, valets and maids can be summoned to the vast bedrooms at the touch of a button.

Connaught

16 Carlos Pl, W1Y 6AL. **Map** 12 E3.
[0171-499 7070. **FAX** 0171-495 3262. **Rooms:** 90. *MC, V.* **£)£)£)£)£)**

So self-confident is this famous hotel that it provides neither a brochure nor a rate list. (Terms – not the highest in Mayfair – are available "on application.") The hotel is not large and its decor is unshowy. Utter discretion is the watchword: guests' privacy is jealously guarded, and every whim is noted for future reference. Those outside the charmed circle may feel they are being exluded from the club of Connaught residents. Many are gently informed that the hotel is quite full. To make a reservation, don't call – and don't dream of just turning up! Write, courteously, well in advance.

Dorchester

53 Park Lane, W1A 2HJ. **Map** 12 D3.
[0171-629 8888. **FAX** 0171-495 7342. **TX** 887704 DORCH G. **Rooms:** 252. *AE, DC, MC, V, JCB.* **£)£)£)£)£)**

Soft, pale gold gleams on marble pillars and scalloped ceiling domes; towering arrangements of flowers deck the Promenade, where teas are served; and all is conspicuous, flamboyant grandeur in this old hotel. Eating places include the famous Grill Room, the calmer Terrace and the exotically themed Oriental restaurants. Suites and bedrooms, which have triple-glazing on the Park Lane side, are – needless to say – luxurious.

Dukes

35 St. James's Pl, SW1A 1NY.
Map 12 F4. **[** 0171-491 4840.
FAX 0171-493 1264. **TX** 28283.
Rooms: 64. *AE, DC, MC, V.* **£)£)£)£)£)**

This fine Edwardian building is wedged into a tiny secluded courtyard where the gas lamps are still lit by hand. Though expensive and exclusive, Dukes is notably friendly and comfortable. The bar has a masculine look: monumentally priced cognacs are dispensed beneath the stern gaze of three ducal portraits (Wellington, Marlborough, Norfolk). Children over 5 are welcome.

Forty-seven Park Street

47 Park St, W1Y 4EB. **Map** 12 D2.
[0171-491 7282. **FAX** 0171-491 7281. **TX** 22116 LUXURY. **Rooms:** 52. *AE, DC, MC, V, JCB.* **£)£)£)£)£)**

Many have heard of the Roux's celebrated restaurant, Le Gavroche. Fewer realize that you can, if you are wealthy enough, stagger just next door to recover from gastronomic excess. Here the luxurious suites, each unique, feature French-style clocks and bronzes on fireplaces, finely crafted furniture, downy duvets, and thick fluffy towels. Room service from the restaurant is also available.

Grosvenor House

86–90 Park Lane, W1A 3AA. **Map** 12 D3. **[** 0171-499 6363. **FAX** 0171-493 3341. **TX** 24871. **Rooms:** 454. *AE, DC, MC, V, JCB.* **£)£)£)£)£)**

This establishment is perhaps most famous as host to grand occasions. The Great Room is the largest banqueting hall in Europe, with space for 2,000. Behind the Lutyens façade overlooking Hyde Park, the hotel is formal and luxurious but thoroughly comfortable. Several very different restaurants include the suavely elegant Nico at 90 *(see p296).*

Ritz

Piccadilly, W1V 9DG. **Map** 12 F3.
[0171-493 8181. **FAX** 0171-493 2687. **TX** 267200. **Rooms:** 129. *AE, DC, MC, V.* **£)£)£)£)£)** *See p91.*

Cunard's flagship still draws the crowds, especially for afternoon teas in the Palm Court – perhaps the closest most of us can get to sampling Life at the Top. The Ritz's marbled, French-style rooms are undeniably grand – especially the restaurant, where gilded chandeliers are suspended from a fresco of clouds, well worth a look up. There is also an attractive Italian Garden toward the tree-filled oasis of Green Park.

SOHO
LEICESTER SQUARE
OXFORD STREET

Concorde

50 Great Cumberland Pl, W1H 7FD.
Map 11 C1. **[** *0171-402 6169.*
FAX *0171-724 1184.* **TX** *262076.*
Rooms: *27.* 🛏 1 ♨ ☒ 🛄
🔋 ☗ 🕿 *AE, DC, MC, V.* ⓔ

This hotel shares the pleasantly
bygone but cared-for ambience
of its bigger sister next door *(see
Bryanston Court).* Facilities,
however, are simpler, and the
rates are correspondingly lower –
a remarkably good buy this close
to Oxford Street.

Edward Lear

28–30 Seymour St, W1H 5WD.
Map 11 C2. **[** *0171-402 5401.*
FAX *0171-706 3766.* **Rooms:** *31.* 🛏
4. 1 ♨ ☒ ☗ 🔋 *MC, V.* ⓔ

Once the home of humorist Edward
Lear, this clean, simple bed-and-
breakfast is not too far from Oxford
Street. Here one may find both
business travelers and tourists, in
groups or traveling alone. There are
two small lounges (one full of
Edward Lear books and limericks),
plus a light breakfast room. Rear
rooms are quieter.

Parkwood

4 Stanhope Pl, W2 2HB. **Map** 11 B2.
[*0171-402 2241.* **FAX** *0171-402
1574.* **Rooms:** *18.* 🛏 12. 1 ☒
🔋 🔋 *MC, V.* ⓔ

This friendly family bed-and-
breakfast is in a tidy house, with a
classical portico and black
railings, just a block from Marble
Arch. The lounge-cum-reception
area has a gracious air, but
bedrooms are not at all luxurious
and show signs of wear.
Downstairs is a small but cheerful
breakfast room with simple
bentwood chairs.

Bryanston Court

56–60 Great Cumberland Pl, W1H 7FD.
Map 11 C1. **[** *0171-262 3141.*
FAX *0171-262 7248.* **Rooms:** *56.* 🛏
1 ♨ ☒ 🔋 🔋 🕿
🔋 *AE, DC, MC, V.* ⓔⓔ

Blue awnings add a continental
jauntiness to this well-kept hotel.
Inside, soft lighting gleams on oil
portraits and gently battered
brown leather. The atmosphere is
civilized and old-fashioned but
personal – as few West End hotels
are these days. Bedrooms are
simple, smallish and functional.

Durrants

George St, W1H 6BJ. **Map** 11 R1
[*0171-935 8131.* **FAX** *0171-487
3510.* **Rooms:** *96.* 🛏 86 1 ♨ 24
☒ 🔋 🔋 🕿 🍽 🔋 *AE,
MC, V.* ⓔⓔⓔ

This well-loved Georgian hotel
still has the feel of the country
coaching inn it once was. The
restaurant features crisp linen and
silver-domed tureens. Bars and
sitting rooms full of leather and
oak paneling reinforce the
impression of old-fashioned
masculine taste. Bedrooms are
unfussy, and smallish at the rear.

Hazlitt's

6 Frith St, W1V 5TZ. **Map** 13 A2.
[*0171-434 1771.* **FAX** *0171-439
1524.* **Closed** *24–26 Dec.* **Rooms:**
23. 🛏 1 ♨ ☒ 🔋 *AE, DC, MC,
V.* ⓔⓔⓔ

One of London's most beguiling
and individual hotels is set in
three 18th-century houses – the
critic and essayist William Hazlitt
(1778–1830) once lived in one of
them. Although not luxurious, it
has an air of refinement. Pictures
deck every wall, but bedrooms
are restfully plain in greens and
creams, with interesting antiques.
Palms and ferns, and sometimes a
classical bust, perch on Victorian
baths with claw feet. Apart from a
small sitting room behind the
reception areas, there are no
public areas.

Marble Arch Marriott

134 George St, W1H 6DN.
Map 11 B1. **[** *0171-723 1277.*
FAX *0171-402 0666.* **TX** *27983.*
Rooms: *239.* 🛏 1 ♨ 24 ☒ 🔋
🍽 🔋 🔋 🔋 🔋 🔋 🕿
P 🕿 🍽 🔋 *AE, DC, MC, V, JCB.*
ⓔⓔⓔⓔ

This modern box just off Edgware
Road has remarkably good and
clean facilities and a relaxing
atmosphere. Rooms contain one
or two comfortable queen-sized
beds. There is also a health club
with gym and swimming pool,
plus – unusual for the center of
town – free parking.

Hampshire

Leicester Sq, WC2H 7LH. **Map** 13 B3.
[*0171-839 9399.* **FAX** *0171-930
8122.* **TX** *814848 HAMPS G.*
Rooms: *124.* 🛏 1 ♨ 24 ☒ 🕿
🍽 🔋 🔋 🔋 🔋 🕿 🍽 🔋
🔋 *AE, DC, MC, V, JCB.* ⓔⓔⓔⓔ

Few would suspect such
lavishness could possibly be
concealed on one of London's
seediest squares in the unlikely
setting of the former Dental

Hospital. Inside, this imposing
brick building is plush enough to
please the most exacting of
American executives (the core of
its trade). It is a chain hotel (part
of the Edwardian group), that's
stylishly immaculate. A slightly
colonial air prevails among the
ceiling fans and vast Chinese jars.

REGENT'S PARK
MARYLEBONE

Blandford

80 Chiltern St, W1M 1PS.
Map 4 D5. **[** *0171-486 3103.*
FAX *0171-487 2786.* **TX** *262594
BLANFD G.* **Rooms** *33.* 🛏 1 ♨
☒ 🔋 🕿 🔋 *AE, DC, MC, V.*
ⓔⓔ

The Blandford has won numerous
awards for its welcoming brand of
inexpensive bed-and-breakfast. It
is a family-run establishment
offering simple, unassuming and
practical accommodations, plus a
lavish breakfast, in a quiet side
street near Baker Street station.

La Place

17 Nottingham Pl, W1M 3FB.
Map 4 D5. **[** *0171-486 2323.*
FAX *0171-486 4335.* **Rooms:** *23.* 🛏
1 ♨ 24 ☒ 🕿 🔋 🔋 🔋
🕿 🔋 🔋 *DC, MC, V.* ⓔⓔ

Just a stone's throw from Madame
Tussauds, this is a rare commodity
in central London: a pleasant,
affordable bed-and-breakfast. In
fact, La Place is more than that,
since it also serves simple meals in
its basement restaurant. A plant-
filled bar of blond bentwood and
rattan skillfully suggests a garden
setting. Bedrooms are well-
furnished and equipped with
many more features than you
would expect for these prices. The
care that is taken about security
makes this an attractive hotel for
women traveling alone.

Dorset Square

39–40 Dorset Sq, NW1 6QN.
Map 3 C5. **[** *0171-723 7874.*
FAX *0171-724 3328.* **TX** *263964.*
Rooms: *37.* 🛏 1 ♨ 24 ☒ 🕿
🍽 🔋 🔋 🔋 🔋 🕿 🍽 🔋 *AE,
MC, V.* ⓔⓔⓔ

This beautifully restored Regency
building has enormous panache:
antiques, bold fabrics, objets d'art,
and interesting paintings happily
mingle. Each room is unique.
Downstairs, a restaurant and bar,
with games like backgammon in
progress, provide a relaxed
alternative to the carefully
plumped sitting rooms.

White House

Albany St, NW1 3UP. **Map** 4 E4.
[📞] *0171-387 1200.* **FAX** *0171-388 0091.* [TX] *24111.* **Rooms:** *576.* [icons] *AE, DC, MC, V, JCB.* ⓔⓔⓔ

Once touched by the Profumo Affair (a political sex scandal of the 1960s), this large complex of suites and apartments today provides high standards of accommodation and a varied range of public rooms. The smart classic restaurant and comfortable cocktail lounge are complemented by a popular basement wine bar with beams and copper knickknacks, as well as the spacious Garden Café. An extra advantage is the hotel's proximity to the Euston mainline railway station (*see p358–9*).

Langham Hilton

1 Portland Pl, W1N 3AA. **Map** 4 E5.
[📞] *0171-636 1000.* **FAX** *0171-323 2340.* **Rooms:** *387.* [icons] *AE, DC, MC, V, JCB.* ⓔⓔⓔⓔⓔ See p221.

Reopened as a hotel in 1991, after long tenure by the BBC, which used it for radio broadcasting, the Langham offers a lavish Hilton-style re-creation of its former Victorian splendor, in addition to all the contemporary "mod cons" anyone could possibly wish for. The public rooms reflect a fashionable nostalgia for the days of the British Empire. The spacious bedrooms are indeed sumptuous, as is the famous ballroom, boasting glittering Italian chandeliers and pompously ornate plasterwork.

BLOOMSBURY
FITZROVIA
COVENT GARDEN
THE STRAND

Mabledon Court

10–11 Mabledon Pl, WC1H 9BA.
Map 5 B3. [📞] *0171-388 3866.* **FAX** *0171-387 5686.* **Rooms:** *33.* [icons] *MC, V.* ⓔ

There's nothing fancy about this rather plain building or its surroundings, but the rates aren't high and the hotel is handily placed for both King's Cross and St. Pancras railway stations. The small rooms are clean and neat, with a tiny lounge and a stylishly modern breakfast room situated in the basement.

Academy

17–21 Gower St, WC1E 6HG.
Map 5 A5. [📞] *0171-631 4115.* **FAX** *0171-636 3442.* **Rooms:** *33.* [icons] *AE, DC, MC, V, JCB.* ⓔⓔ

Sentinel bay trees mark these three Georgian town houses near the heart of London University. Inside the Academy, the ambience is sophisticated without excess. French doors by the bookshelves of a cozy, inviting sitting room lead to an inviting patio garden. A basement restaurant offers interesting food in intimate surroundings, sometimes accompanied by live music.

Fielding

4 Broad Court, Bow St, WC2B 5QZ.
Map 13 C2. [📞] *0171-836 8305.* **FAX** *0171-497 0064.* **Rooms:** *26.* [icons] *AE, DC, MC, V.* ⓔⓔ

As an inexpensive, personally run bed-and-breakfast in a fascinating part of London, the Fielding is hard to beat. Smoky the parrot may well be the first to greet you in a small bar of pink plush. Upstairs, a miscellany of bedrooms rambles in all directions, some split-level and oddly shaped, all small, none luxurious. Several have useful desks for working visitors; shower rooms with minuscule basins are ingeniously squeezed into impossible spaces.

Bonnington

92 Southampton Row, WC1B 4BH.
Map 5 C5. [📞] *0171-242 2828.* **FAX** *0171-831 9170.* **Rooms:** *215.* [icons] *AE, DC, MC, V.* ⓔⓔⓔ

This family-run hotel is one of the most useful in Bloomsbury. The furnishings are mostly unremarkable, but the managerial style is personal and quietly assured. The lounge bar and restaurant are pleasant and modern. Weekend deals are excellent value for families.

Russell

Russell Sq, WC1B 5BE. **Map** 5 B5.
[📞] *0171-837 6470.* **FAX** *0171-837 2857.* [TX] *24615.* **Rooms:** *328.* [icons] *AE, DC, MC, V, JCB.* ⓔⓔⓔ

The formal exterior of this grand late-Victorian pile is matched by the foyer, a maze of tawny marble with an imposing stairway. Wood paneling, leather chesterfields, rich dark fabrics and chandeliers set

the tone elsewhere. The nicest rooms overlook the gardens. The Virginia Woolf brasserie serves before-theater dinners.

Mountbatten

20 Monmouth St, WC2H 9HD.
Map 13 B2. [📞] *0171-836 4300.* **Rooms:** *127.* [icons] *AE, MC, V, JCB.* ⓔⓔⓔⓔ

Well-located near theaters and Covent Garden, the hotel is filled with memorabilia of World War II veteran Lord Mountbatten. Public areas have the ease and style of Edwardian drawing rooms and are pleasantly filled with colonial and Oriental touches: ceiling fans, rugs, huge potted palms. The popular wine bar downstairs serves a very good range of snacks in pleasing surroundings, and before-theater dinners can be arranged.

Waldorf

Aldwych, WC2B 4DD. **Map** 14 D2.
[📞] *0171-836 2400.* **FAX** *0171-836 7244.* [TX] *24574.* **Rooms:** *292.* [icons] *AE, DC, MC, V, JCB.* ⓔⓔⓔ

Still elegant, this superior Forte hotel is no longer the exclusive haunt of its heyday. However, the tea dances for which it was once so famous still take place on weekends, and afternoon tea beneath the famous scrolled balcony where the band plays is a popular pastime. The Aldwych Brasserie provides a less formal setting for before-theater dinners. Some of the bedroom decor is dated, but rooms are gradually being refurbished.

Howard

Temple Pl, Strand, WC2R 2PR.
Map 14 D2. [📞] *0171-836 3555.* **FAX** *0171-379 4547.* [TX] *268047.* **Rooms:** *135.* [icons] *AE, DC, MC, V, JCB.* ⓔⓔⓔⓔⓔ

The building is unmistakably modern, but the authoritative polish of the hotel's staff soon transports you to a bygone era. The foyer is an ornate classical pastiche, with diamanté chandeliers and elaborate plaster-work painted in pastels. Other notable features are a landscaped interior garden, which is visible from the restaurant and bar. There are also splendid river views from many of the pleasant, traditionally furnished bedrooms.

Savoy

Strand, WC2R 0EU. **Map** 13 C2.
📞 *0171-836 4343.* FAX *0171-240 6040.* TX *24234.* **Rooms:** *200.* 🛏
1️⃣ 🎯 24 📺 📶 🔽 🅿️ 🔁 🛗 🎱 🍴 ⬛ 🔌 🔽 🅿️ 🔁 🍴 *AE, DC, MC, V, JCB.* €€€€€
See p116.

On its dais above the Thames, Richard D'Oyly Carte's dream hotel still lords it over this part of London. Inside, the Savoy Grill is a time-honored institution for political and journalistic tête-à-têtes, and piano-accompanied tea in the lovely Thames Foyer is always popular. Art Deco features give the Savoy much of its distinctive elegance. Many of the bedrooms have old-fashioned bathrooms with enormous watering-can showerheads. Some particularly appealing balconied singles have views upriver. The little touches give the Savoy its excellent reputation: those mattresses with 836 springs, the bells by the beds for instant service and the managing director's quaint belief that "standardization is not part of hotel-keeping." The skylighted rooftop swimming pool and the fitness center are as stylish as one would expect.

THE CITY

Great Eastern

Liverpool St, EC2M 7QN. **Map** 15 C1.
📞 *0171-283 4363.* FAX *0171-283 4897.* TX *886812.* **Rooms:** *161.* 🛏
126 1️⃣ 🎯 24 📺 🔽 ⬛ 🔽 🍴 🔌 *AE, DC, MC, V.* €€€

This old Victorian railway hotel next to the Liverpool Street station is, amazingly, the only hotel within the old City area. Its good points include several restaurants: Café Pierre, a French-style sandwich bar; L'Entrecôte, a windowless sanctum where business people meet; and Bowlers in the City, with Classical columns and a stained-glass dome. Food in all these conforms to conservative City norms, and the bedrooms present no surprises.

Tower Thistle

St. Katharine's Way, E1 9LD.
Map 16 E3. 📞 *0171-481 2575.*
FAX *0171-481 3799.* TX *885934.*
Rooms: *808.* 🛏 1️⃣ 🎯 24 📺 🔽 🌿 🛗 ⬛ 🔽 🅿️ 🔁 🍴 🔌 *AE, DC, MC, V, JCB.* €€€€

This 1970s concrete pyramid commands a splendid piece of river frontage, just below Tower Bridge and looking across to Butler's Wharf. Inside, the foyer is cool and spacious, with running water and plants. Restaurants range from the expensive Princes and a hearty Carvery to the chic Which Way West, which transforms into a nightclub. Bedrooms are not very large, but all have good views, modern decor and excellent facilities.

FARTHER AFIELD

Chase Lodge

10 Park Rd, Hampton Wick, KT1 4AS.
📞 *0181-943 1862.* **Rooms:** *9.* 🛏 *7.* 1️⃣ 🎯 📺 🔽 🛗 🔽 🅿️ 🔁 🍴 🔌 *AE, DC, MC, V.* €

This modest Victorian house has an airy conservatory where excellent breakfasts and dinners are served. There are also a small, smart bar and a sitting room. The bedrooms, though small, are prettily done in cottagey styles with pine or Victorian furnishings, and bathrooms are fitted in wherever possible.

La Reserve

422–8 Fulham Rd, SW6 1DU.
Map 18 D5. 📞 *0171-385 8561.*
FAX *0171-385 7662.* **Rooms:** *40.* 🛏
1️⃣ 🎯 24 📺 📶 🔽 🔽 🔁 🛗 🍴 🔌 *AE, DC, MC, V.* €€€

Although the frontage is Classical, the hotel is determinedly different inside. The austere, ultramodern furnishings may not appeal to everyone, but the minimalist bedrooms have fine bedspreads and good bathrooms. The restaurant serves a short but spirited menu of ethnic specialties all day long.

Swiss Cottage

4 Adamson Rd, NW3 3HP.
📞 *0171-722 2281.* FAX *0171-483 4588.* TX *297232 SWISSCO G.*
Rooms: *80.* 🛏 *76.* 1️⃣ 🎯 24 📺 🔽 🛗 🔽 🍴 🔌 *AE, DC, MC, V.* €€

This well-kept Victorian house on a quiet street not far from the Swiss Cottage Underground station offers a pleasantly old-fashioned stay. Antiques and a grand piano mingle with the reproduction furniture and an interestingly unusual collection of paintings and antique wallpapers. Bedrooms are spacious and comfortable, the more expensive rooms boasting velvet sofas or chaises lounges. The restaurant's short menu is supplemented by sandwiches and simple snacks served in the bar and lounge.

Cannizaro House

West Side, Wimbledon Common, SW19 4UF. 📞 *0181-879 1464.*
FAX *0181-879 7338.* TX *941 3837.*
Rooms: *46.* 🛏 1️⃣ 🎯 24 📺 🔽 🛗 🔽 🅿️ 🔁 🛗 🍴 🔌 *AE, DC, MC, V, JCB.* €€€

King George III (reigned 1760–1820) once breakfasted in this merchant's mansion, originally dating from 1705, and the hotel has an ostentatious style that is appropriate to its royal connection. Plaster ceilings, imposing fireplaces, huge flower arrangements and windows ornamented with swagged curtains all add to an air of grandeur. The splendor continues upstairs in the bedrooms. But the best feature of Cannizaro House is its splendid secluded gardens, which give it the pleasing feel of a traditional country house.

Kingston Lodge

Kingston Hill, Kingston-upon-Thames, KT2 7NP. 📞 *0181-541 4481.* FAX *0181-547 1013.* TX *936034.* **Rooms:** *62.*
🛏 1️⃣ 24 📺 🔽 🛗 🔽 🔁 🍴 🔌 *AE, DC, MC, V.* €€€

This small-scale suburban hotel, which is part of the Forte chain, is light and homey. It is on a fairly busy road, but there are plenty of quiet rooms at the rear. The open-plan but nicely intimate split-level public areas ramble from the reception desk. A gas fire burns cheerfully in a wooden fireplace and billowy blinds shield diners from the sun in the glass-walled restaurant. There are a few visible signs of wear and tear, but generally the hotel is comfortable throughout its rooms.

Sheraton Skyline, Heathrow Airport

Bath Rd, Hayes, Middlesex, UB3 5BP.
📞 *0181-759 2535.* FAX *0181-750 9150.* TX *934254.* **Rooms:** *354.* 🛏
1️⃣ 🎯 24 📺 🔽 🛗 🎱 🔽 🔽 🅿️ 🔁 🛗 🍴 🔌 *AE, DC, MC, V, JCB.* €€€€€

If you are looking in the vicinity of Heathrow Airport for something that is more than just an air-conditioned, soundproofed box, try the Sheraton Skyline. One of its main attractions is the Patio Caribe, an extraordinary indoor pool amid tropical foliage, which makes a nice setting for cocktails or buffet lunch. Other features conform to the chain hotel pattern. Courtesy transportation to the airport and free parking are provided.
For a list of other hotels that are close to Gatwick or Heathrow airports see pages 356–7.

RESTAURANTS AND PUBS

EATING OUT IN London is like taking a gastronomic world tour. In the space of just a few days you can travel from America to Africa, taking in all the European countries and the Near, Middle and Far East on the way. Over the past 30 years, particularly the last decade, London has been transformed into a veritable United Nations of cuisine.

A pre-theater menu board

have also been included. *Choosing a Restaurant* on pages 292 – 294 summarizes the key features of the restaurants and is organized by area so that you can locate one close by. More details can be found in the individual listings on pages 295 to 305, grouped according to cuisine type.

CHOOSING YOUR TABLE

The restaurants listed in this book offer a high standard of cooking, value for money and an enjoyable evening out, and represent a huge range of styles and prices. They are spread throughout the main tourist areas; a few that merit a special trip farther afield

In recent years, London's cafés have taken on a new look and are among the most lively places in town. As for pubs, for which Britain is famed, many now serve tasty meals, ranging from simple snacks to popular ethnic dishes. Some more informal places to eat and drink, including pubs, are on pages 306 to 309.

LONDON RESTAURANTS

COVENT GARDEN, Piccadilly Circus, Soho and Leicester Square are the areas where you will find the widest choice of eating places. Kensington and Chelsea also boast a good range of restaurants, and the Docklands area, east of the City, also houses some stylish establishments.

You can still get traditional British roast beef and stodgy puddings at the likes of Simpson's *(see p295)*, but the most significant trend is a new style of British cooking that marries a lighter approach to

Commissionaire at the Hard Rock Café *(see p302)*

a variety of culinary influences. Home-grown chefs like Sally Clarke (of Clarke's, *see p297*), Gary Rhodes (The Greenhouse, *see p295*) and Marco Pierre White (The Restaurant, *see p298*) lead the way.

London is a real paradise for lovers of Indian food, with countless tandoori, balti and bhel poori houses serving cheap food. Two very popular cuisines are Thai and Italian; Soho has a couple of the best-known Thai venues, alongside Japanese, Indonesian, and some of the best Chinese chefs and restaurants outside Hong Kong. Some modern Italian restaurants, epitomized by Riva *(see p299)* and the River Café *(see p299)*, offer a lighter style of cooking than the traditional trattorias. French cooking, the longest-established "guest" cuisine in the city, accounts for a sizable percentage of the high-class establishments in The City and around Mayfair.

Most restaurants, notably Leith's *(see p 298)*, provide a vegetarian option and some offer a separate vegetarian menu. A number of specialist vegetarian restaurants offer more adventurous dishes, such as The Place Below *(see p302)*. Seafood is a London specialty, with both new-style and traditional fish restaurants being well represented.

La Famiglia *(see p299)*

OTHER PLACES TO EAT

MANY LONDON hotels have excellent restaurants open to nonresidents. Some hotel restaurants can be stuffy and a bit overpriced, but others offer top-quality food prepared by star chefs.

Several pizza-and-pasta chains serve decent meals in branches across the city, and some pubs now rival wine bars, serving a range of food from standard British dishes to exotic curries, quiches and lasagne – though the best pub lunches are not to be found in central London. French-style café-brasseries are catching on, and a number of coffee-house-pâtisseries are worth a visit. Otherwise, you can grab a quick, cheap snack from a sandwich bar, pizza stand or all-night bagel bakery.

Bibendum *(see p297)*

Tips on Eating Out

MOST LONDON restaurants serve lunch between 12:30 and 2:30pm and dinner from 7 until 11pm. Last orders are usually at 10:30pm. Ethnic restaurants usually stay open longer – often until midnight or even later. Unfortunately, many restaurants close on Sunday and Monday. All-day café-brasseries (11am–11pm) may be allowed to serve alcohol only at certain times or with a meal. The traditional British Sunday lunch *(see p289)* appears in almost every pub and many restaurants – always check first, unless that's what you want, as even high-class restaurants may suspend their normal menu on Sundays.

Only the most expensive spots demand jackets and ties; the preferred dress is "smart casual." Making reservations is advisable, especially at places like the Connaught *(see p295)* and Bibendum *(see p297)*.

Price and Service

AN AVERAGE three-course meal with wine at a medium-price restaurant in central London can be had for between £25 and £35 per head. Lower prices (£5–£15 a head) prevail at small ethnic and vegetarian cafés, wine bars and pubs. Many smarter restaurants have brasseries where you can sample fare similar to that of the main restaurant, but at a cheaper price and in more informal

circumstances. Before ordering, check the small print at the bottom of the menu. Prices should include value-added tax (VAT) but not necessarily the service charge (between 10% and 15%). In addition, some restaurants impose a cover charge (£1–£2 a head); some have a minimum charge during their busiest periods, and some refuse to take certain credit cards. Beware of the old trick where service is included in the bill but staff leave the "total" box on your credit slip blank, hoping you will add another 10%.

Expect different types of service in different types of restaurants: cheerful and breezy in fast-food joints, discreet yet attentive in high-class places. At peak times you will have to wait longer, though some restaurants offer special before-theater meals geared for quick service.

Eating with Children

EXCEPT IN ITALIAN restaurants, fast-food places and a few other places, children are generally tolerated rather than warmly welcomed in London restaurants. However, many do offer a special children's menu, small portions and highchairs *(see pp292–4)*, and some actively encourage children and teenagers with entertainments, music and activities. Turn to page 339 for a list of places that cater particularly well to children of various ages.

Using the Listings
Key to symbols in the listings on pp295–305.

Using the Listings

🍽 fixed-price menu
🚭 no-smoking area
V vegetarian specialties
🧒 children's portions and highchairs
♿ wheelchair access
👔 jacket and tie required
♫ live music
☰ tables outside
🍷 particularly good wine list
★ highly recommended
▣ credit cards accepted:
AE American Express
DC Diners Club
MC MasterCard/Access
V VISA
JCB Japanese Credit Bureau

Price categories for a three-course meal for one including a half-bottle of house wine and all unavoidable extra charges (cover, service, VAT):
£ under £12
££ £12–£20
£££ £20–£30
££££ £30–£40
£££££ over £40

Clarke's Restaurant *(see p297)*

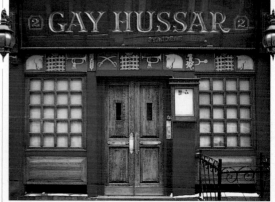

London's top Hungarian restaurant *(see p300)*

What to Eat in London

THE TRADITIONAL SUNDAY lunch displays what is best about British food – good ingredients prepared simply but well. A joint of roast meat (usually lamb or beef) served with appropriate accompaniments (mint sauce or red-currant jelly for lamb, mustard or horseradish sauce for beef) is the centerpiece of the meal;

Fish and Chips
The battered fish (usually haddock or cod) and chips are deep fried.

wonderful homestyle puddings and fine British cheeses served with crackers are obligatory "afters." Sunday lunch is still an institution for Londoners, and you will find versions of it in many restaurants and cafés as well as in hotels and pubs all over the capital. The legendary English breakfast may be less ambitious than the five-course feast enjoyed by the Victorians, but it is still a hearty meal that's the perfect start to a hard day's sightseeing. Afternoon tea (usually taken at around 4pm) is another treat, when the British genius for cakes and their fondness for tea drinking come together. The smell of fish and chips will often greet you as you wander around the city, and this classic British meal is best eaten in the open air, directly from its paper wrapping.

Full English Breakfast
This favorite meal consists of bacon, egg, tomato, fried bread and a variety of sausage.

Toast and Marmalade
Breakfast is usually finished off with slices of toast spread with orange marmalade.

Cheeses
British cheeses are mostly hard or semihard, such as Cheshire, Leicester and the most famous of all, cheddar. Stilton is blue-veined.

Cheddar

Sage Derby

Ploughman's Lunch
Crusty bread, cheese and sweet pickles are at the heart of this simple pub lunch.

Cheshire   **Stilton**   **Red Leicester**

Bread-and-Butter Pudding
Served hot, the layers of bread and dried fruit are baked in a creamy custard.

Strawberries and Cream
Strawberries served with sugar and cream are a favorite summer dessert.

Summer Pudding
The outer bread lining is soaked in the juice of the many soft fruits inside.

Cucumber Sandwiches
Wafer-thin cucumber sandwiches are a traditional part of an English tea.

Jam-and-Cream Scones
Halfway between a cake and a bun, scones are served with cream and jam.

Tea
A cup of tea, served with milk or lemon, is still the British national drink.

Meat dishes are usually served with at least one green vegetable.

Horseradish sauce

Yorkshire pudding

Roast beef

Steak-and-Kidney Pie
Chunks of beef and pigs' kidneys are braised in a thick gravy and topped with a browned pastry crust.

Roast potatoes

Roast Beef and Yorkshire Pudding
Yorkshire pudding, a savory batter baked in the oven, is the traditional accompaniment to roast beef, along with horseradish sauce, roast potatoes and a meat gravy.

Shepherd's Pie
This is made with stewed minced lamb, vegetables and a mashed-potato topping.

What to Drink
Beer is the British drink. The many different kinds (see p308) range from light lager to stout and bitter. Gin originally came from London. Pimms, usually mixed with lemonade, fruit and mint, is a cooling drink on those hot summer days.

Stout (Guinness) **Bitter** **Lager** **Pimms** **Gin and tonic**

London's Best: Restaurants and Pubs

THE SHEER VARIETY OF eating and drinking places in London is overwhelming. There are elegant high-class restaurants offering the most haute of haute cuisine, exotic ethnic specialists (from the Indian subcontinent to the Caribbean), cheap and cheerful cafés, friendly neighborhood pubs and fish-and-chip shops. There is something for every taste, pocket and occasion. See pages 295–305 for the full restaurant listings, pages 306–7 for more informal eating places and pages 308–9 for pubs.

Chutneys
Eat as much as you like, for a few pounds, from a superb lunchtime buffet in this vegetarian Indian restaurant. (See p303.)

Sea Shell
One of the best fish-and-chip shops in London, this busy restaurant has customers who come from far and wide. (See pp306, 307.)

Regent's Park and Marylebone

Kensington and Holland Park

South Kensington and Knightsbridge

Veronica's
This award-winning restaurant serves an intriguing blend of British regional and traditional dishes. (See p296.)

Chelsea

Brown's
Afternoon tea is a specialty of this traditional hotel. (See pp306, 307.)

Le Gavroche
The famous Roux brothers' restaurant is a temple of French haute cuisine. (See p296.)

Bibendum
In the restored Michelin building, diners enjoy sophisticated creations by chef Simon Hopkinson, plus a superb wine list. (See p297.)

The Sun
*This traditional London pub
in the heart of Bloomsbury
has one of the widest ranges
of "real ales" in the capital.*
(See pp308, 309.)

Pâtisserie Valerie
*This busy old-fashioned
pâtisserie serves cakes, coffee
and croissants to an arty
clientele.* (See pp306, 307.)

Bloomsbury
and
Fitzrovia

Smithfield and
Spitalfields

Holborn
and the
Inns of
Court

Covent
Garden and
nd Trafalgar the Strand

The City

N

0 kilometers 1

0 miles 0.5

dilly
St.
's's

RIVER THAMES

South Bank

Southwark and
Bankside

ehall and
tminster

The Place Below
*Vegetarian food is exquisitely
prepared and presented in St.
Mary-le-Bow's crypt.* (See p302.)

New World
*Diners hail passing
trolleys laden with
lunchtime dim sum
at this huge, cheap
restaurant in China-
town.* (See p305.)

The George Inn
*Plays are sometimes
performed in the courtyard
of London's only surviving
coaching inn, now a popular
pub.* (See pp308, 309.)

Choosing a Restaurant

THE RESTAURANTS IN this section have been selected for their good value or exceptional food. This chart highlights some of the main factors that may influence your choice. For more details about the restaurants see pages 295–305; light meals and snack places are on pages 306–7, with pubs on pages 308–9.

	Page Number	Seafood Specialties	Fixed-Price Menu	Late Opening	Children's Facilities	Tables Outside	Quiet Restaurant	Vegetarian Specialties
BAYSWATER, PADDINGTON								
Magic Wok (*Chinese*) ££	305	●	■					
Mega Kalamaras (*Greek*) ££	300		■	●	■			●
L'Accento Italiano (*Italian*) £££	299		■		■	●		
Veronica's (*British*) £££	296		■		■			●
KENSINGTON, HOLLAND PARK, NOTTING HILL								
Malabar (*Indian*) ££	303		■		■			
L'Altro (*Fish*) £££	301	●	■		■	●		
Boyd's (*Modern/International*) £££	297							
Kensington Place (*Modern/International*) ★ £££	298			●	■			
Wodka (*Polish*) £££	301							
Clarke's (*Modern/International*) ★ ££££	297		■					
The Halcyon (*Modern/International*) ££££	297				■	●		
Leith's (*Modern/International*) ★ ££££	298		■				■	●
SOUTH KENSINGTON, GLOUCESTER ROAD								
Bacco (*Italian*) £££	299	●			■			●
St. Quentin (*French*) £££	297		■					
Bibendum (*Modern/International*) ★ £££££	297	●	■	●				
Hilaire (*Modern/International*) £££££	298		■	●	■			
KNIGHTSBRIDGE, BROMPTON, BELGRAVIA								
Ognisko Polskie (*Polish*) ££	301				■			
Bill Bentley's (*Fish*) £££	301	●						
Caravela (*Portuguese*) £££	300	●		●				
Khun Akorn (*Thai*) £££	304				■			●
Le Suquet (*Fish*) £££	301	●		●				
Tui (*Thai*) £££	304	●						
Bombay Brasserie (*Indian*) ££££	303		■	●				●
The English House (*British*) ££££	295		■				■	
L'Incontro (*Italian*) ££££	299	●		●	■			●
Memories of China (*Chinese*) ££££	305	●	■					
Poissonnerie de L'Avenue (*Fish*) ££££	301	●		●	■	●	■	
Salloos (*Indian*) ★ ££££	303		■				■	
The Restaurant (*Modern/International*) £££££	298	●	■				■	
Turner's (*Modern/International*) £££££	298		■				■	
CHELSEA, FULHAM								
Chutney Mary (*Indian*) £££	303		■					●
Eleven Park Walk (*Italian*) £££	299		■		■			
La Famiglia (*Italian*) £££	299			●	■	●		●
Nikita's (*Russian*) ££££	301		■					
La Tante Claire (*French*) ★ £££££	297	●	■				■	
WESTMINSTER, VICTORIA								
Tate Gallery Restaurant (*British*) £££	295				■			
Auberge de Provence (*French*) £££££	296	●	■				■	
Mijanou (*Modern/International*) £££££	298		■			●	■	

Price categories include a three-course meal for one, half a bottle of house wine and all unavoidable extra charges, such as cover, service, VAT.
£ under £12
££ £12–£20
£££ £20–£30
££££ £30–£40
£££££ over £40.

★ Means highly recommended.

SEAFOOD SPECIALTIES
Seafood or fish restaurant, or restaurant with good seafood selection.
LATE OPENING
Last orders taken at or after 11:30pm, excluding Sunday.
CHILDREN'S FACILITIES
Children's portions and/or highchairs.
QUIET RESTAURANT
No piped music; intimate atmosphere.
VEGETARIAN SPECIALTIES
Vegetarian restaurant, or restaurant with at least one vegetarian main course.

	Page Number	Seafood Specialties	Fixed-Price Menu	Late Opening	Children's Facilities	Tables Outside	Quiet Restaurant	Vegetarian Specialties
PICCADILLY, MAYFAIR, BAKER STREET								
Down Mexico Way (Mexican) ££	302			●	■			
Hard Rock Café (American) ££	302			●	■	●		●
Sofra (Turkish) ££	300	●	■	●				●
Stephen Bull (Modern/International) £££	298				■			
Al Hamra (Lebanese) £££	300			●	■	●		
Le Caprice (Modern/International) ££££	297			●				
The Greenhouse (British) ££££	295							
Ikeda (Japanese) ££££	304	●	■					
Mulligan's of Mayfair (Irish) ££££	298							
Miyama (Japanese) ££££	304	●			■		■	
Quaglino's (Modern/International) ££££	298	●	■	●				
The Connaught (British) ★ £££££	295		■				■	
Le Gavroche (French) ★ £££££	296	●	■					
Nico at Ninety (French) ★ £££££	296							
The Oriental (Chinese) £££££	305	●	■		■			
Suntory (Japanese) ★ £££££	304	●	■				■	
SOHO								
Mildred's (Vegetarian) £	302							●
Tokyo Diner (Japanese) £	305			●	■			
Deal's (American) ££	302				■	●		
Fung Shing (Chinese) ££	305	●	■	●				
Harbour City (Chinese) ★ ££	305	●	■		■			
Melati (Indonesian) ££	304	●	■	●				●
New World (Chinese) ££	305		■		■			
Jade Garden (Chinese) ££	305				■			
Bahn Thai (Thai) £££	304	●			■			●
Bistrot Bruno (Modern/International) ★ £££	297	●		●				
Café Fish (Fish) £££	301	●		●				
Chiang Mai (Thai) £££	304	●	■					●
The Gay Hussar (Hungarian) ★ £££	300						■	
Gopal's (Indian) £££	303		■	●				
Grahame's Seafare (Fish) £££	301	●	■		■			
Ming (Chinese) £££	305		■	●				●
Sri Siam (Thai) ★ £££	304	●	■					●
Wheeler's (Fish) £££	301	●			■			
Alastair Little (Modern/International) ★ £££	297		■	●				
COVENT GARDEN, THE STRAND								
Food for Thought (Vegetarian) £	302						●	●
Calabash (African) ££	302							
Plummers (British) ££	295		■	●				
Alfred (British) ★ £££	295	●	■	●	■	●	■	
Joe Allen (American) £££	302			●				
Bertorelli's (Italian) £££	299							●
Café des Amis du Vin (French) £££	296				■	●		
Manzi's (Fish) £££	301	●		●				

Price categories include a three-course meal for one, half a bottle of house wine and all unavoidable extra charges, such as cover, service, VAT.
£ under £12
££ £12–£20
£££ £20–£30
££££ £30–£40
£££££ over £40.

★ Means highly recommended.

SEAFOOD SPECIALTIES
Seafood or fish restaurant, or restaurant with good seafood selection.
LATE OPENING
Last orders taken at or after 11:30pm, excluding Sunday.
CHILDREN'S FACILITIES
Children's portions and/or highchairs.
QUIET RESTAURANT
No piped music; intimate atmosphere.
VEGETARIAN SPECIALTIES
Vegetarian restaurant, or restaurant with at least one vegetarian main course.

	Price	Page Number	Seafood Specialties	Fixed-Price Menu	Late Opening	Children's Facilities	Tables Outside	Quiet Restaurant	Vegetarian Specialties
Mon Plaisir (French)	£££	296		■					
Orso (Italian)	£££	299			●				●
Rules (British)	£££	295							
Simpson's (British)	£££	295		■					
The Ivy (Modern/International) ★	££££	298			●			■	
The Neal Street Restaurant (Italian)	£££££	299						■	
BLOOMSBURY, FITZROVIA									
Chutneys (Indian)	£	303		■					●
Ravi Shankar (Indian)	£	303		■		■			●
Wagamama (Japanese) ★	£	305							●
Mandeer (Indian)	££	303		■					●
Museum Street Café (Modern/International)	£££	298							
Pied-à-Terre (French)	£££££	296	●	■					
CAMDEN TOWN, HAMPSTEAD									
Cottons (Caribbean)	££	303			●				
Daphne (Greek)	££	300			●	■	●		●
Lemonia (Greek)	££	300		■	●	■			●
ISLINGTON									
Anna's Place (Swedish)	£££	300	●			■	●	■	
SPITALFIELDS, CLERKENWELL									
Nazrul (Indian)	£	303			●				●
Bloom's (Jewish)	££	300				■			
The Alba (Italian)	£££	299							●
The Peasant (Italian) ★	£££	299	●			■			
Quality Chop House (British)	£££	295			●	■			
Tatsuso (Japanese)	££££	305	●	■		■			
THE CITY, SOUTH BANK									
The Place Below (Vegetarian) ★	££	302		■					
RSJ (French)	£££	297		■				■	
Le Pont de la Tour (French)	£££££	296	●		●		●		
FURTHER AFIELD									
The Abacus (Chinese)	££	305		■	●	■			●
Istanbul Iskembecisi, N16 (Turkish)	££	300			●	■			
Madhu's Brilliant, Southall (Indian)	££	303		■	●				
Osteria Antica Bologna, SW11 (Italian)	££	299				■	●		●
The Brixtonian, SW9 (Caribbean)	£££	302		■					
Riva, SW13 (Italian) ★	£££	299		■		■		■	●
Spread Eagle, SE10 (French)	£££	297				■			
Wilson's, W14 (Scottish)	£££	296		■		■			
Cibo, W14 (Italian) ★	££££	299		■		■			
River Café, W6 (Italian) ★	££££	299				■	●		

BRITISH

British food has an unenviable reputation and is increasingly irrelevant to the British daily diet, which has become a medley of ingredients and styles from around the world. However, there are restaurants that take pride in producing authentic British food at its best *(see pp288–9)*, and these have a very loyal following.

Alfred

245 Shaftesbury Avenue WC2. **Map** 13 B1. **C** *0171-240 2566.* **Open** *noon–3:30pm, 6–11:30pm Mon–Sat.* **Closed** *Dec 24–Jan 2.* 🌶️🎎♿🏠 ★ 🗝️ *AE, DC, MC, V.* ££££

Opened in 1994, this is one of a new breed of restaurants that avoids the "starch and two veg" formula of many traditional British restaurants. The minimal decor is retro, reminiscent of a post-war café, tastefully decorated with carefully-chosen details in Bakelite and Formica. The menu changes seasonally to make the best use of market produce. Simple classics and imaginative modern dishes are immaculately prepared and presented. Staff are polite and purposeful, and there's a useful bar downstairs in the evening with an excellent list of beers, ciders and English country wines.

The Connaught

16 Carlos Pl W1. **Map** 12 E3. **C** *0171-499 7070.* **Open** *12:30–2:30pm, 6–10:45pm daily.* **Grill open** *12:30–2:30pm, 6–10:45pm Mon–Fri.* **Grill closed** *public hols.* ♿🍴♟️★ 🗝️ *AE, MC.* £££££

The Connaught Hotel houses London's grandest old-fashioned dining room. Here French flair is seamlessly joined with British formality, in both the food and the surroundings. Immaculate staff serve indigenous specialties like filet steak, mixed grill and bread-and-butter pudding; or Gallic treats like *feuilleté d'oeufs brouillés aux truffes* (pastries filled with scrambled eggs and truffles), *homard grillé aux herbes* (grilled lobster with herbs) and crème brûlée. The same menu is served in the Grill Room during the week. You need to reserve well in advance for both restaurants.

The English House

3 Milner St SW3. **Map** 19 C1. **C** *0171-584 3002.* **Open** *12:30–2:30pm & 7:30–11:15pm Mon–Sat, 12:30–2pm & 7:30–10pm Sun.* **Closed** *Dec 25–26.* 🌶️🍴 🗝️ *AE, DC, MC.* ££££

Homey British food is served at this pretty little house in a quiet street close to Harrods. Recommended appetizers are crab cakes and the soup of the day. Best main courses are the traditional roasts (rack of lamb, beef, duck); for dessert, try the steamed sponge if available. This restaurant is particularly good for Sunday lunch, when you get the real flavor of a British domestic occasion.

The Greenhouse

27a Hay's Mews W1. **Map** 12 E3. **C** *0171-499 3331.* **Open** *7–10pm Sun, 7–11pm Mon–Sat.* 🗝️ *AE, DC, MC, V.* ££££

Worth seeking out, in a quiet Mayfair mews this elegant low-ceilinged restaurant, serving British food with confidence. Dishes such as boiled bacon with lentils, faggots (meatballs) in gravy or cod in batter with mushy peas are raised by leading chef Gary Rhodes from their lowly status to the level of smart dinner-party fare. The atmosphere buzzes; the lighting glows warmly; and the steamed sultana, ginger and syrup sponge is delicious.

Plummers

33 King St WC2. **Map** 13 C2. **C** *0171-240 2534.* **Open** *noon–2:30pm, 5:30–11:30pm Mon–Fri, noon–2:30pm, 5:30–11:30pm Sat, 6:00–10pm Sun.* **Closed** *public hols.* 🍽️🌶️🎎 🗝️ *AE, DC, MC, V.* ££

In an area full of transient restaurants, Plummers has stayed in business by serving good food in sizable portions, from a menu that offers set prices for one, two or three courses. Diners can choose from a menu that has changed little over the past 15 years: chunky British food like steak-and-kidney pie and pork-and-apple casserole, alongside equally chunky American dishes such as clam chowder, Cajun meatloaf and hamburgers with an interesting choice of sauces.

Quality Chop House

94 Farringdon Road EC1. **Map** 6 E4. **C** *0171-837 5093.* **Open** *noon–3pm, 6:30pm–11:30pm Mon–Sat, noon–4pm & 7–11:30pm Sun.* **Closed** *Christmas week.* 🎎 ££££

"Progressive working class caterer" says the sign on the etched-glass window of this beautiful Victorian diner with its original 1869 fixtures wonderfully intact. But the workers these days are more likely to hail from the City than the factory. Sausages and mash may still appear on the bill of fare, but the sausages

are meaty veal and the mash is perfectly fluffy and creamy. Other upgraded stalwarts of British cuisine include salmon fishcakes (with sorrel sauce), liver and bacon, scrambled eggs and smoked salmon and, of course, chops. If you're part of a small party you may have to share one of the six-seater booths; if smoke bothers you, this can be a problem.

Rules

35 Maiden La WC2. **Map** 13 C2. **C** *0171-836 5314.* **Open** *noon–midnight daily.* **Closed** *Dec 24–25.* 🗝️ *AE, DC, MC.* £££

London's oldest surviving restaurant has been serving staunchly traditional British food since 1798. Long a haunt of actors and aristocrats (historical cartoons and photographs signed by the great luminaries of British theater cover the walls), it now attracts tourists, businessmen, and a few "hunting-shooting-fishing" types visiting town. Specialties include beef, venison and feathered game (grouse, woodcock, partridge). *(See also p112.)*

Simpson's

110 Strand WC2. **Map** 13 C2. **C** *0171-836 9112.* **Open** *noon–2:30pm, 6–11pm Mon–Sat, noon–2:30pm, 6–9pm Sun.* **Closed** *public hols.* 🌶️♿🍴🎵 🗝️ *AE, DC, MC, V, JCB.* £££

This is a vast open dining hall, with more than a hint of a British public school (men must wear jackets and ties). Go there for the roast beef, carved in thick slices from silver-domed trolleys. A recommended appetizer is the quail's eggs in haddock-and-cheese sauce, and, for the truly British experience, finish with bread-and-butter pudding or spotted dick (sponge pudding). You'll hardly be able to get up from the table.

Tate Gallery Restaurant

Tate Gallery, Millbank SW1. **Map** 21 B2. **C** *0171-887 8877.* **Open** *noon–3pm Mon–Sat.* **Closed** *Christmas & public hols.* 🌶️🎎♿ ♟️ 🗝️ *MC, V.* £££

The food is an interesting mix of traditional old English cooking (roast beef, steak-and-kidney pie) and the very new (scallop mousse with pink grapefruit sauce, veal-and-apricot galantine). A main attraction, apart from the excellent wine list, is the opportunity of dining amid the impressive and unusual setting of the Rex Whistler mural *Expedition in Pursuit of Rare Meats. (See also p82.)*

Veronica's

3 Hereford Rd W2. **Map** 10 D2.
C *0171-229 5079*. **Open** *noon–3pm & 7pm–midnight*. **Closed** *Sat lunch, Sun, public hols.* 🍴 V 🔲 👤 🏧
🍷 *AE, DC, MC, V.* ⓔⓔⓔ

Veronica's specializes in a style of British regional and historical cooking that is unique among London restaurants. Dishes might include calves' liver and beetroot (1940), spring lamb with crabmeat (19th century) or Hannah Woolley chicken and mustard (1644). Every couple of months, proprietress Veronica Shaw changes both the menu and the decor to tie in with a different theme (such as Scottish or Tudor food, the Middle Ages or World War II).

Wilson's

236 Blythe Road, W14. **Map** 17 A1.
C *0171-603 7267*. **Open** *12:30–2:30pm Sun–Fri, 7:30–10:30pm Mon–Sat.* **Closed** *Christmas week, public hols.* 🍴 👤 🍷 *MC, V.* ⓔⓔⓔ

Bob Wilson runs the best "Scottish" restaurant in London. It's not a theme park, though; dishes from the daily-changing menu are mostly Anglo-Gallic, though there are a few Scottish dishes such as haggis, Athol brose (a dessert of cream with oats, whisky and honey), plus of course Scotch beef and salmon. There are also half a dozen malt whiskies to choose from. After dinner Mr. Wilson will play the bagpipes, if requested.

As London's longest established "guest" cuisine, French food is readily available throughout the capital, and the quality can be superb. La Tante Claire and Nico at Ninety Park Lane (three Michelin stars) and Le Gavroche (two), are legendary names on the London restaurant scene, and prices are commensurately high. You'll find most types of French food well represented in London, from *haute cuisine*, through the modern, lighter style, to traditional, regional cuisines.

Auberge de Provence

41 Buckingham Gate SW1.
Map 12 F5. **C** *0171-821 1899*.
Open *12:30–2:30pm Mon–Fri, 7:30–11pm Mon–Sat.* 🔲 🍴 👤
🍷 *AE, DC, MC, V, JCB.*
ⓔⓔⓔⓔⓔ

This white-painted cavernous-but-cozy restaurant is attached to the St. James Court Hotel, near Victoria Station. The combinations of lightly cooked meats and delicate fish, with imaginatively flavored sauces and fresh fruits and vegetables are inspired. This is the best place in London for a taste of Provence.

Café des Amis du Vin

11–14 Hanover Place WC2.
Map 13 C2. **C** *0171-379 3444*.
Open *noon–2:30pm & 6–11:30pm Mon–Sat, noon–10:30pm Sun.* 🍴
👤 🏧 🍷 *AE, DC, MC, V, JCB.* ⓔⓔⓔ

This popular brasserie, just across the road from the Royal Opera House, is usually filled with customers. The food can be simple – omelettes or meaty Toulouse sausages in the bar – or more elaborate, ranging from trout stuffed with spinach and turkey brochettes in the café, to fish terrine, pan-fried calves' liver with lime and chargrilled steaks with piquant sauces in the restaurant.

Le Gavroche

43 Upper Brook St W1. **Map** 12 D2.
C *0171-408 0881or 0171-499 1826*.
Open *noon–2pm, 7–11pm Mon–Fri.*
Closed *public hols.* 🍴 🔲 👤 ★
🍷 *AE, DC, MC, V.* ⓔⓔⓔⓔⓔ

This is the high temple of *haute cuisine*, with prices to match. However, the standard of cooking set by the Roux brothers is consistently superb. The Roux philosophy is to create a perfect marriage between ingredients, cooking methods and flavourings – for example, sautéed scallops in a soy and spice sauce, served with crisp, fried vegetable strips. Décor, like the food, is tasteful and firmly traditional. The service is relentlessly formal, the menu written entirely in French, and the wine list vast and daunting (800 wines). If you want to experience Le Gavroche on a budget, there are set meals which work out half the price of going *à la carte* – two people might even get some change from a hundred quid.

Mon Plaisir

21 Monmouth St WC2. **Map** 13 B2.
C *0171-836 7243*. **Open** *noon–2:15pm, 6–11:15pm daily.* 🍴
🍷 *AE, DC, MC, V, JCB.* ⓔⓔⓔ

A long-standing fixture of Covent Garden's theaterland, Mon Plaisir retains its reputation for reliable, unpretentious French provincial food, cooked and served with care and courtesy. The menu changes, but you will usually find the likes of fish soup, goat's cheese salad, snails in garlic, *coq au vin*, *daube de boeuf* and a marvellous array of cheeses. The pre-theater fixed-price menu is particularly convenient.

Nico at Ninety

90 Park La W1. **Map** 12 D3.
C *0171-409 1290*. **Open** *noon–2pm & 7–11pm Mon–Fri, 7–11pm Sat.*
Closed *public hol eves, 10 days Christmas.* 🍴 👤 🔲 ★ 🍷 *AE, DC, MC, V.* ⓔⓔⓔⓔⓔ

Nico at Ninety is the new three-star Michelin headquarters of volatile superstar chef Nico Ladenis. In these spacious surroundings, Nico's artistry runs riot. Foie gras is a recurring theme, adding a richness and strength of flavor that is balanced by painstakingly delicate touches. Nico's other restaurants, Nico Central on Great Portland Street (0171-436 8846) and Simply Nico near Victoria Station (0171-630 8061), allow you to enjoy less complicated creations in more cramped surroundings. Here, the provençal influence is more peasant- than prince-oriented; dishes might be fish soup, squid salad or duck confit with herb dumplings.

Pied-à-Terre

34 Charlotte St W1. **Map** 13 A1.
C *0171-636 1178*. **Open** *12:15–2:30pm Mon–Fri, 7:15–10:15pm Mon–Sat.* **Closed** *last week Dec–1st week Jan, last 2 weeks Aug.* 🍴
🍷 *AE, DC, MC, V.* ⓔⓔⓔⓔⓔ

In the shadow of the Telecom Tower, this somewhat serious French restaurant is a beacon of quality in a street of mainly cheap-and-cheerful eating houses. Both decor and menu are on the stark side, but the food is rich in the extreme. Appetizers favor seafood (tagliatelle of langoustines, roasted scallops with coriander, crab galette); main courses are meat-orientated – pigeon, lamb, even pig's head. Wines start expensive and go upward.

Le Pont de la Tour

Butlers Wharf SE1. **Map** 16 E4.
C *0171-403 8403*. **Bar and grill open** *noon–midnight daily.*
Restaurant open *noon–3pm daily, 6pm–midnight Mon–Sat, 6–11pm Sun.* 🍴 👤 🎵 🔲 🏧 🍷 *AE, MC, V.* ⓔⓔⓔⓔⓔ

This riverside creation of design mogul Terence Conran boasts, among other things, wonderful views of Tower Bridge. Set in a converted warehouse, the interior of the restaurant has the stylish look of an ocean liner; the food is equally bold and streamlined: pea risotto with mint, scallops with garlic butter, calves' liver with red onions, grilled tuna with coriander. There is also a bar, as well as a grill serving seafood, steaks, and salads. Bread comes from the house bakery.

RSJ

13a Coin St SE1. **Map** 14 E3.
[*0171-928 4554.* **Open** noon–2pm
Mon–Fri, 6–11pm Mon–Sat. **Closed**
public hols. ᵀᵉᴵ ᵫ ᵽ ᵿ AE, MC,
V. ££££

RSJ serves a mixture of unspec-
tacular but well-executed dishes.
Salmon, lamb, duck and chicken
are the most commonly featured,
served both plain and with sauces.
An extraordinarily good wine list
specializes in wines of the Loire
region of France.

St. Quentin Restaurant

243 Brompton Rd SW3. **Map** 19 B1.
[*0171-581 8377.* **Open** noon–3pm
& 7–11:30pm Mon –Sat, noon –3:30pm
& 6:30–10:30pm Sun. ᵀᵉᴵ ᵿ AE,
DC, MC, V. £££

In this many-mirrored meeting
place of well-to-do local residents,
the decor is matched by the rich
food: foie gras, confit of duck,
chicken in cream. It can be
expensive, but the set menus
provide an escape. The Grill St.
Quentin (0171-581 8377), just
around the corner, specializes in
seafood and is more child-friendly
than most London restaurants. The
pâtisserie at both St. Quentin
restaurants is superb.

Spread Eagle

1–2 Stockwell St SE10. **Map** 23 B2.
[*0181-853 2333.* **Open** 6:30–
10:30pm Mon–Sat, noon–3:30pm
Sun. ᵀᵉᴵ ᵫ ⃰ AE, DC, MC, V.
£££

If you're visiting Greenwich, eat at
the Spread Eagle, one of the few
reliable and reasonably-priced
restaurants in the area. Set meals
of hearty, no-nonsense food are
served in this dark and rather
quaint 17th-century coaching inn:
generous mussel soup, seafood
sausage, veal kidneys in mussel
sauce and the excellent lamb
with tomatoes and black olives.

La Tante Claire

68 Royal Hospital Rd SW3.
Map 19 C3. [*0171-351 0227* or
0171-352 6045. **Open** 12:30–2pm &
7–11pm Mon–Fri. **Closed** public hols.
ᵀᵉᴵ ᵫ ᵽ ⃰ ᵿ AE, DC, MC,
V, JCB. £££££

You have to reserve well ahead at
this small, top-notch expensive
establishment. Gascon owner-chef,
Pierre Koffman, likes to cook rich
dishes, using goose fat and foie
gras liberally. Stuffed pig's trotter,
tournedos Rossini and kid (goat)
with chocolate and raspberry-
vinegar sauce represent the typical
cooking style.

MODERN INTERNATIONAL

These restaurants represent an
approach to cooking that has
evolved quite recently. Its main
feature is a willingness to borrow
ingredients and styles from various
cuisines all over the world and to
create something new: a dish might
include a cut of British lamb, some
Oriental herbs and a few sun-dried
tomatoes from Italy. The lightness
of touch and innovative use of
fresh ingredients is much favored
by adventurous new chefs, such
as Sally Clarke and Alastair Little.

Alastair Little

49 Frith St W1. **Map** 13 A2.
[*0171-734 5183.* **Open** noon–3pm
Mon–Fri, 6–11:30pm Mon–Sat.
Closed public hols. ᵀᵉᴵ ᵫ ★ ᵿ
AE, MC, V. £££££

This bastion of innovation in the
heart of Soho serves always
interesting food in a rather spartan
restaurant that perpetually treads
the line between lively and plain
noisy. Star dishes are fish soup,
tournedos with polenta, oysters
with Thai sausages, plus anything
else that sports Alastair Little's
brilliant relishes or garnishes.

Bibendum

Michelin House, 81 Fulham Road
SW3. **Map** 19 A2. [*0171-581 5817.*
Open 12:30–2:30pm Mon–Fri,
7–11:30pm Mon–Sat; 12:30–3pm,
7–10:30pm Sat–Sun. **Closed** Easter
Mon, 4 days Christmas. ᵀᵉᴵ ᵫ ᵽ
★ ᵿ MC, V. £££££

In the glorious stained-glass
setting of the restored Michelin
building, well-heeled diners feast
on the sophisticated creations of
top chef Simon Hopkinson.
Calves' kidneys are matched with
anchovy butter, poached veal with
watercress purée; bacon is used to
wrap a host of meats. There are
sensational risottos, and you can
choose from a splendid wine list.
Reserve well in advance.

Bistrot Bruno

63 Frith Street W1. [*0171-734
4545.* **Open** 12:15–2:30pm Mon–Fri,
6:15–11:30pm Mon–Sat. ★ ᵿ AE,
DC, MC, V. £££

This bare but comfortable canteen
serves Bruno Loubet's eclectic but
uncommonly successful dishes.
The combinations in main courses
might include duck *confit* on
chestnut and celeriac with a red
onion gravy, or jugged hare with
split pea ravioli. Appetizers and
desserts are equally improbable,
but the overall effect is satisfying.

Boyd's

135 Kensington Church St W8.
Map 10 D4. [*0171-727 5452.*
Open 12:30–2:30pm & 7–11pm Mon–
Sat. ᵀᵉᴵ ᵫ ᵿ AE, MC, V. £££

The calling card of chef-owner
Boyd Gilmour is his ability with
sauces: wholegrain mustard sauce
(calves' liver), béarnaise (beef),
pink peppercorn (venison). He
also borrows his flavors from
around the world – lime juice, soy
sauce, ginger and sesame oil.
Desserts have a tendency towards
chocolate and cream.

Le Caprice

Arlington House, Arlington St SW1.
Map 12 F3. [*0171-629 2239.*
Open noon–3pm & 6pm–midnight
daily. **Closed** Dec 24–Jan 2. ᵫ ᵽ
ᵿ AE, DC, MC, V. £££££

This stylish, elder sister of The Ivy
(*see p298*) attracts the same kind
of elegant and celebrity-studded
clientele. The food is simple,
modern and uses influences and
ingredients from all corners of the
globe, with the emphasis on grills
(tuna, rabbit and squid). Gravy
and thick sauces are taboo – clean
lines and clean shirt fronts are
essential in such a high-profile
eaterie. Book well ahead.

Clarke's

124 Kensington Church St W8.
Map 10 D4. [*0171-221 9225.*
Open 12:30–2pm & 7–10pm
Mon–Fri. **Closed** 2 weeks summer,
Christmas, Easter, public hols. ᵀᵉᴵ
ᵫ ᵽ ★ ᵿ MC, V. ££££

Britain, California and Italy meet
over a charcoal grill in the kitchens
of talented chef-proprietress Sally
Clarke. There is a set dinner menu
that changes daily and is always
superb. Food is light but incredibly
tasty; recurring ingredients are
Mediterranean vegetables, corn-fed
chicken, salmon, bream, fresh
herbs and wild plants like
dandelion and elderflower.

The Halcyon

129 Holland Park Ave W11.
Map 9 A4. [*0171-727 7288.*
Open 7–10:30am, noon–2:30pm &
7–10:30pm daily. ᵀᵉᴵ ᵽ ᵿ AE,
DC, MC, V. £££££

Housed at the back of the Halcyon
Hotel (*see p278*), this is a frequent
stopping place of the stars. For an
appetizer, the Japanese-style beef
tataki is marvelous; also try the
marinated scallops and the foie gras
with brioche. The main courses are
always interesting – for example
chicken with eggplant and mint,
duck with honey and almonds.

For key to symbols see p287.

Hilaire

68 Old Brompton Rd SW7.
Map 18 F2. 0171-584 8993. **Open**
12:30–2:30pm & 6:30–11:30pm Mon–
Fri, 6:30–11:30pm Sat.
AE, DC, MC, V. ££££££

Thick drapes and a sweeping glass
frontage welcome diners to this
rather boudoirlike restaurant that
serves similarly sumptuous food.
Rather than use conventional
sauces, owner-chef Bryan Webb
flavors meat and fish with pesto,
chutney, foie gras or herbed or
spiced lentils. His supper menu
(after 9:30pm) is the cheapest way
to get the best out of this most
original of eating places.

The Ivy

1 West St WC2. **Map** 13 B2.
0171-836 4751. **Open** noon–3pm
& 5:30–midnight daily. AE,
DC, MC, V. ££££

The Ivy has long been a landmark of the theater district and
traditional venue for first-night
parties. Stars cluster in the oak-
paneled, leather-benched interior
to dine on fashionable fare like
salmon fishcakes with arugula and
shaved Parmesan salad.

Kensington Place

201–205 Kensington Church St W8.
Map 9 C3. 0171-727 3184.
Open noon–3pm, 6:30–11:45pm
Mon–Sat; noon–3:30pm, 6:30–10:15pm
Sun. **Closed** Aug public hol, Christmas.
MC. £££

This austerely decorated restaurant
attracts a noisy, vibrant crowd. It
combines conventional fare like
steak au poivre and grilled salmon
with the unusual – braised squid
with peas, pigeon crostini (on
toasted or fried bread) with truffle
paste, boiled ox tongue with
lentils and salsa verde, raspberries
with mascarpone cheese.

Leith's

92 Kensington Park Rd W11.
Map 9 B2. 0171-229 4481.
Open 7:30–11:30pm daily.
AE, DC, MC, V.
££££££

Hushed diners explore gourmet
offerings at this elegant restaurant
run by good-food apostle Prue
Leith, proprietor of Leith's School
of Food and Wine. British
specialities include rib of beef and
ox tongue, and there is an all-
British cheeseboard. Small, filled
savoury tartlets are a recurring
feature, along with monkfish,
scallops and guinea fowl. An
outstanding vegetarian menu
offers imaginative dishes and is
very popular with omnivores too.

Mijanou

143 Ebury St SW1. **Map** 20 E2.
0171-730 4099. **Open** noon–2pm
& 7–11pm Mon–Fri. **Closed** 2 weeks
Christmas, 1 week Easter, 3 weeks
Aug, public hols.
AE, MC, V. £££££

Owners Mr. (wine) and Mrs. (food)
Blech pair ingredients and wine
with great care and ingenuity:
quail slices in a foie gras mousse
beside an orange and passion fruit
jelly, or a mousseline of melon
with raisin-stuffed ham slices. The
wine list is one of London's best.

Mulligan's of Mayfair

13–14 Cork St W1. **Map** 12 F3.
0171-409 1370. **Open** noon–
2:15pm Mon–Fri, 6:30–11pm
Mon–Sat. **Closed** public hols. AE,
DC, MC, V. ££££

Dishes tend to be hearty at this
Irish basement restaurant – turnip
and brown bread soup, black
pudding, ox tongue, and a good
range of fish dishes. Sample
specialities such as colcannon
(mashed cabbage and potatoes)
and boxty (potato pancake).

Museum Street Café

47 Museum St WC1. **Map** 13 B1.
0171-405 3211. **Open** 12:30–
2:30pm, 6:30–9:30pm Mon–Fri.
£££

The student-dive decor and the
blackboard-only menu are more
than made up for by the excellent
cooking, which makes good use
of Californian charcoal grilling and
trendy Italian ingredients such as
bresaola, arugula (rocket) and
pesto. Bring your own liquor.

Quaglino's

16 Bury Street SW1. **Map** 12 F3.
0171-930 6767. **Open**
noon–3pm daily, 5.30–midnight
Mon–Thu, 5:30pm–1am Fri–Sun.
Closed Christmas, New Year.
AE, DC, MC, V. ££££

Terence Conran's flagship in the
center of town has great elegance
and attention to detail. This is a
bustling barn of a place though,
and not the place for a discreet
and relaxing meal. The seafood is
particularly recommended; the
service can be brusque.

The Restaurant

Hyde Park Hotel, 66 Knightsbridge
SW1. **Map** 11 C5. 0171-259
5380. **Open** noon–2:15pm Mon–Fri,
7-11pm Mon–Sat. **Closed** public
hols, Christmas–New Year.
AE, DC, MC, V. £££££

Food critics have showered praise
and awards on the talented and
temperamental chef Marco Pierre
White. White moved to these new
premises from the less imposing
Harvey's in Wandsworth during
1994 – and has added his third
Michelin star. His sauces travel
from the subtle to the exquisite,
ranging from Sauternes to soy-
based, with foie gras and truffles
featuring prominently. Fish and
seafood are particular strengths,
and his desserts are sublime.
There's a three-course set lunch
costing under £30, but dinner will
cost more than double this.

Stephen Bull

5–7 Blandford St W1. **Map** 12 D1.
0171-486 9696. **Open** 12:15–
2:30pm Mon–Fri, 6:30–10:30pm
Mon–Sat. MC, V.
£££

This immaculate and stylish
modern restaurant offers delicate,
rather than sturdy, fare: crab-and-
orange ravioli with basil cream,
cuttlefish risotto with saffron and
lemon, grilled baby chicken with
citrus fruit. The fish dishes are
particularly well executed, and an
interesting wine list offers good
value. There's also a bistro and
bar (0171-490 1750) near Smithfield
Market (see p164), offering
cheaper food in a striking setting.

Turner's

87–9 Walton St SW3. **Map** 19 B2.
0171-584 6711. **Open** 12:30–
2:30pm & 7:30–11pm Sun–Fri,
7:30–11pm Sat. **Closed** Dec 25–31.
AE, DC, MC.
£££££

This highly acclaimed restaurant
serves clever but unpretentious
food to its fashionable clientele:
guinea fowl terrine with pistachio
nuts, roast turbot with butter-bean
ragôut, grilled beef with bone-
marrow sauce, lamb with duck
liver in black olive sauce. Other
distinctive features are a long
Chablis list (there are 15 types)
and burly owner-chef Brian
Turner, who is often to be seen
out among the diners.

ITALIAN

Italian cuisine in London is
undergoing a renaissance. A
move away from the pizza, pasta
and veal standards, toward a
style that combines traditional
home cooking with a modern
lightness of touch, has captivated
the capital's gourmets. Seafood,
beans, mixed-leaf salads, charcoal
grilled vegetables and pan-roasted
meats, stuffed breads, polenta and
wild mushrooms feature strongly.

L'Accento Italiano

16 Garway Rd W2. **Map** 10 D2.
📞 0171-243 2201. **Open** 12:30–
2:30pm & 6:30–11:30pm daily. 🍽️🅶
🚼 ♿ 🔲 🔳 *MC, V.* £££
This popular restaurant offers
stylish new-wave Italian food. It
has one of the best-value set
menus in town which might
feature saffron risotto with
sausages, followed by a warm
salad of octopus and potato. A
typical dessert is sweet fritters with
a fruit sauce. The menu changes
frequently, but standards remain
high. Reserve ahead.

The Alba

107 Whitecross St EC1. **Map** 7 A4.
📞 0171-588 1798. **Open** noon–3pm
& 6–11pm Mon–Fri. **Closed** public
hols. 🆅 🔲 *AE, DC, MC, V, JCB.*
£££
Stark and clean, this place offers an
interesting range of meat, fish and
vegetable dishes. Italian cheeses,
wild mushrooms and fresh herbs
feature strongly, and the pasta and
sausages – both homemade – are
particularly good. Eat in the wine
bar if you don't want a full meal.

Bertorelli's

44a Floral St WC2. **Map** 13 C2.
📞 0171-836 3969. **Open** noon–3pm
& 5:30–11:30pm Mon–Sat. 🆅 ♿
restaurant only. 🔲 *AE, DC, MC, V,
JCB.* £££
This slick operation near the
Opera House is used to dealing
with rushed pre-theatre diners.
Upstairs there is a grander
restaurant, while downstairs a
simpler café concentrates on
reliable pasta and pizza dishes.
Booking is essential.

Cibo

3 Russell Gdns W14. **Map** 9 A5.
📞 0171-371 2085. **Open** noon–3pm
Sun–Fri, 7–11pm Mon–Sat. 🍽️🅶
🚼 ♿ ★ 🔲 *AE, DC, MC, V.*
££££
This is one of the leaders in the
move toward traditional Italian
home cooking. Pasta here is stuffed
with wild mushrooms, broad beans
or sea bass and spinach. Salads are
red, green and orange, and there
are charcoal grilled lamb cutlets
and sautéed calves' liver. Noisy,
trendy and bright.

Eleven Park Walk

11 Park Walk SW10. **Map** 18 F4.
📞 0171-352 3449. **Open** noon–
3pm daily, 7pm–11pm Mon–Sat.
Closed public hols. 🍽️🅶 🚼 ♿ 🔲
🔲 *AE, MC, V, JCB.* £££

With well-spaced tables, mirrors
and potted plants, this reliable, if
somewhat conventional, restaurant
is patronized by a band of local
devotees. Go for standards like
ravioli with tomato and basil,
scallops with wine sauce and
spaghetti with fresh lobster.

La Famiglia

7 Langton St SW7. **Map** 18 F4.
📞 0171-351 0761. **Open** noon–3pm
& 7pm–midnight daily. **Closed**
Christmas, Easter. 🆅 🚼 ♿ 🔲
🔲 *AE, DC, MC, V.* £££
This bright, noisy, for-all-the-family
place has a fresh blue-and-white-
tiled interior and large awnings in
the back garden – eating outside is
a particular treat. The grilled and
baked fish and traditional appetizers
such as mozzarella salad and *pasta
e fagioli* (pasta with white beans),
are highly recommended.

L'Incontro

87 Pimlico Rd SW1. **Map** 20 D2.
📞 0171-730 6327 or 0171-730 3663.
Open 12:30–11:30pm Mon–Fri, 7–
11:30pm Sat, Sun. 🚼 ♿ 🔲 🔲
🔲 *AE, DC, MC, V, JCB.* ££££
Clean and gleaming, there is a
distinct leaning towards Venetian
food – fish in particular – in this
startlingly designed establishment.
Try the salt cod with olive oil and
milk or the squid-in-its-own-ink.
The fresh pasta is legendary.

Neal Street Restaurant

26 Neal St WC2. **Map** 13 B1.
📞 0171-836 8368. **Open** 12:30–
2:30pm & 7:30–11pm Mon–Sat.
Closed public hols, 1 week Christmas,
New Year. 🍽️🅶 ♿ 🔲 🔲 🔲 *AE,
DC, MC, V* £££££
Famed for his passion for fungi,
owner Antonio Carluccio makes
sure a mushroomy theme runs
through the menu at this stylish
eating place. There's wild
mushroom soup, warm mushroom
and bacon salad, venison with
morels and beef medallions with
wild mushrooms. Make sure to ask
how much the seasonal mushroom
special costs before you order it:
the prices can be astronomical.

Orso

27 Wellington St WC2. **Map** 13 C2.
📞 0171-240 5269. **Open** noon–
midnight daily. **Closed** Christmas,
public hols. 🔲 £££
At this gathering point for media
and theater types, the food is
modern and constantly changing.
It is particularly noted for
innovative pasta and meat and fish
in bold sauces. Service is brisk.

Osteria Antica Bologna

23 Northcote Rd SW11.
📞 0171-978 4771. **Open** 6–11pm
Mon–Tue, noon–11pm Wed–Sat,
12:30–10:30pm Sun. 🍽️🅶 🆅
🚼 ♿ 🔲 🔲 *AE, MC, V.*
££
This is an ideal venue for parties;
friends can enjoy a cheap but
satisfying meal by sharing a
selection of small dishes *(assagi)* –
delicious vegetable and fish
combinations for a few pounds.
Otherwise, there's an impressive
selection of innovative salads,
pastas and meat and fish.

The Peasant

240 St. John Street EC1.
Map 6 F3. 📞 0171-336 7726.
Open 12:30–2:30pm Mon–Fri,
6:30–10:45pm Mon–Sat. **Closed**
public hols, Dec 24–Jan 3. ★ 🆅 🚼
🔲 *MC, V.* £££
This converted pub produces
modern Italianate meals that put
many grander Italian restaurants to
shame. Fresh ingredients are
cooked without cream or alcohol
sauces to produce simple, robust
dishes served in generous portions.
The bottled beers are interesting
too. Prices seem high for a pub,
but this is pub food like no other.

River Café

Thames Wharf Studios, Rainville Rd W6.
📞 0171-381 8824. **Open** 12:30–
2:30pm & 7:30–11pm Mon–Fri,
1–2:30pm & 7:30–11pm Sat,
1–2:30pm Sun. **Closed** public hols.
🚼 ♿ 🔲 🔲 ★ 🔲 *MC, V.*
££££
Praise has been heaped on this
headquarters of the Italian new-
wave movement. Both the food
and the surroundings are clean,
light and crisp. Mozzarella, sage,
sun-dried tomatoes, Parmesan,
pine nuts, basil, thyme and garlic
are the recurring flavors that
accompany delicious charcoal
grilled fish and meats.

Riva

169 Church Road SW13.
📞 0181-748 0434. **Open**
12–2:30pm Sun–Fri, 7–11pm
Mon–Sat, 7–9:30pm Sun.
🆅 🚼 ♿ ★ 🔲 *MC, V.* £££
Barnes is a long way out from the
center of town, but residents of
southwest London are devoted to
the regional Italian cooking served
here. The emphasis is on top-
quality ingredients combined in
imaginative ways. Seafood and fish
are always well-represented on the
menu, which changes regularly.
Quiet, civilized, and great value.

For key to symbols see p287.

GREEK
MIDDLE EASTERN

Cuisines from all over the Middle East (Greece, Turkey, Lebanon and North Africa) have a lot in common. Dishes tend to be lightly rather than heavily spiced – barbecued meats, herby stews, salads and vegetable dips such as *taramasalata* (cod's roe), *hummus* (chick pea) and *tzatziki* (yogurt and cucumber) feature strongly. The cheapest way to eat is with a set-price *meze* – a selection of such dishes: it's a sociable affair and particularly good for those new to this food.

Daphne

83 Bayham St NW1. **Map** 4 F1.
(0171-267 7322. **Open** noon–2:30pm & 6–11:30pm daily. **Closed** Jan 1 & Dec 25–26. V ⚑ & ⚑ ⚑ MC, V. £££

Daphne is a welcoming and friendly place. It offers all that's best about good Greek food: simple and fresh ingredients, carefully flavored with herbs and at a reasonable price. Good meat and fish dishes predominate, but there is also a changing list of vegetarian specials. The *meze* is superb value.

Al Hamra

31–33 Shepherd Market W1.
Map 12 E4. (0171-493 1954.
Open noon–11:45pm daily. V ⚑ ⚑ ⚑ AE, DC, MC, V. ££££

On arrival at this smart Lebanese restaurant you will be brought a plate of olives, fresh Middle Eastern bread and raw vegetables to accompany the *meze* dishes, of which there are over 40. Try the *moutabal*, made with eggplant and sesame, or for a warm dish, the *houmous kawarmah* (chick pea paste topped with lamb and pine nuts). The service is formal.

Istanbul Iskembecisi

9 Stoke Newington Road N16.
(0171-254 7291. **Open** 5pm–5am Mon–Sat, 2pm–5am Sun. ⚑ ⚑ ⚑ MC, V. £££

Istanbul Iskembecisi specializes in Turkish home-cooking, including several authentic offal dishes, such as grilled lamb intestines and boiled brains with salad. It also serves excellent dishes for the fainter of heart, such as char-grilled meats. It's lively, with charming staff and low prices.

Lemonia

89 Regents Park Road NW1.
Map 3 C1. (0171-586 7454. **Open** noon–3pm Sun–Fri, 6–11:30pm Mon–Sat. V ⚑ & £££

This enormously popular Greek restaurant serves beautifully prepared food in a bustling atmosphere. The menu includes such good vegetarian options as stuffed vegetables and bean and lentil dishes; the *meze* dishes include a fine *tabouleh* (a bulgar wheat salad) and eggplant dip. Reserve evenings well in advance.

Mega Kalamaras

76 Inverness Mews W2. **Map** 10 E2.
(0171-727 9122. **Open** 7pm–midnight Mon–Sat. **Closed** public hols. ⚑ ⚑ V ⚑ & ⚑ on request. ⚑ AE, DC, MC, V. £££

This is the best Greek cooking in London, served in spacious surroundings with a pleasantly laid-back atmosphere. The menu includes a wide and creative choice of vegetarian dishes. Seafood and casserole dishes are also well represented, but choosing the *meze* often makes the most interesting meal. Micro Kalamaras next door is a bring-your-own-booze basement taverna that packs out with merry bargain hunters.

Sofra

18 Shepherd St W1. **Map** 12 E4.
(0171-493 3320. **Open** noon–midnight daily. ⚑ ⚑ V ⚑ AE, DC, MC. ££££

Sofra is one of the best-known and most expensive Turkish restaurants in London. The meat grills are good, but the real attraction is the delicious but tiny *meze* dishes: *kisir* (a crushed-wheat salad), *imam biyaldi* (stuffed aubergine), *böreks* (filled pastries) and so on. The desserts are superb, too.

OTHER
EUROPEAN

Although most international cuisine can be found in London, some are restricted to only one or two establishments of any note. The British generally favor food from climates more southern and exotic than their own, but there are a few Northern and Eastern European restaurants well worth a visit.

Anna's Place

90 Mildmay Pk N1. (0171-249 9379. **Open** 12:15–2:15pm & 7:15–10:30pm Tue–Sat. **Closed** Christmas, 2 wks Easter, Aug. ⚑ ⚑ £££

Virtually everything in this airy Swedish restaurant is homemade, including the bread and the sorbets. With the attentive service, and Anna herself as often as not stopping by your table for a chat, it is like eating in a friend's kitchen. The menu is short, with marinated fish and meat featuring strongly. The main courses include some quite simple dishes – roast lamb in a herb crust, grilled fish and more traditional Swedish specialties. The desserts, in particular, are not to be missed. Reserving in advance is essential, especially if you want to sit outside on the very pretty terrace.

Bloom's

90 Whitechapel High St E1.
Map 16 E1. (0171-247 6001 or 0171-247 6835. **Open** 11am–9:30pm Mon–Thu, 11am–3pm Fri. **Closed** Dec 25, Jewish hols. ⚑ & & AE, DC, MC, V. ££

After a Sunday morning spent bargain hunting among the stalls of nearby Petticoat Lane, you can have lunch at London's most famous Jewish eating house. The food and decor are a throwback to the city's old East End. Start with a good, thick beetroot, barley or butter-bean soup and continue with the chopped liver or the salt beef. The traditional accompaniments to these are fried potato latkes and dill pickles.

Caravela

39 Beauchamp Place SW3.
Map 19 B1. (0171-581 2366.
Open noon–3pm Mon–Sat, 7pm–11:30pm daily. ⚑ ⚑ AE, DC, MC, V. ££££

In the evenings a serenading guitarist and *fado* singer add to the holiday atmosphere in this lively Portuguese restaurant. The food draws on a tradition of simple peasant cooking dominated by seafood – salt cod, grilled fish and shellfish – plus soups, marinated meats and fresh vegetables and salads.

The Gay Hussar

2 Greek St W1. **Map** 13 B2.
(0171-437 0973. **Open** 12:30–2:30pm & 5:30–11pm Mon–Sat. **Closed** public hols. ⚑ ⚑ ★ ⚑ AE. £££

The atmosphere in the city's only Hungarian restaurant is masculine and library like. For many years politicians and literary figures have gathered in the wood-paneled and velvet-upholstered interior to feast on such specialties as the renowned chilled wild cherry soup; stuffed cabbage; pork Schnitzel with smoked sausage; cold pike; and, of course, the rich goulash with egg dumplings, spiked with Hungarian paprika.

Nikita's

65 Ifield Rd SW10. **Map** 18 E4.
(0171-352 6326. **Open** 7:30–
11:30pm Mon–Sat. **Closed** public
hols. **⚫ ⚫ ⚫** AE, MC, V. **€€€€**

This exotic basement restaurant
serves excellent Russian food:
borscht (beetroot soup), *pirozhki*
(meat pastries), *blinis* (yeast
pancakes) with smoked salmon
and sour cream, chicken Kiev,
beef Stroganoff and salmon
coulibiac (stuffed with rice and
egg and encased in pastry). Stars
of the show are the vodkas in
17 different flavors, such as
pepper, lemon and tarragon; the
carafes come spectacularly
encased in ice.

Ognisko Polskie

55 Prince's Gate, SW7.
Map 11 A5. **(** 0171-589 4635.
Open noon–3pm, 6–11pm daily.
⚫ ⚫ €€€

This Polish restaurant and bar are
set together in a rather grand old
Knightsbridge building. The Polish
dishes consist of the usual hearty
combinations of heavy dumplings,
sauerkraut and bits and pieces of
meat, but cooked more deftly than
you'll find in Warsaw. The bar is
open all afternoon and serves a
good selection of vodkas, popular
with the many Polish regulars.

Wodka

12 St. Albans Gro W8. **Map** 10 E5.
(0171-937 6513. **Open** 12:30–
2:30pm & 7–11:15pm Mon–Fri,
7–11pm Sat, 1–3:30pm Sun. **⚫** AE,
MC, V. **€€€**

A mixture of heavy traditional and
light modern Polish food is served
in this small, bare, but friendly
setting. Alongside the bulky
standards – meat-stuffed cabbage
(*golabki*) and olive-stuffed beef
(*zrazy*) – you can find vegetable
timbale with couscous, blinis with
eggplant mousse and chicken with
lentils and mustard sauce.

FISH AND SEAFOOD

London boasts a thriving, though
fairly small, collection of fish
restaurants, the best of which get
their produce fresh every morning
from local markets. Solid, old-
fashioned establishments like
Manzi's and Wheeler's serve a
traditional mix of grilled, poached,
fried and steamed plaice, cod,
haddock, sole and salmon, plus
richer dishes with cream and
butter sauces. Others have a
range of allegiances from Jewish
(Grahame's) to French (Le Suquet)
and Italian (L'Altro).

L'Altro

210 Kensington Park Road W11.
Map 9 B2. **(** 0171-792 1066 or 0171-
792 1077. **Open** noon–2:30pm &
7–11pm Mon–Thu, noon–2:30pm &
7–11:30pm Fri, Sat, noon–3pm Sun.
⚫ ⚫ ⚫ ⚫ ⚫ AE, DC, MC.
€€€

In this busy spin-off of Cibo (*see
p299*) highlights include seafood
risotto, octopus-and-arugula salad,
roast sea bass with rosemary-
dotted potatoes and *gratinata di
mare* (shellfish in olive oil, lemon
and breadcrumbs). The wine list is
informative and friendly.

Bill Bentley's

31 Beauchamp Pl SW3. **Map** 19 B1.
(0171-589 5080. **Open** 11:30am–
2:30pm & 6–10:30pm Mon–Sat.
⚫ MC. **€€€**

Standing in Knightsbridge's main
restaurant street, this busy eating
place has a pleasant open-air
patio. The short Anglo-French
menu includes traditional dishes
like oysters, smoked salmon and
Dover sole, alongside up-to-date,
more adventurous offerings such
as cod in a herb crust and grilled
red mullet with balsamic vinegar
and coriander.

Café Fish

39 Panton St SW1. **Map** 13 A3.
(0171-930 3999. **Open** noon–3pm
Mon–Fri, 5:45–11:30pm Mon–Sat.
Wine bar open 11:30am–11pm
Mon–Sat. **⚫ ⚫** restaurant only. **⚫**
⚫ ⚫ AE, DC, MC, JCB. **€€€**

This large, bustling, sea-green-
colored restaurant and wine bar is
a convenient two-minute walk
from Piccadilly. Appetizers are
straightforward (oysters, whitebait,
smoked salmon, fish soup), but
the main courses lean toward
cream and butter sauces. A short
wine list has one of the cheapest
house champagnes in London.

Grahame's Seafare

38 Poland St W1. **Map** 12 F1.
(0171-437 0975 or 0171-437 3788.
Open noon–2:45pm & 5:30–9pm
Sun–Thu, noon–2:45pm & 5:30–8pm
Fri & Sat. **Closed** public hols, 2 weeks
Christmas. **⚫ ⚫ ⚫ ⚫ ⚫** AE,
DC, MC. **€€€**

This Jewish restaurant serves
kosher specialties such as gefilte
fish, followed by gigantic portions
of plainly grilled, steamed or
deep-fried fish. Tables are packed
at lunchtime, but evening trade is
slower (note the early closing
times). The decor is minimal and
the cooking unsophisticated, but
the fish is fresh every day.

Manzi's

1–2 Leicester St WC2. **Map** 13 A2.
(0171-734 0224. **Open** noon–
2:30pm Mon–Sat, 5:30–11:30pm
daily. **Closed** Dec 25–26. **⚫** AE, DC,
MC, V, JCB. **€€€**

This grand, old-fashioned family-
run (since 1928) restaurant is
situated near Leicester Square. You
can ask for your fish poached or
grilled and your eels jellied,
smoked or served in a parsley
sauce. It can be expensive unless
you stick to house wine and mid-
priced dishes.

Poissonnerie de L'Avenue

82 Sloane Ave SW3. **Map** 19 B2.
(0171-589 5774 or 0171-589 2457.
Open 12:30–3pm & 7–11:30pm
Mon–Sat. **Closed** public hols. **⚫ ⚫**
⚫ ⚫ AE, DC, V. **€€€€**

At this smart, oak-paneled,
congenial establishment there are
some plain dishes (oysters, grilled
sole or scallops), but rich dishes
involving cream, butter and
mayonnnaise are more common,
flavored with such ingredients as
tarragon, fennel and Pernod. Its
restful, old-world atmosphere
makes it an ideal place for a
discreet lunch.

Le Suquet

104 Draycott Ave SW3. **Map** 19 B2.
(0171-581 1785. **Open** noon–
2:30pm & 7–11:30pm daily. **⚫** AE,
DC, MC, V. **€€€**

Le Suquet is a lively but relaxed
French hang-out. It is at its best on
summer nights, when the windows
open out onto Draycott Avenue.
Highlights are foil-wrapped sea
bream (bluegill); scallops in garlic;
and the spectacular seafood
platter – a seaweed-fronded
marine cornucopia.

Wheeler's

19–21 Old Compton St W1.
Map 13 A2. **(** 0171-437 2706.
Open 12:30–2:30pm, 6–11:15pm
Mon–Sat, 12:30–2:30pm, 7–10:30pm
Sun. **Closed** Dec 25. **⚫ ⚫ ⚫**
⚫ ⚫ AE, DC, MC, V, JCB.
€€€

The accent at Wheeler's is on large
helpings of plain, traditional fish
dishes served in old-fashioned,
comfortable surroundings. Oysters
are a specialty appetizer, as are fried
sole, plaice (flounder) and lobster
thermidor for the main course.
Wheeler's has been a London
institution for decades, and there
are several branches throughout the
London area. (Check the phone
directory for details.)

For key to symbols *see p287*.

VEGETARIAN

Vegetarians can eat well at many London restaurants, but there are still relatively few places that offer a completely vegetarian menu. The restaurants in this section specialize in food without meat or fish, though Mildred's sneaks in the occasional seafood dish. Menus often indicate which dishes are suitable for vegetarians.

Food for Thought

31 Neal St WC2. **Map** 13 B2.
C 0171-836 0239 or 9072. **Open** noon–8pm Mon–Sat, noon–4pm Sun.
🌱 Ⓥ 🏠 Ⓔ

The short but imaginative menu features stir-fries, Japanese tofu dishes and European casseroles and soups, plus interesting quiches (leek, cauliflower) and indulgent puddings and cakes (raspberry scrunch, apple crumble, orange-and-coconut scones with whipped cream). It's very cheap for Covent Garden, which partly explains the crowds, especially at lunchtimes.

Mildred's

58 Greek St W1. **Map** 13 B2.
C 0171-494 1634. **Open** noon–11pm Mon–Sat. 🌱 Ⓥ 🏠 Ⓔ

This is one of the few vegetarian restaurants that offer a range of dishes to match their meat-serving rivals. Soups range from Japanese miso to Polish vegetable and barley (*krupnik*), main courses from Brazilian vegetable-and-coconut casserole to Chinese black-bean vegetables with fresh pineapple and noodles. Cramped surroundings mean you may be asked to share tables; staff are happy to come and get you from the pub opposite if you want to have a drink while you wait.

The Place Below

St. Mary-Le-Bow Church EC2.
Map 15 A2. **C** 0171-329 0789.
Open 7:30am–2:30pm Mon–Fri, 6:30–9:30pm Thu & Fri. 🌱 only.
🍽 Ⓥ ★ ⒺⒺ

At lunchtimes, city workers pack the crypt of Wren's famous "Bow Bells" church (*see p147*) for tasty soups, quiches and hot dishes. After olive bread, there might be red-pepper-and-almond soup, then cucumber, fetta and mint tartlets with tomato gravy and an avocado-and-plum-tomato salad. This can be followed by a dessert of seasonal fruits, homemade ice cream or something indulgent like dark and white chocolate truffle cake. You can bring your own wine (free corkage) or even sample some of the delicious homemade lemonade.

AMERICAN

MEXICAN

Apart from the long-standing flood of burger bars (*see pp306–7*), American food – especially of a reasonable standard – is comparatively new to London. Places like the Hard Rock Café make some concessions to the healthy-eating trend, but as a rule big is beautiful. Standard fare is hamburgers, fried chicken, barbecued spareribs and BLTs (bacon, lettuce and tomato sandwiches), all under a mountain of French fries and followed by rich cakes and ice-cream sundaes. Most of the restaurants offer a few dishes from Mexico and Louisiana.

Deal's

14–16 Fouberts Pl W1. **Map** 12 F2.
C 0171-287 1001. **Open** noon–11pm Mon–Sat, noon–4pm Sun. 🧍
♿ 🎵 🏠 🌱 AE, MC, V. ⒺⒺ

The young clientele at this lively eating place are served typically American food (burgers, spare ribs, T-bone steaks) with a strong Oriental slant (Thai curries, steak teriyaki, delicious seafood spring rolls). The Chelsea Harbour branch (0171-352 5887) is also worth a visit.

Down Mexico Way

25 Swallow St W1. **Map** 12 F3.
C 0171-437 9895. **Open** noon–midnight Mon–Sat, noon–10pm Sun.
Closed Dec 25–26. 🍽 groups of six or more. 🧍 🎵 🌱 AE, DC, MC, V, JCB. ⒺⒺ

The most attractive Mexican restaurant in London has a menu that is much less orientated to fast food than most. It has all the standard nachos (tortilla chips with various toppings and sauces) and empanaditas (pasties with corn or spiced-meat fillings), but it's also got the more interesting possibilities of fish in chili and almond sauce, lime-cooked chicken, stuffed cucumbers and shark with tabasco butter.

Hard Rock Café

150 Old Park Lane W1. **Map** 12 E4.
C 0171-629 0382. **Open** 11:30am–12:30am Sun–Thu, 11:30am–1am Fri & Sat. **Closed** Dec 25–26. 🌱 Ⓥ 🧍 🏠 🌱 AE, MC, V. ⒺⒺ

This is the only eating place in London where a line is a permanent feature. Rock fans flock from all over the planet to eat burgers here beneath Jimi Hendrix's old guitar or beside Ozzie Osborne's white leather shoes. A rock museum, a place of pilgrimage, a marketing outlet –

this is a place people either love or hate. There is a surprisingly good selection of vegetarian dishes – devised by Linda McCartney, of course.

Joe Allen

13 Exeter St WC2. **Map** 13 C2.
C 0171-836 0651. **Open** noon–1am Mon–Sat, noon–midnight Sun.
Closed Dec 24–25. Ⓥ ⒺⒺⒺ

At this hard-nosed haunt of the famous, the menu used to be all-American chopped steak and cold shoulder, but now has a strong Italian influence. Recommended are the spaghetti with prawns, tomato, garlic and red pepper; the baked John Dory with tomato, capers, black olives and garlic; and pasta with roast chicken and peppers. Reserve ahead.

AFRO-CARIBBEAN

Given London's multiethnic population, there are fewer Afro-Caribbean restaurants than you might expect; the style of cooking has not caught on like Indian and Chinese. African and Caribbean cooking have basic foods in common – fibrous root vegetables like sweet potato and cassava, rice and flat breads, pumpkin, beans and peas and sweet, fleshy fruits like guava and mango. Common dishes are fried plantain (a type of banana) with a hot sauce, spicy stews and soups and curried goat.

The Brixtonian

11 Dorrell Place SW9.
C 0171-978 8870. **Open** 7–11pm Tue–Sat, 6pm–midnight Mon. 🌱
🍽 🎵 🌱 MC, V. ⒺⒺⒺ

This sophisticated Caribbean specialist features dishes from different Antillean islands each month. Everything is immaculately prepared and presented, albeit rather expensive. The atmosphere is enhanced by the sound of live jazz escaping from the downstairs bar, which serves lunches and is popular for the widest selection of rum in London. A sister restaurant, the Brixtonian Backyard, is in Covent Garden (0171-240 2769).

Calabash

The Africa Centre, 38 King St WC2.
Map 13 C2. **C** 0171-836 1976.
Open 12:30–3pm Mon–Fri, 6–11:30pm Mon–Sat. **Closed** public hols. 🧍 🌱 AE, DC, MC, V. ⒺⒺ

On a side street just off Covent Garden's Piazza, one of London's premier African restaurants is hidden down a flight of stairs.

By day, its soothing lunchtime atmosphere comes as a relief from the market's crowds. By night, especially on weekends, the place comes alive. A carefully explained menu demystifies exotic dishes like *yassa* – Senegalese chicken cooked with onions in a special lemon sauce.

Cottons Rhum Shop, Bar and Restaurant

55 Chalk Farm Rd NW1.
[0171-482 1096. **Open** noon–midnight daily. **Closed** Dec 25–26.
☰ MC, V. **£££**

The loud reggae music announcing Cottons' presence doesn't bother the smart young crowd that flocks to this intimately lit bar-restaurant for cocktails every night. On the menu, jokily named dishes such as "rasta pasta" and "ragga prawns" sit beside such staples of Jamaican cooking as curried goat and fried chicken. The desserts are positively wicked.

INDIAN

Indian food is a true delight of eating out in London. There is a vast number of Indian restaurants, and many of them specialize in specific styles of food. Dishes range from mildly spicy *(korma)* through medium-hot *(bhuna, dansak, dopiaza)* to very hot *(madras, vindaloo)*. Indian meals in the West may begin with soup or a appetizer and main course dishes (with rice or flat breads such as *chapati* or *nan*) are often shared. "Balti" dishes, fast-cooked dishes served in a small wok, are a recent import from the Midlands.

Bombay Brasserie

Courtfield Cl, Courtfield Rd SW7.
Map 18 E2. **[** 0171-370 4040. **Open** noon–3pm & 7pm–midnight daily.
Closed Dec 25–26. **[|]** **V** **&** **♫**
☰ DC, MC, V. **££££**

This is one of the most acclaimed Indian restaurants outside Asia. It has an impressive colonial atmosphere, redolent of the Raj. The mainly North Indian menu includes some unusual regional specialties. The execution of the regional dishes (including Parsi and Goan) is second to none. If you visit at lunchtime, there's a much less expensive buffet.

Chutney Mary

Plaza 535, Kings Rd SW10.
Map 18 E5. **[** 0171-351 3113.
Open 12:30–2:30pm, 7–11:30pm Mon–Sat, 12:30–3:30pm (buffet), 7–10:30pm Sun. **[|]** **V** **☰** AE, DC, MC, V. **£££**

"Chutney Mary" is an Indian term used to describe women who straddle two cultures: Indian and British. It neatly sums up the cookery of this smart restaurant. There are such standard Indian staples as *roghan josh* (lamb braised in yogurt or cream and colored with beetroot or tomato) and *chicken tikka* (cubed, marinated and baked), but the majority of the cooking is a unique – and very successful – blend of Indian and Western tastes.

Chutneys

124 Drummond St NW1. **Map** 4 F4.
[0171-388 0604. **Open** noon–2:45pm & 6–11:30pm daily. **Closed** Christmas. **[|]** **V** **☰** MC. **£**

Pale and cool, this is the smartest of the clutch of Indian restaurants that line Drummond Street, and it is superb value. At the buffet lunches you can help yourself to as much as you like from a table groaning with *dals* (lentils), vegetable curries, rice, chutneys, breads and a dessert – all for about £4 (available all day Sunday).

Gopal's

12 Bateman St W1. **Map** 13 A2.
[0171-434 1621 or 0840. **Open** noon–3pm & 6–11:30pm daily.
Closed Dec 25–26. **[|]** **&** **T** **☰** AE, DC, MC, V. **££££**

This is one of the best new-wave Indian restaurants, with dishes freshly prepared for the serious tandoori and curry lover. There are a few unusual dishes on the menu, such as a *meenu* (fish curry) from Karnataka.

Madhu's Brilliant

39 South Rd, Southall, Middx UB1.
[0181-574 1897 or 0181-571 6380.
Open 12:30–3pm, 6–11:30pm Mon–Fri, 6–11:30pm Sat, Sun.
Closed Tue. **[|]** **♣** **☰** AE, DC, MC, V. **££**

Madhu's Brilliant may not look like much, but the cooking is authentic and an outstanding value – half the price (or less) than you might expect. The accent is on strongly flavored Indian and Pakistani meat dishes, and it is well worth the effort of making the trip to this peripheral location.

Malabar

27 Uxbridge St W8. **Map** 9 C3.
[0171-727 8800. **Open** noon–3pm & 6–11:30pm daily. **Closed** 1 week following Aug public hol, 4 days Christmas. **[|]** **♣** **☰** MC, V. **££**

A stylish little place situated in a quiet mews, the Malabar is one of very few Indian restaurants in the area that offers outstanding North-Indian/Pakistani-style cookery. Try, for example, the venison or charcoal grilled chicken livers – both marinated.

Mandeer

21 Hanway Place W1. **Map** 13 A1.
[0171-323 0660 or 0171-580 3470.
Open noon–3pm & 5:30–10pm Mon–Sat. **Closed** public hols. **[|]** **V** **♫** **☰** AE, DC, MC, V. **££**

Easily the most elegant Indian vegetarian restaurant in London, and also the priciest, it serves a good selection of dishes, from run-of-the-mill South Indian fare to less common Gujarati-inspired dishes (puffed lotus seeds, a yellow-pea dal, even tofu curry).

Nazrul

130 Brick Lane E1. **Map** 8 E5.
[0171-247 2505. **Open** noon–3pm & 5:30pm–midnight Mon–Thu, noon–3pm & 5:30pm–1am Fri & Sat, noon–midnight Sun **£**

Nazrul is one of the scores of cheap Bangladeshi-run cafés and restaurants in the Brick Lane area. Decor and furnishings are very basic, prices very low and the atmosphere very lively. Portion sizes can be big, so take it easy when ordering. It's unlicensed, but you can bring your own alcohol.

Ravi Shankar

133–5 Drummond St NW1.
Map 4 F4. **[** 0171-388 6458.
Open noon–10:45pm daily. **[|]** **V** **♣** **&** MC, V. **£**

This South Indian restaurant serves vegetarian *bhel poori* (South Indian) fare from the kitchens of Chutneys *(see above)*. The *dosas* (pancakes) and *thalis* (set meals) are especially good, and the fresh carrot juice is wonderful. There is also a branch on St. John Street (0171-833 5897), handy for Sadler's Wells *(see p243)*.

Salloos

62–4 Kinnerton St SW1. **Map** 11 C5.
[0171-235 4444. **Open** noon–2:30pm & 7–11:15pm Mon–Sat.
Closed public hols. **[|]** **★** **☰** AE, DC, MC, V. **££££**

Almost certainly the best Indian restaurant in town isn't Indian at all – it's Pakistani. There's a predominance of meat (lamb, chicken, quails) grilled, baked in the tandoori oven and curried. The wine list is impressive, and the cooking is precise and fresh, but the prices reflect this. Try the bargain set lunch. The atmosphere here is elegant and almost somber, with service that is faultlessly professional.

For key to symbols *see p287*.

SOUTHEAST ASIAN

Southeast Asian food, especially Thai, has made a distinctive mark on the London restaurant scene. The majority of restaurants in this section tend to emphasize Thai, Singaporean, Malaysian or Indonesian cuisine but also offer a combination of all of them. A sharp, tangy taste comes from lime juice, kaffir lime leaves and lemongrass; a sour note from tamarind; ginger and garlic; chillies provide the fire, coconut milk the coolant. Rice or noodles are the basis of any Southeast Asian meal, the preferred cooking methods are steaming and stir-frying, and the food is usually served lukewarm.

Bahn Thai

21a Frith St W1. **Map** 13 A2.
[0171-437 8504. **Open** noon–2:45pm & 6–11:15pm Mon–Sat, 11am–1:30pm & 6:30–10:30pm Sun. **Closed** Christmas, Easter, public hols.
V ⫘ ⌀ AE, DC, MC, V.
£££

Bahn Thai offers many dishes which are rarely found outside Thailand. Thai-style pigs' trotters, frogs' legs and chicken liver appear on the menu, but the more mainstream dishes are also excellent; try the *tom yum* (hot soup spiced with lemongrass) or the *kwaitiew pad Thai* (a quickly fried noodle dish). Vegetarian dishes are clearly marked on the menu and so is the heat (chili) of dishes. The wine list is unusually good, but Singha beer tends to complement the food better.

Chiang Mai

48 Frith St W1. **Map** 13 A2.
[0171-437 7444. **Open** noon–3pm Mon–Sat, 6–11pm daily. **Closed** public hols. ⫙⫘ V ⫙ ⌀ AE, MC, V. £££

This prominent Thai restaurant has an airy dining room and separate vegetarian menu, which helps it stand apart from others of its kind. It is particularly renowned for its delicious noodles and unusual *yams* (spicy salads). The *som tam* (fresh papaya salad) and *kow soy* (chicken noodle soup), both very popular dishes from northern Thailand, are faithfully reproduced at this restaurant.

Khun Akorn

136 Brompton Rd SW3. **Map** 11 C5.
[0171-225 2688. **Open** noon–3pm daily, 6:30–11pm, Mon–Thu, 6:30–11pm Fri–Sat. ⫙⫘ V ⫙ ⌀ AE, DC, MC, V. £££

Diagonally across the road from Harrods, Khun Akron is an elegant, calm and comfortable dining room owned by Imperial Hotels, Tailand's luxury hotel chain. Most dishes are Tai classics – aromatic curries, stir-fried noodles, and plenty of seafood, chicken and beef dishes. The flavors and scents of lemongrass, holy basil, coconut, coriander chilli and fish sauce predominate. Both cooking and presentation are immaculate. The set lunches are strongly recommended because of their outstanding value.

Melati

21 Gt Windmill St W1. **Map** 13 A2.
[0171-734 6964 or 0171-437 2745. **Open** noon–11:30pm Sun–Thu, noon–12:30am Fri, Sat. **Closed** Christmas. ⫙⫘ V ⫙ ♫ ⌀ AE, DC, MC, V, JCB. ££

Reservations are advisable in this bustling Indonesian restaurant if you don't want to wait in line. The service is swift and polite but a little rushed and the preparation of dishes very authentic. The Singapore *laksa* – an aromatic vermicelli noodle soup – is particularly good, the *satés* (small spicy kebabs) are moist and tasty and desserts such as *kue dadar* (a green pancake roll stuffed with coconut) are unmissable.

Sri Siam

14 Old Compton St W1. **Map** 13 A2.
[0171-434 3544. **Open** noon–3pm & 6–11:15pm Mon–Sat, 6–10:30pm Sun. **Closed** Jan 1, Dec 24–26. ⫙⫘ V ★ ⌀ AE, DC, MC, V. ££

This stylish restaurant is a perfect place for your first taste of Thai food. Try the mixed appetizers and any of the seafood dishes. There is an extensive vegetarian menu, which contains exquisite hot-and-sour soups and salads, as well as *saté*, curries, deep-fried beancurd, and more. The set-lunch menu is very good value.

Tui

19 Exhibition Rd SW10. **Map** 19 A1.
[0171-584 8359. **Open** noon–2:30pm & 6:30–11pm Mon–Sat, 12:30–3pm & 7–10:30pm Sun. **Closed** public hols. ⫙ ⌀ AE, DC, MC, V. £££

Tui looks cool and modern in contrast to the neo-Gothic facade of the Victoria and Albert Museum just opposite. The menu is a conservative but reliable selection of Thai staples; portions of the expertly prepared soups (such as seafood *pob tak*, which simmers at your table) are generous.

JAPANESE

Japanese restaurants are renowned for being simply but stylishly decorated. Some have teppan yaki tables (where diners surround a chef who cooks on a hotplate) and a bar where you can snack on sushi – raw fish or vegetable on vinegared rice. The most expensive have tatami rooms, where parties eat seated on straw mats.

Ikeda

30 Brook St W1. **Map** 12 E2.
[0171-629 2730. **Open** 12:30–2:30pm Mon–Fri, 6:30–10pm daily. ⫙ ⫘ ⌀ AE, DC, MC, V, JCB. ££££

Prices are reasonable and the food is delicious at this small but comfortable *yakitori* and *sushi* bar. The reasonably priced set lunches are particularly appealing; the chicken *yakitori* meal is centered on bamboo skewers of grilled chicken, while the sashimi (raw fish) is prepared as you wait. A seaweed appetizer, miso soup, fresh orange dessert and green tea are also included in the price.

Miyama

38 Clarges St W1. **Map** 12 E3.
[0171-499 2443. **Open** noon–2:30pm Mon–Fri, 6–10:30pm daily. ⫙⫘ ⫙ ⌀ AE, DC, MC, V, JCB. ££££

Just off Piccadilly, Miyama is an elegant place for meticulously prepared and presented Japanese food. Besides the sushi and sashimi meals, the teppan yaki counter is popular for meats and seafood grilled as you watch.

Suntory

72–73 St. James's St SW1. **Map** 12 F3.
[0171-409 0201. **Open** noon–2pm & 6–9:30pm Mon–Sat. **Closed** public hols. ⫙⫘ ⫙ ★ ⌀ AE, DC, MC, V, JCB. £££££

Britain's top Japanese restaurant with a much-deserved Michelin star is as professionally run as you might expect. It has several dining areas, including private tatami rooms, teppan yaki tables and a simply decorated main dining area. The atmosphere is only as formal as you want it to be, and the presentation is immaculate.

Tatsuso

32 Broadgate Circle, Broadgate EC2. **Map** 7 C5. [0171-256 9304. **Open** 11:30am–2:30pm & 6:30–9:30pm Mon–Fri. **Closed** public hols. ⫙⫘ ⫙ ⫘ ⌀ AE, DC, MC, V, JCB. £££££

Tatsuso is discreetly tucked under the sweeping curves of the Broadgate Circle. The quality is superb, but be warned that the prices are strictly expense-account territory.

Tokyo Diner

2 Newport Place WC1. **Map** 13 B2.
[0171-287 8777. **Open** noon–midnight daily. 🍷 **V** 🏃 🍽 MC, V. ⓔ

The handy location (just behind Leicester Square) and the low prices make this restaurant a very useful bolt-hole. In true Japanese fashion, the door is electric, the taps in the restrooms automatic, and tips are not expected or accepted. The menu is extensive and clearly annotated, covering sushi, sashimi, noodle soups, and Japanese curries; accompany these with Japanese lager. The cooking may not be first-rate, but the bill is a pleasant surprise.

Wagamama

4 Streatham St, off Coptic St WC1.
Map 13 B1. [0171-323 9223.
Open noon–2:30pm, 5:45–11pm Mon–Sat, 12:30–3pm, 6–10pm Sun.
🍷 only. **V** ★ ⓔ

This basement noodle bar near the British Museum is immensely popular. The bustling interior is decorated in a minimalist style. The food is cheap, filling and interesting: large bowls of soup, or pan-fried noodles or rice with seafood and vegetables. Studiously cool waiting staff take orders on handsets which resemble Nintendo Game Boys. The queue looks very daunting as it can stretch out into the street, but it's fast-moving.

CHINESE

The cuisine most common to London's Chinese restaurants is Cantonese, which has rice as its staple food and favors steaming or light frying. However, most also offer Peking dishes, which rely more on deep-fried crispiness and may replace rice with bread, and Shanghai dishes, which have more starch, fat and spices and may be noodle-based. The highly spiced Szechuan or Hunan food is popular here, too. At lunchtime in many Cantonese restaurants you can eat dim sum, a series of delicious snacks, mostly steamed or deep-fried dumplings, which you choose from heated trolleys wheeled from table to table.

The Abacus

38 Clapham High St SW4. [0171-497 0376. **Open** noon–2:30pm, 6pm–midnight Mon–Sat; 6pm–midnight Sun.
🍷 **V** 🏃 🍽 AE, DC, MC, V.
ⓔⓔ

This is one of the best Chinese restaurants south of the Thames, but is very reasonably priced. It specializes in Peking dishes, such as duck served with pancakes and plum sauce. For those who prefer spicier food, there are Szechuan standards like twice-cooked beef or pork, or kung-po king prawns. From the large choice of appetizers, try the deep-fried shredded smoked chicken. And don't miss the ginseng beer, served ice cold.

Fung Shing

15 Lisle St WC2. **Map** 13 A2.
[0171-437 1539. **Open** noon–11:30pm daily. **Closed** Dec 24–25.
🍷 🍽 AE, DC, MC, V. ⓔⓔ

For many, Fung Shing is Chinatown's best restaurant. Furnishings are markedly more elegant than many you'll find in the vicinity, and food from the breadth of the Cantonese repertoire is on the menu. The hot-pot dishes (hearty stews in delicious stock) are recommended.

Harbour City

46 Gerrard Street W1. **Map** 13 A2.
[0171-439 7859. **Open** noon–11.30pm Mon–Thurs, noon–midnight Fri, Sat, 11am–10.30pm Sun. 🍷 🏃
★ 🍽 AE, DC, MC, V. ⓔⓔ

One of many establishments on Gerrard Street serving an extensive *dim sum* selection, Harbour City stands out because the *dim sum* menu is carefully translated into English, and because the staff are very gracious. As with all Chinese food vegetarian dishes are limited, but all the dishes taste superb.

Jade Garden

15 Wardour St W1. **Map** 13 A2.
[0171-437 5065. **Open** noon–11:45pm Mon–Sat, 11:30am–10:45pm Sun. **Closed** Christmas.
🍷 🏃 🍽 AE, MC, V. ⓔⓔ

The Jade Garden has long been a favorite dim sum venue for London's Cantonese. Well-spaced round tables lend themselves to communal feasting, service is patient and the dim sum are of top quality and include elaborate delicacies such as quail's eggs with prawn dumplings. Try the fish dishes on the à la carte menu.

Magic Wok

100 Queensway W2. **Map** 10 D2.
Open noon–11pm daily. 🍷 lunch only. **V** 🏃 🍽 AE, DC, MC, V. ⓔ

Magic Wok is one of the finest of Queensway's many Chinese restaurants. The list of specials changes regularly yet invariably

contains the most interesting Cantonese dishes. Deep-fried soft-shell crab with garlic and spicy chilli makes an excellent appetizer.

Memories of China

67–69 Ebury St SW1. **Map** 20 E1.
[0171-730 7734. **Open** noon–2:15pm & 7–10:45pm Mon–Sat.
Closed public hols. 🍷 🏃 🍽 AE, DC, MC, V, JCB. ⓔⓔⓔ

At this restaurant decorated in a light minimalist style, the menu aims to guide Western diners through China's major cuisines. Set meals provide a sound (if expensive) introduction to regional food, tailored to Western tastes.

Ming

35–36 Greek St W1. **Map** 13 A1.
[0171-437 0292. **Open** noon–11:45pm Mon–Sat, Chinese New Year (Sun). **Closed** Dec 24–25. 🍷 🍷
V 🍽 AE, DC, MC, V, JCB. ⓔⓔⓔ

Ming offers a soothing alternative to the bustle of nearby Chinatown. Food includes interesting dishes from north China; try *ta tsai mi*, lamb cooked to an 18th-century recipe. Unusually for a Chinese restaurant, vegetarians have been thoughtfully considered.

New World

1 Gerrard Pl W1. **Map** 13 B2.
[0171-434 2508. **Open** 11am–12:30am daily, 11am–11pm Sun.
Closed Dec 25–26. 🍷 🏃 🏃
🍽 AE, DC, MC, V, JCB. ⓔⓔ

This is one of the most authentic restaurants serving dim sum in Chinatown. Flag down a trolley and take your pick. Many staff have shaky English, so there's an element of chance in what you'll receive, adding to the fun. The full menu is as long as the Great Wall, accommodating both the meek and the daring diner.

The Oriental

The Dorchester Hotel, 53 Park La W1. **Map** 12 D4. [0171-629 8888.
Open noon–2:30pm Mon–Fri, 7–11pm Mon–Sat. 🍷 🏃 🏃
T 🍽 AE, DC, MC, V, JCB.
ⓔⓔⓔⓔⓔ

The Dorchester Hotel unveiled its Chinese restaurant with much aplomb in 1991. Battalions of skillful chefs were shipped in to prepare the Cantonese food meticulously. The expensive ingredients and exquisite presentation find favor with the business and social elite that gather here. Don't miss the full Chinese tea service. Parties of up to 12 can rent the sumptuous private rooms.

For key to symbols see p287.

Light Meals and Snacks

SOMETIMES YOU HAVE neither the time nor the money to sit down for a full meal. Fortunately, London has a wonderful range of places offering simple, quick and sometimes cheap food. The places listed here are ideal for hungry tourists on a tight sightseeing schedule.

BREAKFAST

A GOOD BREAKFAST IS essential preparation for a hard day's sightseeing. Many hotels *(see pp272–85)* will serve breakfast to nonresidents, and you can get a taste of luxury by breakfasting in one, such as the **Savoy** *(see p285)*. Here wonderful English breakfasts *(see pp288–9)* are served from silver trays and tureens for £10 to £20. If a mug of tea with eggs and baked beans on toast is more to your taste, there are "greasy spoons" all over the city. A more cosmopolitan option is a pastry and a cappuccino from a café. If you're late to bed or early to rise, **Harry's** is open from 11pm to 6am, and several pubs around Smithfield market, including the **Cock Tavern**, serve inexpensive fare from 5:30am.

COFFEE AND TEA

I F YOU'RE OUT SHOPPING, you'll note that many department stores have their own cafés, the most stylish being the new-wave Italian **Emporio Armani Express**. There are also good coffeehouses; **Bar Italia** stays open over the weekend. Patisseries such as **Patisserie Valerie** and **Maison Bertaux** are a particular delight, with mouthwatering window displays. Afternoon tea is an English institution not to be missed. Top hotels like the **Ritz** and **Brown's** *(see p282)* offer pots of tea, scones with jam and cream, delicious cucumber sandwiches and cakes galore. **Fortnum and Mason** *(see p311)* serves both afternoon and high teas (a more substantial meal). In Greenwich, try **Peter de Wit's**, a toyshop that serves tea-time treats. On the other side of London, the **Kew Greenhouse** serves

homestyle food, and the **Maids of Honour** tea room offers pastries, reputedly enjoyed here by King Henry VIII.

GALLERY AND THEATER CAFÉS

M OST GALLERIES HAVE cafés: the one at **Whitechapel Art Gallery** *(see p169)* has lots of vegetarian dishes; the **Café de Colombia** at the Museum of Mankind *(see p91)* offers excellent coffee accompanied by chocolate coffee beans. At the **Tate Gallery** there is a splendid restaurant *(see pp82–5)* as well as a café. If you intend seeing a film at the **Everyman** cinema *(see pp328–9)*, visit the delightful basement café. If you're visiting the Institute of Contemporary Arts *(see p92)*, enjoy the ambience of the trendy **ICAfé**. The **Arts Theatre Café** and the lively **Almeida Theatre** café bar also serve excellent food.

DINERS

L ONDON HAS MANY BURGER bars, where the food consists of burgers, fries, fried chicken, apple pie, milk shakes and cola. **Fatboy's Diner** is an authentic 1940s trailer brought from the United States, and at the **Rock Island Diner** staff leap onto tables for rock-and-roll routines. Try the tasty burgers and fun atmosphere at the branches of **Ed's Easy Diner**.

PIZZA AND PASTA

I TALIAN FAST FOOD IS sold all over London. The best pizza chain is **Pizza Express**; try its branches in a converted dairy *(see p122)* as well as at the elegant **Kettners**. For pasta, go for family-run trattorias like **Centrale, Lorelei** and **Pollo**; these have character and are reasonably priced.

VEGETARIAN

T HERE ARE many vegetarian cafés in London selling tasty food in informal settings. Increasingly, they are run by special-interest groups: sample the food at **Country Life**, a self-service café run by Seventh-Day Adventists; a curry that has been cooked by Radha Krishnas at **Govinda's**; or a healthy salad and a wicked dessert served by Buddhist women at **Cherry Orchard**. Neal's Yard *(see p115)* is home to several vegetarian restaurants and take-out places.

FISH AND CHIPS

F ISH AND CHIPS is a British experience you should not miss. Visit local "chippies" for fish deep-fried in batter, with thick potato chips smothered in salt and vinegar. Traditional accompaniments are bread baps (buns) and pickled onions. For a higher-class supper, try a sit-down restaurant that offers a range of fresh fish, such as lemon sole, skate and cod. The best are the **Sea Shell**, **Faulkner's** and the **Upper Street Fish Shop**.

BARS

I F YOU WANT A DRINK, the obvious venue is a pub *(see pp308–9)*. A more elegant option is to visit a hotel like **Claridge's** and relax in a comfortable armchair in the foyer while a waiter brings the drinks. Wine bars are good if you want a snack, a meal or just a glass of wine. The **Cork and Bottle** is popular and always full, and the **Brackenbury** serves a variety of outstanding international food. Bar-brasseries are convenient places to drop in for food and drink at any time. The **Dôme** chain of cafés emphasizes a European style. If rum is a passion, then Afro-Caribbean **Cottons** *(see p303)* and the **Brixtonian** *(see p302)* both have large selections. *Tapas* bars are also fun. Drink Spanish beer and wine and eat tasty snacks while enjoying live flamenco music. West London's Spanish community has spawned some of the best – try **Galicia** or **Los Remos**; for after-pub hours, the basement **Bar Sol Ona**, open until 2am – but be prepared for a crowd.

STREET FOOD

HOT ROASTED CHESTNUTS are an autumnal delight. Shellfish stalls, which sell ready-to-eat potted shrimps, crab, whelks and jellied eels are a feature of every street market. At Camden Lock and Spitalfields you can wander from stall to stall choosing falafels, satay chicken, vegeburgers, Chinese noodles or honey balls. If you're in the East End, Jewish bakeries such as **Brick Lane Beigel Bake** and **Ridley Bagel Bakery** are open 24 hours a day; they're great fun and very cheap. London is not generally geared toward hot weather, but try **Marine Ices**, which serves some of the best ice cream in town.

PIE AND MASH

You won't find pie-and-mash shops in smart areas, but they are worth trying for a true Cockney experience. Have eels and potatoes or meat pie with mashed potato and liquor (green parsley sauce) for only a few pounds. They should be eaten with vinegar and washed down with tea. Worth a visit is **F. Cooke and Sons**.

DIRECTORY

BREAKFAST

Cock Tavern
East Poultry Market, Smithfield Market EC1.
Map 6 F5.

Harry's Bar
19 Kingly St W1.
Map 12 F2.

Savoy Hotel
Strand WC2. **Map** 13 C2.

COFFEE AND TEA

Bar Italia
22 Frith St W1.
Map 13 A2.

Brown's Hotel
Albermarle St W1.
Map 12 F3.

Emporio Armani Express
191 Brompton Rd SW3.
Map 19 B1.

Fortnum and Mason
181 Piccadilly W1.
Map 12 F3.

Kew Greenhouse
1 Station Parade, Richmond.

Maids of Honour
288 Kew Rd, Richmond.

Maison Bertaux
28 Greek St W1.
Map 13 A1.

Patisserie Valerie
215 Brompton Rd SW3.
Map 19 B1.

Peter de Wit
21 Greenwich Church St SE10. **Map** 23 B2.

Ritz
Piccadilly W1. Palm Court.
Ritz Bar. **Map** 12 F3.

GALLERY AND THEATER CAFÉS

Almeida Theatre Wine Bar
1 Almeida St N1.

Arts Theatre Café
6 Great Newport St WC2.
Map 13 B2.

Café de Colombia
Museum of Mankind, 6 Burlington Gardens W1.
Map 12 F3.

Everyman Café
Holly Bush Vale NW3.
Map 1 A5.

ICAfé
The Mall SW1. **Map** 13 A4.

Tate Gallery Coffee Shop
Millbank SW1. **Map** 21 B2.

Whitechapel Café
Whitechapel Gallery, 80 Whitechapel High St E1.
Map 16 E1.

DINERS

Ed's Easy Diner
12 Moor St W1. **Map** 13 B2.
One of several branches.

Fatboy's Diner
21–22 Maiden La WC2.
Map 13 C2.

Rock Island Diner
2nd Floor, London Pavilion, Piccadilly Circus W1.
Map 13 A3.

PIZZA AND PASTA

Centrale
16 Moor St W1.
Map 13 B2.

Kettners
(Pizza Express) 29 Romilly St W1. **Map** 13 A2.

Lorelei
21 Bateman St W1.
Map 13 A2.

Pizza Express
30 Coptic St WC1.
Map 13 B1.
One of several branches.

Pollo
20 Old Compton St W1.
Map 13 A2.

VEGETARIAN

Cherry Orchard
241–245 Globe Rd E2.

Country Life
1b Heddon St W1. **Map** 12 F2.

Govinda's
9–10 Soho St W1.
Map 13 A1.

FISH AND CHIPS

Faulkner's
424–426 Kingsland Rd E8.

Sea Shell
49–51 Lisson Grove NW1.
Map 3 B5.

Upper St Fish Shop
324 Upper St N1.
Map 6 F1.

BARS

Bar Sol Ona
17 Old Compton St W1.
Map 13 A2.

Brackenbury
129 Brackenbury Rd W6.

Brixtonian
11 Dorrell Pl, off Nursery Rd SW9.

Claridge's
Brook St W1.
Map 12 E2.

Cork and Bottle
44 46 Cranbourn St WC2. **Map** 13 B2.

Cottons Rhum Shop, Bar and Restaurant
55 Chalk Farm Rd NW1.

Dôme
38 Long Acre WC2.
Map 13 C2.
One of several branches.

Galicia
323 Portobello Rd W10.
Map 9 B2.

Los Remos
38a Southwick St W2.
Map 11 A1.

STREET FOOD

Brick Lane Beigel Bake
159 Brick La E1.
Map 8 E5.

Marine Ices
8 Haverstock Hill NW3.

Ridley Bagel Bakery
13–15 Ridley Rd E8.

PIE AND MASH

F. Cooke and Sons
41 Kingsland High St E8.

London Pubs

PUBLIC HOUSES, OR PUBS, were originally just that – houses where the public could eat, drink and stay the night. Large inns with courtyards, like the **George Inn** (see p176), were the interchanges for horse-drawn coach services. Some pubs stand on age-old ale-house sites, like the **Ship**, the **Lamb and Flag** (see p116) and the **City Barge** (see p254). But many of the finest pubs date from the emergence in the late 1800s of "gin palaces," where Londoners escaped from the misery of the slums into lavish interiors, often with stunning mirrors (the **Salisbury**) and elaborate decoration (the **Tottenham** and the **Princess Louise**). Near Little Venice (see pp262–3) you will find **Crockers**, probably the finest of London's surviving gin palaces.

RULES AND CONVENTIONS

IN THEORY, PUBS are open from 11am to 11pm Monday to Saturday and noon to 3pm and 7 to 10:30pm Sunday, but some close in the afternoon or early evening and also on weekends. You must be at least 18 to buy or drink alcohol and at least 14 to enter a pub without an adult. Children can be taken into pubs that serve food or can use outside areas. Order at the bar and pay when you are served; tips are not usual unless you are served food and drink at a table. "Last orders" are called five minutes before closing. When "time" is called a further 10 minutes are allowed to finish drinks.

BRITISH BEER

THE MOST TRADITIONAL British beers come in many different strengths and tastes, are flat (not fizzy) and are only lightly cooled. The spectrum of bottled beers goes from "light" ale, through "pale," "brown" and "old," up to the particularly potent "barley wine." A sweeter lower-alcohol alternative is shandy, a mixture of draft beer or lager with lemonade.

Many traditional methods of brewing and serving beer have been preserved over the years, and there is a great variety of "real ale" in London pubs. Some ale pubs, such as the **Sun** in Bloomsbury, pride themselves on a gimmick-free atmosphere, with bare wooden floors and tables. The Sun serves 20 different beers – one of the widest selections in London. Serious beer drinkers should also try the **Princess Louise**; the **Anglesea Arms**; or pubs run by local brewers, like Young's (try the very strong "Winter Warmer" beer) or Fuller's, who produce a beer called London Pride. "Free houses" are pubs that are not tied to any particular brewery.

OTHER DRINKS

ANOTHER TRADITIONAL English drink found in every London pub is cider. Made from apples, it comes in a range of strengths and levels of dryness. A truly local London spirit is gin, usually mixed with tonic water. In winter, mulled wine (warm and spicy) or hot toddies (brandy or whisky with hot water and sugar) may be served. Non-alcoholic drinks like mineral water and fruit juices are always available, too.

FOOD IN PUBS

PUB FOOD is at its best at lunchtime (though some pubs serve meals in the evenings). Many still offer traditional fare (see pp288–9), such as ploughman's lunch (cheese, salad and bread), shepherd's pie, and roast beef lunch on Sundays. Others now offer newer, more ad-venturous food. The beautiful **Warrington**, for example, has a Thai restaurant.

TYPES OF PUBS

OLD-FASHIONED London pubs still exist in a few places (try the **White Lion**), but they are rare. Today, pubs cater for many different tastes. Plain but stylish, with a better choice of wine and excellent food, are the **Eagle** and the **Crown and Goose**. Team darts are still played at the **Angel** and **City Darts**. Pool tables can be found in some pubs, including **Jack Straw's Castle** (see p228), and the **Freemasons' Arms** has a traditional skittle alley and lawn billiards.

HISTORIC PUBS

NEARLY EVERY PUB in London has a fascinating history. The buildings might contain beamed medieval snugs, extravagant Victorian fantasies or the stunning Arts and Crafts-style interior of the **Black Friar**. At the **Bunch of Grapes** (SW3), the bar is divided by "snobscreens," a feature once found in many pubs that allowed the upper classes to enjoy a drink without having to mix with their servants. The 16th-century **King's Head and Eight Bells** has a display of antiques. Many pubs have strong literary associations, such as the **Fitzroy Tavern** (a meeting place for writers and artists: see p131); **Ye Olde Cheshire Cheese** (associated with Dr. Johnson: see p140); and the **Trafalgar Tavern** (see p238), where Charles Dickens was a regular customer. On a less literary note, the **Bull and Bush** in North London was the subject of an old music-hall song.

Other pubs have more violent associations – victims of Jack the Ripper were found near the **Roebuck** and the **Ten Bells**. The 18th-century highwayman Dick Turpin refreshed himself between robberies at **Spaniards Inn** in North London (see p231), and the **French House** (see p109) in Soho was once a meeting point for the French Resistance in World War II.

OUTDOOR DRINKING

THERE ARE FEW pubs in the center of London with outdoor areas; the better choices tend to be farther out of town. The **Freemasons Arms** has a pleasant garden; the **Bunch of Grapes** in Southwark welcomes families. Some pubs enjoy riverside locations with fine views. From the **Grapes** down in Limehouse to the **White Cross** in Richmond, there are many choices along the length of the Thames in London.

PUBS WITH ENTERTAINMENT

ENTERTAINMENT is offered in many London pubs. There are theater productions at the **King's Head**, the **Bush**, the **Latchmere** and the **Prince Albert**. Other pubs have live music (*see pp333–5*): rock at the **Half Moon**, country at the **Prospect of Whitby**, English folk at the **Archway Tavern** and modern jazz at the **Bulls Head**; the **Mean Fiddler** draws full houses for a wide variety of styles.

PUB NAMES

Signs have hung outside public houses since 1393, when King Richard II decided they should replace the older practice of having a bush outside the door. Most people were illiterate, so names were chosen that could easily be pictured: coats of arms (Freemasons Arms), historical figures (Princess Louise) or heraldic animals (White Lion).

DIRECTORY

Key to symbols:
🍺 stage in bar area or special room for live performers (phone for details)
🍴 offers more than standard bar snacks
🎵 regular live music (phone for details)
🍺 outside drinking area

SOHO, TRAFALGAR SQUARE

French House
49 Dean St W1.
Map 13 A2. 🍴

Tottenham
6 Oxford St W1.
Map 13 A1.

COVENT GARDEN, STRAND

Lamb and Flag
33 Rose St WC2.
Map 13 B2. 🍴

Angel
61 St. Giles High St
WC2. **Map 13 B1.**

Salisbury
90 St. Martin's Lane
WC2. **Map 13 B2.**

BLOOMSBURY, FITZROVIA

Fitzroy Tavern
16 Charlotte St W1.
Map 13 A1. 🍴

Sun
63 Lamb's Conduit St WC1.
Map 5 C4. 🍴

HOLBORN, FLEET STREET

Princess Louise
208 High Holborn WC1.
Map 13 C1. 🍴

Ye Olde Cheshire Cheese
145 Fleet St EC4.
Map 14 E1. 🍴

THE CITY, CLERKENWELL

Black Friar
174 Queen Victoria St EC4.
Map 14 F2.

City Darts
40 Commercial St E1.
Map 16 E1.

Eagle
159 Farringdon Rd EC1.
Map 6 E4. 🍴

Ship
23 Lime St EC3. **Map 15 C2.**

Ten Bells
84 Commercial St E1.
Map 16 E1.

White Lion
37 Central St EC1.
Map 7 A3.

SOUTHWARK

Bunch of Grapes
St. Thomas St SE1.
Map 15 C4. 🍺 🍴

George Inn
77 Borough High St SE1.
Map 15 B4. 🍺 🍴

CHELSEA, SOUTH KENSINGTON

Anglesea Arms
15 Selwood Ter SW7.
Map 18 F3.

Bunch of Grapes
207 Brompton Rd SW3.
Map 19 B1.

King's Head and Eight Bells
50 Cheyne Walk SW3.
Map 19 A5. 🍴

CAMDEN TOWN, HAMPSTEAD

Crown and Goose
100 Arlington Rd NW1.
Map 4 F1. 🍴

Freemasons Arms
32 Downshire Hill NW3.
Map 1 C5. 🍺

Jack Straw's Castle
North End Way NW3.
Map 1 A3. 🍴

Bull and Bush
North End Way NW3.
Map 1 A3.

Spaniards Inn
Spaniards Rd NW3.
Map 1 A3. 🍺

NOTTING HILL, MAIDA VALE

Crockers
24 Aberdeen Pl NW8.

Prince Albert
11 Pembridge Rd W11.
Map 9 C3. Gate Theatre:
📞 0171-229 0706. 🍺

Warrington
93 Warrington Cres W9. 🍴

GREENWICH

Trafalgar Tavern
Park Row SE10.
Map 23 C1. 🎵 🍴

FARTHER AFIELD

Archway Tavern
1 Archway Close N19. 🎵

Bull's Head
373 Lonsdale Rd SW13.
🎵

Bush
Shepherd's Bush Green
W12. Theater: 📞 0181-
743 3388. 🍺

City Barge
27 Strand-on-the-Green
W4. 🍺 🍴

Grapes
76 Narrow St E14. 🍺

Half Moon
93 Lower Richmond Rd
SW15. 🎵

King's Head
115 Upper St N1. **Map 6**
F1. Theater 📞 0171-
226 1916. 🍺 🎵 🍴

Latchmere
503 Battersea Park Rd
SW11. Grace Theatre:
📞 0171-228 2620. 🍺

Mean Fiddler
28a High St NW10. 🎵

Prospect of Whitby
57 Wapping Wall E1.
🎵 🍴

Roebuck
27 Brady St E1.

White Cross
Cholmondeley Walk,
Richmond. 🍺 🍴

SHOPS AND MARKETS

Bags from two of the most famous West End shops

L ONDON IS STILL one of the most lively shopping cities in the world. Within just a few minutes' walk, you can find both vast department stores, with glittering window displays, and tiny cluttered rooms where one customer fills almost the entire shop. Many of the most famous London shops are in Knightsbridge or Regent Street, where prices can be steep, but Oxford Street, which is packed with a huge number of shops offering quality goods at a range of prices, is also worth a visit. All over London, there are plenty of places tucked away down side streets – and don't forget to try the markets for antiques, crafts, household goods, food and clothing. You can buy virtually anything in London; specialties include clothes (from Burberry raincoats and traditional tweeds to "street fashion"); floral scents and soaps; art and antiques; and craft goods such as jewelry, ceramics and leather.

WHEN TO SHOP

I N CENTRAL LONDON, most shops open somewhere between 9 and 10am and close between 5 and 6pm on weekdays; some close earlier on Saturdays. The "late night" shopping (until 7 or 8pm) is on Thursdays in Oxford Street and the rest of the West End and on Wednesdays in Knightsbridge and Chelsea. Some shops in tourist areas, such as Covent Garden *(see pp110–19)* and the Trocadero, are open until 7pm or later every day, including Sundays. A few street markets *(see pp322–3)* and a growing number of other shops are also open on Sundays.

HOW TO PAY

M OST SHOPS WILL accept the following major credit cards: Access (MasterCard), American Express, Diners Club, Japanese Credit Bureau and VISA. Some, however, do not, notably the John Lewis stores and Marks & Spencer, as well as street markets and some smaller shops. Some of the stores do accept traveler's checks, especially if they're in sterling; for other currencies the rate of exchange is less favorable than in a bank. You need your passport with you. Very few shops accept personal checks drawn against foreign banks, unless they are Eurocheques.

RIGHTS AND SERVICES

I F YOUR PURCHASE is defective you are usually entitled to a refund if you have proof of purchase and return the goods. This isn't always the case with sales goods, so inspect them carefully before you buy.

Most large stores, and some small ones, will pack goods up for you and also send them anywhere in the world.

VAT EXEMPTION

V AT (VALUE-ADDED TAX) is a sales tax of 17.5% that is charged on virtually all goods sold in Britain (the notable exceptions are books, food and all children's clothes). VAT is nearly always included in the advertised or marked price, although often business suppliers, including some stationers and electrical goods shops, charge it separately.

Non-European Community visitors to Britain who stay no longer than three months may claim back VAT. If you plan to do this, make sure you take along your passport when shopping. You must complete a form in the store when you buy the goods and then give a copy to Customs when you leave the country. (You may have to show your purchases to customs, so do pack them somewhere accessible.) The tax refund may be returned to you by check or attributed to your credit card, but then a service charge will usually be

Harrods' elaborate Edwardian tiled food halls

deducted, and most stores have a minimum purchase threshold (often £50 or £75). If you arrange to have your goods shipped directly home from the store, VAT should be deducted before you pay.

TWICE-YEARLY SALES

THE TRADITIONAL sale season is from January to February and June to July, when virtually every shop cuts its prices and sells off imperfect or unwanted stock. The department stores have some of the best reductions; one of the most famous sales is at **Harrods** *(see p207)*, where lines start to form outside long before opening.

BEST OF THE DEPARTMENT STORES

THE KING OF London's department stores, by tradition, is **Harrods**, with its 300 departments and staff of 4,000. Prices are not always as high as you may expect. The spectacular food hall, decorated with Edwardian tiles, has splendid displays of fish, cheese, fruit and vegetables; other specialties include fashions for all ages, china, glass, electronics and kitchenware. Though Harrods is still just as popular, especially with well-heeled visitors, Londoners often head instead for nearby **Harvey Nichols**, which aims to stock the best of everything with the price tags to match. Clothes are featured, with the emphasis firmly on very high fashion; many talented British, European and American names are represented. There is also an impressive menswear section. The food hall, opened in 1992, is one of the most stylish in London.

Selfridges vast building on Oxford Street houses everything from Gucci bags and Hermès scarves to household gadgets and bed linen. **Miss Selfridge**, the popular high street fashion chain, also has a branch in the store.

The original **John Lewis** was a draper, and his shop still has a gorgeous selection of fabrics and haberdashery. Its china, glass and household items make John Lewis, and its well-known Sloane Square partner, Peter Jones, equally popular with Londoners.

Liberty *(see p109)*, the last privately owned department store in London, still sells the hand-blocked silks and other Oriental goods it was famed for when it opened in 1875. Look for the famous scarf department.

Fortnum and Mason's ground-floor provisions department is so engrossing that the upper floors of classic fashion remain peaceful. The food section stocks everything from baked beans to beautifully prepared hampers.

Some of the best-known names in British clothes design today

DEPARTMENT STORES

Fortnum and Mason
181 Piccadilly W1. **Map** 12 F3.
(0171-734 8040.

Harrods
87–135 Brompton Rd SW1.
Map 11 C5.
(0171-730 1234.

Harvey Nichols
109–25 Knightsbridge SW1.
Map 11 C5.
(0171-235 5000.

John Lewis
278–306 Oxford St W1. **Map** 12 E1.
(0171-629 7711.

Liberty
210–20 Regent St W1. **Map** 12 F2.
(0171-734 1234.

Selfridges
400 Oxford St W1. **Map** 12 D2.
(0171-629 1234.

Doorman at Fortnum and Mason

MARKS AND SPENCER

MARKS AND SPENCER has come a long way since 1882, when Russian emigré Michael Marks had a stall in Leeds's Kirkgate market under the sign, "Don't ask the price – it's a penny!" It now has over 680 stores worldwide, and everything in them is "own label." It stocks reliable versions of more expensive clothes – Marks and Spencer's underwear, in particular, is a staple of the British wardrobe. The food department concentrates entirely on elegant convenience foods. The main Oxford Street branches at the Pantheon (near Oxford Circus) and Marble Arch are the most interesting and well-stocked.

Penhaligon's for perfume *(see p318)*

London's Best: Shopping Streets and Markets

LONDON'S BEST shopping areas range from the elegance of Knightsbridge, where the highest-priced porcelain, jewelry and couture clothes are found to colorful markets such as Brick Lane and Portobello Road. Meccas for those who enjoy searching for a bargain, London's outdoor markets reflect the vibrant street life of its enterprising multiracial community. The city is fertile ground for specialty shoppers: there are streets crammed with antiques shops, antiquarian booksellers and art galleries. Seee pages 316 to 323 for more details of shops, grouped according to category.

Kensington Church Street
The small book and furniture shops on this winding street still provide old-fashioned service. (See p321.)

Regent's Park and Marylebone

Portobello Road Market
Over 200 stalls sell objets d'art, jewelry, medals, paintings and silverware—plus fresh fruit and vegetables. (See p323.)

Kensington and Holland Park

South Kensington and Knightsbridge

See inset map

Piccadı and S James

Knightsbridge
Exclusive designer-wear is on sale here, at Harrods as well as smaller stores. (See p207.)

Chelsea

King's Road
A center for avant-garde fashion in the 1960s and 1970s, the street is still popular with West London shoppers. There is also a good antiques market. (See p192.)

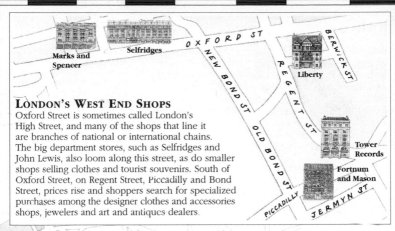

LONDON'S WEST END SHOPS

Oxford Street is sometimes called London's High Street, and many of the shops that line it are branches of national or international chains. The big department stores, such as Selfridges and John Lewis, also loom along this street, as do smaller shops selling clothes and tourist souvenirs. South of Oxford Street, on Regent Street, Piccadilly and Bond Street, prices rise and shoppers search for specialized purchases among the designer clothes and accessories shops, jewelers and art and antiques dealers.

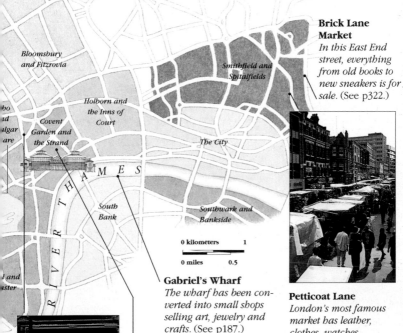

Brick Lane Market
In this East End street, everything from old books to new sneakers is for sale. (See p322.)

Gabriel's Wharf
The wharf has been converted into small shops selling art, jewelry and crafts. (See p187.)

Petticoat Lane
London's most famous market has leather, clothes, watches, jewelry and toys. (See p323.)

Charing Cross Road
Crammed shops selling old and new books line this long street. (See p316.)

Covent Garden and Neal Street
Street entertainers perform in this lively and historic market. The specialty shops of Neal Street are nearby. (See p115.)

Clothes

LONDON OFFERS the clothes shopper a seemingly endless variety of styles, price levels, quality and areas to shop in. The world's top designers are here, clustered around Knightsbridge, Bond Street and Chelsea, as are such familiar chains as Benetton and The Gap. But it is the wealth of home-based style that makes London such an exciting place to buy clothes. British designers excel in the opposite extremes of the market – traditional tailoring and street fashions.

TRADITIONAL CLOTHING

THE RUGGED country look is best found in the Regent Street/Piccadilly area. Waxed Barbour jackets are available from Farlow's *(see Royal Opera Arcade p92)* of Pall Mall and riding accessories from **Swaine Adeney**. Go to **Kent and Curwen** for cricket sweaters and to **Captain Watts** for guernsey sweaters and oil-skins. Try the Knightsbridge branch of **The Scotch House** for traditional tartan clothing, cashmere, Aran jerseys and Shetland shawls.

Classic town and business wear is another speciality of this area. **Burberry** sells its famous trenchcoats as well as checked clothing and some distinctive luggage from its shop on Haymarket. **Hackett** stocks traditionally tailored men's clothing. For shirts visit Jermyn Street, where you can order them made-to-measure or choose the more reasonably priced off-the-shelf ones. Many manufacturers now also sell classic women's blouses.

Liberty *(see p109)* use its famous patterned prints to make scarves, ties, blouses, pretty English rose dresses and some unusual trimmed denim jackets. **Laura Ashley** is also renowned for its floral-print dresses and frilly blouses.

For the ultimate suits, visit Savile Row, home of **Gieves and Hawkes** and other tailors.

AVANT-GARDE AND STREET FASHION

LONDON IS one of the world's capitals for street fashion – designer **Jean Paul Gaultier** prefers it to Paris because he says, the street fashion is "free from the constraints of good taste." In Britain, quirky

Vivienne Westwood won the Fashion Designer of the Year Award (1991). Other over-the-top British designers can be found in **Browns**. For more wearable styles, try the shops around Newburgh Street, West Soho. Most are predominantly for women, but **The Duffer of St George** is among the trail-blazers for men. New designers often start with a small stall at **Hyper Hyper**, **Kensington Market** or **The Garage** – all good for whacky or unusual clothing. Nowadays Oxford Street shops like **Top Shop** and **Mash** excel at copying street fashions at very low

prices. For British high fashion, **Paul Smith** is one of the best shops for men. For women, try **Browns, Whistles, Jasper Conran, Katharine Hamnett** and finally **Caroline Charles**.

KNITWEAR

FROM Fair Isle sweaters to Aran knits, the traditional British knitwear is famous. The best places for these are in Piccadilly – where you will find **N. Peal** – and in Regent Street and Knightsbridge. Such top designers as **Patricia Roberts** and **Joseph Tricot** and such small shops as **Jane and Dada**, stock a range of quite unusual and innovative machine- and hand-knits.

CHILDREN'S CLOTHES

YOU can get traditional hand-smocked dresses and romper suits from Liberty, **Young England** and **The White House**, which stock

SIZE CHART
For Australian sizes follow British and American convention.

Children's clothing

British	· 2–3	4–5	6–7	8–9	10–11	12	14	14+ (years)
American	2–3	4–5	6–6X	7–8	10		12	14	16 (size)
Continental	2–3	4–5	6–7	8–9	10–11	12	14	14+ (years)

Children's shoes

British	7¹/	8	9	10	11	12	13	1	2
American	7½	8½	9½	10½	11½	12½	13½	1½	2½
Continental	24	25½	27	28	29	30	32	33	34

Women's dresses coats and skirts

British	6	8	10	12	14	16	18	20
American	4	6	8	10	12	14	16	18
Continental	38	40	42	44	46	48	50	52

Women's blouses and sweaters

British	30	32	34	36	38	40	42
American	6	8	10	12	14	16	18
Continental	40	42	44	46	48	50	52

Women's shoes

British	3	4	5	6	7	8
American	5	6	7	8	9	10
Continental	36	37	38	39	40	41

Men's suits

British	34	36	38	40	42	44	46	48
American	34	36	38	40	42	44	46	48
Continental	44	46	48	50	52	54	56	58

Men's shirts

British	14	15	15½	16	16½	17	17½	18
American	14	15	15½	16	16½	17	17½	18
Continental	36	38	39	41	42	43	44	45

Men's shoes

British	7	7½	8	9	10	11	12
American	7½	8	8½	9½	10½	11	11½
Continental	40	41	42	43	44	45	46

nostalgically styled clothes such as smocks, gowns and tweed coats with smart velvet collars. **Trotters**, just behind Sloane Square, offers everything from shoes to haircuts.

SHOES

WITH SHOES, again it's the very traditional or the very trendy British designers and manufacturers who excel.

Their ready-made traditional brogues and Oxfords are the mainstay of **Church's Shoes**. For handmade classic footwear, try the Royal Family's shoemaker **John Lobb**. At the other end of the scale, **Shelly's** sells the utilitarian, trendy Dr. Martens, originally designed as hard-wearing work boots but now the shoe to be seen in. **Red or Dead** designs and produces some

really extravagant shoes as well as clothes, while for something a little more elegant, try **Johnny Moke** of the King's Road or **Emma Hope** in East London. If you are on the lookout for more exquisite women's shoes, visit **Manolo Blahnik**. Cheaper and less exclusive but often equally original designs can be found in either **Hobbs** or **Pied à Terre.**

DIRECTORY

TRADITIONAL

Burberry
18–22 Haymarket SW1.
Map 13 A3.
【 0171-930 3343.
One of two branches.

Captain Watts
7 Dover St W1.
Map 12 F3.
【 0171-493 4633

Gieves & Hawkes
1 Savile Row W1.
Map 12 E3.
【 0171-434 2001.

Hackett
87 Jermyn St SW1.
Map 13 A3.
【 0171-930 1300.
One of several branches.

Kent and Curwen
39 St James's St SW1.
Map 12 F3.
【 0171-409 1955.

Laura Ashley
256–258 Regent St W1.
Map 12 F1.
【 0171-437 9760.
One of several branches.

The Scotch House
2 Brompton Rd SW1.
Map 11 C5.
【 0171-581 2151.
One of several branches.

Swaine Adeney
185 Piccadilly W1.
Map 12 F3.
【 0171-734 4277.

MODERN/STREET FASHION

Browns
23–27 South Molton St W1. **Map** 12 E2.
【 0171-491 7833.
One of several branches.

Caroline Charles
56–57 Beauchamp Pl SW3.
Map 19 B1.
【 0171-589 5850.

The Duffer of St George
27 D'Arblay St W1.
Map 13 A2.
【 0171-439 0996.

The Garage
350 King's Rd SW3.
Map 19 A4.
【 0171 352 8653.

Hyper Hyper
26–40 Kensington High St W8. **Map** 10 D5.
【 0171-938 4343.
One of two branches.

Jean-Paul Gaultier
171–5 Draycott Ave SW3.
Map 19 B2.
【 0171-584 4648.

Katharine Hamnett
20 Sloane St SW1.
Map 11 C5.
【 0171 823 1002.

Kensington Market
49–53 Kensington High St W8. **Map** 10 D5.
【 0171-938 4343.

Mash
73 Oxford St W1.
Map 13 A1.
【 0171-434 9609.

Koh Samui
50 Monmouth St WC2.
Map 13 B2.
【 0171-240 4280.

Nicole Farhi
158 New Bond St W1.
Map 12 E2.
【 0171-499 8368.

Paul Smith
41–44 Floral St WC2.
Map 13 B2.
【 0171-379 7133.

Top Shop
Oxford Circus W1.
Map 12 F1.
【 0171-636 7700.
One of several branches.

Vivienne Westwood
6 Davies St W1.
Map 12 E2.
【 0171-629 3757.

Whistles
12–14 St Christopher's Pl W1. **Map** 12 D1
【 0171-487 4484.

KNITWEAR

Jane and Dada
20–21 St Christopher's Pl W1. **Map** 12 D1.
【 0171-486 0977.

Joseph Tricot
28 Brook St W1.
Map 12 E2.
【 0171-629 6077.

N Peal
Burlington Arcade,
Piccadilly, W1. **Map** 12 F3.
【 0171-493 9220.
One of several branches.

Patricia Roberts
60 Kinnerton St SW1.
Map 11 C5.
【 0171-235 4742.

CHILDREN'S

Trotters
34 King's Rd SW3.
Map 19 C2.
【 0171-259 9620.

The White House
51–52 New Bond St W1.
Map 12 E2.
【 0171-629 3521.

Young England
47 Elizabeth St SW1.
Map 20 E2.
【 0171-259 9003.

SHOES

Church's Shoes
163 New Bond St W1.
Map 12 E2.
【 0171-499 9449.
One of several branches.

Emma Hope
33 Amwell St EC1.
Map 6 E3.
【 0171-833 2367.

Hobbs
47 South Molton St W1.
Map 12 E2
【 0171-629 0750.
One of several branches.

Johnny Moke
396 King's Rd SW10.
Map 18 F4.
【 0171-351 2232.

John Lobb
9 St James's St SW1.
Map 12 F4.
【 0171-930 3664.

Manolo Blahnik
49–51 Old Church St,
Kings Road SW3.
Map 19 A4.
【 0171-352 8622.

Pied à Terre
19 South Molton St W1
Map 12 E2.
【 0171-629 1362.
One of several branches.

Red or Dead
33 Neal St WC2.
Map 13 B2.
【 0171-379 7571.
One of several branches.

Shelly's
19–21 Foubert's Pl,
Carnaby Street, W1.
Map 12 F2.
【 0171-287 0593.
One of several branches.

Specialty Shops

LONDON MAY BE famed for grand department stores such as Harrods, but there are many specialty shops that should be included in the visitor's itinerary. Some have expertise built up over a century or more, while others cater to the new and fashionable.

FOODS

BRITISH FOOD may be much maligned, but there are many specialties that are well worth sampling, such as teas, cheeses, chocolates, biscuits and preserves (see pp288–9). The food halls of Fortnum and Mason, Harrods and Selfridges are good for all of these. Otherwise, head for **Paxton and Whitfield**, a delightful shop dating from 1830 and stocking over 300 cheeses, including baby Stiltons and Cheshire cheeses, along with pork pies, elegant biscuits, oils and preserves.

For chocolates, the ultimate extravagance is **Charbonnel et Walker**. Despite the name it is an English manufacturer, and the chocolates are all handmade. **Bendicks** on Curzon Street stands 50 yards from the original 1921 premises. They make dark chocolates in Winchester by hand, and the classic dessert mint is still the specialty.

TEAS

THAT MOST famous of British drinks comes in all kinds of flavors, from the delicate gunpowder green to the rich, strong and dark English breakfast types. An interesting selection, including fruit-flavored teas, is available at the **Tea House** in Covent Garden. Teapots are also stocked here. The **Algerian Coffee Stores** sells more teas than coffee, including herbal and fruity ones. The selection of coffees is excellent, however, and there are many luxury grocery items in stock.

ONE-OFFS

THERE ARE hundreds of odd shops in London that specialize in just one sort of thing. **The Bead Shop**, for example, sells a massive selection of beads and also stocks the equipment for making them into jewelry. **The Candle Shop** supplies candles of every imaginable shape and size, along with candle holders and candle-making equipment. Demonstrations of the art take place outside. **Halcyon Days** specializes in little enamelled copper boxes, a revived English 18th-century craft.

Astleys sells pipes but not tobacco; the range is quite bewildering, from simple handturned straightgrains to weird-looking slope-domed calabashes and Sherlock Holmesian meerschaums. For serious collectors of antique scientific instruments, **Arthur Middleton** has a fascinatingly cluttered shop full of ancient globes and early microscopes. For equally serious collectors of dolls' houses, the **Singing Tree** has the ultimate in English dolls' houses, plus many beautifully crafted tiny things to put inside them, all replicated to precise scale in accurate period style.

Finally, at the **Left-Handed Shop** in Soho, everything is designed to make life easier for the left-hander. Scissors, corkscrews, cutlery, pens and kitchen and garden tools are the main sellers.

BOOKS AND MAGAZINES

BOOKSHOPS ARE high among London's specialties. Charing Cross Road (see p108) is the focal point for those searching for new, antiquarian and second-hand volumes, and it is the home of **Foyle's**, with massive but notoriously badly organized stock. Large branches of such chains as **Books Etc.** and **Waterstone's** are also here; so are many theme shops, such as **Murder One** for crime books, **Silver Moon** for women's and feminist writing,

Books for a Change for green politics and **Zwemmer** for art books. **Stanford's** (see p112), with maps and guides to cover the globe, is in Long Acre; other travel books can be found at the **Travel Bookshop**. Nearby is **Books for Cooks**, whose well-informed staff can offer advice. Adult comics are the specialty at the Neal Street shop **Comic Showcase**, which also has books by well-known cartoonists. For gay and lesbian writing, **Sisterwrite** in Islington caters to women and **Gay's The Word**, near Russell Square, to men. The best selection of books on the cinema is at the **Cinema Bookshop**.

The **PC Bookshop** sells a huge range of books on all aspects of computers, while its sister shop nearby stocks multimedia packages.

Two of the best general bookshops are **Hatchard's** in Piccadilly and the flagship **Dillons** store in Gower Street, both of which offer a well-organized and extensive choice. **Compendium**, an alternative bookstore near Camden Market, features interesting and hard-to-obtain titles, while the **Penguin Bookshop** and its children's branch, the **Puffin Bookshop**, stock a fine range of very recent paperbacks.

The Charing Cross Road area is the best hunting ground for antiquarian books. Many shops offer a book-finding service if the title you want is no longer in print.

If you're looking for newspapers and magazines from abroad, the basement of **Tower Records** has the best selection of U.S. newspapers, while **Capital Newsagents** stocks (among others) Italian, French, Spanish and Middle Eastern publications. **Gray's Inn News** is also worth a visit (see pp352–3).

RECORDS AND MUSIC

AS ONE OF the world's greatest centers of recorded music, London has a huge and excellent selection of record shops catering to all manner of musical styles. The **Music Discount Centre** has a very good range of classical music, as do such megastores as **HMV**, **Virgin** and **Tower Records**, which are best for mainstream adult-oriented rock and easy listening. The small specialty shops tend to cater to the more esoteric tastes. For jazz try **Ray's Jazz** and **Honest Jon's**, while reggae fans should jam down to **Daddy Kool**. **HMV** has a good selection of world music, and **Stern's** has no competition when it comes to African music. For 12-inch singles, the medium of club and dance music, **Trax** and **Black Market** are two of the most central places to look.

DIRECTORY

FOODS

Bendicks of Mayfair
7 Aldwych WC2.
Map 13 C2.
☏ 0171-836 1846.

Charbonnel et Walker
1 Royal Arcade, 28 Old Bond St W1. **Map** 12 F3.
☏ 0171-491 0939.

Paxton and Whitfield
93 Jermyn St SW1.
Map 12 F3.
☏ 0171-930 0250.

TEAS

Algerian Coffee Stores
52 Old Compton St W1.
Map 13 A2.
☏ 0171-437 2480.

The Tea House
15 Neal St WC2.
Map 13 B2.
☏ 0171-240 7539.

ONE-OFFS

Astleys
16 Piccadilly Arcade SW1.
Map 13 A3.
☏ 0171-499 9950.

Arthur Middleton
12 New Row, Covent Garden WC2.
Map 13 B2.
☏ 0171-836 7042.

The Bead Shop
43 Neal Street WC2.
Map 13 B1.
☏ 0171-240 0931.

The Candle Shop
30 The Market, Covent Garden Piazza WC2.
Map 13 C2.
☏ 0171-836 9815.

Halcyon Days
14 Brook St W1.
Map 12 E2.
☏ 0171-629 8811.

The Left-Handed Shop
57 Brewer St W1.
Map 13 A2.
☏ 0171-437 3910.

The Singing Tree
69 New King's Rd SW6.
☏ 0171-736 4527.

BOOKS AND MAGAZINES

Books Etc
120 Charing Cross Rd WC2.
Map 13 B1
☏ 0171-379 6838.

Books for a Change
52 Charing Cross Rd WC2.
Map 13 B2.
☏ 0171-836 2315.

Books for Cooks
4 Blenheim Crescent W11.
Map 9 B2.
☏ 0171-221 1992.

Capital Newsagents
48 Old Compton St W1.
Map 13 A2.
☏ 0171-437 2479.

Cinema Bookshop
13–14 Great Russell St WC1. **Map** 13 B1.
☏ 0171-637 0206.

Comic Showcase
76 Neal St WC2. **Map** 13 B1.
☏ 0171-240 3664.

Compendium
234 Camden High St NW1.
☏ 0171-485 8944.

Dillons
82 Gower St WC1.
Map 5 A5.
☏ 0171-636 1577.

Forbidden Planet
71 New Oxford St WC1.
Map 13 B1.
☏ 0171-836 4179.

Foyle's
113–119 Charing Cross Rd WC2. **Map** 13 B1.
☏ 0171-437 5660.

Gay's The Word
66 Marchmont St WC1.
Map 5 B4.
☏ 0171-278 7654.

Gray's Inn News
50 Theobald's Rd WC1.
Map 6 D5.
☏ 0171-405 5241.

Hatchard's
187 Piccadilly W1.
Map 12 F3.
☏ 0171-439 9921.

Murder One
71 Charing Cross Rd WC2.
Map 13 B2.
☏ 0171-734 3485.

PC Bookshop
11 Sicilian Ave WC1.
Map 13 1C.
☏ 0171-831 0022.
(Multimedia at No. 25)

Penguin/Puffin Bookshop
10 The Market, Covent Garden Piazza WC2.
Map 13 C2.
☏ 0171-379 7650.

Silver Moon
64–68 Charing Cross Rd WC2. **Map** 13 B2.
☏ 0171-836 7906.

Stanford's
12–14 Long Acre WC2.
Map 13 B2.
☏ 0171-836 1321.

Travel Bookshop
13 Blenheim Crescent W11. **Map** 9 B2.
☏ 0171-229 5260.

Waterstone's
121–125 Charing Cross Rd WC2. **Map** 13 B1.
☏ 0171-434 4291.

The Women's Book Club
45–6 Poland St W1.
Map 13 A2.
☏ 0171-437 1019.

Zwemmer
26 Litchfield St WC2.
Map 13 B2.
☏ 0171-379 7886.

RECORDS AND MUSIC

Black Market
25 D'Arblay St W1.
Map 13 A2.
☏ 0171-437 0478.

Daddy Kool Music
12 Berwick St W1.
Map 13 A2.
☏ 0171-437 3535.

HMV
150 Oxford St W1.
Map 13 A1.
☏ 0171-631 3423.

Honest Jon's Records
278 Portobello Rd W10.
Map 9 A1.
☏ 0181-969 9822.

The Music Discount Centre
33–34 Rathbone Pl W1.
Map 13 A1.
☏ 0171-637 4700.

Ray's Jazz
180 Shaftesbury Ave WC2. **Map** 13 B1.
☏ 0171-240 3969.

Rough Trade
130 Talbot Rd W11.
Map 9 C1.
☏ 0171-229 8541.

Stern's
116 Whitfield St W1.
Map 4 F4.
☏ 0171-387 5550.

Tower Records
1 Piccadilly Circus W1.
Map 13 A3.
☏ 0171-439 2500.

Trax
55 Greek St W1.
Map 13 A2.
☏ 0171-734 0795.

Virgin Megastore
14–30 Oxford St W1.
Map 13 A1.
☏ 0171-631 1234.

Gifts and Souvenirs

LONDON IS A WONDERFUL PLACE to shop for presents. In addition to an impressive array of original ceramics, jewelry, perfume and glassware, there is exotic merchandise from around the world, including jewelry from India and Africa, stationery from Europe and kitchenware from France and Italy. The elegant Regency-period Burlington Arcade (see p91) is a popular shopping destination selling high-quality gifts, clothes, art and crafts, many made in the United Kingdom.

The shops at big museums, such as the Victoria and Albert (see p198–201), the Natural History (see p204–5) and the Science Museum (see p208–9), often have unusual and original items to take home as mementoes of your visit, while **Contemporary Applied Arts** and the market in Covent Garden Piazza (see p114) have a selection of British pottery, jewelry, knitwear and other crafts. If you want to buy all your presents under one roof, go to Liberty (see p311), where beautiful stock from all over the globe fills every department.

JEWELRY

JEWELRY SHOPS in London range from the extremely traditional to the tiny shops and stalls that huddle in areas like Covent Garden (see pp110–19), Gabriel's Wharf (see p187) and Camden Lock (see p322), which specialize in unusual pieces. **Butler and Wilson** has some of the most eye-catching costume jewelry in town, while next door **Electrum** keeps less bold but equally innovative pieces.

Past Times sells modern reproductions of ancient British designs, including Celtic, Roman and Tudor, as do the shops at the British Museum (see pp126–9) and the V&A. The **Leslie Craze Gallery** sells new designs, while **Contemporary Applied Arts** has stylish craft jewelry. The essential place for Gothic jewelry is **The Great Frog** on Carnaby Street. Liberty stocks spectacular ethnic, costume and fashion jewelry. **Manquette** is also worth visiting for its elegant, unique pieces in lapis lazuli, amber, coral, gold and silver.

HATS AND ACCESSORIES

TRADITIONAL MEN'S hats, from flat caps to bowlers and pith helmets, can be found at **Edward Bates** and **Herbert Johnson**. For women, truly distinctive creations come from **Herald and Heart Hatters**, while **Stephen Jones** has a wide range of designs from the everyday to the extravagant and will make hats to match any outfit if you supply your own fabric.

For a selection of the best in British accessories, try the shops on Jermyn Street or in the arcades off Piccadilly. Elsewhere, **James Smith & Sons** produces wonderful umbrellas, ideal for wet London weather. For walking sticks, canes and riding crops, pay a visit to Swaine Adeney (see p315).

Mulberry Company stocks classically English luggage, as well as accessories such as belts, purses and wallets, and **Janet Fitch** sells a wide range of bags, belts, jewelery, hats and other essential accessories.

At the cheaper end of the market, the **Accessorize** chain sells all manner of beads and baubles, grouped by color to help co-ordinate your outfit.

PERFUMES AND TOILETRIES

MANY BRITISH perfumeries use recipes that are hundreds of years old. **Floris** and **Penhaligon's**, for example, still manufacture the same flower-based scents and toiletries for men and women that they sold in the 19th century. The same goes for **Czech and Speake**, as well as for men's specialists **Truefitt and Hill** and **George F. Trumper**, where you can buy some wonderful reproductions of antique shaving equipment. Both **Culpeper** and **Neal's Yard Remedies** employ traditional herbal and floral remedies as bases for their therapeutic, natural toiletries.

Other manufacturers have a more contemporary approach to their wares; the **Body Shop**, for example, uses recyclable plastic packaging for its natural cosmetics and toiletries and encourages staff and customers alike to take an interest in environmental issues. **Molton Brown** sells a variety of natural cosmetics, body and haircare products, from both its own shops in South Molton Street and Hampstead and from other outlets.

STATIONERY

SOME OF THE most interesting wrapping paper on sale in London is designed by **Tessa Fantoni**, whose paper-covered boxes, photo frames and albums are sold in several specialty stationery and gift shops, as well as the Conran Shop and her own shop in Clapham. **Falkiner Fine Papers** stocks a range of handmade and decorative papers. Their marbled paper makes glorious giftwrapping for a very special gift. To find luxurious writing paper, pens, pencils and desk accessories, try the Queen's stationer, **Smythson** of Bond Street. **Fortnum and Mason** (see p311) does handsome leather-bound diaries, blotters and pencil holders, while Liberty embellishes desk accessories with its famous Art Deco prints. For personal organizers covered in anything from vinyl to iguana skin, there's the **Filofax Centre** or the more original **Lefax**. The minuscule shop **Pencraft** is the place for pens by Mont Blanc, Watermans, Parker or Sheaffer. Finally, for cards, pens, wrapping paper and stationery, pop into one of the branches of **Paperchase**.

INTERIORS

WEDGWOOD STILL makes the famous pale-blue Jasper china that Josiah Wedgwood designed in the 18th century. You can buy it, as well as Irish Waterford crystal and Coalport bone china, at **Waterford Wedgwood** on Piccadilly. Adventurous contemporary tableware is available at **Anta**, which produces stoneware handpainted in various colorful Scottish tartans. For a fine selection of original pottery, visit the **Craftsmen Potters Association** of Great Britain and **Contemporary Applied Arts**. Quirky ceramics are the specialty of **Mildred Pearce**, offering a trendy new slant on everything from candlesticks to clocks. Personalized gifts are also available. **Heal's**, the **Conran Shop**, **Gore Booker** and **Freud's** all offer a great selection of stylish, well-designed accessories for the home. For good-quality kitchen and household items, **Divertimenti** and **David Mellor** are the places to go.

DIRECTORY

JEWELRY

Butler & Wilson
20 South Molton St W1.
Map 12 E2.
(0171-409 2955.

Contemporary Applied Arts
43 Earlham St WC2.
Map 13 B2.
(0171-836 6993.

Electrum Gallery
21 South Molton St W1
Map 12 E2.
(0171-629 6325.

The Great Frog
51 Carnaby St W1.
Map 12 F2.
(0171-734 1900.

Leslie Craze Gallery
34 Clerkenwell Green
EC1. **Map** 6 E4.
(0171-608 0393.

Manquette
20a Kensington Church
Walk W8. **Map** 10 D5.
(0171-937 2897.

Past Times
146 Brompton Rd SW3.
Map 11 C5.
(0171-581 7616.

HATS AND ACCESSORIES

Accessorize
42 Carnaby St W1.
Map 12 F2.
(0171-437 4766.

Edward Bates
21a Jermyn St SW1.
Map 13 A3.
(0171-734 2722.

Herald & Heart Hatters
131 St Philip St SW8.
(0171-627 2414.

Herbert Johnson
30 New Bond St W1.
Map 12 F2.
(0171-408 1174.

James Smith & Sons
53 New Oxford St WC1.
Map 13 C1.
(0171-836 4731.

Janet Fitch
2 Percy St, W1. **Map** 13 A1.
(0171-580 8710.

Mulberry Company
11–12 Gees Court, St
Christopher's Pl W1.
Map 12 D1.
(0171-493 2546.

Stephen Jones
29 Heddon St, W1.
Map 12 F2.
(0171-734 9666.

PERFUMES AND TOILETRIES

The Body Shop
32–34 Great Marlborough
St W1. **Map** 12 F2. Branches
throughout London.
(0171-437 5137.

Culpeper Ltd
21 Bruton St W1.
Map 12 E3.
(0171-629 4559.

Czech & Speake
39c Jermyn St SW1.
Map 13 A3.
(0171-439 0216.

Floris
89 Jermyn St SW1.
Map 13 A3.
(0171-930 2885.

Molton Brown
58 South Molton St W1.
Map 12 E2.
(0171-629 1872.

Neal's Yard Remedies
15 Neal's Yard WC2.

Map 13 B1.
(0171-379 7222.

Penhaligon's
41 Wellington St WC2.
Map 13 C2.
(0171 836 2150.

Truefitt & Hill
71 St James's St SW1.
Map 12 F3.
(0171-493 2961.

George F Trumper
9 Curzon St W1.
Map 12 E3.
(0171-499 1850.

STATIONERY

Falkiner Fine Papers
76 Southampton Row
WC1. **Map** 5 C5.
(0171-831 1157.

The Filofax Centre
21 Conduit St W1.
Map 12 F2.
(0171-499 0457.

Lefax
69 Neal St WC2.
Map 13 B2.
(0171-836 1977.

Paperchase
213 Tottenham Court Rd
W1. **Map** 5 A5.
(0171-580 8496.

Pencraft
91 Kingsway WC2.
Map 13 C1.
(0171-405 3639.

Smythson of Bond Street
44 New Bond St W1.
Map 12 E2.
(0171-629 8558.

Tessa Fantoni
77 Abbeville Rd SW4.
(0181-673 1253.

INTERIORS

Anta
46 Crispin St E1.

Map 8 D5.
(0171-247 1643.

Conran Shop
Michelin House, 81
Fulham Rd SW3.
Map 19 A2.
(0171-589 7401.

Craftsmen Potters Association of Great Britain
7 Marshall St W1.
Map 12 F2.
(0171-437 7605.

David Mellor
4 Sloane Sq SW1.
Map 20 D2.
(0171-730 4259.

Divertimenti
45–47 Wigmore St W1.
Map 12 E1.
(0171-935 0689.

Freud's
198 Shaftesbury Ave
WC2. **Map** 13 B1.
(0171-831 1071.

The Glasshouse
21 St Albans Place N1.
Map 6 E2.
(0171-836 9785.

Gore Booker
41 Bedford St WC2.
Map 13 C3.
(0171-497 1254.

Heal's
196 Tottenham Court Rd
W1. **Map** 5 A5.
(0171-636 1666.

Mildred Pearce
33 Earlham St WC2.
Map 13 B2.
(0171-738 0055 .

Waterford Wedgwood
173 Piccadilly W1.
Map 12 F3.
(0171-629 2614.

Art and Antiques

L ONDON'S ART AND antiques shops are spread across the capital. While the more fashionable (and more expensive) dealers are concentrated in a relatively small area bounded by Mayfair and St. James's, other shops and galleries catering to a more modest budget are scattered over the rest of the city. Whether your taste is for Old Masters or young modern artists, Boule or Bauhaus, you are bound to find in London something of beauty that is within your financial means.

MAYFAIR

C ORK STREET is the center of the British contemporary art world. Walk up from Piccadilly and pass, on your left, the **Piccadilly Gallery**, which sells modern British pictures. Next come several galleries, including **Raab** and **Salama-Caro**, offering contemporary art in varying degrees of the avant-garde. The biggest name to watch for is **Waddington**, and if you want to discover the flavor of the month, a stop here is a must. However, purchasing is only for the serious (and rich) collector. **Chat Noir**, in nearby Albemarle, Street is committed to selling contemporary work at a more affordable price. Before retracing your steps down Cork Street, look into Clifford Street, where **Jeremy Maas** excels in Victorian masters. Return passing a wide variety of art, from traditional British sporting pictures and sculpture at **Tryon and Morland** and the Scottish themes of **William Jackson** to **Mayor's** Surrealism and the mainstream art of **Redfern**.

Nearby, Old Bond Street is the center of the fine antiques trade in London. If it's Turner watercolors or Louis XV furniture you're after, this is the place. A walk up from Piccadilly takes you past the lush portals of **Richard Green** and the **Fine Art Society**, among other extremely smart galleries. For furniture and decorative arts, visit **Bond Street Antiques Centre** and **Asprey**; for silver, go to **S. J. Phillips**; and for Victorian art, try **Christopher Wood's** gallery. Even if you are not a buyer, these galleries are fascinating places to visit,

so don't be afraid to walk in – you can learn more from an hour spent here than you can from weeks of studying textbooks. Also on Old Bond Street you will find two of the big four London auction houses, **Phillips** and **Sotheby's**.

ST. JAMES'S

S OUTH OF Piccadilly lies a maze of 18th-century streets. This is gentlemen's club country (see Pall Mall p92), and the galleries mostly reflect the traditional nature of the area. The center is Duke Street, home of Old Master dealers **Johnny van Haeften** and **Harari and Johns**. At the bottom is King Street, with that leviathan of antiques dealers, **Spink**. A few doors down you will find the main salerooms of **Christie's**, the well-known auction house where Van Goghs and Picassos sell for millions.

Walk back up Bury Street, past several interesting galleries, and duck into Ryder Street to visit **Chris Beetle's** gallery of works by illustrators and caricaturists.

WALTON STREET

C LOSE TO fashionable and expensive Knightsbridge, the art galleries and antique shops along this elegant little street have prices to match. Here the well-heeled visit galleries such as **Malcolm Innes**, where there are sporting watercolors on show. A short walk away in nearby Montpelier Street is **Bonham's** the auctioneers, fourth in line of the big four and recently redecorated in chic style. You may be lucky enough to find a bargain here.

PIMLICO ROAD

T HE ANTIQUES shops that line this road tend to cater predominantly to the pricey requirements of the interior decorator – this is where to come if you are searching for an Italian leather screen or a silver-encrusted ram's skull. Of particular interest is **Westenholz**. Nearby, **Henry Sotheran** offers fine prints.

BELGRAVIA

T HIS AREA HAS a reputation for good British pictures. The hub of art activity is Motcomb Street, which caters for most tastes. Those seeking fine but well-priced British pictures should visit **Michael Parkin's** gallery, while Oriental-art enthusiasts will revel in the **Mathaf Gallery**, with its 19th-century British and European paintings of the Arab world.

AFFORDABLE ART

T HE HUGELY popular Contemporary Art Society's market takes place every autumn at **Smith's Galleries** in Covent Garden, with work on sale from £100. The three galleries here also show (and sell) excellent work throughout the year. London's East End, a growth area for contemporary art, is home to a host of small galleries as well as the magnificent **Flowers East**, which is strong on work by young artists. For sometimes brilliant shows of contemporary art, step along to Portobello and the **East-West Gallery**. A lot of the work here is reasonably-priced, too.

PHOTOGRAPHY

T HE LARGEST collection of original photographs for sale in the country is at the **Photographers' Gallery**. The **Special Photographers' Company** is well known for selling top-quality work – by unknown artists as well as famous photographic names. **Hamilton's** is worth visiting during its major exhibitions.

BRIC-A-BRAC

For smaller, more affordable pieces, it's worth going to one of the outdoor markets, such as Camden Lock (see p322), Camden Passage (p322) or Bermondsey (p322), which is the main antiques market, catering to the trade. Many high streets out of the center of town have covered markets of specialty stalls. Finally, a browse along Kensington Church Street in west London will turn up everything from handcrafted furniture to Staffordshire dogs, in a concentration of small emporia.

AUCTIONS

If you are confident enough, auctions are a cheaper way to buy art or antiques, but be sure to read the small print in the catalog (which usually costs around £15). Bidding is simple – you simply register, take a number, then raise your hand when the lot you want comes up. The auctioneer will see your bid. It's as easy as that and can be great fun. The main auction houses are Christie's, Sotheby's, Phillips and Bonham's. Don't forget Christie's salesroom in South Kensington, which offers art and antiques for the more modest budget.

Markets

LONDON STREET MARKETS have an air of exuberant irreverence that in itself provides sufficient reason to pay them a visit. At many you'll also find some of the best prices in the capital. Stay alert and keep an eye on your purse or wallet and join in the fun.

Bermondsey Market (New Caledonian Market)

Long Lane and Bermondsey St SE1. **Map** 15 C5. 🚇 *London Bridge, Borough.* **Open** *5am–2pm Fri.* **Starts closing** *midday. See p179.*

Bermondsey is the gathering point for London's antiques traders every Friday. Serious collectors start early and scrutinize the paintings, the silver and the vast array of old jewelry. Browsers might uncover some interesting curiosities, but most bargains go before 9am.

Berwick Street Market

Berwick St W1. **Map** 13 A1. 🚇 *Piccadilly Circus, Leicester Sq.* **Open** *9am–6pm Mon–Sat. See p108.*

The spirited hawkers of Soho's Berwick Street sell the cheapest and most attractive fruit and vegetables in the West End. Spanish black radish, star fruit and Italian plum tomatoes are among the produce you might find here; Dennis's vegetable stall sells a massive range of interesting edible fungi, all immaculately presented. The market is good for fabrics and cheap household goods, too, as well as for leather handbags and delicatessen items. Separated from Berwick Street by a seedy passage-way is Rupert Street market, where prices tend to be higher and the traders quieter.

Brick Lane Market

Brick Lane E1. **Map** 8 E5. 🚇 *Shoreditch, Liverpool St, Aldgate East.* **Open** *daybreak to 1pm Sun. See pp170–1.*

This massively popular East End jamboree is at its best around its gloriously frayed edges. Explore the little shops on Cheshire Street, packed with tatty furniture and old books, or the mish-mash of junk sold on Bethnal Green Road. East End street vendors huddle together on Bacon Street proffering gold rings and watches, while much of Sclater Street is given over to pet foods and provisions. On the wasteland off Cygnet Street, new bicycles, fresh meat and frozen food are among the myriad of goods for sale. Brick Lane itself is rather more prosaic, with new goods such as handbags, sports shoes and jeans on sale, but look for the wonderful range of spice shops and curry restaurants in this vital, active center of London's Bangladeshi community.

Brixton Market

Electric Ave SW9. 🚇 *Brixton.* **Open** *8:30am–5:30pm Mon, Tue & Thu–Sat; 8:30am–1pm Wed.*

This market offers a wonderful assortment of Afro-Caribbean food, from goats' meat, pigs' tails and salt fish to plantain, yams and breadfruit. The best food is to be found in the old Granville and Market Row arcades, where exotic fish are a highlight. Afro-style wigs, strange herbs and potions, religious tracts sold by Rastafarian priests and, on Brixton Station Road, cheap second-hand clothes are also to be had. From record stalls, the bass of raw reggae pounds through this cosmopolitan market like a heartbeat.

Camden Lock Market

Buck St NW1. 🚇 *Camden Town.* **Open** *9am–5pm Thu and Fri, 10am–6pm Sat & Sun.*

Camden Lock Market has grown swiftly since its opening in 1974. Handmade crafts, new and second-hand street fashions, wholefoods, books, records and antiques form the bulk of the goods that are on sale, although thousands of young people come here simply for the atmosphere, especially on weekends. This is enhanced by the hawkers and street performers who draw the crowds to the attractive cobbled area around the canal.

Camden Passage Market

Camden Passage N1. **Map** 6 F1. 🚇 *Angel.* **Open** *10am–2pm Wed, 10am–5pm Sat.*

Camden Passage is a quiet walk-way where bookshops and restaurants nestle among bijou antiques shops. Prints, silverware, 19th-century magazines, jewelry and toys are among the many collectibles displayed. There aren't very many bargains to be picked up here, as most of the traders tend to be specialists. However, it is an ideal market for those who just want to indulge in some genteel browsing.

Chapel Market

Chapel Market N1. **Map** 6 E2. 🚇 *Angel.* **Open** *9am–3:30pm Tue, Wed, Fri & Sat; 9am–1pm Thu & Sun.*

This is one of London's most traditional and exuberant street markets. Weekends are best; the fruit and vegetables are varied and cheap, the fish stalls are the finest in the area, and there's a wealth of bargain household goods and clothing to be had.

Church Street and Bell Street Markets

Church St NW8 and Bell St NW1. **Map** 3 A5. 🚇 *Edgware Rd.* **Open** *8:30am–4pm Mon–Thu, 8:30am–5pm Fri & Sat.*

Like many of London's markets, Church Street reaches a crescendo on the weekend. On Friday, stalls selling electrical goods, cheap clothes, household goods, fish, cheese and antiques join the everyday fruit-and-vegetable stalls. Alfie's Antique Market at Nos. 13 to 25 houses over 300 small stalls selling everything from jewelry to old radios and gramophones. Bell Street, running parallel, has its own market where second-hand clothes, records and antiquated electrical goods are sold for a song on Saturdays.

Columbia Road Market

Columbia Rd E2. **Map** 8 D3. 🚇 *Shoreditch, Old St.* **Open** *8am–12:30pm Sun. See p171.*

This is the place to come to buy greenery and flowers or just to enjoy the fragrances and colors. Cut flowers, plants, shrubs, seedlings and pots are all sold at about half the normal prices in this charming Victorian street on a Sunday morning.

East Street Market

East St SE17. 🚇 *Elephant and Castle.* **Open** *8am–5pm Tue, Wed, Fri & Sat; 8am–2pm Thu & Sun.*

East Street Market's high spot is Sunday, when over 250 stalls fill the narrow street and a small plant-and-flower market is set up on Blackwood Street. Fruit-and-vegetable stalls are in a minority as traders of clothes (mainly new), electrical and household goods swing into action, while furtive street hawkers proffer shoelaces and razor blades from old suitcases. Many locals come here more for the entertainment than to buy, as did the young Charlie Chaplin *(see p37)* at the beginning of the century.

Gabriel's Wharf and Riverside Walk Markets

56 Upper Ground and Riverside Walk SE1. **Map** 14 E3. ⊖ *Waterloo.* **Gabriel's Wharf open** *9:30am–6pm Fri–Sun;* **Riverside Walk open** *10am–5pm Sat & Sun and irregular weekdays. See p187.*

Little shops filled with ceramics, paintings and jewelry surround a bandstand in Gabriel's Wharf where jazz groups sometimes play in the summer. A few stalls are set up around the courtyard, selling ethnic clothing and handmade jewelry and pottery. The nearby book market, to be found under Waterloo Bridge, includes a good selection of new and old Penguin paperbacks, as well as new and second-hand hardcover books.

Greenwich Market

College Approach SE10. **Map** 23 B2. � *Greenwich.* **Open** *9am–6pm Sat & Sun.*

On weekends, the area west of the Hotel Ibis accommodates dozens of trestle tables piled with coins, medals, banknotes, second-hand books, Art Deco furniture and assorted bric-a-brac. The covered crafts market specializes in wooden toys, clothes made by young designers, handmade jewelry and accessories.

Jubilee and Apple Markets

Covent Gdn Piazza WC2. **Map** 13 C2. ⊖ *Covent Gdn.* **Open** *9am–5pm daily.*

Covent Garden has become the center of London street life, with some of the capital's best street entertainers. Both these markets sell many interesting crafts and designs. The Apple Market, inside the Piazza where the famous fruit-and-vegetable market was housed (*see p114*), has chunky knitwear, leather jewelry and novelty goods; a nearby open-air section has cheap army-surplus clothes, old prints and more jewelry. Jubilee Hall sells antiques on Monday; crafts on the weekend; and a large selection of clothes, handbags, cosmetics and tacky mementoes in between.

Leadenhall Market

Whittington Ave EC3. **Map** 15 C2. ⊖ *Bank, Monument.* **Open** *7am–4pm Mon–Fri. See p159.*

Leadenhall Market is a welcome culinary oasis in the City and houses some of the best food shops in the capital. The market's

traditional strengths of poultry and game have been maintained: mallard, teal, partridge and woodcock are all available in season. There is also a fabulous display of seafood, including excellent oysters, at Ashdown. Other stores stock high-class delicatessen items, cheeses and chocolate – an expensive but mouth-watering display of goods that is hard to beat.

Leather Lane Market

Leather Lane EC1. **Map** 6 E5. ⊖ *Chancery Lane.* **Open** *10:30am–2pm Mon–Fri.*

This ancient street has played host to a market for over 300 years. The history of the Lane has nothing to do with leather (it was originally called Le Vrune Lane), but it is in this commodity that some of the best buys are to be had in modern times. The stalls selling electrical goods, cheap tapes and CDs, clothes and toiletries are also well worth browsing through.

Petticoat Lane Market

Middlesex St E1. **Map** 16 D1. ⊖ *Liverpool St, Aldgate, Aldgate East.* **Open** *9am–2pm Sun (Wentworth St 10am–2:30pm Mon–Fri). See p169.*

Probably the most famous of all London's street markets, Petticoat Lane continues to attract many thousands of visitors and locals every Sunday. The prices may not be as cheap as some of those to be found elsewhere, but the sheer volume of leather goods, clothes (the Lane's traditional strong point), watches, cheap jewelry and toys more than makes up for that. Various fast-food sellers do a brisk trade catering to the appetites of the bustling crowds.

Piccadilly Crafts Market

St. James's Church, Piccadilly W1. **Map** 13 A3. ⊖ *Piccadilly Circus, Green Park.* **Open** *10am–5pm Thu–Sat.*

Many of the markets in the Middle Ages were held in churchyards, and Piccadilly Crafts Market is rekindling that ancient tradition. It is aimed mostly at visitors to London rather than locals, and the merchandise on display ranges from tacky T-shirts to genuine 19th-century prints. Warm Aran woolens, handmade greeting cards and, on a few of the stalls, antiques also compete for custom and attention. All are spread out in the shadow of Wren's beautiful church (*see p90*).

Portobello Road Market

Portobello Rd W10. **Map** 9 C3. ⊖ *Notting Hill Gate, Ladbroke Grove.* **Open** *antiques and junk: 7am–5:30pm Sat. General market: 9am–5pm Mon–Wed, Fri & Sat; 9am–1pm Thu. See p215.*

Portobello Road is really three or four markets rolled into one. The Notting Hill end has over 2,000 stalls displaying a compendium of objets d'art, jewelry, old medals, paintings and silverware. Most stalls are managed by experts, so bargains are rare. Farther down the gentle hill, antiques give way to fruit and vegetables. The selection changes again beneath the Westway overpass, where cheap clothes, bric-a-brac and tacky jewelry take over. From this point on the market becomes increasingly rundown.

Ridley Road Market

Ridley Rd E8. ⊖JR *Dalston.* **Open** *9am–3pm Mon–Wed. 9am–noon Thu. 9am–5pm Fri, Sat.*

Early this century Ridley Road was a center of the Jewish community. Since then, Asians, Greeks, Turks and West Indians have also settled in the area, and the market is a lively celebration of this cultural mix. Highlights include the 24-hour bagel bakery, the shanty-town shacks selling green bananas and reggae records, the colorful drapery stalls and the very cheap fruit and vegetables.

St. Martin-in-the-Fields Market

St. Martin-in-the-Fields Churchyard WC2. **Map** 13 B3. ⊖ *Charing Cross.* **Open** *11am–5pm Mon–Sat, noon–5pm Sun. See p102.*

This crafts market was started in the late 1980s. T-shirts and football scarves are among the unremarkable selection of London mementoes; more interesting are the Russian dolls, the South American handicrafts and the assorted knitwear.

Shepherd's Bush Market

Goldhawk Rd W12. ⊖ *Goldhawk Road, Shepherd's Bush.* **Open** *9:30am–5pm Mon–Wed, Fri & Sat. 9:30am–2:30pm Thu.*

Like Ridley Road and Brixton, Shepherd's Bush Market is a focal point for many of the local ethnic communities. West Indian food, Afro wigs, Asian spices and cheap household and electrical goods are just some of the attractions.

ENTERTAINMENT IN LONDON

Café sign advertising free live music

LONDON HAS THE ENORMOUS, multilayered variety of entertainment that only the great cities of the world can provide, and, as always, the city's historical backdrop adds depth to the experience. While few things could be more contemporary than dancing the night away in style at a famed disco such as Stringfellows or Heaven, you could also spend the evening in London's theater district. The West End theaters offer everything from the world's best blockbuster musicals to new drama by leading playwrights to the familiar Shakespeare play. There's a healthy, innovative fringe theater scene, too, plus world-class ballet and opera in such fabled venues as Sadler's Wells, the Royal Opera House and the Coliseum. In London you can hear the best music, ranging from classical, jazz and rock to rhythm and blues, while dedicated movie buffs can choose from hundreds of films each night, in both large multiscreen complexes and small independent theaters. Sports fans can catch a game of cricket at Lords, cheer on the oarsmen rowing on the Thames or eat strawberries and cream while watching an exciting game of tennis at Wimbledon. Should you feel adventurous yourself, you can try going on a horse ride along Rotten Row in Hyde Park. There are numerous festivals, celebrations and sports events to attend, and there's plenty for children to do, too. Whatever you want, you'll be sure to find it in London; it's just a question of knowing where to start to look.

Cultural classics: a concert at Kenwood House *(top)*; open-air theater at Regent's Park *(above left)*; *The Mikado* at the Coliseum *(above right)*

INFORMATION SOURCES

FOR DETAILS OF events in London, check the comprehensive weekly listings and review magazine *Time Out* (published every Wednesday), sold at most newsstands and many bookshops; this publication also includes news, features, a travel section, advertisements, and interesting personal columns. The weekly *What's On and Where to Go in London* (Wednesdays) is also useful, and London's evening newspaper, the *Evening Standard*, gives daily listings (less comprehensive). The

Independent has daily listings and reviews a different arts sector every day, while the *Guardian* has arts reviews in its G2 section every day and weekly listings on Saturday; the *Independent*, the *Guardian* and *The Times* all have lists of ticket availability.

Special announcements, brochures and schedules are distributed free in the foyers of theaters, concert halls, movie theaters and such arts complexes as the South Bank and Barbican. Tourist information offices and hotel foyers often have the same publications. Flyers advertise forthcoming events.

The Society of West End Theatres (SWET) publishes an informative free schedule every two weeks, available in many theater foyers. It tends to concentrate on mainstream theaters but does provide invaluable information about what's going on. The National Theatre and the Royal Shakespeare Company also publish free announcements of future performances, distributed at the theaters.

Each SWET theater has a phone-in "Theaterline" with details of seat availability updated daily. Note that these calls cost three times as much as a standard local call and five times as much in peak hours. The general SWET line (0171-836 0971) provides daily updates on seat availability as well as more general information on choice of shows.

RESERVING TICKETS

S OME OF THE more popular shows and plays in London's West End – the latest Lloyd Webber musical for instance – can be totally sold out for weeks and even months ahead, and you will find it impossible to purchase any tickets. This is not the norm, though, and most tickets will be available on the night, especially if you are prepared to line up in front of the theater for returns. However, for a stressfree holiday it helps if you reserve tickets in advance; this will ensure that you get the day, time and seats you want. You can reserve tickets at the box office in person, by telephone or by mail. Quite a few hotels have concierges or porters who will give advice on where to go and arrange to get some tickets for you.

Box offices are usually open from about 10am to 8pm, and accept payment by cash, credit card, traveler's check or a personal UK check when

Lineup from the Royal Ballet, onstage at Covent Garden

supported by a check guarantee card. Many venues will now sell unclaimed or returned tickets just before the performance; ask at the box office for the times to get in line. To reserve seats by telephone, call the box office and either pay on arrival or send payment – seats are usually held for three days. Some venues now have separate phone numbers for those with credit cards – check before you call. Reserve your seat and always take your credit card with you when you get your ticket. Some smaller venues do not accept credit cards.

Palace Theatre plaque

DISABLED VISITORS

M ANY LONDON venues are old buildings that were not originally designed with disabled visitors in mind, but recently many facilities have been updated, particularly to give access to those using wheelchairs or for those with hearing difficulties.

Telephone the box office prior to your visit to reserve the special seating places or equipment, which are often limited. It is also worth your while to inquire about any special discounts that might be available for disabled people and for their party.

TRANSPORTATION

N IGHT BUSES are now the preferred late-night transportation, or you can phone for a cab from the venue. If you find yourself outside the city center late at night, do not rely on hailing a taxi quickly in the street. The Underground usually runs until just after midnight, but the times of last trains vary according to the lines. Check timetables in the stations (*see p362–3*).

RESERVATION AGENCIES

Tickets are also available from agencies. Try the theater box office first; if no seats are available there, find out the standard prices before going to an agency. Most, but not all, are reputable. Agencies advertising top show tickets for "tonight" may really have them and at a fair price. If you order by phone, tickets will be sent to you or to the theater for **The major listings magazines** you to pick up. The agency fee should be a standard 22%. Some shows waive the fee by paying the charge themselves; this is usually advertised, and agencies should then charge standard box office prices. Always compare prices, try to avoid agencies in bureaus de change and buy from ticket scalpers in the street only in desperation.

Ticket booth in Shaftesbury Avenue

London's Theaters

LONDON OFFERS AN extraordinary range of theatrical entertainment – this city is one of the world's great stages, and standards of quality are extremely high. Despite their legendary reputation for reserve, the British are passionate about theater and London's theaters reflect every nuance of this passion. You can stroll along a street of West End theaters and find a somber Samuel Beckett, Brecht or Chekhov play showing next door to some absurdly frothy farce like *No Sex Please, We're British!* Amid such diversity there is always something to appeal to everyone.

WEST END THEATER

THERE IS a distinct glamour to the West End theaters. Perhaps it is the glittering lights of the foyers and the impressively ornate interiors, or maybe it is their hallowed reputations – but whatever it is, the old theaters retain a magic all of their own.

The West End always features a generous sprinkling of world-famous performers, such as Judi Dench, Vanessa Redgrave, John Malkovich, Richard Harris and Peter O'Toole.

The major commercial theaters cluster along Shaftesbury Avenue and the Haymarket and around Covent Garden and Charing Cross Road. Unlike the national theaters, most West End theaters survive only on profits; they do not receive any state subsidy. They rely on an army of ever-hopeful "angels" (financial backers) and producers to keep the old traditions alive.

Many theaters are historical landmarks, such as the classic **Theatre Royal Drury Lane**, established in 1663 *(see p115)*, and the elegant **Theatre Royal Haymarket** – both superb examples of early 19th-century buildings. Another to note is the **Palace** *(see p108)*, with its terra-cotta exterior and imposing position right on Cambridge Circus.

NATIONAL THEATER

THE **Royal National Theatre** is based in the South Bank Center *(see p330)*. Here, the large open-staged Olivier, the proscenium-staged Lyttelton and the small, flexible Cottesloe offer a range of size and style, making it possible to stage every kind of theater from extravagant works to miniature masterpieces. The complex is also a lively social center. Enjoy a drink with your friends before your play begins; watch the crowds and the river drift by; wander around the many free art exhibitions; relax during the free early-evening concerts in the foyer; or browse through the theater bookshop.

The **Royal Shakespeare Company**, Britain's national theater company, has its London home at the Barbican Centre. While this unique company centers its work on Shakespeare's many plays, its repertoire also includes some classic Greek tragedies, gems of the Restoration theater and a multitude of modern works. Vast productions of superb quality are staged in the magnificent Barbican Theatre, and smaller performances can be seen on the more intimate stage of The Pit, which is contained in the same complex. The center's layout is known to be somewhat confusing so go a little early to ensure you arrive before the performance. Use any spare time to enjoy the free arts-and-crafts exhibitions in the foyer, often complementary to the plays being staged at the time, and the free musical entertainments that range from classical opera to chamber music, samba to the sound of the big brass band.

The Barbican can also supply information about RSC productions at their theaters in Stratford-upon-Avon.

NATIONAL THEATER RESERVATION ADDRESSES

Royal National Theatre
(Lyttelton, Cottesloe, Olivier) South Bank SE1. **Map** 14 D3.
📞 *0171-928 2252.*

Royal Shakespeare Company
Barbican Centre, Silk St EC2.
Map 7 A5.
📞 *0171-638 8891.*

PANTOMIME

SHOULD YOU HAPPEN to be visiting London between December and February, one exciting experience for the whole family is pantomime. Part of nearly every British child's upbringing, "panto" is an absurd tradition in which major female characters are played by men and principal male roles are played by women. The audience is known to participate, shouting encouragement and stage directions to a set formula. Adults may find the whole experience rather strange, but most children are delighted.

OPEN-AIR THEATER

A PERFORMANCE OF one of Shakespeare's airier creations – such as *Comedy of Errors*, *As You Like It* or *A Midsummer Night's Dream* – takes on an atmosphere of pure enchantment and magic among the green vistas of Regent's Park *(see p220)* or Holland Park *(see p214)*. Be sure to take a blanket and, to be safe, an umbrella. Refreshments are available, or you can take a picnic basket.

OPEN-AIR THEATER RESERVATION ADDRESSES

Holland Park Theatre
Holland Park. **Map** 9 B4.
📞 *0171-602 7856.*
Open Jun–Aug.

Open-Air Theater
Inner Circle, Regent's Park NW1.
Map 4 D3.
📞 *0171-486 2431.*
📠 *0171-486 1933.*
Open May–Sep.

WEST END THEATERS

Adelphi ⓭
Strand WC2.
☎ 0171-344 0055.

Albery ❶
St. Martin's Lane WC2.
☎ 0171-867 1115.

Aldwych ⓱
Aldwych WC2.
☎ 0171-836 6404.

Ambassadors ㉔
West St WC2.
☎ 0171-836 6111.

Apollo ⓴
Shaftesbury Ave W1.
☎ 0171-494 5070.

Cambridge ㉒
Earlham St WC2.
☎ 0171-379 5299.

Comedy ❽
Panton St SW1.
☎ 0171-867 1045.

Criterion ❼
Piccadilly Circus W1.
☎ 0171-839 4488.

Duchess ⓯
Catherine St WC2.
☎ 0171-494 5075.

Duke of York's ❹
St. Martin's Lane WC2.
☎ 0171-836 5122.

Fortune ⓳
Russell St WC2.
☎ 0171-836 2238.

Garrick ❺
Charing Cross Rd WC2.
☎ 0171-494 5085.

Gielgud ㉙
Shaftesbury Ave W1.
☎ 0171-494 5065.

Her Majesty's ❿
Haymarket SW1.
☎ 0171-494 5050.

Lyric ㉛
Shaftesbury Ave W1.
☎ 0171-494 5045.

New London ⓴
Drury Lane WC2.
☎ 0171-405 0072.

Palace ㉖
Shaftesbury Ave W1.
☎ 0171-434 0909.

Phoenix ㉕
Charing Cross Rd WC2.
☎ 0171-867 1044 .

Piccadilly ㉜
Denman St W1.
☎ 0171-867 1118.

Playhouse ⓬
Northumberland Ave WC2.
☎ 0171-839 4401.

Prince Edward ㉗
Old Compton St W1.
☎ 0171-734 8951.

Prince of Wales ❻
Coventry St W1.
☎ 0171-839 5972.

Queen's ㉘
Shaftesbury Ave W1.
☎ 0171-494 5040.

Shaftesbury ㉑
Shaftesbury Ave WC2.
☎ 0171-379 5399.

Strand ⓰
Aldwych WC2.
☎ 0171-930 8800.

St. Martin's ㉓
West St WC2.
☎ 0171-836 1443.

Theater Royal:
–Drury Lane ⓲
Catherine St WC2.
☎ 0171-494 5062.
–Haymarket ❾
Haymarket SW1.
☎ 0171-930 8800.

Vaudeville ⓮
Strand WC2.
☎ 0171-836 9987.

Whitehall ⓫
Whitehall SW1.
☎ 0171-867 1119.

Wyndham's ❸
Charing Cross Rd WC2.
☎ 0171-867 1116.

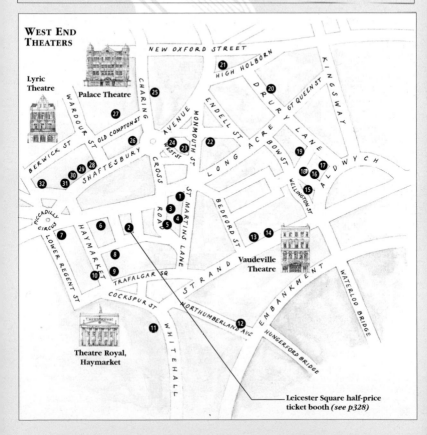

WEST END THEATERS

Leicester Square half-price ticket booth *(see p328)*

FRINGE THEATER

L ONDON'S FRINGE theater provides an outlet for new, adventurous writing and for writers from other cultures and lifestyles – works by Irish writers, by Caribbean and Latin American authors and by feminist and gay and lesbian writers.

The plays are usually staged in tiny theaters based in pubs – such as the **Gate Theatre** above the Prince Albert pub in Notting Hill, the **King's Head** in Islington and the **Grace** in the Latchmere pub in Battersea (see p309) – or in warehouses and spare space in larger theaters, such as the **Studio** in the Lyric.

Venues like the **Bush**, the **Almeida** and the **Theatre Upstairs** at the Royal Court have earned their reputations for discovering outstanding new works, some of which have been subsequently transferred to the West End.

Foreign-language plays are sometimes performed at national cultural institutes; for example, you might be able to catch Molière at the **French Institute** or Brecht at the **Goethe Institute**; check the listings magazines.

For alternative stand-up comedy and cabaret, where you can encounter the sharp edge of satire with its brash, newsy style, try the **Comedy Store**, the birthplace of so-called "alternative" comedy; the **Hackney Empire** (a former Victorian music hall well worth visiting for its magnificent well-preserved interior); and also the **Canal Café Theatre** in Little Venice.

BUDGET TICKETS

T HERE IS A wide range of prices for seats in London theaters. The cheaper West End tickets, for example, can cost under £10, whereas the best seats for musicals hover around the £30 mark. However, it is quite possible to obtain cheaper tickets.

The Leicester Square half-price ticket booth (see p327) sells tickets on the day of the performance for a wide range of mainstream shows. Situated in Leicester Square, the booth is open Monday to Saturday, from noon for matinees and from 2:30 to 6:30pm for evening performances. Payment is by cash, and there is a strict limit of only four tickets for each purchaser. There is also a small service charge to be paid.

You can sometimes get reduced-price seats for matinee performances, press and preview nights – it is always worth checking with the box office to see what they currently have to offer.

CHOOSING SEATS

I F YOU GO TO the theater in person, you will be able to see its seating plan and note where you can get a good view at an affordable price. If you reserve by telephone, you should note the following: stalls are in front of the stage and expensive. The back stalls are slightly cheaper; dress, grand and royal circles are above the stalls and cheaper again; the upper circle and balcony are the cheapest seats, but you will have to climb several flights of

stairs; the slips are seats that run along the very edges of the theater; boxes are the most expensive option.

You should also remember that some of the cheapest seats may have a restricted view of the stage.

THEATER-RELATED ACTIVITIES

I F YOU ARE curious about how the mechanics of the theater work, you will probably enjoy a backstage tour. The National Theatre and the RSC both organize these tours (contact the box office – see p326 – for details). If you enjoy a good walk, London Theatre Walks (0171-839 7438) may interest you. The Theatre Museum (see p115) is well worth a visit.

IRATE GHOSTS

Many London theaters are reputed to have ghosts; however, the two most famous specters haunt the environs of the Garrick and the Duke of York's (see p327). The Garrick is heavily atmospheric, and the ghost of Arthur Bourchier, a manager at the turn of the century, is reputed to make fairly regular appearances. He hated critics, and many believe he is still trying to frighten them away. The ghost occupying the Duke of York's theater was Violet Melnotte, an 1890s actress manager who was famed for her extremely fiery temper.

FRINGE THEATER

Almeida
Almeida St N1.
[C] 0171-359 4404.

Bush
Shepherds Bush Green W12.
[C] 0181-743 3388.

Canal Café Theatre
The Bridge House
Delamere Ter W2.
[C] 0171-289 6054.

Comedy Store
28a Leicester Sq WC2.
Map 13 B3.
[C] 0171-839 6642.

French Institute
17 Queensberry Pl SW7.
Map 18 F2.
[C] 0171-589 6211.

Gate Theatre
The Prince Albert,
11 Pembridge Rd W11.
Map 9 C3.
[C] 0171-229 0706.

Goethe Institute
50 Prince's Gate, Exhibition
Rd SW7. **Map** 11 A5.
[C] 0171-411 3400.

Grace
503 Battersea Park Rd SW11.
[C] 0171-228 2620.

Hackney Empire
291 Mare St E8.
[C] 0181-985 2424.

King's Head
115 Upper St N1.
Map 6 F1.

[C] 0171-226 8561.
[Cf] 0171-226 1916.

Studio
Lyric, Hammersmith,
King St W6.
[C] 0181-741 8701.
[C] 0171-836 3464.

Theatre Upstairs
Royal Court,
Sloane Sq SW1.
Map 19 C2.
[C] 0171-730 2554.
[C] 0171-836 2428.

Movies

IF YOU CAN'T FIND a movie you like in London, then you don't like movies. The huge choice of British, American, foreign-language, new, classic, popular and special-interest films makes London a major international film center, with about 250 different films showing at any one time. There are about 50 movie theaters in the central district of London alone, many ultramodern multiscreened complexes. The big commercial chains show current smash hits, and a healthy number of independent theaters offer some inventive programs drawing on the whole history of film. London's listings magazines carry full details of what's on and where.

WEST END THEATERS

WEST END is a loose term for the main movie theaters in the West End of London that show new releases, such as the **Odeon Leicester Square** and the **MGM** Shaftesbury Avenue, but it also includes the theaters found in Chelsea, Fulham and Notting Hill. Programs normally begin around midday and are then repeated every two or three hours, with the last show around 8:30pm; there are late-night screenings on Fridays and Saturdays at most of the central theaters.

West End theaters are very expensive, and a seat in front of the best screens will cost you twice what you would pay to see the same film at a local theater outside central London. The price of admission is often cheaper for the afternoon performances or on Mondays. It is a good idea to reserve your seats well in advance for screenings of the more popular films on Friday and Saturday evenings and Sunday afternoon. Most of the larger theaters now take credit card seat reservations over the telephone.

REPERTORY THEATERS

THESE THEATERS OFTEN show foreign-language and slightly more "off-beat" art films and sometimes change programs daily or even several times each day. Some theaters show two or three films, often on the same theme, for one entrance charge.

These include the **Prince Charles**, which is situated centrally; close to Leicester Square; the **Everyman** in north London; the ICA in the Mall; the **Electric** in west London; the **Ritzy**; and the National Film Theatre.

NATIONAL FILM THEATRE

THE NATIONAL FILM Theatre (NFT) *(see p182)* and the Museum of the Moving Image (MOMI) *(see p184)* are both located in the South Bank Arts Complex, near Waterloo Station. The NFT has two theaters of its own, both of which offer a huge and diverse selection of films. The NFT also holds regular screenings of rare and restored films and television programs taken from the National Film Archive. A must for movie buffs.

FOREIGN-LANGUAGE FILMS

THESE ARE screened at the repertory and independent movie houses, including the **Renoir**, the **Prince Charles**, the **Lumière**, the Curzon in Shaftesbury Avenue, the **Minema** and the **Screen** chain. Films are shown in their original language, with English subtitles.

FILM CERTIFICATES

CHILDREN ARE ALLOWED to go to a movie theater unaccompanied by an adult to see films that have been awarded either a U (universal) or a PG (parental guidance advised) certificate for viewing.

With other films, the numbers 12, 15 and 18 simply denote the minimum ages allowed for admission to the theater. These classifications are always clearly advertised in the publicity for the film.

LONDON FILM FESTIVAL

THE MOST important film event in Britain is held every November, when over 100 films – some of which will have already won awards abroad – from a number of countries are screened. The NFT, several of the repertory theaters and some of the big West End theaters will have special showings of these films. Details are published in the listings magazines. Tickets are quite hard to come by, but some "standby" tickets will generally be available to the public 30 minutes before the start of a performance.

MOVIE THEATERS

Electric
191 Portobello Road W11.
📞 0171-792 2020.
📠 0171-792 0328.

Everyman
Hollybush Vale NW3.
Map 1 A5.
📞 0171-435 1525.

Lumière
49 St. Martin's Lane WC2.
Map 13 B2.
📞 0171-836 0691.
📠 0171-379 3014.

MGM
135 Shaftesbury Ave WC2.
Map 13 B2.
📠 0171-836 6279.

Minema
45 Knightsbridge SW1.

Map 12 D5.
📞 0171-235 4225.

Odeon Leicester Sq
Leicester Sq WC2.
Map 13 B2.
📞 0171-930 3232.
📠 01426-915 683.

Prince Charles
Leicester Pl WC2.
Map 13 B2
📞 0171-437 8181.

Renoir
Brunswick Sq WC1.
Map 5 C4.
📞 0171-837 8402.

Ritzy
Brixton Rd SW2.
📞 0171-737 2121.

Screen Cinemas
96 Baker St NW1
Map 3 C5.
📞 0171-935 2772.

Opera, Classical and Contemporary Music

UNTIL RECENTLY, OPERA and classical music have suffered from an elitist reputation. However, televised concerts and free outdoor concerts in Hyde Park and the Piazza, Covent Garden, have greatly increased their popularity. London is home to five world-class orchestras and a host of smaller music companies and contemporary music ensembles; it also houses three permanent opera companies and numerous smaller opera groups and world-renowned period orchestras. It is a major center for the classical recording industry, supporting a large community of musicians and singers. Mainstream, obscure, traditional and innovative music can be found in profusion. *Time Out (see p324)* has the most comprehensive listings of the classical music offerings.

Royal Opera House

Floral St WC2. **Map** 13 C2.
[0171-240 1066. See p115.

The building, with its opulent red, white and gold interior, is very glamorous; it looks, and is, expensive. It is the home of the Royal Opera, but very often visiting opera and ballet companies also perform here. Many productions are shared with foreign opera houses, so if you are a visitor to England check that you haven't already seen the same production at home. Works are always performed in the original language, but English translations are flashed up above the stage.

Seats are usually reserved well in advance, particularly for major stars such as Placido Domingo, Luciano Pavarotti and Kiri Te Kanawa. The sound is best in the seats in front of center stage. Tickets range from about £5 to £200 or more for a world-class star. The cheapest seats tend to be bought first, although a number are reserved for sale on the day of the performance. (Some of the cheaper seats in the Royal Opera House have restricted views of the stage.) Standing passes can often be obtained up to curtain time. Standby information is available on the day of the performance on 0171-836 6903, and there are often concessions on tickets. It is also worthwhile getting in line for last-minute returns.

London Coliseum

St. Martin's Lane WC2. **Map** 13 B3.
[0171-836 3161.
[0171-240 5258. See p119.

The Coliseum, home of the English National Opera (ENO), has rather faded decor, but the musical standards are extremely high. The company trains its own singers for its productions, and they rehearse in the setting in which they will perform. ENO productions of the classics are nearly all sung in English. The productions are often adventurous, and critics have been known to complain that the clarity of the storyline is impaired. The audiences tend to be younger than those at the Royal Opera House, the seats are much cheaper, and there is less corporate entertaining. The cheapest seats are infamous for being real backbreakers.

Sadler's Wells

Rosebery Ave EC1. **Map** 6 E3.
[0171-278 8916.

Less glamorous, expensive and central than the other opera houses, Sadler's Wells does not have its own company but provides a useful venue for many visiting companies. Among these, three have a regular season here, each presenting two works: the D'Oyly Carte company, formed in 1875 specifically to perform works by Gilbert and Sullivan, has its season in April and May; Opera 80, with a cast of 22 singers and an orchestra of 27, offers opera in English in the last two weeks of May; and the British Youth Opera performs here each year in early September.

South Bank Centre

South Bank Centre SE1. **Map** 14 D4.
[0171-928 8800. See p182.

The South Bank Centre houses the Royal Festival Hall (RFH), the Queen Elizabeth Hall and the Purcell Room. There are nightly performances, mostly of classical music, interspersed with opera, ballet and modern dance seasons, jazz, festivals of contemporary and ethnic music and other special events running throughout the year. The largest concert hall on the South Bank is the RFH, which is ideal for the major national and international orchestras and large-scale choral works. The Purcell Room is comparatively small and often hosts string quartets and contemporary music in addition to many debut recitals of young artists. The Queen Elizabeth Hall lies somewhere in between. It stages medium-size ensembles whose audiences, while too large for the Purcell Room, would not fill the Festival Hall. Jazz and ethnic music are performed here, and the very innovative and often controversial Opera Factory makes several appearances throughout the year. It performs a range of modern interpretations of the classics and often also commissions and performs new works. The acoustics are very good throughout the complex.

The London Philharmonic Orchestra is resident at the South Bank. The Royal Philharmonic, the Philharmonia and the BBC Symphony Orchestra are frequent visitors, along with leading ensembles and soloists, such as Shura Cherkassky, Stephen Kovacevich and Anne-Sofie von Otter.

The Academy of St. Martin-in-the-Fields, the London Festival Orchestra, Opera Factory, the London Classical Players and the London Mozart Players all have

LONDON MUSIC FESTIVALS

The London Opera Festival takes place in June. Venues include the Place Theatre, the Lilian Baylis Theatre (Sadler's Wells), the Purcell Room, St. John's Smith Square and the Royalty Theatre. Singers and companies from all over the world come to London to perform in this festival. For tickets and general information, contact the individual theaters.

The City of London Festival is held annually in July, when churches and public buildings in the City host a range of varied musical events. Venues such as the Tower of London *(see p154)* and Goldsmiths' Hall can themselves lend much atmosphere to the events. Many concerts are free. For more details, call the box office (0171-248 4260) from May onward.

regular seasons. There are also frequent free foyer concerts, and throughout the summer the center is worth visiting since musical events take place on the terraces, weather permitting.

Barbican Concert Hall

Silk St EC2. **Map** 7 A5.
☎ 0171-638 8891. See p165.

This stark concrete building is the permanent home of the London Symphony Orchestra (LSO), which concentrates on the work of one composer each season. The LSO Summer Pops features an impressive line-up of stars from stage, television, movies and the recording world, which in the past has included such famous artists as Victor Borge and the jazz singer Barbara Cook.

The English National Opera makes regular appearances, and the Royal Philharmonic Orchestra has a spring season.

The Barbican is also renowned for its concerts of contemporary music: the BBC Symphony Orchestra holds an annual festival of 20th-century composers here; the London Sinfonietta, which specializes in 20th-century music, performs most of its London concerts at the same venue. There are free foyer concerts, too.

Royal Albert Hall

Kensington Gore SW7. **Map** 10 F5.
☎ 0171-589 8212. See p203.

The beautiful Royal Albert Hall is the venue for a wide variety of events – from fashion and pop shows to wrestling. However, from mid-July to mid-September it is devoted solely to the Henry Wood Promenade Concerts, the "Proms." Organized by the BBC, the season features the BBC Philharmonic Orchestra, which performs some modern symphonic music as well as classics. Visiting orchestras from around the United Kingdom and worldwide, such as the City of Birmingham Orchestra, the Chicago Symphony Orchestra and the Boston Symphony Orchestra, make up a very varied program. Tickets for the Proms can be bought on the day of the performance but long lines form early in the day, so experienced Promenaders take cushions to sit on. Tickets sell out weeks ahead for the "Last Night of the Proms," which has become a national institution. The audience wave flags and sing. Some people may consider it an evening of nationalistic fervor, although the majority who sing the traditional *Land of Hope and Glory* without giving much thought to the jingoistic words.

OUTDOOR MUSIC

London has many outdoor musical events in summer. At Kenwood House on Hampstead Heath *(see p230)*, a grassy hill leads down to a lake, beyond which is the concert platform. Arrive early since the concerts are popular, particularly if fireworks are to accompany the music. Deckchairs tend to be taken early, so most people sit on the grass. Take a sweater and a picnic. Purists beware – people walk around, eat and talk throughout, and the music is amplified so it can be a little distorted. You don't get your money back if it rains: they have never abandoned a performance yet.

Other venues include Marble Hill House in Twickenham *(see p248)*, with practices similar to Kenwood, Crystal Palace Park and Holland Park.

Wigmore Hall

36 Wigmore St W1. **Map** 12 E1.
☎ 0171-935 2141. See p222.

Because of its excellent acoustics, the Wigmore Hall is a favorite with visiting artists and attracts such international names as Jessye Norman and Julian Bream for a very wide-ranging program of events. It presents seven evening concerts a week, plus a Sunday morning concert from September through to July.

St. Martin-in-the-Fields

Trafalgar Sq WC2. **Map** 13 B3.
☎ 0171-930 1862. See p102.

This elegant Gibbs church is home to the Academy of St. Martin-in-the-Fields and the famous choir of the same name. These and orchestras as disparate as the Henry Wood Chamber Orchestra, the Penguin Café Orchestra and the St. Martin-in-the-Fields Sinfonia provide evening concerts. The choice of each program is, to a degree, dictated by the religious year; for example, Bach's *St. John Passion* is played at Ascensiontide and Handel's *Messiah* at Christmas. Free lunchtime concerts are given on Mondays, Tuesdays and Fridays by young artists.

St. John's, Smith Square

Smith Sq SW1. **Map** 21 B1.
☎ 0171-222 1061. See p81.

This converted Baroque church has good acoustics and provides comfortable seating, making it a marvelous setting. It hosts varied concerts and recitals by groups such as the Wren Orchestra, the Vanbrugh String Quartet and the London Sonata Group. A daily series of BBC Radio lunchtime concerts covers the music and song recitals.

Broadgate Arena

3 Broadgate EC2. **Map** 7 C5.
☎ 0171-588 6565. See p169.

This is the new City-based venue for a summer season of lunchtime concerts offering varied programs, often from innovative and up-and-coming musicians.

MUSIC VENUES

Orchestral
Barbican Concert Hall
Broadgate Arena
Queen Elizabeth Hall
Royal Albert Hall
Royal Festival Hall
St. Martin-in-the-Fields
St. John's, Smith Square

Chamber and Ensemble
Barbican Concert Hall
Broadgate Arena
Purcell Room
Royal Festival Hall foyer
St. Martin-in-the-Fields
St. John's, Smith Square
Wigmore Hall

Soloists and Recitals
Barbican Concert Hall
Purcell Room
Royal Albert Hall
St. Martin-in-the-Fields
St. John's, Smith Square
Wigmore Hall

Children's
Barbican Concert Hall
Royal Festival Hall

Free
Barbican Concert Hall
National Theatre foyer *(see p326)*
Royal Festival Hall foyer
St. Martin-in-the-Fields (lunchtime)

Early Music
Purcell Room
Wigmore Hall

Contemporary Music
Barbican Concert Hall
South Bank Complex

Dance

LONDON-BASED DANCE companies present a range of styles from classical ballet to mime, jazz, experimental and ethnic dance. London is also host to visiting companies as diverse as the classic Bolshoi Ballet and the innovative Jaleo Flamenco. Most dance companies (with the exception of the resident ballets) have short seasons that seldom last longer than two weeks and often less than a week – check the listings magazines for details *(see pp324)*. Theaters that regularly feature dance are the **Royal Opera House**, the **London Coliseum**, **Sadler's Wells** and **The Place Theatre**. There are also performances at the **South Bank Centre** and other arts centers throughout the city.

workshops in April at the **Riverside Studios**. Other locations that are sometimes used include the **Institute of Contemporary Arts** (ICA) *(see p92)* and the **Shaw Theatre**, as well as a new East End venue, the **Chisenhale Dance Space**, a center for small independent companies currently regarded as on the experimental fringe of contemporary dance.

BALLET

THE **Royal Opera House** *(see p115)* and the **London Coliseum** on St. Martin's Lane are by far the best venues for classical ballet, providing the stage for foreign companies when they visit London. The Opera House is home to the Royal Ballet, which usually invites major international artists to take up residence. Reserve well in advance for such classics as *Swan Lake* and *Giselle*. The company also has an unusual repertoire of modern ballet; triple bills provide a mixture of new and old, and seats are normally readily available.

The English National Ballet holds its summer season at the **London Coliseum**. It has a similar repertoire to that of the Royal Ballet and stages very popular productions.

Visiting companies also perform at **Sadler's Wells** *(see p243)*, where the London City Ballet has its annual season during December and January. This company has a mainly classical repertoire.

CONTEMPORARY

A PLETHORA OF new and young companies is flourishing in London, each with its own distinctive style. **Sadler's Wells** is one of the main venues, with short seasons featuring visiting and local companies. Attached to Sadler's Wells is the Lilian Baylis Studio, a venue for smaller and often more experimental productions.

The Place Theatre, the home of contemporary and ethnic dance companies, has a year-round program of performances from these and visiting dancers. The London Contemporary Dance Theatre, the largest of Britain's contemporary dance companies, is based here.

The **Island Theatre** was designed as a theater/movie theater and has only recently been used for dance. During the summer, Rambert Dance performs its season of works by internationally acclaimed choreographers. Rambert has another short season and runs a week of choreographic

ETHNIC

THERE IS A constant stream of visiting groups coming to perform traditional dance from all over the world. Both **Sadler's Wells** and the **Riverside Studios** are major venues, while classical ethnic dance companies, including Indian and Far Eastern, have seasons at the South Bank Centre, often in the **Queen Elizabeth Hall**. Check the listings magazines for details.

DANCE FESTIVALS

THERE ARE TWO major contemporary dance festivals each year in London, featuring many different companies. Spring Loaded runs from February to April, while Dance Umbrella runs from early October to early November. The listings magazines carry all details.

Other, smaller festivals include Almeida Dance, from the end of April to the first week of May at the **Almeida Theatre**, and The Turning World, a festival in April and May offering dance from all over the world.

DANCE VENUES

Almeida Theatre
Almeida St N1.
☏ 0171-359 4404.

Chisenhale Dance Space
64 Chisenhale Rd E3.
☏ 0181-981 6617.

ICA
Nash House,
Carlton House Terrace,

The Mall SW1.
Map 13 A4.
☏ 0171-930 3647.

Island Theatre
Portugal St WC2.
Map 14 D1.
☏ 0171-494 5090.

London Coliseum
St. Martin's Lane WC2.
Map 13 B3.
☏ 0171-836 3161.
✉ 0171-240 5258.

The Place Theatre
17 Duke's Rd WC1.
Map 5 B3.
☏ 0171-387 0031.

Queen Elizabeth Hall
South Bank Centre SE1.
Map 14 D4.
☏ 0171-928 8800.

Riverside Studios
Crisp Rd W6.
☏ 0181-741 2255.

Royal Opera House
Floral St WC2. **Map** 13 C2.
☏ 0171-240 1066 or
0171-240 1911.

Sadler's Wells
Rosebery Ave EC1.
Map 6 E3.
☏ 0171-278 8916.

Shaw Theatre
100 Euston Rd NW1.
Map 5 B3.
☏ 0171-388 1394.

Rock, Pop, Jazz and Ethnic Music

YOU WILL FIND THE WHOLE range of popular music being strummed and hummed, howled, growled or synthesized in London. There may be as many as 80 listed concerts on an ordinary weeknight, featuring rock, reggae, soul, folk, country, jazz, Latin and world music. In addition, there are various music festivals in the summer at parks, pubs, halls and stadiums throughout the capital (see p335). Check the listings magazines and publicity posters (see p324).

MAJOR ARENAS

THE LARGEST arenas in London are host to an extraordinary variety of music. Stars who are guaranteed to fill thousands of seats play **Wembley Stadium** in the summer, when the soccer season is over. In winter, the pop idols tend to prefer the cavernous indoor **Wembley Arena**; the **Hammersmith Odeon**; or, if they take themselves seriously, the **Royal Albert Hall**.

The **Brixton Academy** and the **Town and Country Club** are next in prominence and size. Each can hold over 1,000, and for many Londoners these former movie theaters are the best venues, with seating upstairs, large dance floors downstairs and accessible bars.

ROCK AND POP

INDIE MUSIC is one of the mainstays of London's live music scene. It has also now encompassed goth rock, where pallid fans in black clothing gaze at bands playing ponderous power chords (Kentish Town's **Bull and Gate** and the **Powerhaus** in Islington are the places for this). The newer Manchester Sound is popular with latter-day psychedelics (try the **Astoria** in the West End and the **National Ballroom Kilburn**, among many others). The **Marquee** on Charing Cross Road has long been a major rock-and-pop scene. The **Grand** in Clapham, a former music hall, has recently been renovated as a rock venue, run by the same management as the **Mean Fiddler** in Harlesden, one of the best of the mid-size clubs.

London is the home of pub-rock, which is an odd blend of rhythm and blues, heavy rock and punk that has been developing since the 1960s. The **Station Tavern** in West London hosts many of the best pub-rock bands around; while there's usually no entrance charge, drinks are surcharged. The **Sir George Robey** near Finsbury Park and dozens of other pubs across the city follow suit.

New bands have a popular showcase at the **Rock Garden** in Covent Garden on most nights of the week; **Borderline,** near Leicester Square, is known to be frequented often by record company talent scouts.

Subterania in Ladbroke Grove holds new songwriter nights, often with some session musicians backing. The **Camden Palace** is very good, especially on Tuesdays, with the finest indie pop both before and after live performances from up-and-coming indie bands.

JAZZ

THE NUMBER of jazz venues in London has grown in the last few years. **Ronnie Scott's** in the West End is still the pick of the old crop; since the 1950s some of the finest performers in the world have played here. The **100 Club** on Oxford Street is another very popular venue for jazz lovers.

The **Bass Clef** in Hoxton was a great success in the 1980s and gets very crowded on weekends. Located in the same building, a sister club called the **Tenor Clef** stages Latin and African jazz in smaller and more upscale surroundings. Jazz and food have formed a partnership at

many venues, such as the **Palookaville** in Covent Garden, the **Dover Street Wine Bar** and the largely vegetarian **Jazz Café**, which are among the best; others include the **Pizza Express** on Dean Street and the **Pizza on the Park**, which is by Hyde Park Corner.

The **South Bank Centre** (see p182) and also the **Barbican** (see p165) feature formal jazz concerts and free jazz in the foyers.

REGGAE

LONDON'S LARGE West Indian community has made the city the European reggae capital. At the **Notting Hill Carnival** (see p57), in late August, many top bands perform free.

Reggae has now become integrated with the mainstream rock music scene, and bands appear at most of London's rock venues.

WORLD MUSIC

MUSICIANS FROM every corner of the globe live in London. "World music" includes African, Latin and South American, and its popularity has sparked a revitalization of British and Irish folk music. **Cecil Sharp House** has regular shows for folk purists, while the **ICA** (see p92) hosts innovative acts. Many pubs in Kilburn and Willesden now have regular nights for Irish folk music, as does the Acoustic Room at the **Mean Fiddler.**

The **Weavers Arms,** near Newington Green, has a reputation for Cajun, African and Latin American music. Hot Latin nights can be found at **Down Mexico Way** near Piccadilly and at **Cuba Libre** in Islington. For all-French Caribbean and African sounds you could check **Le Café de Piaf** inside Waterloo Station; and for the widest selection of African sounds and food in town, try visiting the **Africa Centre** in Covent Garden.

Clubs

The old cliché that London dies when the pubs shut no longer holds true. Europe has long scoffed at Londoners going to bed at 11pm, when the night is only just beginning in Paris, Madrid and Rome; but London has caught on at last, and you can revel all night if you want to. The best clubs are not all confined to the city's center – initial disappointment that your hotel is a half-hour tube ride from Leicester Square can be offset by the discovery of a trendy club right on your doorstep.

ETIQUETTE

Fashions and club nights change very rapidly, and nightspots open and close down all the time. Some of the best club nights are one-nighters – check the listings magazines (see p324). Style magazines like *The Face* can help you avoid humiliating comments from bouncers who don't like your appearance. Some clubs change the dress policy with each evening, so it is best to check in advance.

A few clubs require that you arrange membership 48 hours in advance, and you may have to be introduced by a member. Again, check these details in the listings magazines. Groups of men may not be welcome, so they should split up and find a woman to go in with; expect to line up to get in. Entrance fees may seem reasonable, but drinks tend to be overpriced.

Opening times are usually 10pm to 3am Monday to Saturday, although many clubs stay open until 6am on weekends, and some open on Sunday from 8pm to midnight.

MAINSTREAM

London is home to one of the best-known discos in the world: **Stringfellows** is as much a part of the tourist circuit as Madame Tussaud's. It's glitzy and expensive, so jeans are out of the question. The nearby **Hippodrome** is similar. One of the world's largest discos, it has stunning lighting and several bars, plus serves food.

Most of the more upscale nightclubs in London, for example, **Annabel's**, have a strict members-only policy; they require nominations by current members and have long waiting lists, so unless you mix in privileged circles you are unlikely to get in.

Traditional West End disco-type clubs that are easier to enter include the sleek club **Legends** and **Café de Paris**, where you can waltz and foxtrot all night.

Further north, the **Forum** hosts popular club nights, which feature classic soul, funk and rhythm and blues. Similar clubs are **Equinox** in Leicester Square and **Tattershall Castle**, a disco boat moored on the Thames.

FASHIONABLE VENUES AND CLUB NIGHTS

Over the last few years, London has become one of the most innovative club capitals in the world, a major stage where trends are set. "House music" is very popular, and **Heaven** hosts England's premier house night. With its huge dance floor, excellent lasers, sound systems and lightshows, it's very popular, so get in line early. A new venue, the **Ministry of Sound**, is a New York-style club that has set the pattern for others to follow in the nineties, but it has no alcohol license and is very hard to get into. House nights are also run at **Maximus** (cheaper and wilder after 3am); the **Gardening Club**, home to garage as well as hardcore house; and the young and trendy **Wag Club**.

"Talkin' Loud" club night at the **Fridge** offers some of the funkiest jazz-based sounds. **Turnmills** is London's first 24-hour club; it is cheap, plays funky jazz and also boasts a decent restaurant.

For 1970s nostalgia, try **Le Scandale's** hosts "Carwash" – disco was never as trashy or fun. There is cheaper admission for those who dress up in seventies style. For more Earth, Wind and Fire, head for "Boogie Wonderland" at **79 Club** in Oxford Street.

There are surprisingly few regular reggae nights. **Gossips** has the best dance reggae on Saturday, with ska, classic soul and R&B on Thursday.

GAY AND LESBIAN

London has a number of gay and lesbian nightclubs. The most popular is **Heaven**, with its huge dance floor and bar and video lounge. Islington's **Paradise** hosts a men-only leather-and-rubber night and has transvestite shows as well as games rooms and two discos. **Club Copa** in Earl's Court is a relaxed venue for gay men. The **Fridge** and the **Gardening Club** host gay and lesbian nights, and the Fridge holds women-only nights.

TRANSVESTITE

Watch for the occasional "Kinky Gerlinky" night in the listings magazines, an outrageously kitsch collection of drag queens and assorted exotica. In Soho, **Madame Jojo**'s revue is a fabulous whirl of glittering colour and extreme high camp.

CASINOS

To gamble in London you must be a member, or at least the guest of a member of a licensed gaming club. Most clubs are happy to let you join, but membership must be arranged 48 hours in advance. Many will let you in to use facilities other than the gambling tables until about 4am, when most close. Try the excellent restaurants and bars, which are often subject to the usual licensing laws (see p308). Many clubs also have "hostesses" – beware the cost of their company.

DIRECTORY

MAJOR MUSIC VENUES

Brixton Academy
211 Stockwell Rd SW9.
📞 0171-924 9999.

Hammersmith Odeon
Queen Caroline St W6.
📞 0181-741 4868.

Royal Albert Hall
See p203.

Forum
9–17 Highgate Rd NW5.
📞 0171-284 1001.
📠 0171-284 2200.

Wembley Arena and Stadium
Empire Way, Wembley, Middlesex.
📞 0181-900 1234.

ROCK AND POP VENUES

Astoria
157 Charing Cross Rd WC2. **Map** 13 B1.
📞 0171-434 0403.

Borderline
Orange Yard, Manette St WC2. **Map** 13 B1.
📞 0171-734 2095.

Bull and Gate
389 Kentish Town Rd NW5. 📞 0171-485 5358.

Camden Palace
1a Camden High St NW1. **Map** 4 F2.
📞 0171-387 0428.

Grand
Clapham Junction, St John's Hill SW11.
📞 0171-738 9000.

LA2
157 Charing Cross Rd WC2. **Map** 13 B2.
📞 0171-734 6963.

Limelight
136 Shaftesbury Ave WC2. **Map** 13 B2.
📞 0171-434 0572.

Marquee
105 Charing Cross Rd WC2. **Map** 13 B2.
📞 0171-437 6601.

Mean Fiddler
24–28a High St NW10.

📞 0181-961 5490.
📠 0181-963 0940.

National Ballroom Kilburn
234 Kilburn High Rd NW6.
📞 0171-328 3141.

Powerhaus N1
1 Liverpool Rd N1.
Map 6 E2.
📞 0171-837 3218.
📠 0171-284 2200.

Rock Garden
6–7 The Piazza, Covent Garden WC2. **Map** 13 C2.
📞 0171-240 3961.

79 Club
79 Oxford St W1.
Map 13 A1.
📞 0171-439 7250.

Sir George Robey
240 Seven Sisters Rd N4.
📞 0171-263 4581.

Station Tavern
41 Bramley Rd W10.
📞 0171-727 4053.

Subterania
12 Acklam Rd W10.
📞 0181-960 4590.
📠 0171-284 2200.

Woody's
41–43 Woodfield Rd W9.
📞 0171-286 5574.

JAZZ VENUES

100 Club
100 Oxford St W1.
Map 13 A1.
📞 0171-636 0933.

Barbican Hall
See p165.

Bass Clef
35 Coronet St N1.
Map 7 C3.
📞 0171-729 2476.

Dover Street Wine Bar
8 Dover St W1. **Map** 12 F3.
📞 0171-629 9813.

Jazz Café
5 Parkway NW1. **Map** 4 E1.
📞 0171-916 6000.

Pizza Express
10 Dean St W1. **Map** 13 A1.
📞 0171-437 9595.

Pizza on the Park
11 Knightsbridge SW1.
Map 12 D5.
📞 0171-235 5550.

Ronnie Scott's
47 Frith St W1.
Map 13 A2.
📞 0171-439 0747

Royal Festival Hall
See p184.

Tenor Clef
1 Hoxton Sq N1.
Map 7 C3.
📞 0171-729 2440.

Vortex
Stoke Newington Church St N16. 📞 0171-254 6516.

WORLD MUSIC VENUES

Africa Centre
38 King St WC2.
Map 13 C2.
📞 0171-836 1973.

Cecil Sharp House
2 Regent's Park Rd NW1.
Map 4 D1.
📞 0171-485 2206.

Cuba Libre
72 Upper St N1. **Map** 6 F1.
📞 0171-354 9998.

Down Mexico Way
25 Swallow St W1.
Map 12 F3.
📞 0171-437 9895.

ICA
See p92.

Mean Fiddler
24-28A High St NW10.
📞 0181-961 5490.

Weavers Arms
98 Newington Green Rd N1.
📞 0171-226 6911.

CLUBS

Annabel's
44 Berkeley Sq W1.
Map 12 E3.
📞 0171-629 1096.

Café de Paris
3 Coventry St W1.
Map 13 A3.
📞 0171-287 3481.

Club Copa
180 Earl's Court Rd SW5.
Map 18 D2.
📞 0171-373 3407.

Equinox
Leicester Sq WC2.
Map 13 B2.
📞 0171-437 1446

Fridge
Town Hall Parade, Brixton Hill SW2.
📞 0171-326 5100.

Gardening Club
4 The Piazza, Covent Garden WC2.
Map 13 C2.
📞 0171-497 3154.

Gossips
69 Dean St W1.
Map 13 A2.
📞 0171-434 4480.

Heaven
Under the Arches, Villiers St WC2. **Map** 13 C3.
📞 0171-839 3852.

Hippodrome
Cranbourn St WC2.
Map 13 B2.
📞 0171-437 4311.

Legends
29 Old Burlington St W1.
Map 12 F3.
📞 0171-437 9933.

Madame Jojo
8–10 Brewer St W1.
Map 13 A2.
📞 0171-734 2473.

Maximus
14 Leicester Sq WC2.
Map 13 B2.
📞 0171-734 4111.

Ministry of Sound
103 Gaunt St SE1.
📞 0171-378 6528.

Paradise Club
1–5 Parkfield St N1.
Map 6 E2.
📞 0171-354 9993.

Scandale
53–54 Berwick St W1.
Map 13 A1.
📞 0171-437 6830.

Stringfellows
16 Upper St Martin's Lane WC2. **Map** 13 B2.
📞 0171-240 5534.

Tattershall Castle
Victoria Embankment, SW1. **Map** 13 C3.
📞 0171-839 6548.

Turnmills
63 Clerkenwell Road EC1
Map 6 E5.
📞 0171-250 3409.

Wag Club
35 Wardour St W1.
Map 13 A2.
📞 0171-437 5534.

Sports

THE RANGE OF SPORTS available in London is quite phenomenal. Whether your urge is to watch a game of medieval tennis or scuba-dive, you've come to the right place. You can also swim or ice skate, watch a football (called soccer in the US) or rugby match or play tennis in a park. With far more public facilities than most European capitals, London is truly an ideal place to enjoy cheap, accessible sports.

AMERICAN FOOTBALL

THE LONDON MONARCHS play teams from Europe and America at **Wembley** in March and April. The NFL Bowl, in which two top U.S. football teams compete in an exhibition match, is held in August.

ATHLETICS

ATHLETES WILL find a good choice of running tracks, often with free admission. **West London Stadium** has good facilities; **Regent's Park** is free; try also **Parliament Hill Fields**. For a sociable jog, meet the Bow Street Runners at **Jubilee Hall** on Tuesdays at 6pm.

CRICKET

TEST CRICKET is played in the summer at **Lord's** *(see p242)* and the **Oval**. Tickets have to be reserved well in advance, though those for one-day internationals are easier to get. Middlesex and Surrey play first-class county matches at Lord's and the Oval. You can also take a tour of the Long Room and Pavilion at Lord's.

FOOTBALL (US: SOCCER)

THE MOST popular spectator sport in Britain is soccer. The season runs from August to May, with matches starting at 3pm on Saturdays. Although the FA Cup Final at **Wembley** sells out in advance, tickets for international matches are usually available from the box office. The biggest London soccer clubs are **Arsenal** and **Tottenham Hotspur**, and, unless admission is by advanced reservations only, admission on the day should not be a problem.

GOLF

THERE ARE NO golf courses in Central London, but a few are scattered around the outskirts. The most accessible public courses are **Hounslow Heath**, **Chessington** (nine holes, train from Waterloo) and **Richmond Park** (two courses, computerized indoor teaching room). If you didn't pack your clubs, sets can be rented at a reasonable price.

GREYHOUND RACING

AT A NIGHT "down the dogs," you can follow the races on a screen in the bar, stand by the track or watch from the restaurant (reserve first) at **Walthamstow Stadium**, **The Embassy London Stadium** or **Wimbledon Stadium**.

HORSE RIDING

FOR CENTURIES, fashionable riders have exercised their steeds in Hyde Park; **Ross Nye** will provide you with a horse so that you can follow a long tradition.

ICE SKATING

ICE SKATERS SHOULD head for London's best-known rink, **Queens**, where you can rent skates. The most attractive ice rink, open only in winter, is in the **Broadgate** complex in the heart of the City.

RUGBY

THE PROFESSIONAL Rugby League has 13 players a side and plays cup final matches at **Wembley** stadium; Rugby Union, or rugger, is a 15-a-side amateur game, and its international matches are played at **Twickenham Rugby Football Ground**. The season runs from September to April, and you can watch "friendly" weekend games at local sports grounds. Top London teams **Saracens** and **Rosslyn Park** can be seen at their own sports grounds outside the center of town.

SQUASH

SQUASH COURTS tend to be busy, so reserve one at least two days ahead. Many sports centers have squash facilities and will rent out equipment, including **Swiss Cottage Sports Centre** and **Saddlers Sports Centre**.

STOCK CAR RACING

STOCK CAR RACING can be found at **Wimbledon Stadium**. It is an extremely noisy sport, but spectators can always forsake the racket, the wrecks and the fumes for the calm of the restaurant.

SWIMMING

BEST INDOOR pools include **Chelsea Sports Centre** and **Porchester Baths**; for outdoor, try **Highgate** (men), **Kenwood** (women) and **Hampstead** (mixed bathing).

TENNIS

THERE ARE hundreds of tennis courts in London's public parks, most of them cheap and easily reserved. They can be busy in summer, so reserve a court two or three days ahead. You must supply your own racquet and balls. Good public tennis courts include **Holland Park**, **Parliament Hill** and **Swiss Cottage**.

Tickets for the Centre Court of the **All England Lawn Tennis Club** at Wimbledon are hard to obtain – it is possibly easier to enter the tournament as a player than to obtain tickets for Centre Court; try lining up overnight, or getting in line for return tickets after lunch on the match day – for a bargain price, you can enjoy a good four hours of tennis. *(See p247.)*

TRADITIONAL SPORTS

A N OLD LONDON tradition is the University Boat Race, held in March or April, when Oxford and Cambridge row from Putney to Mortlake (*see p56*); a newer tradition is the Marathon, which is run from Greenwich to Big Ben at Westminster (*see p56*) on an April Sunday. You can watch croquet at the **Hurlingham Club**, polo at the **Guards Polo Club** and medieval tennis at **Queen's Club**.

WATER SPORTS

T HERE ARE FACILITIES for a wide variety of water sports at the **Docklands Sailing and Water Sports Centre** (windsurfing, dinghy sailing, powerboating and canoeing), **Docklands Water Sports Club**, **Peter Chilvers Windsurfing School** and **Royal Docks Waterski Club**. Boats are also available for rent on the calmer waters of the **Serpentine** in Hyde Park and on **Regent's Park Lake**.

WORKING OUT

M OST SPORTS CENTERS have gymnasiums, workout studios and health clubs. If you are a member of the YMCA, you'll be able to use the excellent facilities at the **Central YMCA**. **Jubilee Hall** and **Swiss Cottage Sports Centre** both offer a variety of fitness and aerobic classes, and weight training. For those who have overdone it, the **Chelsea Sports Centre** has a sports injury clinic.

DIRECTORY

General Sports Information Line
(0171-222 8000.

Greater London Sports Council
(0181-778 8600.

All England Lawn Tennis and Croquet Club
Church Rd, Wimbledon SW19. (0181-946 2244.

Arsenal
Avenell Rd, Highbury N5.
(0171-359 0131.

Broadgate Ice Rink
Eldon St EC2. **Map 7** C5.
(0171-588 6565.

Central YMCA
112 Great Russell St WC1. **Map 13** B1.
(0171-637 8131.

Chelsea Sports Centre
Chelsea Manor St SW3.
Map 19 B3.
(0171-352 6985.

Chessington Golf Course
Garrison Lane, Surrey.
(0181-391 0948.

Docklands Sailing and Watersports Centre
235a Westferry Rd, E14.
(0171-537 2626.

Docklands Water Sports Club
King George V Dock, Woolwich Manor Way E16. (0171-511 5000.

The Embassy London Stadium
Waterden Rd, E15 2EQ.
(0181-986 3511.

Guards Polo Club
Windsor Great Park, Englefield Green, Egham, Surrey.
(01784-434212.

Hampstead Ponds
off East Heath Rd NW3.
Map 1 C4.
(0171-435 2366.

Holland Park Lawn Tennis Courts
Kensington High St W8.
Map 9 B5.
(0171-602 2226.

Hounslow Heath Golf
Staines Rd, Hounslow, Middlesex.
(0181-570 5271.

Hurlingham Club
Ranelagh Gdns SW6.
(0171-736 3148.

Jubilee Hall Sports Centre
30 The Piazza, Covent Garden WC2. **Map 13** C2.
(0171-836 4835.

Kenwood and Highgate Ponds
off Millfield Lane N6.
Map 2 E3.
(0181-340 4044.

Lord's Cricket Ground
St. John's Wood NW8.
Map 3 A3.
(0171-289 1611.

Oval Cricket Ground
Kennington Oval SE11.
Map 22 D4.
(0171-582 6660.

Parliament Hill
Highgate Rd NW5.
Map 2 E4.

(0171-435 8998
(athletics).
(0171-485 4491 (tennis).

Peter Chilvers Windsurfing Centre
Gate 6, Tidal Basin, Royal Victoria Docks E16.
(0171-474 2500.

Porchester Centre
Queensway W2.
Map 10 D1.
(0171-792 2919.

Queen's Club Real Tennis
Palliser Rd W14.
Map 17 A3.
(0171-385 3421.

Queens Ice Skating Club
17 Queensway W2.
Map 10 E2.
(0171-229 0172.

Regent's Park Lake
Regent's Park NW1.
Map 3 C3.
(0171-486 4759.

Richmond Park Golf
Roehampton Gate, Priory Lane SW15.
(0181-876 3205.

Rosslyn Park Rugby
Priory Lane, Upper Richmond Rd SW15.
(0181-876 1879.

Ross Nye
8 Bathurst Mews W2. **Map 11** A2.
(0171-262 3791.

Royal Docks Waterski Club
Gate 16, King George V Dock, Woolwich Manor Way E16.
(0171-511 2000.

Saddlers Sports Centre
Goswell Rd EC1.
Map 6 F3.
(0171-253 9285.

Saracens Rugby
Dale Green Rd N14.
(0181-449 3770.

Serpentine
Hyde Park W2.
Map 11 B4.
(0171-262 3751.

Swiss Cottage Sports Centre
Winchester Rd NW3.
(0171-413 6490.

Tottenham Hotspur
White Hart Lane, 748 High Rd N17.
(0171-396 4567.

Twickenham Rugby Ground
Whitton Rd, Twickenham, Middlesex.
(0181-892 8161.

Walthamstow Stadium
Chingford Rd E4.
(0181-531 4255.

Wembley Stadium
Wembley, Middlesex.
(0181-900 1234.

Linford Christie Stadium
Du Cane Rd W12.
(0181-749 5505.

Wimbledon Stadium
Plough Lane SW19.
(0181-946 5361.

CHILDREN'S LONDON

LONDON OFFERS children a potential gold mine of fun, excitement and adventure. Each year finds new attractions and sights opening constantly, and older ones being updated.

First-time visitors may want to watch traditional ceremonies *(see pp52–5)* or visit famous buildings *(see p35)*, but these are merely the tip of the iceberg. London's parks, zoos and imaginative

Humpty Dumpty doll

playgrounds provide outdoor activities, but there are also loads of workshops, activity centers and museums featuring delightful hands-on experiments and interactive displays. A day out needn't be costly: children are entitled to reduced fares on London Transport and lower admission prices at museums. Some of London's star attractions – for instance, all the ceremonies – are free.

PRACTICAL ADVICE

A LITTLE PLANNING is the key to a successful outing. In advance, you may want to phone to check the opening hours of the places you plan to visit. Work out your journey thoroughly using the subway (called the Underground or tube) map at the end of this book. If you are traveling with very young children, remember that there will be lines at the Underground stations or bus stops near popular sights. These will be long during peak hours, so buy your tickets or a Travelcard in advance *(see p360)*.

Children under 5 can travel free on buses and tubes, and there are reduced fares for children between 5 and 15. (Children of 14 and 15, and those who look older than they are, need to have a Photocard.) Children very often enjoy using public

Punch and Judy show in the Piazza, Covent Garden

transportation, especially when it's a novelty, so plan your outing carefully using one form of transportation to go out sightseeing and another going home. You can get around London easily by bus, Underground, taxi, train and riverboat *(see pp 360–7)*.

Visiting exhibitions and museums as a

Covent Garden clowns

family doesn't have to be expensive. An annual family season ticket, usually for two adults and up to four children, is available at many museums and often costs only marginally more than the initial visit. In some cases you can buy a family ticket that covers a group of museums – for instance, the Science, Natural History, and Victoria and Albert Museums in South Kensington *(see pp194–209)*. Being able to visit a sight more than once means you won't exhaust your children and turn them against museums for life by trying to see absolutely everything in one long, tiring day.

If your children want a break from sightseeing, most borough councils provide information on activities for children, such as playgroups, theaters, fairs and activity centers in their area. Leaflets are usually available from libraries and public recreation centers, as well as local town halls. During the summer school holidays (July to the beginning of September), there are organized activities all over London.

CHILDREN AND THE LAW

C HILDREN UNDER 14 are not allowed into British pubs and wine bars (unless there is a special family room or garden), and you must be over 18 to drink or buy liquor. In restaurants, however, those over 16 can drink wine and beer with their meal (over 18 for liquor).

EATING OUT WITH CHILDREN

The chart *(see pp292–4)* in the front of the restaurants section of this book shows establishments that welcome children. But as long as your offspring are reasonably well behaved, most of London's more informal and ethnic restaurants will be happy to serve a family. Some can also provide highchairs and booster cushions, as well as coloring placemats to keep children quiet while waiting for their food to arrive. Many

will also offer special children's menus with small helpings; these, although fairly unadventurous, will cut the cost of your meal.

On weekends some restaurants (such as **Smollensky's Balloon** and **Sweeny Todds**) provide live entertainment for children in the form of clowns, storytellers and magicians. Some places accept reservations for children's parties. It is always worth trying to reserve in advance (especially for Sunday lunch), so you don't have to hang around waiting with tired and hungry children.

London has a number of restaurants ideal for older children. Among these are the Rock Island Diner *(see p306)* and the **Hard Rock Café** on Old Park Lane. For budget eating, try the Café in the Crypt, St. Martin-in-the-Fields *(see p102).*

Coming up for air at Smollensky's Balloon

USEFUL ADDRESSES

Häagen-Dazs
14 Leicester Square WC2. **Map** 13 B2.
℡ 0171-287 9577.

Hard Rock Café
150 Old Park Lane W1. **Map** 12 E4.
℡ 0171-629 0382.

Smollensky's Balloon
1 Dover St W1. **Map** 12 F3.
℡ 0171-491 1199.

Sweeny Todds
3–5 Tooley St SE1. **Map** 15 C3.
℡ 0171-407 5267.

Colorful service at the Rock Island Diner

Some films are classed as unsuitable for children *(see p329)*, and young children are rarely welcome anywhere they might create a nuisance.

If you want to take your children by car, you must use seat belts wherever they are provided. Babies will need a special child seat. If you are in doubt, ask at any police station.

GETTING THEM OFF YOUR HANDS

MANY OF London's great museums *(see pp40–3)* and theaters *(see pp326–8)* provide weekend and holiday activities and workshops where you can leave children for a few hours or even for a whole day, and the children's theaters are a great way to spend a rainy afternoon. A day at the fair is always a success – try Hampstead fair on summer bank holidays.

London has a great many sports centers *(see pp336–7)*, which usually open daily and

often have special clubs and activities to occupy children of every age.

From 4 to 6pm Kids Line (0171-222 8070) details children's events in London.

If you want a total break, contact **Childminders**; **Babysitters Unlimited**; **Universal Aunts**; or **Pippa Pop-Ins**, London's hotel for children between 2 and 12.

BABY-SITTING

Babysitters Unlimited
2 Napoleon Rd, Twickenham.
℡ 0181-892 8888.

Childminders
9 Paddington St W1.
Map 4 D5.
℡ 0171-487 5040.

Pippa Pop-Ins
430 Fulham Rd SW6.
Map 18 D5.
℡ 0171-385 2458.

Universal Aunts
PO Box 304, SW4.
℡ 0171-738 8937.

Airborne at the Hampstead fair

Bathtime fun at Pippa Pop-Ins

SHOPPING

All children love a visit to **Hamleys** toy shop or **Harrods** toy department *(see p311)*. **Davenport's Magic Shop** and **The Doll's House** are smaller and more specialized.

The **Early Learning Centre**, the **Children's Book Centre** and the **Puffin Book Shop** all have good selections of books. Some bookshops organize readings and signings by children's authors, especially during Children's Book Week during October.

Useful numbers Children's Book Centre [0171-937 7497; Davenport's Magic Shop [0171-836 0408; The Doll's House [0171-379 7243; Early Learning Centre [0171-937 0419; Hamleys [0171-734 3161; Puffin Book Shop [0171-379 7650.

Bears at Hamleys toy shop

MUSEUMS AND GALLERIES

LONDON HAS a wealth of museums, exhibitions and galleries; more information on those listed here is to be found on pages 40 to 43. Most have been updated over the last few years to incorporate many exciting modern display techniques. It's unlikely that you'll have to drag reluctant children around an assortment of lifeless and stuffy exhibits.

The Bethnal Green Museum of Childhood (the children's branch of the Victoria and Albert Museum); the London Toy and Model Museum, with its garden and steam railroad; and Pollock's Toy Museum are especially good for young children.

For older children, try one of London's Brass Rubbing Centres: the great Brass Rubbing Centre in the Crypt of St. Martin-in-the-Fields *(p102)*, Westminster Abbey *(pp76–9)* or St. James's Church, Piccadilly *(p90)*. The Guinness World of Records Exhibitions *(p100)* at the Trocadero, the Museum of the Moving Image *(p184)*, Madame Tussaud's *(p220)* or Tower Bridge *(p153)* are all favorites with children, too.

The British Museum has fabulous treasures from all over the world, and the Commonwealth Institute, Horniman Museum and Museum of Mankind have colorful displays from many different cultures. The Science Museum, with over 600 working exhibits, is one of London's best attractions for children – its Launch Pad gallery will help keep them amused for hours. If you have the stamina, the Natural History Museum next door contains hundreds of amazing objects and animals from the world of nature, including a new Dinosaur Exhibition

complete with sound effects. Suits of armor built for knights and monarchs can be seen at the Tower of London. More up-to-date armory and weapons, including aircraft and the tools of modern warfare, can be seen at the National Army Museum and the Imperial War Museum. Also worth a visit is the Guards' Museum located on Birdcage Walk. London's colorful past is brought alive at the Museum of London. Its new offshoot, the Tower Hill Pageant, manages to cover 2,000 years of the capital's history, complete with many realistic sights, sounds and smells.

Shirley Temple doll at Bethnal Green Museum

THE GREAT OUTDOORS

LONDON IS FORTUNATE in having many parks and open spaces *(see pp48–51)*. Most local parks contain conventional playgrounds for children, many with safe modern equipment. Some parks also have One O'Clock Clubs (specially enclosed areas for children under 5 with activities supervised by play-workers) as well as

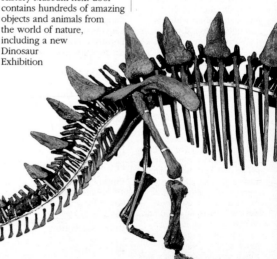

Puppets at the Little Angel Marionette Theatre, Highbury

Playground at Gunnersbury Park

adventure playgrounds, nature trails, boating ponds and athletic tracks for older children and energetic adults.

Kiteflying on Blackheath (p239), Hampstead Heath or Parliament Hill can be great fun, as can boating in Regent's Park. A trip to Primrose Hill (pp262–3) can be combined with a visit to London Zoo and Regent's Canal (p223).

The large parks are one of London's greatest assets for parents who have energetic children. For a good walk or cycle ride, there is quite an abundance of parks all over London. For instance, there's Hyde Park in the city center; Hampstead Heath up in the north; Wimbledon Common in southwest London; and Gunnersbury Park in west London. Cyclists should be sure to watch for pedestrians and remember that some paths may be off-limits.

Battersea Park has a children's zoo, and Crystal Palace Park (Thicket Rd, Penge SE20) has a children's farm. Greenwich and Richmond Parks have herds of deer. If you want a relaxing trip, why not go and feed the ducks on the pond in St. James's Park?

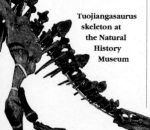
Tuojiangasaurus skeleton at the Natural History Museum

CHILDREN'S THEATER

INTRODUCING CHILDREN to the theater can be great fun for adults, too. Try the **Little Angel Marionette Theatre** or the floating fantasy of the **Puppet Theatre Barge** in Little Venice. **The Unicorn Theatre** offers the best range of children's theater, and the **Polka Children's Theatre** also presents good and varied entertainment.
Useful numbers Little Angel Marionette Theatre [C] 0171-226 1787; Polka Children's Theatre [C] 0181-543 4888; Puppet Theatre Barge [C] 0171-249 6876; The Unicorn Theatre [C] 0171-836 3334.

Deer at Richmond Park

SIGHTSEEING

FOR SEEING the sights of London, you can't beat the top of a double-decker bus (see pp364–5). It's a cheap and easy way of entertaining children, and if they get restless you can always jump off the bus at the next stop. London's colorful ceremonies are detailed on pages 52 to 55.

Children will also enjoy such spectacles as the summer fun fairs in London's parks, the fireworks displays throughout London on

Boating lake near Winfield House in Regent's Park

Guy Fawkes Night (every November 5) and the Christmas decorations in Regent Street and Trafalgar Square.

BEHIND THE SCENES

OLDER CHILDREN in particular will love the opportunity to look "behind the scenes" and see how famous events or institutions are run.

If you have a brood of sports enthusiasts, you should visit the impressive Wembley Stadium, Twickenham Rugby Football Ground (see p337), Lord's Cricket Ground (p242) or the Wimbledon Lawn Tennis Museum (p247).

For budding theater buffs, the Royal National Theatre (p184), the Royal Opera House (p115) and Sadler's Wells (p243) all offer tours.

Other good buildings to visit include the Tower of London (pp154–7), the Old Bailey law courts (p147) and the distinguished Houses of Parliament (pp72–3).

If none of the above satisfies the children, the London Fire Brigade (0171-587 4063) and the London Diamond Centre (0171-629 5511) offer more unusual guided tours.

SURVIVAL
GUIDE

PRACTICAL INFORMATION

Lᴏɴᴅᴏɴ ʜᴀꜱ ʀᴇꜱᴘᴏɴᴅᴇᴅ well to the demands of tourism. The range of facilities available for travelers, from cash machines and bureaux de change to medical care and late-night transportation, has expanded rapidly over the last few years. Whether you find London an expensive city will depend on the prevailing exchange rate between the pound and the US

dollar. London is known for its high hotel prices, but even here there are budget options *(see pp272–5)*. Also, you need not spend a lot on food if you choose carefully: for the price of a single meal at some Mayfair restaurants, you could feed yourself, albeit modestly, for several days *(see pp306–7)*. The following tips will help you make the most of your visit.

A walking tour of the City

Aᴠᴏɪᴅɪɴɢ ᴛʜᴇ Cʀᴏᴡᴅꜱ

Mᴜꜱᴇᴜᴍꜱ ᴀɴᴅ ɢᴀʟʟᴇʀɪᴇꜱ can be crowded with school groups, particularly at the end of terms, so it might be best to plan your visit to start after 2:30pm during the school year. At other times, visit early in the day and try and avoid weekends if you can.

Bus tours are another source of congestion. They do, however, tend to follow a predictable path. To avoid them, it is wise to stay away from Westminster Abbey in

the morning and St. Paul's in the afternoon. The Tower of London is usually busy all day.

A lot of London can be seen on foot. Brown signs indicate sights and facilities of interest to tourists. Watch, too, for the blue plaques attached to many buildings *(see p39)* showing where famous citizens have lived in the past.

Gᴜɪᴅᴇᴅ Tᴏᴜʀꜱ

A ɢᴏᴏᴅ ᴡᴀʏ to enjoy London, weather permitting, is from the top of a traditional open-topped double-decker bus. The **London Transport Sight-seeing Tour** lasts around 90 minutes and leaves every half hour or so (10am–6pm) from various central locations. Commercial rivals, including **Frames Rickards**, **Harrods** and **Cityrama**, offer tours lasting anything from an hour to a full day. You can buy your tickets just before boarding or in advance (sometimes more cheaply) at Tourist Information Centres. Private tours can also be arranged with many companies, for instance, **Tour Guides Ltd** or **British Tours.** The best tour guides receive a Blue Badge qualification from the London Tourist Board.

You can also explore London by joining a walking tour *(see p259)*. Themed tours range from pub crawls to a jaunt in the steps of Charles Dickens. Check for details at tourist offices or in listings magazines *(see p324)*.

Cruise boats operate on the River Thames – an excellent way of traveling the breadth of London *(see pp60–5)*.
Useful numbers British Tours [C] 0171 629 5267; Cityrama [C] 0171-720 6663; Frames Rickards [C] 0171-837 3111; Harrods [C] 0171-581 3603; London Transport Sightseeing Tour [C] 0171-828 7395; Tour Guides Ltd [C] 0171-495 5505; information for the disabled: [C] 0171-495 5505.

Oᴘᴇɴɪɴɢ Hᴏᴜʀꜱ

Oᴘᴇɴɪɴɢ ᴛɪᴍᴇꜱ for sights have been listed in the *Area by Area* section of this book. Core visiting times in London are 10am to 5pm daily, though many places stay open longer, especially in summer. Some major sights, like the British Museum, also stay open late on certain evenings. There are variations on weekends and public holidays. Opening times on Sundays are often restricted, and a few museums close on Mondays.

-decker sightseeing bus with an open top

Lining up for a bus

ADMISSION CHARGES

Many major sights, including London's cathedrals and some churches, have recently begun either to charge for admission or to ask for a voluntary contribution upon entry. Charges vary greatly, from the cheap (only a few pounds for the Florence Nightingale Museum, *see p185*) to the more expensive (over £6.00 for the Tower of London, *see pp154–7*). The *Area by Area* listings tell you which museums charge for admission.

Some sights have reduced-price visiting times and offer concessions. It is best to telephone if you think you might be eligible.

Signposted information for tourists

ETIQUETTE

Smoking is now forbidden in many of London's public places. These include the bus and Underground systems, taxis, some British Rail stations, all theaters and most movie theaters. Many London restaurants now have no-smoking sections. The exception to the anti-smoking trend is pubs. ASH (Action on Smoking and Health) can give advice on smoke-free venues (0171-935 3519). Consult the Hotels and Restaurants listings (*pp278–85* and *pp295–305*) for details of places that cater to nonsmokers.

Londoners line up for anything from shops, buses and post offices to theater tickets,

takeout food and taxis. Anyone barging in will encounter frosty glares and acid comments. The exceptions are commuter rail and rush-hour tube services, when the laws of the jungle prevail.

The words *please*, *thank you* and *sorry* are used regularly in London; people sometimes apologize if you step on their feet. It may seem unnecessary to thank a barman for simply doing his job, but it should improve your chances of good service.

Like any big city, London can seem alienating to newcomers, but Londoners are usually helpful, and most will respond generously to your request for directions. The stalwart British bobby (police constable on the beat) is also always ready to patiently help stranded tourists (*see p346*).

DISABLED VISITORS

Most sights have access for wheelchairs. Again, this information is listed in the *Area by Area* section of this book, but phone first to check that your special needs are catered to. Useful guides to buy include *Access in London*, published by Nicholson; *London for All*, published by the London Tourist Board; and a booklet from London Transport called *Access to the Underground*, available at main tube stations. **Artsline** gives free information on facilities for disabled people at cultural events and venues. **Holiday Care Service** offers many facts on hotel facilities for the disabled. **Tripscope** provides free information on transportation for the elderly and the disabled.
Useful numbers Artsline [0171-388 2227; Holiday Care Service [01293 774535; Tripscope [0181-994 9294.

Box for voluntary contributions in lieu of admission charges

TOURIST INFORMATION CENTERS

These offer advice on anything from day trips and guided tours to accommodation choices.

Tourist information symbol

If you need tourist information, including free leaflets on current events, look for the large blue symbol at the following locations:

Heathrow Airport
Location The Underground station. Heathrow, 1, 2, 3. **Open** 8am–6pm daily.

Liverpool Street Station
EC2. **Map** 7 C5.
Location The Underground station. Liverpool Street. **Open** 8:15am–7pm Mon, 8:15am–6pm Tue–Sat, 8:15am–4:45pm Sun.

Selfridges
400 Oxford St W1. **Map** 12 D2.
Location The basement. Bond Street. **Open** 9:30am–7pm Fri–Wed, 9:30–8pm Thu.

Victoria Station
SW1. **Map** 20 F1.
Location The railway station forecourt. Victoria. **Open** 8am–7pm daily.

You can also telephone the London Tourist Board at [0171-971 0026.

Another service exists for information about the City of London area only (see pp143–59):

City of London Information Centre
St. Paul's Churchyard EC4. **Map** 15 A1. [0171-606 3030. St. Paul's. **Open** Apr–Oct: 9:30am–5pm daily; Nov–Mar: 9:30am–12:30pm Sat only.

Personal Security and Health

PERSONAL PROPERTY

London is a large city which, like any other, has had its recent share of urban problems. It has also often been a terrorist target, and London life is sometimes disrupted by security alerts. Nearly all of these turn out to be false alarms, but they should always still be taken seriously. Never hesitate to approach one of London's many police constables for assistance – they are trained to help the public with any problems.

SUITABLE PRECAUTIONS

There is little likelihood that your stay in London will be disrupted at all by the spectre of violent crime if you are careful. The risk of having your pocket picked, or your bag stolen, even in the run-down and rougher parts of the town, is not actually very great. It is far more likely to happen right in the middle of shopping crowds in areas like Oxford Street or Camden Lock, or perhaps on a very busy tube platform.

Muggers and rapists prefer poorly lit or isolated places like back streets, parks and unstaffed railroad stations. Avoid these, especially at night, travel around in a group and know where you are at all times.

Pickpockets and thieves pose a much more immediate problem. Keep your valuables securely concealed. If you carry a purse or a briefcase, never let it out of your sight – particularly in restaurants, theaters and movie houses, where bags have been known to vanish from between the feet of their owners.

London has a small number of homeless people but they do not present a threat. At worst all they will do is request your spare change.

WOMEN TRAVELING ALONE

Unlike some European cities, it is considered quite normal in London for women to eat out on their own or go out in a group, perhaps to a pub or a bar. However, risks do exist, and caution is essential. Stick to well-lit streets with plenty of traffic. Even women in groups avoid traveling on the tube late

Mounted police

at night, and it is best not to travel alone on trains. If you have no companions, try to find an occupied car – preferably one with more than one group of people. Better yet, take a taxi *(see p367).*

Many forms of self-defense are restricted in the UK, and it is illegal for anyone to carry various offensive weapons in public places. These include knives, clubs, guns and tear-gas canisters, all of which are strictly prohibited. Personal alarm systems are permitted.

Take sensible precautions with personal property at all times. Make sure that your possessions are adequately insured before you arrive, since it is difficult for visitors to obtain once in the UK.

Don't carry your valuables around with you; take just as much cash as you need, and leave the rest in a hotel safe or lock it up in your suitcase. Traveler's checks are the safest method of carrying large amounts of money *(see p349).* Never leave bags or briefcases unattended in tube or train stations – they will either be stolen or suspected of being bombs and therefore cause a security alert.

Report all lost items to the nearest police station (get the necessary paperwork if you plan an insurance claim). Each of the main rail stations has a lost property office on the premises. If you do leave something on a bus or tube, it may be better to call in at the address given below rather than to telephone.

Lost Property

Lost Property Offices
London Transport Lost Property Office, 200 Baker Street W1. *Open weekday mornings only.* 📞 0171-486 2496, enquiries should be made in person; Black Cab Lost Property Office. 📞 0171-833 0996.

Woman Police Constable

Traffic Police Officer

Police Constable

Typical London police car

London ambulance

London fire engine

EMERGENCIES

Lᴏɴᴅᴏɴ's ᴇᴍᴇʀɢᴇɴᴄʏ police, ambulance and fire services are on call 24 hours a day. These, like the London hospital casualty services, are strictly for emergencies only.

Other services are also available to offer help in emergencies, for instance in case of rape. If there is no appropriate number in the Crisis Information box *(see right)* you can obtain one from the directory enquiries service (dial 142). Police stations plus hospitals with casualty wards are shown on the Street Finder maps *(see pp368–9)*.

MEDICAL TREATMENT

Vɪsɪᴛᴏʀs ᴛᴏ ʟᴏɴᴅᴏɴ from all countries outside the European Community (EC) are strongly advised to take out medical insurance against the cost of any emergency hospital care, specialists' fees and repatriation. Emergency treatment in a British casualty ward is free, but additional medical care may be costly.

Residents of the EC and nationals of other European and Commonwealth countries are entitled to receive free medical treatment under the

National Health Service (NHS), the free, state-run medical service available to all UK residents. Before traveling, you should obtain a form confirming that your country of origin has a reciprocal health arrangement with Britain. Without this form free medical treatment can still be obtained if you offer proof of nationality, but there are exceptions for certain kinds of treatment so medical insurance is always advisable.

If you need to see a dentist in London, you will have to pay for either all or part of the treatment, depending on your NHS entitlement and whether you can find an NHS dentist. Various institutions offer 24-hour dental treatment *(see addresses right)*, but if you wish to visit a private dental surgeon, try looking in the Yellow Pages *(see p352)*.

MEDICINES

Yᴏᴜ ᴄᴀɴ ʙᴜʏ most medical supplies from chemists (drugstores) and supermarkets throughout London. However, many medicines are available only with a doctor's prescription. If you are likely to require drugs, bring your own or get your doctor to write out the generic name of the drug, as opposed to the brand name. If you have no NHS entitlement you will be charged for the medicine, so keep your receipt to support any medical insurance claim.

Boots, a chain of drugstores

CRISIS INFORMATION

Police, fire and ambulance services
[*Dial 999 or 112. Calls are free.*

Emergency Dental Care
[*0171-837 3646 (24-hour phoneline).*

London Rape Crisis Centre
[*0171-837 1600 (24-hour phoneline).*

Samaritans
[*0171-734 2800 (24-hour helpline). For all emotional problems. Check in local telephone directory for nearest branch.*

Chelsea and Westminster Hospital
369 Fulham Rd SW10. **Map** 18 F4.
[*0181-746 8000.*

St. Thomas's Hospital
Lambeth Palace Rd SE1.
Map 13 C5. [*0171-928 9292.*

University College Hospital
Gower St WC1. **Map** 5 A4.
[*0171-387 9300.*

Medical Express (Private Casualty Clinic)
117A Harley St W1.
Map 4 E5. [*0171-499 1991. Treatment guaranteed within 30 minutes, but a fee is charged for consultations and tests.*

Eastman Dental School
256 Gray's Inn Rd WC1.
Map 6 D4. [*0171-837 3646. Private and NHS dental care.*

Guy's Hospital Dental School
St. Thomas's St SE1. **Map** 15 B4.
[*0171-955 5000.*

Late-opening drugstores
Contact your local London police station for a comprehensive list.

Bliss Chemist
5 Marble Arch W1. **Map** 11 C2.
[*0171-723 6116.*
Open *until midnight daily.*

Boots the Chemist
Piccadilly Circus W1. **Map** 13 A3.
[*0171-734 6126.* **Open** *8:30am–8pm Mon–Fri, 9am–8pm Sat, noon–6pm Sun.*

Banking and Local Currency

Visitors to London will find that banks usually offer them the best rates of exchange. Privately owned bureaux de change have variable exchange rates, and care should be taken to check the small-print details relating to commission and minimum charges before completing any transaction. Bureaux de change do, however, offer the advantage of staying open long after the banks have closed.

Cashpoint machine

BANKING

Banking hours vary in London. The minimum opening hours are, without exception, 9:30am–3:30pm on Monday to Friday, but many stay open longer than this, especially those in the center of London. Saturday-morning opening is also more common now. Banks close on public holidays (known as bank holidays in the UK, *see* p59), and some close early the day before.

Many major banks have cash machines that will allow you to obtain money by using your credit card and a PIN (personal identification number); some machines have clear computerized instructions in several languages. American Express cards may be used in 24-hour Lloyds Bank and Royal Bank of Scotland cash machines in London, but you must arrange to have your PIN linked by code to your personal account before you leave home. There is a 2% charge for each transaction.

You can also change your traveler's checks at **Thomas Cook** and **American Express** offices or the bank-operated bureaux de change, which can usually be found at airports and major railroad stations. Don't forget to bring along a passport if you want to change checks.

BUREAUX DE CHANGE

American Express
6 Haymarket SW1. **Map** 13 A3.
[*0171-930 4411*.

Chequepoint
13–15 Davies St W1.
Map 12 E2. [*0171-409 1122*.

Exchange International
Victoria Station SW1.
Map 20 E1. [*0171-630 1107*.

Thomas Cook
45 Berkeley St
W1. **Map** 12 F3.
[*0171-408 4179*.

Ways of paying accepted at bureaux de change

You can find facilities for changing money all over the city center; at main stations and tourist information offices, and in most large stores. **Chequepoint** is one of the largest bureaux de change in Britain; **Exchange International** has a number of useful late-opening branches. There is no UK consumer organization to regulate the activities of the privately run bureaux de change, so their prices need to be examined carefully.

CREDIT CARDS

It is worth bringing a credit card with you, particularly for hotel and restaurant bills, shopping, car rental and reserving tickets by phone. VISA, MasterCard (its local name is Access), American Express, Diners Club and JCB are all accepted.

It is possible to obtain cash advances (up to your credit limit) with an internationally recognized credit card at any London bank displaying the appropriate card sign. You will be charged the credit card company's interest rate, which will appear on your statement along with the amount advanced.

MAIN BANKS IN LONDON

England's main clearing banks (those whose dealings are processed through a single clearing house) are Barclays, Lloyds, Midland and National Westminster (NatWest). Each bank can be easily identified by a distinctively styled sign bearing its name. The Royal Bank of Scotland also has a number of branches in London with exchange facilities. Commissions charged by each bank for changing money vary, so check before going ahead with your transaction.

CASH AND TRAVELER'S CHECKS

Britain's currency is the pound sterling (£), which is divided into 100 pence (p). Since there are no exchange controls in Britain, there is no limit to how much cash you may import or export.

Traveler's checks are the safest alternative to carrying large amounts of cash. Keep receipts from your traveler's checks separately and also make a note of offices where you will be able to obtain a refund if the checks are lost or stolen. Some banks issue traveler's checks free of commission to established customers, but the normal rate is about 1%. It is sensible to change some money into sterling before arriving in Britain, since lines at airport exchange offices can be long. Obtain some smaller denominations: shopkeepers may refuse to accept £20 notes for small purchases.

English bank notes of all denominations always feature the Queen's head on one side.

Bank Notes

English notes used in the UK are £5, £10, £20 and £50. Scotland has its own notes that, despite being legal tender throughout the UK, are not always accepted.

£50 note

£20 note

£10 note

£5 note

Coins of the Realm

Coins in circulation are £1, 50p, 20p, 10p, 5p, 2p and 1p (shown here at actual sizes). They all have the Queen's head on one side. Some, such as the 10p and 5p, have recently been changed.

1 pound (£1)   50 pence (50p)   20 pence (20p)

10 pence (10p)   5 pence (5p)   2 pence (2p)   1 penny (1p)

Using London's Phones

You will find a phonebox on many street corners in central London and in every British Rail station. Rather than always searching your pockets to find loose change to make a call, you can buy prepaid phonecards. Both British Telecom (BT) and Mercury phonecards come in £2, £4 and £10 denominations and can be purchased from some newsagents as well as post offices.

Old BT phonebox

New BT phonebox

Phoneboxes
There are three different types of phoneboxes in London: old and new BT phoneboxes and Mercury phoneboxes. All Mercury public phones will accept Mercury phonecards and credit cards but not coins. Some BT phones accept BT credit cards and phonecards, some accept only BT phonecards, and some take only coins.

Mercury phonebox

Using a BT Card Phone

1 Lift the receiver and wait for a dial tone.

2 Insert a BT phonecard, green side up and in the direction of the arrows on the card.

3 The display shows how many units are left. The minimum charge is one unit.

4 Some BT phones accept credit cards as well as phonecards. Insert the card, with the black stripe to the right and away from you and slide it through.

5 Dial the number and wait to be connected.

6 When your phonecard runs out you will hear a rapid beeping noise. To continue, press the button and the old card will come out. Remove it and put a new card in.

7 If you want to make another call, do not replace the receiver; press the follow-on call button.

BT phonecards come from shops with this sign

Using a Mercury Phone

1 Lift the receiver and wait for a dial tone.

2 Insert a Mercury phonecard, with the picture face up, in the direction of the arrows on the card.

Credit card slot

3 The display shows how much credit is left.

4 Mercury phones accept credit cards as well as phonecards. Insert the card, with black stripe face up on the left and slide it through.

5 Dial the number and wait to be connected.

Mercury card slot

6 When the phonecard runs out, it automatically ejects.

7 If you want to make another call, do not replace the receiver; press the follow-on call button.

Some Mercury cards are now collector's items

REACHING THE RIGHT NUMBER

- Central London areas use the prefix 0171.
- Outer areas use 0181.

To call Greenwich from Covent Garden, for example, you must first dial 0181; for Covent Garden from Greenwich, dial 0171.

- Internal directory inquiries are on 192.
- If you have any problems contacting a number, call the operator on 100.

Inland calls are charged according to the time of day. They are most expensive from 9am to 1pm on weekdays. Cheap rate applies before 8am or after 6pm on weekdays, and all day at weekends.

- To make an international call, dial 00 followed by the country code (USA and Canada: 1; Australia: 61; New Zealand: 64), area code and the number.
- The international operator is on 155.
- International directory inquiries are on 153. You need a phonecard with at least £2 credit to make an international call.

Cheap times for overseas calls vary from country to country, but in general they tend to be on weekends and in evenings.

- **In an emergency, dial 999 or 112.**

USING A BT COIN PHONE

1 Lift the receiver and wait for a dial tone.

2 Insert any combination of the coins below (the illuminated display shows the minimum amount you must put in).

3 Dial the number and wait to be connected.

4 The display indicates how much money you have put in and the credit left. A rapid bleeping noise means your money has run out. Insert more coins.

5 If you want to make another call, do not re-place the receiver, press the follow-on call button.

6 When you've finished speaking, replace the receiver. Any coins that were not used will be in the chute. Pay phones do not give change, so use 10p and 20p coins.

£1   50p   20p   10p

Sending a Letter

Post Office sign

BESIDES MAIN post offices, London has many sub post offices, which often double as newsagents. These are open from 9am until 5:30pm on week-days, and 9am–12:30pm on Saturdays. London's most central post office is in King Edward Street EC1A 1AA (Map 9 A3), where there is a *poste restante*. Stamps can be bought from outlets with the "stamps sold here" sign. First-class

Shops sell stamps

stamps can be used for letters and cards to the European Community. Always include the post code when writing to a UK address. Main post offices are shown on the *Street Finder* maps (see pp368–9).

Books of 10 stamps

UK Post

Letters within the UK can be sent first- or second-class. First-class is more expensive, but most first-class letters reach their UK destinations the following day (except Sunday).

Second-class stamp   **First-class stamp**

Aerogrames (air letters) go first-class anywhere in the world. They cost the same for all destinations.

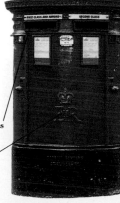

New-style post box

First-class and overseas mail has its own slot on many post boxes.

Initials show who was monarch when the post box was built.

EXTRA INFORMATION

SHOULD YOU require any services that are not listed in this guide, try consulting one of London's telephone directories. The Yellow Pages comprehensively lists services throughout London and should be available at your hotel. **Talking Pages** is a telephone service operated by British Telecom. It gives you the telephone number of someone who offers the service you want in any part of London (or the UK) that you specify.

Directory inquiries (dial 192) can be dialed free from pay phones and will give you any telephone number in the directory. You need to know the name and address of the person or business.

CUSTOMS AND IMMIGRATION

A VALID PASSPORT is needed to enter the United Kingdom. Visitors from the EU, the United States, Canada, Australia and New Zealand do not need a visa or any inoculations or vaccinations.

When you arrive at one of Britain's airports or seaports, you will find separate lines at immigration control – one for European Union (EU) nationals, several others for everyone else.

European union has led to changes in UK Customs and immigration policy. Travelers entering the UK from outside the EU still have to pass through Customs channels: red exit routes for people carrying goods on which a duty has to be paid; green routes for those with no payment to make (nothing to "declare"). If, however, you are traveling from within the EU, you will find that these have been replaced by a blue channel – EU residents no longer have to "declare" goods. Random checks will still be made to guard against the likes of drug traffickers.

EU residents are no longer entitled to a VAT (value-added tax) refund on goods bought in the UK Travelers from outside the EU can obtain one if they leave the UK within three months of the purchase date *(see p310)*.

International Student Identity Card

STUDENT TRAVELERS

A N ISIC CARD (International Student Identity Card) entitles full-time students to discounts on things from travel to sports events. For US students, the ISIC also includes some medical coverage, though

this alone may not be sufficient. If you don't have an ISIC, it can be obtained (with proof of student status) from the **University of London Union** (ULU) or branches of **STA Travel**. ULU offers many social and sports facilities to valid union card holders and reciprocating educational establishments. **International Youth Hostel Federation** membership is also worth having for cheap accommodations in London.

EU nationals do not require a permit to work in the UK. Commonwealth citizens under 27 are allowed to do parttime work in the UK for up to two years. Visiting US students can get a blue card that enables them to work for up to six months (you must get this before you arrive). **BUNAC** is a student club organizing work-exchange schemes for students from Australia, the United States, Canada and Jamaica.

USEFUL ADDRESSES AND TELEPHONE NUMBERS

BUNAC
16 Bowling Green Lane EC1.
Map 6 E4. 📞 *0171-251 3472.*

International Youth Hostel Federation
📞 *01707-332 487.*

STA Travel
74 and 86 Old Brompton Rd SW7.
Map 18 F2. 📞 *0171-937 9962.*

Talking Pages
📞 *0800-600 900.*

University of London Union
Malet St WC1. **Map** 5 A5.
📞 *0171-580 9551.*

NEWSPAPERS, TELEVISION AND RADIO

L ONDON'S PRINCIPAL news-paper is the *Evening Standard*, available from about midday on Monday to Friday.

PUBLIC TOILETS

Although many older-style, supervised public conveniences still exist, these have largely been replaced by coin-operated "Superloos." Young children should never use these devices on their own – they will find it almost impossible to operate the inner door handle.

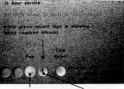

"Vacant" light   Coin slot

1 If the green "vacant" light is shown, insert the required fee. Enter when the door on your left slides open.

2 The door will slide closed behind you.

3 To exit, pull down the inner door handle.

London newspaper stand

The Friday edition is worth getting for its listings section and reviews. International newspapers are sold at many newsstands. The *International Herald Tribune* is available on the day it's issued; others may appear a day or more later. Four television channels can be seen with conventional receiving equipment: two run by the BBC (called BBC1 and BBC2) and two independent (ITV and Channel 4). Satellite and cable networks are both available in the UK, and some hotels have installed these facilities for their guests.

The BBC's local and national radio stations are supplemented by many independent local companies,

EMBASSIES AND CONSULATES

Australian High Commission
Australia House, The Strand
WC2. **Map** 13 C2.
(0171-379 4334.

Canadian High Commission
Haut Commissariat du Canada,
Macdonald House,1 Grosvenor
Square W1. **Map** 12 D2.
(0171-258 6600.

New Zealand High Commission
New Zealand House,
80 Haymarket SW1. **Map** 13 A3.
(0171-930 8422.

United States Embassy
24 Grosvenor Square W1.
Map 12 D2. (0171-499 9000.

like London's Capital Radio (194m/1548kHz MW; 95.8mHz FM), a pop music station.

INTERNATIONAL NEWSSTANDS

Gray's Inn News
50 Theobald's Rd WC1. **Map** 5 C5.
(0171-405 5241.

A. Moroni and Son
68 Old Compton St W1.
Map 13 A2. (0171-437 2847.

D. S. Radford
61 Fleet St EC4. **Map** 14 E1.
(0171-583 7166.

ELECTRICAL ADAPTERS

THE ELECTRICAL supply in London is 240V AC and plugs have three square pins. An adaptor plug and convertor are needed for other format appliances; these can be bought with you. Most hotels have two-pronged European-style sockets for shavers in the bathroom.

Standard British plug

LONDON TIME

DIAL 123 TO CHECK the time on London's 24-hour **Speaking Clock** service. Clocks change for summer and winter time.

CONVERSION CHART

OFFICIALLY THE metric system is used, but imperial measures are still common.

Imperial to metric
1 inch = 2.5 centimeters
1 foot = 30 centimeters
1 mile = 1.6 kilometers
1 ounce = 28 grams
1 pound = 454 grams
1 pint = 0.5 liter
1 US gallon = 3.8 liters
(1 UK gallon = 1.2 US gallon)

Metric to imperial
1 millimeter = 0.04 inch
1 centimeter = 0.4 inch
1 meter = 3 feet 3 inches
1 kilometer = 0.6 mile
1 kilogram = 2.2 pounds

RELIGIOUS SERVICES

THE FOLLOWING organizations can help you find a place to worship.

Baptist
London Baptist Association,
1 Merchant St E3.
(0181-980 6818.

Buddhist
The Buddhist Society,
58 Eccleston Sq SW1.
Map 20 F2. (0171-834 5858.

Church of England
St. Paul's Cathedral EC4.
Map 15 A2. (0171-248 2705.

Evangelical
Whitefield House, 186
Kennington Park Rd SE11.
Map 22 E4. (0171-582 0228.

Jewish
Liberal Jewish Synagogue,
28 St. John's Wood Rd NW8.
Map 3 A3. (0171-286 5181.
United Synagogue (Orthodox)
Woburn House, Tavistock Square
WC1. **Map** 5 B4.
(0171-387 4300.

Moslem
Islamic Cultural Centre,
146 Park Rd NW8. **Map** 3 B3.
(0171-724 3363.

Quakers
Religious Society of Friends,
173–7 Euston Rd NW1.
Map 5 A4. (0171-387 3601.

Roman Catholic
Westminster Cathedral,
Victoria St SW1. **Map** 20 F1.
(0171-834 7452.

**St. Martin-in-the-Fields,
Trafalgar Square** *(see p102)*

GETTING TO LONDON

LONDON IS ONE of Europe's central routing points for international air and sea travel. Air travelers face a bewildering choice of carriers serving North America, Europe and Australasia. Stiff competition on some routes means that low fares are occasionally introduced to attract new passengers. British Airways has a Concorde service boasting the fastest flights in the world between London and New York or Washington. Long-distance sea travel is, however, a different proposition because so few transatlantic liners now operate.

Concorde

Cunard currently offers the only regular service, which may soon change. There are efficient and regular ferry services from Europe, but these, too, will be subject to change once the Channel Tunnel opens. About 20 passenger and car ferry routes, served by large ferries, hovercrafts, jetfoils and catamarans, cross the North Sea and the English Channel to Britain. When it is eventually operating at full capacity, the Channel Tunnel will provide an efficient high-speed train link running between Europe and the United Kingdom.

AIR TRAVEL

THE MAIN US airlines offering scheduled flights to London include **Delta**, **United**, **American Airlines** and **USAir**. Two major British operators are **British Airways** and **Virgin Atlantic**. From Canada, the main carriers are **Canadian Airlines** (now incorporating WardAir) and **Air Canada**. Fierce competition for these prestigious transatlantic routes means that there are some excellent deals available. The flight time from New York is about six and a half hours (less on Concorde), and from Los Angeles about 10 hours.

There are regular scheduled flights to London from all the major European cities, as well as from numerous other parts of the UK itself, including northern England, Scotland and Northern Ireland.

The choice of carriers from Australasia is enormous. Well

Passenger jet landing at Heathrow

over 20 airlines share around two dozen different routes. Journey times can vary from just over 20 hours on a big modern jet to over 100 hours via China. The more indirect your route, the cheaper the fare; but remember that three days' jet travel is bound to be stressful. Qantas, Air New Zealand and British Airways may be your first thoughts for comfort and speed, but all the Far Eastern operators and several European airlines offer interesting alternatives.

Getting a good deal

Cheap deals are available from good travel agents and package operators and are advertised in newspapers and travel magazines. Airlines will quote you the regular price, but they often reduce this if seats are unsold. Students, senior citizens and regular or business travelers may well be able to obtain a discount. Children under two (who do not occupy a separate seat) pay 10% of the adult fare; older children up to 12 also travel at lower fares.

Ticket types

APEX (advanced purchase excursion) tickets can be good buys, but they must be reserved up to a month in advance, are subject to restrictions and cannot be changed without penalty.

There may be minimum (and maximum) stay requirements. Fares on scheduled flights are available through discount travel agencies at much lower rates. Charter flights offer even cheaper seats, are not restricted in terms of minimum and maximum stay but may require payment in full to reserve.

If you arrange a deal with a discount agency, check whether you will get a refund if the agency goes out of business, and don't pay the full fare until you see the ticket. You will have to pay a deposit. Check with the relevant airline to confirm your seat.

AIRLINE NUMBERS

Major Carriers

Air Canada
℆ 1-800-776-3000.

American Airlines
℆ 1-800-433-7300.

British Airways
℆ 1-800-Airways

Canadian Airlines
℆ 1-800-426-7000.

Delta
℆ 1-800-221-1212.

United
℆ 1-800-241-6522.

USAir
℆ 1-800-428-4322.

Virgin Atlantic
℆ 1-800-862-8621.

TRAVELING BY RAIL

L ONDON HAS EIGHT main train stations at which InterCity express trains terminate (for information, call 0171-928 5100). These are scattered in a ring around the city center *(see pp358–9)*. Paddington in west London serves the West Country, Wales and the South Midlands; Liverpool Street in the City covers East Anglia and Essex. In north London, Euston, St. Pancras and King's Cross serve northern and central Britain. In the south, Charing Cross, Victoria and Waterloo serve the whole of southern England and are also the termini for travel by ferry and train from Europe.

All these stations have had recent facelifts and are now smart and modern with many facilities for the traveler, such as bureaux de change and shops selling books and

Station concourse at Liverpool Street

BR information point *(see p345)*

candy. There are bars and cafés serving a range of refreshments, but, like the buffet service on some long-distance trains, these can be very expensive.

Information about British Rail (BR) services is now easy to find; most rail stations have an information point detailing times, prices and destinations.

In addition, constantly updated details of services are either screened on monitors found throughout the stations or written up on information boards located at platform entrances. BR staff are usually helpful and courteous.

If your ferry ticket does not include the price of rail travel to the center of London, tickets can be bought at the clearly signposted ticket offices or automatic machines *(see p366)*. You may decide to buy a Travelcard from the first day you are in London *(see p360)*.

COACH SERVICES

T HE MAIN COACH (bus) station in London is on Buckingham Palace Road (about 10 minutes' walk from Victoria railroad station). You can travel to London by coach from many European cities, but the majority of services traveling through London are from within the UK National Express run to about 1,000 British destinations, but other companies depart from this station, too. Coach travel is cheaper than the railroad, but journeys are longer and arrival times can be unpredictable if there are problems on the roads. National Express Rapide coaches can be very comfortable and normally have sophisticated facilities. Green Line buses operate within 40 miles (64 km) of London.
Coach numbers Green Line [0181-668 7261; Rapide [0171-730 0202.

CROSSING THE CHANNEL BY SEA

Britain's sea links with Europe were finally joined by a landlink in late 1994 when the Channel Tunnel opened. At present, a network of ferry services operates between 13 British ports and over 20 Continental ports. Many of the vessels on these routes have recently been refurbished. The ferry services presently offered may change, depending on the impact of the tunnel. Ferry crossings from the Continent are operated by **Sealink Stena**, **P&O European Ferries**, **Sally Line**, the **Olau Line** and **Brittany Ferries**. Fast hovercraft services between Dover and Calais or Boulogne are run by **Hoverspeed**. A **Seacat** service crosses between Folkestone and Boulogne *(see pp358–9)*. From 1995 another will operate between Newhaven and Dieppe. The shortest crossings are not necessarily the cheapest –

Cross-channel ferry

you pay for both the speed of your journey and the convenience. If you are traveling with your car, check your insurance coverage.
Useful numbers Brittany Ferries [01705 827701; Hoverspeed [01304 240241; Olau Line [01795 666666; P&O European Ferries [0181-575 8555; Sally Line [01843 595522; Seacat [01304 240241; Sealink Stenna [01233 647047.

London's Airports

Passenger jet

Lᴏɴᴅᴏɴ's ᴛᴡᴏ ᴍᴀɪɴ airports, Heathrow and Gatwick, are supported by Luton, Stansted and London City airport *(see pp358–9)*. Heathrow and Gatwick are both well connected with the city center and have a range of facilities – from banks and bureaux de change to hotels, shops and restaurants. Find out which airport you'll be landing at so you can plan the last stages of your journey.

Customs channels at Heathrow

Hᴇᴀᴛʜʀᴏᴡ (LHR)

Hᴇᴀᴛʜʀᴏᴡ ɪɴ ᴡᴇsᴛ London (airport information 0181-759 4321) is the world's busiest international airport. Mainly, scheduled long-haul aircraft land there, and a fifth terminal is being planned to cope with the rising levels of air traffic to the UK. Money exchanging facilities are also found in all terminals.

All of the four terminals are linked to the Underground system by a variety of moving walkways, passageways and elevators. Follow the clearly marked directions posted throughout the terminals and

you can't go wrong. London Underground runs a regular service on the Piccadilly line. The tube journey into central London normally takes about 40 minutes (add 10 minutes more from terminal 4).

Regular Airbus services travel from Heathrow into the

Signs for exits in Heathrow

center of London. Services stop outside each terminal. The Airbus costs more than the Underground, but it involves less struggling with luggage. A taxi ride into central London takes about 45 minutes and costs about £25.

Aɪʀᴘᴏʀᴛ Hᴏᴛᴇʟs

Forte Crest
℄ *0181-759 2323.*

Holiday Inn
℄ *01895-445555.*

Sheraton Skyline
See p285.

London Heathrow Hilton
℄ *0181-759 7755.*

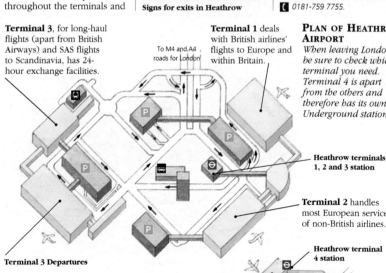

Terminal 3, for long-haul flights (apart from British Airways) and SAS flights to Scandinavia, has 24-hour exchange facilities.

To M4 and A4 roads for London

Terminal 1 deals with British airlines' flights to Europe and within Britain.

Terminal 3 Departures

Heathrow terminals 1, 2 and 3 station

Terminal 2 handles most European services of non-British airlines.

Heathrow terminal 4 station

A30 road

Sterling Hotel

Terminal 4 serves Concorde; British Airways intercontinental flights; and some flights to Paris, Athens and Amsterdam.

Pʟᴀɴ ᴏꜰ Hᴇᴀᴛʜʀᴏᴡ Aɪʀᴘᴏʀᴛ
When leaving London, be sure to check which terminal you need. Terminal 4 is apart from the others and therefore has its own Underground station.

Kᴇʏ

Ⓔ Underground station
🚌 Bus terminal (local services)
🚍 Coach station
🅿 Shortterm parking
⇒ Direction of traffic flow

GATWICK (LGW)

GATWICK AIRPORT (airport information 01293-535 353) is located south of London, on the Surrey–Sussex border. Unlike Heathrow, it handles scheduled and charter flights.

A large volume of package holiday traffic passes through Gatwick. This can cause long lines at immigration desks and security checks, so make sure to leave plenty of time in which to check in on your return journey if you want to avoid being rushed. Make

PLAN OF GATWICK AIRPORT

There are two terminals at Gatwick: north and south. They are linked by a free monorail service, and the journey between them takes only a couple of minutes. Near the British Rail station entrance (which, if you are not arriving by rail, is clearly marked) you will find boards that state which terminal serves your carrier.

Gatwick Express

Trains to London
Services to Victoria Station every
15 minutes; hourly throughout the night

Platform indicator for express railway service to London

certain, too, that you know which terminal your flight home leaves from.

Gatwick has fewer business facilities than Heathrow. On the positive side, however, it has a number of 24-hour restaurants, banks, exchange

KEY

🚆	British Rail station
🚌	Coach station
P	Shortterm parking
🚓	Police station
⇉	Direction of traffic flow

facilities and duty-free shops located in both the north and the south terminals.

Gatwick has convenient rail links with the capital, including BR's Thameslink. The Gatwick Express train provides a fast, regular service into Victoria station. Allow about half an hour for the journey, but check *(see p366)* to find off-peak variations.

Driving from Gatwick to central London can take a couple of hours. A taxi will cost from £50 to £60.

AIRPORT HOTELS

Chequers Thistle
(01293-786992.

Forte Crest
(01293-567070.

Hilton International
(01293-518080.

To A23 and M23 roads for London

Hilton International

Railway line

A23 road

Inter-terminal monorail link

To A23 and M23 roads for London

Forte Crest Hotel

P

Taxi stand

Arrivals pickup (lower level)

Coach station and arrivals pick-up (lower level)

North terminal

South terminal

OTHER AIRPORTS SERVING LONDON

Luton and Stansted airports, both located to the north of London, are at present used principally by charter flights. Both airports have future plans for expansion. From Luton, connecting buses take passengers to the railroad station, and from there trains run to King's Cross station. Alternatively, take a coach to Victoria. The half-hourly Stansted Express train terminates at Liverpool Street station, and there is a regular and efficient coach service to Victoria.

The relatively new London City Airport, in Docklands, is designed mainly for business travelers and operates short flights to Europe. It has particularly good business facilities and is only a short taxi (or helicopter) journey from the City.

One of two large hotels at Gatwick

Arriving in London

THIS MAP SHOWS the bus, rail and Underground
links between London's airports and its mainline
railroad stations. It also shows not only rail
connections between these stations and
the southeastern seaports but also those
linking London with the rest of the UK
Travel information, including journey
times for rail, bus and coach services,
is listed in each information box.
Details of how to reach London by car
from the seaports is also given.

KEY

✈ Airport see pp356–7

⚓ Seaport see p355

🚆 British Rail see p366

🚌 Coach link see p355

🚍 Bus service see pp364–5

🔵 Underground link see pp362–3

── British Rail link see p355

── British Rail Thameslink
see p366

── Piccadilly line see p356

── Bus link see p355

N

0 kilometers   1

0 miles   0.5

🚆 **East Midlands**
Links with St. Pancras station.
Leicester (1 hr 10 mins),
Nottingham (1 hr 45 mins),
Sheffield (2 hrs 20 mins).

🚆 **West Midlands, the North
West and West Scotland**
Links with Euston station.
Birmingham (1 hr 40 mins),
Glasgow (5 hrs),
Liverpool (2 hrs 40mins),
Manchester (2 hrs 30 mins).

🚆 **The West and South Wales**
Links with Paddington station.
Bristol (1 hr 45 mins), **Cardiff**
(2 hrs), **Oxford** (55 mins),
Plymouth (3 hrs 30 mins).

✈ **HEATHROW**
Underground service to the city
center every 5 minutes. Bus services
to the city center.
🔵 **Piccadilly line** through city
center (40 mins).
🚍 **Airbus** A1 to **Victoria** (1 hr).
🚍 **Airbus** A2 to **Russell Sq** (1 hr).

🚆 **The South**
Links with Waterloo station.
Winchester (1 hr 5 mins).

⚓ **SOUTHAMPTON**
Ferry links with **Cherbourg**.
Take M3 motorway for
the city center.

⚓ **PORTSMOUTH**
Ferry links with **Caen**, **St. Malo**,
Le Havre and **Cherbourg**.
Take A3 trunk road for the
city center.

*Regent's Park
and
Marylebone*

Euston 🚆

Soho
and Trafalg
Square

Paddington 🚆 🔵

Piccadilly Circus 🔵

*Kensington
and
Holland Park*

*South
Kensington
and
Knightsbridge*

Piccadilly
and St.
James's

Victoria 🚆

Chelsea

Victoria Coach Station

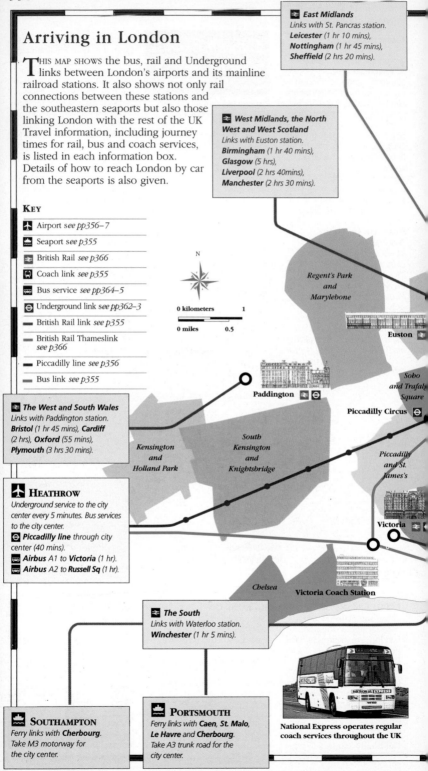

**National Express operates regular
coach services throughout the UK**

The North East and Scotland
Links with King's Cross station.
Aberdeen (7 hrs), **Durham**
(3 hrs), **Edinburgh** (4 hrs 30 mins),
Leeds (2 hrs 30 mins),
York (2 hrs).

STANSTED
Bus and train services to the city
center every 30 mins. Underground from **Tottenham Hale**.
to **Liverpool Street** (45 mins).
National Express to Victoria
(1 hr 25 mins).

LUTON
Direct bus services. Train services
from **Luton town** to the center of
London every 15–30 mins. Bus
services to **Luton railway
station**.
to **King's Cross** (30 mins).
Greenline to Victoria
(1 hr 15 mins).

Tottenham
Hale

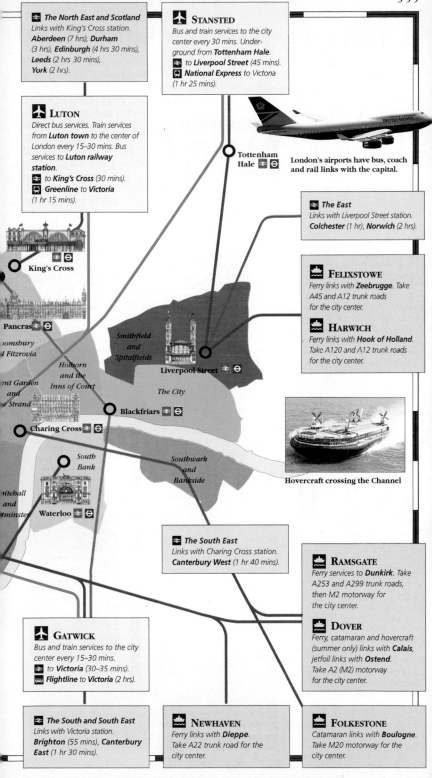

London's airports have bus, coach
and rail links with the capital.

The East
Links with Liverpool Street station.
Colchester (1 hr), **Norwich** (2 hrs).

King's Cross

FELIXSTOWE
Ferry links with **Zeebrugge**. Take
A45 and A12 trunk roads
for the city center.

Pancras

Bloomsbury
and Fitzrovia

Smithfield
and
Spitalfields

HARWICH
Ferry links with **Hook of Holland**.
Take A120 and A12 trunk roads
for the city center.

Holborn
and the
Inns of Court

Covent Garden
and
the Strand

Liverpool Street

The City

Blackfriars

Charing Cross

South
Bank

Southwark
and
Bankside

Hovercraft crossing the Channel

Whitehall
and
Westminster

Waterloo

The South East
Links with Charing Cross station.
Canterbury West (1 hr 40 mins).

RAMSGATE
Ferry services to **Dunkirk**. Take
A253 and A299 trunk roads,
then M2 motorway for
the city center.

DOVER
Ferry, catamaran and hovercraft
(summer only) links with **Calais**,
jetfoil links with **Ostend**.
Take A2 (M2) motorway
for the city center.

GATWICK
Bus and train services to the city
center every 15–30 mins.
to **Victoria** (30–35 mins).
Flightline to **Victoria** (2 hrs).

The South and South East
Links with Victoria station.
Brighton (55 mins), **Canterbury
East** (1 hr 30 mins).

NEWHAVEN
Ferry links with **Dieppe**.
Take A22 trunk road for the
city center.

FOLKESTONE
Catamaran links with **Boulogne**.
Take M20 motorway for the
city center.

GETTING AROUND LONDON

ONDON'S PUBLIC TRANSPORTATION system must be one of the busiest and largest in Europe, and it has all the overcrowding problems to match. The worst and busiest times to travel are in the two rush hours, between 8 and 9:30am or later, and from 4:30 to 6:30pm. Within London and its suburbs, most of the public transportation is provided by London Regional Transport (LRT). This consists of various types of buses, the

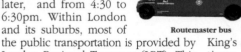

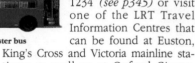

Routemaster bus

Underground system and Network SouthEast (an overland train system that is operated by British Rail). For any information you require about fares, routes and timings of the various transportation services, phone 0171-222 1234 *(see p345)* or visit one of the LRT Travel Information Centres that can be found at Euston, King's Cross and Victoria mainline stations as well as at Oxford Circus, Piccadilly Circus and Heathrow Airport.

PUBLIC TRANSPORTATION

THE UNDERGROUND (the "tube") is usually by far the quickest way of traveling around London. Services are, however, prone to delays, and the trains are often crowded. Changing lines may involve a longish walk at some stations.

London is so large that some sights are a long way, even a bus journey, from any Underground station. There are also areas, often in the south, with no Underground service. Bus travel can be slow, so walking may be quicker.

Photocard and Weekly Travelcard

TRAVELCARDS

PUBLIC TRANSPORTATION in London is expensive compared with that of many cities in Europe because government subsidies are low and distances are great. Short trips are relatively more expensive than the longer journeys; it is rarely worthwhile taking the tube to travel just one stop.

By far the most economical tickets are Travelcards – daily, weekly or monthly passes that allow unlimited travel on all forms of transportation in

the zones you require. (Six bands, called travel zones, extend into the outer suburbs; most of London's main sights are located in zone one.)

Travelcards can be bought in train or Underground stations *(see p362)* and at newsstands displaying a red "pass agent" sign. For weekly and monthly tickets, you need

a passport-sized photo for a Photocard. One-day Travelcards cannot be used before 9:30am from Monday to Friday. There are no restrictions on when you can use your weekly or monthly Travelcards. If you are in London for four days or more, a one- or two-zone weekly Travelcard is probably the most suitable pass.

LONDON ON FOOT

Once you get used to traffic driving on the left, London can be safely explored on foot – but take care when crossing the street. There are two types of pedestrian crossing in London: striped zebra crossings marked by beacons and push-button crossings at traffic lights. Traffic should stop for you if you are waiting at a zebra crossing, but at push-button crossings cars will not stop until the green man lights up. Watch for instructions written on the pavement: these tell you from which direction you can expect the traffic to come.

Beacons mark London's older-style zebra crossings.

Pushing the button makes the red man, located on a pillar across the road, turn into a green man.

Zebra crossing

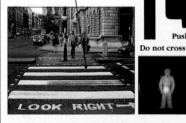

Push-button control

Do not cross   Cross the road

Driving a Car in London

Sign for a car park

MOST VISITORS ARE better off not driving in central London. Traffic moves at an average speed of about 11 mph (18 km/h) during the rush hour, and parking is hard to find. Many Londoners only take their cars out on weekends and after 6:30pm on weekdays, when you are allowed to park in some single yellow-line areas and at parking meters free of charge. Remember, you must drive on the left.

Double yellow lines on road, meaning no parking at any time

PARKING REGULATIONS

Parking meter

PARKING IN London is scarce, and you should read carefully any restrictions (usually posted on lampposts). Meters close to the center are expensive during working hours (usually 8:00am–6:30pm Mon–Sat). You will also need plenty of coins *(see p349)* to feed them. Two hours is usually the maximum time you can stay at any meter. National Car Parks (marked with the logo NCP) are available in central areas and are easy to find. NCP produces a free London Parking Guide showing its parks; write to 21 Bryanston Street, W1A 4NH, or call 0171-499 7050.

You are not allowed to park along red routes or on double yellow lines at any time. Parking on single yellow lines is prohibited during working hours, but you can park on them during the evening or on Sundays provided you are not causing an obstruction. Resident permit zones are unenforceable outside office hours, but remove your car before 8am. Steer clear of any parking areas marked "Card-holders Only." Parking on pedestrian crossings is always forbidden. In "Pay-and-Display" areas, you should buy a ticket for the appropriate time span to display on your windshield.

slapped across your windshield will inform you which Payment Centre you need to visit to get your car released (after paying a hefty fine). If you can't find your car at all, it is quite likely to have been removed by a team of London's feared and hated car impounders. Their speed and efficiency are remarkable, the cost and inconvenience to drivers enormous: it is rarely worth taking the risk. The main car pounds are at Hyde Park, Kensington and Camden Town. Call 0171-747 7474 and you will be told if they do have your car and where it is being held.

TRAFFIC SIGNS

Every driver should read the UK Highway Code *manual (available from bookshops) and familiarize themselves with London's traffic signs.*

No stopping

30 mph (48 km/h) speed limit

No entry

GIVE WAY
Yield to all vehicles

One-way traffic

No right turn allowed

CLAMPING AND TOWING

IF YOU PARK illegally or allow a meter to run out, you may well find your car has been clamped. A large notice

Illegally parked car immobilized by wheel clamp

CAR RENTAL AGENCIES

Avis
(0171-917 6700.

Eurodollar
(0171-278 2273.

Europcar
(0171-387 2276.

Hertz
(0171-278 1588.

BICYCLING AROUND LONDON

London's roads can be quite hazardous for bicyclists, but the parks and quieter districts make excellent cycling routes. Use a solid lock to deter thieves and wear weatherproof reflective clothing. Cycle helmets are not compulsory but are strongly recommended. Bikes can be rented from **On Your Bike** and **Portobello Cycles**. **Rental shop numbers and addresses** On Your Bike, 52–54 Tooley St SE1. (0171-357 6958. Portobello Cycles, 69 Golborne Rd W10. (0181-960 0444.

Traveling by Underground

BAKER STREET

Underground sign outside a station

THE UNDERGROUND system, or subway, known as the "tube" to Londoners, has 273 stations, each clearly marked with the Underground logo. Tube trains run every day, except Christmas Day, from about 5:30am until just after midnight, but a few lines or sections of lines provide a more irregular service. Check when the last train leaves if you are relying on it after 11:30pm. Fewer trains run on Sundays. It can occasionally be unpleasant traveling on the tube late at night.

London Underground train

Reading the Underground Map

The 11 Underground lines are color-coded, and maps (see inside cover) called Journey Planners are posted at every station. Maps of the central section are displayed in the trains. The map shows how to change lines to travel from where you are to any station on the Underground system. Some lines, such as the Victoria and Jubilee, are simple single-branch routes; others, such as the Northern line, have more than one branch. The Circle line is a continuous loop around central London. Distances shown on the map are not to scale, and the routes that lines are seen to take should not be relied on for directions.

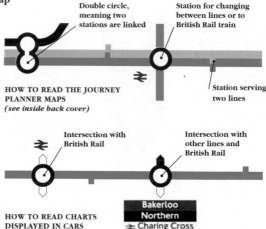

Double circle, meaning two stations are linked

Station for changing between lines or to British Rail train

HOW TO READ THE JOURNEY PLANNER MAPS
(see inside back cover)

Station serving two lines

Intersection with British Rail

Intersection with other lines and British Rail

HOW TO READ CHARTS DISPLAYED IN CARS

Bakerloo
Northern
⇌ Charing Cross

BUYING A TICKET

If you are likely to be making more than two journeys a day on London's Underground, the best ticket to buy is a Travelcard *(see p360)*. You can also buy single tickets or return tickets either from the ticket office in each station or from one of the two types of automatic machines that are found in most stations. The large machines *(see below)* take coins and £5 or £10 notes and normally give

change. You select the ticket type you need and then the station you are traveling to, and the cost of the fare is automatically displayed. The smaller machines show a choice of fare prices from which you select the correct one for your journey. They do not take notes, seldom give change and are geared toward regular travelers who know the cost of their journey in advance.

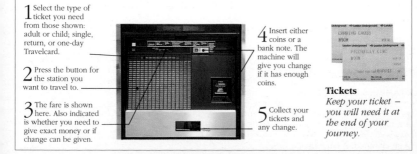

1 Select the type of ticket you need from those shown: adult or child; single, return, or one-day Travelcard.

2 Press the button for the station you want to travel to.

3 The fare is shown here. Also indicated is whether you need to give exact money or if change can be given.

4 Insert either coins or a bank note. The machine will give you change if it has enough coins.

5 Collect your tickets and any change.

Tickets
Keep your ticket – you will need it at the end of your journey.

MAKING A JOURNEY BY UNDERGROUND

1 When you first enter the station, check which line, or lines, you will need to take. If you have any difficulty planning your route, ask the clerk at the ticket office for help.

⊖ **Journey planner**

Feed your ticket or Travelcard into the slot found at the front of the machine.

As soon as your ticket emerges, withdraw it and the gate will open.

2 Buy your ticket or Travelcard from one of the automatic machines *(see facing page)* or the ticket office located in each station. If you wish to make a return journey by Underground, you will normally be given one ticket that you must keep until you have completed both journeys.

TRAVELCARD Z123456
OFF PEAK Z123456

TRAVELCARD Z123456
OFF PEAK Z123456

3 The platforms are on the other side of the ticket barriers. These are easy to use if you follow the correct procedure.

Central line →

4 Follow the directions to the line on which you need to travel. In some cases this can be a complicated route, so keep your eyes open.

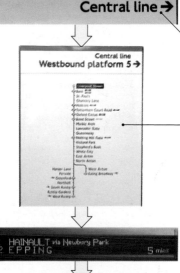
Central line
Westbound platform 5 →

Liverpool Street
Bank
St. Paul's
Chancery Lane
Holborn
Tottenham Court Road
Oxford Circus
Bond Street
Marble Arch
Lancaster Gate
Queensway
Notting Hill Gate
Holland Park
Shepherd's Bush
White City
East Acton
North Acton
Hanger Lane   West Acton
Perivale   Ealing Broadway
Greenford
Northolt
South Ruislip
Ruislip Gardens
West Ruislip

5 You will eventually find yourself with a choice of platforms for the line you want. Look at the list of stations if you are not sure which direction to take.

The ticket office is near the ticket barriers in most stations.

6 Most platforms now have electronic indicators displaying the destination of the next two or three trains and the length of time that you will have to wait before they arrive.

1 HAINAULT via Newbury Park
2 EPPING   5 mins

On some trains, you must push a button to open the carriage doors.

7 Once you have boarded the train and begun your journey, you can check on your progress using the line chart displayed in every carriage. As you pull into each station, you will see its name posted along the length of the walls.

Way out →
⇌ British Rail

Hammersmith & City →
Metropolitan and Circle lines

8 After leaving the train, look for signs giving directions to exits or to platforms for any connecting lines.

London's Buses

LONDON BUSES

London Regional Transport symbol

ONE OF LONDON'S most recognizable symbols is the old-fashioned red double-decker Routemaster bus, but it is a less common sight today than it once was. As a result of deregulation and privatization of the city's bus system, there are now many smaller modern buses, some single-decker and some not even red, carrying passengers on London's streets. If you are able to get a seat, a bus journey is an undemanding and enjoyable way of seeing London. If you are in a hurry, however, it can be frustrating. London's traffic is notoriously congested and slow-moving, and bus journeys can take a long time, especially during rush hours (8–9:30am and 4:30–6:30pm).

FINDING THE RIGHT BUS

EACH BUS STOP in central London has a list of main destinations showing the bus routes. There may also be a local street plan with each nearby bus stop letter-coded. Make sure you catch a bus going in the right direction; if in doubt, check with the bus conductor or driver.

USING LONDON'S BUSES

BUSES PAUSE, even if nobody wants to get on or off, at stops marked with the LRT symbol (*see above*), unless they are labeled "request" stops. Route numbers and destinations are displayed clearly on the front and rear of the buses. The newer buses have only a driver, who takes fares as passengers board. Routemaster services have both a driver and a conductor who collects fares during the journey. The driver or conductor will tell you the fare for your destination and give change (but not for large notes). You will be given a ticket valid only for that journey – if you change buses you have to pay again. Keep your ticket until the end of your journey

in case an inspector boards. Buying a Travelcard (*see p360*) is more convenient, especially if you are making several journeys.

When you want to get off the bus, ring the bell as the bus approaches the stop you require; on Routemasters the conductor will do this for you. Never get on or off a bus unless it is standing at a bus stop. If you are not sure which stop you need, ask the conductor or driver.

Bus Conductor
Conductors sell tickets on London's Routemaster buses.

Bus Stops
Buses always pause at stops marked with the LRT symbol (far left). At request stops (below), hail the driver by raising your arm. In practice it pays to do this at any stop.

Tickets on Routemasters
The conductor will issue you the right ticket for your journey. Try not to pay with a large note.

USEFUL BUS ROUTES
Several of London's bus routes are convenient for many of the capital's main sights and shops. If you arm yourself with a Travelcard and are in no particular hurry, sightseeing or shopping by bus can be great fun. The cost of a journey by public transportation is far less than any of the charges levied by tour operators, but you won't have the commentary that tour companies give you as you pass sights (*see p344*).

There are also some sights or areas in London that are inaccessible by Underground. Buses run regularly from the city center to, for instance, the Albert Hall (*see p203*), Chelsea (*see pp188–93*) and Clerkenwell (*see p243*).

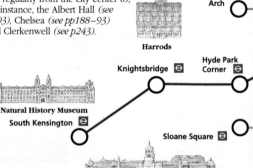

To stop the bus, press the bell located by the doors or near the stairs, just once.

Destinations are shown on the front and rear of buses.

To buy a ticket, have your money ready before you board.

Routemaster Bus
Board these buses at the rear. The conductor asks for your fare after you have boarded and found a seat.

Night Buses
These services run through the night from stops with this logo. One-day Travelcards are not valid on them.

New-Style Bus
These buses are controlled by the driver and do not have a conductor. The driver collects fares as passengers board.

NIGHT BUSES

LONDON'S NIGHTTIME services run on several popular routes from 11pm until 6am. The routes are prefixed with the letter *N* before blue or yellow numbers. All these services pass through Trafalgar Square, so if you are out late, head there to get a ride at least part of the way home. Be sure to plan your journey carefully; London is so big that even if you board a bus going in the right direction, you could end up completely lost or a long walk from your accommodations. As always, make sure that you employ a little common sense when traveling on a night bus. Sitting all alone on the top deck is not a good idea; night buses never have a conductor. Travel information centers can supply you with details of routes and time-tables for night buses, which are also posted at bus stops.

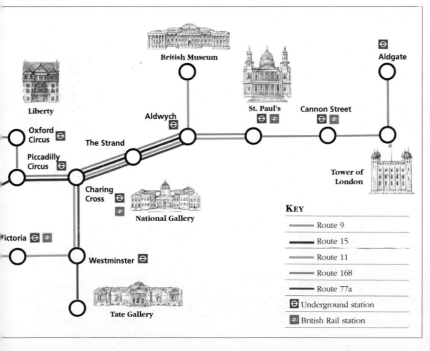

Seeing London by British Rail

British Rail station sign

BRITISH RAIL'S train service is used by many hundreds of thousands of commuters each day. As far as visitors to London are concerned, BR services are useful for trips to the outskirts of the capital, especially south of the river, where the Underground hardly extends. You may also decide to take a train for much longer excursions around Britain *(see pp358–9).*

USEFUL ROUTES

PERHAPS THE MOST useful BR line for visitors to London is the one that starts off from Charing Cross or Cannon Street station (services from here only run on weekdays) and goes via London Bridge to Greenwich *(see pp232–9).*

The Thameslink service also connects Luton Airport with south London, Gatwick Airport and Brighton via West Hampstead and Blackfriars.

USING THE TRAINS

LONDON HAS EIGHT main railroad stations serving the whole of the southeast and beyond *(see pp358–9).* BR services travel overground and vary between slow stopping trains, express services to major towns and Intercity trains that travel throughout the UK. Make sure you study the platform indicators carefully so that you get on the most direct train to the correct destination.

Some train doors will open automatically, others at the touch of a button or by means of a handle. To open the older-style manual doors from inside, you need to pull down the window and reach outside. Keep well away from the doors while the train is traveling, and if you have to stand, make sure you hold on firmly to a strap or hand rail.

BR TICKETS

All tickets must be bought in person, either from a travel agent or from a BR station. Most credit cards are accepted. Lines for ticket offices can often be long, so use the automatic machines that operate similarly to those on the Underground *(see p362).*

A bewildering range of train tickets exists, but two main options stand out: for travel within Greater London, Travelcards *(see p360)* offer the most flexibility, while for longer journeys, Cheap Day Return tickets offer excellent value compared to the standard return fares. However, these are both obtainable and usable only after 9:30am.

Cheap Day Return tickets

DAY TRIPS

Southeast England has a lot more besides the capital to offer visitors. Getting out of London is fast and very easy with British Rail. For details of sights, call the English Tourist Board *(see p345).* BR Passenger Enquiries (0171-928 5100) will give you details of all their services.

Boating on the River Thames at Windsor Castle

Audley End
Village with a stunning Jacobean mansion nearby.
≥ *from Liverpool Street. 40 miles (64 km); 1 hr.*

Bath
Beautiful Georgian city that has escaped redevelopment. It also has Roman remains.
≥ *from Paddington. 107 miles (172 km); 1 hr 25 mins.*

Brighton
Lively and attractive seaside resort. See the Royal Pavilion.
≥ *from Victoria. 53 miles (85 km); 1 hr.*

Cambridge
University city with fine art gallery and ancient colleges.
≥ *from Liverpool Street or King's Cross. 54 miles (86 km); 1 hr.*

Canterbury
Its cathedral is one of England's oldest and greatest sights.
≥ *from Victoria. 84 miles (98 km); 1 hr 25 mins.*

Hatfield House
Elizabethan palace with remarkable contents.
≥ *from King's Cross or Moorgate. 21 miles (33 km); 20 mins.*

Oxford
Like Cambridge, famous for its ancient university.
≥ *from Paddington. 56 miles (86 km); 1 hr.*

Salisbury
Famous for its cathedral, Salisbury is within driving distance of Stonehenge.
≥ *from Waterloo. 84 miles (135 km); 1 hr 40 mins.*

St. Albans
Once a great Roman city.
≥ *from King's Cross or Moorgate. 25 miles (40 km); 30 mins.*

Windsor
Riverside town; royal castle damaged by fire in 1992.
≥ *from Paddington, change Slough. 20 miles (32 km); 30 mins.*

Getting a Taxi

LONDON'S WELL-KNOWN black cabs are almost as much of an institution as its red buses. But they, too, are being modernized, and you may well see blue, green, red or even white cabs, with some carrying advertising. Black-cab drivers have to take a stringent test on their knowledge of London's streets and its quickest traffic routes before they are awarded a license. Contrary to popular opinion, they are also among London's safest drivers, if only because they are forbidden to drive a cab with damaged bodywork.

The modern colors of traditional London cabs

London taxi rank

FINDING A CAB

LICENSED CABS MUST carry a "For Hire" sign that is lit up whenever they are free. You can phone for them; hail them on the streets; or find them gathered in "ranks" (stands), especially near large stations and major hotels. Raise your arm and wave purposefully. The cab will stop, and you simply tell the driver your destination. If a cab stops, it must take you anywhere within a radius of 6 miles (9.6 km) as long as it is in the Metropolitan Police district, which includes most of the Greater London area and Heathrow Airport.

An alternative to black cabs are minicabs, sedans summoned by calling a firm or going into one of their offices, which are usually open 24 hours a day. Do not take a minicab in the street since they often operate illegally, without proper insurance. Negotiate your fare before setting off. Minicab firms are listed in the Yellow Pages *(see p352)*.

TAXI FARES

ALL LICENSED CABS have meters that will start ticking at around £1 as soon as the driver accepts your request. The fare increases by minute or for each 340 yds (311 m) traveled. Surcharges are then added for pieces of luggage; extra passengers; and off-hours, such as late at night. Fares should be on display.

USEFUL NUMBERS

Computer Cabs (licensed)
(0171-286 0286.

Radio Taxis (licensed)
(0171-272 0272.

Ladycabs
(0171-254 3501.

My Fare Lady
(0181-458 9200.

Lost property
(0171-833 0996.
Open 9am–4pm Mon–Fri.

Complaints
(0171-230 1631
You will need to know the cab's serial number.

The light, when lit, shows the cab is available and whether there is wheelchair access.

The meter displays your fare as it increases, plus surcharges for extra passengers, luggage or off-hours. Fares are the same in all licensed cabs.

Fare / Surcharges /

Licensed Cabs
London's cabs are a safe way of traveling around the capital. They have two fold-down seats, can carry a maximum of five passengers and have ample luggage space.

STREET FINDER

THE MAP REFERENCES given with all sights, hotels, restaurants, shops and entertainment venues described in this book refer to the maps in this section *(see* How the Map References Work, *opposite).* A complete index of street names and all the places of interest marked on the maps can be found on the following pages.

The key map shows the area of London covered by the *Street Finder,* with the postal codes of all the various districts. The maps include the sightseeing areas (which are color-coded), as well as the whole of central London with all the districts important for hotels, restaurants, pubs and entertainment venues.

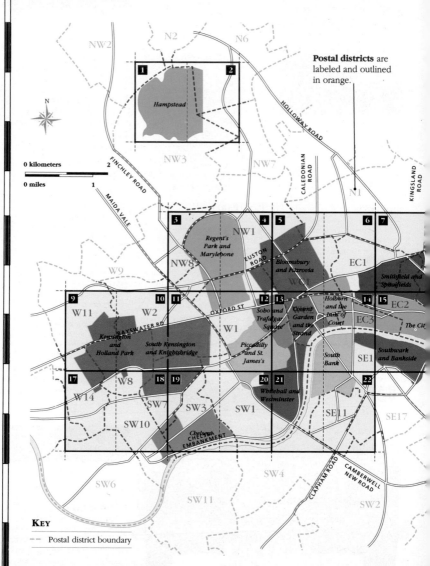

Postal districts are labeled and outlined in orange.

KEY

- - - Postal district boundary

How the Map References Work

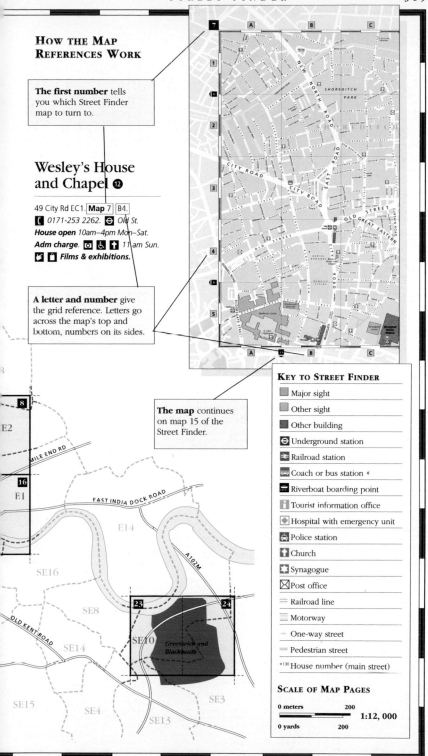

The first number tells you which Street Finder map to turn to.

Wesley's House and Chapel ⓬

49 City Rd EC1. **Map** 7 B4.
☎ 0171-253 2262. ⊖ Old St.
House open 10am–4pm Mon–Sat.
Adm charge. ◎ ⬥ ✝ 11 am Sun.
▮ ▯ **Films & exhibitions.**

A letter and number give the grid reference. Letters go across the map's top and bottom, numbers on its sides.

The map continues on map 15 of the Street Finder.

KEY TO STREET FINDER

▮ Major sight
▮ Other sight
▮ Other building
⊖ Underground station
⊕ Railroad station
▭ Coach or bus station *
▭ Riverboat boarding point
ℹ Tourist information office
✚ Hospital with emergency unit
▭ Police station
✝ Church
✡ Synagogue
⊠ Post office
= Railroad line
▬ Motorway
– One-way street
– Pedestrian street
*130 House number (main street)

SCALE OF MAP PAGES

0 meters	200
0 yards	200

1:12, 000

Street Finder Index

Each place name is followed by its postal district and then by its Street Finder reference.

Each place name is followed by its postal district and then by its Street Finder reference.

Each place name is followed by its postal district and then by its Street Finder reference.

Upper Terr NW3 1 A4
Upper Belgrave Street SW1 20 E1
Upper Berkeley St W1 11 C1
Upper Brook St W1 12 D2
Upper Cheyne Row SW3 19 B4
Upper Grosvenor St W1 12 D3
Upper Ground SE1 14 E3
Upper Marsh SE1 14 D5
Upper Montagu St W1 3 C5
Upper Phillimore Gdns W8 9 C5
Upper St. Martin's La WC2 13 B2
Upper Thames St EC4 15 A2
Upper Wimpole St W1 4 D5
Upper Woburn Pl WC1 5 B4
US Embassy W1 12 D2
Uxbridge St W8 9 C3

V

Vale,The SW3 19 A4
Vale of Health NW3 1 B3
Valentine Pl SE1 14 F5
Vallance Rd E1,E2 8 F4
Vanbrugh Fields SE3 24 E3
Vanbrugh Hill SE3 24 E2
Vanbrugh Hill SE10 24 E1
Vanbrugh Pk SE3 24 E3
Vanbrugh Pk Rd SE3 24 F3
Vanbrugh Pk Rd West SE3 24 E3
Vanbrugh Terr SE3 24 F4
Vane Clo NW3 1 B5
Vanston Pl SW6 17 C5
Varndell St NW1 4 F3
Vassall Rd SW9 22 E5
Vaughan Way E1 16 F3
Vauxhall Bridge SW1 21 B3
Vauxhall Bridge Rd SW1, SE1 20 F1 / 21 A2
Vauxhall Gro SW8 21 C4
Vauxhall Park SW8 21 C4
Vauxhall St SE11 22 D3
Vauxhall Wlk SE11 21 C3
Vere St W1 12 E1
Vereker Rd W14 17 A3
Vernon Rise WC1 6 D3
Vernon St W14 17 A2
Vestry St N1 7 B3
Vicarage Gate W8 10 D4
Victoria & Albert Museum SW7 19 A1
Victoria Embankment EC4 14 E2
Victoria Embankment SW1 13 C4
Victoria Embankment WC2 13 C3
Victoria Embankment Gdns WC2 13 C3
Victoria Gro W8 18 E1
Victoria Rd W8 10 E5 / 18 E1
Victoria St SW1 13 B5 / 20 F1 / 21 A1
Victoria Tower Gardens SW1 21 C1
Villiers St WC2 13 C3
Vince St EC1 7 C3
Vincent Sq SW1 21 A2
Vincent St SW1 21 A2
Vincent Terr N1 6 F2
Vine La SE1 16 D4
Vine St EC3 16 D2
Vintner's Pl EC4 15 A2
Virginia Rd E2 8 D3
Voss St E2 8 F3

W

Wakefield St WC1 5 C4
Wakley St EC1 6 F3
Walbrook EC4 15 B2
Walcot Sq SE11 22 E1
Waldorf Hotel WC2 13 C2
Walham Gro SW6 17 C5
Wallace Collection W1 12 D1
Walmer Rd W11 9 A3
Walnut Tree Rd SE10 24 E1
Walnut Tree Wlk SE11 22 D1
Walpole St SW3 19 C3
Walton Pl SW3 19 C1
Walton St SW3 19 B2
Wandon Rd SW6 18 E5
Wandsworth Rd SW8 21 B5
Wansdown Pl SW6 18 D5
Wapping High St E1 16 F4
Wardour St W1 13 A2
Warham St SE5 22 F5
Warner Pl E2 8 F2
Warner St EC1 6 F4
Warren St W1 4 F4
Warwick Gdns W14 17 B1
Warwick La EC4 14 F1
Warwick Rd SW5 18 D3
Warwick Rd W14 17 B1
Warwick Sq SW1 20 F2
Warwick St W1 12 F2
Warwick Way SW1 20 F2
Wat Tyler Rd SE10 23 B5
Waterford Rd SW6 18 D5
Waterloo Bridge SE1,WC2 14 D3
Waterloo Pl SW1 13 A3
Waterloo Rd SE1 14 E4
Waterson St E2 8 D3
Watling St EC4 15 A2
Weaver St E1 8 E4
Weavers La SE1 16 D4
Webb Rd SE3 24 E2
Webber Row SE1 14 E5
Webber St SE1 14 E4 / 15 A5
Weighouse St W1 12 D2
Welbeck St W1 12 D1
Well Rd NW3 1 B4
Well Wlk NW3 1 B4
Welland St SE10 23 B2
Weller St SE1 15 A5
Wellesley Terr N1 7 A3
Wellington Arch W1 12 D4
Wellington Bldgs SW1 20 E3
Wellington Pl NW8 3 A3
Wellington Rd NW8 3 A2
Wellington Row E2 8 E3
Wellington Sq SW3 19 C3
Wellington St WC2 13 C2
Wells Rise NW8 3 C1
Wells St W1 12 F1
Wenlock Basin N1 7 A2
Wenlock Rd N1 7 A2
Wenlock St N1 7 B2
Wentworth St E1 16 D1
Werrington St NW1 5 A2
Wesley's House & Chapel EC1 7 B4
West Sq SE11 22 F1
West St WC2 13 B2
West Cromwell Rd SW5,W14 17 B3
West Eaton Pl SW1 20 D1
West Ferry Rd E14 23 A1
West Gro SE10 23 B4
West Harding St EC4 14 E1
West Heath NW3 1 A3
West Heath Rd NW3 1 A4
West Hill Ct NW6 2 E3
West Hill Pk N6 2 E2
West Pier E1 16 F4
West Smithfield EC1 14 F1
West Tenter St E1 16 E2
Westbourne Cres W2 10 F2
Westbourne Gdns W2 10 D1

Westbourne Gro W2 10 D2
Westbourne Gro W11 9 B2
Westbourne Pk Rd W2 10 D1
Westbourne Pk Rd W11 9 B1
Westbourne Pk Vlls W2 10 D1
Westbourne St W2 11 A2
Westbourne Terr W2 10 E1
Westcombe Hill SE10 24 F1
Westcombe Pk Rd SE3 24 E2
Westcott Rd SE17 22 F4
Westerdale Rd SE10 24 F1
Westgate Terr SW10 18 D3
Westgrove La SE10 23 B4
Westland Pl N1 7 B3
Westminster Abbey SW1 13 B5
Westminster Bridge SE1, SW1 13 C5
Westminster Bridge Rd SE1 14 D5
Westminster Cathedral SW1 20 F1
Westminster Hospital SW1 21 B1
Westminster School Playing Fields SW1 21 A2
Westmoreland Pl SW1 20 E3
Westmoreland St W1 4 D5
Westmoreland Terr SW1 20 E3
Weston Rise WC1 6 D3
Weston St SE1 15 C4
Westway A40(M) W10 9 A1
Wetherby Gdns SW5 18 E2
Wetherby Pl SW7 18 E2
Weymouth Ms W1 4 E5
Weymouth St W1 4 E5
Weymouth Terr E2 8 E2
Wharf Pl E2 8 F1
Wharf Rd N1 7 A2
Wharfdale Rd N1 5 C2
Wharton St WC1 6 D3
Wheatsheaf La SW8 21 C5
Wheler St E1 8 D4
Whetstone Pk WC2 14 D1
Whiston Rd E2 8 D1
Whitbread Brewery EC2 7 B5
Whitcomb St WC2 13 A3
White Lion St N1 6 E2
White's Row E1 8 D5
Whitechapel Art Gallery E1 16 E1
Whitechapel High St E1 16 E1
Whitechapel Rd E1 8 F5 / 16 E1
Whitechurch La E1 16 E1
Whitecross St EC1,EC2 7 A4
Whitfield St W1 4 F4
Whitefriars St EC4 14 E2
Whitehall SW1 13 B3
Whitehall Ct SW1 13 C4
Whitehall Pl SW1 13 B4
Whitehall Theatre SW1 13 B3
Whitehead's Gro SW3 19 B2
White's Grounds SE1 16 D4
Whitfield Rd SE3 23 C5
Whitfield St W1 5 A5
Whitgift St SE11 21 C2
Whitmore Rd N1 7 C1
Whitworth St SE10 24 D1
Wicker St E1 16 F2
Wickham St SE11 22 D3
Wicklow St WC1 5 C3
Wigmore Hall W1 12 E1
Wigmore St W1 12 D1
Wilcox Rd SW8 21 B5
Wild Ct WC2 13 C1
Wild St WC2 13 C1
Wild's Rents SE1 15 C5
Wildwood Gro NW3 1 A2

Wildwood Rise NW11 1 A1
Wildwood Rd NW11 1 A1
Wilfred St SW1 12 F5
Wilkinson St SW8 21 C5
William St SW1 11 C5
William IV St WC2 13 B3
William Rd NW1 4 F3
Willoughby Rd NW3 1 B5
Willow Pl SW1 20 F2
Willow Rd NW3 1 C4
Willow St EC2 7 C4
Wilmer Gdns N1 7 C1
Wilmer Gdns N1 8 D1
Wilmington Ms SW1 11 C5
Wilmington Sq WC1 6 E3
Wilsham St W11 9 A3
Wilkes St E1 8 E5
Wilson Gro SE16 16 F5
Wilson St EC2 7 C5
Wilton Cres SW1 12 D5
Wilton Pl SW1 12 D5
Wilton Rd SW1 20 F1
Wilton Row SW1 12 D5
Wilton Sq N1 7 B1
Wiltshire Row N1 7 B1
Wimborne St N1 7 B2
Wimpole Ms W1 4 E5
Wimpole St W1 4 E5
Winchester Clo SE17 22 F2
Winchester St SW1 20 E3
Wincott St SE11 22 E1
Windmill Hill NW3 1 A4
Windmill Wlk SE1 14 E4
Windsor Terr N1 7 A3
Winfield House NW1 3 B3
Winforton St SE10 23 B4
Winnington Rd N2 1 B1
Winsland St W2 10 F1
· 11 A1
Woburn Pl WC1 5 B4
Woburn Sq WC1 5 B4
Woburn Wlk WC1 5 B4
Wolseley St SE1 16 E5
Wood Clo E2 8 F4
Wood St EC2 15 A1
Woodbridge St EC1 6 F4
Woodland Gro SE10 24 D1
Woodlands Pk Rd SE10 24 D2
Woods Ms W1 12 D2
Woodseer St E1 8 E5
Woodsford Sq W14 9 A4
Woodsome Rd NW5 2 F4
Woodstock St W1 12 E2
Woolwich Rd SE10 24 E1
Wootton St SE1 14 E4
Worfield St SW11 19 B5
World's End Pas SW10 18 F5
Wormwood St EC2 15 C1
Woronzow Rd NW8 3 A1
Worship St EC2 7 C4
Wren St WC1 6 D4
Wright's La W8 10 D5
Wycherley Clo SE3 24 E3
Wyclif St EC1 6 F3
Wyldes Clo NW11 1 A2
Wynan Rd E14 23 A1
Wyndham Rd SE5 22 F5
Wyndham St W1 3 C5
Wynford Rd N1 6 D2
Wynyatt St EC1 6 F3
Wyvil Rd SW8 21 B5

Y

Yardley St WC1 6 E4
Yeoman's Row SW3 19 B1
York Gate NW1 4 D4
York House Pl W8 10 D4
York Rd SE1 14 D4
York St W1 3 B5
York Ter East NW1 4 D4
York Ter West NW1 4 D4
York Way N1 5 C1
Yorkton St E2 8 E2
Young St W8 10 D5

Each place name is followed by its postal district and then by its Street Finder reference.

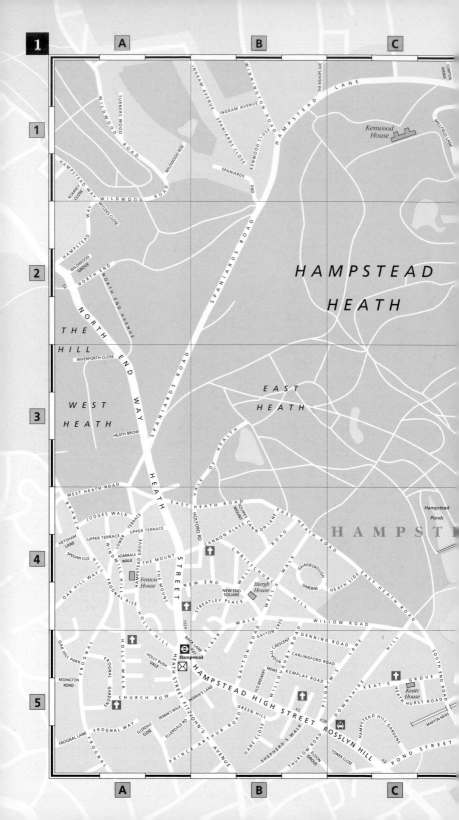

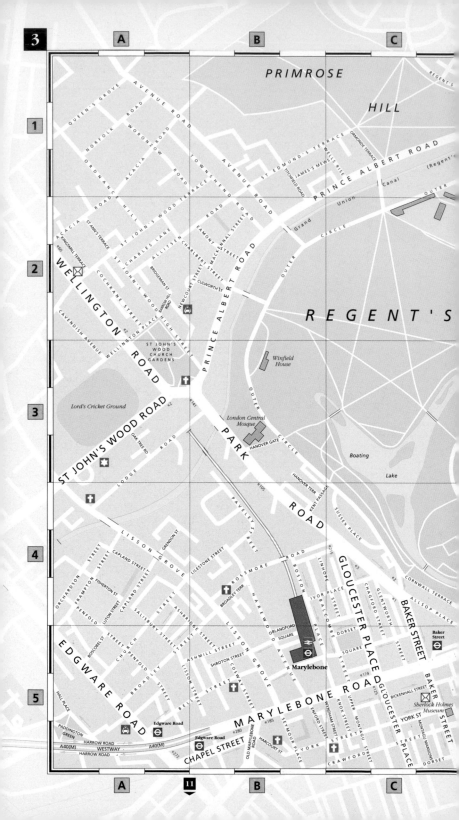

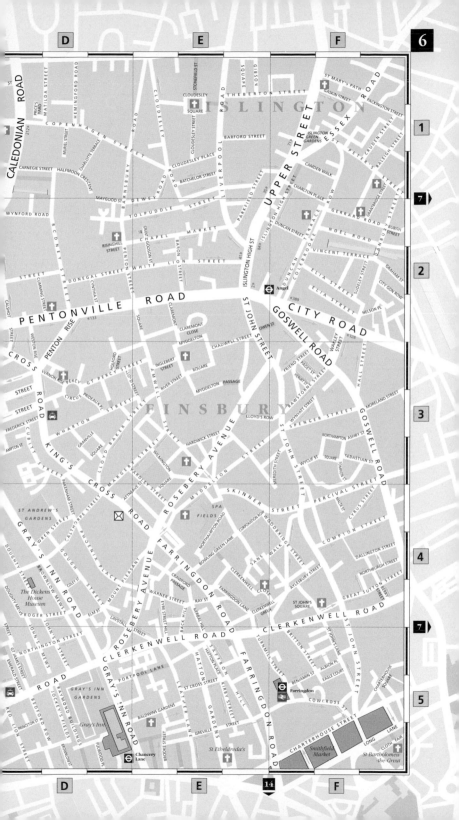

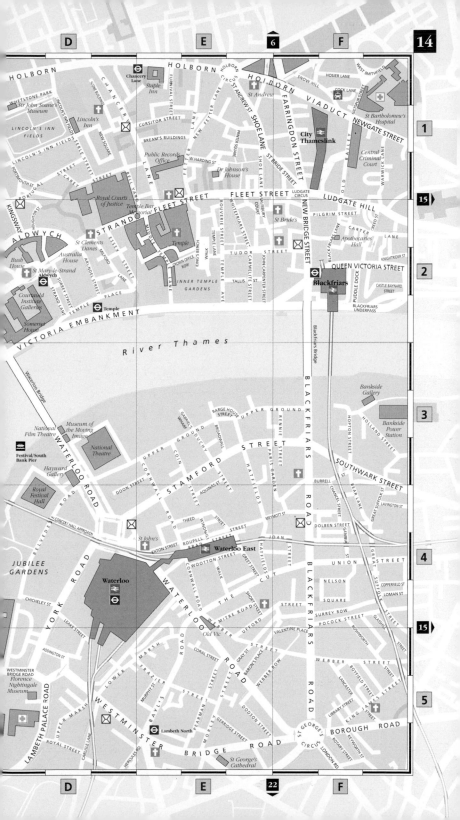

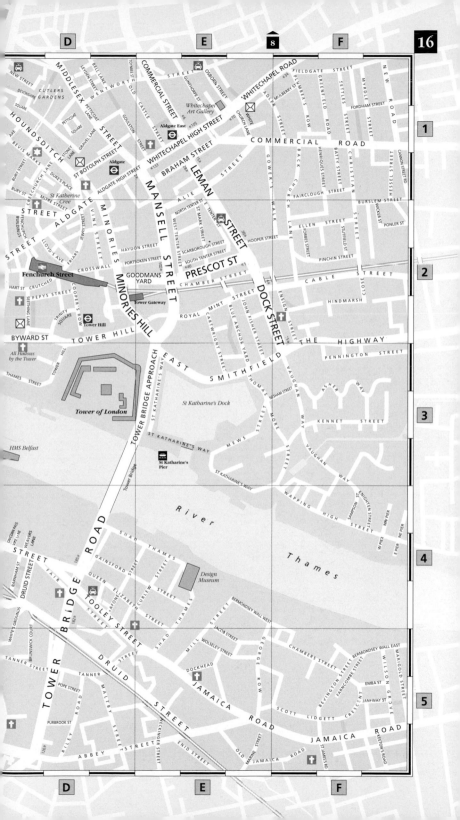

D   E   F

1

NEW STREET
DEVONSHIRE SQUARE
CUTLERS GARDENS
MIDDLESEX STREET
BELL LANE
LEYDEN STREET
WENTWORTH STREET
TOYNBEE ST
OLD CASTLE STREET
COMMERCIAL STREET
STREET
GUNTHORPE STREET
OSBORN STREET
WHITECHAPEL ROAD
FIELDGATE STREET
PLUMBER'S ROW
GREENFIELD ROAD
SETTLES STREET
MYRDLE STREET
FORDHAM STREET
NEW ROAD

HOUNDSDITCH
AXE STREET
BEVIS STREET
BURY STREET
GRAVEL LANE
PETTICOAT LANE
GOULSTON STREET
Whitechapel Art Gallery
Aldgate East
WHITECHAPEL HIGH STREET
WHITE CHURCH LANE
ADLER STREET
COMMERCIAL   ROAD
GOWER'S WALK
BACK CHURCH LANE
HENRIQUES STREET
BATTY STREET
CHRISTIAN STREET
BURSLEM STREET
WICKER ST
CANNON STREET RD
HESSEL STREET
PONLER ST

BURY ST
CREECHURCH LANE
DUKE'S PLACE
St Botolph
Aldgate
WHITECHAPEL HIGH STREET
BRAHAM STREET
ALDGATE HIGH STREET
LEMAN STREET
ALIE STREET
FAIRCLOUGH STREET

ST KATHARINE CREE
MITRE STREET
St Katherine Cree
ALDGATE
MINORIES
VINE STREET
JEWRY STREET
NORTH TENTER ST
ST TENTER ST
WEST TENTER STREET
ST MARK STREET
HOOPER STREET
ELLEN STREET
FORBES STREET
STUTFIELD ST
PINCHIN STREET

STREET
KENNINGTON
BUILDING
LLOYD'S AVE
FRIARS
CROSSWALL
MANSELL STREET
HAYDON STREET
PORTSOKEN STREET
SCARBOROUGH STREET
SOUTH TENTER STREET
PRESCOT ST
CHAMBER STREET
CABLE   STREET

2

Fenchurch Street
HART ST
PEPYS STREET
COOPER'S ROW
GOODMANS YARD
Tower Gateway
ROYAL MINT STREET
CARTWRIGHT STREET
JOHN FISHER STREET
BLUE ANCHOR YARD
ENSIGN STREET
DOCK STREET
HINDMARSH

CRUTCHED
SEETHING LANE
TRINITY SQUARE
Tower Hill
TOWER HILL
BYWARD ST
EAST SMITHFIELD
THE   HIGHWAY
PENNINGTON STREET

All Hallows by the Tower
THAMES STREET
TOWER HILL
TOWER BRIDGE APPROACH
ST KATHARINE'S WAY
THOMAS MORE STREET
NESHAM STREET
VAUGHAN WAY
ASHER WAY

3

Tower of London
St Katharine's Dock
KENNET   STREET

HMS Belfast
Tower Bridge
St Katharine's Pier
ST KATHARINE'S WAY
MEWS STREET
VAUGHAN WAY
SANDON STREET
KNIGHTEN STREET

ST KATHARINE'S WAY
River   Thames
WAPPING HIGH STREET
W PIER   NW PIER
W PIER   E PIER   NE PIER

4

STREET
CINNAMON
WEAVERS LANE
LANE
GAINSFORD STREET
SHAD THAMES
QUEEN ELIZABETH STREET
CURLEW STREET
Design Museum
Thames

BARNHAM ST
DRUID STREET
TOWER   BRIDGE   ROAD
FAIR STREET
TOOLEY STREET
SHAD THAMES
BERMONDSEY WALL WEST
GEORGE ROW
CHAMBERS STREET

WHITE'S GROUNDS
BRUNSWICK COURT
DRUID STREET
JACOB STREET
MILL STREET
WOLSELEY STREET
BEVINGTON STREET
FARNCOMBE STREET
ST JAMES'S RD
BERMONDSEY WALL EAST
WILSON GROVE
MARIGOLD STREET

TANNER STREET
POPE STREET
TANNER STREET
DOCKHEAD
JAMAICA   ROAD
SCOTT LIDGETT CRESCENT
EMBA ST
JANWAY ST

5

PURBROOK ST
RILEY ROAD
MALTBY STREET
DRUID   STREET
ABBEY STREET
NECKINGER STREET
ENID STREET
OLD JAMAICA ROAD
MARINE STREET
JAMAICA   ROAD
KEETON'S ROAD

D   E   F

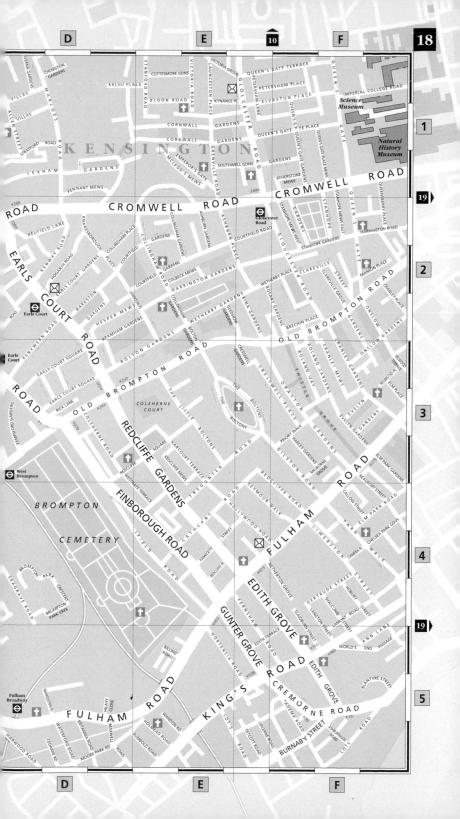

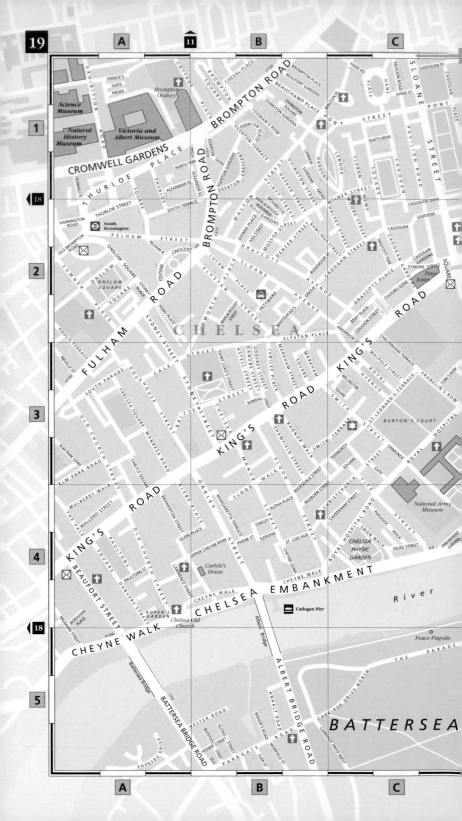

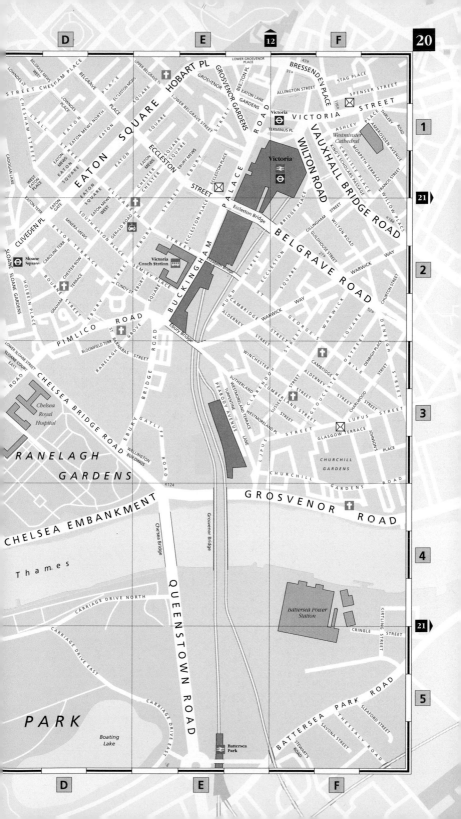

General Index

Acknowledgments

DORLING KINDERSLEY would like to thank the following people whose help and assistance contributed to the preparation of this book.

MAIN CONTRIBUTOR

Michael Leapman was born in London in 1938 and has been a professional journalist since he was 20. He has worked for most British national newspapers and now writes about travel and other subjects for several publications, among them *The Independent, Independent on Sunday, The Economist* and *Country Life.* He has written ten books, including *London's River* (published 1991) and the award-winning *Companion Guide to New York* (1983, revised 1991). In 1989, he edited the widely praised *Book of London.*

CONTRIBUTORS

Yvonne Deutch, Guy Dimond, George Foster, Iain Gale, Fiona Holman, Phil Hariss, Christopher Middleton, Steven Parissien, Bazyli Solowij, Mark Wareham, Jude Welton.

DORLING KINDERSLEY wishes to thank the following editors and researchers at Webster's International Publishers: Sandy Carr, Matthew Barrell, Siobhan Bremner, Serena Cross, Annie Galpin, Miriam Lloyd, Ava-Lee Tanner.

ADDITIONAL PHOTOGRAPHY

Max Alexander, Peter Anderson, June Buck, Peter Chadwick, Michael Dent, Philip Dowell, Mike Dunning, Andreas Einsiedel, Steve Gorton, Christi Graham, Alison Harris, Peter Hayman, Stephen Hayward, Roger Hilton, Ed Ironside, Colin Keates, Dave King, Neil Mersh, Nick Nichols, Vincent Oliver, John Parker, Tim Ridley, Kim Sayer, Chris Stevens, James Stevenson, James Strachan, Doug Traverso, David Ward, Mathew Ward, Steven Wooster, Nick Wright.

ADDITIONAL ILLUSTRATIONS

Ann Child, Tim Hayward, Fiona M. Macpherson, Janos Marffy, David More, Chris D. Orr, Richard Phipps, Michelle Ross, John Woodcock.

CARTOGRAPHY

Advanced Illustration (Cheshire), Contour Publishing (Derby), Euromap Limited (Berkshire). Street Finder maps: ERA Maptec Ltd (Dublin) adapted with permission from original survey and mapping from Shobunsha (Japan).

CARTOGRAPHIC RESEARCH

James Anderson, Roger Bullen, Tony Chambers, Ruth Duxbury, Jason Gough, Ailsa Heritage, Jayne Parsons, Donna Rispoli, Jill Tinsley, Andrew Thompson, Iorwerth Watkins.

RESEARCH ASSISTANCE

Chris Lascelles, Kathryn Steve.

DESIGN AND EDITORIAL ASSISTANCE

Keith Addison, Oliver Bennett, Julee Binder, Ron Boudreau, Michelle Clark, Carey Combe, Vanessa Courtier, Lorna Damms, Simon Farbrother, Marcus Hardy, Sasha Heseltine, Stephanie Jackson, Stephen Knowlden, Jeanette Leung, Stephen McClure, Jane Middleton, Fiona Morgan, Louise Parsons, Leigh Priest, Liz Rowe, Simon Ryder, Anna Streiffert, Andrew Szudek, Diana Vowles, Andy Wilkinson.

SPECIAL ASSISTANCE

Christine Brandt at Kew Gardens; Shelia Brown at The Bank of England; John Cattermole at London Buses Northern; the DK picture department, especially Jenny Rayner; Pippa Grimes at the V&A; Emma Healy at Bethnal Green Museum of Childhood; Alan Hills at the British Museum; Emma Hutton and Cooling Brown Partnership; Gavin Morgan at the Musuem of London, Clare Murphy at Historic Royal Palaces; Ali Naqei at the Science Museum; Patrizio Semproni; Caroline Shaw at the Natural History Museum; Gary Smith at British Rail; Monica Thurnauer at The Tate; Alistair Wardle.

PHOTOGRAPHIC REFERENCE

The London Aerial Photo Library and P. and P. F. James.

PHOTOGRAPHY PERMISSIONS

DORLING KINDERSLEY would like to thank the following for their kind permission to photograph at their establishments:
All Souls Church, Banqueting House (Crown Copyright by kind permission of Historic Royal Palaces), Barbican Centre, Burgh

House Trust, Cabinet War Rooms, Chapter House (English Heritage), Charlton House, Chelsea Physic Garden, Clink Exhibition, Maritime Trust (Cutty Sark), Design Museum, Gatwick Airport Ltd., Geffrye Museum, Hamleys and Merrythought, Heathrow Airport Ltd., Imperial War Museum, Dr. Johnson's House, Keats House (the London Borough of Camden), London Underground Ltd., Madame Tussaud's, Old St. Thomas's Operating Theatre, Patisserie Valerie, Place Below Vegetarian Restaurant, Royal Naval College, St. Alfege's, St. Bartholomew-the-Great, St. Bartholomew-the-Less, St. Botolph's Aldersgate, St. James's, St. John's Smith Square, The Rector and Churchwardens of St Magnus the Martyr, St. Mary le Strand, St. Marylebone Parish Church, St. Paul's Cathedral, the Master and Wardens of the Worshipful Company of Skinners, Smollensky's Restaurants, Southbank Centre, Provost and Chapter of Southwark Cathedral, HM Tower of London, Wellington Museum, Wesley Chapel, the Dean and Chapter of Westminster, Westminster Cathedral, and Hugh Hales, General Manager of the Whitehall Theatre (part of the Maybox Theatre group). Dorling Kindersley would also like to thank all the other museums, galleries, churches, restaurants, shops, and other sights who aided us with photography at their establishments. These are too numerous to thank individually.

PICTURE CREDITS

t = top; tl = top left; tc = top center; tr = top right; cla = center left above; ca = center above; cra = center right above; cl = center left; c = center; cr = center right; clb = center left below; cb = center below; crb = center right below; bl = bottom left; b = bottom; bc = bottom center; br = bottom right.

Every effort has been made to trace the copyright holders, and we apologize in advance for any unintentional omissions. We would be pleased to insert the appropriate acknowledgments in any subsequent edition of this publication.

Works of art have been reproduced with the permission of the following copyright holders: © ADAGP, Paris and DACS, London 1993: 83br, 85c; © DACS 1993: 82cr; © D. HOCKNEY 1970 1: 85b; © the family of ERIC H. KENNINGTON,

RA: 151bl; © ROY LICHTENSTEIN DACS 1993: 83ca. The works illustrated on pages 45c, 206b, 266cb have been reproduced by kind permission of the HENRY MOORE FOUNDATION.

The Publishers are grateful to the following individuals, companies and picture libraries for permission to reproduce their photographs:

Printed by kind permission of MOHAMED AL FAYED: 310b; GOVERNOR AND COMPANY OF THE BANK OF ENGLAND: 145tr; BRIDGEMAN ART LIBRARY, London: 21t, 28t; British Library, London 14, 19tr, (detail) 21br, 24cb, (detail) 32tl, 32bl; Courtesy of the Institute of Directors, London 29cla; Guildhall Art Gallery, Corporation of London (detail) 26t; Guildhall Library, Corporation of London 24br, 76c; M.L. Holmes Jamestown – Yorktown Educational Trust, VA (detail) 17bc; Master and Fellows, Magdalene College, Cambridge (detail) 23clb; Marylebone Cricket Club, London 242c; William Morris Gallery, Walthamstow 19tl, 247tl; Museum of London 22–3; O'Shea Gallery, London (detail) 22cl; Royal Holloway & Bedford New College 157bl; Russell Cotes Art Gallery and Museum, Bournemouth 38tr; Thyssen-Bornemisza Collection, Lugano Casta 253b; Westminster Abbey, London (detail) 32bc; White House, Bond Street, London 28cb.

BRITISH AIRWAYS: 354t, 356tl, 359t; reproduced with permission of the BRITISH LIBRARY BOARD: 127b; © THE BRITISH MUSEUM: 16t, 16ca, 17tl, 40t, 91c, 126–7 all pics except 126t & 127b, 128–9 all pics.

CAMERA PRESS, London: P. Abbey – LNS 73cb; Cecil Beaton 79tl; HRH Prince Andrew 95bl; Allan Warren 31cb; COLORIFIC!: Steve Benbow 55t; David Levenson 66–7; THOMAS CORAM FOUNDATION FOR CHILDREN: 125b; Courtesy of the CORPORATION OF LONDON: 55c, 146t; COURTAULD INSTITUTE GALLERIES, London: 41c, 117b.

PERCIVAL DAVID FOUNDATION OF CHINESE ART: 130c; DEPARTMENT OF TRANSPORT (Crown Copyright): 361b; Courtesy of the GOVERNORS AND THE DIRECTORS DULWICH PICTURE GALLERY: 43bl, 248bl.

ENGLISH HERITAGE: 254b, 256b; ENGLISH LIFE PUBLICATIONS LTD.: 255b; PHILIP ENTICKNAP: 247tr; E.T. ARCHIVE: 19bl, 26c, 26bc, 27bl, 28br,

29cra, 29clb, 33tc, 33cr, 36bl, 185tl; British Library, London 18cr; Imperial War Museum, London 30bc; Museum of London 15b, 27br, 28bl; Science Museum, London 27cla; Stoke Museum Staffordshire Polytechnic 23bl, 25cl; 33bc; Victoria and Albert Museum, London 20c, 21bc, 25tr; MARY EVANS PICTURE LIBRARY: 16bl, 16br, 17bl, 17br, 20bl, 22bl, 24t, 25bc, 25br, 27t, 27cb, 27bc, 30bl, 32br, 33tl, 33cl, 33bl, 33br, 36t, 36c, 38tl, 39bl, 72cb, 72b, 90b, 112b, 114b, 116c, 135t, 139t, 155bl, 159t, 162ca, 174ca, 178b, 203b, 212t, 222b.

Courtesy of the FAN MUSEUM (The Helene Alexander Collection) 239b; FREUD MUSEUM, London: 242t.

THE GORE HOTEL, London: 273.

ROBERT HARDING PICTURE LIBRARY: 31ca, 42c, 52ca, 169tl, 325t, 347cb, 366b; Philip Craven 206t; Brian Hawkes 21clb; Michael Jenner 21cra, 238t; 58t, 223t; HEATHROW AIRPORT LTD.: 356tr; Reproduced with permission of HER MAJESTY'S STATIONARY OFFICE (Crown Copyright): 156 all pics; JOHN HESELTINE: 12tr, 13tl, 13tr, 13cb, 13br, 51tr, 63br, 98, 124b, 132, 142, 172, 216; FRIENDS OF HIGHGATE CEMETERY: 37tr, 240, 242b; HISTORIC ROYAL PALACES (Crown Copyright): 5t, 35tc, 250–51 all except 250br, 252–3 all except 253br; THE HORNIMAN MUSEUM, London: 248br; HOVERSPEED LTD: 359b; HULTON-DEUTSCH COLLECTION: 24bl, 124tl, 228t.

THE IMAGE BANK, London: Gio Barto 55b; Derek Berwin 31t, 272t, Romilly Lockyer 72t, 94br; Leo Mason 56t; Simon Wilkinson 197t; Terry Williams 139b; Courtesy of ISIC, UK: 352t.

PETER JACKSON COLLECTION: 24–5.

ROYAL BOTANIC GARDENS, KEW: Andrew McRob 48cl, 56b, 244–5 all pics except 245t & 245br.

LEIGHTON HOUSE, ROYAL BOROUGH OF KENSINGTON: 212b; LITTLE ANGEL MARIONETTE THEATRE: 341tl; LONDON AMBULANCE SERVICE: 347ca; LONDON TOY AND MODEL MUSEUM: 257t; LONDON TRANSPORT MUSEUM: 28ca; 362–3 all maps and tickets.

MADAME TUSSAUD'S: 218c, 220t; MANSELL COLLECTION: 19br, 20t, 20br, 21bl, 22t, 22cl, 23br, 27ca, 32tr; METROPOLITAN POLICE SERVICE: 346t, 347t, MUSEUM OF LONDON: 16cb, 17tr, 17cb, 18t, 21crb, 41tc, 166–7 all pics.

NATIONAL EXPRESS LTD.: 358; Reproduced by courtesy of the TRUSTEES, THE NATIONAL GALLERY, London: (detail) 35c, 104–5 all except 104t, 106–7 all except 107t; NATIONAL PORTRAIT GALLERY, London: 4t, 41tl, 101cb, (detail) 102b; NATIONAL POSTAL MUSEUM, London: 26bl, 164t; By permission of the KEEPER OF THE NATIONAL RAILWAY MUSEUM, York: 28–9; NATIONAL SOUND ARCHIVE, London – The trademark HIS MASTER'S VOICE is reproduced with the kind permission of EMI RECORDS LIMITED: 197cl; NATIONAL TRUST PHOTOGRAPHIC LIBRARY: Wendy Aldiss 23ca; John Bethal 254t, 255t; Michael Boys 38b; NATURAL HISTORY MUSEUM, LONDON: 205t; Derek Adams 204b; John Downs 204c; NEW SHAKESPEARE THEATRE CO.: 324bl.

PALACE THEATRE ARCHIVE: 108t; PICTOR INTERNATIONAL, London: 61t; PIPPA POP-INS CHILDREN'S HOTEL, London: 339b.

PITSHANGER MANOR MUSEUM: 256c; POPPERFOTO: 29tl, 29crb, 30tl, 30tr, 30c, 33tr, 39br; PRESS ASSOCIATION LTD: 29bl, 29br; PUBLIC RECORD OFFICE (Crown Copyright): 18b.

BILL RAFFERTY: 324br; REX FEATURES LTD.: 53tl; Peter Brooker 53tr; Andrew Laenen 54c; THE RITZ, London: 91t; ROCK CIRCUS: 100cb; ROCK ISLAND DINER: 339ca; ROYAL ACADEMY OF ARTS, London: 90tr; THE BOARD OF TRUSTEES OF THE ROYAL ARMOURIES: 41tr, 155tl, 157tl, 157c, 157br; ROYAL COLLECTION, ST. JAMES'S PALACE © HM THE QUEEN: 8–9, 53b, 88t, 93t, 94–5 all pics except 94br & 95bl, 96t, 250br; ROYAL COLLEGE OF MUSIC, London: 196c, 202c.

THE SAVOY GROUP: 274t, 274b; SCIENCE MUSEUM, London: 208cr, 208b, 209cla, 209cb; SCIENCE PHOTO LIBRARY: Maptec International Ltd 10b; SEALINK PLC: 355b; SPENCER HOUSE LTD: 88b; SOUTHBANK PRESS OFFICE: 182bl; SYNDICATION INTERNATIONAL: 31bl, 35tr, 52cb, 53c, 58bl, 59t, 136; Library of Congress 25bl.

TATE GALLERY: 43br, 82–3 all pics except 82t & 83t, 84–5 all pics.

Courtesy of the BOARD OF TRUSTEES OF THE VICTORIA AND ALBERT MUSEUM: 35br, 40b, 198–9 all except 198t, 200–1 all pics, 246b, 340t.

THE WALDORF, London: 272b; THE WALLACE COLLECTION, London: 40ca, 222c; Courtesy of the TRUSTEES OF THE WEDGWOOD MUSEUM, Barlaston, Stoke-on-Trent, Staffs, England: 26br; VIVIENNE WESTWOOD: Patrick Fetherstonhaugh 31br; THE WIMBLEDON LAWN TENNIS MUSEUM: Micky White 249t; Photo © WOODMANSTERNE: Jeremy Marks 35tl, 149t.

YOUTH HOSTEL ASSOCIATION: 275.

ZEFA: 10t, 52b, 54br, 324c; Bob Croxford 57t; Clive Sawyer 57b.

Front Endpaper: all special or additional photography except THE IMAGE BANK, London: Romilly Lockyer bl, crb; MUSEUM OF LONDON: bcr; NATURAL HISTORY MUSEUM: John Downs cl; TATE GALLERY: bcl; Courtesy of the BOARD OF TRUSTEES OF THE VICTORIA AND ALBERT MUSEUM: cla.

The London Underground

UNDERGROUND